# Jonathan Edwards

Jonathan Edwards, ca. 1750–55

# Jonathan Edwards
## *A Life*

## George M. Marsden

*Yale University Press*
New Haven & London

B
EDWARDS
M
7-2003

Published with assistance from the Annie Burr Lewis Fund.

Designed by James J. Johnson and set in Adobe Caslon type by Keystone Typesetting, Inc., Orwigsburg, Pennsylvania.
Printed in the United States of America by R. R. Donnelley and Sons, Harrisonburg, Virginia.

*Library of Congress Cataloging-in-Publication Data*

Marsden, George M., 1939–
   Jonathan Edwards : a life / George M. Marsden.
     p. cm.
   Includes bibliographical references and index.
   ISBN 0-300-09693-3 (alk. paper)

   1. Edwards, Jonathan, 1703–1758. 2. Congregational churches—
United States—Clergy—Biography. I. Title.
BX7260.E3M412 2003
285.8'092—dc21
[B]                                2002013611

A catalogue record for this book is available from the British Library.

10  9  8  7  6  5  4  3  2  1

*To a generation of Edwards scholars who made this work possible*

But we have this treasure in earthen vessels, that the excellency of
the power may be of God, and not of us.

—II Corinthians 4:7

# Contents

List of Maps ........................................................... ix

Cotton Mather's Map of New England ....................... x

Chronology of Edwards' Life and Times .................... xiii

Preface ................................................................ xvii

Note on the Text .................................................. xxi

Introduction ......................................................... 1

Chapter  1.  A Time to Be Born ............................... 11

Chapter  2.  The Overwhelming Question .................. 25

Chapter  3.  The Pilgrim's Progress .......................... 44

Chapter  4.  The Harmony of All Knowledge .............. 59

Chapter  5.  Anxieties ........................................... 82

Chapter  6.  "A Low, Sunk Estate and Condition" ....... 101

Chapter  7.  On Solomon Stoddard's Stage ............... 114

Chapter  8.  And on a Wider Stage .......................... 133

Chapter  9.  The Mighty Works of God and of Satan .... 150

Chapter 10.  The Politics of the Kingdom ................. 170

Chapter 11.  "A City Set on a Hill" .......................... 184

Chapter 12.  God "Will Revive the Flame Again,
             Even in the Darkest Times" .................... 201

Chapter 13.  The Hands of God and the Hand of Christ ... 214

Chapter 14. "He That Is Not with Us Is Against Us"                227

Chapter 15. "Heavenly Elysium"                                   239

Chapter 16. Conservative Revolutionary                           253

Chapter 17. A House Divided                                       268

Chapter 18. A Model Town No More                                 291

Chapter 19. Colonial Wars                                        306

Chapter 20. "Thy Will Be Done"                                   320

Chapter 21. "I Am Born to Be a Man of Strife"                    341

Chapter 22. The Crucible                                         357

Chapter 23. The Mission                                          375

Chapter 24. Frontier Struggles                                   395

Chapter 25. Wartime                                              414

Chapter 26. Against an "Almost Inconceivably Pernicious"
             Doctrine                                            432

Chapter 27. Original Sin "in This Happy Age of Light
             and Liberty"                                        447

Chapter 28. Challenging the Presumptions of the Age              459

Chapter 29. The Unfinished Masterworks                           472

Chapter 30. The Transitory and the Enduring                      490


Appendix A. Genealogical Table of Edwards' Relatives             507

Appendix B. Edwards' Sisters                                     510

Appendix C. Edwards' Immediate Family, from His Family Bible     511

Notes                                                            513

Credits                                                          601

Index                                                            603

# Maps

Southeastern Section of Cotton Mather's Map of New England, 1696     x

Central New Haven, 1748     92

Edwards' World as the Embattled American West     384

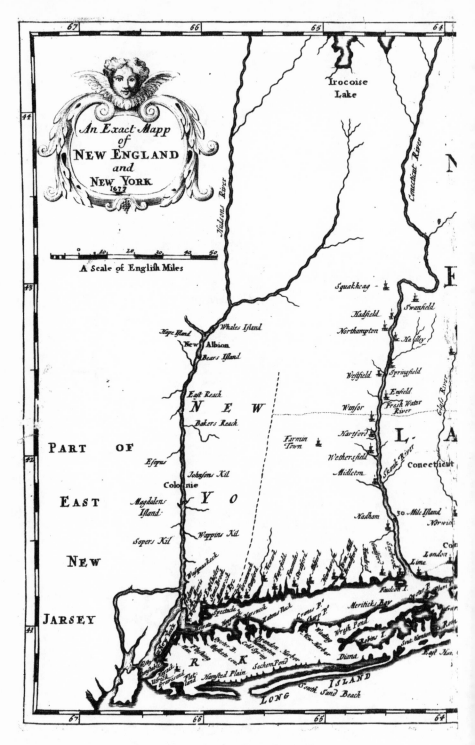

Southeastern section of Cotton Mather's map of New England, 1696

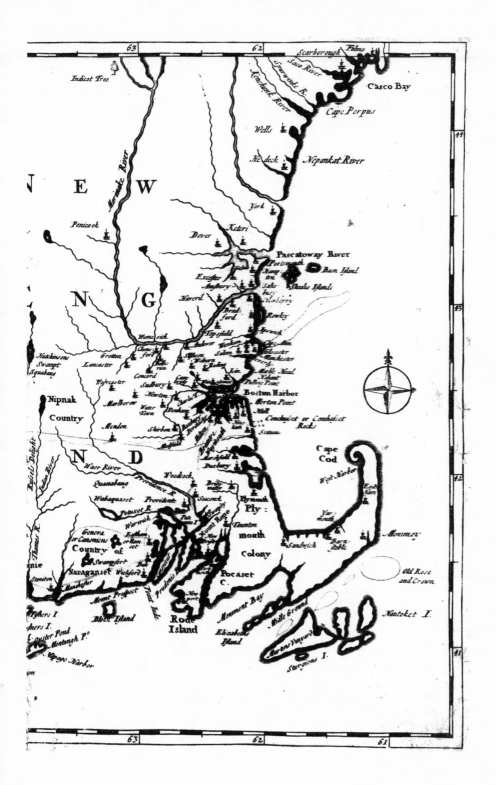

# Chronology of Edwards' Life and Times

EDWARDS' LIFE

1703   Born October 5, East Windsor, Connecticut

1716–20   Undergraduate at Yale College

1720–22   M.A. student at Yale

1721   (spring) Intense religious experiences begin

1722   (August) to 1723 (April) Pastor of church in New York City

1723   (summer) Home at East Windsor

1723   (November) to 1724 (May) Pastor of church at Bolton, Connecticut

EDWARDS' TIMES

1685   Louis XIV revokes Edict of Nantes, Protestants persecuted, many flee

1688–89   "Glorious Revolution": William and Mary succeed James II of England, a Catholic

1701   Founding of Yale

1702–13   Queen Anne's War

1704   Indians sack Deerfield, Massachusetts

1706   Birth of Benjamin Franklin

1707   Union of England and Scotland under the name Great Britain

1712   Slave uprising in New York City

1714   George I of the Protestant House of Hanover succeeds to English throne

1715–16   Jacobite rebellion in Scotland, to place James III (the "Pretender") on the throne, suppressed

1721   Cotton Mather promotes smallpox vaccinations in Boston

EDWARDS' LIFE

1724–26   Tutor at Yale (illness fall 1725)

1726   Called to assist his grandfather Solomon Stoddard in Northampton

1727   (July) Marries Sarah Pierpont

1729   Death of Solomon Stoddard; Edwards becomes full pastor

1734   *A Divine and Supernatural Light* preached

1734–35   Northampton and Connecticut Valley awakening

1734–35   Breck Case

1737   *A Faithful Narrative* brings revival international attention

1738   *Charity and Its Fruits* preached

1740   George Whitefield's tour of New England sparks Great Awakening

1741   *Sinners in the Hands of an Angry God* preached

1741   *Distinguishing Marks of the Work of the Spirit of God*

1742   *Some Thoughts Concerning the Present Revival of Religion in New England*

1742   Sarah's ecstatic experience

1742   Northampton covenant

1744   "Young folks' Bible" case

1746   *Religious Affections*

1747   *An Humble Attempt*

1747   Visit and death of David Brainerd

1748   Death of daughter Jerusha

1749   *Life of David Brainerd*

1750   Dismissed from Northampton pastorate

1751   Settles in Stockbridge, Massachusetts, as pastor and missionary to Indians

EDWARDS' TIMES

1724–25   New England vs. French and Abenakis in Father Râle's War

1727–60 King George II

1730–41   Jonathan Belcher governor of Massachusetts

1735   Treaty at Deerfield prepares for founding of Stockbridge

1738   John Wesley begins Methodist revivals in England

1740–41   Land Bank agitation in Massachusetts

1742   Great revivals begin in Scotland

1744–48   French phase of King George's War

1745   Capture of French fortress, Louisbourg

1745–46   "Young Pretender," Charles Edward Stuart, is defeated after invading Scotland and England

1746–57   Jonathan Belcher governor of New Jersey

1746   College of New Jersey founded

| EDWARDS' LIFE | EDWARDS' TIMES |
|---|---|
| | 1752    Franklin's electrical experiment with kite |
| | 1752    Georgian calendar adopted by English |
| 1754    *Freedom of the Will* | |
| 1755    Drafted *The End for Which God Created* and *The Nature of True Virtue* (pub. 1765) | 1755    Lisbon earthquake |
| | 1755–63    French and Indian War |
| 1758    *Original Sin* | |
| 1758    Installed as president of the College of New Jersey (now Princeton University) | |
| 1758    Dies of smallpox inoculation | |

# Preface

A number of people of common sense have asked me something like, "Isn't there a good bit written on Jonathan Edwards already?" or "Aren't there quite a few other biographies of Edwards?" Their implication, I believe—since they are people of common sense—has been, "Why would anyone spend years working on a subject that has been so well covered?"

Part of the answer is that, despite the vast specialized literature about Edwards, there is no recent full critical biography. The last was Ola Winslow's Pulitzer Prize–winning *Jonathan Edwards, 1703–1758*, published in 1940. Perry Miller's influential, brilliant, and often misleading *Jonathan Edwards* (1949) was a sketch of Edwards' intellectual life. Patricia Tracy's *Jonathan Edwards: Pastor* (1980) dealt only with his years in Northampton. Iain Murray's *Jonathan Edwards: A New Biography* (1987) provides a well-documented updating of biographies in the honorable but uncritical tradition of Edwards' earlier admirers.

Further, a revolution in Edwards studies, especially during the past decade, has made a full critical biography feasible in a way that it never was before. In recent years The Works of Jonathan Edwards project at Yale University has brought to fruition a generation of scholarship begun under Perry Miller in the 1950s. Since the early 1990s, the project has transcribed most of Edwards' enormous corpus of previously unpublished writings. Most of these works were known to Edwards specialists and were available in principle to anyone who had the patience to decipher his nearly illegible handwriting. Today the transcriptions can be perused by computer in ways that were unthinkable a generation ago. Further, the volumes of the Yale edition of *The Works of Jonathan Edwards* provide not only definitive editions of familiar writings, but also much that was not previously available and extensive introductions that fill in many of the gaps of earlier scholarship. In the meantime, scholars continue to add to an enormous literature about Edwards. The works published through just 1993 fill two volumes of M. X. Lesser's annotated bibliographies (*Jonathan Edwards: A Reference Guide*, 1981, and *Jonathan Edwards: An Annotated Bibliography, 1979–1993*, 1994) and the pace has not slackened. These efforts have made it possible to write a more comprehensive life of Edwards than was practicable before.

This book, then, is a tribute to a generation of scholars. Particularly all those who have participated in The Works of Jonathan Edwards project at Yale University have been essential to this enterprise. Every Edwards scholar today benefits from the decades of work by Thomas A. Schafer in dating Edwards' previously undated writings, typically by painstaking analysis of changes in paper, ink, and handwriting. George S. Claghorn, similarly, spent decades collecting all the extant correspondence of Edwards (now published) as well as collecting and transcribing letters to and about Edwards. He has been immensely helpful to me in making available transcriptions and information, in answering questions, in checking quotations from the correspondence, and in making numerous suggestions. Without the exhaustive archival work by Schafer, Claghorn, and others, we would not be able to reconstruct the details of Edwards' life and thought as we now can. Kenneth P. Minkema, the executive editor of The Works of Jonathan Edwards, who has become a legend in his own time for his skills in advancing such research, is another person without whom a volume like this would not have been possible. He has been immensely helpful at every stage of this process, providing me with complete access to all the materials the project has transcribed or collected and untiringly answering questions, offering information about details, and providing criticism of my work. My close friend Harry S. Stout, the general editor of *The Works of Jonathan Edwards*, has played an incalculable role. Although this volume is not connected with *The Works* as such, he brought me into contact with Yale University Press and has been a seemingly inexhaustible source of shrewd advice, enthusiasm, and goodwill. My wife, Lucie, and I are particularly grateful to Skip and his wife, Sue, for their wonderful hospitality whenever we were in New Haven.

Numerous others who have been part of The Works of Jonathan Edwards project have also contributed directly or indirectly to this volume. Douglas A. Sweeney, Ava Chamberlain, and Kyle Farley were especially helpful while they were on the staff of The Works. I am also deeply grateful to all the individual editors of the Yale University Press edition of *The Works*. Without their researches and analyses, I would not have been able to proceed as I did. I am particularly grateful for the work of the former general editor, John E. Smith, and for that of the late Perry Miller, who was a major force in bringing about the publication of a definitive edition of Edwards' work. Although I am sometimes critical of Miller's specific interpretations of Edwards, Miller has always been one of my intellectual heroes.

I am grateful to the staffs of the Beinecke Rare Book and Manuscript Library, Yale University; Storrs Library, Longmeadow, Massachusetts; the Forbes Library, Northampton, Massachusetts (particularly to Elise Feeley); and the Library of the University of Notre Dame for their gracious help. I am also indebted for the indirect help of other libraries, especially the Franklin Trask Library, Andover Newton Theological School, Newton Centre, Massachusetts, from which I have received transcriptions of materials collected through the research of others.

Among my largest debts are to the many readers of earlier drafts of this book. These include Ava Chamberlain, George S. Claghorn, David D. Hall, Mark Noll, Kenneth P. Minkema, Amy Plantinga Pauw, Stephen J. Stein, Harry S. Stout, and Grant Wacker. Thomas S. Kidd, my graduate assistant throughout most of the project, provided much help and insightful advice. R. Bryan Bademan and Kristin Kobes DuMez served as my editors in the latter stages, checking many quotations and offering astute suggestions on style and content. Joe Creech collected bibliographical materials for me at the early stages. The class members of my graduate course, "Puritanism and the Culture of Colonial New England," Grant Brodrecht, Ángel Cortes, Timothy Gloege, Matthew Grow, Michael Lee, and Tammy Van Dyken, also read a late draft and made valuable suggestions. Collectively, these readers contributed tremendously to improving this volume. I am also indebted to my editors at Yale University Press, Lara Heimert and Susan Laity, for their skillful oversight. John Long, also of Yale University Press, worked beyond the call of duty in finding illustrations. Eliza Childs improved the work through her excellent copyediting.

I am especially grateful for support from the Francis A. McAnaney Chair in History at the University of Notre Dame, and to the Peter B. and Adeline W. Ruffin Foundation in funding that chair. Officials of the University of Notre Dame have always been most helpful in encouraging this book. I am particularly grateful to the chairs of the History Department, Wilson Miscamble, Christopher Hamlin, and Thomas Kselman, for their help during the time I have been working on this project. Provost Nathan O. Hatch, himself a distinguished scholar of eighteenth-century religion and culture, has provided personal encouragement and leadership for the university.

My sincere thanks go also to the John Simon Guggenheim Memorial Foundation for their award of a fellowship that supported this project in its early stages.

As always by far my greatest debt is to Lucie. A keen critic, her assurance that she genuinely enjoyed the chapters I gave her to read was a great encouragement. Far more important, her love and friendship has fostered an "uncommon union" that has grown even better with the years.

# Note on the Text

Quotations have been modernized in spelling and sometimes in grammar, except in rare cases where the sense or tone would be changed.

Dates before September 1752 (when the date was advanced by eleven days in the British world) are old style, except that dual listings for winter months are treated as though the new year began on January 1 (e.g., February 1750–51 is translated as February 1751).

All biblical quotations are from the King James Version.

# Introduction

Edwards was extraordinary. By many estimates, he was the most acute early American philosopher and the most brilliant of all American theologians. At least three of his many works—*Religious Affections, Freedom of the Will,* and *The Nature of True Virtue*—stand as masterpieces in the larger history of Christian literature. The appeal of his thought endures. Every year several new books and scores of academic articles, reviews, and dissertations appear about him. Yet he also wrote effectively for popular audiences. His celebrated biography of David Brainerd was a best-selling religious text in nineteenth-century America and encouraged countless Christians to seek lives of disinterested sacrifice and missionary service. His writings, including some of his more substantial works, continue to inspire many lay readers.[1]

His pen brought lasting influence, but Edwards' life involved far more. An activist at the center of the most important religious and social movement of his day, he oversaw an amazing local revival, which became a prototype for one of America's most influential religious practices. He worked vigorously both in promoting and in attempting to delimit the momentous colonial and international awakenings that soon followed. A heralded preacher, he delivered what became America's most famous sermon, *Sinners in the Hands of an Angry God.* In his pastorate, he spent years shepherding parishioners through awakenings and declines, and he struggled to define the role of the church in a town and region that were making the transition from a Puritan heritage toward a revolutionary destiny. He sustained deep interests in politics and the military, especially as they bore on the international Protestant cause. In the midst of everything else, he spent much time in disciplined devotion and is sometimes most admired as a contemplative. For seven years Edwards served as a missionary to Indians in a dangerous frontier village. At his death, at age fifty-four, he was the president of the College of New Jersey at Princeton. Throughout his life his experiences were shaped by his relationships to his large immediate and extended family. His wife, Sarah, also became a legendary figure. They reared eleven children and nurtured what became an American dynasty.

In writing this life of Edwards, one of my goals has been to understand him as a real person in his own time. Because he became such a monumental figure, it has often been difficult to find the person behind the monuments. Further, as a leading controversialist in a vigorous religious movement, Edwards invites strong reactions. He has many ardent admirers, many detractors, and many who attempt to rehabilitate him by making him over in their own images. My aspiration, which I am sure has been only partially realized, is to make Edwards intelligible to widely diverse audiences by first attempting to depict him in his own time and in his own terms.

Readers might also begin by thinking about Edwards as an *eighteenth-century* figure and about how that context should shape their understanding of him. The most fascinating question that framed this book is "What was it like to live in western New England in the first half of the eighteenth century?" (or "How was that time different from our own?"). This second version of the question suggests, of course, a twenty-first-century viewpoint. My task as an historian is to make intelligible the outlook of another time, which demands taking into account the various perspectives of readers and also what has transpired since the eighteenth century. Yet it would be a failure of imagination if we were to start out—as today's histories sometimes do—by simply judging people of the past for having outlooks that are not like our own. Rather, we must first try to enter sympathetically into an earlier world and to understand its people. Once we do that we will be in a far better position both to learn from them and to evaluate their outlooks critically.

A number of things will be particularly striking to twenty-first-century readers about early eighteenth-century New England. First, the world into which Edwards was born will make a lot more sense if we think of it as British rather than American. It was, of course, significantly American, yet by the time of Edwards' death in 1758, it had not yet manifested most of the traits that were soon to be associated with "America." The American Revolution was not yet on anyone's horizon, even if with hindsight we can see that many of the potentialities were there. Edwards lived in a thoroughly pre-Revolutionary British province.

Its British or Old World character was most conspicuously evident in its rigid hierarchical structures. We might think of eighteenth-century or early nineteenth-century English novels to get some sense of the social hierarchy taken for granted in eighteenth-century British America. New England, having been shaped by seventeenth-century Puritanism, had its own version of such hierarchism. Edwards was an aristocrat by New England standards. Clergymen in New England wielded more authority and could expect more deference to their opinions than in most other parts of the British World. Further, Edwards belonged to an elite extended family that was part of the ruling class of clergy, magistrates, judges, military leaders, village squires, and merchants. The Stoddards and Williamses, along with a few other families with whom they intermarried, ruled the Connecticut River Valley, or western Massachusetts (Hampshire County) and parts of Connecticut.

Eighteenth-century Britons viewed their world as monarchical and controlled by hierarchies of personal relationships.[2] On both these counts, their assumptions were almost opposite of those of most Westerners today, who tend to think of society as in principle egalitarian and in fact controlled by impersonal forces. Eighteenth-century British-American society depended on patriarchy. One's most significant relationships were likely to be vertical rather than horizontal. Fathers had authority over families and households, the cornerstones of good order. Women, children, hired servants, indentures, and African slaves were all dependent on persons directly above them. Society was conceived of as an extended household. In this arrangement paternalism was a virtue, not a term of opprobrium. Although British people spoke much of "liberty," few had personal freedom in a modern sense. Gentlemen ruled largely through a hierarchical system of patronage extending from the king down. Good order, especially for the lower ranks of society, was enforced by strict surveillance and stern punishments. Ordinary life under any circumstances was often cruel, plagued by epidemics, unrelieved pain, and constant uncertainties about life itself. Many essential tasks were painfully difficult and time-consuming. Personal dependency was one way of dealing with a harsh and insecure world and was often taken as a matter of course.

Adding to the distresses and periodic terror in western New England was its location on the frontier of British settlements in an era of frequent warfare. Edwards lived at the vortex of conflict among three civilizations—the British Protestant, the French Catholic, and the Indian. Each was fiercely struggling to control North America. We now know how those contests turned out, but the outcome was not apparent to Edwards' generation. This international context was enormously important to Edwards. He spent vast amounts of time concerned about both Roman Catholicism and the Indians and their respective and very different places in God's plans. Edwards framed his fundamental theological concerns and especially his view of history in the context of his perceptions of world wars, which he viewed as intimately linked to the prospects for the Gospel.

To make sense of Edwards' life, one must take seriously his religious outlook on his own terms. That might be said of any figure with strongly held views, but the point needs to be underscored regarding Edwards for several reasons. Because Edwards is associated with a number of living Christian traditions, current opinions about him are likely to be shaped by our reactions to those religious movements. Edwards was loyal to the theology inherited from the seventeenth-century Puritans and their continental "Reformed," or Calvinistic, counterparts and he was pivotal in the emergence of international evangelicalism in the eighteenth century.[3] Puritanism and Calvinism have always elicited strong reactions regarding their role in American history. Evangelicalism now comes in so many energetic varieties that it is difficult to view one of its progenitors without looking through the lens of later popularizations. Edwards anticipated some traits of later evangelicals, but the facts that he was a Calvinistic thinker, that he was rigorously intellectual, and that he was working in an eighteenth-century context make him very different from his evangelical heirs. Our challenge is to try to step into his world and to understand it in terms that he himself would recognize.

The central principle in Edwards' thought, true to his Calvinistic heritage, was the sovereignty of God. The triune eternally loving God, as revealed in Scripture, created and ruled everything in the universe. Most simply put, the sovereignty of God meant that if there were a question as to whether God or humans should be given credit for anything good, particularly in matters of salvation, the benefit of the doubt should always go to God. Edwards avoided allowing God's rule to be thought of as a distant abstraction, as it could become. Rather, he emphasized that God's very purpose in creation was the great work of redemption in Christ. Everything in the universe pointed ultimately to the loving character of the triune God.

If the central principle of Edwards' thought was the sovereignty of God, the central *practical* motive in his life and work was his conviction that nothing was more momentous personally than one's eternal relationship to God. Many Christians affirm this proposition, yet most have not followed its implications for personal relationships with utter seriousness. Most who have taken it seriously have been activists rather than thinkers. Edwards was both.

He built his life around disciplines designed constantly to renew that eternal perspective. In his sermons and writings he turned his immense intellectual powers to rigorously following out the implications of God's sovereignty for understanding humans' eternal destinies, as defined by his biblicist and Calvinistic heritage.[4] If there is an emphasis that appears difficult, or harsh, or overstated in Edwards, often the reader can better appreciate his perspective by asking the question: "How would this issue look if it really were the case that bliss or punishment for a literal *eternity* was at stake?"

Presenting Edwards' life in terms that he would recognize and a wide variety of readers can understand may be a sufficient end in itself. If we can enter imaginatively into another time and place and into the experiences of people different from ourselves, we have achieved one of the goals of literature. For that reason I have tried to tell the story of Edwards and his family with relatively few interpretive intrusions. I hope I have done this in a way that is, as much as possible, objective in the sense of fair-minded and true to the evidence.

Nonetheless, we all have points of view. As one astute historian has recently reminded us, "objectivity is not neutrality."[5] Even the fairest observers have biases and blind spots. They have (and they ought to have) interests. The best way to deal with these universal phenomena is to acknowledge one's point of view rather than posing as a neutral observer. That way readers can take an author's viewpoint into account, discount it if they wish, and learn from it to the extent they can. At the same time, authors who are self-conscious about their points of view can use such self-knowledge to limit unintended or unfair warping of the evidence to fit their perspectives.

That being said, I find that after spending countless hours with Edwards, my point of view regarding him is complex. He was such a multisided person and thinker that the answer to the question of what I think about him depends on the particular aspect of his life or thought we are talking about. I find him to be a person of immense personal integrity. He was intensely pious and disciplined, admirably but dauntingly so for those of more ordinary religious faith. His unrelenting intensity led him to follow the logic of his faith to its conclusions. His accompanying seriousness made him not an easy person to spend time with as a casual acquaintance, although he would have been fascinating to talk to about matters that concerned him. His prowess as a logician made him exceedingly sure of his opinions, sometimes given to pride, overconfidence, tactlessness, and an inability to credit opposing views. At the same time, he was often aware of his pride and was constantly trying—and apparently often succeeding—to subdue his arrogant spirit and to cultivate such Christian virtues as meekness, gentleness, and charity. As was common for eighteenth-century leaders, he was authoritarian, yet he was also extremely caring. He was much loved by those closest to him. His opponents found him aloof, opinionated, and intolerant. For a time he won the hearts of almost everyone in his Northampton parish; then he lost them again in a bitter dispute, a quarrel of former lovers.

My assessments of his theological views are similarly varied. My interest in Edwards arises from my admiration for aspects of his theology. As one committed to a Christian faith in a tradition that is a branch of the same Augustinian and Reformed tree, I find some of Edwards' emphases awe-inspiring. Other aspects seem to me to be brilliant analysis based on false premises. Much else falls in between. Some of his views seem dated. Others are valuable just because they come from another era and challenge assumptions that are today too easily taken for granted. Overall, since I have learned from many of his insights, my attitude toward Edwards' theology is more sympathetic than not. I try to employ that sympathy in providing readers clear accounts of his thought, usually without arguing with him, though sometimes pointing out assumptions or implications I think he did not see. My overall sympathy, then, should not be mistaken for an endorsement of all his views. One reason for careful study of great persons of the past is to be able to learn from them in a discriminating way. Excepting a few comments on the concluding pages, I have attempted to follow my working principle of explaining as best I can Edwards' thought in its historical context, pointing out what I see as especially significant but also allowing readers to make most of their own critical judgments.

In writing a *life* of Edwards I am not attempting a theological work nor even an essentially intellectual biography. While I hope I have adequately integrated his theology and his thought into his life, my approach also reflects my interests as a historian of American culture. My focus is primarily on understanding Edwards as a person, a public figure, and a thinker in his own time and place. Implicit in my presentation is my fascination with how Edwards fits or does not fit with the larger patterns of religion in American life. Since I do not often interrupt the narrative to make such points explicit, I can here suggest to readers some themes to keep in mind.

The largest theme concerns a question that has always been near the center of American experience, but one that is not well integrated into our histories. How does a religion that claims universal and exclusive truth fit into a pluralistic environment? This, of course, is not at all a uniquely American issue. Arguably it was also the central question for British culture in the first half of the eighteenth century. Much of the "Enlightenment" thought of that time was a direct reaction to the conflicting absolutist claims of the preceding era of deadly religious wars. The most explosive issue in British politics was still whether the monarchy would remain Anglican or revert to Roman Catholicism as it had been as recently as 1688 under James II. If Anglican, how should the nation treat Protestant dissenters, whose Puritan forebears had fought a holy war against the Anglican monarch in the 1640s, prospered under Cromwell's dictatorial Commonwealth in the 1650s, and been harshly repressed with the Restoration of Charles II in the 1660s? In the early 1700s all that was hardly forgotten. English dissenters, such as Congregationalists and Presbyterians, enjoyed toleration but were excluded from political office and the universities. In Scotland, joined with England to form the United Kingdom in 1707, the established church was Presbyterian. In this more pluralistic environment many of the leading champions of a more liberal rational Christianity were the heirs to militant Calvinists of the previous era.

Edwards came of age at a time and place that would give him an acute sense of the juxtaposition of old and new outlooks in this revolution taking place in British culture. The son of a strict Calvinistic pastor in the river town of East Windsor, Connecticut, Edwards grew up in a world where many of the ways of seventeenth-century New England Puritanism were preserved pretty much intact. Seventeenth-century Puritanism in turn was in many respects closer to the world of medieval Christendom than it was to that of even nineteenth-century America. Puritanism was part of an international Calvinistic movement to *reform* Christendom, not to destroy it. Its goal had been to establish one pure church supported by each Christian state.

A precocious teenage intellectual who immersed himself in the literature of the emerging British Enlightenment, the world of Locke and Newton and of Addison and Steele, Edwards was confronted with how hopelessly quaint, dated, and even laughable the provincial world of East Windsor would look to British sophisticates. Yet the New Englanders, unlike most provincials, were products of an intellectual tradition that until recently had been as formidable as any in the world and was—as notably represented, for instance by the Edwardses' family acquaintance Cotton Mather—still making heroic efforts to keep in touch. Jonathan, after an early intellectual and spiritual crisis, emerged intensely committed to demonstrating how his heritage was not only viable but *the* answer to all the questions posed by the new world of his day. Those answers were not only intellectual, but also practical, built around awakenings and missions as the engines through which the triune God would eventually bring the modern world to his love in Christ.

Edwards' life presents a particularly dramatic and influential instance of a perennial American story. Countless Americans reared in conservative religious traditions have confronted the troubling issue of how their exclusive faith should relate to a pluralistic modern American environment. That tension has been felt especially among persons in ethno-religious communities— of which the English Puritans were one of the first instances—who brought with them Old World ideals concerning the one true religion. Much of the history of religion in America has been written to emphasize the triumph of pluralism. Perhaps rightly so. That has meant, however, that those who have never conceded the premise that all or most religions, or even most Christian denominations, are more or less equal, have not been taken as seriously in our histories as they might. Even today there are vast numbers of Americans who, although committed to live at peace with other religious groups, believe it is a matter of eternal life or death to convert members of those groups to their own faith. Like it or not, such evangelistic religion has been and continues to be a major part of the experiences of many ordinary Americans. The dynamics of such religious experience need to be understood if one is to understand large tracts of American culture. Indeed, the tensions between religious exclusivism and pluralism are among the leading unresolved issues shaping the twenty-first-century world.

Edwards' eighteenth-century Calvinistic evangelicalism is significant not merely as an early instance of a wider phenomenon, but also because it played a prominent role in subsequent American history. After the American Revolution, New England Calvinism with a deep Edwardsian imprint emerged as one of the most influential movements shaping the new American voluntary religious culture. Edwards' grandson Timothy Dwight was an early leader of resurgent evangelical Calvinism, and Lyman Beecher, progenitor of the famous Beecher family, was one of Dwight's most effective lieutenants. New England Congregationalists and their Presbyterian allies carried the evangelical Calvinist campaigns into the upper "west" (now upper Midwest). By the 1830s their voluntary organizations for missions, evangelism, and reform had combined budgets larger than that of the federal government. Before the Civil War these heirs to the now-contested Edwardsian heritage or their near counterparts controlled most of the nation's leading colleges, including the state "universities." They were leaders in the reform movements, including temperance and antislavery, and were leading figures in the moral reform wing of the Whig Party and then in Republicanism. To cite the best-known example, Harriet Beecher Stowe often wrote about and agonized over her Edwardsian heritage, from which she only gradually departed. On the eve of the Civil War she published a theological novel whose leading character was Edwards' protégé and first biographer, Samuel Hopkins.[6]

Edwards' early eighteenth-century version of the tensions between a rigorous exclusivist Christianity and modern life were very different from those of his nineteenth-century heirs, yet the latter can hardly be understood without knowing about the former. If we are comparing Edwards' wrestlings with such issues to those of his more recent counterparts, the differences are still greater, even if the comparisons may be illuminating. Our sense of encountering perennial cultural themes, or even perennial human themes, always needs to be tempered by a sense of differences among eras.

Historians of the United States have been prone to give much more attention to Benjamin Franklin than to Edwards as a progenitor of modern America. That is understandable since Franklin seems so congenially to represent tendencies that triumph in mainstream American life and politics. Yet a good case can be made that stories of America are deficient if they do not at least temper emphasis on the Franklins of the heritage with a serious reckoning with its Edwardses.[7] Most strikingly, the standard narratives fail to account for why levels of religious practice came to be much higher in the United States than in other modernized nations. They also do little to explain why evangelical Christianity flourished in American and why its revivalist style became one of America's leading exports. The particularities of Edwards' life—so different in many ways from what followed—do not explain all that, even if they shed light on it. Nonetheless, the larger point is that histories of America—or of the modern world for that matter—need to integrate people like Edwards into their accounts.

I have been here emphasizing Edwards' significance in the history of American religion and culture, yet I realize that many readers will also be concerned with something larger. Edwards is, after all, most important as a figure in the history of Christianity. For one thing, although much of his influence has been mediated by his American setting, one should not forget that Edwards was a citizen of the British Empire and part of an international Reformed movement. He is still a revered figure in those circles and in

broader evangelicalism. Theologians continue to debate his insights. How
he is to be evaluated at those levels will depend largely on one's religious
commitments.

The first goal of a biographer, it seems to me, should be to tell a good
story that illuminates not only the subject, but also the landscapes surrounding that person and the horizons of the readers. Unlike specialized studies
that analyze every intellectual issue and historical debate, much of the illumination should come simply from the telling a *story*. That story should
reveal a real person whose successes were achieved in the midst of anxieties,
weaknesses, and failings. The tensions of a life are often what cast most light,
not only on the person but also on the culture and on wider human experience. In the case of renowned thinkers, we also want to understand and learn
from their thought. Once again it is the tensions, both within the thinker's
own tradition and between that tradition and its competitors, that are most
illuminating for understanding the creativity and the limits of the person's
thought.

Edwards was involved with many of the most momentous issues of his
day, and his life does not lack for drama and intrigue. I hope I have successfully uncovered and recounted some of that. A biographer's problem is
that the goal of being comprehensive sometimes competes with the main
story lines. In any life many things are going on at the same time, and some
significant things do not contribute to dramatic narrative as well as others. Yet
the understanding of a life can also be enriched by taking into account the
interconnections among seemingly disparate themes.

I have tried to keep in view Edwards as a person, especially as a person in a
family setting, as I deal with the larger issues. That is more of a challenge than
it would be for some well-documented lives because the overwhelming proportion of his surviving writings deal with theological or ecclesiastical matters. Even his family letters seldom deal with personal matters outside of a
theological framework. That underscores the point that for Edwards one
cannot draw a line between his theological or ecclesiastical roles and the
person in some more essential sense. Edwards' roles were so integrated in his
life that they were basic to who he was. Even so, we know that there was more
beneath that formidable surface and sometimes we do see it. Behind the roles
of theologian, pastor, and preacher that shaped most of his writings, we can
also get enough intimate glimpses of him and his family to gain a sense that
we are dealing with a real person with weaknesses and strengths.

CHAPTER 1

## A Time to Be Born

God accompanied his blessings with warnings of his judgments. Solomon Stoddard, pastor of the river town of Northampton, Massachusetts, knew that well and preached it often. Although he was the most renowned man in the promising valley of the Connecticut River, he knew that no mortal could guarantee the survival of the English on this beleaguered frontier. In 1703 the little towns stretched out along the river were not the peaceful New England villages of later postcards. Many of them looked more like armed garrisons, especially from Northampton north to Deerfield, the region most vulnerable to Indian attacks. Part of Northampton itself was surrounded by a stockade wall and the town was divided into "military divisions."[1] Some families picketed their homes as well, creating an ominous effect almost the reverse of the next century's white picket fences.

Stoddard often served as a spokesman for the western half of Massachusetts. According to legend, the witticism in this hyper-Protestant land was that Stoddard aspired to be the "pope" of the Connecticut Valley.[2] He was at least a formidable presence. Every year he traveled 120 miles to Boston, the capital city, a horseback journey of two-and-a-half days, often preaching at a major public event, either the Harvard commencement or election day. Stoddard was a large, impressive man and a powerful preacher famed for speaking without notes. Sixty years old in 1703, he had come of age in Boston when Oliver Cromwell ruled in England, and he still dressed in the austere Puritan manner.[3] Stoddard disdained the modern fashion of gentlemen wearing wigs. Some of Boston's Congregational clergy now affected such English manners. To him their wigs made them look "as if they were more disposed to court a maid, than to bear upon their hearts the weighty concernments of God's Kingdom."[4] Yet Stoddard was also a man of affairs: his brother was a leading

Boston merchant, the influential Judge Samuel Sewall was a close friend, and governors sought his advice on matters concerning the western regions of the colony.

On May 26, 1703, election day, Stoddard preached "before his excellency, the governour, the honoured Council and Assembly," and his fellow clergy on "The way for a People to Live Long in the Land that God hath Given Them." The subject was survival. The text was the Fifth Commandment: "Honour thy father and thy mother, that thy days may be long upon the land which the Lord thy God giveth thee" (Exodus 20:12). The commandment taught, as the Puritans had conventionally argued, to honor not only parents but "all who are in authority," including civil rulers and clergy. These were God's representatives on earth.[5] To honor them was to honor God. Survival and prosperity depended on honoring God.

The latest threats to New England arose because England was, for the second time in a decade, at war with France. Queen Anne's War renewed two deadly conflicts for the colonists. Most monumental in New Englanders' minds was the contest with Roman Catholicism, with the Antichrist. Under Louis XIV, Catholic France was at its zenith, and New France was on New England's borders. The Sun King revoked the Edict of Nantes in 1685 and drove French Protestants from their homeland. Huguenot refugees in the Boston audience were ready with tales of Catholic cruelty. England, too, it was feared, could revert to becoming a Catholic domain. Although Protestants had ousted the openly Catholic James II in 1688, the question of succession was still in a turmoil. Parliament had declared in 1701 that only Protestants might succeed to the throne, but Queen Anne (r. 1702–14), a Protestant daughter of James, had no surviving children, and Louis XIV supported James' Catholic son, James III, or the "Pretender," as the rightful "King of Great Britain and Ireland." In New England, heirs to the Puritans knew that their liberty and their destiny as a people depended on the triumph of the Protestant cause.

War with France also renewed the more immediate deadly threat of Indian attacks on the colonial frontiers. The New Englanders' most conspicuous failure was their relationship to the natives they were displacing. King Philip's War of 1675–76, the most destructive war in losses per capita in American history, ended early hopes for peaceful relations and successful missions. Many of the surviving Indians were driven into the arms of the French and—worse—their Jesuit missionaries. The 15,000 French residents of New France would have been little threat to the far more numerous New Englanders, except for their Indian allies. Because the French population was small, it had not displaced Indians from their lands, making relations with the natives generally more harmonious and missionary work more effective.[6]

In this wartime setting Stoddard's message to the royal governor and the Massachusetts legislators was what would become classic advice from the American west: keep taxes low and defenses strong. "Do not lay unnecessary burdens on the people, yet be willing to expend what is necessary." "People are in a bad condition" when those who are "to preserve them" are "pillaging of them themselves: when their shepherds prove like evening wolves." Yet at the same time the government "may not decline any necessary [expense for] the safety of the land," lest New England go the way of Carthage and Constantinople, which were lost "through the penuriousness of the people."

The far deeper problem, Stoddard declared, was moral and spiritual. God was punishing New England because its people violated his commandments. The evidence was clear. "God has had a great controversy with the country for many years," Stoddard warned in familiar terms. Stoddard, who could have been a businessman himself, had calculated the economic consequences of God's judgments: "I do judge that a third part of that income, that the country had or might with an ordinary blessing have had, has been taken away by the judgements of God." The only solution was "the work of reformation." "We live in a corrupt age, and multitudes of men take a licentious liberty, in their drinking and apparel, and company, and recreations, and unsavory discourses," Stoddard warned in vintage style. Perhaps with a glance at the powered wigs among the assembled clergy, he added ominously, "and ministers living in an infectious air, are in danger to be infected also." Many people of the land made a "profession of godliness." The clergy must now "labour after their sincere conversion" more effectively.[7]

Stoddard believed that God had brought this people to this promising land with an eternal purpose. God had designed all their earthly blessings and punishments, promises and warnings, to teach them of their need for a higher citizenship, to accept God's free gift of an eternal kingdom. New Englanders should thank God for their temporal blessings, yet they must always bear in mind that they were no better than the people of Old Testament Israel. God, like a loving father, taught them by chastisements as much as by blessings. Israel, New England's model, had lost its land and been carried into captivity.

## Northampton, October 1703

Solomon Stoddard knew well, then, how he should interpret the juxtaposition of earthly emotions that confronted him in early October 1703. Within a week he heard the news from down river, from East Windsor, Connecticut, that his daughter Esther Stoddard Edwards had borne a child—finally a son after four daughters—and he also received an alarming report that threatened family members closer to home. At Deerfield, just fifteen miles to the north, Indians had ambushed two young men and carried them captive into Canada. John Williams, Deerfield's pastor and the Stoddards' son-in-law, had narrowly escaped a similar fate.[8]

Deerfield was in a panic. Stoddard wrote to Governor Joseph Dudley urging further protection and tax relief for the already overburdened town. He also proposed a controversial innovation that was later widely adopted: the colonial government might authorize the training of dogs to help track Indians, who were skilled at disappearing into the woods.[9]

Stoddard had a deep personal stake in the protection of Deerfield in the winter of 1703–4. His stepdaughter, Eunice Mather Williams, had grown up in Stoddard's household after he had married Esther Warham Mather, the widow of Eleazar Mather, Solomon's predecessor at the church in Northampton.[10] Her husband, John Williams, was a leading ministerial ally and a member of the most influential clan in the region. He and Eunice had seven children whom Solomon regarded as his own grandchildren.

## Deerfield, February 1704

John Stoddard was probably as brave as any Harvard graduate was likely to be. Unlike an older brother and many of his classmates who had entered the ministry, the multitalented twenty-two-year-old son of Solomon Stoddard was now a young soldier heading toward a career in which he would eventually become commander of the military and the leading magistrate of the region. Whatever his bravery, when he was startled awake before dawn on February 29, 1704, he knew that the better part of valor was to run. No sooner did he hear the desperate call of his brother-in-law, the Reverend John Williams, than he realized that the house was overrun with Indian warriors—perhaps twenty. He must escape. Grabbing only his greatcoat, he was out the back, barefoot, in two feet of snow. Once he made his way across the Deerfield River, he stopped long enough to cut off the bottom of his coat to cover his nearly frozen feet. He arrived completely exhausted at Hatfield, more than ten miles to the south, with the first news confirming the attack. The river towns had already sounded their alarms when they saw the sky ominously aglow with the fires at Deerfield.[11]

The militia roused to aid the beleaguered town returned with grisly news. The Indians and their French officers had killed 39 of Deerfield's some 300 residents and carried away another 112 through the deep snows as captives to Canada. For the Stoddards, the news, when it was all pieced together, was especially grim. In the early assault the Indians killed two of the Williams' children, six-week-old Jerusha and six-year-old John Jr. in front of their horrified parents. Their mother, Eunice (the Stoddards' daughter), recovering from childbirth and now further burdened by inexpressible grief, faltered and fell crossing a river on the second day of the trek to Canada. An Indian warrior put her out of her misery "with his hatchet at one stroke." The Reverend John Williams and his surviving children were taken as captives to Canada.[12]

The attack on Deerfield—to New Englanders, a terrorist massacre of innocents (even if the displaced Indians saw it as a justified act of war)—was the defining event of the era, especially for families of the victims, such as the Stoddards.[13] Over a year later Esther Mather Stoddard was still reeling from images of the slaughter of her daughter and two grandchildren. These losses were compounded by the sudden death of a son and by more recent news that another close family member, taken captive at sea, had died in France. "What shall I say?" she wrote to her daughter Esther Stoddard Edwards in East Windsor. "It becomes me Aaron-like to hold my peace. God grant that I may, with Job, come as gold out of the fire when I have been tried." The mother went on to remind her daughter to be prepared for death at any moment. "The time is short, and it may be very short to us that remains, as was to your sister and brother. One day made a great change in my dear daughter's condition." Her best consolation was that her son-in-law the Reverend John Williams, though still in captivity, had sent a letter assuring the family of the spiritual condition of his slain wife. "Son Williams is satisfied that she is now in glory."[14]

## East Windsor: Later That Same Era

Jonathan Edwards' earliest memories were shaped in this wartime setting. Although East Windsor, a small river town near Hartford, Connecticut, was far enough from the frontier to be safe from attack, the continuing war was ever present in defining who he, his family, and his people were. The family gathered for prayers several times a day. In their repeated entreaties he learned not only of distant conflicts, but also that the encounters were not simply

An East Windsor house dating from the era when Edwards was growing up

among the English, the French, and their Indian allies. The real war was among spiritual powers, a nation God had favored with true religion versus peoples in Satan's grip, Catholics and pagans.

Retellings of the Deerfield massacre vividly reinforced this understanding of the cosmic significance of the international struggles. Since before Jonathan could remember, family prayers included petitions for his Uncle Williams of Deerfield and cousins, captive in Canada. After Williams and two of his three remaining captive children returned in fall 1706, petitions continued for the one remaining child, Eunice (aged seven at the time of her capture), still with the Indians and, far worse, reportedly under Romish delusions.

By the time the precocious Jonathan was old enough to read, he would have discovered that one of the most fascinating books in his father's library was his uncle's *The Redeemed Captive, Returning to Zion*. John Williams' best-selling narrative vividly recounted the horrors of the Indian attack, the agony of seeing two children killed and losing his wife, and the pain of his long captivity among the Indians and French in Canada. Williams' story highlighted the deviltry of the inventions of Rome, the judgment of God on papal superstitions, and the awful plight of the souls of the poor Indians subject to the deceptions of the Antichrist.[15]

Queen Anne's War (which lasted until 1713) touched the Edwards family directly and almost disastrously. In summer 1711, when Jonathan was in his eighth year, his father, the Reverend Timothy Edwards, set out from home to serve as a chaplain for a colonial military expedition against Canada. Timothy Edwards was an extraordinarily meticulous, careful man, always concerned to control every detail. He was not suited for military life. Almost immediately he fell ill with a nervous stomach. He started to keep a campaign diary, but he soon became so preoccupied with the symptoms of his illness and his spiritual well-being that he recorded little about the campaign. By the time the army reached its staging ground in Albany, he was too ill to go on and feared he might die. Eventually he was shipped by wagon back to East Windsor where he soon recovered.[16]

Although the Reverend Timothy Edwards' time "in the queen's service" was less than glorious, he was a formidable figure in his own domains—his home and his church. Jonathan, his only son, followed closely in his father's footsteps. One might think of Leopold and Wolfgang Amadeus Mozart, later in the century, for a partial analogy. The father was accomplished in his own right and controlling. The son was precocious and eventually outshone his father, but his achievements were also a tribute to the father's careful tutelage and continuing looming influence.

## The Edwards Household

Timothy Edwards' letters home while he was serving as chaplain in 1711 provide our best picture of the Edwards household. The first of these letters, written to his wife, Esther, within a week of leaving home, is filled with admonitions. At the top of the list is the instruction for Jonathan's schooling: "I desire you to take care that Jonathan don't lose what he has learned but that as he has got the accidence, and above two sides of *propria Quae moribus* by heart so that he keep what he has got." The older sisters were helping in the Latin lessons and learning that language, which usually set apart the class of educated men, primarily for their brother's benefit. So their father continues, "I would therefore have him say pretty often to the girls; I would also have the girls keep what they have learned of the grammar, and get by heart as far as Jonathan has learned: he can help them to read as far as he has learned: and would have both him and them keep their writing, and therefore write much oftener than they did when I was at home."[17]

The scene that this letter depicts reminds us also that, while Timothy Edwards was unquestionably the head of the household, Jonathan was growing up in a home that was, practically speaking, a world of women. In addition to his mother, he had four older sisters in 1711 and three younger. Eventually he would have six younger sisters. All eleven children would, remarkably, survive childhood. Timothy Edwards, who was more given to witticisms than the son, later referred to them as his "sixty-feet of daughters." Even allowing room for exaggeration, this was a tall family in an era when the average heights were far less than today. Jonathan, who would grow to be over six feet but strikingly thin as an adult, was probably spindly as a child.

We can only speculate as to what effect living in such a feminine environment had on Jonathan. He did have several male cousins, including one his age, living next door, and there were many other boys in East Windsor, a village of close to a hundred households of large families. Nevertheless, he seems to have been close to his sisters. They were an accomplished group. New England's elite encouraged their daughters to develop their intellectual gifts as these were useful for religion. The biblical figure of Mary who listened to Jesus' discourses, rather than helping her sister Martha in the kitchen, was a favorite Puritan model for women's learning—even though the care of family and home was their primary calling. Collegiate education was reserved strictly for men, yet in a pastor's household girls might be encouraged to learn all they could appropriate to their station. The Edwardses also sent all but one of Jonathan's sisters to Boston for finishing school. The eldest daughter, Esther, apparently wrote a satirical piece called "The Soul," which was long attributed to Jonathan.[18] A younger sister, Jerusha, was said to have great delight in books and especially in theology.[19] Another younger sister, Hannah, who did not marry until her thirties, remarked that women may find the single state a great advantage "if they can make religion and knowledge their chief end." One of the other younger sisters, Martha, apparently was not so easy to get along with. When a clergyman suitor asked Timothy for her hand, the father warned him of her temperament. The suitor persisted, pointing out that he had heard Martha had received God's converting grace. "Oh yes, yes," Timothy replied, "Martha is a good girl but . . . the grace of God will dwell where you or I cannot!"[20]

While we would like to know more about the sisters, especially about the older girls who took care of Jonathan, we can be sure that as the family's only boy in a culture where males had many prerogatives, he was doted over and soon deferred to. One of the overarching rules of life was that everyone must respect God-ordained orders of society. Puritans did insist on the spiritual equality of all before God, but they carefully limited the applications of that potentially revolutionary doctrine in their social relationships. They also stressed the bonds of affection between superiors and inferiors. The affections and piety of some of his sisters may have been early lessons in his own cultivation of such sensibilities. Many commentators on Edwards have remarked on how often, in his later accounts of true religious affections and remarkable piety, he used women or girls to illustrate his point.

Jonathan's mother, Esther Stoddard Edwards, was a formidable presence in her own right, but it is symptomatic of those times that we know little about her. What we do know is largely from what was recalled from much later in her long life (she outlived both her husband and her son by twelve years). East Windsor villagers remembered her as "tall, dignified and commanding in appearance" yet "affable and gentle in her manners" and as of impressive intelligence, learning, and theological acumen. Solomon Stoddard had sent his daughter to finishing school in Boston. As a young mother Esther assisted her husband in teaching their children and those of the town in a small school that occupied one of the two large downstairs rooms in their farmhouse. As an old woman, after her husband died, she remained an avid reader and teacher. Until she was in her nineties, women of East Windsor regularly came to afternoon sessions in the old parlor–school room for readings of the Bible and theological writers punctuated by her acute commentary.[21]

Nevertheless, whatever the talents of Solomon Stoddard's daughter, it went without saying that Esther was a subordinate in Timothy Edwards' household. For Puritans, as for almost everyone else, the axiom that the world was hierarchical was as unquestionable as that the sun rose in the east. Fathers were the heads of their households and their rule was law. The household was also an economy in which everyone shared. The Edwardses farmed a number of acres of land to supplement their income. They used some of this land for orchards and some for crops such as flax, which the women could make into linen yarn, and they kept some cattle.[22] Hospitality was an important virtue and the crowded household often included guests.

To help with this work, the Edwardses always had an African slave. Household slaves were particularly common among New England clergy, both because of a pastor's social status and because the head of the house was not primarily engaged in physical labor. The enslavement of Africans could take root in seventeenth-century New England not only because even the most pious were not exempt from human cupidity but also because other sorts of enslavements had been common for so long and were taken for granted in Scripture. Even so, by 1700 at least some whites recognized the unusual inequities of African slavery. Solomon Stoddard's Boston friend Judge Samuel Sewall raised the issue most forcefully in *The Selling of Joseph: A Memorial* (Boston, 1700). Yet Sewall's unusual views created only a ripple. Cotton Mather, whom Timothy Edwards knew and admired, probably represented the majority when he justified slavery as an opportunity for converting Africans to the Gospel. Mather also campaigned for treating slaves kindly as fellow humans.[23] If some New England slave owners had uneasy consciences, their most common way of dealing with the subject was to avoid it; so the topic received little more public discussion until the era of the American Revolution.

In a household economy where family members shared many tasks, Puritan fathers—as Timothy Edwards' wartime letters suggests—played a significant role in overseeing the discipline and spiritual nurture of the children. Children's natural selfishness, greed, and disobedience were everyday reminders that the human race was corrupt, inheriting sinful natures from their first parents, Adam and Eve. Likely the elder Edwardses subscribed to the principle of suppressing any signs of willfulness, although Puritan practices of childrearing varied and often included more displays of warm affection than is sometimes depicted. For those whose first concern was to prepare their children for salvation, the most loving thing a parent could do was to teach children the disciplines that would open them to receive a truly submissive spirit. Ultimately that could come only through the regenerating grace of God, but habits of obedience to God's commands could pave the way. As John Wesley, who was also born in 1703 and reared with similar rigor in an English parsonage, put it, "Break their wills that you may save their souls."[24]

Timothy's wartime letters reveal that Jonathan at age seven was not the perfect child. "I hope you will take special care of Jonathan," Timothy urged Esther, "that he doesn't learn to be rude and naught[y] etc. of which you and I have lately discoursed. I wouldn't have you venture him to ride out into the woods with Tim." This same letter is especially revealing of some characteristics of the father that shaped the son. No detail is too small to escape Timothy's attention and advice. "Let care be taken that the cattle don't get into the orchard and wrong the trees. And that the barn door ben't left open to the cattle." Be sure the "dung be carried out and laid in the orchard where there is most need before winter and that the flax be not spoiled." And so on and so forth. One suspects the family had heard these admonitions before. Or that, "if any of the children should at any time go over the river to meeting I would have them be exceedingly careful, how they sit or stand in the boat lest they should fall in the river." Even what we might assumed would be his wife's domain comes under his purview: "And let Esther and Betty [the two oldest girls] take their powders as soon as the dog days are over, and if they don't help Esther, talk further with the doctor about her. . . . Something also should be done for Anne who as thou knowest is weakly: and take care of thyself, and don't suckle little Jerusha too long."[25]

If such advice suggests overmanaging, even in matters that might be thought Esther's domain, it also reveals an affectionate father who is homesick and is thinking about everyone. Timothy's letters are filled with expressions of deep love for Esther and the children. In one he writes, "Remember my love to each of the children," and then mentions each of the first seven by name, "Esther, Elizabeth, Anne, Mary, Jonathan, Eunice and Abigail." He goes on: "The Lord have mercy on and eternally save them all, with our dear little Jerusha. The Lord bind up their souls with thine and mine in the bundle of life." Ask the children, he continues, "if they desire to see their father again, to pray daily for me in secret; and above all things to seek the grace and favor of God in Christ, and that while they are young."[26] In a later sermon Timothy preached that a husband's love for his wife should be a "singular peculiar thing," that displayed the "honor and respect" she deserved. He should "not act magisterial or lordly, but in a loving manner with due respect to his wife."[27]

At the same time the loving father was not indulgent to his children. After his own father died in 1718, Timothy made the best of his grief by writing privately for his "soul's profit and comfort" an eighty-eight-page tribute and spiritual biography. He observed approvingly that his father did not "favor" his children: "Yea his spirit (though he loved them dearly) was more stirred against that which is evil in them than in such as were but neighbors."[28] Everything we know about Timothy Edwards suggests an intensely disciplined perfectionist, a worrier about details, a firm authoritarian who was nonetheless capable of good humor and warm affections toward his family.[29] Jonathan Edwards never entirely escaped the hold this demanding yet affectionate father had over him. He followed closely in his father's footsteps and, except for greater reserve, closely resembled his father in standards and attitudes.

It is not hard to guess one source of the family's perfectionist discipline. Timothy had learned from *his* father to use exacting discipline to overcome adversity. Timothy's great-grandfather had been a clergyman in Wales and then rector of a school in England, but his death in 1625 had brought the family into poverty. In 1635 the family migrated to Massachusetts and settled in Hartford, joining Thomas Hooker's migration to the new western colony. Timothy's father, Richard, born in Hartford in 1647, brought the family back to some financial success, turning a cooper's trade into a prosperous merchant business.

Timothy's mother, however, was a scandal and a disgrace. Three months after she married Richard Edwards, in 1667, Elizabeth Tuthill (or Tuttle) revealed that she was pregnant by another man. Richard nonetheless protected her by paying the fine for fornication himself and arranging to have the child raised by her parents. The problem proved to be much deeper. Elizabeth was afflicted with a serious psychosis. She was given to fits of perversity "too grievous to forget and too much here to relate," repeated infidelities, rages, and threats of violence, including the threat to cut Richard's throat while he was asleep. The Tuthill family was evidence that New England was not the staid place that we might imagine, but rather one where humans suffered the same horrors found in any era. One of Elizabeth's sisters murdered her own child, and a brother killed another sister with an ax.[30] Jonathan Edwards is sometimes criticized for having too dim a view of human nature, but it may be helpful to be reminded that his grandmother was an incorrigible profligate, his great-aunt committed infanticide, and his great-uncle was an ax-murderer.

Elizabeth Tuthill Edwards' condition worsened with the burden of bearing six children to Richard, of whom Timothy was the eldest. Eventually she deserted her family for a number of years, staying away from Richard's bed when she returned. By 1688 her behavior became so erratic that Richard did something almost unheard of in New England: he sued for divorce. He had suffered, he told the court, from "afflictions, discontents, jealousies, the rage of man, with horrible confusions, distractions, with intricate, heart-breaking miseries, the most pinching pressures of spirit that have been my meat day and night."[31]

Despite these agonizing circumstances, the court refused Richard's request. After more years of suffering, he presented his case again, and this time the court relented, granting the divorce on the advice of a council of ministers. From then on Richard's situation improved dramatically. He joined the Hartford church. Still in his forties, he married a second wife, who bore him six more children. Richard, always a man of learning as well of piety, read law and in 1708 was appointed "Queen's attorney." He became particularly noted for some cases he pleaded for the Pequot Indians.[32]

In the meantime Timothy, who came by his apprehensive disposition honestly, had been groomed by his father to go to college to prepare for the ministry. He entered Harvard in 1686. Early in 1688 he left the college, apparently expelled. All we know is that an "ominous" mark was entered next to his name in the "Severe Punishments" column of the Harvard records. The best guess is that this had something to do with his father's first divorce proceedings, which began about the same time. Everything else we know about Timothy is of a meticulously disciplined perfectionist, and this episode did not ruin his reputation in the long run or divert him from his plans for a ministerial career. He continued his studies under the private tutelage of the Reverend Peletiah Glover in Springfield, Massachusetts, just north of Hartford. Timothy was a most able student, and in 1694 Harvard recognized his accomplishments by granting him both his belated B.A. and a M.A. (the latter a degree routinely granted for three years of some study, usually on one's own, beyond the four-year B.A.).[33]

Timothy was proving himself to all who knew him and fast overcoming any stigma that may have been attached to his family background or the Harvard episode. Puritans were strict, but they were also strictly forgiving if the circumstances warranted. Timothy's dramatic rise in status came with the imprimatur of none other than Solomon Stoddard, who in 1694 granted him permission to marry his second daughter, Esther. By this time the Stoddards knew Timothy well because he was teaching school in Northampton. Everything quickly fell into place for the promising young man: Harvard granted him his degrees, and a new parish, called Windsor Farms or East Windsor, across the Connecticut River from Windsor and not far from his native Hartford, called him to be its pastor.

Esther, the new bride, was the granddaughter of John Warham, well remembered as the sometimes controversial first pastor in Windsor, so she was already part of one of the leading families of the original town. Richard Edwards, who must have been delighted not only to have his children settled nearby but also with this second great upturn in the family's position, gave the new couple farmlands and a very adequate house. Their home stood along the one long road of East Windsor, paralleling the Connecticut and overlooking the fertile floodplain, the river in the distance and the roofs of Windsor beyond that. Soon there were grandchildren much the same age as Richard's second family. Timothy and Esther named Jonathan after the first son of Richard's second marriage, a child who had died in infancy.[34]

# CHAPTER 2

# The Overwhelming Question

Timothy Edwards was an effective preacher of revival. According to Jonathan's later estimation, of all the pastors in the region, only his grandfather, Solomon Stoddard, oversaw more local awakenings. In his famous account of the "Surprising Work of God" of 1734–35 in Northampton, Jonathan recorded that there had been "four or five" outpourings of the Spirit in "my honored father's parish, which has in times past been a place favored with mercies of this nature above any on this western side of New England, excepting Northampton."[1] So the father more directly than the grandfather set the footsteps in which Jonathan would try to follow. Timothy's reputation as a revivalist eventually faded in the light of his son's prominence. One difference was that he did not publicize his successes. Like many locally influential persons who are later forgotten, he relied on personal presence and the spoken word.

In 1712 and 1713, about a year after Timothy Edwards returned from the war, his preaching precipitated one of these awakenings. Jonathan marked the beginning of his own notable spiritual experiences from the time of this revival. His account, written much later, when he was a renowned evangelist, is inevitably stylized. Nonetheless, it provides evidence not only of the events themselves but also of Edwards' critical understanding of the meanings of his youthful experiences. When he was only nine years old, he recounted, he experienced the first of "two more remarkable seasons of awakening, before I met that change, by which I was brought to those new dispositions, and that new sense of things, that I have had since." For months the nine-year-old was a model of sanctity. He prayed secretly five times a day, spoke much of religion to other boys, and organized prayer meetings with them. "My mind was much engaged in it," he recalled, "and had much self-righteous pleasure;

and it was my delight to abound in religious duties." He and his schoolmates "built a booth in a swamp, in a very secret and retired place, for a place of prayer." He also had his own secret places in the woods where he would retire "and used to be from time to time much affected." Eventually, the nine-year-old lad "entirely lost all those affections and delights" and "returned like a dog to his vomit, and went on in ways of sin."[2]

Timothy Edwards was an expert on the science of conversion. Nothing was more challenging than to be able to tell what was truly a work of God and what was self-deception. Nothing had more resting on it. Conversion was not just an euphoria of enthusiasm; emotions were deceptive and sure to change. Evidences of God's work had to be substantial and lasting. Like eighteenth-century observers of nature, Timothy kept records of the indications of spiritual experiences among his parishioners and knew exactly what to look for. In observing the state of souls, the East Windsor pastor was drawing on more than a century of highly developed Puritan science. Yet the object of this science—whether an apparent spiritual experience was a work of God or a Satanic imitation—was notoriously elusive. Satan's favorite device was self-deception. Self-generated religious enthusiasm could look like the real thing for a time but soon would fade away. So Timothy Edwards would not have been at all surprised by his nine-year-old son's falling from his self-generated enthusiasm for spiritual things or at finding that Jonathan and the other boys had reverted to pretending to fight Indians from their secret hideout in the woods.

Timothy Edwards, following Puritan precedents, emphasized three principal steps toward true conversion. First was "conviction" or "an awakening sense of a person's sad estate with reference to eternity."[3] The term that the Reverend Edwards used for this first, but insufficient, step was "awakening." We must notice that usage because "awakening" is the most common term used for periodic outbreaks of religious enthusiasm in New England congregations. An "awakening" was no guarantee of salvation. Jonathan described his ephemeral boyhood experience as one of "two more remarkable seasons of *awakening*."

Recognition of the precariousness of both life and death, a "sense of a person's sad estate with reference to eternity," as Timothy Edwards phrased it, often precipitated an initial awakening. Much of Puritan upbringing was designed to teach children to recognize how insecure their lives were. Every child knew of brothers, sisters, cousins, or friends who had suddenly died. Cotton Mather, under whose preaching Timothy had once sat, eventually lost thirteen of his fifteen children. Parents nightly reminded their children that sleep was a type of death and taught them such prayers as "This day is past; but tell me who can say / That I shall surely live another day." The *New England Primer* illustrated the letter "T" with "Time cuts down all, both great and small" and a woodcut of the grim reaper. "Y" was "Youth forward slips, Death soonest nips" with a woodcut of Death holding a large arrow at a child's head.[4] One of the Edwards children's surviving writing exercises reads, "Nothing is more certain than death. Take no delay in the great work of preparing for death."[5]

If life was uncertain and frightening, eternity was more so. Parents who themselves experienced God's saving grace and who lost children in infancy might have hopes in God's covenant promises of mercy from generation to generation. Young children might have saving grace, even if they did not live long enough for it to come to fruition in identifiable signs of conversion. One nighttime prayer (a form of which has long survived) was "Lord, if my Soul this night away thou take, / Let me by morning then in Heav'n awake."[6] Yet no child was innocent or worthy of anything but eternal damnation. All were totally depraved. Not only would they sin as soon as they could, but they were also born guilty of the sins of the race. "In Adam's fall, we sinned all," was the first lesson in the *New England Primer*. Children soon learned that in their natural state they deserved the flames of hell. Only God's mysterious grace might rescue them.

Timothy Edwards, like the vast majority of New England's preachers, was convinced he must not flinch from warning sinners of the dangers of falling into unending hellish tortures. Timothy recorded how a parishioner named Abigail Rockwell had been first awakened "from hearing such a question expressed in a sermon to unconverted sinners, namely, can you bear to live half an hour in fire, and if not how can you bear to live in hell to all eternity." Joshua Wallis Jr., a local farmer, reported how he was "stirred . . . to take more pains for an interest in Christ" by "fears of falling into the hands of an angry God."[7]

To benefit from these awful warnings sinners had to reach the second step toward true conversion, which was humiliation. Normally, following the first enthusiasm of their awakening, they would experience a backsliding into sin that would lead them to realize the terribleness of their sins and that God would be entirely just in condemning them to hell. Sometimes this stage was described as involving a sense of "terror." Puritan authors offered many complex lists of steps, and Timothy's standard was relatively flexible and simple in emphasizing only three essential steps—but he does seem to have insisted on these, particularly this one. Potential converts not only had to recognize their guilt deserving eternal flames, but be "truly humbled" by a total sense of their unworthiness.[8]

Only then was one sufficiently prepared to reach the third step—if God graciously granted it—of receiving God's regenerating "light," or a "new spirit created in them," so that they truly repented and sin would no longer reign in them, but rather they would be guided by the Holy Spirit "dwelling in them" and they would receive the gift of faith in Christ alone as their hope of salvation and would experience a "glorious change" to a life dedicated to serving God. Following stricter Puritan practice, Timothy Edwards required prospective communicant church members to give a public profession of their experience, which would follow this essential pattern.[9]

It is essential to notice that in this Calvinist scheme of things God's grace could not be controlled. Puritans, like others in the Reformed tradition, were insistent on giving God credit for everything. God's saving grace was in no way a reward for good works. Truly good works, or works motivated by true love to God, were possible only for the regenerate, and even then they were tinged by the remnants of one's inherited sinful nature. Even faith itself, though a positive act of receiving God's free gift of salvation, was not the efficient cause of salvation but only a necessary means by which one received the gift as one's own.[10]

Unable to control God's grace, one could at best prepare oneself to be in a position to receive it. So the steps leading through the gradual process of conversion were steps of "preparation." The irony of the rigorous discipline was that one could not take any pride in successfully following it. One sign of being on the road to conversion was to strive fervently to keep God's law, but it was only when sinners came to realize their total inability to succeed in keeping that law that they would be prepared truly to depend on God's grace. Seldom has there been a spiritual discipline where so much effort was put into recognizing the worthlessness of one's own efforts.

Rigorous disciplines combined with a recognition of one's inability to follow them also characterized the lives of Christians after conversion. Like John Bunyan's pilgrim, one would constantly be discovering one's wayward-ness and the deceitfulness of one's residual old self even after the change of heart in regeneration.[11] Following the straight and narrow was hard work, but ultimately any success in it was a matter of God's grace. So Timothy Edwards and his contemporaries often used the prescription of "preparation" not only regarding the steps toward conversion, but also to describe how to seek God's grace at other stages in Christian experience. One needed to be properly submitted to God or "prepared" for the Sabbath, or for partaking of the Lord's Supper, or when seeking the Holy Spirit in prayer. All of life was preparation for death and eternal judgment.[12]

Despite their doctrines of grace, New England Calvinists, such as the Edwardses, worked constantly at trying to regulate their own lives and those of others by God's law. Keeping the law of God was part of God's original "covenant of works" with Adam and the human race. Nations and individuals were still blessed or punished according to that standard. Civil law accordingly should reflect God's commands, as in upholding true religion or requiring Sabbath observance. God's moral law, as summarized in the Ten Commandments, was also an essential guide to unregenerate persons seeking salvation. The law was a "schoolmaster" showing how far short of fulfilling God's covenant one's efforts came. Those under the "covenant of grace," whose salvation was purchased by Christ's perfect obedience and sacrifice, still had to be guided by the law. Even though they too would be reminded daily of their imperfections, their willingness to strive to keep God's commands would be an important evidence of conversion.[13]

## The Church and Its Sacraments

Although Puritans aspired to make all of life a ritual of obedience to God's commands, they drastically reduced the formal rituals of the church. Rigorously following the principle that "the Bible alone" should guide Christian life and worship, they observed only two formal sacraments, baptism and the Lord's Supper. These were, as the authoritative Westminster Confession of Faith of 1646 put it, "holy signs and seals of the covenant of grace."[14] These holy signs and seals were also the gateways to membership in the church, which was to be made up of those persons who were under the covenant of grace, as much as that could be determined. Since seventeenth-century New England Puritans found it so difficult to determine who was truly converted, they were never able to settle entirely the questions of who should have access to the sacraments or be regarded as part of the church.

Much of the problem arose from conflicting traditions that shaped their determinations of who should receive the two sacraments. Baptizing infants, based on the analogy to Old Testament circumcision and reflecting the long heritage of Christendom, suggested an inclusive Christian nation. Restricting the Lord's Supper to visible saints, or those who could give evidence of conversion, suggested a New Testament church separated from the rest of the nation. In the early days of Massachusetts, Roger Williams had pointed out what he saw as a contradiction in these two models and had attempted to resolve the tensions by following only the *New Testament* example of a separated church, denying that God any longer dealt with nations as such. After his exile to Rhode Island in 1636, he followed the logic of his position by becoming, at least briefly, a Baptist, or one who refused to baptize infants and confined that rite only to converted adults.[15]

The dominant early New England leadership successfully marginalized Williams and the Baptists, but the inherent tensions in their views of the sacraments (and of the church and society) soon led to sharp disputes over the emotionally charged question of whose children to baptize. Under the initial impulse to institute a pure church, the early New Englanders baptized children only if the parents were full communicant members of the church. But they soon faced a troubling question. What happened if those baptized children grew to adulthood but were never certifiably converted, even though they might be upstanding in other respects? Should the children of these half-way (baptized) church members be baptized? If God's covenant, as the Old Testament clearly said, extended to many generations, how could the grandchildren of the regenerate be denied the sacrament? After much debate, a synod of clergy declared in 1662 that children of half-way members could be baptized. New England churches, however, were congregational and so were not subject to synods. Practice might differ from one church to the next or one pastor to the next. It took much more debate before this "half-way covenant" was generally accepted by New England clergy, as it was even by the conservative Timothy Edwards.[16]

By 1700 the sacramental debate had shifted to a new front, the question of communicant membership or of who should partake of the Lord's Supper, and at the center of this new controversy was Timothy's father-in-law, the redoubtable Solomon Stoddard. Northampton's renowned pastor shocked the New England establishment by challenging their practice of allowing only those who showed convincing evidence of conversion to become communicants or full members of a congregation. Instead, he adopted the practice followed by some Presbyterian and Reformed churches of opening the table to persons who professed Christian belief and whose lives were free from scandal. Stoddard offered several reasons. First, it was too hard to tell exactly who was converted. The external church would never be perfectly coextensive with the body of believers anyway. Second, the Lord's Supper was a means of grace, so that opening it to sincere upright people might foster their conversions. Stoddard, a proven champion of revival in Northampton, insisted that the sacrament itself could be "a converting ordinance."

Stoddard saw opening up communicant membership as part of a larger program of strengthening the role of the church and the clergy in the community. The concern was a common one for clergy, especially in the period after Massachusetts lost its original charter in the 1680s. Although the colony secured a new charter in 1692, it was now under a royal governor. No longer, as in the early Puritan days, could the church look to the state to do its bidding. To strengthen the role of the clergy, Stoddard favored a more "Presbyterian" form of church government, or government by regional associations of clergy rather than by congregations. Unlike most Presbyterians, though, he followed a New England trend toward diminishing the role of lay ruling elders.[17] Extending communicant church membership to most citizens in a town would also strengthen the control of the clergy over the citizens.

Solomon Stoddard's proposed solution to New England's conundrum regarding the sacraments, the church, and society cut through the knot from almost the opposite direction of Roger Williams. Instead of putting all the emphasis on the New Testament church, Stoddard insisted that the church and society should be modeled even more than before on the Old Testament. Not only were the people under a national covenant, but the church and the people of the nation (or, in this case, a province,) should be, more or less, coextensive. In other words, the essence of a nation should be a true national church.

Virtually everyone in a parish would be baptized and hence under the direct discipline of the church and its pastor. As Stoddard put it in his fullest exposition of his plan, *The Doctrine of the Instituted Churches* (1700), "If a Christian live in a Town where there is a church, he is immediately bound to join with that church; and that church is bound to him to govern him."[18]

New England was almost as divided over Stoddard's opening up of communicant membership as it had been over the half-way covenant. While most of the clergy shared Stoddard's concerns about strengthening their roles and retaining a national covenant, New Englanders took their sacraments seriously. At communion services New England pastors read the warning text (I Corinthians 11:29): "For he that eateth and drinketh unworthily, eateth and drinketh damnation to himself, not discerning the Lord's body." Partaking unworthily could imperil one's soul. Many laypeople, even when urged to become communicants by their pastors, refused to do so on the ground that they feared they might not be truly converted.[19]

One of Stoddard's ministerial critics was Edward Taylor (ca. 1645–1729) of Westfield, Massachusetts, some twenty miles north and west of East Windsor. Taylor is remembered for his remarkable poetry, written for his own edification, often in preparation for communion. "Lord, blow the Coal," Taylor prayed in a typical communion prayer, "Thy Love Enflame in me."[20] Such intense communion piety was common among laity as well as clergy.[21] To Taylor, Stoddard was demeaning the sacrament by encouraging people to partake, when there was no live coal in their heart that could be so inflamed. Taylor publicly attacked Stoddard's views and admonished him personally for proposing to open the Lord's Supper to "all above fourteen years of age, that live morally, and have catechisical knowledge of the principals of religion."[22] Privately he confided to his poetry notebooks the greater danger of returning to the degeneracy of the national Church of England, ruled by bishops or prelates:

> Apostasy wherewith thou art thus driven
> Unto the tents of Presbyterianism
> (Which is refined Prelacy at best) . . .
>
> Where open Sinners vile unmasked indeed
> Are welcome Guests (if they can say the Creed)
> Unto Christ's Table.[23]

In Boston Stoddard's leading opponents were the Mathers, Increase and his irrepressible son Cotton, who also hinted that Stoddard was on the road toward making himself into a "congregational Pope."[24] During the first decade of the century the Mathers helped keep the local printers in business as they hammered away at the dangers of "brother" Stoddard's opening of communion to the merely upright. Increase referred to Stoddard as "brother" not only in the Christian sense but because the Northampton pastor was married to Esther Warham Mather, widow of Increase's brother Eleazar. In 1714, after years of controversy and a dozen titles on the two sides, the two "brothers" made peace, although they could not settle the controversy. As with much else in New England church policy, the matter was left to the potentially contentious vicissitudes of local option.[25]

Timothy Edwards was caught in the middle of all this. He had been influenced by the Mathers, whose works he continued to revere, and he shared their views on requiring credible evidence of conversion for communicant church membership. He also shared with his ministerial neighbor and friend Edward Taylor a strong sense of the necessity of guarding the sanctity of the sacrament. His difference with Solomon Stoddard on the issue was both a question of theology and a family matter. Apparently the son-in-law and the father-in-law found enough in common on other matters, such as zeal for revival and a strong role for the clergy, that they could live with their differences over the sacrament. Timothy Edwards, however, was not one to give in to his formidable father-in-law, or to anyone else, on a matter of high principle.[26]

## The Quest

Even after his boyish religious experience proved ephemeral, Jonathan remained fascinated by the eternally momentous question of conversion. The first writing we have from him is a letter, written in 1716, when he was twelve, to his next oldest and favorite sister, Mary, recounting the remarkable awakening going on in their father's parish. "Through the wonderful mercy and goodness of God," he wrote, "there hath in this place been a very remarkable stirring and pouring out of the Spirit of God, and likewise now is, but I think I have reason to think it is in some measure diminished, but I hope not much. About thirteen have been joined to the church in an estate of full communion."[27]

The East Windsor awakening was more than an ordinary event. Stephen Williams, who as a boy had been one of the Deerfield captives in Canada and was now a young pastor in the neighboring town of Longmeadow, Massachusetts, noted in his diary that there was "an extraordinary stir among the people at East Windsor—many were crying what shall we do to be saved."[28] Jonathan's own account records that "commonly a-Mondays above thirty persons to speak with father about the conditions of their souls." A good proportion of the some hundreds of townspeople were seeking grace, even though, at the time Jonathan wrote, only thirteen had met Timothy Edwards' high standards and "joined to the church in an estate of full communion."[29]

As in his relationship to his family, Timothy Edwards as pastor tempered meticulous rigor with engaging warmth. Even in ordinary times, Timothy spent considerable time counseling, reflecting a sociable trait that his son did not acquire.[30] He was also an effective preacher. Unlike his son, he was first of all a speaker, rather than a writer. In East Windsor, the "customary remark" of those who later often heard the son as well as the father preach was that

"Mr. Jonathan was the deeper preacher" yet "Mr. Edwards was perhaps the more learned man, and more animated in his manner."[31]

Timothy Edwards was also a disciplinarian who set high standards for everyone. His reputation for learning was based on his library that contained many spiritual classics, on his mastery of Scripture, and on being a skilled teacher of the classics who successfully prepared a number of the boys of the town for college. One of his former students recalled that when he arrived at college the officers remarked that they had no need to examine Mr. Edwards' students.[32]

Such perfectionism could be a mixed blessing when expressed in the official capacity of God's ordained overseer of the morals of the community. He was remembered in East Windsor as a formal and fastidious man who would never be seen in public without his full clerical garb.[33] He took seriously his role as the guardian of the behavior of the village. Like other Puritan clergy, he railed against the inevitable vices of drunkenness, lasciviousness, "a rude vain conversation in any respect," and such sins of youth as "nightwalking," and "vain company-keeping." He also followed the custom of reinforcing community standards by bringing notorious violators before the congregation where they were publicly shamed as he read their confessions.[34] Although it was not out of the ordinary for ministers to play such authoritarian roles, it meant that villagers' affections toward them could easily change from love to hate. In later years Timothy Edwards enjoyed other revivals, but he also sometimes saw his relationship with the town deteriorate into bitter antagonisms—once again setting a course his son would follow.[35]

We can imagine the strict attentions that such an exacting mentor must have directed toward preparing his only son for the ministry. In matters academic the two were well matched. The son's precocious aptitudes suited the father's perfectionist demands. Far more difficult for Jonathan was meeting the high standards his father set for true spirituality. No amount of discipline and striving could satisfy. For a boy who took great satisfaction in his own superior standing and achievements, the challenge of attaining superior humility was truly daunting. Yet God—and Timothy Edwards, the expert in God's standard—would accept nothing less. Twelve-year-old Jonathan's zeal for the revival of 1716 was transparent and he may have shown hopeful signs of seeking grace, yet he was not among those who could make profession. His next years would be spiritually troubled.

In the fall of that year, just as he was turning thirteen, Jonathan left home to begin college. The average age for beginning college was closer to sixteen, but it was not unusual for younger boys to attend as soon as they had mastered the necessary languages. Connecticut's fledgling Collegiate School, which had been founded on a shoestring in 1701, now had three tiny rival branches. Jonathan and nine or ten other students attended the branch at Wethersfield, near Hartford and only ten miles down river from East Windsor. This arrangement kept him in the family orbit. The principal tutor was Elisha Williams, a very talented half-cousin of the Williams-Stoddard clan, only nine years Jonathan's senior and a person who would long play important roles in his life. Jonathan probably boarded either with Elisha or with the family of his Aunt Mary, his mother's next oldest sister, and Uncle Stephen Mix, the local pastor.

By Jonathan's third year, in 1718, New Haven was beginning to prevail in the complex rivalries among Connecticut's regions as the future location of the Collegiate School. Cotton Mather, a tireless friend of the Connecticut college ever since Harvard had fallen out of the Mathers' control in 1701, had recently secured a gift from the English merchant Elihu Yale. The college trustees used this money to build a fine building in New Haven to house the students and a handsome collection of books earlier secured by Jeremiah Dummer, Massachusetts' agent in London. In September 1718 when the New Haven group marked the commencement of the school year by celebrating these events and renaming the college for Yale, the Wethersfield group held rival ceremonies. The Connecticut General Assembly then ordered the Wethersfield students to move to New Haven. They did so, apparently with a chip on their collective shoulders, and soon filed a list of complaints, centering on the poor teaching of the principal tutor, Samuel Johnson. Although only twenty-one, Johnson did not lack for intellectual firepower. Later he would become president of King's College (Columbia) in New York and be known as "the American Samuel Johnson." The perceptions of his deficiencies as a fledgling teacher may have been accentuated by his lack of enthusiasm for some Calvinistic doctrines. Johnson would soon be among a group of young New Englanders who would defect to the great Puritan nemesis, Anglicanism. Whatever the source of the Wethersfield students' complaints, after a month they packed up and returned to Wethersfield and Elisha Williams.

Jonathan reported to his sister Mary in March 1719 that they were doing well in Wethersfield yet soon expected to return to New Haven since the college trustees had recently "removed that which was the cause of our coming away, viz. Mr. [Samuel] Johnson, from the place of a tutor, and have put in Mr. [Timothy] Cutler, pastor of Canterbury, [as] president."[36] When

Jonathan and others moved to New Haven later that spring, he found Cutler, the new president, to be an impressive man in his mid-thirties. In mid-July he wrote to his father, "Mr. Cutler is extraordinary courteous to us, has a very good spirit of government, keeps the school in excellent order, seems to increase in learning, and is loved and feared by all that are under him."[37] These were just the qualities the fifteen-year-old had long since learned to admire.

Studying under Cutler and, above all, having access to a library of modern books was an exhilarating adventure for the precocious scholar, and he would graduate as the valedictorian of his class; yet something even more important was going on in his spiritual life. During his senior year he fell deathly ill with pleurisy; he was not prepared to die and was terrified. As he later recalled, it was as though God "shook me over the pit of hell." Having peered over the edge of the abyss, Jonathan resolved to give himself up to God and for a time had the delight of believing himself reconciled to God. Soon after his recovery, however, the same thing happened as after his childhood experience, he "fell again into my old ways of sin."[38]

Self-discipline had failed as much as it had succeeded. Self-examination was not encouraging either. As early as he could remember, he had resented much of the endless tedium of his parents' teaching and discipline. Holiness seemed "a melancholy, morose, sour and unpleasant thing."[39] He did not find delight in lengthy church services. He still had a rebellious nature. He was proud. He had a difficult and unsociable personality, and he did not have signs of charity that were evidence of grace. He struggled with sexual lusts which, despite prodigious efforts, he could not wholly control.[40]

The sixteen-year-old returned to his old ways, but this time God would not let him go and Jonathan would not give up. He stayed on in New Haven the next year to read for a M.A. degree. It was a time of immense intellectual growth, yet once again that was overshadowed by intense spiritual struggles without much satisfaction. "God would not suffer me to go on with any quietness; but I had great and violent struggles: till after many conflicts with wicked inclinations, and repeated resolutions, and bonds that I laid myself under by a kind of vows to God, I was brought wholly to break off all former wicked ways, and all ways of known outward sin; and to apply myself to seek my salvation, and practice the duties of religion: but without that kind of affection and delight, that I had formerly experienced."[41]

Further distressing him were his personal relationships to other students. Although adults lauded his intellectual achievements, that did not translate into being liked by his peers. His struggles to right himself with the deity at the same time he was intensely engaged in trying to comprehend the essence of reality probably accentuated his naturally shy and antisocial habit.

First he had a terrible falling out with his roommate and cousin Elisha Mix. Jonathan knew Elisha well because Elisha's father was Stephen Mix, the pastor at Wethersfield. Elisha was only two years younger than Jonathan, but he was no scholar and only beginning his freshman year during Jonathan's first M.A. year. Apparently the father had encouraged the rooming arrangement in the hope that Jonathan would be able to watch over Elisha in his studies. The arrangement went badly almost immediately. Elisha loved to play, detested living with someone so unrelentingly serious, and ignored Jonathan's efforts to prod him to study. To make matters worse, as a freshman, Elisha had to do the bidding of the more advanced students. This was a standard arrangement in colleges: spending one's first year as an errand boy was what an apprentice to any craft or profession at the time would expect. The sudden disparity in status did not work between these cousins. Jonathan, nonetheless, saw a principle involved and was jealous of his prerogatives.

Not wanting to be distracted from his studies and spiritual exercises, Jonathan would as often as ten times a day order Elisha to draw cider for him from the basement immediately below their room in the new Yale building. Late one evening Jonathan gave such an order, but Elisha acted as though he did not hear. Jonathan demanded whether he had heard and, if so, why he did not come. Jonathan described the issue in a complaint to his uncle. "He answered with some earnestness that he did [not] love to be called from play to draw cider. I was astonished at his answer, and it is the first instance I have known of a freshman's absolutely refusing his senior, whether graduate or undergraduate." Jonathan went on, with characteristic thoroughness, to observe that he demanded relatively little of Elisha and that "the burthen of his freshmanship *caeteris paribus* is no greater than of other freshmen."[42]

Jonathan apparently sent this complaint by way of his own father who added his own considerably less deferential admonishments to his brother-in-law. Elisha's behavior, Timothy suggested, reflected Stephen's laxness. Not one to allow tact to stand in the way of principle, Timothy added that he intended soon "to write my mind concerning some things that I have observed in you and met with from you, that have not been very pleasant . . . and I am verily persuaded are not justifiable in you."[43]

We can see Jonathan as his father's son in a second incident during the same school year. On March 1, 1721, Jonathan wrote to his father, reassuring him that he had no part in a small student uprising that had become the talk of the colony. He began by thanking his father "from the bottom of my heart for your wholesome advice, and counsel and the abundance of fatherlike tenderness therein expressed." Far from needing such advice, Jonathan assured, he was the model of rectitude throughout the entire affair. What had happened, he wrote, was that "Every undergraduate, one and all, that had anything to do with the college commons," announced that they had made a pact never to eat there again nor to pay for the service. Edwards was not a party to this "cabal." One reason was that he was the college butler, an attractive position he would not want to jeopardize, even if he had been sympathetic to the other students. Jonathan believed that the undergraduates' pernicious agreement had been made "before Mr. Cutler [the rector] or (I believe) anybody knew that they were discontented." When the next meal was served, none of the some fifty students of the college appeared. Jonathan allowed that "the commons at some times have not been sufficient as to quality, yet I think there has been very little occasion for such an insurrection as this."

What comes through in this account, aside from his scrupulous respect for authority, is that Jonathan appears to have had miserable relationships with his fellow students. Not only was he the outsider, but he was not reticent to express his adultlike opinions. Particularly, he told his father, he had done so to his fellow East Windsorite, Isaac Stiles. Stiles was six years older than Jonathan. Timothy Edwards had noticed the intelligence of this farmer's son (who later became father to a famous Yale president). Jonathan, who was superior in status to Isaac, took the older student under his wing. Stiles, said Jonathan, had been strongly pressured by his colleagues to enter into this bond, without time to consider. Jonathan was quick with his advice: "As soon as I understood him to be one of them, I told him that I thought he had done exceedingly unadvisedly, and I told him also which I thought of the ill consequences of it would be, and quickly made him sorry that he did not take advice in the matter, I am apt to think that this thing will be the greatest obstacle of any to Stiles' being butler."

While the rebellion was "speedily quashed," the disturbances were "succeeded by much worse and greater, and I believe greater than ever were in the college before." As Jonathan reported in shocked tones, "some monstrous impieties, and acts of immorality lately committed in the College, particularly stealing of hens, geese, turkeys, pigs, meat, wood, etc., unseasonable night-walking, breaking people's windows, playing at cards, cursing, swearing, and damning, and using all manner of ill language, which never were at such a pitch in the College as they now are." Rector Cutler had called a meeting of the trustees, and "'tis thought the upshot will be the expulsion of some, and the public admonition of others." Jonathan, however, had remained pure. "Through the goodness of God," he attested, "I am perfectly free of all their janglings."

He went on to assure that "I live in very good amity and agreement with my chambermate." While that conflict at the college may have been resolved, Edwards' relationships with other students remained poor and he continued to look to adults for justice. The best he could report was, "There has no new quarrels broke out betwixt me and any of the scholars, though they still persist in their former combination but I am not without hopes that it will be abolished by this meeting of the Trustees."[44]

Jonathan's alienation from his fellow students and his revulsion at their escapades can be better understood if we recognize that he was undergoing the most intense spiritual journey of his life. He was living like a young monk seeking sainthood in a school of rowdy boys. By March 1, 1721, the date he was reporting on the college shenanigans, he was on the verge of, or perhaps already in the midst of, discovering some of the marvels that he would eventually recognize as the essence of his conversion.[45] During this academic year he was also engaged in what for a seventeen-year-old were prodigious philosophical and theological speculations. If we take seriously the level of profundity he was reaching in his search to understand the harmonies of God's reality and the sense of beauty toward which he was reaching, it is easier to see why he was out of tune with his foul-minded and rambunctious schoolmates. Temperamentally he was never at ease in the midst of secular male camaraderie. He expected others to sustain the serious intensity of which he himself was capable. He had no middle gears. He could not abide inconsistencies, such as seeing fellow students, many training for the ministry, flaunting the moral order. Further, he was a boy who had much to learn about himself and about human relationships, not all of which he ever quite learned. Nonetheless, we must take into account that, like a great artist, he was exploring dimensions of reality that were beyond the imagination of most of his peers.

Until his intense experiences began, the year was one of excruciating spiritual struggles for Jonathan. He later described his efforts, in a conventional phrase, as "miserable seeking." He wondered whether his efforts could have been of any value at all, yet through them, he recalled, "I was brought to seek salvation, in a manner that I never was before." Even though since his illness the year before he had "felt a spirit to part with all things in the world, for an interest in Christ," he seemed not to have made real progress.

While one part of him was powerfully drawn toward full commitment, another part stiffly resisted. The resistance built its bastion in his intellect. Since childhood, as he later depicted it, he had been "full of objections against the doctrine of God's sovereignty, in choosing whom he would to eternal life, and rejecting whom he please; leaving them eternally to perish, and be everlastingly tormented in hell. It used to appear like a horrible doctrine to me."[46]

This brief passage is crucial for understanding not only the young Edwards, but also his entire later career. As a young man he was, if the difference of the two eras is taken into account, like the intensely saintly Aloysha Karamazov, disciplining himself in the quest to know God; but he was also the skeptical Ivan. His moral outrage against God's sovereignty reflected his youthful rebellious spirit, which despite his outward conformity had long reserved a place for secret inward resistance to his parents, their schooling, and to church indoctrination. His resourceful intellect provided a powerful weapon for this resistance. Like many other of the great thinkers of the era, he attacked Calvinist teachings at their most vulnerable point: that the sovereignty of God meant that by God's decree many humans were predestined to the horrors of eternal punishment. As he read widely he found such objections reinforced by the new humanitarian spirit of the age. Part of him was ready, as so many of the greatest thinkers of the age had done, to overthrow the dogmas of his heritage. Yet he also recognized his frailty before eternity, and another side of him believed that his rebellious spirit must be repressed. Once he had stared death in the face, once he been shaken over the pit of hell, he could not rest until his heart rested in God.

His heart and his intellect were not separable in this quest. His reason and his moral sensibilities had put a huge obstacle in his path. These objections were manifestations of a rebelliousness against the orthodoxy of his parents, dating to his childhood. He could not believe in God's total sovereignty, the doctrine at the very foundation of Calvinist teaching. Yet he was sure also that he had no hope on his own. What good would it do him if "he gain the whole world, and lose his own soul" (Matthew 16:26)? Earth's pleasures were fleeting and would turn to dust. Even if he thought it was repulsively unfair, he deeply feared that the fires of hell awaited those who rebelled against God.[47] He desperately wanted to trust in God, yet he could not believe in, let alone submit to, such a tyrant.

In the midst of this turmoil, he had a breakthrough. Suddenly he became convinced that indeed God was just in "eternally disposing of men, according to his sovereign pleasure." The tortuous obstacle was removed. Later he remembered clearly when he had reached this conviction, but "never could give an account, how, or by what means, I was thus convinced; not in the least imagining, in the time of it, nor a long time after, that there was any extraordinary influence of God's Spirit in it: but only that now I saw further, and my reason apprehended the justice and reasonableness of it."[48]

Attributing all to God's grace, as he did in his later narrative, Edwards played down the extent to which his reasoning had been crucial in reconciling himself to his heritage. We, of course, cannot tell what brought him to overcome this hurdle, since he says he himself did not fully understand. Yet we do know that around this time he was beginning to formulate his most characteristic and profound insights on God's character and relationship to the entire universe. These insights were for him like a Copernican revolution, providing a whole new perspective for understanding God's relation to reality and putting questions of God's relation to humans in an entirely new framework.

This intellectual breakthrough later seemed the work of the Holy Spirit because it soon had an overwhelming spiritual manifestation. At first Jonathan's mind simply "rested" in his insights, "and it put an end to all those cavils and objections, that I had till then abode with me, all the preceding part of my life." Then one day came a wondrous response, far beyond what his intellect could produce. He was reading I Timothy 1:17, "Now unto the King eternal, invisible, the only wise God, be honor and glory forever and ever, Amen." He had heard these words countless times and long since repeated catechism answers cataloguing such attributions of the deity and emphasizing that people existed to "glorify and enjoy" (or be in a state of joy with) God.[49] Now the implications of the incomprehensible greatness of the God of the vast universe who was truly eternal and all wise flamed out at him. As he read these words, he recalled, "there came into my soul, and was as it were diffused through it, a sense of the glory of the divine being; a new sense, quite different from anything I ever experienced before." He was so much enraptured that, as he put it, "I thought with myself, how excellent a Being that was; and how happy I should be, if I might enjoy that God, and be wrapped up to God in heaven, and be as it were swallowed up in him." He kept repeating the verse "and as it were singing over these words of Scripture to myself . . . and prayed in a manner quite different from what I used to do; with a new sort of affection."

Even so, the introspective and keenly observant young man remained deeply suspicious of his own affections, having been twice fooled by what had seemed like the strongest spiritual emotions that disappeared when the crisis was past. So he added immediately to the above account the remarkable observation "But it never came into my thought, that there was anything spiritual, or of a saving nature in this."

This time was different. The new sensibilities grew during the spring. As he wandered in the fields, woods, and hills near New Haven for his meditations he repeatedly saw the glory and beauty of God's love in Christ. He experienced an "inward sweet sense" of Christ's love expressed in "the work of redemption, and the glorious way of salvation by him." He spent much time reading the love poetry of the Canticles or Song of Songs. In the fields he would often contemplate the words "I am the rose of Sharon, the lily of the valleys" (Cant. 2:1). "The words seemed to me, sweetly to represent the loveliness and beauty of Jesus Christ." Such contemplations would carry him away "from all the concerns of the world" into "a kind of vision . . . of being alone in the mountains, or some solitary wilderness, far from all mankind, sweetly conversing with Christ, and wrapped and swallowed up in God." This new sense of divine things "would often of a sudden as it were, kindle up a sweet burning in my heart; an ardor of my soul, that I know not how to express."

Not long after he began having these experiences, they reached a memorable peak. He was at home for vacation in the spring and had been talking to his father about what was happening. Jonathan recalled that he was "pretty much affected" by this conversation, and when it ended he walked alone into the fields for contemplation. "And as I was walking there," he reported, "and looked up on the sky and clouds; there came into my mind, a sweet sense of the glorious majesty and grace of God, that I know not how to express." What overwhelmed him was two seemingly opposite attributes of the triune God "in a sweet conjunction: majesty and meekness joined together: it was a sweet and gentle, and holy majesty; and also a majestic meekness; an awful sweetness; a high, and great, and holy gentleness."[50]

A crude interpretation of Jonathan's experience might suggest that his vision of God was a cosmic projection of his father.[51] While there is always a grain of truth in such reductionist observations, the essence of the matter is nearly the opposite. So long as Jonathan's God was substantially a projection of his father or of other human analogies, he could not believe. If God were simply a cosmic version of the greatest imaginable human, God would still be by human standards a capricious and unreasonable tyrant, the father whose love turned out to be petty control, harsh judgments, tenderness mixed with fits of anger, unyielding disciplines, and punishments.[52] In fact, it was only when Jonathan's vision expanded to appreciate that the triune God who controlled this vast universe must be ineffably good, beautiful, and loving beyond human comprehension that he could lose himself in God.

# CHAPTER 3

# The Pilgrim's Progress

A fter this," Edwards recalled in his spiritual autobiography, "my sense of divine things gradually increased, and became more and more lively, and had more of that inward sweetness. The appearance of everything was altered: there seemed to be, as it were, a calm, sweet cast, or appearance of divine glory, in almost everything. God's excellency, his wisdom, his purity and love, seemed to appear in everything; in the sun, moon and stars; in the clouds, and blue sky; in the grass, flowers, trees; in the water, and all nature."

One might think, from this account, written almost twenty years later, that Jonathan lived happily ever after, enraptured in God's love and enthralled by God's glory. He described himself as often lost in contemplations of nature. Before his spiritual transformation, he noted, he had been "uncommonly terrified" by thunderstorms; afterward they inspired "sweet and glorious contemplations of my great and glorious God." It became natural for him "to sing or chant forth my meditations; to speak my thoughts in soliloquies, and speak with a singing voice."

True, once he experienced these ecstasies his life would never be the same. The exhilaration of having encountered the light of God's love, being enthralled by the beauty of Christ, and being filled by "an infinite fountain of divine glory and sweetness" was almost more than he could describe.[1] His new "sense of divine things," an overwhelming sense of the wondrous beauty and love of the triune God, would often be renewed. Even when such experiences were absent, their object remained the polestar of his life and thought. Without an appreciation of the intensity of these life-transforming experiences and their monumental implications for all else that he did, it is impossible to make sense of Edwards.

Yet Edwards' experiences were not simply those of a born mystic who at will could lose himself in contemplations of divine beauties. He was not a saint by nature. Even his stylized account in the later "Personal Narrative" reveals that his spiritual life was often an immense struggle. Despite his massive intellect and heroic disciplines, he was, like everyone else, a person with frailties and contradictions. That becomes apparent, as we shall soon see, from reading his private spiritual diary, in which he confided during his early years as a spiritual pilgrim. In the "Personal Narrative" he was writing as a famed revival preacher to a younger admirer.[2] So he was, in effect, preaching, using his experience as a model. Without changing the facts (he had the diary before him), he put them into a conventional theological framework.

His Calvinist framework itself demanded that even the greatest saints acknowledge their ongoing sinfulness. So in the "Personal Narrative," after several pages of describing the overwhelming joys of the heart whose affections are fully turned to God, Edwards turned back to an acknowledgment of his terrible failings. "My wickedness, as I am in myself, has long appeared to me perfectly ineffable. . . . When I look into my heart, and take a view of my wickedness, it looks like an abyss infinitely deeper than hell."

In this context of declaring his exceeding sinfulness, Edwards offered some reflections on the differences between his mature faith and that of his early years. "It is affecting to me," he remarked, "to think, how ignorant I was, when I was a young Christian, of the bottomless, infinite depths of wickedness, pride, hypocrisy and deceit left in my heart." Particularly, the mature Edwards lamented, with insight on his most besetting sin (which he was not the only one to notice), "I am greatly afflicted with a proud and self-righteous spirit; much more sensibly, than I used to be formerly. I see that serpent rising and putting forth its head, continually, everywhere, all around me."[3]

Edwards immediately followed this confession of his pride in his "Personal Narrative" with a particularly important interpretation of the difference between his early and his mature years: "Though it seems to me," he wrote, "that in some respects I was a far better Christian, for two or three years after my first conversion, than I am now; and lived in a more constant delight and pleasure: yet of late years, I have had a more full and constant sense of the absolute sovereignty of God, and a delight in that sovereignty; and have had more of a sense of the glory of Christ, as a mediator, as revealed in the gospel."[4]

What does this passage and its theological framework tell us about his first two or three years as a convert? And what do these early years reveal about the mature Edwards? To answer these questions we must turn to the

New York City was a thriving seaport when Edwards lived there in 1722–23. This engraving is from around 1719.

evidence from those years. We do not have much of a written record of the first year and a half of this intense time, when Jonathan was still an M.A. student at Yale. The only contemporary evidence comes from a number of sermons he preached during that time of preparation for the ministry. These cover a range of conventional Calvinistic topics. One revealing tendency is that the young convert sometimes adopted a balance-sheet approach to matters eternal, apparently reflecting a persistent theme in his own spiritual struggles. Worldly pleasures, wealth, and honors all soon turn to dust. It would be very foolish to invest in them. Sensual pleasures, from which people expect so much, "are like shadows and phantoms which vanish as we endeavor to embrace them." Only one of these early sermons, *Glorious Grace,* expresses much of the enthusiasm later recalled in the "Personal Narrative."[5] We get a much fuller picture of the latter part of his early years as a fervent convert because in December 1722 he began to keep his spiritual diary. First, we need to look at the setting.

In August 1722, still not quite nineteen, Jonathan went to New York City to minister as an unordained "supply" pastor to a small Presbyterian church that had broken away from the larger Presbyterian church of the town. The conflict was of the sort that plagued American Presbyterianism for much of its history. The Presbyterian Church of the Middle Colonies was made up of two principal groups, Scots-Irish and New Englanders of English heritage. They shared the same theology but had developed differing ecclesiastical traditions and styles. In New York City the two groups had formed a Presbyterian congregation in 1716 and built a building at Wall Street and Broadway. The

New Englanders, however, believed that the Scottish pastor, James Anderson, overstepped his pastoral authority, and withdrew to form their own group. They found a meeting place on Williams Street, near the docks, and invited the young Edwards to serve them, in hope that if they survived as a congregation he might become their regular pastor.[6]

During the eight months he lived in New York, from August 1722 to May 1723, Jonathan lived with a Madam Susanna Smith and her son, John. The Smiths, recent immigrants from England, were ardent Calvinists. Jonathan came to know them through the oldest son, William, an outstanding student in the class ahead of him at Yale.[7] The little Presbyterian congregation was small enough to be like a family, and Jonathan became deeply attached to the Smiths, who seemed to him models of Christian piety.

New York City, though a town of only seven to ten thousand inhabitants, was already far more cosmopolitan than anywhere Jonathan had lived. The city's Dutch origins and populace gave it a European tone still much in evidence less than sixty years after the British takeover. The British who lived in this seaport were themselves far more diverse than he had encountered in New England. The city also had a closely watched African slave population. A decade earlier nineteen participants in a bloody slave insurrection had been brutally executed in retaliation for killing nine whites. Jonathan also encountered French Huguenots, Protestant refugees from Louis XIV's revocation of the Edict of Nantes in 1685. Such refugees were constant reminders of the dangers of coming under the rule of the Catholic Antichrist and his minions. Jonathan also saw many people who were openly of no religion, and for the first time he was seriously confronted with the realities of another faith. As he later recalled, "I once lived for many months next to a Jew (the houses adjoining one to another) and had much opportunity daily to observe him; who appeared to me the devoutest person that ever I saw in my life; great part of his time being spent in acts of devotion, at his eastern window, which opened next to mine, seeming to be most earnestly engaged, not only in the daytime, but sometimes whole nights."[8]

The town at the tip of Manhattan Island was also one of the most beautiful settings in British North America. Jonathan loved to walk along the banks of the Hudson well north of the city to seek a solitary place where he could revel not just in the natural beauty but in the beauty of the sacrificial compassion of Christ to which all of nature pointed. Jonathan also found in Madam Smith's twenty-year-old son John a spiritual brother and soul mate. John would sometimes accompany Jonathan on his walks along the wilds of the Hudson's shore and, as Jonathan fondly recalled, "our conversation used much to turn on the advancement of Christ's kingdom in the world, and the glorious things that God would accomplish for his church in the latter days."

Living near the docks in this seaport town enhanced Jonathan's keen interest in world affairs. As with everything else, he saw world events as merely outward signs of spiritual realities, of what God was doing through human history. During his stay in New York he began making entries in his notebooks on the mysterious revelations of the last book of the Bible as a framework for understanding current events. This subject soon became a lifetime preoccupation. As he recalled of his New York days: "If I heard the least hint of any thing that happened in any part of the world, that appeared to me, in some respect or other, to have a favorable aspect on the interest of Christ's kingdom, my soul eagerly catched at it; and it would much animate and refresh me. I used to be earnest to read public news-letters, mainly for that end; to see if I could not find some news favorable to the interest of religion in the world."[9]

What is especially striking amid all this spiritual exuberance in these

---

Detail of view of New York in Edwards' day. The original Trinity Church (Anglican) overshadows City Hall. The harborside pavilion, known as "The Exchange," is at the end of Wall Street, where a slave market was sometimes held. The original Presbyterian meetinghouse was on Wall Street, and the break-off group met nearby.

early—and in some ways best—days of his journey as a convert was how rocky the road was. In Edwards' reconstruction he reported that in New York he felt a "sense of divine things" in "a much higher degree, than I had done before." He did confess that during these months he was also in "continual strife day and night, and constant inquiry, how I should be more holy."[10] Nevertheless, that representation glosses over the depth of the struggle as revealed in his original record.

Probably in late fall 1722, perhaps in response to the difficulties in sustaining high levels of spiritual intensity, Jonathan undertook the Puritan practice of framing a set of resolutions to discipline himself, adding new entries as needed. Shortly later, in December 1722, he also started a spiritual diary, which he kept fairly regularly at first and then sporadically over the next three years. These documents are worth careful scrutiny because they are almost the only sources from his entire career that provide a direct window into Edwards' interior life.[11] In his mature years he left no such candid record. Nevertheless, we may presume that throughout the rest of his life, beneath the discipline and genuine exterior of the model saint, there were also painful struggles for grace and for control amid uncertainties and vicissitudes.

The diary begins on a note of uncertainty, raising the question that was still plaguing him during these years, as to whether he was truly converted. In his first entry he listed a number of reasons why, despite his intense experiences, he might "question my interest in God's love and favor." He worried, probably reflecting the concerns of his father, that his experiences did not fit the exact steps of which the Puritan divines spoke. More seriously, he questioned whether his experiences themselves were "sufficiently inward, full, sincere, entire and hearty." He knew he was "sometimes guilty of sins of omission and commission." Were his spiritual sensibilities, he asked, "wrought into my very nature," or were they simply "hypocritical outside affections, which wicked men may feel." Was he once again in love with his own raptures?

Jonathan directed his "Resolutions" toward plugging every gap that would allow distraction from what he saw as his only worthy activity, to glorify God. In his fourth resolution, which is a briefer summary of the first three, he determined "never to do any manner of thing, whether in soul or body, less or more, but what tends to the glory of God; nor be, nor suffer it, if I can avoid it." Many of the resolutions are directed toward trying never to lose focus on spiritual things. In a number of them he reminded himself, as he had been taught since childhood, to think of his own dying, or to live as though he had only an hour left before his death or "before I should hear the last trump."

Sometimes he went beyond typical Puritan rigor. He resolved "to maintain the strictest temperance in eating and drinking." On this he was constantly experimenting with himself, seeing how much he needed to eat out of necessity and avoiding all excesses that would dull his mind or rouse his passions. Throughout his life observers commented on his strict eating habits and often emaciated appearance. Though he lived in the midst of the world, he did so as an ascetic. Few better illustrated the Protestant ideal of what Max Weber called "worldly asceticism."

True to his Puritan heritage, he often came back to the use of time. He early resolved, "never to lose one moment of time; but improve it the most profitable way I possibly can." In one later entry he observed that "a minute, gained in times of confusion, conversation, or in a journey, is as good as a minute gained in my study." In an early resolution, perhaps after being slowed down by a stalled horse in Manhattan traffic, he determined, "Resolved, never to suffer the least motions of anger to irrational beings."

Many of his resolutions and diary entries have to do with cultivating practical Christian virtues. He resolved, for instance, "to be endeavoring to find out fit objects of charity and liberality." In another entry he determined "always to do what I can towards making, maintaining and establishing peace, when it can be without over-balancing detriment in other respects."

Most of the specifically practical resolutions have to do, however, with correcting personal faults, especially irritability, pride, and evil-speaking. Typically, he related these tendencies to his pride and resolved to view himself in the perspectives of others and not to think himself better than others. In a New York sermon on "poverty of spirit" he attempted to show of what "an excellent, lovely temper and disposition true Christians" possess if the self-denying spirit of Christ truly dwells in them. A Christian was "at all times to esteem others better than himself, to place himself last in his own esteem."[12] He was preaching first of all to himself. He knew he was proud, yet he was resolved to fight pride every step of the way. In an early resolution he determined "to act in all respects . . . as if nobody had been so vile as I, and as if I had committed the same sins, or had the same infirmities or failings as others."

A. C. McGiffert, writing of the rigor of these resolutions in an early twentieth-century biography of Edwards, observes that "deliberately he set about to temper his character into steel."[13] That is a helpful way of getting a modern sense of what he was doing, but we also have to take into account that "character" suggests a typically twentieth-century idea of self-development as a primary motive. Edwards' resolutions are even a far cry from those of Benjamin Franklin, which were designed as practical disciplines for a life of success. In spite of the preoccupation with self that Puritan piety inevitably entailed, Edwards was desperately trying to keep God in the forefront of his consciousness. Unlike Franklin, he was concerned with law and duty more than with what would work. High among his priorities were reminders not to omit his regular times of Scripture study and prayer and to control those passions that would distract his focus on God. He was indeed honing a character of steel, but his goal was also to subordinate his natural self so that he would be pliable to the demands of God's law and will.

Like both Franklin and Cotton Mather before him, Edwards literally kept score of how well he did or, as he would put it, of the evidence of God's grace. Late in December 1723, near the beginning of his diary he "Concluded to observe, at the end of every month, the number of breaches of resolutions, to see whether they increase or diminish, to begin from this day, and to compute from that the weekly account, my monthly increase, and, out of the whole, my yearly increase, beginning from new year days."

In his diary he also kept track of his spiritual highs and lows. On Saturday, December 22, 1722, he noted that he was particularly "affected with the sense of the excellency of holiness" and that he "felt more exercise of love to Christ than usual." On Monday the twenty-fourth he had "higher thoughts than usual of the excellency of Jesus Christ and his kingdom." The next day he "was hindered by the headache all day." By Saturday sunset, the time when the Sabbath began, he was "dull and lifeless." The next Tuesday the dullness persisted, despite the fact that he could not think of any "negligence" of which he was guilty. On Wednesday he reflected how without the Spirit of God, no amount of resolution could help him. Nevertheless, he also believed the inverse. Without the firmest resolution, he would not find the Spirit. So when finding that the tally of his "weekly account" had fallen low, he "Resolved, that I have been negligent in two things: in not striving enough in duty; and in not forcing myself upon religious thoughts."

By the following Tuesday he had "Higher thoughts than usual of the excellency of Christ, and felt an unusual repentance of sin therefrom." But by Wednesday night he reported: "Decayed. I am sometimes apt to think, I have a great deal more of holiness than I have. I find now and then, that abominable corruption which is directly contrary to what I read of eminent Christians." On Thursday he was "reviving" again and concluded that he was "much more sprightly and healthy, both in body and mind, for my self-denial in eating, drinking, and sleeping."

He was still on the upswing on Saturday, January 12, which became a milestone in his spiritual autobiography. In the morning he "solemnly renewed my baptismal covenant" and then spent the rest of the day in spiritual disciplines and reflections.[14] He debated with himself the *"Query"* whether he ought ever to delight in anything other than that which had a specifically religious purpose. He concluded that he might because otherwise one could not rejoice in seeing friends or even take the pleasure in eating necessary for good digestion. So he made a resolution that was just slightly more lenient: he "never ought to allow any joy or sorrow, but what helps religion." That same evening, he observed: "it is suggested to me" (one suspects by Madam Smith) that "too constant a mortification, and too vigorous application to religion, may be prejudicial to health." He resolved, however, not to give in "no matter how much tired and weary I am, if my health is not impaired."

Despite the spiritual heights of the weekend, by Tuesday, January 15, he was "decaying" again. On Thursday he reported being "overwhelmed with melancholy." Five days after being at a peak, he was in a dark valley. Friday night he thought he was "beginning to endeavor to recover out of the death I have been in for these several days." So his diary goes back and froth from spiritual highs to dreadful lows. On Tuesday February 5 he was considering "that this being so exceedingly careful, and so particularly anxious, to force myself to think of religion, at all leisure moments, has exceedingly distracted my mind, and made me altogether unfit for that, and everything else." That excessive discipline, he determined, may have "caused the dreadful, low condition I was in on the 15th of January." Yet in the very same entry he lamented that "I do not seem so greatly and constantly to mortify and deny myself, as the mortification of which they [the apostles] speak." So, rather than relaxing his discipline he concluded he must do more: "I am again grown too careless about eating, drinking and sleeping—not careful enough about evil speaking."

The mature Edwards looked back on this rigor as involving "too great a dependence on my own strength; which afterwards proved a great damage to me."[15] Yet he never abandoned his belief in the value of strict spiritual disciplines, as his later *Life of David Brainerd* would reveal.

His theological explanation in his "Personal Narrative" for the difference between his early and his mature experiences as a convert was that he now had "a more full and constant sense of the absolute sovereignty of God, and a delight in that sovereignty; and have had more of the sense of the glory of Christ, as a mediator." Both of these sensibilities, that one must trust more in God's care and in Christ's intercession, fit with his self-criticism that he had earlier depended too much on his own efforts.

At the same time, if we notice that it was in his early years after conversion that he "lived in a more constant delight and pleasure" than afterward, then we must also recognize that his time of *more constant* delight was also a time of moving back and forth between his spiritual mountains and deep valleys. Only steady habits of spiritual disciplines kept his emotional swings under control. Edwards later explained the distinction involved when writing about David Brainerd, whose intense spirituality was tempered by even deeper bouts of "melancholy," or what we might call depression. True religion for Brainerd, Edwards wrote, "did not consist in unaccountable *flights* and *vehement* pangs," but was "like the steady lights of heaven, constant principles of light, though sometimes hid with clouds." Faith is then an abiding "principle" or habit that persists in spite of a "natural temper" prone to "the disease" of "melancholy and dejection of spirit."[16]

In the winter of 1723 in New York, Jonathan must have appeared as an extraordinarily pious and intense young man to his parishioners in his little Presbyterian congregation. They could not but feel the power of his penetrating intellect. His carefully memorized sermons already had the relentless quality that characterized his later preaching. He left no loophole in his logic as he deduced his conclusions from his Scriptural premises (the "doctrine" portion of a Puritan sermon) and then showed how this set of proven truths must apply to his hearers (the "use" or "application"). The most conspicuous themes, not surprisingly, reflected his personal struggles. Quite a few of the sermons are on self-renunciation and total dedication to God. "God will not accept of any if we keep back a part. The flesh, the world, and the devil are God's most irreconcilable enemies."[17] Constantly he reminded his hearers of the inversion of values that Christianity involves. They must be renouncing all worldly ambitions and counting as gain only time spent in devotion and service to God.

In other sermons Edwards' almost poetic sensibilities begin to emerge in mature form. The sermon *Jesus Christ the Light of the World* is a gem of his early writing, sustaining his favorite metaphor of light throughout. Light is a primary biblical image to describe God's love. Light was also a familiar theme in both the preaching and philosophizing of an era so concerned with enlightenment. No one looked more intensely at the biblical meaning of light for his day than did Edwards. For him, light was the most powerful image of how God communicated his love to his creation. *Regeneration* meant to be given eyes to see the light of Christ in hearts that had been hopelessly darkened by sin.[18]

As spring was reaching its height in late April 1723 (early May by our modern calendars, which add eleven days), Jonathan reluctantly had to leave New York. Timothy Edwards was trying to get his son back to Connecticut and more under his wing. The previous fall Timothy had engineered a call for Jonathan to be pastor of the village of Bolton, Connecticut, only fifteen miles from East Windsor. Jonathan had responded in December to the Bolton search committee that he was not yet certain as to whether he might settle as pastor in New York, although he thought it unlikely in light of the congregation's circumstances and "my father's inclinations to the contrary." If he returned to New England in the spring, he might consider their call again, should they care to wait.[19]

Leaving his friends in New York was one of the most bittersweet moments in his life. He remembered it vividly when he wrote his "Personal Narrative." "I came away from New York in the month of April 1723, and had a most bitter parting with Madam Smith and her son. My heart seemed to sink within me, at leaving the family and city, where I had enjoyed so many sweet and pleasant days. I went from New York to Wethersfield by water. As I sailed away, I kept sight of the city as long as I could; and when I was out of sight of it, it would affect me much to look that way, with a kind of melancholy mixed with sweetness." Characteristically, he turned such earthly emotions into a spiritual lesson, reflecting in his diary on how they anticipated heavenly love "where these persons that appear so lovely in this world, will really be inexpressibly more lovely, and full of love to us. And how sweetly will the mutual lovers join together to sing the praises of God and the Lamb." So fondly did he recall these sentiments that he copied them from his diary into his "Personal Narrative."[20]

He faced the prospects of a summer at home with mixed emotions. On the day he arrived, May 1, he reminded himself not to wish he were with his faraway friends but to dwell on the heavenly love in the passage quoted above. During the summer he continued to enjoy some intense spiritual contemplations, but he also noted that his fervor was diminishing. Early in the summer he wrote that he had "lost that relish of the Scriptures and other good books, which I had five or six months ago" (May 12). In July he admonished himself for being "too impatient" at a church meeting (July 11). In August he observed, "There are many things which I should really think to be my duty, if I had the same affections, as when I first came from New York; which now I think not so to be."

He continued to work on cultivating a good nature and reducing his fretfulness. He resolved "to wear a benign aspect, and air of acting and speaking, in all companies, except it should so happen, that duty requires it otherwise" (July 22). He continued to wrestle with evil-speaking, apparently a fault to which he was particularly prone. Early in his stay at home he experimented with eliminating evil-speaking entirely for a week and then resolved that it "is a duty to be observed forever" (May 18, 1723). He also resolved not to hear sarcastic remarks about others (July 31, 1723).

His fretful disposition plus his pride and the resultant attitude toward others were the sins he combated most openly, but we can be sure that he was also fighting sexual desires, even if he did not directly record his struggles with those temptations.[21] One possible allusion to such enticements is in an entry on a Saturday morning in July: "When I am violently beset with temptation, or cannot rid myself of evil thoughts, to do some sum in arithmetic, or geometry, or some other study, which necessarily engages all my thoughts, and unavoidably keeps them from wandering" (July 27).

The problems of sustaining his spiritual intensity through the summer were compounded by the irritations of living under the rule of his parents. In a July 19 diary entry he quoted I Peter 2:18, which tells servants to be subject to their masters, even if the masters are hard to please. Jonathan observed that the same must apply in children's duties to their parents. He went on, significantly, to reflect on the next two verses in which Peter says that it is pleasing to God if we "endure grief, suffering wrongfully." A few weeks later, on the morning of August 13, he confessed that he had "sinned, in not being careful enough to please my parents." Later that same day he added: "I find it would be very much to advantage, to be thoroughly acquainted with the Scriptures. When I am reading doctrinal books or books of controversy, I can proceed with abundantly more confidence; can see upon what footing and foundation I stand."

What was the source of this conflict? Part of it may have been that his parents were insisting that he fill the vacancy in the pastorate at Bolton, a prospect Jonathan did not relish. If that were the main issue, though, one would wonder why he would resolve to be better acquainted with Scripture as a tool for assessing doctrinal "books of controversy."

The previous day's entry suggests the immediate source of open contention. Jonathan was still worrying about his eternal estate because of "my not
having experienced conversion in those particular steps, wherein the people
of New England, and anciently the Dissenters of Old England, used to
experience it." As far as we know, Jonathan had not yet become a full communicant church member—oddly we have no record of when he did. That lacuna
leaves the door open to speculation as to whether his dramatic spiritual
experiences and subsequent heroic efforts to do good still seemed unsatisfac-
tory to him (despite his later estimate that they marked his conversion). Or
perhaps he and his parents saw the matter differently. If we may conjecture,
perhaps he had proposed that he was ready for communicant membership
and Timothy Edwards, learned in such matters and always setting the highest
standards for his son, had said no.

Whether or not communicant membership was at stake, the dispute
seems to have been going on for over a month and to have been about the
steps to conversion. Jonathan's diary entry of July 4 is especially revealing of
the mentality of those who cultivated a consciousness of the precariousness of
this life and the urgency of questions of eternal destiny. He began matter-of-
factly, "Last night, in bed, when thinking of death . . . ," as though that was his
usual nightly concern. He went on to say that the only reason he would face
death "in the least degree fearfully, would be, the want of a trusting and
relying on Jesus Christ, so distinctly and plainly, as has been described by
divines." In particular, he worried that he might not be "entirely trusting my
soul on Christ, after the fears of hell, and terrors of the Lord, encouraged by
the mercy, faithfulness and promises, of God, and the gracious invitations of
Christ." After some further reflections on this issue he added: "Resolved,
for the future, to observe rather more of meekness, moderation and temper,
in disputes."

Possibly Jonathan had recounted his spiritual experiences to his parents,
but they were not entirely convinced that this was not just a later version of
building the secret prayer booth in the woods. All the fervor in the world, all
the religious discipline in the world, would do no good, if one did not have the
true marks of conversion. Considering what we know of his efforts to cultivate
spiritual and moral rigors, such doubt may seem difficult to imagine. Yet his
spirituality was marked by bright peaks and dismal valleys, and Jonathan
himself kept coming back to the possibility that his parents might be right.[22]

Apparently the dispute involved Timothy Edwards' emphasis on a preparatory step toward conversion that some Puritans had described as the

experience of "legal terrors." Timothy's views seem to have been influenced by the Elizabethan Puritan writer William Perkins (1558–1602), who insisted that undergoing "legal terrors" was a necessary step in preparation for conversion. One had to be so overcome by one's sinfulness as to experience the terror of total "humiliation" before knowing total dependence on God's grace. In a 1695 sermon Timothy had declared, "No person that is not truly humbled whatever change is wrought in him is not, can not be, savingly changed or truly converted." Years later in his "Personal Narrative," Jonathan was still concerned about the topic and made a point of remarking that "it never seemed to be proper to express my concern that I had by the name of terror."[23]

Whatever the exact details of the dispute, both parents were involved and it was sometimes heated. One or both of the learned parents had outgunned their brilliant son in mastery of Scripture and the Puritan authors. Jonathan resolved to show proper deference to his parents and to endure wrongful suffering. Yet Jonathan never gave up on an argument. At the same time that he deferred to his parents he was determining to be more thoroughly prepared with knowledge of Scripture, the one authority that could trump Puritan divines. He also privately "resolved, never to leave searching, till I have satisfyingly found out the very bottom and foundation, the real reason, why they used to be converted in those steps."[24]

Out of his disconcerting religious struggles—which were by no means over—arose one of the major agendas of his later career. How could one tell the difference between true and false religious affections? At age nineteen he had already determined to apply his philosophical or scientific talents to the task of setting the world right on that topic. That question touched him at the center of his being. Not only was his eternal destiny of agonizing personal importance, how he answered the question was deeply tied to his relationship to his parents, his extended family, his community, his church, and his career. In the light of all the ink already poured into that most difficult question by earlier divines, the task of once and for all resolving it might have seemed a formidable life's work in itself. Yet for the young Jonathan it was only one part of a far larger design that he was already drafting to redirect the thought of Christendom.

# CHAPTER 4

## The Harmony of All Knowledge

For we know that Antichrist is to be destroyed by clear light, by the breath of Christ's mouth, [by the] brightness of his coming, that is, by plain reason and demonstration, deduced from the Word of God.

"Exposition on the Apocalypse," 1723

Amid both the exhilarations of New York and the tensions of the summer back at East Windsor, the nineteen-year-old Jonathan was laying out a monumental design. At the same time that he was pursuing his spiritual goals with such intensity he was organizing his views on everything. To do this, he began what would become great notebooks, formed from carefully sewn folded pages. At Yale during his graduate years he had begun to put together his thoughts on natural science (then called "natural philosophy"), a subject that particularly excited him in his late teen years and one that would remain a lifelong interest. In New York he began a notebook of "Miscellanies," in which he placed his thoughts on theology and philosophy. By the end of 1723 he had added three more notebooks: "Notes on the Apocalypse," "Notes on Scripture," and "The Mind."[1] The pastorate was his calling, yet he was resolved that his life's work would not be just local. He was determined to be an international figure. This was part ambition—of which he had a lot—yet he also saw it as his larger calling, if God granted him the grace, to play a role in promoting God's earthly kingdom at a crucial moment in the history of redemption.

Occasionally he reflected on his grand expectations explicitly. On the cover of one of his earliest notebooks he wrote rules for writing. He advised himself, for instance, to display modesty of style and to try to gain readers rather than to silence opposition. Perhaps he thought of Cotton Mather, the most conspicuous model of colonial ambition, who hurt his cause by an affected and self-conscious display of style. Consistent with his resolution of modesty, Edwards put the last of his original set of rules, written in 1723, in shorthand: "6. *The world will expect more modesty because of my circumstances— in America, young, etc. Let there be a superabundance of modesty, and though perhaps 'twill otherwise be needless, it will wonderfully make way for its reception in the world. Mankind are by nature proud and exceeding envious, and ever jealous of such upstarts; and it exceedingly irritates and affronts 'em to see 'em appear in print. Yet the modesty ought not to be affected and foolish, but decent and natural.*"[2] A few years later he added another shorthand note on how, if he hoped to get published in London, he might first need to experiment in his own country.[3] It is possible that he had earlier, perhaps before he went to New York, broached the subject of personally going to London. On a manuscript sermon from 1722 Timothy Edwards doodled the following words in this order: "Jonathan. London. Corruption."[4] What was behind this we can only guess, though we know that the ever-anxious Timothy was eager to keep Jonathan close to home.

Jonathan never traveled widely, yet he saw himself in the midst of an international upheaval of immense significance. While he remained intensely loyal to his Puritan heritage, he was also part of the first generation of New Englanders who had to face the revolutionary scientific and philosophical thought of the era. New Englanders had long been friendly to scientific advances and were confident that discoveries of God's ways of governing the natural world would only confirm what they knew from Scripture. Cotton Mather, for instance, had done much to transmit the latest in contemporary natural philosophy to New England audiences, incorporating summaries of recent texts into his voluminous writings. The younger educated New Englanders—mostly clergy, of course—of the early decades of the century had a passing acquaintance with Newton, Locke, and other British luminaries. Précis of recent publications were available in periodicals and in books of the day.[5] Still, the implications of the new science had not been fully integrated into New England intellectual life. Educated New Englanders took a Copernican viewpoint and the new science for granted, yet the college curricula of the early 1700s included Aristotle but not Newton.

It is easy to misconceive the intellectual situation in which the young Edwards found himself. It is especially easy because such a misconception has been so eloquently presented by Perry Miller, the most influential historian of New England. Miller, who let his creativity get the best of him in his biography of Edwards, depicted young Jonathan as a revolutionary intellectual prodigy who, upon reading Locke, "grasped in a flash" the implications of modern thought. That placed him so far ahead of his generation that his genius could never be fully appreciated in his own time. According to Miller, who adopted the romantic image of the "lonely genius," this "backwoods adolescent" had no more preparation for this insight than the contemplation of God in his father's field. Similarly, when reading Newton he "saw in a glance that no theology would any longer survive unless it could be integrated with the *Principia*." Edwards was "the last great American, perhaps the last European, for whom there could be no warfare between religion and science, or between ethics and nature." The young genius "cast off habits of mind formed in feudalism, and entered abruptly into modernity, where facts rather than prescriptive rights and charters were henceforth to be the arbiters of human affairs."[6]

Miller's portrait is to Edwards what *Hamlet* is to the actual Danish prince, a triumph of the imagination. Edwards thoroughly grounded his early thought, as we now know in exhaustive detail, in the international trends of the era.[7] He was part of a New England culture that was much enamored of things British and, as Mather's example itself illustrates, much concerned with staying current. Early New England had been ruled, perhaps more than any culture in history, by the educated. Despite their predominantly theological interests, many influential New England clergy made considerable efforts to learn about the international trends of the day. Harvard College and later Yale were indeed slow in incorporating some of the new natural philosophy into their curricula, but that was because these institutions were a cross between boys' Latin schools and theological seminaries. Much of their curricula was based on centuries of medieval assumptions as to what education should be. "Education" without Aristotle was almost unthinkable. Even so, particularly at Harvard, modern thought had made significant inroads. Harvard graduates of the late decades of the seventeenth century were familiar, for instance, with the thought of Descartes, who was a dominant figure in mid-seventeenth-century natural science as well as in other aspects of philosophy. Solomon Stoddard owned Descartes' works as a Harvard student in the 1660s.

Sophisticated New Englanders of the early 1700s subscribed to British journals to keep in touch with the international "republic of letters," especially England, France, and Holland, during an extraordinarily creative period. They would have known about Pierre Bayle's encyclopedic and sometimes skeptical *Dictionaire historique et critique* (1697–1702) soon after it was translated into English in 1710. They were familiar with the English "latitudinarians" and such Anglican writers as the popular preacher John Tillotson (1630–94), who used reason to disparage many Calvinist dogmas, and they would have quickly learned of the Third Earl of Shaftesbury's celebration of a sense of divine beauty, published in *The Moralist* in 1709. They might spend an evening over pipes discussing the latest intelligence from the periodicals, such as Joseph Addison's and Richard Steele's witty and sophisticated *Spectator*.

Young Edwards eagerly engaged all these writers. He early became an avid reader of *The Spectator*, which contained the latest in contemporary thought. At Yale College he was one of the first beneficiaries of the library's impressive Dummer collection, to which Isaac Newton and Richard Steele were among the English contributors. Edwards devoured everything from natural philosophy to polite literature. He was profoundly influenced by Isaac Newton, probably the most important thinker of the era.[8] Like many men of his time Edwards was determined to know everything and how it all fit together in God's universe.

Miller's myth about Edwards' single-handed appropriation of the insights of John Locke had, like any distortion, a plausible basis. One of Edwards' earliest memorialists, apparently someone who knew him in college, recalled, "He seemed to be of a logician and a metaphysician by nature; but greatly improved by art and study. He had imbibed the sentiments of the great Mr. Locke; these grew in him as in native soil."[9] Edwards' first biographer, his younger friend and associate Samuel Hopkins, reported:

> In his second year at college, and the thirteenth of his age, he read Locke on human understanding, with great delight and profit. His uncommon genius, by which he was, as it were by nature, formed for closeness of thought and deep penetration, now began to exercise and discover itself. Taking that book into his hand, upon some occasion, not long before his death, he said to some of his select friends . . . that he was beyond expression entertained and pleased with it, when he read it in his youth at college; that he was as much engaged and had more satisfaction and pleasure in studying it, than the most greedy miser in gathering up handsful of silver and gold from some new discovered treasure.[10]

If this discovery of Locke happened as early as Hopkins alleges, it would have been in 1717 while Edwards was still studying at Wethersfield under his cousin Elisha Williams. Some question has been raised about the early date, since no copy of Locke's *Essay Concerning Human Understanding* (1690) is known to have been in New England by that time.[11] Still, it is conceivable that a young intellectual like Elisha Williams had acquired the volume. Williams was a recent Harvard graduate and brought with him from the more cosmopolitan Boston some philosophical sophistication.[12] In any case, by 1719 when Jonathan went to study in New Haven under Timothy Cutler, he had access not only to Locke but to the whole treasure trove of modern writers in the library's new Dummer collection. The college was also in the process of updating its curriculum, which had been based largely on Aristotelian science and what would soon become known as the "old logic" of Petrus Ramus (1515–72). The Ramist scheme, a seventeenth-century Puritan staple, was largely a matter of arranging all knowledge in logically distinct categories that would at least dimly reflect the archetypal logic of the divine mind.[13] By 1718–19 the Yale curriculum began to include a little of Locke and (to the extent that they could handle the mathematics) Newton and other popular interpreters of contemporary science.[14]

Jonathan's exhilarating reading of Locke, Newton, and a host of other modern thinkers convinced him that he stood at a pivotal point in New England's history. This sense grew out of his personal experience. During the early years of such reading, his orthodoxy stood on shaky ground. Almost all modern thinkers professed and defended Christianity; yet virtually all, like Locke, endorsed a broader, more tolerant, and more "reasonable" religion than Jonathan had learned in Connecticut. As a young teenager he had thought of many reasons to doubt the Calvinist teaching of the total sovereignty of God, and these new authors may have reinforced those doubts.

Soon, however, their effect became almost the opposite. Somehow in the midst of this study and his agonizing spiritual searching, his doubts about divine sovereignty dissolved without his quite knowing why.[15] By the time of the electrifying ecstasies of his conversion experience in the spring of his first graduate year, he was also enthralled by a sense of a special calling. He felt called to use the new learning in defense of God's eternal word.

His attitude toward Locke provides the best example. Locke opened up exciting new ways of looking at things, especially regarding the relation between ideas and reality. Locke was crucial in setting Edwards' philosophical agenda and shaping some of his categories. Yet Edwards was no Lockean in any strict sense. When, as a tutor at Yale a few years later, he recorded his views of Locke in his notebooks, it was to refute him or go far beyond him.[16] As others have observed, Edwards was "a miser who critically appraised his treasure."[17]

## God and Natural Philosophy

Edwards' early enthusiasm for natural science is hardly surprising for a boy who was in his mid-teens in an era when natural philosophy was changing dramatically and had become a much-respected avocation among educated men. Natural philosophy for such eighteenth-century gentlemen meant not so much experimentation as keen observation of natural phenomena. The *Philosophical Transactions* of the famous Royal Society in London were filled with scientific trivia from all over the world. The contributors constituted a worldwide network of observers who were constantly looking out for any phenomena not yet heard of or explained. Isaac Newton himself still presided over the Royal Society. Being published in its *Philosophical Transactions* would mark one as having a part in this great international enterprise.

When he was sixteen or perhaps earlier, Edwards became fascinated with the behavior of spiders, one of the creatures with which New Englanders were constantly surrounded. During his senior year in college, at age seventeen, he wrote an engaging account of his observations.[18] His admiration for spiders is apparent throughout. "Of all insects," he began, "no one is more wonderful than the spider, especially with respect to their sagacity and admirable way of working." Like any New Englander well trained in the Ramist method of separating things into categories, he began by distinguishing house spiders from those he was interested in, which lived on trees and bushes in his favorite haunt, the forest. These seemed to be able to fly great distances from tree to tree and could, upon close observation, be seen to be "swimming" high in the air. "The appearance is truly very pretty and pleasing, and it was so pleasing, as well as surprising, to me, that I resolved to endeavor to satisfy my curiosity about it."

By close observation and a little experimentation in shaking spiders off sticks, Jonathan saw exactly how they could fly. The filament they released from their tails was lighter than air, so that by simply letting enough of it out they could ascend or simply float in the air. Drawing on his experience as a swimmer, Jonathan explained that the spiders' movement was like a man at the bottom of the sea who could arise, descend, or maintain an equilibrium by holding onto an object of the appropriate weight. Spiders could thus float at will in light breezes by letting out or contracting the vast filament on which they rode. "And without doubt," he added, "they do it with a great deal of their sort of pleasure." In good New England fashion, which suggested that the Calvinist God was not against joy in recreation, he added the "Corollary" that "We hence see the exuberant goodness of the Creator, who hath not only provided for all the necessities, but also for the pleasure and recreation of all sorts of creatures, and even the insects and those that are most despicable."

Edwards' analysis combined piety with the latest contemporary thought. He addressed the question of why, if the filaments of the web are so small that they can hardly be seen in close observation, they sometimes appear so clearly at "prodigious height" when they are between us and the sun. Optics was another scientific field in which he had great interest, and he explained the spider web phenomenon in those terms: it was like a candle flame that appears far larger than it should at a long distance, or the distant stars appearing larger than their actual proportion of the sky. Particularly, Sir Isaac Newton's demonstration of the "incurvation of the rays passing by the edge of any body" explained the distant visibility of the webs.

A final set of pious observations not only reveals some characteristic patterns in Edwards' thinking but also reflects the state of the art in relating science to religion at that time. Edwards observed that spiders did their flying only on fair days in the fall when the breezes were blowing from the west. Asserting that in all countries fair weather came only "when the wind blows from the midland parts, and so toward the sea," he surmised that those spiders not eaten by birds and so forth must eventually reach the sea and be drowned.

From this analysis he drew two pious "corollaries." First, "we may behold and admire the wisdom of the Creator, and be convinced that is exercised about such little things, in this wonderful contrivance of annually carrying off and burying the corrupting nauseousness of our air, of which flying insects are little collections, in the bottom of the ocean where it will do no harm." So the Creator uses the pleasure and recreation of these creatures for the "greater end," which is their destruction. If, as was commonly supposed, they merely hibernated through the winter, the world would soon be overrun by insects. The second corollary was that we should "admire also the Creator in so nicely and mathematically adjusting their multiplying nature" so that "taking one year with another, there is always just an equal number of them."[19]

Although Jonathan's science became speculative on how the spiders met their end, his pieties were not out of the ordinary. The greatest philosophers of the day agreed that the more one explored the ingenuities of nature, the more one must admire the genius of the Creator. Only an all-wise Governor of the universe could account for such marvels. There was no other way to explain them.[20]

Jonathan's youthful work on spiders, though indeed our best glimpse of him as a close observer of nature, has received inordinate attention because his nineteenth-century biographer and great-grandson, Sereno Dwight, incorrectly dated it from 1716, when Jonathan was twelve. This mistake created a legend about Edwards' scientific precocity, analogous to the myth of George Washington's moral precocity in confessing to cutting down the cherry tree.[21]

The actual story is one more typical of the times but nonetheless revealing. Jonathan continued his scientific pursuits through his college and M.A. years, although he put them aside when he was pastoring in New York. In summer 1723, when he was at home, he picked them up again. Timothy Edwards had an amateur interest in natural philosophy and had recently sent to Judge Paul Dudley, a Massachusetts member of the Royal Society of London, an account of a prodigious pumpkin. He had it on good authority that in 1669 a stray pumpkin vine in a New England field had borne 260 pumpkins, not counting those small or unripe. Dudley sent this information on to the *Philosophical Transactions,* where it was recounted on the authority of a "worthy divine," "the Reverend Mr. Edwards of Windsor." In thanking Timothy, Dudley added that he would welcome any other remarkable observations of nature. Timothy showed this letter to Jonathan, who in fall 1723 carefully polished his paper on spiders and sent it on to Dudley. Nothing more came of it. A reader jotted the name "Lister" on the last page, referring to the English naturalist Martin Lister, who had earlier published on flying spiders, perhaps accounting for not publishing Jonathan's otherwise worthy and original work.[22]

In the meantime, Jonathan's scientific interests had soared to airy heights. "Natural philosophy" in his day was not detached from "philosophy," as it has been since the nineteenth century. Only in the later Victorian era did "science" come to mean natural science, a verbal triumph of momentous proportions. In Edwards' day, by contrast, every serious thinker believed that natural philosophy and philosophy generally (and hence theology) must be of one piece. Natural science had a bearing on the larger sciences of reality, but only later was it widely thought that "nature" was the highest form of reality and hence natural science the definitive mode of thought. Few of Edwards' contemporaries would have thought of natural science and theology as being in conflict.

Natural philosophy was sparking wide questioning of some features of *tradi-tional* Christianity. Nonetheless, the greatest philosophers, mathematicians, and natural philosophers of the day typically combined the highest metaphysical and theological speculations with their down-to-earth concerns.

Edwards' earliest notebooks on natural science, begun in his graduate years at Yale, suggest that he was sketching long-range plans for a great scientific and metaphysical treatise. He titled some of the earliest entries: "Things to Be Considered and Written Fully About." This list, which he continued until he went to Northampton, eventually grew to nearly one hundred short expositions of puzzling natural phenomena or their philosophical implications. Many are thoroughly practical. Why is air necessary to preserve a fire? Why are all mountains pitched westward? Why are no two trees exactly alike? What makes a bubble break? Why is the heat of the sun's rays greater near the surface of earth than higher up? Why do waves form as they do? Why does lightning not travel in a straight line and why do repeated flashes follow the same pattern?[23]

A fair number of these entries reflect his special interest in optics. As a young man enthralled by the spiritual dimensions of light, he was keenly interested in knowing about its mechanics. One of his earliest entries expresses his resolve "to show, from Isaac Newton's principles of light and colors, why the sky is blue, the sun is not perfectly white," and so forth. Edwards avidly studied Newton's great work *Opticks*. In his graduate years he drafted papers on rainbows and on light rays coming from distant stars. He found the phenomenon that colors did not reside in their objects especially fascinating. When he sat under a tree reading a book he noticed that the sunlight filtered through the leaves was a reddish-purplish color, which he attributed to the green rays being filtered out as they passed over the edges of leaves.[24] The insight—common among students of Locke and Newton—that colors were phenomena that existed nowhere but in the minds that experienced them was a crucial stimulant to much wider philosophical reflections.

Edwards' discussions contain sophisticated reflections on the scientific explanations of the day, occasional keen observations, a recognition of difficulties in current explanations of some natural phenomena, and fascination with scientific explanations. Samuel Hopkins reported that "he made good proficiency in all the arts and sciences, and had an uncommon taste for natural philosophy, which he cultivated to the end of his life, with that justness and accuracy of thought which was peculiar to him."[25] Because his love of theology and metaphysics eventually overwhelmed his scholarly interests in natural science, one can easily lose sight of this practical side. Persons who met him did not find someone whose head was only in the clouds, but rather someone who, despite his preoccupation with the spiritual meaning of things, knew many practical things about nature and mechanics. Like many eighteenth-century philosophers, Edwards was a polymath interested in all knowledge and fascinated by how things worked.

New England clergy, being the best educated persons in their communities, were often the chief interpreters of the new science. Jonathan knew well and apparently admired Cotton Mather's daring stance in urging inoculations during a devastating smallpox epidemic in Boston during 1721 and 1722. Probably at least one of Jonathan's sisters was studying there when the epidemic broke out. Mather's stance brought bitter popular opposition. Someone even attempted to bomb his house. James Franklin, who could not resist opposing whatever Mather proposed, attacked inoculation in his irreverent *New England Courant* as a way to fan anticlerical sentiments.[26]

Although science and religion among New England's clergy were firm allies, the characteristic ways of relating God's providential control to his laws of nature had subtly changed. As early as 1683 Increase Mather, almost an exact contemporary of Isaac Newton, helped found the Boston Philosophical Society, patterned after the Royal Society of London.[27] His precocious son Cotton, who was twenty in 1683, soon surpassed his father as a transmitter of the new science to the colonies, and eventually the Royal Society itself honored him with membership. Cotton Mather, however, came of age in a world different from that which young Edwards would find. New Englanders of the 1680s still lived in "an enchanted universe" filled with ghosts, devils, witches, and the preternatural, where one expected to see signs from God and wonders from a vast invisible world.[28] Increase Mather, in good scientific fashion, collected and republished accounts of preternatural providences, of people struck dead for disobeying God, of pacts with the devil, witchcraft, monstrous births, even a man who stole sheep and then had a sheep's horn grow out of his mouth. New England was hardly different from England in such beliefs. Even the pages of the *Transactions* of the Royal Society in these early days were a mix of the scientific and the preternatural.[29]

In the 1690s Cotton Mather paid dearly for attempting to preserve the preternatural as an area for scientific inquiry when he defended "The Wonders of the Invisible World" at the height of the Salem witchcraft convulsions. The hysteria and miscarriage of justice, even by the standards of the time, eventually led the Mathers to help bring the prosecutions to a halt. The fiasco also chastened clerical attempts to identify specific demonic powers in the succeeding years. By Edwards' time witchcraft and the preternatural had almost disappeared from clerical attention. In 1690 Cotton Mather could preach about a prodigious cabbage root he had seen that had one branch shaped like a cutlass, another like a rapier, and another like an Indian club, and pronounce that this was a special providential warning to New England. By the next generation such interpretations of prodigies would be a bit of an embarrassment.

Still, the educated of the early eighteenth century did not abandon their firm belief that God held New England and everything else in his providential care and that he might arrange nature to provide signs of how he was guiding history. One could still read providential signs, such as comets, earthquakes, natural disasters, or sudden deaths, as the Bible said one should, as warnings and judgments on specific sins. Typical of the mentality was a pamphlet published in 1719 by Mather's fellow evangelical preacher Thomas Prince on a wonderful aurora borealis he had seen in England three years earlier. Although the cosmic display was so spectacular that Prince briefly reconsidered his disposition not to look for prodigies, his considered view was that it was explainable both in terms of natural causes and as a divine sign, probably to remind people of the last judgment. His account, he noted, had received the imprimatur of the renowned observer of comets, Edmund Halley.[30]

This was the philosophical world in which young Edwards came of age. Thomas Prince became one of his closest friends. Edwards' attitudes on the dual character of natural phenomena were typical of the orthodox clergy of his generation. He was as eager as anyone to find God's hand in history or nature, but he also expected God to work through secondary, or natural, causes. While he often spoke of Satan as a personal agent, he almost never mentioned witches. This silence, characteristic of his generation, suggests their embarrassment over their immediate predecessors' overreading of the wonders of the invisible world.

Edwards was also cautious about reading everyday successes or failures as precise messages from God. Early in his diary, in January 1723, reflecting on a time of spiritual dullness, he wrote: "I find also by experience, that there is no guessing out the ends of providence, in particular dispensations towards me." He recognized that in a general way "afflictions come as corrections for sin" and should remind one to repent of "all our sin." Further, one should be reminded "that all things shall work together for our good; not knowing in what way, indeed, but trusting in God."[31]

Although New England clergy successfully made the transition from the Aristotelian to Newtonian views of nature, the new science had implications for understanding the nature of God's providential care. During the long era when Aristotelian physics held sway, divine or demonic interventions created no theoretical problem. Aristotelians assumed that physical objects were naturally at rest and that motion was an acquired quality. So motion could be explained by the intervention of a personal mover, such as a spiritual being, without any disruption of the system of physical laws. Newtonians, by contrast, viewed the physical universe as a constantly moving system of interlocking mechanisms. If everything was in motion and exercised a gravitational pull on everything else, then one could not alter one part in the process without influencing the rest. As a teenage student Edwards recognized this problem and never turned away from its amazing implications. One of his early "Things to Be Considered and Written Fully About" was "To shew how the motion, rest and direction of the least atom has an influence on the motion, rest and direction of every body in the universe." That meant that "the least wrong step in a mote, may, in eternity, subvert the order of the universe." So one should "take notice of the great wisdom that is necessary in order thus to dispose every atom at first, as that they should go for the best throughout all eternity; and in the adjusting by an exact computation, and a nice allowance to be made for the miracles which should be needful." The vast computations necessary for all this testified to the necessity that God "be omniscient" and wise beyond our imaginings.[32]

A God of this magnitude, one who created and governed such an immense universe, could, of course, easily plan for miracles and arrange for any number of coincidences that would have special providential meanings. Nothing in the new conception of an automated mechanical universe necessitated a diminishing of God's immediate involvement. God saw every sequence of cause and effect from the vantage point of eternity. He saw beginning and end simultaneously. Yet he also governed the universe through an amazing system of sequential natural laws within which he could, as easily as not, make occasional prearranged adjustments for miracles.

The basis for this reconciliation of God's care with a largely automated universe was nothing new. Greek and medieval thinkers had long made distinctions among complementary levels of causation. God could be the ultimate cause of everything and could use the secondary causes, seen in natural laws, to bring about anything he wanted. Almost all thinkers of the new scientific age made this ancient distinction. They could affirm both that God governed everything and that he did so through a vast system of secondary causes, or natural laws.

Yet for many who had accepted the world of Newton's mechanics and of a God who worked through secondary causes, God's personal interventions could easily seem superfluous. Some of the best thinkers advocated "rational religion" and Deism, which made just this point. In England, John Toland, a disciple of Locke, led the way in popularizing such views in his *Christianity Not Mysterious* (1696). God, said Toland and a number of other influential deistic writers, was an all-wise Creator who established universal natural laws and universal moral laws for free creatures. According to reason, such a God would be wise enough to design a universe of laws that operated on its own, so that he would not have to intervene personally to make miraculous adjustments.[33]

The deists are sometimes almost equated with eighteenth-century enlightened thought, but it is often forgotten how many other renowned thinkers, especially at the dawn of that century, were resisting this dismissal of God's intimate involvement with the physical world. The most prominent was Isaac Newton himself. Newton was a pious, if unorthodox, Anglican with deep theological interests and an expert knowledge of the Bible. At one point before he published *Principia* (1687), he put aside his work in physics because he was more fascinated with his studies in theology and biblical prophecy. Though he questioned the Nicene formula on the Trinity, he did so on the basis of his study of Scripture, and he kept his heterodoxy largely to himself. Throughout his career he kept notebooks on prophecies, typologies, church history, and related topics, devoting himself particularly to deciphering the meanings of mysterious biblical prophecies.

In Newton's own Newtonian universe there was plenty of room for God not just as creator, but as sustainer of physical reality. Early in his career he became particularly alarmed by what he saw as an absurd dualism in Descartes' philosophy that separated matter from spirit and thus, in Newton's view, could lead to an atheism in which matter operated independently of God.[34] Newton's conception of gravity kept God immediately in the picture. Since gravity was simply a property of all matter, without any mechanical explanation, Newton attributed it to the will and action of God the creator and sustainer of matter. What was matter after all but a place in the universe that God had infused with certain powers, such as the power of resistance to other matter trying to pass through it and the power of attraction to other matter even at a distance?[35] In *Opticks* Newton asked, "does it not appear from phenomena that there is a Being incorporeal, living, intelligent, omnipresent, who in infinite space, as it were in his sensory [sense organs], sees the things themselves intimately, and thoroughly perceives them, and comprehends them wholly by their immediate presence to himself."[36]

Newton had derived much of his philosophy from the Cambridge Platonist Henry More (1614–87), who became his elder colleague and friend at Cambridge University. More preceded Newton in his adamant opposition to what they saw as the materialism inherent in Descartes' dualism. As a Neo-Platonist, More insisted that the universe was a single, basically spiritual, reality. He insisted that God was intimately involved with all beings since only through God's action could anything possess the powers that defined it as being.[37]

For New Englanders, Henry More provided a bridge to Newton. Cambridge had been a Puritan stronghold, and even though the Cambridge Platonists put more emphasis on reason as an independent source of religious knowledge than did the stricter Calvinists, More became well known at Harvard before the end of the century. New Englanders, who were schooled in pagan classics, were used to appropriating authors selectively, and they could read More critically, yet with much appreciation. More was so influential because Platonic traditions that emphasized physical reality as a copy or shadow of a purer spiritual reality existing in the mind of God had always had a prominent place in New England thought.[38] So it was not unusual that Edwards had read More by his senior year at Yale or that More's ideas should be evident in his appropriation of the new science.[39]

## The Universe as God's Language

Far from being the frontier boy who, after reading a few works, spun out a whole new conception of Western thought, Edwards could have gleaned his basic views from any number of sources. Indeed, although he displayed originality and genius as he worked out his own exact formulations, his fundamental outlook was strikingly akin to that of a group of late seventeenth- and early eighteenth-century thinkers who have been characterized as "theocentric metaphysicians."[40] When Edwards was coming of age, for instance, one prototypical philosopher was Gottfried Wilhelm Leibniz (1646–1716), a German ecumenical Christian who rivaled Newton in the discovery of calculus and was renowned for a theory of God's constant action in the universe and for his *Theodicy* (1710) justifying God's ways in maintaining the best of possible worlds. Leibniz does not seem to have influenced Edwards directly, but their ideas bore resemblances because they were working in the same field of discourse. Edwards' thought also has some similarities to the views of Nicholas Malebranche (1638–1715), a French Augustinian Catholic philosopher and theologian who held that things are really God's ideas and that the unity of the soul with God is the proper source of knowledge.[41]

Interpreters of Edwards have long noticed parallels between his philosophical idealism and aspects of that of Bishop George Berkeley (1685–1753). Berkeley, an Irish Anglican, argued that Locke's empiricism would lead to skepticism if some things had essentially material existence, yet we knew them only as ideas in our minds. Things truly exist, he countered, as ideas in God's mind. Berkeley had published his views by 1710, but Edwards seems not to have read him directly before the mid-1720s, after his own philosophy was well in place.[42] Berkeley ministered in Newport, Rhode Island, from 1729 to 1731 and became a benefactor to Yale College; Edwards may have even met Berkeley on a trip to Newport in 1731.[43] Edwards appropriated some of Berkeley's views once he read them, but their similarities grew mainly from their common concerns with the most demanding philosophical and theological questions of the era.

The young Edwards was aligning himself with some formidable philosophers who were taking a stand against those who would draw a line between the material and the spiritual and thus distance God from a direct role in creation. Not only Cartesians but many Newtonians, despite Newton himself, were moving in this dualistic direction. The countermovement asserted that the new science was fully compatible with God's most intimate involvement with every moment of existence. Not only could they point, as everyone else did, to the marvels of the intelligent design of this immense creation, but they were attempting to show why it was logically necessary that God's immediate power must sustain creation even in its most minute detail.

When Edwards began his notebook on these topics while still a graduate student at Yale, his main concern was to head off the materialist philosophies that the scientific revolution might invite. The most direct advocate of such views was Thomas Hobbes (1588–1679), the enfant terrible of seventeenth-century English philosophy, who unlike his more pious contemporaries, suggested what later became a triumphant modern view, that material being is the essence of reality. Edwards, who had not studied Hobbes directly, nonetheless recorded a reminder for the book he was planning "to bring in an observation somewhere in a proper place, that instead of Hobbes' notion that

God is matter and that all substance is matter; that nothing that is matter can possibly be God, and that no matter is, in the most proper sense, matter."[44]

This comment was related to other themes he was developing concerning the basic nature of created reality. Following a suggestion of Newton,[45] Edwards argued in a very early set of entries concerning atoms, that the essence of these smallest particles must be their indivisibility, that is, they cannot be made any smaller. This resistance to division must be, in turn, the essence of solidity. So solidity did not have to do most basically with taking up a certain amount of space ("extension" the Cartesians called it), but was rather essentially a power, the power of resistance. This power must, of course, arise ultimately from God, the Creator. A corollary was, "We by this also clearly see that creation of the corporeal universe is nothing but the first causing resistance in such parts of space as God thought fit."[46]

Creation was thus not something that happened just long ago, it also was ongoing. "The first creation," he wrote, is "only the first exertion of this power to cause such resistance." God must continue to preserve these powers or the universe would cease to be. "The universe is created out of nothing every moment," said Edwards, "and if it were not for our imaginations, which hinder us, we might see that wonderful work performed continually."[47] So this "power of being [is] communicated successively from one part of space to another, according to such stated conditions as his infinite wisdom directed." In other words, as he put it in the next corollary, God's ongoing creative power was communicated by "that we call the laws of nature in bodies, to wit: the stated methods of God's acting with respect to bodies."[48]

Gravity, for instance, was not something for which one should expect to find a mechanical cause; it was an inherent quality or power of solidity. It was a power closely related to the power of resistance, and these two powers determined the harmonious relations of bodies to each other. Although gravity operated according to predictable laws, it was no less the direct action of God. So Edwards, reflecting the opinion of Newton and many popular scientific writers of his day, asserted, "it is universally allowed that gravity depends immediately on the divine influence." It followed then, that "if gravity should be withdrawn, the whole universe would in a moment vanish into nothing."[49]

By summer 1723, when Edwards had returned home from New York and resumed work on his scientific notebooks, he had developed much more radical implications of these ideas. His thinking up to that time had not strayed far from the Lockean and Newtonian principles found in the contemporary scientific literature. That summer, however, he extended this line of thought to a momentous conclusion that some other philosophers of the era had also reached, that "nothing has any existence anywhere else but in consciousness." To prove this startling point he suggested that we think of "another universe only of bodies, created at a great distance from this." Only God would know its wondrous motions and spectacular beauties because this universe contained no other intelligence. So where else, he asked, do these beauties and relationships of motions exist other than in the divine consciousness? Suppose the divine consciousness were also removed for a moment. Then, said Edwards, that universe would cease to be, not only because God would not be maintaining it, but because God knew nothing of it. This might be counterintuitive, but Edwards stated confidently that "this will appear to be truly so to anyone that thinks of it with the whole united strength of his mind."

To illustrate this difficult point, he asked his supposed reader to imagine that the world were deprived of light. In that case all color would cease to exist. The color green did not abide in the leaf but existed only when there was both light and someone to perceive those reflected rays as green. This was a fairly conventional point of the day, but it pushed Edwards to his more radical implication. The solidity of bodies was the same sort of thing as colors, something that did not exist in itself but only as a power that could be perceived under certain conditions. If bodies were essentially the power of resistance to other bodies, then suppose the universe were deprived of motion. Then that power would never truly exist because it was something that could not be experienced any more than color could be experienced in a world without light. So then:

> Put both these suppositions together, that is, deprive the world of light and motion, and the case would stand thus with the world: There would be neither white nor black, neither blue nor brown, bright nor shaded, sellucid nor opaque; no noise or sound, neither heat nor cold, neither fluid nor wet nor dry, hard nor soft, nor solidity, nor extension, nor figure, nor magnitude, nor proportion; nor body, nor spirit. What then is become of the universe? Certainly, it exists nowhere but in the divine mind. This will be abundantly clearer to one after having read what I have further to say of solidity, etc. [i.e, that solidity is resistance]. So that we see that a world without motion can exist nowhere else but in the mind, either infinite or finite.

From this it followed, as he immediately added, "that those beings which have knowledge and consciousness are the only proper and real and substantial beings, in as much as the being of other things is only by these." So, he concluded triumphantly, materialism is defeated: "From hence we may see the gross mistake of those who think material things the most substantial beings, and spirits more like a shadow; whereas spirits only are properly substance."[50]

This point may seem hard to grasp and will remain particularly elusive unless one recognizes that Edwards was developing his physics and his metaphysics in relation to the central component of his thought, his theology. He was not, like Locke, trying to build a philosophy from the ground up, starting with human experience. Nor was he, like Descartes, trying to deduce a universe by starting with the dictates of human reason. Rather he was developing his thought in rigorous Calvinist fashion, from the top down, starting with an absolutely sovereign triune Creator who was in control of all things. The universe was a universe of relationships and the ultimate relationship was always to the Creator.

Everything in his religious training and in the Calvinist theologians, whom he studied as assiduously as he studied Locke or Newton, disposed him to think in this holistic way. The "old logic" of Ramism was built around this principle of a universe of relationships in which everything had its place. This outlook had set his habits of thought since he was a child, and as an adult he never departed from its essentials.[51] Edwards, like his New England predecessors, imbibed this comprehensive view of things from William Ames' *Technometria* (1631), a Ramist handbook "which adequately circumscribes the boundaries and the ends of all the arts and of every individual art."[52] Ultimately, everything existed as archetypes in the divine mind. Humans see only the signs and shadows of this perfect reality.[53]

Ramism, of which much has been made regarding seventeenth-century New England thought, was only one tool in the service of much larger ideal of establishing an "encylopedia" or, literally, a "circle of learning." Edwards inherited this ideal from the impressive world of seventeenth-century international Reformed or Calvinist thinkers, which shaped him as much as did purely British writers. A standard work in New England libraries, for instance, was John Alsted's *Encyclopedia Scientiarum Omnium* (1630), which was a compendium of nothing less than, as its title said, "the circle of all knowledge." All things in God's universe were related, and the goal of learning was to recognize the circle of relationships. If one started from the right premises, drawn from Scripture, reason, and observation, one could be confident in the ability to discover the order of reality because it was a manifestation of the perfect patterns in the divine mind. Though Edwards' version of the ideal was shaped by Reformed sources, variations on the encylopedic idea were commonplace in European thought.[54]

What Edwards took from this tradition, following his Calvinist and Augustinian predecessors, was not a static Platonic idealism in which the material world was a copy of fixed ideals that existed in an ultimate Mind. Rather, his universe most essentially consisted of persons and relationships. The Creator was a *personal* acting God. God in this tradition was a trinity, a social being of interrelated persons. The doctrine of the trinity, which set Christianity apart from abstract Greek and Deist theism, was a subject of extraordinary interest to Edwards. In his "Miscellanies" notebooks, he constantly returned to this theme. The very end for which this supremely social being created the universe was, as he wrote in an early entry, "the communication of happiness" to his creatures.[55]

If the universe is most essentially intended for the communication of God's love, beauty, and happiness to his creatures, Edwards believed, then it also makes sense to view physical objects as existing most essentially in minds rather than as independent material objects. Physical creation is a communication of God's love and beauty, but love and beauty require persons to share or appreciate them. With the eyes to see reality as it truly is one can see in nature types of the highest expression of the beauty of divine love, the sacrifice of Christ for the undeserving.

Typology, long a staple of Christian thought, was central to Edwards' conception of the universe. God had created lower things to be signs that poined to higher spiritual realities. The universe, then, was a complex language of God. Nothing in it was accidental. Everything pointed to higher meaning. Scripture, which itself was filled with types, was the key to reading the true meaning of everything else. The types in Scripture (for example, Joshua leading the people of Israel into the promised land) all pointed ultimately to the redemptive work of Christ. Nature needed to be interpreted as containing this same message. Everything was a symbol pointing either to the need for redemption or to some aspect of God's character and the redemptive love in Christ.

Jonathan's contemplative joys were of a piece with his philosophy and theology. His ineffable experiences as he walked alone in the fields were of the beauties of God's love communicated in nature. That created world was the very language of God. As Psalm 19 said, "The heavens declare the glory of God." The beauty of nature proclaimed the beauty and love of Christ. Indeed, in creation, as the Lord declared to Job, "the morning stars sang together, and all the sons of God shouted for joy" (Job 38:7). Enraptured by the beauties of God's ongoing creation, Jonathan recorded, "it was always my manner, at such times, to sing forth my contemplations."[56]

By fall 1723 Edwards was developing this sense of beauty into a creative line of thought that he believed might become the basis for a great masterwork. He started a new notebook, designed to be the basis for a treatise on "The Mind," or "The Natural History of the Mental World, or of the Internal World," and began with the subject of "excellency." Drawing on his Platonic and Augustinian heritage and current theories of beauty, he reflected on why some things appear more beautiful or excellent to us than do others.[57] In contrast to the later notion that "beauty is in the eye of the beholder," he took for granted that beauty originated from God who communicated various degrees of "excellency" in creation. Edwards' question was: "Wherein is one thing excellent and another evil, one beautiful and another deformed?" Thus equating excellency, beauty, and good, he concluded that these qualities had to do with right proportions. Things were excellent if they stood in proper relation to each other. This was illustrated not only by the simple harmonies of symmetrical proportions, but also in exceedingly complex harmonious relationships. For example, "That sort of beauty which is called 'natural,' as of vines, plants, trees, etc., consists of a very complicated harmony; and all the natural motions and tendencies and figures of bodies in the universe are done according to proportion, and therein is their beauty. Particular disproportions sometimes greatly add to the general beauty, and must necessarily be, in order to a more universal proportion."

So beauty or excellency consisted in right relationships to the whole picture, ultimately to the whole of being. All of reality was, as commonly held, a great chain of being. God, the essence of being, was perfectly spiritual and had created a hierarchy of other beings—angels, humans, animals, plants, inanimate things, and so on—with varying capacities to glorify God. Excellency, as Edwards defined it, was "the consent of being to being.... The more the consent is, and the more extensive, the greater is the excellency."[58]

"Consent of being to being" was the essence of love and hence of excellency and beauty. "One of the highest excellencies is love," Edwards wrote. "As nothing else has a proper being but spirits, and as bodies are but the shadow of being, therefore, the consent of bodies to one another, and the harmony that is among them, is but the shadow of excellency. The highest excellency, therefore, must be the consent of spirits one to another."

Physical beauties, whether in nature, human bodies, or the like, could be wonderfully good insofar as they were properly related to higher spiritual realities. On the other hand, physical relationships that were controlled only by the fleeting pleasures derived from limited lower parts of being could be "odious" because they often involved a "deformity," out of proper relation to the whole.

Perhaps the most helpful analogy for understanding Edwards' view of excellency and beauty is to music. One of his favorite terms was "harmony," which he often used as synonymous with "proportion." Reflecting eighteenth-century views of music, he considered how musical harmonies are inherent in various proper relationships of notes to each other. Extending this thought, he wrote: "Spiritual harmonies are of vastly larger extent; i.e., the proportions are vastly oftener redoubled, and respect more beings, and require a vastly larger view to comprehend them, as some simple notes do more affect one who has not a comprehensive understanding of music."[59]

To fully appreciate this analogy one should recall that Edwards was writing at the time when J. S. Bach (1685–1750) was at the height of his creative powers. In 1723 Bach had just arrived in Leipzig to assume his post as cantor and music director and was in the midst of putting together the first of his astonishing cycles of cantatas to be performed in the city's churches. Though Bach was Lutheran and German, he and Edwards were working in similar worlds of discourse where ineffable beauties that pointed to the divine were found in the harmonies of complex relationships. Bach had a keen sense of the fervent affective meanings of biblical texts. Perhaps the best-known example from this period is the *St. John Passion,* performed during Easter season 1724.[60] While Edwards probably never heard the works of Bach, he had heard other eighteenth-century music and knew enough about it to understand how complex harmonies, both challenging to the intellect and overwhelming to the affections, could point toward the divine.

Edwards' integration of his experiences of the sublime with his theology and the latest natural philosophy meant that he was strenuously resisting any desacralization of the New England worldview. Even though he took for granted a certain kind of disenchantment of the world since the days of preternatural powers, he was reasserting the immediate presence of God in everything. Rather than allowing the Newtonian universe to lead to a distancing of God from creation, Edwards insisted that the recently discovered immensities and complexities of the universe confirmed God's ongoing intimate expressions of his art and language in all that had being.

Edwards realized that his underlying metaphysics, that things existed essentially only in consciousness, was difficult for most people to grasp. One of his diary entries as a young preacher was "Remember to act according to Prov. 12:23, 'A prudent man concealeth knowledge.'"[61] While he continued to plan major treatises built on his profound insights, he did not yet venture to unveil his philosophy in public, let alone in preaching. He recognized that in everyday life, as in natural science, people can appropriately talk about things in the commonsense terms of their appearances. "Though we suppose that the existence of the whole material universe is absolutely dependent on idea," he observed, "yet we may speak in the old way, and as properly and truly as ever."[62]

In Edwards' view it would have been entirely beside the point to try to refute his idealism as the English Samuel Johnson was supposed to have attempted to answer George Berkeley's immaterialism by kicking a rock. The very starting point of Edwards' explanation was that God endowed rocks with the power of resistance, so that we will have the painful experience of such resistance if we try to kick one. Commonsense ways of analyzing physical realities—even if limited—would work perfectly well.

The problem with thinking that commonsense experience was ultimate, he was convinced, was a failure of imagination. At the very beginning of his notes for his projected work on natural science he wrote, "Of the Prejudices of Imagination." He subtitled this, "Lemma to the whole," meaning it would be a recurring theme or refrain. "Imagination" at the time meant literally the faculty by which one forms images of things. The source of prejudices, said Edwards, was that people get so used to perceiving things in common ways that they "make what they can actually perceive by their senses, or by immediate and outside reflection into their own souls, the standard of possibility or impossibility; so that there must be no body, forsooth, bigger than they can conceive of, or less than they can see with their eyes; nor motion either much swifter or slower than they can imagine." So, for instance, "some men will yet say they cannot conceive how the fixed stars can be so distant as that the earth's annual revolution should cause no parallax among them, and so are almost ready to fall back into antiquated Ptolemy, his system, merely to ease their imagination."[63]

In his diary in September 1723 he resolved never to close his mind to new scientific discoveries: "I observe that old men seldom have any advantage of new discoveries, because they are beside a way of thinking, they have been so long used to. Resolved, if ever I live to years, that I will be impartial to hear the reasons of all pretended discoveries, and receive them if rational, how long so ever I have been used to another way of thinking."[64]

Prejudices of the imagination were not confined to the old or the unlettered. A "very learned man and sagacious astronomer," whom Edwards had read, supposed the universe must be infinite because it was so immensely large. The astronomer had let the limits of his imagination get the best of him. "Suppose he had discovered the visible world, so vast as it is, to be a globule of water to another," Edwards retorted in his notebook, "the case is the same." Just because one can not imagine how large something is does not imply that it is infinite.[65]

People who limited their sensibilities to what they base on their sense experience were condemned to a shortsighted view of things. Reason needed to correct mere experience. That was what the Copernican revolution had taught. Humans had not been able to conceive of the earth as in motion because all observation confirmed it was at rest. Once people got beyond their crude images of things and examined them by reason as well as observation, they discovered a universe far beyond their imaginations.

Edwards believed that he could develop a unified account of all knowledge, but it could not be discovered by experience and reason alone. God might speak in all of nature and in all of life, but the only place where one could find the key to unlock the whole system was in Scripture. All knowledge must begin there. Scripture was not just a source of information but the necessary guide to a radical life-changing perspective. As every New England child was taught: "The fear of the Lord is the beginning of knowledge" (Proverbs 1:7). The starting point for unraveling the mysteries of the universe must be the shattering revelation of one's total inadequacy and a recognition of God's love in Jesus Christ. One who was so changed could then experience how all creation was one harmonious hymn of praise to the glories of the Creator and the mercies of Christ. Without the grace that gave sinful and rebellious people ears to hear, they would never hear the sublime Christ-like choruses or see how the particular notes of reality all fit together.

# CHAPTER 5

# Anxieties

As the summer of 1723 wore into its dog days and Jonathan continued to be absorbed at his East Windsor home in his many spiritual and intellectual projects, he was becoming anxious. On three occasions in late summer he confided to his diary his worries about failure. "With respect to the important business which I have now on hand," he wrote in the most explicit entry, "resolved, to do whatever I think to be duty, prudence and diligence in the matter, and to avoid ostentation; and if I succeed not, and how many disappointments soever I meet with, to be entirely easy; only to take occasion to acknowledge my unworthiness; and if it should actually not succeed, and should not find acceptance, as I expected, yet not to afflict myself about it, according to the 57th Resolution." Resolution 57 reads, "Resolved, when I fear misfortunes and adversities, to examine whether I have done my duty, and resolve to do it; and let it be just as providence orders it, I will as far as I can, be concerned about nothing but my duty and my sin." Rather than fear failure or let it gnaw away at him, he must learn simply to accept God's providence.[1]

The "important business" appears to have been the M.A. oration he was to deliver at the Yale commencement on September 20. We might wonder why so superb a student should feel so much anxiety over success, failure, or even rejection. M.A. students needed only to study on their own for three years and then present a Latin defense of a thesis. This oration, called a *Quaestio,* took the medieval form of a syllogistic disputation in defense of a proposition. Disputations were the most engaging part of the college curriculum, and no one could have surpassed the relentlessly logical young Edwards in this syllogistic form. He had been honored at the commencement three years earlier by being asked to deliver the Latin valedictory oration, a privilege usually reserved for M.A. candidates.[2] So why the anxiety? Why the fears of possible "disappointments"? He was not going to be denied his degree. Something else rested on this. A future Yale tutorship? A church in the New Haven vicinity? In any case he seemed to have seen his public acceptance as a crucial matter.

"Commencement Quarter Days" were major public occasions marking the end of summer.[3] In a society that, in reaction to Catholic and Anglican traditions, had rid itself of religious holidays excepting the rigorous Sabbath, Commencement Day was a time for the colony to gather in celebration. For the common people it was like a market day in the normally placid village, a day when New Haven, once the capital of its own colony, came into its own. For the educated, the commencement was also serious business, involving a full day of Latin theses presentations, examination of candidates, and ceremonies. The college published the theses in advance, and even in ordinary times educated men all over New England took note of the propositions to be defended.[4]

The commencement of 1723 was no ordinary time, and the people who mattered would be hanging on every word. The colony was still reeling from the aftershocks of the words everyone had heard at commencement the previous year. On that occasion, the Reverend Timothy Cutler, the impressive rector, had closed the ceremonies with a prayer that ended with the shocking phrase: "*and let all the people say, amen.*"

This information resounded as though lightning had struck the podium. Some of the crowd might not have been surprised if lightning *had* struck the rector. It was as though, in a later era, at an NAACP rally, the president had unfurled a Confederate flag, or the commencement preacher at Bob Jones University had closed with a prayer to the Blessed Virgin. Cutler's words were straight out of the Anglican Book of Common Prayer. They were a signal that the very man chosen to be the chief guardian of New England orthodoxy had declared himself in the camp of the enemy.

This great "apostasy," as it became known, was recognized immediately. Storm clouds had been building and tension already filled the atmosphere. Anglicanism had been technically legal for decades in Connecticut, but no Anglican priest had successfully established a mission in the colony. Cosmopolitan Boston had learned to live with an Anglican presence, but every Connecticut town had resisted this Puritan nemesis. Strenuous efforts by the Society for the Propagation of the Gospel (the missionary wing of the Church of England) to plant churches in Connecticut found only stony soil.

People still living remembered Puritans in England who had suffered grievously for their faith when Charles II and Anglicanism were reestablished in
1660. For most Connecticut people, recounting such awful events still helped
define who they were.

Timothy Cutler had been brought from eastern Massachusetts to Connecticut in 1709 to counteract Anglican efforts attempting to gain a foothold
in the town of Stratford. His reputation as pastor there was so commendable
that a decade later the newly united Yale called him to be rector. When
shortly after his apostasy the stunned Yale trustees questioned him on his
betrayal, he confessed, to their dismay, that one of his reasons for leaving the
pastorate for the college was that he was already leaning toward Anglicanism.
During his tenure at Yale he had been meeting regularly with a group of
dissident clergy, including former Yale tutor Samuel Johnson and tutor
Daniel Brown, to read Anglican works and discuss the merits of episcopal
church government. The availability of the Dummer collection of books,
which included Anglican works of every stripe, provided grist for their high
church mill. When Cutler announced his apostasy, six of this group openly
joined the rebellion and may have been heard in the New Haven crowd
intoning their "amens."[5]

The consternation this caused may be difficult to appreciate. Nevertheless
the evidence is abundant. As far away as Boston it was the talk of the town.
Judge Samuel Sewall, friend of both Solomon Stoddard and the Mathers,
described it as "thunder-claps" from Yale. "The colony, the town, the society
from whence it came accented every sound." Connecticut, New Haven, and
Yale were supposed to be bastions of orthodoxy. Sewall wrote to Connecticut's Governor Saltonstall that the event put him in mind of the pouring out
of the vials of judgment predicted in Revelation 16. "I am fully of Mr. [John]
Cotton's opinion; that Episcopacy is that upon which the Fifth Vial [of God's
wrath] is poured out." Cutler "could not easily have lit upon a subject so
indefensible, as that of the English Episcopacy," which was "perfectly the
King's creature" and thus clearly a human invention.[6]

The Mathers, who saw this betrayal of the founders' principles in equally
cosmic terms, were up in arms. At Cotton Mather's Old North Church, they
held a Tuesday fast for "the pouring out of God's Spirit on New England,
especially the rising generation." Aging Increase Mather, in virtually his
last public utterance, "prayed, much bewailed the Connecticut apostasy" as
Sewall reported it.[7] Though Increase was failing, Cotton Mather still served
as the general at headquarters. The orthodox Connecticut clergy immediately

turned to him for help, urging him accept the Yale rectorship. "Our fountain, hoped to have been and continued the repository of truth, and the reserve of pure and sound principles, doctrine and education, in case of a change in our mother Harvard," they lamented, "shews itself in so little time so corrupt."[8] Cotton Mather was not prepared to leave Boston at this late point in his career. Always trusting in the power of the pen, however, he sent a circular letter to the Connecticut clergy urging them "to trace the pious steps of their forefathers."[9]

Meanwhile, the Mathers' opponents in Boston were having a field day. The virulent outbreak of anticlericalism of the previous year, spearheaded by James Franklin and the *New England Courant*, who opposed the Mathers' championing of smallpox inoculations, had just subsided. In spring 1722, the *Courant* was still comparing Mather to "a peevish mongrel," "dunghill cocks," and a "baboon." About this time, James' sixteen-year-old brother Benjamin entered the fray with a memorable pen name that caricatured Cotton, Silence Dogood.[10]

When the news from Connecticut broke, widow Dogood weighed in with her views on the virtues of religious moderation. Playing the role of a critic of the apostasy, she remarked that the Anglican rebels in Connecticut had displayed an "indiscreet zeal" in declaring that ordination except by bishops was invalid. That meant that all ordinations in New England by mere presbyters were invalid, including the rebels' own. Hence "we may justly expect a suitable manifesto of their repentance for invading the priest's office." There were "blind zealots among every denomination of Christians," she observed, but excessive zeal always hurt a cause.

In the same issue a rustic, "Jethro Standfast" of "Nuhaven" lamented the "most grevous rout and hurle-burle amung us." "Sum of owr pepel danse after thare pipe," he went on, "and tel us that owr Ministurs formurlay ware ordan'd by Midwives and Coblurs, but others sa that this is folce Doktrin, and belongs to the Church of Rume." A few weeks later a "Nausawlander" wrote to the *Courant* that "it behooves all men . . . to love and cherish their wives" since their marriages may be declared invalid because they had not been performed by clergy of apostolic succession. So great was the outcry, genuine as well as mocked, that three of the Anglican rebels—James Whetmore, Samuel Johnson, and Daniel Brown—wrote to the *Courant* denying that Mr. Cutler had ever claimed there was no salvation outside the Church of England and deploring the common equation of the Church of England with "popery."[11]

The issue was profoundly political, not simply a matter of religious preference. New England's identity was built around an established church that was Congregational or Presbyterian. New England's churches were not just tolerated "dissenters" as Congregationalists and Presbyterians were in England, they were the state church. If Anglicans became strong in New England, it was not hard to imagine the day when the colonies would be brought into conformity with the mother country, with an Anglican episcopal establishment. The current royal governor of Massachusetts, Samuel Shute, although from an English dissenter family, had recently come out of the closet as an Anglican, adjourning the Council for Christmas—an extra-biblical Anglican holy day that Puritans abhorred—and partaking in Anglican communion. Rumors flew in an ongoing pamphlet war. Some even accused high church Anglicans of being sympathetic to the Jacobite effort, most recently attempted in 1715, of placing the Roman Catholic Stuart "Pretender" back on the British throne.[12]

While real and exaggerated political fears made the Anglican apostasy at Yale a sensation, serious doctrinal issues worried the Reformed clergy just as much. If crypto-Anglicans had been teaching at the Connecticut college, they may have been subtly undermining the Calvinist orthodoxy of their young wards, including a future generation of clergy. For the Mathers and their allies, Anglicanism meant opening the floodgates to "Arminianism."

"Arminianism," named for the sixteenth-century Dutch Protestant theologian Jacobus Arminius, had become a catch-all term for most challenges to strict Calvinist teachings. Although Arminians affirmed that God's grace was essential to salvation, they also believed that people retained some natural ability to choose God's grace or to resist it. Salvation was not simply the result of God's sovereign decree from eternity to save some and not others.

"Calvinism" is and was an imprecise term also. New Englanders did not often use the word nor concern themselves much with the precise teachings of John Calvin. Rather they saw themselves as the heirs to what they considered the truly biblical outlook of "the Reformers." That tradition included Puritan, Presbyterian, and continental "Reformed" authors and came in many varieties. Despite the variations, those who considered themselves orthodox held to a core set of doctrines regarding God's sovereignty that contrasted with the "Arminian" view.[13]

New Englands' champions of orthodoxy thought of most Anglicans as Arminian—although they knew there were also Anglican Calvinists as well. In seventeenth-century England, Puritan efforts to purify the Anglican establishment had included opposition to Arminians, especially in high places. Now, in the eighteenth century, optimism regarding human abilities had grown widely within fashionable Anglicanism and even among some dissenters. In eighteenth-century New England one of the appeals of Anglicanism was as a refuge for those fleeing Calvinist rigors.

Yale was the last place to expect heresy. Connecticut's clergy, loyal to the essential doctrines of their Puritan forebears, had founded their own college partly in reaction to fears that Harvard would lose its orthodoxy after Increase Mather was ousted from its presidency in 1701. Cotton Mather, expecting the worst, had supported their efforts. Yet while Harvard had indeed become more cosmopolitan, it remained essentially orthodox, as did Boston's Congregational clergy.[14] Now it was a shock to find that Yale in conservative Connecticut had turned out to be the real hotbed of apostasy.

Yale's trustees made sure no such thing would happen again. All future rectors, tutors, and trustees, they declared, would have to subscribe the Confession of Faith in the Saybrook Platform of the Connecticut churches (essentially the Westminster Confession of Faith) and give satisfaction "of the soundness of their faith and opposition to Arminian and prelatical corruptions or any other of dangerous consequences to the purity and peace of our churches." In the absence of a rector, they appointed two young men of unquestioned orthodoxy, James Pierpont Jr. and William Smith, to serve as tutors.[15] Both had graduated from the college just before Cutler arrived. Pierpont (Yale 1718) was the son of James Pierpont Sr., the late revered pastor New Haven's First Church, who until his death in 1714 had been the principal trustee of the college. William Smith (Yale 1719) was the older brother of Jonathan's dear New York friend, John Smith. Edwards was very much in the same circle as the new tutors.

In the midst of the aftershocks from the previous commencement, we can sense the drama of the occasion for which young Jonathan was preparing his address in 1723. He was addressing one of *the* subjects, Arminianism. He may have viewed this as an important public declaration so far as his future was concerned. After all, he had studied with Cutler. He had admired the impressive rector and been a star pupil. He had read the Dummer books, including many controversial Anglican works, probably more than any other student. Yet he was going to prove that he had come through the test all the wiser. If it was not clear already, he was declaring himself unmistakably in the party of orthodoxy.

Typically, Jonathan not only saw his future at stake, but he viewed the

The
Commencement
at New Haven
in 1718

Drawing of an early Yale commencement

issue in cosmic terms. Like Judge Sewall and most New England clergy, he considered this world a transient stage where a cosmic drama was being carried out. The key to this drama—the key to *history*—was the mysterious writings of the Apocalypse, or the biblical Book of Revelation. Early in the summer he had written an outline commentary on the Book of Revelation and had begun adding to this new notebook expositions of particular verses and topics. This was one of his principal projects that summer, one that he would resume immediately after his M.A. oration.

Like almost all Protestants, he saw the Church of Rome as the Antichrist that would be defeated in the last epoch of human history before the millennium. Guided by other expositors, he had made literal calculations from biblical prophecies and worked out a scheme for when these events were likely to take place. One conventional Protestant interpretation of prophesies concerning "the beast" in Daniel and the Apocalypse, for example, was that Antichrist or the papacy would be defeated 1,260 years after the rise of the papacy. Edwards followed those who said that A.D. 606 marked the Pope's ascendancy, so that meant the decisive blow against papal power was likely to occur around 1866.[16]

In assessing such apocalyptic thinking, we must be reminded that such expositions of biblical prophecies were commonplace among some of the best thinkers of the era. Isaac Newton is the most prominent example. Newton was as antipapist as Edwards and shared the Protestant assumption that the Church of Rome was Antichrist. Because the Bible was accepted as an authoritative text, it made sense to subject it to scientific and mathematical analysis, just as one might analyze God's secondary revelation in nature. Questions on how biblical prophecies fit with history and the future were topics that the best-educated people might argue about endlessly. In Newton's younger days his elder friend Henry More, the Cambridge Platonist and greatest English philosopher of his era, had calculated the date of the rise of the papacy to as early as the reign of Theodosius, around the year 400. Newton thought it should date from the rise of papal apostasy, which he dated at 607.[17] Newton took up the subject again in old age. We can imagine that at some moment in the summer of 1723 both Newton and Edwards may have been sitting in their respective gardens, working to crack the prophetic code.

New England's spiritual leaders almost universally interpreted contemporary history in such apocalyptic lights, and they continued to do so through the Revolutionary era.[18] Typically they reminded their audiences of this larger meaning in their fast day and militia day sermons. Wars with the Roman Catholic Spanish or French powers and their allies were not merely international rivalries or colonial power struggles but were also scenes in the later acts of the struggles between Christ and Antichrist.

We must consider how the world looked to New Englanders of the early eighteenth century if we are to understand their apocalyptic interpretations of contemporary events. Most of Europe's wars of the past two centuries, as Protestants of New England perceived them, were best understood as part of this fundamental struggle for reform of Christendom. Although in retrospect we know that in the eighteenth century the religious dimensions of the European struggles would diminish as they became clearly subordinate to interests of nation-states, that was not self-evident in the 1720s. It still made sense to believe that, even though reasons of state were always present, an era of predominately religious conflict would continue into the indefinite future.

Edwards had a keen sense of participating in this world historical drama. His early memories were of Queen Anne's War, of his father going away to serve as a military chaplain in the struggle against the Catholic menace. More recently, as his religious experience deepened, so did his partisanship for "the Protestant interest." In New York he acquired the habit of eagerly searching newspapers for any "news favorable to the interest of religion in the world."[19]

The Reformation was the great turning point that defined his calling on the world scene. It was the beginning of the defeat of the Antichrist of Rome. When Revelation 14 depicted an angel "having the everlasting gospel to preach unto them that dwell on the earth, and to every nation and kindred and tongue and people, saying with a loud voice, 'Fear God and give him the glory,'" Edwards commented, "this is doubtless at the Reformation."[20] When New Englanders said they were "Reformed," they were identifying with what they saw as the purest expression of the larger international Protestant cause.

Although perhaps his highest dream was to be among those who would preach "the everlasting gospel" to "every nation," Edwards also saw his talents as suited to an important intellectual role in the spiritual combat. His commencement oration would be a first foray. In his notebook exposition of the Apocalypse, he had interpreted one of the prophecies as predicting a heroic role for the logician in the latter days. In the last verse of Revelation 16, in connection with the pouring out of the final and seventh vial on apostate Babylon, the vision revealed that "there fell upon men a great hail out of heaven, every stone about the weight of a talent." Edwards' gloss was: "by this hail seems chiefly to be meant such strong reasons and forcible arguments and demonstrations, that nothing will withstand them; and [they] will irresistibly beat down and immediately batter to pieces the kingdom of Antichrist, and kill men as to popery, as at one blow, as if they were dashed to pieces by stones from heaven."[21] Although it might take more than a hundred years (if the decisive blow were to be struck around 1866) for these arguments to have their accumulated devastating effects, that was not long in an era when theological works had life spans of many centuries. Whatever Edwards' role in stocking the Reformation arsenal, already well supplied with the scholastic works of the past century, he was confident that the triumph was sure.[22]

To understand Edwards throughout his career, we must appreciate the premium that he and other educated eighteenth-century people placed on logic. Along with the study of language and the classics, logic was the bedrock of the educational system. Every schoolboy was trained in the basics of dialectic. In New England, ordinary parishioners had cut their eyeteeth on the logic of carefully argued sermons. Many eighteenth-century philosophers believed that most major philosophical disputes could be permanently settled if only they could get their premises straight and think clearly about them. Many eighteenth-century citizens, laymen as well as clergy like Timothy Cutler and his friends, were willing to risk their careers on matters they regarded as demonstrated principle. In such a setting, a penetrating intellect such as Edwards' was a powerful weapon. No one trusted in it more than he. But like any source of power, it was also a source of danger. Sometimes oblivious to danger, from this first day of his public career to his last, he would wield this weapon relentlessly in the service of the Lord.

In his commencement oration Edwards was entering the lists to prove himself worthy to fight for the true Protestant cause in two respects: he would demonstrate his loyalty to the orthodox party, and he would display his syllogistic skills, suited to play a leading role in the battle for the truth. The proposition he was defending was most basic to "Reformed religion": "a sinner is not justified in the sight of God except through the righteousness of Christ obtained by faith." Arminian opponents of this Reformed formula argued that God justified sinners, at least in part, on the basis of their sincere repentance and reformation. Edwards countered that, in addition to such a doctrine being inconsistent with Scripture, it involved a number of plain contradictions that could be demonstrated by logic alone.[23]

The commencement examiners may have also quizzed Edwards in Latin on the other of *the* subjects—whether "God has left many things in worship to human determination." At least he hastily sketched some Latin syllogistic arguments on this topic on the back of his oration manuscript. While these jottings are not complete, he had commented on this issue in his "Miscellanies" earlier in the summer. The strict Reformed view was that worship must be guided by biblical principles alone. If the ceremonies of the Church of England were valid and legally binding, even though extrabiblical human inventions, Edwards argued, then the prior laws of the Church of Rome would be binding so that one would be required "not at all to obey the Church of England but the Church of Rome." That was, of course, absurd. Hence the claims that the Church of England was the true apostolic church could be laid to rest.[24]

Although we must imagine that Jonathan succeeded admirably in the

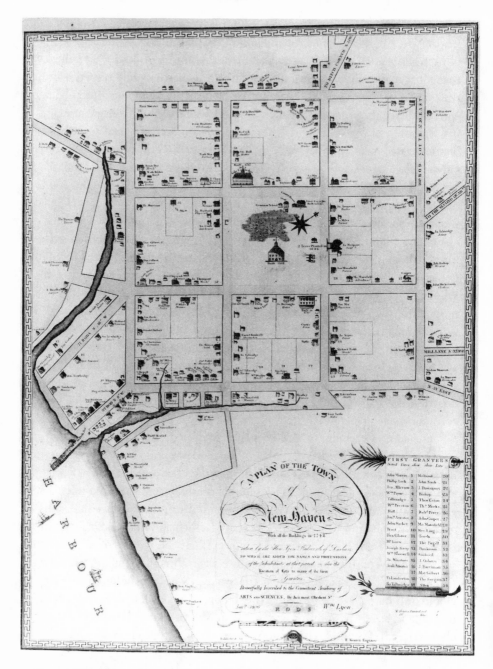

Central New Haven, from a 1748 map. The Pierpont home is next to the green on the right, within sight of Yale College.

syllogistic jousting before the Latin speakers of the commencement crowd, we do have a clue as to why he feared failure and rejection, despite his obvious skills. Far more rode on the performance than a mere degree. He had resolved particularly "to avoid ostentation," perhaps realizing that in New Haven he had a reputation for being being aloof and proud. A good impression could open up an ideal career opportunity. For one thing, the Anglican apostasy had left a number of churches open in the New Haven area. That such possibilities were in the air we know from a letter written by Tutor James Pierpont. Loyal to his illustrious father's memory, James was determined to keep Yale orthodox. Having completed his B.A. two years before Edwards, he was one of New Haven's bright young men and knew Edwards well enough to vouch for him. In early November he wrote to Yale trustee Timothy Woodbridge, suggesting that Edwards would be just the sort of person to be settled at the nearby church in North Haven. It would be, he urged, "both for the interest of the trustees and safety of the college to have the neighboring clergy both able and well principled both which in my account Mr. Edwards bids very fair for."[25] From Jonathan's point of view, to be located in North Haven near the Yale library, rather than at the crossroads hamlet of Bolton, where he seemed headed otherwise, must have been an alluring prospect.

The Yale library may not have been all for which he pined. James Pierpont Jr. had a younger sister, Sarah. In 1723 she was thirteen and Jonathan had known her at least since he moved to New Haven in 1719. He attended New Haven's First Church where he would see the family of the former pastor every week. Sarah's mother, Mary Hooker Pierpont, came from one of the most distinguished ministerial families in Connecticut and was the granddaughter of the renowned founder of Hartford, Thomas Hooker. Timothy Edwards had been an ally of the staunchly orthodox James Pierpont Sr. and would have paid his respects to the widow when in New Haven. Possibly Jonathan was a regular visitor in their home, which was diagonally across the green from the college building.

If tradition is correct, she was already much in his thoughts. What we do know is that he wrote a prose poem about her. Though the original is now lost, it is supposed to have been written in 1723 on a blank endpaper of a book he presented to her.[26]

> They say there is a young lady in [New Haven] who is beloved of that almighty Being, who made and rules the world, and that there are certain seasons in which this great Being, in some way or other invisible, comes to her and fills her mind with exceeding sweet delight, and that she

hardly cares for anything, except to meditate on him—that she expects after a while to be received up where he is, to be raised out of the world and caught up into heaven; being assured that he loves her too well to let her remain at a distance from him always. There she is to dwell with him, and to be ravished with his love, favor and delight, forever. Therefore, if you present all the world before her, with the richest of its treasures, she disregards it and cares not for it, and is unmindful of any pain or affliction. She has a strange sweetness in her mind, and sweetness of temper, uncommon purity in her affections; is most just and praiseworthy in all her actions; and you could not persuade her to do anything thought wrong or sinful, if you would give her all the world, lest she should offend this great Being. She is of a wonderful sweetness, calmness and universal benevolence of mind; especially after those times in which this great God has manifested himself to her mind. She will sometimes go about, singing sweetly, from place to [place]; and seems to be always full of joy and pleasure; and no one knows for what. She loves to be alone, and to wander in the fields and on the mountains, and seems to have someone invisible always conversing with her.[27]

This was quintessential Jonathan. Whatever his underlying emotions, he expressed them as pure platonic Christian love. Sarah was his Beatrice. Indeed, Edwards lived in a world of spiritual realities that was in some respects closer to the medieval Dante's than to our own. Sarah was the perfectly embodied ideal of all that he aspired to be, the pure spiritual being, sweet tempered, singing sweetly, always full of joy and pleasure. The last sentence— of conversing with God in the fields—is strikingly a mirror image of himself. Perhaps he had heard her speak of this delight; perhaps he had heard it from others. Sarah was the same age as Jonathan's most pious younger sister, Jerusha. It is possible Jerusha had accompanied her father and Jonathan to New Haven and reported to her brother of this soul mate. In any case, Jonathan was sure that in Sarah he had found a kindred spirit.

On the Sabbath evening, September 22, the day after his return home from New Haven, he wrote in his diary, "To praise God, by singing psalms in prose, and by singing forth the meditations of my heart in prose."[28] Singing God's praises, already his practice, was to reflect the harmonies of the spiritual universe in which all dimensions of reality were balanced. Everything was good if kept to its proper proportions in this universe of relationships and of loves. To sing spiritual songs, best expressed in the words of the sweet singer of Israel, was to be in tune with the Creator-Redeemer. Jonathan could also think of those harmonies as putting him in tune with the sweet young singer of New Haven, yet his burden for the next four years would be to think of her as essentially spirit.

The next day he was back at work on his notebooks. "My time is so short," he wrote in his diary, "that I have not time to perfect myself in all studies: wherefore resolved, to omit and put off, all but the most important and needful studies."[29] His time was short because he would soon have to take a position somewhere, at Bolton if nothing else opened up. Probably what he most urgently wished to work on were his complex reflections on the "excellency," as emanating in God's beauty and love and designed to elicit rightly proportioned harmonious responses from all spiritual beings. It was around this time that he deleted the beginning of an entry of his "Miscellanies" on "excellency" and rewrote it as the beginning of a new notebook on "The Mind."[30] The spiritual nature of love, beauty, and harmonies seen in his ode to Sarah Pierpont fit exactly with these deeper thoughts on the nature of the cosmos. As usual, he was working on many fronts at once, giving as close attention to the mundane as to the sublime. One of the last things he did during the ensuing month was to complete and carefully transcribe his "Spider" letter, dated from Windsor, October 31, 1723.

Apparently he was not so happy about the prospect of accepting the pastorate at Bolton. The town was only recently settled, mostly by people from Windsor and East Windsor.[31] Taking this modest position near to home seems to have been mainly his father's idea. On October 4, he confided to his diary: "Have this day fixed and established it, that Christ Jesus has promised me faithfully, that, if I will do what is my duty." He resolved to accept God's will no matter what his condition in life and "if I find need of faith in the matter, that I will confess it as impiety before God. Vid. Resolution 57, and June 9." Resolution 57 and the June 9 entry were resolves to do his "duty," even "when I fear misfortunes and adversities."[32]

Two weeks later, October 18, he determined, "To follow the example of Mr. B— who, though he meets with great difficulties, yet undertakes them with a smiling countenance, as though he thought them but little; and speaks of them as if they were very small." By this time the inevitability of going to Bolton for lack of an alternative was closing in. He had been clinging onto the possibility of going back to New York, but recently it became clear there was no position there. In the meantime, his expressions of continuing interest in New York had hurt his chances in the New Haven area.[33] By early November he dutifully moved to Bolton and on November 11 signed the town book agreeing to be their pastor.

Two weeks later he confided to his diary: "Nov. 26. 'Tis a most evil and pernicious practice in meditations on afflictions, to sit ruminating on the aggravations of the affliction, and reckoning up the evil, dark circumstances thereof, and dwelling long on the dark side; it doubles and trebles the affliction." The cure, he decided, was to think positively. "If we dwelt on the light side of things in our thoughts, and extenuated them all that possibly we could, when speaking of them, we should think little of them ourselves; and the affliction would really, in a great measure, vanish away."

This resolution to accentuate the positive seems to have carried over to his preaching. His sermons written at Bolton were among his most consistently in cheerful major keys. His own needs may have been a factor. One of the first sermons, which remained a favorite with him, was on *The Pleasantness of Religion*. His theme was, "Religion does not deny a man the pleasures of sense, only taken moderately and with temperance and in a reasonable manner." One of the first things his new parishioners must have noticed about the spindly twenty-year-old was how abstemiously he ate, even when they set great quantities of home cooking in front of him.[34] Nonetheless, he wanted to assure them that Christianity had a place for the proper pleasures of the flesh. "Religion allows us to take the full comfort of our meat and drink, all reasonable pleasures are to be enjoyed in conversation or recreation; allows of the gratification of all our natural appetites." The secret for keeping these pleasures reasonable was to enjoy them in the perspective of the far greater pleasures of spiritual things. Reason showed the vast superiority of things eternal, so it would be folly to enjoy pleasures of the flesh for their own sake. The righteous, by contrast, subordinate earthly passions to higher spiritual enjoyments so that they live in harmony with themselves, "all the powers are of one consent, and there is peace among them, and they all concur in the same thing."[35]

In another early sermon at Bolton, Edwards developed one of his most characteristic themes, drawing on a motif in the Puritan heritage and his own religious experience. Preaching on *A Spiritual Understanding of Divine Things Denied to the Unregenerate*, he emphasized that when "the eyes of believers are opened" in regeneration, "they do as it were see divine things." It is as though the work of the Holy Spirit gives them a sixth sense so that they not only know about divine things, but can experience their beauty directly. "Thus," in his most repeated illustration, "it is not he that has heard a long description of the sweetness of honey that can be said to have the greatest understanding of it, but he that has tasted." In a touching passage, he drew on his own longings:

"Thus with respect to earthly beauty, 'tis not the hearing of elegant descriptions of a beautiful face that can ever make a person have a sense of the sweetness and amiableness of the beauty; 'tis not the slight notion of beauty by hearsay that causes love to burn in the heart: but it is the sight of the eye. One glance of the eye doth more than all the most particular descriptions that can be given."

Like everything, the "glance of the eye" that causes "love to burn in the heart" must point toward higher spiritual things. Spiritual sensibilities counter the disabling shortsightedness of the worldly-minded. "Wicked men" have only "a low and narrow sort of knowledge" based on their immediate senses. Rather than knowing about only "the appurtenances of this clod of dirt," he urged the country folk of Bolton, they should seek the excellency of "the great Creator, the first and the last."[36]

Spiritual harmony, he quickly discovered, was not any more characteristic of the people of Bolton than was broadness of vision. They were at each other's throats. In one particularly blunt sermon preached in late December he practically pleaded with his congregation to live peaceably with one another: "We are but a little handful, Christ has but a little flock; and shall his sheep devour one another?" Typically, he argued his case in terms of a sort of Platonic view of human nature, in which reason teaches people to seek the spiritual rather than being subject to their animal passions. "We are all reasonable creatures," he urged. " 'Tis the part of beasts, of wolves, tigers, dogs and the beasts of the forest to bite and devour one another. 'Tis exceeding hateful amongst creatures that have reason and understanding, and of such a noble make."

Edwards' call for peace was so strong that he sounded almost like one of Boston's Calvinist moderates. "The gospel spirit is a catholic spirit, a noble and unconfined benevolence, like unto that of our Creator, not confined to any particular part of mankind exclusive of others." Christians should hate the sin but love the sinner: "To make the wickedness of men the cause of contention and strife in us, is to make one sin the cause of another. We cannot please the devil better than by hating men's persons under pretense of duty." Even doctrinal differences are no excuse for hatred. People can not help what they believe. " 'Tis as unreasonable to strive with others because they can't be in everything of our minds, as to quarrel with another because he differs in the color of his hair or the features of his face. . . . However pernicious his tenets, yet we ought, as much as in us lies, [to] endeavor to live peaceably with him."

The fledgling pastor, who had a lot of personal experience in suppressing resentments, even presented some homely advice: "By stepping a little back when we are resisted, the blow of the enemy loses its force, as a woolsack stops and deadens a bullet sooner than an oak tree because it gives way. So a man of a meek and mild temper kills strife sooner than he that resists."[37]

Edwards would never be the Poor Richard of the pulpit, but he did work hard at communicating. It was around this time that he wrote in his diary, for Friday, January 10, "Remember to act according to Prov. 12:23, 'A prudent man concealeth knowledge.'" In his Bolton sermons we can sense his Herculean efforts to make some of his most profound ideas intelligible to ordinary people. Imagery and analogy were his most powerful weapons. In a sermon titled *Nothing upon Earth can Represent the Glories of Heaven*, for instance, he used the text Revelation 21:18, "And the city was pure gold, like unto clear glass." We can imagine the tall, intense young man lecturing in a freezing meetinghouse to the huddled farm families on the glories of the heavenly city. The very setting of the unadorned room made the biblical pictures all the more important for exciting the imagination. One by one, Edwards recounted the similes used in Scripture to describe heaven—a crown, a kingdom, a treasure, a city, and so forth. His larger point was that, however wonderful it might be to imagine these things, earthly images are not really adequate. So the text provides an image that is like nothing on earth, gold that is clear as glass.

These biblical images, he explained, are "very faint shadows" that represent the joys of heaven humans are intended to enjoy. Here Edwards attempted to bring in the central thought of one of his most important recent "Miscellanies" entries. "God created man for nothing else but happiness," he assured his congregation. "He created him only that he might communicate happiness to him." His parishioners would have learned that "Man's chief end is to glorify God and to enjoy him forever," as the first question of the Westminster Catechism put it. Edwards assured them, "this is not different: for he created them that he might glorify himself this way, by making them blessed, and communicate his goodness to them."

The abstractions that followed in explaining this point may have sailed over the heads of some of his parishioners, but he came back down to earth with a theme he never tired of hammering home. How absurd would it be, he asked, to be satisfied with merely "earthly pleasures," "the same kinds of things that the beasts enjoy." The lesson for the farmers should be plain. "What reasonable [persons] cannot see the folly of groveling on the ground for a little dirt and dung, and all the while disregarding such manner of things as we have heard of, which are eternal and are offered even unto them, and they are urged to accept of? How dreadfully will such persons in torment cry out of this folly, how will they accuse and curse themselves forever for such neglects."[38]

Even though he spoke boldly from the pulpit, Jonathan had to remind himself not to lose his own eternal perspectives in his everyday efforts to be pleasing to others. In his diary he worried: "Monday, Jan. 20. I have been very much to blame, in that I have not been as full, and plain and downright, in my standing up for virtue and religion, when I have had fair occasion, before those who seemed to take no delight in such things." He was, he feared, being too tactful in not speaking of religious matters to those who scorned such conversation. "I have in some degree," he confessed, "minced the matter, that I might not displease, and might not speak right against the grain, more than I should have loved to have done with others, to whom it would be agreeable to speak directly for religion. I ought to be exceedingly bold with such persons, not talking in a melancholy strain, but in one confident and fearless, assured of the truth and excellence of the cause."

While he worried about his role as a country pastor through the lonely winter of 1724, at least once, probably in the spring, the old spiritual ecstasy flamed forth. In his "Personal Narrative" (in his only surviving mention of Bolton), he recalled: "having one special season of uncommon sweetness: particularly once at Bolton, in a journey from Boston, walking out alone in the fields."

Perhaps in connection with this experience he wrote in his "Miscellanies" one of his most beautiful meditations on the spiritual glories of nature. It begins with what must be a contemplation on Sarah, but which, as all else in nature, points to "the excellencies of Christ." "When we behold a beautiful body, a lovely proportion, a beautiful harmony of features of face, delightful airs of countenance and voice, and sweet motion and gesture, we are charmed with it; not under the notion of a corporeal, but a mental beauty. For if there could be a statue that should have exactly the same, could be made to have the same sound, and have the same motions precisely, we should not be so delighted with it; we should not fall entirely in love with the image, if we knew certainly that it had no perception or understanding." The highest raptures by which "when we love the person for the airs of voice, countenance and gesture; which have much greater power upon us" have to do with our resonating with the "excellencies of the mind." Physical beauties only point to those higher spiritual excellencies.

Edwards was captivated by the idea that God's purpose in creating the universe is to bring harmonious communications among minds, or spiritual beings, and every detail of physical creation points to that loving reality, epitomized in Christ. In this enthralling framework, he continued his meditation:

> When we are delighted with flowery meadows and gentle breezes of wind, we may consider that we only see the emanations of the sweet benevolence of Jesus Christ; when we behold the fragrant rose and lily, we see his love and purity. So the green trees and fields, and singing of birds, are the emanations of his infinite joy and benignity; the easiness and naturalness of trees and vines [are] shadows of his infinite beauty and loveliness; the crystal rivers and murmuring streams have the footsteps of his sweet grace and bounty. . . . That beauteous light with which the world is filled in a clear day is a lively shadow of his spotless holiness and happiness, and delight in communicating himself.[39]

Yet young Calvinist that he was, he was too well trained in the hermeneutics of self-suspicion to ever rest easy in his own experience, no matter how profound. Even contemplating the beauties of nature could be a temptation. So in Bolton, as spring was arriving, he wrote in his diary: "Monday, March 16. To practice this sort of self-denial, when at sometimes on fair days, I find myself more particularly disposed to regard the glories of the world, than to betake myself to the study of serious religion."

# CHAPTER 6

## "A Low, Sunk Estate and Condition"

In late May, Edwards received news that provided escape from Bolton—Yale had offered him a position as tutor. Apparently he and the people of Bolton had an understanding that his pastorate was provisional, because within two weeks he was on his way to New Haven. Yet, characteristic of someone for whom no silver lining lacked a cloud, getting the position he wanted proved a trial. He wrote wearily soon after his arrival in New Haven: "Saturday night, June 6. This week has been a remarkable week with me with respect to despondencies, fears, perplexities, multitudes of cares and distraction of mind; being the week I came hither to New Haven, in order to entrance upon the office of Tutor of the College. I have now abundant reason to be convinced of the troublesomeness and vexation of the world, and that it never will be another kind of world."[1]

We can only guess at these severe distractions. The most obvious were the disruptions of becoming a tutor, a position he would hold for a little more than two years. When Edwards arrived in June 1724, Yale College was struggling. It had been almost two years since Timothy Cutler's defection, and the trustees had still not managed to find a new rector. They were working their way through a list of Connecticut ministers but could pry none from their parishes. The college limped on without real leadership. The board designed a stopgap system of having local ministers serve as acting rectors on a monthly rotating basis, hardly an effective arrangement. That left the school, forty to fifty mostly teenage boys, in the hands of two tutors who were only a few years older.

College students could be unruly, as Jonathan already well knew. Even though the students were to be the future clergy or magistrates of the colony, many took advantage of the freedom from their families to cut loose in the meantime. Yale had perennial problems with drinking and rowdiness. The sudden exodus of Rector Cutler at a commencement season made the situation worse. The trustees strengthened penalties for frequenting taverns, bringing rum into the dorms without permission, and contempt for tutors.[2]

The college was particularly out of hand during Jonathan's years as tutor. According to the earliest college history, when in 1726 Yale finally got a resident rector (Jonathan's cousin and former tutor, Elisha Williams), he "began by degrees, more effectually to suppress vice and disorder among the students; and to introduce and settle a number of good customs." The reformation took some time because "the ill habits formerly contracted by the students were not easily and suddenly eradicated."[3]

One can imagine Jonathan striving with deadly earnest to enforce the strict college rules with students who had long since established their lax ways and were not about to give up their independence to the latest and the youngest in a series of tutors. Yale's rules were designed to suppress vice and cultivate piety, two goals Jonathan viewed as demonstrated by all reason to be of overriding eternal importance. A number of his diary entries suggest his concerns with student discipline. In one he commented, "If I had more of an air of gentleness, I should be much mended." In another he resolved, "When I reprove for faults, whereby I am in any way injured, to defer, till the thing is quite over and done with."[4]

Added to the irritations of disciplining were the burdens of teaching. Tutors taught the whole range of subjects, hearing all the recitations of a class (freshmen, sophomores, etc.) of students. Presumably Jonathan had charge of two classes. The day began at sunrise or at 6 A.M. in the winter, with chapel (prayers, Scripture, and exposition). Then the tutors heard recitations all day, with an hour and a half break for lunch. Evening prayers were from four to five in the afternoon. Then supper, free time, and time for study before lights out at eleven. The college maintained this schedule six days a week. The curriculum for Friday afternoon and Saturday focused on theological study. The Sabbath included the usual two lengthy church services, morning and afternoon, supplemented by explications of Puritan works, such as William Ames' *Cases of Conscience.*[5] For the students it was a day of rest mainly in the sense that they must abstain from the sports and diversions permitted on other days.

Adjustment to this time-consuming schedule, plus the distractions of discipline, must have been nerve-racking for Jonathan, especially since when left to himself he could easily fill a long day with intellectual pursuits and spiritual disciplines. Apparently he drove himself relentlessly. From his note-books we know that during these years he was especially productive in broad-ening his reading and preparing for his own works. During the first year, the college paid him and his fellow tutor, Robert Treat (Yale 1718), extra for organizing and cataloging the library. Edwards doubtless relished this oppor-tunity to peruse so much of the literature of his time and he developed a lengthy catalogue of books he needed to read.

Especially important for him was the opportunity to engage contempo-rary authors as he continued laying his plans to write a comprehensive defense of Christianity. He is credited with reintroducing Locke's *Essay Concerning Human Understanding* into the Yale curriculum. His notebooks, especially "The Mind," reveal that he was deeply engaged with Locke, from whom he learned much, despite his essential disagreements. He still sometimes called his "Miscellanies" his "Rational Account," referring to the major comprehen-sive apology for the Christian religion that he was preparing to write. In this notebook he was dealing with a wide range of theological and philosophical themes. He was making, for instance, a new set of entries on "Deism," which he recognized as one of the primary religious-intellectual challenges of the era. He also continued to prepare for treatises on natural science and on "the Mind," and he was still developing his "Notes on the Apocalypse." At Bolton he had begun his "Notes on Scripture," which would become one of his largest and most essential studies.[6]

Without a resident rector, commencement was particularly demanding for the tutors. Graduating students had to be prepared to defend their theses in Latin. Discipline was the greater problem because commencement week was a traditional time for the students to kick over the traces. After the "Commencement Quarter Days" of the previous year (when Jonathan de-fended his M.A. thesis), the trustees had to assess students for broken glass in the dormitories. No doubt mortified by the students' rowdiness at the very moment when the eyes of all New England were on Yale, the trustees voted fines for "any public disturbance by hallooing, singing or ringing of the bell unseasonably, firing guns, or otherways."[7]

Commencement week of 1724 precipitated a monumental spiritual crisis for the young tutor. Something happened that cast him into spiritual dol-drums from which he did not escape for three distressing years. He recog-nized the disaster immediately and recalled it long after, but he never indi-cated its source. Writing at the end of commencement week, he confided to his diary: "Saturday night, Sept. 12. Crosses of the nature of that, which I met with this week, thrust me quite below all comforts in religion. They appear no more than vanity and stubble, especially when I meet with them so unprepared for them. I shall not be fit to encounter them, except I have a far stronger, and more permanent faith, hope and love."

What thrust him "quite below all comforts in religion," it is difficult to guess. On September 30 he noted in his diary that "the hurries of commencement, and diversion of the vacancy, has been the occasion of my sinking so exceedingly, as in the last three weeks. The "diversion of the vacancy," probably referred to the two-week vacation after each quarter. Or it could have referred to the vacancy of the rectorship and the difficulty of policing his sometimes riotous charges. Still, as he carefully stated his problem, these were only the *occasion* of his being pushed below the comforts of his spiritual resources.[8] In his "Personal Narrative," written fifteen years later, he remarked, "After I went to New Haven, I sunk in religion; my mind being diverted from my eager and violent pursuits after holiness, by some affairs that greatly perplexed and distracted my mind."

His diary does not offer much to fill in the details. In the months immediately after the spiritual collapse, we get only a few glimpses of his struggles. Once again he was facing the dread of gnawing doubts that his conversion might be a delusion. In November he had some revival of hope: "Friday, Nov. 6. Felt sensibly, somewhat of that trust and affiance in Christ, and with delight committing of my soul to him, of which our divines used to speak, and about which, I have been somewhat in doubt." Still he soon found himself back in a spiritual wasteland. Within two weeks he was attempting to deal with his inability to concentrate in prayer: "Sabbath, Nov. 15. Determined, when I am indisposed to prayer, always to premeditate what to pray for; and that it is better, that the prayer should be of almost any shortness, than that my mind should be almost continually off from what I say."

As the crisis went on he turned less often to his diary. In February 1725 he made a rare entry that intimated that his spiritual deadness might have an intellectual component: "The very thing I now want," he wrote, "to give me a clear and more immediate view of the perfections and glory of God, is a clear knowledge of the manner of God's exerting himself, with respect to spirits and mind, as I have, of his operations concerning matters and bodies." Whether this issue could amount to the "affairs that greatly perplexed and distracted my mind" is not clear.

Giving up Calvinism entirely was not beyond his thoughts. "If ever I am inclined to turn to the opinion of any other sect," he wrote on May 21, 1725, "resolved . . . privately to desire all the help that can possibly be afforded me from some of the most judicious men in the country, together with the prayers of wise and holy men, however strongly persuaded I may seem to be that I am right."[9]

Finally, on May 28 he wrote in resignation: "It seems to me, that whether I am now converted or not, I am so settled in the state I am in, that I shall go on in it all my life. But, however settled I may be, yet I will continue to pray to God, not to suffer me to be deceived about it, nor to sleep in an unsafe condition; and ever and anon, will call all into question and try myself, using for helps, some of our old divines, that God may have opportunities to answer my prayers, and the spirit of God to show me my error, if I am in one."

The settled state was not one of despair. Rather it was one of guarded hope and firm resolve. We also know from his notebooks that he was still capable of reflecting on spiritual sensibilities much beyond the ordinary. Yet he seems to have lost the raptures, the ability to become lost in the direct experience of the divine.

Meanwhile, the light of his earthly love for Sarah Pierpont shone ever more luminously. By the spring 1725 their relationship had blossomed into a suit for her hand. Sarah was still only fifteen but by May or June they were engaged to be married.[10] The wedding would be in two years. Sarah would be considerably younger than the average New England bride, but such an early engagement was within the bounds of propriety.[11] The approval of James Pierpont Jr., sometimes his colleague as tutor at Yale, may have helped speed the courtship and provided ready access for Jonathan to socialize at the widow Pierpont's home.[12]

We have a rare glimpse from this summer of Jonathan in the company of other young people, in a happy mood sharing their ordinary joys. Writing in his "Miscellanies," he observed that it is good to set aside times for festivity. "Thus our elections are times of pleasure and rejoicing; and what an influence has it on the mind of the youth all over the Colony, to think this time is by general agreement made a time of mirth. How uneasy are they if they are alone and not in company, and han't opportunity to be merry as well as others; how extraordinarily unnatural and unpleasant does serious business and solitude seem at such a time, which would seem pleasant at another time; and how does it promote mirth, to think that the whole country are then merry. This abundantly convinces me of the rational foundation of sabbaths, and holy days of fasts and thanksgivings."[13]

Although he seems to have lost his immediate sense of divine things, he still could see the higher spiritual meaning of the most sublime of human experiences. During the spring of his courtship, in 1725, he wrote a series of meditations on love and heaven in his "Miscellanies." Their theme is much like the entry of the previous spring on "The Excellencies of Christ," though without the poetic flourishes. Whatever "ravishing" beauties one encountered in this life, he observed, whether in right proportions of light, sound, or motions of a body, would be perfected in heaven when there would be perfect harmony of minds.

Jonathan and Sarah both loved to sing, and Jonathan wrote that music pointed especially well toward the coming perfections of a universe of harmonious relationships. Music, he believed, was the highest way of communicating among persons. "The best, most beautiful, and most perfect way that we have of expressing a sweet concord of mind to each other, is by music. When I would form in my mind an idea of a society in the highest degree happy, I think of them as expressing their love, their joy, and the inward concord and harmony and spiritual beauty of their souls by sweetly singing to each other." The young lovers also enjoyed the complex harmonies of the music of the day. Yet their delights in earthly harmonies were only dim anticipations of the heavenly communication of spiritually fulfilled persons. "Then perhaps we shall be able fully and easily to apprehend the beauty, where respect is to be had to thousands of different ratios at once to make up the harmony. Such kind of beauties, when fully perceived, are far the sweetest."[14]

In the last of these entries "On the Love of Christ," Jonathan explored the usual typological meaning of human love as pointing to Christ's love of his bride, the church. In doing so he expressed his enthusiasm for human sexuality within, of course, its properly spiritual bounds. "We see how great love the human nature is capable of, not only to God but fellow creatures. How greatly are we inclined to the other sex! Nor doth an exalted and fervent love to God hinder this, but only refines and purifies it. God has created the human nature to love fellow creatures, which he wisely has principally turned to the other sex; and the more exalted the nature is, the greater love of that kind that is laudable is it susceptive of; and the purer and better natured, the more is it inclined to it."[15]

Much as he tried to turn his love for Sarah into the purely spiritual assent of minds, the problem of his sexuality must have been a source of deep tension for Jonathan as long as he was unmarried. Whether it had anything to do with his continuing in a low spiritual state, we can only speculate. Viewing the human condition as a warfare between flesh and spirit, he had a firm conviction that sexual impurity was incompatible with the spiritual sensibilities he sought. Indeed, he often preached that to be driven by short-term pleasures of physical lust was the epitome of self-love. The devil used such inclinations, not evil in themselves, to blind people to spiritual love to others and to God. As Jonathan had put it to the people of Bolton in a typical exhortation, those who indulged "the lusts of the flesh" could find no spiritual light. "They love sinful pleasures, carnal and sensual delights, which do becloud their souls and muddy their understanding, so that no light can enter in it."[16]

Although Jonathan was guarded in his diary, he occasionally alluded to the problem. In November 1725 he observed, "When one suppresses thoughts that tend to divert the run of the mind's operations from religion, whether they are melancholy, or anxious, or passionate, or any others; there is this good effect of it, that it keeps the mind in its freedom. Those thoughts are stopped in the beginning, that would have set the mind a-going in that stream."[17]

In dealing with any of these three recurrent psychic distractions, "melancholy, anxious, and passionate," his most typical cure was to keep driving himself to work his way out of it. So in a particularly revealing diary entry, for June 6, 1725, presumably at the height of his courtship, he observed of himself: "I am sometimes in a frame so listless, that there is no other way of profitably improving time, but conversation, visiting, or recreation, or some bodily exercise." Sensible as this advice might appear, he resolved not to give in to it so easily. "However," he concluded, "it may be best in the first place, before resorting to either of these, to try the whole circle of my mental employments."

His continuing strict diet was another way of suppressing the physical to enhance the mental and to get more work done. At the beginning of September 1724, his first year as tutor, he set down reasons to eat only lightly, which he believed would lengthen his life, help him think more clearly, study more, sleep less, and give him fewer troubles with "the headache."[18]

Constantly driving himself in so many ways was taking a toll on his health. His June 6, 1725, resolve to try overcome his listlessness by working "the whole circle of my mental employments" before resorting to conversation, visiting, or recreation, or some bodily exercise was his last entry before a severe physical collapse.

Once again the strains of commencement week seem to have been the last straw. After commencement in September 1725 Jonathan set out to visit his parents in East Windsor. He got as far as North Haven and collapsed, too ill to be moved. He stayed in the home of his fellow East Windsorite, Isaac Stiles, who had just filled the vacancy as North Haven's pastor. Jonathan's illness was serious enough that his mother Esther came to care for him. In his "Personal Narrative" he recalled this time as a hiatus in the spiritual lethargy of his years as tutor. "And in this sickness, God was pleased to visit me again with the sweet influences of his spirit. My mind was greatly engaged there on divine, pleasant contemplations, and longings of soul. I observed that those who watched with me, would often be looking out for the morning, and seemed to wish for it. Which brought to my mind those words of the Psalmist, which my soul with sweetness made its own language, 'My soul waiteth for the Lord more than they that watch for the morning: I say, more than they that watch for the morning' [Psalms 130:6]."

He must have again been near death since his nurses were sitting up with him through the nights. His mother stayed longer than she had expected and presumably Sarah was sometimes there also. He recalled: "about that time, I used greatly to long for the conversion of some that I was concerned with. It seemed to me, I could gladly honor them, and with delight be a servant to them, and lie at their feet, if they were but truly holy."

Sarah may have been among those for whom he was concerned. Sarah has long been romanticized as a saint since her childhood, as though she were always in sweet communion with the divine. Yet, if we learn anything from Jonathan's diary, Calvinist saints never sailed long on smooth waters with steady spiritual winds. Rather, faith was a constant struggle as God tested them and allowed Satan to toss them on stormy seas. Often it seemed to them that God had deserted them. Often they saw themselves as the greatest of sinners. Just as Jonathan was anything but secure or steady in his faith, so too was Sarah. Though Jonathan later judged she had been truly converted at an early age, he also noted that she, when "in lower degrees of grace," had "many ups and downs." She had, he explained, "a vapory habit of body" (a tendency toward depression—which he had also) and was "often subject to melancholy" and sometimes "almost overborne with it, it having been so even from early youth." At age sixteen, whatever her considerable virtues, she was much different from the idealized thirteen-year-old Jonathan had pictured as a purely spiritual being singing God's praises in the field. Like Jonathan—and as was expected in the tradition—she may have had deep doubts as to whether she had found saving grace. In the long run Jonathan admired her as the truest of saints, yet from the little candid information that survives and from what we know of human nature, we can be sure that her path was not always smooth.[19]

By November 16, 1725, Jonathan was well enough to resume his diary and was studying again. He resolved in his first entry: "to observe this rule: To let half a day's, or at most, a day's study in other things, be succeeded, by half a day's, or a day's study in divinity." At the same time, he resolved to be more sociable, observing that he erred in the social duties of writing letters to friends and visiting friends and relations.[20] At the insistence of the ever-cautious Timothy, rather than immediately resuming his tutoring duties, he returned to East Windsor to complete his recovery.[21] Once again he took up some work on his "Miscellanies" and other notebooks, mostly on usual topics, amassing evidences to confirm the truth of Christianity.

In one notable entry, he again placed his longing for Sarah in its larger spiritual context: "Happiness. How soon do earthly lovers come to an end of their discoveries of each other's beauty; how soon do they see all that is to be seen! Are they united as near as 'tis possible, and have communion as intimate as possible? How soon do they come to the most endearing expressions of love that 'tis possible to give, so that no new ways can be invented given or received." Once again, he contrasted the easily reached limits of human love with the infinitely progressing heavenly love between Christ and the saints: "And how happy is that love, in which there is an eternal progress in all these things; wherein new beauties are continually discovered, and more and more loveliness, and in which we shall forever increase in beauty ourselves; where we shall be made capable of finding out and giving, and shall receive, more and more endearing expressions of love forever: our union will become more close, and communion more intimate."[22]

By the winter term of 1726 he was back in New Haven to be reunited with Sarah and to resume his duties. At Yale there was still no resident rector, and he and his uncle of nearly his own age, Daniel Edwards (his grandfather's son by his second marriage) were the two tutors who tried to hold the disorderly college together.

Once again the Yale atmosphere and a multitude of concerns brought him back into the valley of spiritual emptiness. In his "Personal Narrative" he recalled: "I was again greatly diverted in my mind, with some temporal concerns, that exceedingly took up my thoughts, greatly to the wounding of my soul: and went on through various exercises, that it would be tedious to relate, that gave me much more experience of my own heart, than ever I had before."

What these "temporal concerns" were, we do not know. He did have a long dispute with the Yale trustees as to whether he should be paid his salary for the time he was ill. That would hardly seem sufficient, however, to give him the unprecedented self-knowledge that he described.[23]

A more substantial distraction and anxiety during this whole period was the question of his own career and ambition. Jonathan was intensely ambitious. He viewed himself as having a high calling from God, nothing less than to present the definitive defense of the Christian religion in relation to all knowledge and all possible objections. But what would be the platform from which he would speak? Being a college tutor was a short-term occupation. And, as the difficulties in a finding a leader for Yale showed, even being the rector of a college could be seen as a step down from an attractive parish.

By spring 1726 a great opportunity was on the horizon. Probably during the vacation between the winter and spring terms he traveled to Northampton to preach in his grandfather's church.[24] Doubtless this added to his anxieties. Solomon Stoddard was now in his eighties, and in the fall of 1725 the town had voted to hire an assistant. Possibly Stoddard had already had his grandson in mind but was prevented by Jonathan's illness from pursuing the matter. In the meantime, the town chose a young Harvard graduate from a distinguished family, Israel Chauncy, to fill the position temporarily. Jonathan's notebooks show that he was reflecting on his grandfather's writings. In August the town of Northampton formally invited Jonathan to come to serve as assistant. Jonathan apparently finished out his commencement duties and arrived by early October. On November 21, 1726, the town meeting voted, "by a very great majority" on the basis of "what experience we have had of him by his preaching and conversation and also from his character from other places" to settle permanently as a pastor to assist Stoddard. He was ordained February 15, 1727.[25]

Five months later Jonathan traveled to New Haven, where he and Sarah were married on Friday, July 28, 1727. We have only one hint about the occasion. Years later, in Stockbridge, Jonathan wrote part of a sermon to the Indians on a scrap of paper he apparently had saved for years. It was a bill to "Rev. Sir," from Boston, January 26, 1727, that included charges for silver buckles, white gloves, and a lute string.[26] We can guess that these items were for the wedding and that he would have seen music, the "most perfect way that we have of expressing a sweet concord of mind to each other," as especially appropriate to celebrating their union.

Marriage brought fulfillment to a courtship that we know little about except that it coincided with the time he was spiritually troubled. Whether that was simply coincidence is not clear. When Jonathan referred to the spiritual crisis of these years he usually related it to events connected to Yale, never to the stresses of courtship, unless they were the "temporal concerns" by which he was so distracted.

Jonathan and Sarah celebrated sexuality in the context of viewing it as ultimately a spiritual experience, pointing to the much higher bliss of Christ's relation to his church. A "Miscellanies" entry on the incarnation written around the time of his marriage is perhaps a commentary on the challenge for ordinary mortals to keep the spiritual thoughts supreme. When Christ was conceived in Mary's womb, Edwards observed, her "mind was filled with a divine and holy pleasure instead of sensual pleasure."[27]

By fall 1727 Jonathan had dramatically recovered his spiritual bearings, specifically his ability to find the spiritual intensity he had lost for three years. In a rare diary entry he wrote: "'Tis just about three years, that I have been for the most part in a low, sunk estate and condition, miserably senseless to what I used to be, about spiritual things. 'Twas three years ago, the week before commencement; just about the same time this year, I began to be somewhat as I used to be."

Exactly how this recovery was related to his marriage, we can not be sure.[28] We do know that Jonathan's renewed spiritual intensity shaped the way he experienced marriage. About a year after their marriage he started a new notebook, "Shadows of Divine Things" (later "Images of Divine Things"), dedicated to the reinvigorated spirituality. In it he collected his reflections on the spiritual meanings of nature, doubtless in part to share these with Sarah, who like himself had long been attuned to listening for this "language of God."[29] God's manner of speaking in creation was "to make inferior things shadows of the superior and most excellent, outward things shadows of spiritual."[30] In several very early entries he reiterated that "marriage signifies the spiritual union and communion of Christ and the church." This explicit biblical typology provided a basis for extending to all of life the principle of finding spiritual analogies. "If God designed this [marriage] for a type of what is spiritual, why not many other things in the constitution and ordinary state of human society, and the world of mankind."[31]

On August 25, 1728, Sarah bore their first child, another Sarah. Childbirth, a biblical image, was especially typical of the afflictive way God dealt with fallen humanity, even in bringing them the best things personally, spiritually, or through history. "Women travail and suffer great pains in bringing children, which is to represent the great persecutions and sufferings of the church in bringing forth Christ and in increasing the number of his children; and a type of those spiritual pains that are in the soul when bringing forth Christ."[32] Jonathan himself had just gone through years of the agonies of a sort of spiritual childbirth.

While noting the relationship between his marriage and his renewed spiritual intensity, we need also to keep in mind the larger theological lens through which Jonathan himself viewed his recovery. In his "Personal Narrative," he wrote: "Since I came to this town [Northampton], I have often had sweet complacency in God in views of his glorious perfections, and the excellency of Jesus Christ. God has appeared to me, a glorious and lively being chiefly on the account of his holiness. The holiness of God has always appeared to me the most lovely of all his attributes. The doctrines of God's absolute sovereignty, and free grace, in showing mercy to whom he would show mercy; and man's absolute dependence on the operations of God's Holy Spirit, have very often appeared to me as sweet and glorious doctrines."

Edwards' representation here of the sequel to the years of his "low, sunk estate," may be a clue to one of its multiple components—a recurrence of his inability to rest in the doctrine of God's sovereignty in saving whom God would. Only when he could bring himself to accept the premise of God's perfect holiness could he accept the teaching that human rebellion against such perfection could be so infinitely evil as to warrant eternal punishment. Only when he could sustain a view of God's holiness that was infinitely beyond human standards could he delight in God's arbitrary but perfectly good sovereignty.

Jonathan emerged from his three years of spiritual depression not only with a renewed sense of the "images and shadows of divine things" but also with the zeal of a convert to defend strict Calvinist orthodoxy. So far as we can judge from his notebooks, he had in the meantime never worked in any other framework. Yet often during those three agonizing years there had been a disconcerting disjunction between head and heart.

After he moved to Northampton, Jonathan very rarely made diary entries, so there is no longer a candid record of his spiritual struggles. In his "Personal Narrative" he indicated that for at least the next decade he sustained his ability to be enraptured by God's holiness and perfections. Nevertheless, we know that he also suffered from depressions throughout his life. In trying to imagine what someone who could be so enraptured by the holiness of God was really like during his years of ministry, it is important to recall what he was like during the time for which we have a more complete record. In Northampton he recovered to "somewhat as I used to be" at the height of his early spiritual experience. Yet as he "used to be," as in his fondly remembered days in New York, was a time of constant struggle. Even as he kept the disciplines of the faith, he was frequently afflicted by times of spiritual deadness and very human imperfections. Probably he never again sank as low, or at least not nearly for so long, as he did in his years in New Haven. Yet, whatever the spiritual forces working in him, it would be a mistake to think of him as someone for whom saintliness came easily.

# CHAPTER 7

# On Solomon Stoddard's Stage

To move to Northampton was to move into the seat of family power. Solomon Stoddard, the patriarch, now eighty-three, though somewhat feeble and nearly blind was still sharp of mind, strong of opinion, and a formidable presence. The people of Northampton, Edwards later recalled, regarded Stoddard "almost as a sort of deity."[1] Not only in Northampton but throughout the region, Stoddard was a force. Like a feudal baron whose power depended on personal allegiances, he had used kinship ties to connect with other powerful clergy, merchants, and magistrates—with the other "river gods," as they sometimes were collectively known.[2] Having his hand-picked grandson as his successor was one more link that would help secure the future after he relinquished command.

Many other links in this network of leadership were already firmly in place. For Jonathan, the magistrate-patron of crucial importance was his uncle, Colonel John Stoddard. Second son of the patriarch, Colonel Stoddard was the man of affairs, a military commander, political leader, and wealthy real estate merchant. Aged forty-four in 1726, he still resided with his parents in the family home, which sat on a prominence that overlooked the town. After his father's death, John married in 1731 and continued to live in this home, which signaled his inheritance and his baronial authority as the richest man in the town and its most influential magistrate.[3] The first year Jonathan lived in Northampton, he presumably lived with his grandparents and his uncle. John, a Harvard graduate of some learning and a man of piety, took his young nephew under his wing and remained his most important ally and patron.

John Stoddard's narrow escape at Deerfield in 1704 had been a defining moment. Throughout his life his greatest challenge would be to cope with western Massachusetts' agonizing relations with the Indians. He first gained prominence as a military leader in the Indian wars. During Queen Anne's War he rose to be a commander in the field. At the end of the war in 1713, he and his now-famous brother-in-law, the Reverend John Williams of Deerfield, were the colony's envoys to Canada who negotiated the return of many of the captives. Throughout the rest of his career, when he was not fighting in wars, he trying to keep the peace. Eventually he became the colony's leading figure both in fortifying western Massachusetts' frontier and in attempting to reestablish Indian missions.

John Stoddard was, in effect, the village squire and was sometimes referred to as such. He was Northampton's most frequently elected representative to the Massachusetts General Court, although he was also at the center of the town's political contentions. He sometimes served as a member of the Governor's Council. His loyalty to the royal governors was rewarded with various local judicial posts and control of the patronage in Hampshire County. As one historian put it, "everyone—county residents and provincial governors alike—knew that whatever was distributed in Hampshire County came only with the approval of Colonel Stoddard."[4] He was a pillar of the church, and he frequently presided over town meetings, as he had over the one that called his nephew to assist his father.

In 1726 Colonel Stoddard was dealing with the aftermath of another round of ugly warfare with the Indians, which had kept the frontier towns in turmoil during the previous three years. The colonists called the conflict Father Râle's War after a French Jesuit missionary who they believed had incited the Abenaki Indians of Maine to attack France's New England enemies. In western Massachusetts the conflict was led by a renegade leader of the displaced Abenakis known as Grey Lock. The elusive Grey Lock and his men made hit-and-run guerrilla raids in and around the Connecticut Valley settlements. Stoddard had overseen the building of a new garrison fort up the river and an improved watch for Northampton. Possibly when Jonathan first moved there, the Stoddard house itself was protected with a palisade.[5]

The other pivotal link in the chain of family relationships was Solomon Stoddard's son-in-law William Williams, pastor of the neighboring town of Hatfield. Although Solomon Stoddard had a son and five sons-in-law among the valley clergy, Williams was by far the most important. William Williams' influence was based on his being the most talented clerical figure in the most prominent clan among the Connecticut Valley gentry. The Williamses had intermarried with just about every leading family in the area and hence were connected with nearly all the leading merchants and political leaders as well as many of the clergy. At age fifty-one in 1726, William Williams was heir apparent to Stoddard's ecclesiastical domain. "Uncle Williams" of Hatfield was the obvious choice to preach the ordination sermon for his young nephew.

There is every reason to believe that William Williams approved the choice of his intensely pious and learned nephew to be Stoddard's successor. There may indeed already have been a minor rivalry between Jonathan and some of his Williams cousins. A few years earlier the Edwards family had been speculating as to whether Uncle Williams' son Solomon might be settled in Northampton. At one point when they thought that was fact, Jonathan had made a note in his diary to "always rejoice in everyone's prosperity."[6] Years later, after the generation of William Williams and John Stoddard was gone, a rivalry emerged among the cousins with all the ugliness of a family feud. In the meantime, the older generation seems to have gotten along. Jonathan's next oldest sister, Mary, to whom he was close, had lived with her aunt and uncle in Hatfield in the early 1720s, before moving to Northampton to take care of her grandparents. Mary was living in the Stoddard home when Jonathan arrived. Uncle Williams seems to have been happy to form an alliance with his nephew, who was closer to him and his generation in many of his principles than were some of Williams' own children.

Though William Williams and Solomon Stoddard did not agree on everything, the two leaders stood firmly together on three points as crucial for the survival and prosperity of their people under God's covenant.[7] First, they were eager to strengthen the hand of the clergy. Second, they were determined to preserve Reformed orthodoxy. Third, they were zealous for evangelism. To foster the first two of these, they had managed in 1714 to take one step in a Presbyterian direction by founding the Hampshire Association of clergy to have oversight of ecclesiastical affairs in the region. Across the border in Connecticut the clergy had gained more regional authority and also adopted a version of the Westminster Confession of Faith, but in independent-minded Massachusetts an association of clergy, with largely advisory functions, was the best they could do. Still, it consolidated clerical influence, and they hoped it might provide some check against heterodox doctrine intruding in their midst.

Zeal for evangelism was the cutting edge of their campaign. Like other pietists springing up throughout the Protestant world in this era, they recognized that amid the vicissitudes of religious-political conflicts, one could not count on state support for churches. During the seemingly endless religious conflicts, one characteristic response among seventeenth-century renewal movements in many traditions—including Catholic and Jewish—had been to emphasize vital heartfelt piety.[8] For New Englanders of Puritan heritage that was nothing new, but with the weakening of state support, they preached it with increasing urgency. Practically speaking, evangelism was essential to gaining the benefits of the social covenant. A predominance of converted people was the only hope for cultivating the collective virtue necessary to ease God's controversy with the region and to bring blessings.

With these concerns in the forefront, Stoddard and Williams cultivated revivals throughout the valley. Spurred by a regional awakening in 1712, they insisted that revival should be the church's top concern. In the ensuing years they found eager support among Boston's leading clergy for such evangelical renewal. In 1714 Increase Mather wrote a preface to Stoddard's new manual on evangelism, *A Guide to Christ*, thus signaling the end of their long controversy over church membership.[9] Similarly, the Mathers had by this time put aside an earlier conflict with Benjamin Colman, pastor of Boston's upstart Brattle Street Church, realizing that Colman was as committed to Calvinism and international awakening as they were. During these years, William Williams joined Stoddard as his right-hand man on his trips to Boston and was clearly heir apparent as western spokesman for the cause. Almost every year he or Stoddard preached in Boston and published treatises on evangelism.[10]

Stoddard took the lead in extending this evangelistic impulse toward missions to the Indians. In a treatise published in 1723, he framed the question in classic covenantal form, *Question Whether God is not Angry with the Country for Doing so Little Towards the Conversion of the Indians?* Stoddard's tract appeared near the onset of Father Râle's War and included the point that a mission would be a strategic counter to the Jesuits. Jesuit missionary success was a reproof to the New Englanders whose missions efforts had been paltry since the disaster of King Philip's War. The Jesuit missions also created a military threat. Yet Stoddard's realism on that score was accompanied by a sharp critique of typical English attitudes toward the Indians. Such attitudes, he proposed, might be the chief reason why God had been punishing the country for "these three score years." True the Indians might be of "a very brutish and sottish spirit." Nonetheless, "they are of mankind, and so objects of compassion." The colonists should remember that the British were no better. "Our fore-fathers . . . were given up unto as brutish a service of the Devil, as any nation under the sun" until missionaries had "pitied them and brought the Gospel among them." A few colonists had attempted Indian missions, but the colony as a whole had done practically nothing. "Many men," Stoddard railed, "have been more careful to make a booty of them, than to give to them the practice of religion."

One learned writer, Stoddard observed, had conjectured that the English on the frontier might "Indianize and become that Gog and Magog spoken of in Revelation 20." As an alternative, he urged, if the Indians "embrace religion, it might provoke us to emulation." The English "make a high profession, but yet religion runs low and iniquity doth abound. There is a great deal of pride, drunkenness, injustice, prophaneness, and koraism [rebelliousness against authority] in the land. And we need to say as David, '*Wilt thou not revive us again.*'"[11]

William Williams shared Stoddard's concern for the Indians and like his mentor viewed the urgency of their conversion in covenantal and millennial terms. Writing in 1728 to their mutual friend Judge Samuel Sewall, thanking him for sending his treatise on the Apocalypse, Williams rejoiced in some recently reported signs of Indians' responsiveness to the Gospel as hope that God's anger with New England might be relaxed.[12] When Edwards settled in western Massachusetts in 1726, the need to convert the Indians was certainly an early topic of conversation. One can imagine the three learned clergy of Northampton and Hatfield, each to be the region's leading cleric of his generation, sitting by the fireplace debating how God might use New England in his millennial plans and agreeing on the urgency of both revival and effective Indian missions.

Stoddard's powerful presence consolidated Jonathan's views in other ways, especially regarding the urgency of evangelism. Jonathan had been reading at least some of his grandfather's works since his youth and had heard his powerful preaching on occasion. In Stoddard he could find themes that resonated with or helped to shape what became his most characteristic views. In *Treatise on Conversion* (1719), for instance, Stoddard emphasized the theme of "*spiritual light,*" or of having eyes opened to see the glory and excellency of God as the essence of conversion. "When men know the excellency of God, they must chose him. The glory of God is such, that it captivates the heart; where it is seen, it has a magnetic power; it irresistibly conquers the will; there is a necessity of loving God, when he is seen."[13] While these were common images that Jonathan could have acquired anywhere, they also indicate that he and his grandfather, despite some differences, were kindred spirits.

Even when years later Edwards turned against his grandfather's views on church membership, he candidly described Stoddard as "a very great man, of strong powers of mind, of great grace, and great authority, of a masterly countenance, speech, and behavior."[14] One sign that in his first years in Northampton, Edwards held his grandfather in the highest regard is an enthusiastic "Miscellanies" entry from 1727. "The best philosophy that I have met with," he wrote, "of original sin and all sinful inclinations, habits and principles, is undoubtedly that of Mr. Stoddard's, of this town of Northampton."[15]

Stoddard's publications were also full of advice to clergy, which he doubtless repeated to his young protégé. He urged ministers not to preach with notes, or if they must, to not let them hinder gestures.[16] For the meticulously thorough Edwards, most comfortable writing in the privacy of his study, this was hard advice. He was not the animated natural conversationalist his grandfather was. Although he practically memorized his sermons, not until late in his career could he manage to abandon writing them out in precise detail and having the security of the text in front of him.

"Ten to one they will know it" if they are converted, Stoddard would say with his typical businesslike dogmatism, cutting through a century of New England debates. Jonathan, who had just spent years in his own quest for assurance, may have seen the odds a little differently. Stoddard admitted exceptions but thought it just encouraged indecisiveness to let the exceptions become the rule. It "is not good preaching" he insisted," to teach "that frequently men are ignorant of the time of their conversion."[17]

Another sign of bad preaching was "when men don't preach much about the danger of damnation."[18] Here was a point on which grandfather and grandson saw eye to eye. Timothy Edwards had taught the same thing, and Jonathan was long familiar with his grandfather's published sermon on *The Efficacy of the Fear of Hell, to Restrain Men from Sin*. Stoddard had preached this sermon in 1712 on "the occasion of a more than ordinary outpouring of the Spirit of God." The forceful Northampton preacher had brought this wonderful effect by piling up lurid images, mostly from Scripture. He compared hell to "where they burnt their children to Moleck" at Tophet. "There they burnt them as sacrifices to the Devil, and made a noise with trumpets, that they might drown the noise of the cries of the poor children, they could not bear their roarings. Hell is worse than all these." Being in hell would be like suffering in the fire and brimstone that fell on Sodom: "men, women, children, all like torches; their bodies blazed; How they scream out in that extremity!"

The difference was that such agony was short-lived, whereas in hell one suffered "everlasting burnings." Stoddard liked to put things in numbers:

"Add thousands to thousands, and multiply millions by millions; fill quires of paper with numbers. . . . When men have suffered never so long there is still an eternity remaining. . . . This makes every part of their misery infinite, their pain will be infinite, the terror infinite."[19]

Stoddard and his peers saw preaching hellfire as a matter of compassion. Given the reality of hell, it would be inhumane not to alert people to the horrible danger they were in. One could hardly doubt hell's reality in a world where the Bible was the highest authority. As Stoddard pointed out, no one insisted on the point more than Jesus.[20] Even the modern philosophers acknowledged that there must be some system of justice in the next life to rectify injustices in this one, although the latitudinarian's God might be lenient in its administration. For Calvinists, who premised every argument on their reading of Scripture, there seemed no choice but to heed the Bible's direct word. The duty of preachers was clear. They must warn people that they trod on the brink of eternal misery. To fail to do so was to lack human feeling. As Stoddard observed regarding the urgency of mission to the Indians, "It is a doleful thing to think, that from generation to generation, they go down to Hell."[21]

Jonathan had had his own problems with the strict Calvinist version of this doctrine—both as a general question of justice and a personal question as to whether it was what his sins deserved—but he agreed entirely as to the usefulness of the teaching in God's wise economy. Ever since the first glimmerings of his own awakening, he was acutely aware that *the* human problem was to see one's condition in its true perspective. Human self-centeredness was so overwhelming and this world was so alluring, that each person was by nature incredibly short-sighted, self-absorbed, and blinded by pride. People had to awaken to their true interests. Over and over again he stressed this point in his early preaching. So even in his first sermons from his teenage years, when he may have had his own doubts, he was scrupulous to give the conventional warnings of hellfire their due place. The dreadful teaching was a gift of God to awaken people who were blindly sleepwalking to their doom.[22]

Stoddard must have been pleased to hear Edwards' early sermon in Northampton on *The Warnings of Future Punishment Don't Seem Real to the Wicked*. The problem, said Edwards, was that many people who affirm belief in hell, believe it is an inherited belief, but it does not seem *real* to them. Developing one of the most characteristic principles in all his preaching, he distinguished between believing something theoretically and having a true sense of it as a personal reality. So he first presented a series of arguments why there must be a hell (for instance, that otherwise "oftentimes it would really be for men's interest to do wickedly," which would be absurd). Yet such theoretical belief would be useless unless people "have a lively or sensible idea" of its eternal horrors. They needed a verbal picture of hell painted for them so that they could, in effect, hear the "shrieks and cries of the damned." Edwards' own sermonic picture, piling up all the Scriptural images, closely resembled the pattern of Stoddard's earlier sermon and would have done Dante proud. In this world (to take just one from the onslaught of images), God *restrains* the devil and his crew, but not in the next. "The devil thirsts for the blood of souls, and 'tis only because God restrains him that he don't lay hold of the soul before death; but as soon as ever the man is dead, God restrains him no more, but then these hell hounds fly upon their prey, these roaring lions dare then lay hold as it were with open mouths."[23]

In late 1727 Stoddard (who still took his turn at preaching) and Edwards received a providential jolt that greatly aided their cause of making the impending judgment seem real. On a Sunday evening, October 29, 1727, a sizable earthquake shook New England, bringing down chimneys and walls and rocking even the strongest houses. The populace was terrified. This was a society where Michael Wigglesworth's doleful *The Day of Doom* (1662) was still a best-seller, ministers endlessly preached impending judgment, and earthquakes were a predicted sign of the end. The next morning colonists crowded into churches for a day of humiliation and fasting. Nine days of aftershocks kept many in a state of dread. Numerous churches experienced awakenings, some adding scores of confessing members. In Northampton, Edwards later recorded, Solomon Stoddard was pleased to see this, the last of his revivals, during which he judged they gained some twenty new converts, even if he was disappointed that they did not have a general awakening as in earlier days nor as many conversions as some towns to the east, nearer the center of the quake.[24]

Many New Englanders regarded the quake as a warning of worse judgments to come. The Massachusetts governor called for a day of repentance and fasting for Thursday, December 21, and in Northampton, Edwards delivered the fast-day sermon. Preaching from the book of Jonah and employing the standard covenantal formula of God's punishments or rewards for communal behavior, he emphasized that the only way to avert impending judgments was by true reformation. As an expert on natural phenomena, he acknowledged in passing that "earthquakes and signs in the heavens may often have natural causes," but he immediately added, "yet they nevertheless be ordered to fall out so as to be forerunners of great changes and threatenings of judgements." God left nothing to chance in his arrangements of natural causes. So this earthquake should be seen as a direct message, especially to the young people of Northampton. The Sabbath ended at sundown, and Sunday evenings were a time for young people to frolic. "It was their manner very frequently to get together in conventions of both sexes, for mirth and jollity, which they called frolics; and they would often spend the greater part of the night in them, without regard to any order in the families they belonged to."[25] It was no accident then that in the midst of such carryings-on the earthquake "lately terrified you in the night." " 'Tis the very probable opinion of some," Edwards reported as though speaking for an older authority, "that the earthquake was sent as a token of God's anger against not only the wickedness of the land in general, but more especially the sin that is committed on a sabbath-day night."[26]

While grandson and grandfather agreed on most subjects, the most difficult transition for Jonathan was from being under his father's sway regarding the much-debated question of conversion and communion to working in his grandfather's domain. Though the controversy between Stoddard and the Mathers had died down, the sensitive issue of who should be allowed to partake of the Lord's Supper had not been settled. Jonathan had studied Stoddard's controversial opinion that the presumption should be that baptized adults should partake, even without evidence of being converted. He had convinced himself (and his grandfather) he could live with the practice. Northampton was worth an open communion.

Stoddard was concerned first of all with fostering conversion through any God-given means possible. Opening the Lord's Supper was a tangible way to bring people into the presence of Christ's sacrifice and a sensibility of the depths of their wickedness for which Christ had died. During the years he spent under Stoddard's tutelage, Jonathan was reading or rereading his grandfather's works and wrestling with whether it was possible to devise a science of identifying visible saints.[27] Unable to settle the issue, he was willing to make the most of Stoddard's practice. In an early communion sermon in Northampton he preached on Jesus' parable in which the master ordered his servants to go to the highways and hedges to compel the poor, the maimed, the lame, and the blind to come to his feast. Applying this to the unconverted, he told them how their poverty, misery, and blindness was far beyond that of the beggars in the parable. "You know not how sweet and satisfying the meat and drink of this feast is, and what abundance and variety there is. If you did, you would need no compelling to come; the sense of it would be wings to your feet. You know not what friendship, what communion, what love and joy there is at God's table. Taste and see that the Lord is gracious: put off your filthy garments; wash yourself from your filthiness; accept of the white raiment Christ offers you; go to Christ and enter with him into his chambers; sit down with him in his feasting and banqueting house."[28] This was pure Stoddardeanism. The Supper would be a converting ordinance.

Allowing himself to be under his grandfather's sway on such a life-or-death issue was a momentous decision for Jonathan. Years later, when it led to the greatest calamity of his career, he confessed that he had never been at ease with Stoddard's approach. In these early days Jonathan's internal anxieties must have been great because, among other things, Timothy Edwards was not so far away—especially not from his son's psyche. Jonathan, despite his creativity, remained remarkably close to his father's opinions on most issues. We do not know how they handled their differences on this much-debated matter, except for one clue. In 1732, after Stoddard was out of the picture, Timothy Edwards had the honor of delivering the election-day sermon in Connecticut. The sermon was one of his few publications. In the midst of a standard covenantal jeremiad about the deplorable state of society, he made a point of saying that people should "scorn and abhor" the practice of allowing ungodly persons who "make a profession of godliness, and are accepted by the people of God to sit with them at the Lord's Table."[29] The once-controlling father was keeping the pressure on.

Family, immediate and extended, was immensely important in shaping Jonathan's life. The worst times of his youth had been when he was in New Haven separated from his immediate family, even if the best had been when he was adopted into the Smith family in New York. After he moved to Northampton, he was once again surrounded by close family, grandfather, grandmother, and sister.

His marriage to Sarah in July 1727 was a step signaling the young assistant's transition to adult and authoritative status. Under the leadership of Squire John Stoddard, the town saw that the young couple were well settled as befit their status. As part of his initial settlement, Edwards was granted ten acres of land for a pasture and another forty acres farther from town that could be used for income. His annual salary was set with an inflation clause, probably reflecting advice from his father, who constantly fought with his town over his declining real income. The Northampton town meeting specifically agreed that "he should have an honorable and suitable maintenance according to the dignity of his office." In addition he was given sufficient funds to purchase a home, so that shortly before his marriage he could acquire a "Mansion house, barn and home lot" of three acres, on King Street near the church.[30]

## "The Falling of a Mighty Spreading Tree"

On February 11, 1729, the earth shook again as the center of family power, indeed the center of gravity in western Massachusetts, shifted with the passing of Solomon Stoddard. In December 1728 Stoddard's old friend Samuel Sewall wrote him a last letter congratulating him on continuing to preach even when in much pain. Sewall, after reporting the death of a mutual friend, Dr. John Clark, could not resist wryly adding, "I have buried very many noble physicians." Sewall urged the eighty-five-year-old Stoddard, especially in the light of the "blessing granted you in the serviceableness of your children and grandchildren" to be ready to pronounce his *Nunc dimittis* [Let now thy servant depart in peace] when the time came.[31] Stoddard did not give up easily. Edwards recalled that "he retained his powers surprisingly to the last." His obituary in the Boston paper noted that to the end he preached without notes and he had written several more sermons that he did not get to deliver.[32]

William Williams, the ecclesiastical heir apparent, preached the principal funeral sermon. At age sixty-four, he was the most influential member of the Hampshire Association as well as the patriarch of the region's leading clan. The "death of a prophet," he proclaimed, was "like the falling of a mighty spreading tree in a forest, which . . . makes all the trees about it to shake, leaves a wide breach where it stood which may be long ere it be filled again." In Boston, Benjamin Colman, Brattle Street Church's eminent pastor, eulogized Stoddard. Alluding to Increase Mather's old accusation that Stoddard wanted to be the first Puritan "pope," Colman turned the criticism into a compliment. He was "a Peter here among the Disciples . . . very much our Primate."[33] A Northampton eulogist recalled the remarkable awakenings under Stoddard when "the Spirit of God so moved upon the heart of the people, that it became almost the general cry of the place, *What must I do to be saved.*"[34]

To step into the hollow where for so long had stood a mighty tree was no easy task. For sixty years, as long as almost anyone could remember, Stoddard had shaped the town by the force of his personality. For sixty years he had had a near monopoly on the most authoritative public speaking. Even in the last two and a half years when he shared the pulpit with his grandson, the frail retiring young man, however attractive, was clearly the apprentice and pro-tégé. In powerful sermons year after year Stoddard had berated the people of Northampton for their sins and fostered their periodic reformations. He had created their identity. "He being our pastor," wrote the anonymous eulogist, "gave a name and reputation to our town."[35]

Edwards may have been determined to do the same, but handling the people of Northampton was no easy matter. Though they were sometimes subject to the heights of revival enthusiasm, they were also fickle. As in any dictatorship, however successful, there were strong emotions and some deep resentments. Edwards later wrote: "The people of Northampton are not the most happy in their natural temper. They have, ever since I can remember, been famed for a high-spirited people, and close, and of a difficult, turbulent temper." Once, during Stoddard's day, a church controversy became so heated that "it came to hand-blows: a number of one party met the head of the opposite party, and assaulted him and beat him unmercifully."

Moreover, for a decade or so before Edwards arrived, Northampton had been torn with a persistent political division, "a sort of settled division of the people into two parties, something like the Court and Country Party in England (if I may compare small things with great)." Edwards explained: "There have been some of the chief men in the town, of chief authority and wealth, that have been great proprietors of their lands, who have had one party with them. And the other party, which commonly has been the greatest, have been of those who have been jealous of them, apt to envy 'em, and afraid of their having too much power and influence in town and church. This has been a foundation of innumerable contentions among the people from time to time."[36]

Some of these conflicts centered around Colonel John Stoddard, who rose to political prominence in the mid-1710s and was known for his "Tory" political views. Stoddard had used his political power to build a fortune in land. Although he was the most powerful politician and the one most often elected to represent the town, as well as the most influential laymen in the church, he was opposed by a more whiggish "country party." The tensions were exacerbated by a gradual transition from the more communal and defer-ential standards of the Puritan era to the more individualistic tendencies of the eighteenth century and by perennial questions of availability of land for the younger generations. The line of division that Edwards referred to may also have reflected some acrimonious contentions in Massachusetts government between the royal governors' "Tory" supporters, such as Stoddard, and the recalcitrant and more popular lower house, debates that dimly presaged issues of the American Revolution a half-century later.[37] Though Edwards considered the "country party" in Northampton the more numerous, they were not often able to find a representative who carried the prestige to displace the aristocratic Stoddard.

To add to the challenge of the transition, the moral behavior, especially of the young people, had become increasingly lax as Solomon Stoddard became too old to oversee it effectively. At church meeting, young people were given to misbehaving, knowing that the enfeebled Stoddard could no longer see them. The late Sunday night frolics had not abated either. Edwards recalled, "just after my grandfather's death, it seemed to be a time of extraordinary dullness in religion: licentiousness for some years greatly prevailed among the youth of the town; they were many of them very much addicted to night-walking, and frequenting the tavern, and lewd practices."[38]

On his own now as the spiritual overseer of a town that was, by old Puritan standards, out of control, Edwards made the most of the memory of the great Stoddard in a classic jeremiad sermon of lament and warning. "God has taken away our Joshua," he declared, "he that was our captain to lead us into the heavenly Canaan, and with him he has taken away many of the elders that were contemporary with him." That was the warning. "It looks darkly upon us that those of that generation are taken away so fast, and that there is a no more hopeful prospect from the rising generation." On the day Stoddard had died, so had Ebenezer Strong, the last of the elders of the church (Stoddard, in consolidating power, had let the office die out). A few months later the venerable John Williams, who had suffered so much as pastor of Deerfield, was taken. In June, Edward Taylor, the conservative ally of Timothy Edwards, passed on, his great poetry safely stored away for only posterity to see.

With that generation disappearing, Edwards found little basis for hope that another generation of saints would be raised up from among the irreverent and pleasure-loving youth of Northampton. As he put it in a sermon: "Licentious and immoral practices seem to get great head amongst young people. And how little appearance is there of a spirit of seriousness and religion to be seen among them? How little concern about their salvation and escaping eternal misery?" Once a generation departs from the old ways, he admonished, there was little hope to reverse the trend. "They who live loosely while young, and give the reins to their lust, it is to be feared they will not hold the reins very taut with respect to their children. When a people have got into a way of declining, they will be likely to wax worse and worse, to revolt more and more."[39]

The people of Northampton, he cautioned in another sermon memorializing Stoddard's work, should consider how much more liable to punishment they were by "living unconverted under an eminent means of grace." Using an image from Jeremiah 6 of a bellows burnt out in attempting to refine "reprobate silver," Edwards chided the Northamptonites for having become "sermon proof" after years of powerful preaching. Northamptonites who might be proud of their heritage should realize that more is required of them having lived under such a means of grace. "Woe to them that go to hell out of Northampton and that lived under Mr. Stoddard's ministry! We are ready to wonder at the wickedness we hear there is in some parts of the world, in the West Indies and in other places; but they han't one half of the sins to answer as obstinate sinners will have that go from this place."[40]

In the spring, shortly after Stoddard's death, Edwards' health once again collapsed. In late April and early May he and his two Sarahs took a trip to New Haven and East Windsor, perhaps for a needed rest.[41] After a few weeks back in the pulpit, he was struck down more severely and could not preach for about a month in the early summer. One of Sarah's brothers, Benjamin Pierpont, supplied the pulpit, though he was soon called to fill the vacancy left by John Williams' death at Deerfield.

Likely Edwards was suffering from anxiety and the strain of too much work. He was now responsible for the spiritual and moral oversight of perhaps thirteen hundred people.[42] A congregation of that size, even under the best of circumstances, could be overwhelming for one man. To make matters worse, he had to wrestle with the disparities between his high spiritual ideals and the coarse realities of an ordinary town, which seemed particularly out of control after Stoddard's death. He could not escape the conclusion that most of his neighbors and parishioners were blindly stumbling their way to perdition. As usual, he was also working himself too hard. In addition to responsibilities of marriage, becoming a father, assuming the full duties as pastor, and often preaching three times a week (Sunday morning, Sunday afternoon, and a weekly Thursday lecture), he was also working on a number of ambitious writing projects.

What we know is that his condition involved loss of voice and "weakness" and that the condition seems to have been recurrent. Near the end of his life he reported, in very similar terms, being subject to "a low tide of spirits; often occasioning a kind of childish weakness and contemptibleness of speech, presence, and demeanor."[43] In this case he was back at work by the summer, but as late as September 1729 his father reported to Jonathan's sister Anne that her brother was still recovering.[44]

Though fear of early death from disease was something that most separates that era from some later times, the Edwards family had been remarkably spared. In his twenty-sixth year, Jonathan had lost only two grandfathers among those closest to him. Timothy and Esther Edwards had reared eleven children without a loss. So the pain may have all the greater for Jonathan in December 1729 when an epidemic of diphtheria or "the throat distemper" took perhaps his dearest youngest sister.

Jerusha Edwards was the same age as Sarah Pierpont and had all the qualities Jonathan idealized in her New Haven counterpart. As much as anyone, she was his model of female piety. She was renowned for her devotion, her solitary contemplations, sweetness of temper, fine understanding and beautiful countenance.

Jonathan must have deeply loved his younger sister because they were so much alike in intellect, temperament, and piety. According to her eulogy in a Boston newspaper, Jerusha "conversed much with books, upon various subjects, but most of all upon divinity, for which she had the greatest relish." Like him, she "often expressed her abhorrence of that conversation which is full of froth and levity." "Discourses rational and weighty were her delight."[45] When Jonathan last saw her at East Windsor in 1729 she had two clergymen suitors. When she died a number of her family wrote tributes to her model of submission.[46] Timothy Edwards recalled that when "my dear daughter" was dying she referred to the story of the foolish virgins who were not prepared for the bridegroom and urged her family gathered around her, "all of you, don't let your lamps go out." When Jonathan and Sarah's second daughter was born the next spring, they named her Jerusha. Seldom would a namesake be so much like the original.

In the meantime, Edwards was back in Northampton in fall 1729, throwing his energies into turning things around. In sermon after sermon he hammered away at themes of hypocrisy, the certainty of judgment, the excellencies of the triune God, the means God has provided for awakening, and the benefits of salvation.[47] Whereas Stoddard's preaching was sometimes blunt in getting directly to the point, Edwards' was intricate, extremely clear, logical, and relentless. He followed the Puritan style of a brief exposition that translated the text into a theme or proposition, then, following Ramist method, divided the proposition into various points of doctrine and recapitulated all these implications in an application. His sermons have been compared to "the extraordinary ceiling and dome paintings of the Renaissance" where it seems as though "the whole visionary distance as far as the eye can see in any direction has been opened."[48] Or they might be compared to Bach's fugues, exploring every variation of a theme. The great difference from those analogies is that Edwards' sermons reveal little attempt at overall artistic design or symmetry. They are the products of a logician who fills in all the implications of each thought. Those who listened would be left little room to escape his web of arguments.

With his grandfather gone, Edwards was troubled that so many communicant members seemed unconverted. He was not giving up the Stoddardean practice, but in his notebooks he was contemplating tightening it up. He was especially concerned about the young people who took communicant membership for granted without worrying about whether they were converted. Those who present themselves for membership, he wrote in his "Miscellanies" notebook, must "often be put in mind of the danger of hypocrisy . . . and before every sacrament, examination should in a more solemn manner be renewed."[49]

In one sermon, probably for a bimonthly communion service, he focused on the theme of hypocrites, building on the image of how Judas betrayed Christ with a kiss. The Church of Rome presented one horrifying model of such betrayal, but Judases could be found closer to home. Partaking of the sacrament itself could be the fatal kiss. "You pretend to be Christ's friend, or else why do you come here? And there are many of you that make a further profession than the generality of men under the gospel do. You are like Judas and the other disciples in that respect, that you appear as disciples: you go along with the rest of the disciples; you profess to forsake all and to follow him; you come to Christ as it were with a kiss; you come to meeting and to the sacrament as though you were friends. Inquire whether you ben't like Judas also in this other respect, that you betray your Lord."[50]

If some of his parishioners were like Judas, England and New England could be compared to ancient Israel and Judah when they turned from the Lord. In a fast-day sermon preached in December 1729 on the occasion of the meeting of the Hampshire County court in Northampton, Edwards once again brought his usual thoroughness to the jeremiad form. Ministers on such public occasions conventionally preached on "the state of the land," enumerating the vices for which God was punishing them. Edwards' account depicts what he saw himself up against. First of all, "our nation" as a whole, meaning Britain, "is at this day exceedingly corrupted and degenerated." Not only had "debauchery and wickedness, profaneness and unbounded licentiousness in sensuality" come in "like a flood" in recent years, all sorts of sects and infidels, including Deists and Freethinkers, had arisen. Such infidelity, Edwards believed, might well presage God's judgments in tribulations and terrible earthquakes that would usher in the last times.

In the meantime there was plenty of vice in Hampshire County to warrant the wrath of a just God. The guilt was all the greater in light of all the Gospel preaching it had been given. People readily laughed and made fun of sacred things. They were given to pride and vanity, "flaunting . . . their buildings, apparel and way of living, many going far beyond their condition." Covetousness and injustice were rife; people would do anything for gain. Those who bought and sold often deceived their neighbors (one of Edwards' most frequent accusations). Drunkenness was commonplace as "multitudes . . . haunt and throng public houses from day to day." Contentiousness appeared among people in suing each other (the court would soon be in session), and it was particularly lamentable "that there is so much contention amongst the leaders." (In late 1729 Massachusetts was between royal governors and its country and court parties were in an uproar).

Edwards' most lengthy exposition in his catalogue of vices had to do, predictably, with the indulgences of the young. The fault lay first of all with parents. Family government and education, the keystone of the old Puritan social system, had fallen badly in decline. Parents, he observed, were reacting against what they felt were too strict upbringings. The most notorious result was "amazing" impurities tolerated among the young in recent years. Not only was lasciviousness encouraged by nightwalking and similar frivolities, but New England parents allowed practices that are "looked upon as shameful and disgraceful at Canada, New York, [and] England." Everyone knew that he referred to the New England practice of "bundling" in which parents allowed young people to spend the night in bed together partly clothed. "I believe there is not a country in the Christian world," Edwards warned, "however debauched and vicious, where parents indulge their children in such liberties in company-keeping as they do in this country—that is, amongst those that pretend to keep the credit of their children. Such things as are commonly winked at by parents here, trusting in their children that they won't give way to temptation, would in almost any other country ruin a person's reputation and be looked upon as sufficient evidences of a prostitute."

Bundling, which was supposed to be a way of getting acquainted without sexual intercourse, did not always work as advertised. Pregnancies before marriage were rising dramatically in New England. Even in well-churched Northampton, where premarital pregnancies were rarer than in some parts the region, the figure had recently risen to one in ten first children born within eight months of marriage.[51] Premarital sex was commonplace. Even when it resulted in pregnancy, so long as the couple married, there was no longer much stigma involved. Alluding to that new attitude, Jonathan perceived another alarming decline. "And there is not that discountenance of such things as there formerly used to be. It is not now such a discredit; 'tis not accounted such a blot and disgrace to a person. Formerly, things were accounted such a wound as a person never could get over as long as he lived. That ben't much minded: now they are so bold and impudent, that they are not ashamed to hold up their heads."[52]

One might suppose that, given Edwards' perfectionist standards demanding not only avoidance of vice but also evidences of Christ-like virtue, his prospects among the factious and self-indulgent Northamptonites would be dim. Yet the heritage of Stoddard's preaching, the orthodox profession of so many of the inhabitants, their uneasiness with their vices, and their anxieties over their eternal destinies gave him much to work with.

Most Northamptonites participated in a lay culture that put some distance between themselves and clerical ideals, while still affirming many of those ideals in principle or in parts of their lives. Typically, families and kinship networks shaped their primary loyalties, and these were interwoven in varying degrees with church loyalties. For unmarried young people the youth culture provided the major buffer against clerical ideals.[53]

Tavern culture offered an especially important alternative to the culture of piety. Taverns played prominent social and political roles in eighteenth-century New England towns. Northampton already had three. Farmers would gather there for social life, relaxation, and to conduct business. Often taverns were centers for popular political activity. We can speculate that the "country party" Edwards described was also the tavern party, opposed by the Stoddard family and their aristocratic allies who were active in suppressing vice and who cultivated the political patronage of the governors and the crown.[54]

Even if family culture, youth culture, and tavern culture provided substantial alternatives to church culture, most Northamptonites did not draw clear or consistent lines between the secular and the sacred. Like most church-going people they had a pious side, an impious side, and a side in daily routines of work that was not especially either. They were constantly negotiating the often contradictory standards of the subcultures of which they were a part.

Amid these contradictions Edwards still had a base of goodwill. He might be constantly scolding the congregation and railing against their vices, but that was what he was expected to do. That was what Stoddard had done and most townspeople revered him for it. Stoddard may have been a difficult act to follow, but in some ways the passing of such a powerful overlord could foster goodwill toward his successor. True, with their Joshua gone, there may have been an increase in open defiance for a time, but the more controlled and gentle Edwards was also a breath of fresh air. His abilities, his piety, and his transparently passionate sincerity could win him respect.

At twenty-six, Edwards was now a man of authority. He was an aristocrat in a hierarchical society that took aristocracy for granted. He was much aware of the authority of his office and the deference it should command. He was God's spokesman in Northampton. He was, in one of his favorite metaphors, "the trumpet of God."[55] His learning, especially his expertise in Scripture but also his superior knowledge of natural philosophy and history, enhanced his authority. Even more important, he realized, was the authority of his piety. As he had written years earlier when he was imagining his calling, the power of following Christ was limitless. "If it was plain to all the world of Christians that I was under the infallible guidance of Christ, and [that] I was sent forth to teach the world the will of Christ, then I should have power in all the world: I should have power to teach them what they ought to do, and they would be obliged to hear me."[56]

By the fall of 1729 Jonathan was already winning the approval of his Northampton parishioners. Timothy Edwards proudly reported to his daughter Anne that Benjamin Pierpont had told him "that the people of Northampton seem to have a great love and respect for him, and that they take great content in his ministry. They continue their usual kindness to him, and have built him a good large barn and almost finished it, since he hath been laid aside by his weakness from his work."[57] The people of Northampton, despite their divisions, could also show the communal spirit that one might hope for in a religiously oriented interdependent farming community.[58] Respecting their young pastor and wishing the best for him and his young family in time of need, they could put on their best face in a barn-raising.

# CHAPTER 8

## And on a Wider Stage

Edwards usually rose at four or five in the morning in order to spend thirteen hours in his study. In his only diary entry during his early years in Northampton he wrote, in January 1728, "I think Christ has recommended rising early in the morning, by his rising from the grave very early." The discipline was part of a constant, heroic effort to make his life a type of Christ. He began the day with private prayers followed by family prayers, by candlelight in winter. Each meal was accompanied by household devotions, and at the end of each day Sarah joined him in his study for prayers. Jonathan kept secret the rest of his daily devotional routine, following Jesus' command to pray in secret. Throughout the day, his goal was to remain constantly with a sense of living in the presence of God, as difficult as that might be. Often he added secret days of fasting and additional prayers.[1]

His work was also a service to God in the many hours each day he devoted to study. As Daniel Walker Howe has observed, if one is looking for the prototype of the work ethic in colonial America, it would be better to look to Edwards than Benjamin Franklin.[2] As Edwards saw it, the discipline of work was part of his worship of God, an offering of his time to God. Moreover, huge amounts work were directed toward knowing the ways of God. In addition to carefully crafting lengthy sermons each week, he was deeply engaged in biblical study, a daily activity that produced several major notebooks filled with his tiny writing. One of these, his "Notes on Scripture," was essentially a commentary. Another was a "Blank Bible" of more than nine hundred pages interleaved with pages of Scripture. His brother-in-law Benjamin Pierpont, who stayed in the Northampton parsonage during parts of 1730, had given it to him, and Edwards used it to develop a ready compendium for his reflections on biblical texts.[3] He also continued his "Notes on the

Apocalypse," which combined interpretations of biblical prophecies with close reading of current events for clues to how the prophecies were being fulfilled.

Edwards was also driven by ambition to serve the coming of God's kingdom in some great way not just in Northampton but throughout the world. He was planning a massive masterwork that would both establish his reputation and strike a blow for Protestant-biblical truth versus its recent detractors. In 1729 or 1730 he drew up a new outline of his ambitious treatise: "A Rational Account of the Main Doctrines of the Christian Religion Attempted." What he sketched out was closer to a systematic theology than most of his plans. It would start with the being, nature, and excellency of the triune God, considering these in relation to the end of creation and the work of redemption. Yet the great work, which he was constantly expanding in his "Miscellanies," would be much more than another systematic theology. It would expound his distinctive philosophical theology of God's dynamic relationship to all created being. It would challenge claims of eighteenth-century philosophers that "natural notions" of God, justice, good, evil, and so on were adequate without biblical revelation. It would be comprehensive. In a note for a "preface," he wrote: "To shew how all arts and sciences, the more they are perfected, the more they issue in divinity, and coincide with it, and appear to be parts of it. And to shew how absurd for Christians to write treatises of ethics distinctly from divinity as revealed in the Gospel."[4]

Such a monumental project, which included not only all of theology but also attention to the arts and sciences and to basic issues in philosophy and ethics, required that Edwards keep up with all the latest authors. This was not easy in an inland town of a province far from the world's intellectual centers, and he kept long lists of books to be searched for and read. Always interested in prophecy and current events, as well as information about publications, he eagerly awaited those who made trips to Boston and could bring back recent periodicals and newspapers. Beginning in 1731, Edwards organized and kept in his home a library for the clergy of the Hampshire Association. The association also served as a sort of debating society where, at each of the twice-a-year meetings, the clergy honed their disputational skills by debating a difficult topic in theology, biblical interpretation, church order, and discipline.[5]

Thirteen hours a day was hardly enough for work on all these fronts and pastoring a large congregation. To ease the latter burden, Edwards decided early on that he should serve God first with his best gifts. Accordingly, except in cases of sicknesses and emergencies, he declined to make pastoral calls on his parishioners as was usually expected of New England clergy. He was not good at small talk, often not of a sociable frame of mind, and such routine calls sapped his meager energies and were too time-consuming. If parishioners had special needs, he welcomed counseling them on spiritual things in his study. He also encouraged neighbors or young people to meet for private religious exercises and would preach to such groups. Normally, however, he believed he could best exercise his extraordinary intellectual gifts as well as best serve his parishioners by staying in his study during the day.[6] Early in 1734, in his first diary entry in six years, he observed: "I judge that it is best, when I am in a good frame for divine contemplation, or engaged in reading the Scriptures, or any study of divine subjects, that ordinarily, I will not be interrupted by going to dinner, but will forego my dinner, rather than be broke off."[7]

In order to work every possible minute, it was essential that he not be unduly distracted. He turned over the management of the house and oversight of the husbandry to Sarah, who must have been working at least as many hours per day as Jonathan. Through the 1730s she was pregnant with great regularity every two years, so that by the end of the decade they had seven children, six girls and a boy. We have little record of how Sarah managed through these years, although she had help from servants, or at least from an African woman slave.[8] White servants or hired laborers may have aided in the farming since the Edwardses had both a large garden plot and the use of some fields outside the village. We are told that Jonathan, unlike his father, paid little attention to daily chores. Samuel Hopkins, his admiring protégé, from whom we learn most of the details of his routine of some years later, remarked, "He was less acquainted with most of his temporal affairs than many of his neighbors; and seldom knew when and by whom his forage for winter was gathered in, or how many milk kine he had; whence his table was furnished, etc."[9]

To preserve his always precarious health, Edwards engaged in recreation necessary to continue his work. In winter he usually chopped wood moderately for a half an hour or more. When the weather permitted, in the afternoons after dinner he would ride two or three miles to a secluded place where he would walk for a while. He had great love of natural beauty and enjoyed the blue mountains that graced the horizon of the river valley, and he loved the views he could gain by climbing the surrounding hills.[10] His walks were in part for contemplation, prayer, and spiritual communion, but so that no time would be wasted, he also carried with him pen and ink to write down his thoughts along the way. For longer horseback rides, he used a memory device. For each insight he wished to remember, he would pin a small piece of paper on a particular part of his clothes, which he would associate with the thought. When he returned home he would unpin these and write down each idea. At the ends of trips of several days, his clothes might be covered with quite a few of these slips of paper.[11] Fashionable appearance apparently was not a high priority.

## "Roses Grow upon Briers"

Riding through the countryside, Edwards was always alert to "Shadows of Divine Things," as he called a recently developed notebook. What he perceived was not sentimentally sweet. Rather, he saw all created reality as bittersweet contrasts, dazzling beauty set against appalling horrors, ephemeral glories pointing to divine perfections. His first entry, characteristically, was on death, that "being eaten with worms (Is. 66:24) is an image of the misery of hell."[12] He loved flowers, but the lesson of flowers was one of great beauty that soon died. His enthusiasm for the flowers of spring, for instance, is indicated inside the back cover of his account book, where he began noting the dates in the spring when their cherry, peach, plum, and apple trees would first bloom. Yet in his contemplations he was not carried away by the romance of physical beauty. There was a more profound lesson: "That of so vast and innumerable a multitude of blossoms that appear on a tree, so few come to ripe fruit; . . . seem to be lively types: how few are saved out of the mass of mankind, and particularly how few are sincere, of professing Christians, that never wither away but endure to the end, and how, of the many that are called, few are chosen."[13]

This bittersweet view of reality, made up of the sharpest contrasts, permeated his view of history as well as individual experience. "'Tis God's manner to make men sensible of their misery and unworthiness before he appears in his mercy and love to them." So Edwards explained to his congregation in the fall of 1730 in a long, carefully designed sermon-exposition, preached over four services. Throughout history, God repeatedly allowed his people to fall into despair as a means to a most wonderful redemption. They fell into slavery in Egypt and misery in the wilderness, their judges and kings failed to bring righteousness or preserve peace, they were taken into the Babylonian captivity, and so forth—all to show them their need for utter dependence on God. "Even the man Christ Jesus was first made sensible of the wrath of

God before his exaltation to that transcendent height of enjoyment of the Father's love."[14]

At the core of Edwards' outlook is a rigorously unsentimental view of love. This attitude is especially difficult to appreciate for those whose sensibilities have been shaped by the sentimentality of the succeeding eras. Edwards starts with the premise that the trinitarian God is essentially loving and creates the universe in order to share that love with others. Yet God permits real and terrible evil in that universe; it is in a state of war because of Satan's rebellion against God. Those on the side of evil in this warfare hate true love and what is ultimately good. So, whatever one's sentiments about such persons, one must view them as those whose commitment to evil is destroying themselves and others. Evil is real and pernicious, and justice demands that God should punish those who promote it.

This outlook may seem alien given the sentimental views of human relationships in our era, but it is helpful to our understanding of them to be reminded that Edwards' universe was similar to that of many of our own moral tales, from *Star Wars* and *Lord of the Rings* to countless lesser entertainments.[15] Edwards' essential outlook was of a piece with perennial human narratives that have explained reality as a struggle between light and darkness, in which the light will eventually triumph and vindicate justice. The astonishing feature of the Christian account, as Edwards emphasized, was that the triune God was not only the great opponent of evil but had also in the incarnate Christ suffered God's own wrath in order to offer redemption.

For the Christian who was to be united with Christ, life remained a struggle of the deepest contrasts. Edwards resolved the highs and lows of his own spiritual experiences into the lessons of this tough-minded theological heritage that did not flinch at the discomforts of a lifetime of struggles, even for the regenerate. As he expressed it in one of the most revealing early entries in his "Shadows of Divine Things" notebook: "Roses grow upon briers, which is to signify that all temporal sweets are mixed with bitter. But what seems more especially to be meant by it, is that true happiness, the crown of glory, is to be come at in no other way than by bearing Christ's cross by a life of mortification, self-denial and labor, and bearing all things for Christ."[16]

## The Arminian Threat

All of life, then, was spiritual warfare. Although Edwards was fighting battles on many fronts, he believed his greatest contribution could be in intellectual combat. Among the enemies—such as Roman Catholicism, latitudinarianism, Deism—none was more important than Calvinism's subtly subversive offspring, Arminianism. For Edwards and his ministerial friends, "Arminianism" usually referred both to the specific anti-Calvinist teachings attributed to Arminius and to broader trends to affirm the ability of humans to contribute to their own salvation. Calvinists believed that such doctrines led to "works righteousness" and to a loss of a sense of absolute dependence on God. Paradoxical as it might seem, they were convinced that only when one recognized that all one's efforts were worthless could one exert the effort appropriate to the demands of God's holiness. Few Christians have emphasized the law more than did these champions of grace. The law showed the unregenerate their true state and was the delight of the converted, driving them toward a holiness they would never perfectly obtain in this life. If Calvinist orthodoxy collapsed in New England, they were convinced, so would vital piety and so would strict morality. Mere moralism would never do because it depended on flawed human efforts rather than on God. In short, the future of their civilization and the light it might provide for the world depended on maintaining the doctrine of the sovereignty of God. Promoting good works depended on undermining belief in their efficacy.

One had only to look to the English homeland, riddled with fashionable heresy and lax morals. This was nothing new. From the beginning of New World settlements, New Englanders had defined themselves against Anglicanism, Arminianism, and moral laxity. Since the Restoration of 1660, at least, English elite culture was, as the heirs to Puritanism viewed it, driven by fashion and degeneracy. Fashion controlled not only styles and manners; it also shaped belief. Arminianism was a beguiling first step. For well over a generation the most popular English preaching had been an attractive Christian moralism, which New Englanders saw as offering easy salvation and false security. Fashionable philosophy affirmed a natural moral sense as an innate basis for cultivating virtue.[17] To orthodox New Englanders, the permissiveness of their homeland and the decline of vital religion were evidences of the folly of urging people to overcome their moral weaknesses by voluntarily exercising resources native to human nature.

Modern intellectual fashion was almost everywhere rising up to challenge inherited authority, presenting an even larger issue. Inspired by the scientific revolution, advanced thinkers increasingly acted as though the newest idea were the most likely to be true. In 1704 Jonathan Swift, an Irish Anglican cleric, in the *Battle of the Books* could still celebrate the ancient champions in his mock epic battle of library volumes, but the very idea that the recent upstarts might take the field against such long-proven authorities signaled a new era. Though the Anglican Church was still bound by law to the authority of the orthodox Thirty-Nine Articles, enforcement of the standards was inconsistent and leading Anglican clergy pushed the boundaries, especially in antitrinitarian teachings.[18] Even in the formerly Puritan nonconformist denominations, Arminianism and Arianism were growing at remarkable rates at the same time these English dissenters were losing ground relative to the population.[19]

In the face of the onslaught of modern fashion, New England orthodoxy could look hopelessly quaint. That Deism and antitrinitarianism should be beyond the New England pale was understandable, but to be still fighting against "Arminianism" in this age of high moral ideals could be seen as pitifully provincial. True, Calvinism remained an international movement to be reckoned with, and in some other provincial strongholds, such as parts of Presbyterian Scotland and Scots-Irish Ulster, it could hold to a strict confessionalist line. Yet in more cosmopolitan centers, such as the enlightened cities of Scotland or among London dissenters, inroads of modern thought had forced tolerance.

In New England the contest between modern fashion and Puritan authority was often literally a battle of the books. Harvard and Yale had both been committed to the principle of theological inoculation, exposing their students to modern authors, but in safe doses and in a controlled environment. When the infection spread, as it had most notoriously in the Anglican apostasy at Yale, one of the first responses was to blame the books. After that defection Jeremiah Dummer, who had secured the original Yale gift for the library, had to assure that in addition to Anglican authors, no "eminent dissenter" had been omitted from the collection.[20] When in 1732, Anglican cleric George Berkeley, the philosopher, then residing in Rhode Island, secured another large gift, including more books for the college, some of the orthodox Calvinists suspected it was Anglican plot. The idea was not entirely fanciful. Yale defector Samuel Johnson encouraged Berkeley to think the school might become Anglican.[21]

In Boston the once controversial Benjamin Colman, pastor of Brattle Street Church since 1699, was among the chief guardians of Yale's orthodoxy. Like many who argued for tolerance on matters indifferent, Colman was alarmed when such tolerance was extended toward what he considered the heart of the matter. Such developments all too readily could be misconstrued to confirm predictions of critics who claimed that moderation was the first step down a slippery slope to heterodoxy. During the Anglican crisis, he had been among those criticizing Dummer for overloading the collection of books with Anglican and Arminian authors.[22] When he got wind of the Berkeley donation he wrote to Rector Elisha Williams inquiring whether the gift came with strings attached. Williams assured him that it had not been "clogged in the manner you hint."[23] Not entirely satisfied, Colman wrote to another Yale trustee, Eliphalet Adams, about the same concerns, urging that Adams "freely write" about his investigations into the rumored "prevalence of Arminianism in the college."[24]

Colman's alarm is especially revealing about the significance of Arminianism for the Massachusetts establishment in the early 1730s. Colman, an innovative upstart in his youth, was by now Boston's leading clergyman. Cotton Mather had died in 1728. Early in the century the Mathers had bitterly opposed Colman and Brattle Street, but they had long since been reconciled, and by the 1720s Colman and Cotton Mather presented a united front on almost everything, including questions of Calvinist orthodoxy.

In 1726 Mather had boasted that "every one knows" that the churches of New England "perfectly adhere to the confession of faith, published by the Assembly of Divines at Westminster." He reassured his readers, "I cannot learn that among all the pastors of two hundred churches, there is one Arminian: much less an Arian, or a Gentilist."[25] Mather exaggerated, although he was technically correct. No congregationalist pastor would publicly deny Westminster or take an open stance for Arminianism, but everyone also knew that for decades some Harvard students toyed with Arminian notions and that a few of the more liberal clergy were rumored to be tainted with Arminian and rationalist tendencies. Increasingly the guardians of the New England establishment were using "Calvinistic" or "Calvinistical" as shorthand for "non-Arminian."[26]

In this setting (though a year before the Berkeley gift) Jonathan Edwards made his Boston debut, delivering the public lecture on Thursday, July 8, 1731, the week of the Harvard commencement, when Boston was filled with clergy. Those who designed the occasion were well aware of the symbolic significance of inviting not only Stoddard's young successor but also a thoroughly orthodox Yale man to address an audience overwhelmingly of Harvard graduates.[27]

Edwards did not disappoint. In "God Glorified in Man's Dependence," he once again took on directly the Arminian threat. Nothing he said was new. Indeed, on such a ceremonial occasion nothing new was expected any more than it would be in a later Fourth of July speech. Yet Edwards said it well. With his usual thoroughness he fashioned his sermonic architecture. At the foundations of his edifice he systematically closed every seam that might allow people to gain a glimmer of a supposition that their salvation was partly their own doing. So he forced them to look toward the dome around which he crafted windows that framed the light of God's ways.

Humans had a greater dependence on God, he pointed out, because of their fall into sin. "We are more apparently dependent on God for happiness, being first miserable, and afterwards happy." "Schemes of divinity" that in any way questioned "an absolute and universal dependence on God, derogate his glory, and thwart the design of our redemption." They "own an entire dependence on God for some things, but not for others." Thus they rob the Gospel of "that which God accounts its lustre and glory." Faith itself includes "a sensibleness and an acknowledgement of absolute dependence on God." Far from being a human work, it "abases men, and exalts God." So the redeemed have no room for pride. "Is any man eminent in holiness," he concluded to his eminent audience, "let him take nothing of the glory of it to himself, but ascribe it to him whose 'workmanship we are, created in Christ Jesus unto good works.'"[28]

Pleased to be so well reminded of their unworthiness, the powerful Boston clergy saw that the sermon was quickly published. In the "Advertisement," or foreword to the publication, Thomas Prince and William Cooper reiterated the point that "vital piety will proportionably languish" if people lose their sense of total dependence on God. Such had been the doctrines that flourished "in the days of our forefathers," and they hoped they "will never grow unfashionable among us." They were delighted that God was raising up "among the children of his people" those who "have still a high value for such principles." And particularly they hoped that "the college in the neighboring colony (as well as our own) may be a fruitful mother of many such sons as the author."[29]

## The International Cause

The Boston sermon marked a turning point in Edwards' career. Aside from providing his first publication (his sponsors claimed, conventionally, "it was with no small difficulty that the author's youth and modesty were prevailed on"), it placed the twenty-seven-year-old within the international network promoting evangelical renewal. His sponsors had an interest in maintaining

Calvinist orthodoxy, but defense of the Reformed faith was inextricably linked for them, as it was for him, to a larger concern. Their great practical hope lay in the growing transatlantic movement to promote heartfelt piety. Inspired by a progressive historical vision, they aspired to be used by God to help usher in his kingdom through a great outpouring of the Holy Spirit and the salvation of countless souls. Although they were looking back with loyalty to their Puritan heritage, they were also looking forward as part of an emerging spiritual movement that we now know as "evangelicalism."[30]

Thomas Prince, the elder of Edwards' immediate sponsors, was one of Boston's leaders in building an international network of Calvinist evangelicals. A 1707 Harvard graduate, he spent most of his time from 1709 to 1717 in England. There he temporarily filled various pulpits and established evangelical contacts. Upon his return he was soon settled at the prestigious Old South Church as a colleague of his classmate Joseph Sewall, son of Judge Samuel Sewall. That put him near the center of what might be called the Boston evangelical network that included the Sewalls, the Mathers, and Solomon Stoddard when he visited his hometown. Prince hoped to move even closer to the inner circle when he asked for the hand of Judge Sewall's daughter, Judith. Judith turned him down and Prince married another. Soon after, Judith married Prince's friend William Cooper.[31]

William Cooper and Thomas Prince had similar tastes in religion as well as in women and remained friends and close allies in the evangelical cause. Cooper (Harvard 1712), a gifted preacher, had accepted a call in 1715 to be Benjamin Colman's colleague at Brattle Street Church. During the next decade and a half, Colman, Cooper, Prince, the Sewalls, and Cotton Mather (until his death) were at the center of a campaign for a revival of vital Calvinist piety. In 1730 Colman became the colonial correspondent for the Society in Scotland for Propagating Christian Knowledge, which supported Indian missions. In 1731 William Cooper established a correspondence with John Maclaurin of Glasgow, a Scottish Calvinist champion of religion of the heart.[32] When Jonathan Edwards visited Boston in 1731, he was incorporated into this internationally oriented circle into which he so naturally fit, both by birth and by disposition.

A shared emphasis on the affections helped unite these sometimes disparate allies. In contrast to some other Boston clergy who were more rationalistic (Charles Chauncy is the best known), Colman and his party shaped their Calvinism more by the strands of modern thought growing out of Henry More and the Cambridge Platonists, stressing the beauty of God's creation and redemption and the role of beauty in rousing the affections. Edwards already belonged to this school of thought. He was also a reader and admirer of Colman's works, though he probably did not agree with the eminent Bostonian in every detail.[33]

Among the most noticeable changes marking the sometimes subtle transformation from Puritanism to Calvinistic evangelicalism that this group was fostering was the reform of singing in worship. New England congregational singing had become chaotic and dissonant. Seventeenth-century Puritans had strictly followed the anti-Anglican principle that nothing should be part of public worship except what was commanded in Scripture. Like others of the Reformed, they would sing only literally translated biblical psalms. Although many Puritans owned musical instruments, they would not think of using them in the meetinghouse. As though to underscore the point that music was incidental to words, they published the metric psalms without musical notes. Congregations sang to any one of a number of familiar psalm tunes. A precentor, or leading singer, would "set the tune" by singing at least the first line, and the congregation would then join in. Over the years the collective memory of the tunes evolved or devolved. Further, members of the congregation sang variations on the original notes as it pleased them. Whereas today this might be regarded as a wonderful folk tradition, by the early eighteenth century the near chaos seemed appalling to those attuned to the refined musical standards of the day.

Judge Samuel Sewall was the precentor at Old South Church from 1694 to 1718. In 1713 he reported in his diary that he started the psalm tune "Windsor" in a key much too high and ended up unintentionally moving into the tune "High Dutch." Twice in 1718, not long before giving up the job, he reported that he was unable to keep the "gallery" from forcing their way "irresistibly" into "St. David's" despite his setting the tune of "York."[34] One early proponent of reform wrote in 1721 that "the tunes are now miserably tortured and twisted and quavered . . . it sounds in the ear of a good judge like five hundred different tunes roared out at the same time with perpetual interferings with one another." The irreverent James Franklin satirized in the *New England Courant* that he was "credibly informed that a certain gentlewoman miscarried at the ungrateful and yelling noise of a deacon" whom he suggested might be employed as a "procurer of abortions."[35]

In the meantime, English dissenters had been reforming sacred singing for nearly a generation. The leading figure was Isaac Watts, a Calvinist clergyman. Watts argued that it was not necessary to use exact biblical words, only that hymns and spiritual songs be based on Scriptural *themes.* On this principle he wrote hymns for private devotional use, publishing them as *Hymns and Spiritual Songs* in 1707. These included, "When I Survey the Wondrous Cross," "Alas and Did My Savior Bleed," and "Jesus Shall Reign Where'er the Sun." In 1719 he added what became very popular paraphrases of the psalms. By the time Edwards was a young man Watts' hymns were being used in New England for family devotions and neighborhood social meetings, and he certainly was familiar with Watts.[36] We might imagine, in light of his musical sensibilities, that the singing in his private meditations, or with Sarah, included such hymns.

At the same time that hymns were being introduced to New England, so was "regular" singing, or singing in parts. Music was not taught at seventeenth-century Harvard, and so musical literacy had been low. In 1713 the first of a number of schools for music and dancing opened in Boston, primarily for women to learn genteel skills. Probably from around this time whatever finishing education Jonathan's sisters received in Boston included education in music, though not dancing.[37]

With enthusiasm for the symmetries of eighteenth-century harmonies sweeping sophisticated Boston, the town's clergy took the lead in calling for an end to the pandemonium of psalm singing at meeting. By 1722 Cotton Mather introduced the new singing into Sunday worship.[38] Soon the reform turned into the "singing controversy." Throughout the 1720s New Englanders hotly debated the subject, and in many outlying areas the debate continued decades later. The Boston clergy used the power of the press, publishing numerous defenses of the superiority of "regular" singing and providing instruction on singing by note and in three-part harmony. Colman, the Mathers, Prince, Cooper, and Joseph Sewall all endorsed the new way. Opposition came principally from the laity who found the familiar individual expression of "the old way" more meaningful. They also had Puritan precedent on their side. Singing by rule seemed a step toward Anglican formalism leading to Popery.[39]

Those who promoted singing reform saw the aestheticism of the age as a way to promote vital piety. "The singing of the sacred Psalms in the flock," said Cotton Mather, "may be made more beautiful, and especially have the *beauties of holiness* more upon it."[40] Orderly harmonies were supremely rational, but like much else in true religion, rational harmonies pointed to God's beauty and were ultimately designed to move the affections.

Although most laypeople, especially in rural communities, had their own ideas of beauty and resisted the innovations, clergy whose leadership was strong enough introduced the reform even in many such outlying towns. Not surprisingly, one of the first to do so was Solomon Stoddard. By the time Jonathan settled in Northampton in 1726 at least some of the parishioners had learned singing in parts. Some churches hired "singing masters" to help acquaint their congregation with the new aesthetic forms.[41] Musical literacy was spreading so rapidly, at least in urban areas, that by 1729 one could hear public concerts in Boston.[42] By the time Jonathan visited there in 1731 he was already an enthusiast for the beauties of regular singing.

Isaac Watts was a central figure in the international network of Reformed clergy who shared concerns for heart-felt revival. Watts was, like Edwards, a sometimes sickly polymath who published widely in a number of fields. Watts was more a popularizer, however, producing texts summarizing the learning of the day on subjects from spelling to astronomy. His textbook on logic, for instance, became a standard at New England colleges for generations. Watts became a regular correspondent with Cotton Mather and other New England clergy. Those who had more recently spent time in England, such as Thomas Prince, knew him personally. As his fame rose, Watts became one of the chief patrons of the colonies. He and Benjamin Colman (who each had at one time been in love with the English poet Elizabeth Singer) corresponded regularly and served as each other's literary agents in their respective cities.[43]

## The Royal Governor and the Kingdom

Among Watts' circle of evangelical friends and correspondents was the new royal governor of Massachusetts, Jonathan Belcher. The son of a Boston merchant, Belcher had graduated from Harvard in 1699, frequently traveled to England, where he made important contacts, and become a leading figure in colonial politics. Usually a defender of royal prerogative but also deeply loyal to the cause of Reformed Christianity, he switched in 1728 to the more popular side in opposition to the new royal governor, William Burnet, an Anglican of ostentatious manners. In early 1729 Belcher traveled to England to oppose a permanent salary for the governor, which would have made the governor less dependent on the colonial assembly.

By this time Massachusetts was in bitter political turmoil. Power struggles, personal rivalries, unsettled imperial issues, and economic uncertainties

Inside the portrait, text reads:

His Excellency
Captain General & Governor in Chief
Massachuset's Bay & New Hampshire
Vice Admiral

JONATHAN BELCHER Esq.
of His Majesty's Provinces of
in NEW ENGLAND and
of the same

Governor Jonathan Belcher (1682–1757) had a vision for the advance of Christian civilization.

combined to create deep divisions between the popular "country" party and the more elite "court" faction. The arrival of Governor Burnet in 1728 brought the crisis to a head. The imperious governor and the country party, which controlled the lower house, were equally intransigent. Overheated political rhetoric on both sides raised a sense of alarm. Burnet threatened to have the colony's charter revoked, a possibility that sparked spasms of anxiety among both the religious establishment and the popular country party. The country party was also jealous to guard the Assembly's power to issue "bills of credit," essential for keeping money available for investments in land for the less wealthy. Then suddenly, in September 1729, Burnet died. No one knew what might happen next, and the colony was thrown into a terrible state of uncertainty. By the spring, as Stephen Williams described it in his diary, the "country" was "in an uproar." "What the event of our struggles will be," Williams worried, "God only knows."[44]

Jonathan Belcher's appointment as governor appeared to most of Massachusetts' establishment as a wonderful providence. His presence in England and some earlier contacts with the royal family put him in the right spot at the right time. In exchange for the appointment, he dropped his opposition to the permanent salary, a deal not difficult for him to accept now that he would be the beneficiary. Although Belcher's ability to play both sides in the political fray had and would cost him some friends, in the summer of 1730 he returned to Boston amid great celebrations. Some of his clerical associates were especially delighted. Benjamin Colman had been one of his earliest sponsors, and Thomas Prince was another friend. Isaac Watts sent an extravagant adulatory poem.[45]

Belcher was an heir to the Puritans in the age of Walpole and hard-nosed politics. He had one foot firmly planted in each world.[46] In religious principles he stood solidly among the Calvinistic evangelicals. While he would defend the rights of Anglicans in the colony, attended Church of England services in England, and even would celebrate Christmas in Christ's Church, Boston, he would not let his daughter marry an Anglican and worried when his son attended Anglican services in England.[47] Though duly circumspect in his public religious pronouncements, in his private correspondence he freely expressed his pious religious sentiments and concern for "vital piety."[48] To Isaac Watts he acknowledged that "the station God has set me in is surrounded with snares and difficulties" and requested that Watts "Bow then your knees with mine to the fountain of grace and wisdom, that I may so conduct my administration as most of all to advance the glory of God with the weal and happiness of his people."[49] Belcher took to heart a favorite Puritan image, often applied to him, as a Nehemiah, raised up by God for the restoration of his people.[50]

The people were not so sure that Belcher was the next Nehemiah, especially when they soon found out that he had attained the governorship at the price of defending royal prerogatives. Once again Massachusetts politics fell into a turmoil as the Assembly became bitterly divided. The court party, cultivated by his patronage, supported Belcher, while the country party blocked his initiatives and called for his removal.

Colonel John Stoddard was one of Belcher's closest allies. They had known each other since Harvard days and shared the same combination of Calvinistic principles and shrewd, mostly conservative, political instincts. Belcher valued Stoddard and the votes the "Squire of Hampshire County" could bring from the west and rewarded him appropriately with various appointments to the local judiciary. Stoddard in any case would have supported Belcher's largely unsuccessful efforts to promote legislation for the suppression of "vice and wickedness," such as "gaming and excessive drinking," which they saw as undermining the morals of the commonwealth.[51] Belcher also valued the westerner's knowledge of Indian affairs. In 1734 the governor and the colonel traveled together to interview the tribes on the western frontier and not long afterward cooperated in a plan for an Indian mission.[52]

The contentions in Massachusetts politics had their counterpart in the long-standing factious and often petty political rivalries in Northampton. Belcher's appointment must have strengthened the Stoddard-Edwards commitment to the court party. He was one of their own, a friend both of the landed elite and of true religion.

Edwards was a champion of prerogative and deference. His office, his "river-gods" clan, his theology, and his disposition all pointed in that direction. Time and again in his sermons of this period he warned against the sin of envy. No one in Northampton could miss the political overtones of "envy" as Edwards used it. It was a trait of those who agitated against their betters. Did they, he asked, really have the welfare of the country in mind, or their own advancement? In a communion sermon on this theme, he deplored the party spirit of Northampton, contrasted it with the spirit of Christian love symbolized by the sacrament, and urged agitators that they had better worry about their salvation.[53] In another political sermon he deplored the terribly "unsettled" state of public affairs and declared that "the very excellency of a public state is its stability." "Old and experienced rulers," he said, in a not-so-veiled reference to persons like Squire John Stoddard, were much to be preferred to new and inexperienced ones. "'Tis no part of public prudence," he declared, "to be often changing the persons in whose hands is the administration of government." Viewing the issue in firmly paternalistic terms, he argued that such political fickleness was as ruinous as it would be to be changing heads of families every few years.[54]

When Colonel Stoddard's nephew preached to the Boston establishment in the still unstable days of 1731, Governor Belcher must have warmly welcomed the young man. The two moved in the same elite circles. Edwards, in turn, would have been pleased by the international connections that this official visit to Boston afforded. Building connections with internationally connected clergy, like Prince, Cooper, and Colman, exactly suited his ambitions to bring God's truth to all the world. That the governor of the colony was sympathetic to the same causes was also important to the aspirations of these clerical leaders. Though committed first to the revival of vital piety, they took for granted that God worked also through political means. England under the Hanoverian kings since 1714 and after the defeat of the Stuart Pretender in 1715 was firmly committed to the Protestant cause. Yet the Protestant cause in England itself clearly needed renewal. The New England colonies represented one of the best hopes for building a spiritual-political base that might provide at least a model, perhaps even a staging center, for the coming revival. Despite cultural and political tides that might have seemed to be running against such ambitions, they were confident of the outcome, since this was God's work. They could well join in the sentiments of Isaac Watts' paraphrase of Psalm 72:

> Jesus shall reign where-'er the sun,
> Does his successive journeys run.
> His kingdom stretch from shore to shore,
> Till moons shall wax and wane no more.[55]

# CHAPTER 9

## The Mighty Works of God and of Satan

I n mid-1731, around the time he was preparing for his sermon in Boston, Edwards began to notice some winds of change in Northampton, winds that would eventually blow into an amazing awakening. That spiritual nor'easter would alter the course of his career. His ambition had long been to do great things for God as an internationally recognized writer. Preaching a public lecture sermon that would be published in the provincial capital was a small step in that direction. Yet Edwards was already deeply involved as pastor of one of the largest churches in western Massachusetts. His work and the remarkable developments there would take precedence over everything else.

It all began with the young people. Their disrespect for authority, which had grown during Solomon Stoddard's last years, reached a peak just after his death. Yet as Edwards gained standing in his own right, his railings against their loose behavior, combined with his evident compassion for their souls, began to have some effect. "In two or three years after Mr. Stoddard's death," as he recounted it, "there began to be a sensible amendment of these evils; the young people shewed more of a disposition to hearken to counsel, and by degrees left off their frolicking, and grew observably more decent in their attendance on the public worship, and there were more that manifested a religious concern than there used to be."[1]

The social conditions for young people in western New England had become trying. Families were large, five to nine children on average.[2] During the seventeenth century the town of Northampton had distributed open land to sons as they came of age. That practice, plus scattering tracts and maintaining meadows for common cultivation, had provided a strong economic base for the communalism integral to the Puritan cultural ideal. But after 1705, there was no more land available in the township except some distributed in 1730 to encourage a new settlement at Southampton, about eight miles away. With the ever-present threat of renewed Indian hostilities, homesteading had to be a communal activity, and even then it was precarious. In Northampton, farmers were consolidating land holdings, and the gap between the well-to-do landowners and the less prosperous was growing, contributing to long-standing political antagonisms. With no new land available, young people were living with their parents. While that did not necessarily cause economic deprivation—farms might prosper from having extra family laborers—it did change social patterns. Young people were postponing marriage about three years longer than had their parents, so that the average age of marriage was about twenty-eight or twenty-nine for men and twenty-five for women.

Young people from their mid-teens until their late twenties were likely to be in this in-between situation. They lived in villages with communal structures, but they were not as likely to be participating responsibly in the community as their grandparents had at the same age. Nor did they have many opportunities to strike off on their own, as entrepreneur farmers, as later generations would. A capitalist economy was beginning to replace the communal one, but this is a lot clearer in retrospect than it was for the people living at the time when the relation of individuals to the community was far from settled. The practical effect was that increasing numbers of young people were living with their parents well into their twenties. As Edwards' sermons against frolicking made clear, unmarried sons and daughters were under the authority of their parents, but—not surprisingly—parental rule was hardly working as he would have liked. For many young people, the official expectation that they postpone all sexual activity until marriage and the disparity between that standard and their actual practices helped create a sense of guilt.[3]

While the pressures of this ill-defined stage of life were major contributors to youthful unrest and eventual openness to religious alternatives, the social tensions that fostered the awakening were probably no more severe than in other eras. The peaceful 1730s had no more tensions than the 1720s or many other decades. Northampton had seen impressive revivals under Stoddard at times when new land was readily available and marriage did not need to be long postponed. In other parts of the European world, many communities had revivals under a variety of conditions, so one cannot generalize concerning external causes. Nonetheless, the revivals in western New England were among the most intense, and the particular social conditions of the

1730s were the occasion for that intensity. Often relatively peaceful times are filled with anxieties as people have time to reflect on a seemingly lost past when meaning was supposedly plainer and more intense in contrast to an uncertain future.

Had some of the specific social contributors to the awakening been pointed out to Edwards, such as the extension of unmarried dependence for many of the young, he would have acknowledged them without placing any strain on his theological explanation of the awakening. God always worked through means. Whether he sent an earthquake or a shortage of available land, God was still acting to remind humans of their spiritual needs. Through such forces God provided the soil for revival. God, through the Holy Spirit, also provided the means of grace, such as preaching the Word and the ordinances of the church, as means of tending the spiritual vineyard, as one biblical image put it.

Even though by 1731 Edwards could sense that the spiritual orchard he was tending might be regaining its vitality, it took nearly three more years of patient pruning and cultivation before it burst into bloom. During these years not only did the mood of the young people gradually change, but their elders showed signs of abandoning the town's notorious "party spirit." Still, as late as March of 1734, Edwards was warning in a sermon on Isaiah 5:4 that God would trample under foot a vineyard that brought forth wild fruit, despite all his loving cultivation.[4]

About this same time Edwards was attempting to deploy the town's communal and paternal traditions in hopes of striking a decisive blow against the custom he found most incompatible with its spiritual heritage. Although the young people had moderated their frolicking and become more attentive at worship services, it "had been their manner of a long time, and for aught I know, always, to make Sabbath-day nights and lecture days to be especially times of diversion and company-keeping." During the winter of 1733–34, sensing perhaps that he might win this battle, he preached once again against "company-keeping" and urged parents to bring it to an end. The next evening he gathered at his house "men that belonged to the several parts of the town." He persuaded them to organize in their several neighborhoods "meetings with heads of households" called in the name of the pastor. The town, as he saw it, was essentially an extended family or clan. Or, more precisely, he viewed it as like a tribe of Israel, with himself as the spiritual and moral authority. Through the town elders, who would work through heads of households, he could extend his moral authority over the entire community.

The effort worked wonderfully. Persuasion had softened hearts that coercion alone would have only hardened. According to Edwards' account, not only did the heads of households readily cooperate, but astonishingly, the parents discovered that "the young people declared themselves convinced by what they had heard, and willing of themselves to comply."[5]

Then the first flame of revival appeared in the tiny hamlet of Pascommuck, about three miles from the main part of Northampton but part of Edwards' congregational domain. The several families of Pascommuck were swept by "a remarkable religious concern," and "a number of persons seemed to be savingly wrought upon." In April 1734 came a dramatic turning point. "There happened," Edwards reported, "a very sudden and awful death of a young man in the bloom of his youth; who being violently seized with a pleurisy and taken immediately very delirious, died in about two days; which (together with what was preached publicly on that occasion) much affected many young people."[6]

Edwards' whole life had prepared him to seize this moment. Having been twice on the verge of death, he had spent much of his own youth reflecting on the folly of loving earthly pleasure when on the brink of eternity. He preached to the stricken mourners on Psalm 90:5–6: "In the morning they are like grass which groweth up. In the morning it flourisheth and groweth up. In the evening it is cut down and withereth." His poignant sermon, elaborating this image, brought many friends of the dead young man to tears.

Everyone in the congregation, Edwards pointed out, could vividly recall from walking in their own fields the experience depicted by the psalmist: "If we walk out in the morning we may behold them green and gay appearing in lively and pleasant colours. Green grass interspersed with beautiful flowers seeming to smile . . . to rejoice and sing and shout for joy. . . . But if we walk out again in the evening we may see the grass and flowers that so pleasantly saluted our eyes in the morning all cut down, suddenly mown down and dead and withered, having lost its beautiful colour and cheerful lively aspect."

Following the psalmist, Edwards portrayed the powerful spiritual meaning of this experience. Appreciating the beauties of youth, which he clearly loved as much as the flowers, Edwards painted a picture of the handsome young man who has suffered a horrible death: "Or it may be he flourishes in the bloom of youth. He is just come to mature age. His faculties have lately blossomed. . . . And he is in his full strength and all the powers of nature are most lively and active and the body is in its greatest beauty and comeliness."

Reiterating the image, in his characteristic fugal development of every variation on a theme, he turned to the perceptions of the young man's friends: "He flourishes in the hopes and expectations of friends. . . . He is happy and cheerful, is encompassed about with smiles of nature and Providence. [He is] like the green grass and flowers of a field in the morning that are covered over with drops of dew and has the beams of sun of the morning pleasantly shining upon it and sends forth a fragrant smell as well as salutes the eyes with a gay and beautiful appearance."

The fragility of such wonderful yet fleeting beauty stood in moving contrast to the horrible distortions of death, which Edwards depicted just as vividly: "While man is under the agonies of death and the conflict with the king of terrors, how are his features distorted: the eyes set and glaring in ghastly manner and the mouth gasping for breath. . . . How those countenances that were most beautiful and delighting to beholders while there was life and health become unpleasant and loathsome to the sight by death. Their beauty consumes away like a moth."

Having so powerfully addressed the affections, Edwards turned to reason to warn the youth of Northampton of squandering their lives in pursuit of vanity. "How unreasonable is it," he argued at length, "for one who is so much like the grass and flowers of the field . . . to spend away the prime of his opportunity in levity and vain mirth in inconsideration and pursuit of carnal and sensual delights and pleasures."

As he developed this point in this funeral sermon, he led his young listeners to *feel* the shock of their unreasonableness: "Consider. If you should die in youth how shocking would the thought of your having spent your youth in such a manner be to them that see it. When others stand by your bedside and see you gasping and breathing your last or come afterward and see you laid out dead by the wall and see you put into the coffin and behold the awful visage which death has given you, how shocking will it be to them to think this is the person that used to be so vain and frothy in conversation. This is he that was so lewd a companion. This is he that used to spend of his time in his leisure hours so much in frolicking."

Edwards concluded by reiterating a central principle in his entire outlook, the same principle he had so often reminded himself of during his own youthful struggles. It was wildly unreasonable, he told the young people, to be misled by the beauties and pleasures of this earthly body when they could look forward to vastly greater pleasures in the world to come: "If you have an interest in Christ your body shall flourish again in a glorious manner. If you should die in the flower of your days when the body is most active and beautiful it will rise again a thousand times more active and beautiful." Their happiness would be far greater than that of simply being fondly remembered for a time. Their glory would last.[7]

Having won a foothold among the young and believing that some of those so deeply affected by his sermon were savingly converted, Edwards pressed toward spreading heavenly concerns among them. Some weeks after the death of the young man, he met with the young people in a "private meeting" for them alone. Alluding to the conclusion of his earlier sermon, he preached on a text he knew they could relate to, Canticles (Song of Songs) 6:1, "Whither is thy beloved gone, O thou fairest among women? whither is thy beloved turned aside? that we may seek him with thee."

For Edwards, as in much of the Christian tradition, this love poetry was read as an image of the love between Christ and his church. Christ's "glorious and lovely person" was "more excellent than all earthly things, better than all other beloveds." Trying to spread the excitement of the awakening, he urged the young people to experience how the love of Christ exceeded earthly loves. The delights of love in this world were designed to point to far higher raptures. Just as lovers spoke of their beloved to others, those already converted should be an encouragement to others to conversion. Today the young people were gathered as friends in one place, but unless those who were not converted followed the example of those who were, a great gulf would eventually be fixed among them.[8]

At nearly this same time the young people were stricken by the death of another of their number, this time a married young woman. At the outset of her illness she had been much distressed over the state of her soul but by the time of her death she "seemed to have satisfying evidences of God's saving mercy . . . so that she died very full of comfort, in a most earnest and moving manner warning and counseling others."[9] In June, perhaps for this occasion, Edwards composed another funeral sermon that contrasted to the doleful lamentation of April, this one extolling the joys and comforts one could take in the death of a saint.[10]

By fall the awakening had spread and was transforming the youth culture of Northampton. The young people now seemed so compliant to Edwards' leadership and so eagerly seeking spiritual joys that he easily convinced them to begin meeting on Thursday evenings after lectures (previously a favorite time for frolicking) for "social religion" in smaller groups, meeting in homes in various parts of the town. Soon the adults adopted a similar plan. By the next spring various groups were voluntarily meeting on Sabbath evenings as well. In contrast to ordinary times when women were most active in religious affairs, the young men now led in bringing almost all of their number to meetings for social religion and prayer.[11]

By persuading the town to organize into smaller, private religious meetings, Edwards resuscitated one of the basic components of the Puritan movement. Such prayer meetings had been held in New England on lecture day evenings since the early English settlements, but they apparently had lost some of their vitality. In Elizabethan England when the original Puritans were frequently oppressed, the neighborhood conventicals were often the heart of the movement. Nothing was more distinctive about Puritanism than its encouragement of lay spirituality. Puritans promoted literacy for all because it was important for private, family, and neighborhood lay devotion. In the social meetings, neighbors prayed, studied together, taught and exhorted each other, and built each other up spiritually. Often women met separately, providing them opportunities outside their own homes for teaching and exercising other spiritual gifts.[12]

The renewal of the lay conventicals tied the Northampton awakening not only to old Puritanism but also to the British and European pietist revivals of their day. Early eighteenth-century stirrings throughout the Protestant world were marked by renewals of lay prayer meetings. Evangelical clergy emphasized that regular prayer—personal, family, and social—was the key to any general awakening. Prayer manuals, such as Isaac Watts' popular *Guide to Prayer* (1715), sold briskly on both sides of the Atlantic.[13]

Edwards promoted the new singing at the now-thriving social prayer meetings. His congregation had been learning regular or three-part singing for some time, and Edwards believed they "excelled all that ever I knew in the external part of the duty before, generally carrying regularly and well three parts of music, and the women a part by themselves."[14] In public worship, they still sang only the psalms. In private meetings they could sing and learn the hymns of Isaac Watts, which added to the joy of the occasions. Learning to sing, Edwards believed, was a spiritual duty. It was a biblically mandated way to encourage the faith of others and had a laudable effect in raising the affections, so essential to true spirituality.[15]

Edwards took care to have published in 1734 one notable sermon of the previous year. Addressing his preface to the people of Northampton, he praised them for the "happy union between us" and for so many who unquestionably exhibited the fruits of the doctrines of which he spoke.[16] Yet as the revival grew he wanted them to reflect again on these crucial teachings, both to strengthen their faith and to stir others to seek light from God. This sermon, *A Divine and Supernatural Light*, encapsulates better than any other single source the essence of his spiritual insight. In it he provided a sort of constitution for any true awakening.

More concisely than anywhere else, in *A Divine and Supernatural Light* he related his most profound theological reflections on his understanding of true Christian experience. God communicates to humans, he explained, in an immediate way that goes beyond anything that natural reason by itself can attain. What distinguishes saints from the unconverted is that the Holy Spirit dwells *within* converted persons and so gives them the power to apprehend the things of God. They have, in effect, a new spiritual sense. This new sense is not an ability to have visions, or to gain new information that goes beyond Scripture, or to experience intense religious emotions. Rather, it is the power necessary to appreciate the spiritual light that radiates from God, the power to hear the communication of God's love that pervades the universe. It is a power to appreciate beauty or excellency, specifically the beauty and excellency of Christ.

Such knowledge, Edwards spelled out to the Northamptonites, is qualitative and affective, not simply rational or theoretical. It is, in a familiar image, like the "difference between having a rational judgment that honey is sweet, and having a sense of its sweetness." Or, more exactly, it is like "the difference between believing a person is beautiful, and having a sense of his beauty." The "spiritually enlightened" person does not "merely rationally believe that God is glorious, but he has a sense of the gloriousness of God in his heart."

In his "improvement," or application of the sermon, Edwards emphasized the egalitarian implications. "Persons of mean capacities and advantages" can apprehend this spiritual light "as well as those that are of the greatest parts and learning." If the Gospel "depended only on history, and such reasonings as learned men only are capable of, it would be above the reach of far the greatest part of mankind." But people of "an ordinary degree of knowledge, are capable, without a long and subtle train of reasoning, to see the divine excellency of the things of religion." When they do, they gain divine wisdom "more excellent than all the knowledge of the greatest philosophers or statesmen." This "sweet and joyful" divine knowledge, goes far beyond the pleasures of human knowledge. It is a seeing of "things that are immensely the most exquisitely beautiful." This overwhelming beauty "reaches to the bottom of the heart, and changes its nature." It is the only power capable of producing the fruit of "universal holiness of life," which is the primary evidence that confirms true conversion and the "intuitive and immediate evidence" that one has encountered the beauty of the divine.[17]

By the time Edwards wrote the preface for the printed version, he could say there was no doubt that many of his Northampton parishioners "clearly exemplified" the remarkable spiritual traits depicted in the sermon. In his view, what he was seeing was not just a fad of religious enthusiasm, not excited claims to faith without evidences of holiness, not shallow arousal of the affections that would not last, but lives that were being permanently changed. He wrote this as one who insisted on the most rigorous spiritual standards and who cultivated the suspicions of a cautious rational observer. Yet there seemed no mistaking it: the fires of the Holy Spirit were sweeping through the hearts of many of the people, spreading from one to another.

His personal role was astonishing. The town seemed to be made over in his image, which was no small feat in light of his perfectionist standards and spiritual intensity. Somehow his combination of transparent spirituality and unrelenting crystal-clear logic was winning the hearts of the community. People identified with this demanding young preacher who set before them an exalted spiritual vision. Every day parishioners filled his home, waiting to see him for counseling. Callow youth and callous farmers were coming under the wonderful spell.

The emerging awakening also create tensions between the generations. One of the few accounts of the revival in Northampton coming from someone other than Edwards himself tells of a man who asked his son to go to the woods to replenish their dwindling supply of firewood. The son refused, an argument ensued, and finally the father, invoking his authority, ordered the young man to go. Instead, the son took his ax and went into the barn where he made such a "hideous mourning and noise" that it alarmed the neighbors. Finally, unable to calm him, they called Edwards, before whom the young man continued in his turmoil. Edwards, as the story went, asked the father to forgo his request since the son was under an extraordinary influence of the Spirit and "*was getting through,*" a phrase used for those seeking conversion. Opponents of the awakening who told such stories saw it as scandalously undermining proper authority and deference.[18]

Toward the end of December the awakening took a dramatic upturn. A young woman, notorious as "one of the greatest company-keepers in the whole town," came to him for counsel. Previously he had not heard that she had become "in any wise serious," but as he listened to her story and carefully questioned her she convinced him "that what she gave an account of was a glorious work of God's infinite power and sovereign grace." So unlikely a convert was this previously coarse-mouthed and flirtatious young woman that Edwards feared the news of her supposed conversion would only raise skepticism. Just the opposite. "The news of it seemed to be almost like a flash of lightening, upon the hearts of young people all over the town, and upon many others." Within a few days four or five more showed up at his study, all showing the most convincing signs of having been savingly converted. God used the young woman's conversion, Edwards supposed, as "the greatest occasion of awakening to others, of anything that ever came to pass in the town." The young woman now was speaking with all her friends, persons "farthest from seriousness" of the town, those who had previously hung out with her at the taverns or frolics. As the stream of converts broadened, people would tell him how this dramatic reformation woke them to their own spiritual needs.[19]

By March and April of 1735 the spiritual rains had turned the stream to a flood. The awakening, though similar in kind to earlier revivals, went far beyond them in extent. Edwards, who had once resolved "in narrations never to speak anything but the pure and simple verity" and now feared that exaggeration could hurt his cause, reported that "a great and earnest concern about the great things of religion and the eternal world became universal in all parts of the town, and among persons of all degrees and all ages."[20] People would talk almost of nothing else. At least that was Edwards' impression. Certainly no one was talking of anything else while *he* was around. Given what we know of human nature and of some of Edwards' later disappointments, we may suspect that awakened Northampton was not nearly as perfect as he represented it to be. Edwards was scrupulously honest, but he was also prone to hyperbole in his zeal to inspire others. He could also be misled by high hopes.

Taking all that into account, the spiritual fervor of the town seems to have gone beyond what anyone had previously seen. "All other talk," Edwards reported, but that "about spiritual and eternal things was soon thrown by; all the conversation in all companies and upon all occasions, was upon these things only, unless so much as was necessary for people, carrying on their ordinary secular business. Other discourse than of the things of religion would scarcely be tolerated in any company." What had once seemed a valley of dry bones now flourished with spiritual life almost with disregard of ordinary affairs. "They seemed to follow their worldly business more as a part of their duty than from any disposition they had to it; the temptation now seemed to lie on that hand, to neglect worldly affairs too much, and to spend too much time in the immediate exercise of religion."[21]

One of the extraordinary manifestations of revival fervor was that illness almost disappeared from the town. In usual times Edwards would receive several "bills" each Sunday asking for prayers for the sick. During the months when the awakening was at its height, "we had not so much as one for many Sabbaths together." Edwards did not cite this verifiable phenomenon as evidence of the validity of the awakening. Rather, he mentioned it only as a providence in which Satan seemed to be restrained for a time.[22]

Edwards could not be sure how many would prove in the long run to be savingly converted, but he had good hopes that within a three-month period 300 townspeople had been so changed. The church, the largest west of Boston, now included 620 communicant members, almost all the adults in the town. The awakening was especially extraordinary because it affected "all sorts, sober and vicious, high and low, rich and poor, wise and unwise." Included were "several Negroes," who "appear to have been truly born again." Some 30 children, fourteen and younger, "seemed to be savingly wrought on." Unlike earlier revivals under Stoddard, as many men were converted as women. Most revivals, he further observed, reached almost only young people. This one included 50 persons over forty years of age and even 2 over seventy.

For the moment, the awakening seemed almost to resolve one of the most troubling dimensions of Edwards' Northampton pastorate—the anomaly created by the Stoddardean policy that unconverted person had been allowed to partake of communion. At the bimonthly communion services at the height of the revival eighty to a hundred at a time made "open explicit profession of faith" which "was very affecting to the congregation." Edwards described these new converts as "received into our communion." Then he added, rather apologetically, that such professions of faith were not actually required for partaking in the communion.[23]

This seemingly almost universal awakening also temporarily relieved one of the deepest tensions within the Puritan and Protestant heritage. Was the church to be a separated communion, called out from the world and made up of believers only? Or was it to be a state church to which all respectable citizens belonged? Edwards' ideal for the church and ultimately for the town was that everyone should follow a virtually monastic standard for all of life. Although such an ideal had often been realized in newer sectarian movements whose members separated from established churches and even from former communities, it was a far more unusual standard for an entire town four or five generations removed from the movement's origins. Now that nearly everyone seemed converted or pressing toward conversion, the town appeared to be on the verge of becoming nearly coextensive with a strictly disciplined church of believers.

An event so remarkable and of such magnitude was soon the talk of New England. Many were skeptical, believing that Edwards had led his people into fanaticism. New England had always included a radical religious fringe, as the established clergy viewed it. They were familiar with various prophets, on both sides of the Atlantic, who stirred up the imagination, encouraged spiritual visions, claimed miracles, fostered strange behaviors, and taught sensational doctrines, such as that the millennium or the Age of the Spirit was at hand. New England's Reformed clergy, reflecting something of the spirit of their "enlightened" times as well as knowing of recurrent excesses within their tradition, were deeply suspicious of "enthusiasm," by which they meant undisciplined religious fervor.[24] Word spread that the extraordinary transformation of Northampton was just such a fanatical outbreak.

Outsider critics were even more severe. On June 5, 1735, Edwards' former teacher, Timothy Cutler, now an Anglican rector in Boston, wrote to a friend in England: "The Calvinistic scheme is in perfection about 100 miles from this place. Conversions are talked of, *ad nauseam usque.* Sixty in a place undergo the work at once. Sadness and horror seize them, and hold them for some days; then they feel an inward joy, and it first shows itself in laughing at meeting. Others are sad for want of experiencing this work; and this takes up for the present the thoughts and talk of that country; and the canting question trumped about is, 'Are you gone through?' i.e. conversion."[25]

Edwards remarked that "there were many that scoffed at and ridiculed" the revival and that its detractors were circulating "exceeding great misrepresentations and innumerable false reports." He had to counter especially the rumor that the Northampton converts were being driven by "vain imaginations" or spiritual visions that went beyond Scripture.

This was a delicate issue for Edwards because the very point of his preaching was to touch the affections, to bring people beyond a merely theoretical knowledge of spiritual realities. To do so, he wanted them to form "lively pictures" of the truth in their mind, so they would have to confront them and react affectively toward them. He believed it proper for people to be placed in "great terrors, through fear of hell" by impressing on their minds "lively ideas of a dreadful furnace." Or people might be affected by Christ's death by forming "a lively idea of Christ hanging upon the cross, and of his blood running from his wounds."[26]

Such intense spiritual affections could easily be confused with more sensational religious impulses. In a few instances Edwards' parishioners had visions that he found "mysterious" and did not know how to evaluate. Nonetheless, he took great pains to teach them the distinction between true biblically based experiences and undisciplined imaginations. As he emphasized in *A Divine and Supernatural Light,* the spiritual light provides qualitative knowledge but no truths beyond Scripture.

Being so careful to make such distinctions, it was not difficult for Edwards to refute the charges of sensationalism, although they persisted in some quarters. He could point out, for instance, that Quaker missionaries, upon hearing the sensational reports from Northampton, came there "hoping to find good waters to fish in." Edwards had, however, well-schooled his parishioners not to be lured by the "inner light" of affections when the real food of Scripture was not also attached to the hook. After several visits, the missionaries left with nothing to show for their efforts.[27]

Northampton's revival fervor was contagious. Skeptical visitors would come to the town and leave impressed or even greatly concerned for the states of their souls. When the court met in Northampton in March 1735, just as the revival was building toward its height, many visitors were deeply affected by seeing the remarkably altered state of the town.[28]

By this time the revival was spreading throughout the Connecticut River Valley and as far as New Haven and the coast of Connecticut. In many cases, Edwards believed, these awakenings resulted from direct contacts with Northampton. Some nearby towns followed the Northampton pattern almost exactly, having nearly universal awakenings in April and May 1735. Many other towns were nearly as remarkably touched. In Edwards' account he mentioned nearly every church in western Massachusetts (Hampshire County) and twenty in Connecticut. Included was his "honored father's parish" of East Windsor. In one instance, two Connecticut pastors, Hezekiah Lord and John Owen, having heard conflicting accounts, traveled to Northampton in May 1735 to see for themselves. Deeply affected, they carried the news of the revival to their home churches, where they sparked notable awakenings. Though other reports confirmed Edwards' account, in some cases it was not clear that the awakenings had any direct connection with Northampton. In Edwards' fullest narrative, written in November 1736, he noted that on a trip to New York and New Jersey in fall 1735 he had heard of remarkable works of God's Spirit in New Jersey, especially under the Dutch Reformed preacher "whose name I remember as Freelinghousa [Theodore Frelinghuysen]" and a Presbyterian evangelist, Gilbert Tennent.[29]

## Satan on the Loose

Edwards had been attempting to harness the lightning of the awakening and (like Benjamin Franklin, who was later knocked out cold during one of his electrical demonstrations) discovered it was even more explosive than he had imagined. On June 1, 1735, the town suddenly was struck directly, and the reverberations sent people scattering down from the spiritual peak they had ascended. Or, in Edwards' own terms, it was a power far more dangerous than mere physical energy. "Satan seemed to be more let loose, and raged in a dreadful manner."[30]

On that Sabbath morning, one of Northampton's elite citizens, Joseph Hawley II, slit his throat and died within a half-hour. Everyone in the town knew Hawley. Forty-two years old when he died, he was a successful merchant who brokered trade in cattle for the market in Boston. He also kept a store, which included such staples as rum, gunpowder, pipes (many people smoked and raised their own tobacco), and also luxuries like silk handkerchiefs. Fashion-conscious Sarah Edwards must have frequented the shop for adornments for her clothes or those of her little girls. Hawley was the first in the town to sell knives and forks, and the Edwardses and the Stoddards probably were among the first to adopt such niceties. Hawley was married to one of Solomon Stoddard's younger daughters, Rebekah, and so he was Jonathan's uncle and Colonel John Stoddard's brother-in-law. Townspeople highly respected Hawley; they had elected him town clerk every year since 1716.[31]

Stunned by his uncle's suicide, Edwards searched for an explanation of this "awful providence."[32] Only two days earlier, on Friday, Edwards had completed a lengthy and glowing account of the awakening in response to an inquiry from Benjamin Colman, Boston's leading pastor. On Tuesday following the suicide he broke open the seal to add the doleful postscript. Eager to put the best explanation on this disheartening sequel, he emphasized that Hawley had been mentally unstable. He had fallen into "deep melancholy, a distemper that the family are very prone to." For the past two months (at the height of the awakening) Hawley had become despairing and unable to sleep, beyond reasoning "till he seemed not to have his faculties in his own power." The coroner's inquest "judged him delirious."

Edwards, characteristically, was interpreting the calamity at several levels. While he emphasized Hawley's mental condition and even its genetic component (Hawley's mother, he later explained, had been killed by depression), the real danger of psychological weakness was that it opened the door for a Satanic attack. Once Hawley was "overpowered" by the melancholic distemper, "the devil took the advantage and drove him into despairing thoughts." In a fuller account, Edwards explained that Hawley, though always an honorable and intelligent gentleman of religious practice and strict morals, had during the height of the awakening become deeply concerned over the state of his soul. Normally such concern would be a hopeful sign of grace, but the devil used his depression to prevent him from holding out any hope for himself and kept him awake nights "meditating terror." Much weakened by loss of sleep, Hawley would no longer listen to reason or take advice. As Edwards summarized his analysis in his first letter to Colman: "Satan seems to be in a great rage, at this extraordinary breaking forth of the work of God. I hope it is because he knows that he has but a short time."[33]

The excruciating pain of Satan's counterstroke was that he had struck when the euphoria of the awakening was at its height and had turned what should have been a means to salvation into destruction. During the golden days of the spring the amazing health of the town had included its mental health. "Persons that before had been involved in melancholy," Edwards recounted, "seemed to be as it were waked up out of it." The first contrary sign had come on March 25, when Thomas Stebbins, "a poor weak man . . . being in great spiritual trouble," attempted to cut his throat, "but did not do it effectually." The episode did not dampen the awakening fires. Stebbins' case could be attributed to his pathetic character. More important, although Stebbins "continued a considerable time exceeding overwhelmed with melancholy," his case did not seem hopeless. Eventually, Edwards reported, Stebbins' anxiety became the occasion for God's healing grace, repentance, and an apparently lasting recovery.[34]

Just after the Stebbins episode, during April and May as the awakening was becoming nearly universal, Joseph Hawley's terrible anxieties brought him debilitating sleeplessness. Edwards counseled Hawley and eventually concluded that he "was in great measure past a capacity of receiving advice, or being reasoned with to any purpose."[35] Yet, Edwards, surrounded as he was that spring by astonishing success on every side, did not believe he should curtail his message for the sake of a few of the fainthearted who remained in turmoil. The travail of the new birth might be excruciating, but that was

God's way of working. The pain was life-giving and the faithful midwife must not artificially relieve it.

Edwards' view that such was his duty is apparent in two sermons preached in May 1735. In retrospect these take on ominous significance if we imagine that the nearly desperate Hawley was in the congregation. One of these awakening sermons was largely positive in tone. Preaching on Ephesians 5:25–27, Edwards presented an attractive account of Christ's perfect love for the church. Christ wished to make his people "holy and without blemish." Even though they would not attain that perfection in this world, Christians' behavior should reflect their love for Christ's excellencies. So the "Hampton converts" must be above reproach. "Let none have occasion to say that we are a close niggardly people ... [or] that we are a contentious people." "Throughout the land there is a great fame of our religion. We are a city set upon a hill. Let us adorn our profession and the force that ere is of us so that other towns may see the purity and beauty of Christianity amongst us."

Still, Edwards warned, the standard of Christ's holiness had a terrifying side for those who continued to wallow in some beloved sin: "There is no expressing the hatefulness and how hateful you are rendered by it in the sight of God. The odiousness of this filth is beyond all account because 'tis infinitely odious. You have seen the filthiness of toads and serpents and filthy vermin and creatures that you have loathed and of putrefied flesh ... but there was but a finite deformity or odiousness in this. .... 'Tis but a shadow. Your filthiness is not the filthiness of toads and serpents or poisonous vermin, but of devils which is a thousand times worse. 'Tis impossible to express or conceive or measure how greatly God detests such defilement."[36]

This passage was only a brief dark counterpoint in an engaging portrait of Christ's holy love for his church, but another May sermon was calculated to drive the anxious to their last extremity and hence to God. In the cycle of his sermons covering the full range of Reformed doctrines, Edwards regularly preached on the horrors of hell. Since the chief use of the doctrine was to wake people to seeing their true state, he was sure to include it in his awakening preaching. Knowing that some of his parishioners were intensely distressed about their sins, Edwards hoped to make the most of even the deepest anxieties. Preaching at the height of the awakening in May 1735, on I Thessalonians 2:16, Edwards explained, "God sometimes expresses his wrath towards wicked men in this world not only outwardly but also in the inward expressions of it on their consciences." Sometimes terrible sufferings in this world, he added, "are but forerunners of their punishment."

In any case, God's restraint in permitting sin without *full* punishment would last only so long and then in the next life God's wrath would be unleashed "to the uttermost." "When few drops or little sprinkling of wrath is so distressing and overbearing to the soul," he admonished, "how must it be when God opens the flood gates and lets the mighty deluge of his wrath come pouring down men's heads and brings in all his waves and billows upon the soul."

Unrepentant sinners had all the greater reason to fear the wrath to come if they realized what a terrible thing it would be to be lost amid one of the greatest outpourings of the Holy Spirit ever known. Edwards here revealed his own astonishing hopes for the awakening when it was at its apex. "God appears amongst us," he declared, "in the most extraordinary manner perhaps that ever he did in New England." Not only that, but he considered such works of the Holy Spirit in the era of the church as greater than even the greatest temporal acts of God in the Old Testament age. "The Children of Israel saw many mighty works of God when God brought them out of Egypt," he proclaimed, "but we see here at this day works of God more mighty and of a more glorious nature." How would it be for the few who had hardened their hearts and so been left behind when surrounded by events "more mighty and of a more glorious nature" than even God's deliverance of his people from Egypt?[37]

Edwards did not design this sermon to let the anxious sleep any easier. Always reminding himself and everyone else that eternal benefits far outweighed temporary comforts, he would have believed himself remiss had he offered easy assurance. He seemed to assume that unassailable reason would help drive people to the painful but life-giving recognition of their true state.[38] So he preached, as he believed he must, that those who despaired were indeed unworthy.

At the same time, no degree of unworthiness made one a hopeless case. He had apparently told his Uncle Hawley that "there were some things in his experience, that appeared very hopefully." Hawley's despair nonetheless remained, and "he durst entertain no hope concerning his own good estate." So, on one hand, Edwards was telling the spiritual stragglers in Northampton that they had every reason to think the worst. They were like those in Scripture who despised the prophets and killed Christ. At the same time there was wonderful relief. Christ offered to accept them anyway. So he ended his sermon with an evangelistic appeal: "Now is the time for you to bestir yourself as you would escape wrath and would not have it come upon you to the uttermost. Now Christ is calling. . . . He hath sent me to call you. I would now call you in his name. Come to him. Fly to this refuge that you may be safe in him, welcome as anyone whatsoever. Therefore make no objection from your unworthiness nor any other way. But haste and come away."[39]

The shock of Hawley's suicide could hardly have been greater. Up to that moment it had seemed that nearly the whole town would join the exodus to the safe haven of God's grace. Satan had used the melancholic weakness of one man to turn the logic of the awakening against itself. The outpouring that for so many seemed a means to salvation became for Hawley a cause for despair and self-destruction.

How could this "awful providence" be explained? Where was the sovereign and good God when such an aberration took place? Edwards called a fast day to clarify for his stunned and bewildered parishioners what God was teaching them in this event. His explanation reflected a part of the Reformed vindication of God's ways that is sometimes overlooked or forgotten.

The crucial point was to take seriously the reality of Satan. For Edwards, Satan was just as necessary to explaining human history as that Prince of Darkness was to John Milton's *Paradise Lost*. In neither case was the great fallen angel just a metaphor or literary trope. Satan was an historical figure, one of the chief actors and causal agents shaping the human drama. God in his unfathomable redemptive councils had permitted the evil rebellion to go on, and every human life was touched by it.

In his fast-day sermon Edwards reminded his perplexed congregation that they needed to recognize that Satan was a real person, far more powerful than they were and bent on destroying each of them. They must remember that, except for God's restraining grace, they would be just as weak as the greatest sinner. They were like little children lost and helpless in the dangerous wilds, who could easily be led to destruction by a "subtile man." They were apt to think of themselves as better than someone who had committed some horrible crime, yet they did not realize that they were just as vulnerable. Only God's "restraining grace," he explained, kept people from following the most wicked inclinations of their hearts. "'Tis surely owing thus to God, and not at all to ourselves, if we han't committed adultery, or sodomy, or buggery, or murder, or blasphemy, as others have done, or that we han't destroyed our own lives."

Except for God's restraining grace, Satan would reign unhindered in the earth and easily prey on everyone. The "wisest and greatest of men, they are but as a leaf that is driven of the wind. . . . They are . . . as a poor infant would be, if it should be cast out on the open field in its blood in the day it was born." The awful lesson was, as always, that people must not trust in the least in themselves.[40]

Edwards' understanding of God's redemptive purpose in his terrible permission of evil included the promise that the devil's days were numbered. Satan's brutal, genocidal reign over most of the peoples of the earth would soon be brought to an end. If God destroyed the powers of evil now, so also would he have to punish all humans still under Satan's dominion. The spread of the Gospel in the Protestant Reformation and the recent awakenings were precursors of the end of the age, when the Gospel light would reach through all the earth and most humans would be wonderfully freed from Satan's rule. Yet, even then, at the end of that millennial age, the last thousand years of human history, as Edwards understood it, Satan was to be "loosed out of his prison for a time" (Revelation 20:7). So likewise, along with every advance of the Gospel that prefigured Christ's ultimate victory, the church must expect Satan to strike back in force. When he remarked that during the summer of his Uncle Hawley's suicide, "Satan seemed to be more let loose, and raged in a dreadful manner," he was alluding to this painful struggle that was at the center of his understanding of history and of each person's life.

Satan's rage in the summer of 1735 took the terrible form of using the power of suggestion against the revival. Much as awakening had swept the region, so now "multitudes" were confronted with the horrible temptation to cut their own throats. "And many," he recorded, "that seemed to be under no melancholy, some pious persons that had no special darkness, or doubts about the goodness of their state, nor were under any special trouble or concern of mind about anything spiritual or temporal, yet had it urged upon 'em, as if somebody had spoke to 'em, 'Cut your own throat, now is good opportunity: *now, NOW!*'"

Edwards did not report how many of these "multitudes" actually attempted suicide or succeeded. His cousin Stephen Williams, who that year also presided over an awakening in Longmeadow, Massachusetts, noted in his diary for Sunday, July 13, the "most awful providence," the suicide of one of his parishioners.

In Northampton and elsewhere in Hampshire County the suicide craze effectively brought the conversions to an end, although some awakenings continued well into the next year in Connecticut. At the former center of the awakening religion remained the primary topic of conversation for several months, but soon people's attentions were diverted by other affairs.[41] By the end of the summer Edwards felt his own health was deteriorating, and he left for an extended trip to New York and New Jersey. As he rode south from Northampton he must have thought much about the meaning of the recent events. He had proclaimed that the awakening was perhaps the foremost act of God since the Reformation and the greatest ever in the Americas. Now he saw some setbacks that might give him pause. Nonetheless, he assured himself and others, Satan's raging counterattacks were just what was to be expected.

# CHAPTER 10

## The Politics of the Kingdom

Individual lives do not fit a single neat story line. Many things happen at once. In Edwards' case, that complexity of his life is especially apparent around the time of the spectacular Connecticut Valley awakening and its aftermath. Although the revival overshadows everything else, we need to be careful not to let it obscure our vision of other events of those years. Edwards, now in his early thirties, was emerging as a significant figure in the New England ecclesiastical and social establishment. In that process, he was involved in a number of campaigns and controversies, each of which helped shape patterns of alliances and commitments that would define much of his career.

### Publicity and Patronage

Edwards knew that awakenings spread by example; he had seen the revival that began in Northampton radiate from town to town and well into Connecticut, and he was eager that others should feel its power. He also knew that it had not spread to Boston and vicinity. Although the revival was the talk of town, that was a mixed blessing because much of the talk was ridicule. Many in the seaport viewed it as rustic sensationalism. To complicate matters, the leading Boston clergy were embroiled in an ugly dispute with their western counterparts in Hampshire County over the attempted settlement of a young easterner, Robert Breck, as pastor of one of the churches in Springfield, a major river town south of Northampton.

Edwards' opportunity to correct any false impressions about the revival came in May, when Benjamin Colman requested an account. Colman had heard many rumors, extravagant claims, and accusations about the awakenings and wished to set the record straight. In the eighteenth-century world, influence depended largely on patronage, and Edwards recognized that Colman's response would be crucial. Since the death of Cotton Mather, Colman had played the key role of uniting Massachusetts to international Calvinistic evangelicalism. Despite their current ecclesiastical arguments with the westerners, Colman and his circle of friends were firmly allied with William Williams and his clan in this larger cause. They shared the deep hope that New England would be a model of genuine awakening.

Edwards' letter to Colman was restrained, scientific, and detailed. He provided a brief account of the transformation of Northampton and of the spread of awakening to other towns. He emphasized that he was giving an accurate account of events "which Satan has so much misrepresented" and which had led to "many odd and strange stories . . . which it is a wonder some wise men should be so ready to believe." Many people were remarkably enraptured by the Spirit and, admittedly, there were occasional excesses. Yet there was no new doctrine, no new way of worship, no prevailing oddity of behavior, no superstition about their clothes, or other alleged innovations. Some of the experiences "have been beyond almost all that ever I heard or read of" but were still within accepted biblical bounds. One Northampton young woman, for instance, and two persons from other towns were so overcome by the Spirit that they believed they might die. Others were almost felled by "a sense of divine wrath." Yet it was all by the book. The only thing new was the near universality of Northampton's awakening.[1]

Colman was impressed. Even the sobering postscript did not change the essential picture. The Boston pastor shared the letter with his associates. Then, in a decision momentous for Edwards, he transmitted much of Edwards' account to one of his London correspondents, the Reverend Dr. John Guyse. Guyse passed it on to Isaac Watts. The letter took on a life of its own.[2]

Suddenly Edwards had the international audience for which he had so longed. He had some concern that any advertisement of the events might be immodest or perceived as such. In his sermon on the fast day after Hawley's death, the same week he had sent off the letter to Colman, he warned the Northamptonites (and reminded himself) that God might be punishing them for being proud and boastful about their awakening.[3] Yet he was also eager that word of the revival might be broadcast.

Isaac Watts and John Guyse were elated by the news. Guyse, a leading dissenting pastor, incorporated Colman's version of Edwards' account into a sermon for his London congregation. By this time, early 1736, London itself was ripe for revival. Later that year, the young George Whitefield would have dazzling success preaching there. In the meantime, Guyse's congregation was moved by the story of distant Northampton and suggested publication of the sermon. Guyse wrote to Colman to request permission to quote from the account. Colman relayed the message to Edwards' uncle William Williams, senior pastor of the Hampshire region and patriarch of the Stoddard-Williams clan. Colman viewed Edwards as subordinate to his powerful uncle. Williams, long a proponent of revivals who had shared in the regional awakening in nearby Hatfield, passed Colman's message to his nephew. It was now August 1736, a terribly hot month when Edwards was distracted by an "awful distemper" afflicting two of his sisters in Windsor and bringing the death of one of them, Lucy, the next to youngest, on August 21. Ten days later, Sarah gave birth to their fifth daughter, another Lucy. As soon as he could, Edwards went to work on the longer account, which is still our principal source for the awakening.[4]

Edwards sent his account to Colman on eight sheets of the tiniest writing. Colman realized that this would be well over a hundred pages in print (here is a clue why Edwards' unpublished works have been nearly indecipherable), and so he prepared an abridgment, about one-fourth the original length, and waited to see if there was any interest in publishing the whole. Still taking for granted the Williams-Edwards equation and needing to save printing costs, Colman appended the Edwards abridgment to two of William Williams' sermons he was seeing through the Boston press, adding a prefatory note that the sermons had been preached during the awakening.

As soon as the work appeared in December 1736, Colman sent copies to Isaac Watts and John Guyse, offering them the whole of the Edwards manuscript for possible publication. Watts replied enthusiastically. "We are of [the] opinion that so strange and surprising work of God that we have not heard anything like it since the Reformation, nor perhaps since the days of the apostles, should be published."[5]

While he was seeing Edwards' *A Faithful Narrative of the Surprising Work of God* through the London press in 1737, Watts was a bit worried that the Northampton pastor might have exaggerated or have been deceived by his own enthusiasm.[6] The account was so amazing that Watts was besieged by questions regarding its authenticity, and in several letters he asked whether some of Edwards' neighboring clergy could send confirmation that could be added to a second edition.

Edwards' astonishing narrative created an immediate stir. It served as an inspiration for revivals in both Scotland and England. John Wesley, who in May 1738 had his history-changing experience of having his "heart strangely warmed," was much impressed by Edwards' *Faithful Narrative*, which he read in October of that same year and which provided one of the models for the revivals he hoped to promote.[7] A few years later, when his own Methodist movement was soaring, he published his own abridgment of Edwards' work, making it standard reading in Wesleyan circles.

In the meantime, Colman secured the confirming testimonies, but not in time for the second London edition. The attestation finally appeared in a third American edition (Boston, 1738). It stated simply "that the account Mr. Edwards has given in his narrative of our several towns or parishes is true; and that much more of the like nature might have been added with respect to some of them." This attestation was signed first by "William Williams, pastor of Hatfield" and by five other local pastors, including Stephen Williams and other close allies of Edwards.

## Reviving Indian Missions

This same alliance of revival-minded clergy was active on another crucial front—the effort to resuscitate the mission to the native peoples. In the west, the mission effort was primarily the work of the Williams-Stoddard clan. In the east, Benjamin Colman and his fellow evangelistically minded clergy organized support from both New England and the home country.

The 1730s marked a rare time of extended peace in Massachusetts, and the leaders in the western part of the colony used this opportunity to address their most conspicuous failure. Massachusetts had always been intended as, among other things, a mission to the Indians, but for two generations, since the disaster of King Philip's War in the 1670s, periodic hostilities and ongoing bitterness had thwarted effective new efforts. In his later years Solomon Stoddard had warned of God's punishment if New England continued to neglect this urgent duty. Stoddard's successors were eager to answer that call.

The Reverend Samuel Hopkins of Springfield, married to Edwards' oldest sister, Esther, took the lead in initiating a mission. Having heard from Benjamin Colman of funds from England designated for evangelizing the Indians, Hopkins traveled to Northampton in March 1734 to meet with John Stoddard. Colonel Stoddard, who had often served as chief negotiator with the Indians, was the English leader most knowledgeable about them as well as the most powerful magistrate in the region. Like his late father, he was an advocate for Indian missions. Edwards likely joined his brother-in-law and uncle in these initial discussions. Stoddard was enthusiastic in his support, and Hopkins next approached his neighboring clergyman, Stephen Williams of Longmeadow, about the project. Williams also was an expert on Indian affairs and had acquired a knowledge of Indian languages during his boyhood captivity. He readily agreed to cosponsor the project. The promoters of the mission, with the approval from the Commissioners for Indian Affairs in Boston, met with leaders of the friendly Mahican Indians on the Housatonic River in far western Massachusetts. These Housatonic Indians had already shown some interest in Christianity, and they now agreed to have mission-aries settle among them. The English quickly secured two young men to begin their work in fall 1734. John Sergeant, a tutor at Yale, headed the mission and Timothy Woodbridge, a great-grandson of the famed mission-ary John Eliot, went as a schoolmaster. During the spring of 1735 the Housa-tonics were intrigued by the awakenings going on around them and re-sponded to Sergeant's preaching with great emotion.

Benjamin Colman kept in close touch with these developments and re-ported them to the Commissioners, his English correspondents, and Gover-nor Jonathan Belcher. The governor was enthusiastic about the plan. Belcher shared with others in the transatlantic evangelical community a genuine zeal for missions. Further, like any colonial governor, he saw the great political advantages of improved relations with the Indians.

In late August 1735, Belcher, Colman, and the western Massachusetts leadership brought these interests together in a dramatic conclave at Deer-field. The symbolism of the place, where there had not been so large a gathering of Indians since the massacre of 1704, was poignant. The governor, with the respected John Stoddard at his side, presided over a treaty with several Indian tribes, including some of the Catholic Mohawks from the Montreal area and some of those who had participated in Father Râle's War, settled only by the uneasy peace of 1725. At the end of four days of highly successful negotiations, the English and many of the Indians gathered at the Deerfield Meetinghouse to witness the ordination of John Sargeant as minis-ter to the Housatonics. In a covenantal ceremony the Housatonics received him as their pastor.

Sargeant's mission to the Housatonics advanced rapidly. Within a year forty of the Indians, including their leaders, were sufficiently advanced in the faith to receive baptism. The mission, in many respects an extension of the awakening, quickly came to be regarded as a model and drew admiring Indian visitors from as far away as the Susquehanna. English donors were enthusiastic. The Massachusetts government ceded a tract of land for establishing an Indian village on the western frontier, eventually incorporated as Stockbridge. The Indians had requested that Colonel John Stoddard represent their interests. He, in turn, oversaw the settlement in the town of several New Englander families who were to provide cultural models for the Indians. Most notably, Ephraim Williams, younger brother of William Williams, assumed the role of the town's squire. John Sargeant, the missionary, soon fell in love with and married Ephraim's intelligent and alluring daughter Abigail —whom we shall encounter again later.[8]

We do not know how directly Edwards was involved in the Stockbridge effort at this time, only that most of his closest colleagues and many of his family were. Presumably his interest in the matter was great, but his only surviving mention of it is in *A Faithful Narrative,* where he noted that the treaty in August 1735 was one of the much-heralded matters that first diverted Northampton people from their former exclusive attention to the awakening. Edwards left for his travels south just before or just after the momentous events in Deerfield.[9]

## The "Great Noise" over Arminianism

The extraordinary Connecticut Valley awakening of 1734–35 took place in the midst of an intense theological controversy. The close connections between these two events raises a number of puzzling questions. The most evident is: what relation did the controversy have to the revival? Then, as now, the conventional wisdom was that theological disputes were great dampers to fires of spirituality. Yet Edwards made a point of saying that the "great noise" over Arminianism and the resulting reemphasis on strict Calvinist doctrines helped spark the awakening. At the same time he recognized that the Arminian controversy, which reached an unedifying peak in fall 1735, "doubtless above all things that have happened, has tended to put a stop to the glorious work here, and to prejudice this country against it, and hinder the propagation of it."[10]

The history of the controversy provides a picture of the dynamics of the ecclesiastical leadership of the Connecticut Valley at this time when assumptions of theological uniformity were still intact. Particularly, it reveals the strong hand of the Williams-Stoddard clan in attempting to control western Massachusetts. Further, it shows how Edwards' role in the region was defined by his intimate relationship to that hierarchical clan in the era of William Williams' ascendancy. That in turn raises intriguing questions concerning his later falling out with Williams' heirs.

In late 1733 and early 1734 Robert Breck, son of a late respected eastern Massachusetts pastor, offered himself as a candidate for a newly organized parish in the thriving town of Windham, Connecticut.[11] The pastor of the town's first parish was Thomas Clap, a champion for the orthodoxy of the Westminster divines. After long conversations with the young man, Clap determined that Breck's views were Arminian and announced that he would block his ordination. Breck, seeing his case as hopeless, gave up and moved across the Connecticut-Massachusetts border to Springfield, Massachusetts, where he preached as a candidate for a recently vacated pulpit.

When by summer 1734 it became apparent that the Springfield congregation was inclined to call Breck, the Williams clan went into action. Eleazer Williams of Mansfield, Connecticut, near Windham, wrote to his brother Stephen Williams of Longmeadow, near Springfield, that Breck was unsuitable for the ministry. Stephen circulated this letter among other ministers in the Hampshire Association. Their uncle William Williams of Hatfield mobilized the association. As heir to Solomon Stoddard's mantle and power, William Williams viewed the guardianship of the purity of the county clergy as a primary function of the Hampshire Association. On the question of Arminianism he could count on the support of his nephew Edwards.

A few years earlier Edwards had encountered the patriarch Williams' power in controlling the county clergy closer to home. In 1730, a year after the death of the venerated redeemed captive John Williams of Deerfield, Benjamin Pierpont, a younger brother of Sarah, received a call from the Deerfield parish to fill that vacancy. Pierpont had been living with the Edwardses and perhaps reading theology with his brother-in-law. They were, however, quite different types. William Williams caught wind from a number of sources, including Stephen Williams, who felt some proprietary concern for his late father's parish, that Pierpont was not "a person of prudent, grave, and sober conversation" but "vain, apish and jovial, particularly among females." What the sober Edwards thought of these accusations, we do not know. In any case Williams stepped in and prevailed on the town to rescind the call. After much intrigue, the Williamses then proposed a successor from their own clan, only to have him rejected by Deerfield, which resisted the family's control. Finally in 1732 they settled on Jonathan Ashley of another powerful regional family.

Ashley was not a Williams relative. Not yet. In 1736 he married one of William Williams' daughters, Dorothy.[12]

When it came to the threat of Arminianism in 1734, Edwards was enthusiastic in lining up with the Williams-Stoddard powers. Two years earlier he had agreed with the majority of the Hampshire Association to make subscription to the Westminster Confession of Faith, or an equivalent, a requirement for ministerial membership.[13] This was controversial. Setting subscription standards was hotly contested among Middle Colonies Presbyterians and in Scotland, Ireland, and England. Already within the Hampshire Association at least one minister was rumored to express Arminian views and had openly declared, "every person is to judge for himself," according to his conscience and reason in accord with "the mind of Christ," rather than "any human determinations."[14]

The Hampshire majority had questions about Breck's character as well as his doctrine. At Harvard he had been dismissed for stealing books, and when Thomas Clap asked him about this, he prevaricated on the grounds that, in a sense, he had left voluntarily.[15] Breck later confessed to his youthful misdemeanors. The real issue was, as a number of witnesses testified, that Breck had taught that it was ridiculous to say God would damn the heathen who had never heard of Christ. God, Breck had allegedly said, would hold people responsible only for that which was in their power to do. Breck reportedly had quoted one of the more liberal English authors, Thomas Chubb, in saying a person might be saved out of love of virtue itself, even without any faith or knowledge of Christ.[16] As was customary, Breck's opponents were using "Arminian" in the broad sense of almost any anti-Calvinistic teaching.

Breck insisted he was not an Arminian and said he was willing to affirm the Westminster Confession. He explained that his controversial expressions were speculations, not his settled doctrines. The majority of the Hampshire Association, meeting in fall 1734, was not satisfied with a mere subscription to the Confession in this case. Given the testimony of Clap and others, they demanded that Breck must be thoroughly examined so as to satisfy his most suspicious critics. On this ground they forestalled the Springfield efforts to call Breck.

Just when the people of the region were in an "unusual ruffle" over Arminianism, Edwards preached a two-part public lecture sermon on "Justification by Faith Alone." According to his account, "great fault was found with meddling with the controversy in the pulpit," and it "was ridiculed by many elsewhere." Yet preaching this doctrine, he later emphasized, proved the spark that set off the nearly unprecedented spiritual fires. The very spread of Arminian views, he believed, encouraged people to reexamine and to take more seriously the Calvinist views they had always heard. "Many" people, he wrote, were awakened "with fear that God was about to withdraw from the land, and that we should be given up to heterodoxy and corrupt principles."[17] He himself may have fanned that fear.

In his first letter to Colman in early summer 1735, Edwards underscored the awakening role of preaching against Arminianism. Although Colman and the dominant party of the eastern Massachusetts clergy were in principle as anti-Arminian as the westerners, a serious breach was opening between the two regions over the Hampshire Association's methods in opposing Breck. The rejected candidate had returned east and obtained certifications of his orthodoxy and character from the powerful friends of his late father. Colman thought Breck should have first told them of the nature of the charges in Hampshire, but he nonetheless was willing to vouch for the young man's fine, if not perfect, reputation. "I beseech you Sir," he wrote to Stephen Williams in August 1735, "to be tender of him."[18]

By now the overriding questions had to do with regional power and polity and could not be resolved by goodwill alone. The eastern Massachusetts clerical establishment was unhappy with the "Presbyterian" manner in which the Hampshire Association was controlling the western side of the province. The debate went back to one of the grievances against Stoddard, that he was establishing a Presbyterian system, or government by associations of clergy, in the west. Stoddard's successors were demonstrating the power of that system to thwart the desires of local congregations. The Springfield parish had expressed its will in choosing a pastor, but the Hampshire Association was attempting to override it. Further, the western clergy were wielding subscription to the Westminster Confession of Faith like the strictest Presbyterians. The Boston clergy who defended Breck were just as orthodox as the Hampshire clergy who opposed him.[19] A striking feature of Massachusetts' ecclesiastical affairs (a feature that eventually proved Edwards' undoing) was that the churches never established uniform polity. The battle of Springfield reached a bizarre climax in October 1735 while Edwards was on his extended trip to New York City and New Jersey. Despite his absence from the worst of the turmoil at Springfield, he became deeply involved when he was asked to draft the principal defenses for the Hampshire Association's actions.

In April 1735 a divided Springfield congregation had issued a call to Breck.

The dissatisfied minority appealed to the Hampshire Association, which discussed the question in August. Breck, however, preempted their deliberations by returning from the east, fortified with eight clerical testimonies concerning his orthodoxy and character, and accepting the call. The Springfield church then constituted an ordination council of four Hampshire clergy (three sympathetic to Breck and William Williams, who declined the honor) and four clergy from Boston. The eastern clergy took the matter so seriously that four of them, led by William Cooper, Colman's associate at Brattle Street, and including Samuel Mather, scion of that dynasty, made the arduous two-day journey to Springfield to convene an ordination council on October 7. The Hampshire Association met them there and insisted on turning the session into a hearing. Thomas Clap came with saddlebags loaded with evidence, and Rector Elisha Williams came all the way from New Haven to add firepower and perhaps to manage the anti-Breck, anti-Arminian, Stoddard-Williams family, and regional cause.

The clergy met for a day and a half, hearing evidence behind closed doors. In the middle of the second day, just after Clap's testimony, the sheriff entered and arrested Breck. This seemed to surprise everyone. The justices of the peace for Hampshire County were John Stoddard, Timothy Dwight, and Seth Pomeroy, all leading members of Edwards' Northampton congregation. Apparently someone, possibly Elisha Williams, had hatched a plan to arrest the visiting clergy on grounds of intrusion outside of their domain. At the last moment Pomeroy apparently thought better of such an audacious move and persuaded the justices to have Breck arrested instead.[20] They charged Breck with violating a Massachusetts statute against atheism and blasphemy.

The next morning, as the justices met for a hearing, the locus of the issue shifted to the court of public opinion. Breck's supporters called the Springfield populace together in front of the Town House to hear a man on horseback read Breck's confession of faith and in the process decry the highhanded tactics of his detractors. The Hampshire Association clerics viewed this as crass demagoguery. Even the horse, as one wag quipped, "stood astonished" at the "vile errors" being propounded. "If he had had the tongue of Balaam's Ass, he would have reproved the madness of the prophet."[21]

The civil case against Breck was dubious on the face of it and was soon dropped. In the meantime, the Springfield church protested to the Massachusetts General Court concerning the interference in their affairs. The House of Representatives rebuked the Hampshire magistrates for intruding in matters beyond their authority.[22] In December 1735, amid much excitement in the Boston press, the House also held hearings on the legality of the eastern participation in the ordination council. Predictably they ruled that the council was legal. Breck was ordained early the next year. Hampshire efforts to bring in magisterial power had backfired. Boston clergy still controlled Massachusetts church affairs, even though they did it in the name of congregational autonomy.

By this time the case was a colony-wide sensation. Boston newspapers were filled with charges and countercharges, often spiced with witty rhetoric and derision of opponents' views. The issue became a standing matter for debate. Edwards, though remaining anonymous, played a leading role. He drafted a "Defence" of the Hampshire Association that was published in Boston in 1736 along with a "Narrative" of the controversy written by his elder brother-in-law, Samuel Hopkins of Springfield.[23] Edwards' brief "Defence" responded to the widespread accusation that the Hampshire Association had acted "tyrannically" and countered that the Boston clergy had meddled beyond their domain. The Boston pastors published a scathing reply authored anonymously by William Cooper.[24] Edwards, again unnamed, fired the last shot in 1737 in a longer polemic answering the Bostonians.

*A Letter to the Author of the Pamphlet Called an Answer to the Hampshire Narrative* (1737) is hardly a timeless classic, but it does reveal something about Edwards and his time. In eighty-four pages of tightly reasoned polemic, it answered page by page Cooper's accusations. William Cooper was a supporter of Edwards and the awakenings, and Edwards was responding to him and his Boston colleagues at the same time that Benjamin Colman, copastor with Cooper at Brattle Street Church, was managing the various publications of Edwards' *Faithful Narrative.* Never minding that primary alliance, Edwards had some sharp words for his eastern counterparts.

That the two sides could launch scathing polemics on an issue of polity and procedure while still remaining allies in the cause of vital religion is indicative of a dimension of the eighteenth century that separates it from our time. It was an age of debate. Higher education was largely learning the art of debate. One could fiercely rail against an opponent's arguments yet see in that nothing personal. In this case, since all the authors remained anonymous (though in such a small world it was not hard to guess who was who), the polemics remained particularly impersonal—as though they were lawyers' briefs.

Edwards' *A Letter* can also be seen as a commentary on the "modern" direction in which eighteenth-century debate was headed. This was the age of acerbic Swiftean wit and satire. As the press increasingly depended on popular audiences, the most admired authors often spiced their polemics with biting humor and amusing ridicule. The strategy of Edwards' counterpolemic was to use the weapons of the easterners against themselves, attempting to shame them for resorting to modern techniques unbecoming of the clergy.

So he began in Pauline manner, "We your brethren in the calling of Jesus Christ, and the ministry of his gospel, of the county of Hampshire," continuing in one long sentence to observe that the westerners have become "the butt of your resentment and obloquy," have been portrayed as "obnoxious," "treated with indignity and contempt," and with "disdain and insult as a set of wicked, contemptible men." The eastern brethren, the sentence continues, have thus "acted much against the honor of Christ, the interest of Christianity, and to the prejudice of the ministerial character." Then, page after page Edwards went on answering specific accusations, but also constantly reverting to the theme that ridicule was inappropriate.

As author of part of the original Hampshire defense, Edwards was particularly stung by the ridicule. From the beginning, the easterners had derided the "country" clergy.[25] William Cooper likewise mocked the westerners' efforts, sometimes saying with irony that an argument was "so pleasant" that he would give it in its own words, adding the derisive comment at the end "What can be finer." Or repeatedly Cooper referred to Yale's rector, Elisha Williams, whom he believed had concocted the idea of having his uncle John Stoddard warrant the arrest of the eastern clergy, derisively as "a person of distinction." "They say," the Harvard graduate scoffed concerning the Yale rector's letter, "it came from a person of distinction, so we think it to be a letter of distinction."

Although the westerners were not above using humor (the horse compared to Balaam's ass), Edwards himself disparaged it. "Ridicule," he chided his sophisticated eastern colleagues, is "cheaper than solid argument, though much less worthy of a gospel minister." Edwards, who pulled no punches as he excoriated his opponents for their alleged misrepresentation, did not mind being stinging himself, but his was stinging sobriety. His attack culminated by paralleling two columns. On one side he quoted Christ's prayer for unity (John 17) "that they may all be one," with which the Boston clergy had closed their polemic. In the other column Edwards reiterated key phrases from their derisive attacks on the western clergy. Then he directly accused the easterners of destroying the unity of the province and called on them "to repair the injuries you have done to us." "Don't let us, reverend sir," he summarized, "try who can conquer at scoff and jeer, but let our arguments fight it out; not that we glory in the strength of our reason, but we glory in the goodness of our cause."[26]

Edwards' primary motive in defending against the inroads of Arminianism in western Massachusetts was his conviction that the cause was just, but he was also acting as the spokesman of the Williams ministerial clan and of the Stoddard Hampshire oligarchy. He and his family viewed western Massachusetts as analogous to a tribe of Israel that must serve God and obey his chosen servants. He stood among the dynasty of ministerial and political leaders who were called to rule this people. He depended on the patronage of William Williams and John Stoddard. All his instincts were hierarchical. As long as he was sure their cause was just, he had no hesitation about wielding oligarchical power. The old familial Stoddard-Williams system for attempting to ensure orthodoxy, promote piety, and enforce social discipline was still in place. His place was as a bright up-and-coming junior member of that family oligarchy.

## Resentments

As in any dynastic system there were resentments and rivalries. Resentments arose especially among the most ambitious in the younger generation. In this case, we do not know the original source of the ill will between Edwards and some of his cousins, but it seems to have surfaced around the time of the awakening and Edwards' rise to international prominence. At the center of the opposition was his younger cousin Israel Williams, son of the patriarch, William Williams. Israel Williams was to William Williams what John Stoddard was to Solomon Stoddard, a younger son who, although a Harvard graduate, aspired to economic, political, and military—rather than ministerial—leadership in the valley. In 1735, when the trouble began, Israel was twenty-six years old and just coming into his own. Though Israel lived only five miles away in Hatfield and frequently rode past Edwards' house, for years to come he would conspicuously avoid the courtesy of a visit.[27]

Initially the hostility seems to have been more personal than principled, though historians have alleged grander issues. Perry Miller followed Sereno Dwight in speculating that the Williams family leaned toward Arminianism.[28] Perhaps that was a factor for Israel Williams, but it surely was not for the family as a whole, given their vigorous campaign against Robert Breck. Nor was the family generally opposed to the awakening.[29] William Williams had long championed revival, and he and other ministerial family members had enjoyed amazing awakenings in their own parishes. In 1736 Elisha Williams sent Isaac Watts a glowing account of the widespread awakening, particularly in his father's parish of Hatfield. There, he said, "it seemed almost the universal cry (among the unconverted) what they should do to be saved." The revival brought "an universal reformation of manners," frequent religious meetings, and many conversions.[30]

Possibly there was some family resentment that the young Edwards had overshadowed the clan's patriarch and taken credit for the Northampton origins of a wider awakening. One critic of the revival reported that William Williams thought Edwards' account had been incautious.[31] Boston's Benjamin Colman had not helped matters when he appended his abridgment of the *Faithful Narrative* to the publication of two of Williams' sermons. Edwards himself wrote to Colman saying he wished that William Williams had been consulted.[32]

Possibly there was simply some personal pique between the cousins. If so, Israel Williams would not have been the first of Edwards' younger cousins with whom there had been such a falling out. The dynamics of his relationship with Elisha Mix at Yale might be a clue toward how Jonathan related to younger relatives who had more worldly interests than his own and whom he thought could use his advice.[33]

Nonetheless, whatever rivalries and petty jealousies may have been brewing, Edwards for the time being remained firmly entrenched as a loyal junior partner in the family hierarchy. He enjoyed the patronage of the leaders and gave them, on the whole, due deference. Were it not for later differences of principle on which he was thought to be betraying the family, these earlier resentments would be forgotten.

In the larger picture, the phenomenal awakenings and the question of whether they could be extended still loomed over everything. On the face of it, it looked as though such spiritual outpourings should provide the best vindication of the old system of personal control by the clerical elite. And on the larger kingdom question he and the Boston oligarchy remained allies, despite the sharp barbs they exchanged in their ecclesiastical disputes over who controlled the west. When the American edition of Edwards' *Faithful Narrative* appeared in 1738, not only was Benjamin Colman the sponsor but William Cooper joined three of his orthodox colleagues in signing the preface.[34]

# CHAPTER 11

# "A City Set on a Hill"

B efore the American edition of *A Faithful Narrative* was available, Edwards found himself in a troubling position. He had gained international prominence, but had he claimed too much? In 1735 he had believed that nearly everyone in Northampton had shown hopeful signs of saving grace. Over a year later, in November 1736, when he was completing *A Faithful Narrative,* he was still proclaiming to the world that "God has evidently made us a new people." Granted, he qualified the claim by acknowledging that there were doubtless some wolves in sheep's clothing and that the town still had many reasons to be humbled and ashamed, "but in the main," he added, "there has been a great and marvellous work of conversion and sanctification among the people here."[1]

In May 1737 Colman wrote him a long letter reporting the enthusiastic reception of *A Faithful Narrative* in England. Edwards responded that, while such news was heartening, "at the same time it is a great damp to that joy to consider how we decline, and what decays that lively spirit in religion suffers amongst us, while others are rejoicing and praising God for us." This gradual decline, he explained, "appears not so much by a return to ways of lewdness and sensuality, among young or old, as by an over-carefulness about, and eagerness after the possessions of this life" and a return of the heated party spirit that had so long plagued the town.[2]

Even a dramatic sign from God failed to reawaken the spirit of two years earlier. In March 1737 an apparent disaster turned out to be, in Edwards' characteristic hyperbole, "one of the most amazing instances of divine preservation, that perhaps was ever known in the land." Edwards so described the event in a letter to Colman, who forwarded it to the *Boston Gazette.* The Northampton meetinghouse was in decrepit condition and the town was building a new one. On the Sabbath of March 13, the old building was crowded for the morning service. The winter of 1736–37 had been extremely severe and the heaving from the frost had shifted the wall so that the joists holding the back gallery were drawn out nearly from their supports. Just as Edwards was beginning his sermon, the packed gallery suddenly split in the middle and crashed, burying the people below, mostly women and children, with heavy shattered timbers and scores of bodies. The sound was like "an amazing clap of thunder." Everyone who saw it and heard the "dolorous shrieking and crying" believed it "was impossible but that great numbers must instantly be crushed to death or dashed in pieces." Yet when they finally dug out the buried, they found that while many were cut and bruised, a few seriously, no one was dead. Not even one bone was broken.[3]

God had sent an awful rebuke to the congregation "by so dangerous and surprising an accident," so that they would "praise his name for so wonderful, and as it were miraculous, a preservation." Although many were truly affected by this amazing event, and remained grateful to God for his mercy, Edwards reported to Colman in May that "it has had in no wise the effect that ten times less things were wont to have two or three years ago."[4]

The return of the town's near blindness to spiritual realities contrasted sharply with the overwhelming clear visions of divine beauty that intensified Edwards' own religious experience. In his "Personal Narrative," probably written about 1740, he described one particularly memorable encounter. "Once, as I rid out into the woods for my health, anno 1737," he recounted, "and having lit from my horse in a retired place, as my manner commonly has been, to walk for divine contemplation and prayer; I had a view, that for me was extraordinary, of the glory of the Son of God. . . . The person of Christ appeared ineffably excellent, with an excellency great enough to swallow up all thought and conception." The ecstasy lasted "about an hour; which kept me, the bigger part of the time, in a flood of tears, and weeping aloud." During this time he felt "an ardency of soul," which he could describe only as "to be emptied and annihilated; to lie in the dust, and to be full of Christ alone; to love him with a holy and pure love." On several other occasions he experienced similar raptures.[5]

The townspeople, far from sharing such ardency and desire for heavenly purity, limped along through a late spring in 1737 followed by an early summer drought.[6] Their contentiousness and the old party spirit increased. In May, about the same time Edwards confessed the town's problems to Colman, he preached a scathing sermon on the party spirit, envy, and backbiting that set neighbor against neighbor in the small town. Many people abroad were now rejoicing in the blessings that had come to Northampton and would be greatly disappointed to hear of the renewal of its old party feuds. "No town in America," he reminded his parishioners in an image he was using frequently, is "so like a city set on a hill."[7]

To add to the embarrassment, the new meetinghouse itself was a source of contention. Like just about everything else in the society, seating in New England meetinghouses was assigned by status. The hierarchically ranked seating plan would have to be redrawn for the new meetinghouse, but that was no easy task in a community with some social mobility. The town's seating committee had to rank each family in relation to every other. The town could not agree on whether to continue the practices of seating men on one side and women on the other (with young people in the balcony) or to seat people on the main floor by families. After much wrangling they decided to do both. The new meetinghouse included thirty-five box-shaped pews around the periphery, some of which were occupied by family units. The rest of the seating continued the traditional separation by gender, women on the opposite side of the aisle from their husbands. Seating by family was more comfortable, and the shift to this practice in eighteenth-century churches sometimes has been seen as a harbinger of the middle-class family of the modern era. It also could accentuate family rivalries when one family was seated more prominently than a near rival. That was particularly so when the town, consistent with Edwards' assessment of it, decided to make wealth the primary criterion in determining seating, to consider age secondarily, and to consider "men's usefullness," as in public service to a lesser degree. Previously, age had been the primary consideration and wealth secondary.[8]

Because New Englanders prided themselves on regulating their worship on the Bible alone, one might think that they would have taken more to heart the biblical condemnation of those who "love the uppermost rooms at feasts, and the chief seats in the synagogues" (Matthew 23:6). That they ignored this instruction reminds us how essentially hierarchical their social assumptions were. Not to honor social distinctions, even in church, was to them as un-thinkable as it would be today for persons in the military not to honor differences in rank.

Although Edwards deplored the wrangles over the meetinghouse and preached against those "who seek after an high seat in God's house above seeking eminent holiness," he took for granted that social hierarchies were God's provision for good order.[9] Like others of his tradition, he assumed that

THIRD MEETING HOUSE—ERECTED 1737.

Northampton's third meetinghouse (1737). The steeple reflected New England's turn toward eighteenth-century English fashion. It also helped set the building apart as a special sacred space, in contrast to the unadorned meetinghouses of a century earlier. (The clock was added later.)

even in a "city set upon a hill," some were ordained by God to rule and others to be in subjection.[10] In his view of the family, he emphasized patriarchal governance. Though his own family was growing as a new daughter was born every two years (Timothy, the seventh child, was their first boy, born July 1738), Edwards gave no indication that he held a modern sentimental view of the family. In fact, when in late 1737 and early 1738 the Hampshire Association considered the meaning of an epidemic—probably the "throat distemper"—that was carrying away many children, it concluded, almost certainly with Edwards' approval, that God was warning them against the sins of parents

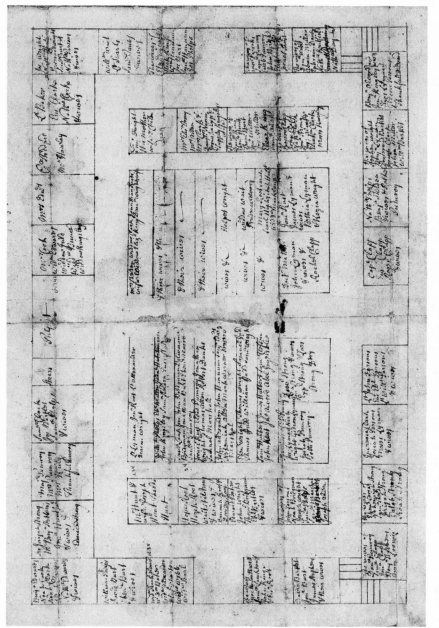

The seating plan for the main floor of the 1737 meetinghouse reflected social rank. Young people were seated in the balcony.

showing immoderate love of children, indulging them, and greedily hoarding up material wealth for them.[11]

An additional source of contention may have been that, almost immediately upon completing the new meetinghouse, the town settled on building a separate town house for town meetings and for the county court. Previously the often rancorous town meetings were held in the same meetinghouse where Edwards preached. The new meetinghouse, unlike its predecessor, was steepled in typical eighteenth-century New England style, suggesting that English tastes had penetrated inland. Perhaps related to this adoption of the European custom of setting the church building apart was the prevailing sentiment to build a separate hall for town meetings and the courts. Whatever the reasons, the decision had symbolic importance. Puritans had built unadorned, unsteepled meetinghouses as a signal that no space was in itself sacred. All of reality was potentially sacred or secular, depending on how it was used. Town meetings were just as appropriate in the meetinghouse as anywhere. Furthermore, civil government, when properly conducted, was a sacred activity. Spiritual and civic leaders were to work hand in hand. In practice, the presence of the empty pulpit during the town meeting may have been a reminder of ministerial and spiritual authority in all matters. The new arrangement can be seen most immediately as a reversion to a more medieval, or at least Anglican, separation of sacred space. In that older arrangement sacred and secular were differentiated but, in theory, should cooperate in harmony. At the same time, the new arrangement can be viewed as a harbinger of a more modern version of the separation of sacred and secular spheres in which, even in theory, they would coexist in uneasy tension.[12]

## Biblical Perspectives

By the late 1730s Edwards was facing the disconcerting reality that just as Northampton was becoming internationally celebrated many of his parishioners were returning to their old ways of greed and constant infighting. He could not escape the evidence that he had overestimated the extent of genuine awakening. Real indications of the Holy Spirit's presence remained, but other evidence suggested that many apparent conversions were the devil's counterfeits. In response, Edwards preached three lengthy sermon series in attempts to correct the course his people were taking.

The first was a nineteen-unit sermon preached in winter 1737–38 on the parable of the wise and foolish virgins of Matthew 25:1–12, the same passage that had been called to mind a decade earlier by his dying sister Jerusha. The wise virgins were prepared for the coming of the bridegroom, while the foolish virgins were not. In this picture of the church, Edwards told his parishioners, the wise and the foolish were mixed together. Not until Christ arrived would it become fully apparent that only half of them were truly prepared. The crucial issue was how to tell the difference between the wise and the foolish. That question, which had plagued him personally in his youth, would preoccupy him for the next decade as a champion of awakening. He warned his parishioners, for instance, that it was "one thing to be much affected in hearing of the dying love of Christ and another thing to . . . see certainly that Christ is supremely excellent." But such a difference between affecting but superficial sentimentality and truly spiritual affections was a subtle one. Or, he advised, "don't content yourself with that that you think you are willing to have Christ for your saviour unless you are willing of free choice and not forced with the threatenings of hell" or the desire of "going to heaven."[13] But how many could be sure about their true motives? Whether or not they were truly prepared would become apparent in how well they would survive trials of their faith. In times of declining faith, such as the Northamptonites were now experiencing, the hypocrites were those who "leave off the laborious parts of religion" and come "secretly to live in ways of known sin."[14]

This sermon series was preparatory to another, *Charity and Its Fruits* which followed almost immediately. Published posthumously, *Charity and Its Fruits* became one of his best-known works. It was an ideal sequel to the sermons on the wise and foolish virgins because many of the applications dealt with how one might tell if an apparent work of the spirit was genuine. To Edwards the biblical principle was clear: "By their fruits ye shall know them." The text, I Corinthians 13:1–8, proclaimed, as Edwards put it, that "all that is distinguishing and saving and true Christianity be summarily comprehended in love." It followed, then, that evidences of love (or their absence) were the best test by which "Christians may try their experience whether it be real Christian experience."[15]

This inescapably biblical test was what was making Edwards so concerned about many of his Northampton "converts" of three years earlier. I Corinthians 13 seemed almost tailored for the town since its fourth and fifth verses ("charity envieth not," etc.) addressed the very vices that so conspicuously plagued the ingrown community. Departing from his usual practice of choosing texts widely to suit various sermon topics, Edwards followed the order of the verses in I Corinthians, spending five sermons working through each phrase of verses four and five. The spirit of love of the truly regenerate, he emphasized to the Northamptonites, was the opposite of (in a sermon for each) envy, pride, selfishness, anger, and censoriousness.

The series, more positive than negative, and always preached in an appropriately gentle tone, concluded with what became one of Edwards' most popular sermons, *Heaven Is a World of Love.* There he depicted through many images the perfectly harmonious society, "no string out of tune," bound together in the perfect love of God. Christ, the bridegroom for whom the church (the wise virgins) had waited, would bring the perfected saints into this eternal, happy society. In this heavenly union they would partake in the fountain of love that overflowed from the perfect love of the triune divine persons, Father, Son, and Holy Spirit, for each other. So consumed would all be by the divine love that no twinge of envy would reduce the love of all whom God loved. Heaven, like everywhere else, would be hierarchical; some would be above others in glory, but such differences would cause no diminishment of happiness because all would wish only fullest happiness for others. In this world, by contrast, humans were never able to love as fully as they should. Everyone was weighed down with "a heavy moulded body, a lump of flesh and blood which is not fitted to be an organ for a soul inflamed with high exercises of divine love. . . . Fain would they fly, but they are held down, as with a dead weight at their feet." In the next life the saints, with spiritual bodies only, would be able fully to express their eternally burning love to God and to each other.[16]

The *Charity* sermons, simple and practical as they were, stood close to the heart of Edwards' theological enterprise. The very essence of reality, he emphasized in his more abstruse theological notebooks, was the intratrinitarian love of the Father, Son, and Holy Spirit. The only possible reason for such a perfect being to create the universe was to extend that love to other, imperfect, beings. So, as he explained briefly to the parishioners of the river town: "There in heaven this fountain of love, this eternal three in one, is set open without any obstacle to hinder access to it. There this glorious God is manifested and shines forth in full glory, in beams of love; there the fountain overflows in streams and rivers of love and delight, enough for all to drink at, and to swim in, yea, so as to overflow the world as it were with a deluge of love."[17]

That God was in essence love was no novelty in Christian or Calvinist theology or in other thought of the era, yet Edwards' emphasis on this theme in a rigorously Reformed context was at the core of his revitalization of that tradition. His theology of love also anticipated, in some ways, later romantic and more liberal theologies of the nineteenth and twentieth centuries. Yet, once again, we must note a vast difference. Because Edwards was so thoroughly Reformed, there was no sentimentality in Edwards' love. To be loving as God loved simply meant that one had to love what God loved and to hate what God hated, which was whatever rebelled against God's love.

Ever since the awakening Edwards was seeing more and more implications of his earlier conviction that what must be central in his theology was not just that God was essentially love, but that God's love toward humans was essentially *redemptive* love. Specifically, he was seeing with increasing clarity that this theme must be the key for unlocking one of the grand mysteries of reality that he had long been thinking about—the mystery of history. Particularly, why would a perfect God be involved in the seeming imperfections of history?

For evangelical Christians that was one of the great questions of the time, an era when Deists were distancing God from history. One might compare Edwards' treatment of this theme and that of Charles Wesley in his famous hymn that begins "And Can It Be," written the same year as the *Charity* sermons. Wesley writes, " 'tis myst'ry all: th'immortal dies! Who can explore his strange design? In vain the first-born seraph tries to sound the depths of love divine."[18] Edwards, though acknowledging the ultimate mystery, still wanted to explore its depths.

That these fundamental theological concerns were much on his mind is indicated in Edwards' choice of his theme when honored to deliver the public lecture in Boston on Thursday, May 24, 1739. Preaching from I Timothy 2:5 on the theme that "Christ is mediator between God and man" he carefully explained the theology of Christ's redemptive mediation, especially as it was an outgrowth of the eternal intratrinitarian love. This eternal origin of Christ's love guaranteed that the union between Christ and the saints effected in salvation would be everlasting. That confirmed the Calvinist doctrine of perseverance of the saints, that once persons were truly united to Christ they could not fall from grace. Further, the very essence of salvation or "the covenant of grace" was nothing less than a true "union of the heart with Jesus Christ."[19]

We have a rare contemporary depiction of Edwards during this Boston visit. Timothy Cutler, Edwards' his former teacher and now Boston's leading

Anglican priest, reported on a call from Edwards. Cutler had recently learned of the death at sea of his youngest son, and Edwards' courtesy may have been related to that news. Cutler took a dim view of the Connecticut Valley awakenings, on which he was preparing a report for the bishop of London. He and Edwards, however, avoided that subject on which they knew they disagreed so totally. Cutler viewed the awakening as mostly "whimsical appearances and fantastic shows." In his account to the bishop he disparaged Edwards' *Narrative* and those who affirmed it. He depicted, for instance, the four leading Boston clergymen who endorsed it as "men of the lowest form in learning and judgement, contracted in their thoughts." Edwards was, of course, a possible exception on this score, but Cutler sketched his learning in a negative light. Cutler allowed that he was "critical, subtil and peculiar" but added, "I think not very solid in disputation." Remembering him as a student, he described him as "always a sober person, but withal pretty recluse, austere and rigid." Too much study, he believed, had taken a striking toll physically. Edwards, he wrote, "continues his application [to study] and in such a degree, that he is very much emaciated, and impaired in his health, and it is doubtful to me whether he will attain the age of forty."[20]

While in his Boston sermon the alarmingly gaunt Edwards spoke of the foundational theological principle of Christ's eternal redemptive love, he was at the time deeply concerned with how that eternal love was expressed in history. In Northampton he was in the midst of his third and by far the largest sermon series, thirty sermons on *A History of the Work of Redemption*, showing how Christ's redemptive love was the key to all history. Edwards' sense that the awakening of 1734–35 had participated in a grand moment of redemptive history had convinced him that his theology should be integrated with the ongoing history of Christ's work. Whereas in the late 1720s Edwards had thought of his projected great theological treatise as "A Rational Account," starting about 1736 he began developing in his notebooks a new historical approach that he believed to be revolutionary. At the end of his life he told the trustees at the College of New Jersey at Princeton that he hoped to write a "great work" called *A History of the Work of Redemption*, which would be "a body of divinity in an entire new method, being thrown into the form of an history."[21] The sermons, which bore the same title as the projected magnum opus and were published posthumously under that name, lacked most of the explicit theological exposition Edwards had in mind for his great work. Rather, these sermons, preached between March and August 1739, were largely historical narratives designed to introduce the Northamptonites to a sense of how they should understand their own history in the perspective of biblical and world history.

Not only was there little explicit theology in the sermons, *A History of the Work of Redemption*—in contrast to the two previous series—also contained relatively little that was directly practical. Almost two-thirds of the sermons were retellings of Old Testament and New Testament events, viewed in the light of the centrality of Christ's redemption. The core assumption was Edwards' typological view of reality. The biblical narratives provided innumerable examples of types of Christ (the destruction of Pharaoh and his hosts in the Red Sea was a type of Christ's defeat of Satan, the water of the sea was a type of the redeeming blood of Christ, also represented today in the waters of baptism, etc.).[22] The subsequent sermons continued the narrative through the basics of church history, showing how that history continued the biblically established patterns and fit specific biblical prophecies.

The constant motif, as in Edwards' view of nearly everything, was the conflict between God and Satan. The stories Edwards told were all variations of this same theme, the major theme of God's redemptive work among his chosen people and the minor theme of Satan's opposition. His text for the series was Isaiah 51:8, "For the moth shall eat them up like a garment, and the worm shall eat them like wool: but my righteousness shall be for ever, and my salvation from generation to generation." In this large perspective one could see "how shortlived the power and prosperity of the church's enemies is." Such transient power and glory is quickly ruined like the garments the moth consumes. The redemptive work of God, which would ultimately triumph, was the only thing of permanent worth.[23]

Edwards constantly urged his parishioners toward grand perspectives to help them overcome the pettiness and self-absorption that went with their low horizons, which hardly reached to the next town. If they could view their recent revival not merely as a local phenomenon, but as an episode in an epic contest between the forces of Christ and Satan, then they might be less likely to be so distracted by more recent local events that were vastly more trivial. Edwards concluded his review of church history by citing "but two" of the recent awakenings. The first, was the "remarkable revival of power and practice of religion in Saxony in Germany" under August Hermann Francke and the Halle pietists. The other was the "remarkable pouring out of the Spirit of God" that his parishioners had just witnessed. Though he did not go into detail, by giving their awakening such a place of honor in his account, Edwards was making sure his parishioners saw the full significance of their recent experience in the history of redemption itself.[24]

Edwards led his people on a journey that would help them see that all history, including their own, was of one piece, centered in Christ's work. If Christ's love was like the fountainhead of a river, then the "beauty" of God's redemptive providence could "be compared to a large and long river, having innumerable branches beginning in different regions and at a great distance one from another, and all comprising one common issue." Because of limited perspectives, people saw only parts of this immense pattern, and they appear "like mere jumble and confusion." It was as though the journey on which Edwards was leading his people was to the top of a high mountain, where, having the divinely revealed perspective of redemption, they could see that these streams, sometimes apparently running in opposite directions, all converge "at one mouth into the same ocean."[25]

Although Edwards' narrative was long and much of it retellings of familiar biblical stories, he was able to sustain a theme and the cumulative impact could be compelling. One Northamptonite, Nehemiah Strong, who was only ten and a half at the time of the sermons, recalled the series as a great event in his life. Strong, who became a professor of mathematics and natural philosophy at Yale, reportedly told Edwards' grandson Timothy Dwight how as the sermon series proceeded he became "more and more engaged." At last when Edwards depicted Christ's second coming, the boy's "mind was wrought up to such a pitch that he expected without one thought to the contrary the awful scene to be unfolded on that day and in that place. Accordingly, he waited with the deepest and the most solemn solicitude to hear the trumpet sound and the archangel call; to see the graves open, the dead arise, and the Judge descend in the glory of his Father, with all his holy angels; and was deeply disappointed when the day terminated and left the world in its usual state of tranquility."[26]

Edwards would have been pleased had all his parishioners reacted as young Nehemiah Strong did. The real application of the lengthy narratives was for the Northamptonites to begin to see themselves as standing directly in the stream of biblical history. *Their* experiences were of a piece with those recorded in the biblical narratives. As he had earlier reminded his hearers, the glimpses of Christ's saving work that they had seen surpassed in some ways the Old Testament types. The Northamptonites, if they could only see themselves in true perspective were participating in salvation history as surely as those who lived in the days of Moses, Samuel, David, or Elijah.[27]

## Looking Toward "the Church's Year of Jubilee"

The sermons of *A History of the Work of Redemption* provide a window into Edwards' perception of world events as of 1739. One striking clue to his framework for understanding his times is the prominence he gave in his history to the formal Christianization of the Roman Empire in the time of Constantine. Four great sets of events, he told his parishioners, made up "Christ's coming in his kingdom." The first was Christ's work on earth, including the defeat of his earthly enemies through the destruction of Jerusalem. The second was the destruction of the heathen Roman Empire in Constantine's time and the establishment of Christendom. The third would be the destruction of the Antichrist, the papacy. The fourth would be Christ's coming again in judgment. This is an amazing set of turning points. Edwards had raised Constantine's triumph to startlingly cosmic proportions. It was a historical turning point comparable to the two comings of Christ![28]

This remarkable elevation of the fourth-century emperor reveals that Edwards assumed that the advance of Christ's kingdom intimately involved politics. Some biblical prophecies, especially those of the book of Daniel, dealt explicitly with the rise and fall of empires, and Edwards' interpretation of Constantine in that framework was not unusual. Nonetheless, he offered a far more positive reading of Constantine than did his most immediate source, a recent commentary on revelation by Moses Lowman.[29] Aside from that, he took for granted, as did most of his religiously minded contemporaries, the spiritual significance of the politics of Christendom. Every stage, or "dispensation," in the coming of Christ's kingdom involved a dark time when Christ or his saints suffered deeply at the hands of Satan, followed by a victory in which Christ the righteous judge avenged the cause of justice. Excepting the final judgment, Christ used human military forces as (sometimes unwitting) agents of his justice.

In taking for granted that God used political agents as central players in his redemptive plans, Edwards was adopting the assumptions of two centuries of Reformation-era interpretations, especially in the Reformed tradition. John Calvin had dedicated his *Institutes of the Christian Religion* to King Francis I of his native France. Christians of almost all sorts assumed that the religious disposition of the ruler was crucial to the religious welfare of the people. In the not-so-distant revolution of 1649, Puritans had committed themselves to the principle that political action may be necessary to protect true religion. New England's survival as a stronghold for Reformed Christianity depended on that principle. New Englanders could not forget the cruel expulsion from France of their Huguenot brethren under Louis XIV in 1685. Catholic France was on New England's borders, and in late 1739 New Englanders would be called to send troops south in a new colonial war with Spain. No one could forget the Catholic political threat to true religion.

Such political assumptions—that religions are tied to nations and empires—are crucial for understanding Edwards' view of history and his place in it. Edwards' outlook on this point is very different from that of Augustine, with whom he is often compared. Augustine projected an ongoing conflict or tension between the City of God, founded on love of God, and the cities of the world, founded on love of temporal things, a conflict that would not be resolved before Christ's return. Edwards had a more progressive view of history marked by increasing revivals and culminating in the millennium.[30] Moreover, as heir to more than a thousand years of "Christendom" and to two centuries of Reformed politics, Edwards took for granted that God was working through national religious wars and revolutions that would facilitate the preaching of the Gospel. Hence progress toward the kingdom would involve the political history of empires. Edwards accordingly emphasized Old Testament models that integrated the spiritual and the political and Old Testament prophecies that depicted history as the history of empires. He did, of course, recognize inevitable tensions between the true church and any nation. As in ancient Israel, a nation might be perilously turning from God even as God was using it for his purposes. Yet he firmly believed that God worked through favored nations.

Although Edwards was thoroughly dedicated to this model, he also emphasized, as he did in all of his thought, the preeminence of the spiritual over the temporal. History was essentially the history of redemption. So the driving force in history was not what princes did, as important as they might be, but rather what "Jesus Christ, the prince and savior of the world" had done and continued to do through his Holy Spirit.[31] Christ did use princes for his redemptive purposes, yet the princes themselves were not the keys to history. At the center of history was Christ's work through the Holy Spirit in saving souls.

The revival of 1734–35 may have solidified Edwards' thinking concerning the characteristic form of the Holy Spirit's work in redemptive history. Ever since his early notebooks on the Apocalypse,[32] Edwards had viewed the spread of the Gospel as the center of redemptive history. Now he was seeing more clearly the role of periodic awakenings as pivotal in that historical process. Biblical history was punctuated by revivals of God's people. So was Christian history, as in the time of Constantine or the Reformation.

Edwards wanted to make sure that his people noticed the role of awakening in the prophetic scenario. Each of the three dispensations beginning with Christ's first coming would involve a "glorious spiritual resurrection of souls," that was "a lively image and type" of the fourth dispensation, when Christ would come in judgment and raise the dead.[33] In the first era, from Christ's ministry until the destruction of Jerusalem, the Gospel was marvelously brought to masses of gentiles. In Constantine's time, the era of widespread persecutions was ended, the blood of the martyrs was avenged (fulfilling the prophecy of the sixth seal in Revelation 6), and the greater part of "the known world" was brought into the church. By identifying Constantine's rule with the opening of the sixth seal, Edwards also advanced the prophetic timetable beyond that of many interpreters, leaving fewer prophecies to be fulfilled before the final triumph. Now, he said, in the approaching last times one could expect another marvelous ingathering preceding the defeat of Antichrist and the establishment of Christ's millennial kingdom on earth. Recent awakenings, such as that at Northampton, were harbingers of that coming day.

Whereas the kingdom of Antichrist, or the rise of the papacy to corrupt Christendom, was Satan's "masterpiece" of the present era, other of the devil's strategies were also to be undone in the last days.[34] On a topic close to home, for instance, Edwards told his people that he had heard that "the occasion of the first peopling America was this: that the devil being alarmed and surprised by the wonderful success of the gospel that was the first three hundred years after Christ, and [by] the downfall of the heathen empire in Constantine's time, and seeing the gospel spread so fast, and fearing that his heathenish kingdom would be wholly overthrown through the world, led away a people from the other continent into America, that they might be quite out of reach of the gospel."[35] The discovery of America, then, was a providential preparation for "the future glorious times of the church" when Satan's work would be undone and "all the inhabitants of this new discovered world shall be brought over into the kingdom of Christ, as well as all the other ends of the earth."[36]

Edwards was sure that the defeat of the Antichrist, the pivotal event in this triumph, would be 1,260 years after the rise of the papacy, but he told his parishioners that we could not be sure what date marked that rise, only that it was after A.D. 479, or else its defeat would have happened already.[37] He also believed that the kingdom of Antichrist would be destroyed before the year 2000, by which time the earth would be 6,000 years old and an era of millennial rest would be due.[38] He had concluded, however, that one could not date these events by exact years. The rise of the papacy had been a gradual process and so would be the Antichrist's demise.[39]

Edwards tallied up for his congregation a balance sheet of the progress of Christ's kingdom as it stood in 1739. On the negative side, first, "The Reformed church is much diminished." The Reformation, he explained, had commenced some 220 years earlier, beginning the era of assault on Antichrist. Catholics had struck back with persecutions and warfare. More serious now, however, than even the Catholic threat was the erosion of the faith within Protestant countries. So the second negative of the age was "the prevailing of licentiousness in principles and opinions." Enthusiasts, such as the Quakers and others, undermined the faith. Meanwhile, Socinians, Arminians, Arians, and Deists were all flourishing. The new unbelief was truly alarming, even unprecedented, because it arose from those reared with the very benefits of Protestant teaching. "And particularly," he proclaimed, "history gives no account of any age wherein there was so great an apostasy of those that had been brought up under the light of the gospel to infidelity, never such a casting off the Christian religion and all revealed religion, never any age wherein was so much scoffing at and ridiculing the gospel of Christ by those that have been brought up under gospel light, nor anything like it as there is at this day."[40]

The last negative, according to Edwards, should be taken as a warning. Even among Reformed people, he cautioned, there was "much less of the prevalency of the power of godliness" than at the beginning of the Reformation. Vital piety was being called enthusiasm, whimsy, and fanaticism. "Those that are truly religious are commonly looked upon as crackbrained."[41]

Balancing the positive against the negative, Edwards listed three hopeful developments since the Reformation. First, "The Pope is much diminished in power and influence." Even many of "the popish princes themselves seem now to regard him very little more than they think will serve their own designs." Second, "there is far less persecution now than there was in the first times of the Reformation." Yet, always especially sensitive to ridicule, Edwards had to add that the new form of persecution is humor "to despise and laugh at all religion and hearken to a spirit of indifference about it." Third, he could point to "a great increase in learning." God had allowed a great era of pagan learning before Christ's coming so that humans might see "the insufficiency of their own wisdom." Now, since the Reformation, was a time of even greater learning. Once again, God's purpose was to show the futility of human learning on its own. "Learned men, and dreadfully divided in their opinions, run into all manner of corrupt opinions and pernicious and foolish errors." Yet the time was coming when people would learn the futility of their own speculations, when they would see "that glorious outpouring of God's Spirit." In that time, Edwards affirmed, "we hope that God will improve this great increase in learning as an handmaid to religion, a means of a glorious advancement of the kingdom of his Son, when human learning shall be subservient to understanding the Scriptures and a clear explaining and glorious defending the doctrines of Christianity."[42]

Edwards' fondest hope, the desire that drove his long days of study and prayer, was that he might have a hand in God's work advancing toward this marvelous vindication of the Gospel. His passion for scholarship and his passion for awakening were of one piece. Eventually the two would triumph together. In the meantime, in an age of conflict, he must do all that he could to promote both. What he longed for most was "the church's year of jubilee." Describing this time to his congregation, he promised, as he was confident Scripture taught, that "there shall be a glorious pouring out of the Spirit with this clear and powerful preaching of the gospel, to make it successful for reviving those holy doctrines of religion that are now chiefly ridiculed in the world, and turning multitudes from heresy, and from popery, and from other false religion, and also for turning many from their vice and profaneness, and for bring vast multitudes savingly home to Christ."[43]

# CHAPTER 12

# God "Will Revive the Flame Again, Even in the Darkest Times"

As Edwards scanned the international horizon, the skies looked dark in many respects, yet he believed he was seeing some glimmers of a coming dawn. He was convinced he had solid biblical reasons to be optimistic, even if there were sure to be trials for the church as the last day approached. Although the once-Reformed nations had become greatly corrupted, the Reformation's assault on the Antichrist marked an irreversible advance of the prophetic clock. Reformed theologians had greatly purified Christian doctrine. Such true Christian teaching would surely prevail, if only hearts were changed.

The real glimmers of the dawn were the scattered lights of awakenings. In 1739 Edwards could point his people to a few distant lights on the horizon that paralleled the flash they had seen close at hand. The glimmer he featured in the *Work of Redemption* sermons was the work of August Hermann Francke (1663–1727), the pietist leader at the University of Halle in Saxony. Francke's work, he told his congregation, had grown out of a simple emphasis on charity that flowered into remarkable orphanages and schools for children of the poor. These had inspired wonderful revivals of religion in Germany and elsewhere. Edwards had also heard hopeful accounts of Gospel preaching in Muscovy and mission successes in Malabar in the East Indies, though he knew little of these.[1]

Edwards viewed himself as part of an international Reformed evangelical movement that saw awakenings as God's greatest works in the current age. Isaac Watts and John Guyse, in their preface to the London edition of *A Faithful Narrative*, had hailed the Northampton events as a sign of "how easy it will be for our blessed Lord to make a full accomplishment of all his predictions concerning his kingdom, and to spread his dominion from sea to sea, through all the nations of the earth." The Connecticut Valley revival, they believed, demonstrated how easy it was for the Lord "to awaken whole countries."[2]

Just as the light from Northampton seemed to be receding and Edwards was finishing his sermon series, wonderful encouragement began to come from across the Atlantic. Moreover, the new light was coming not so much from Watts' dissenters as from, of all places, the Church of England. Up to this time Edwards held a largely dim view of England's established church, particularly its missionaries to the colonies. As recently as 1738 Edwards had written to Benjamin Colman about "the injurious, oppressive designs of the Church of England against us," which helped "to thicken and darken the cloud that hangs over the land."[3]

Now he was hearing something remarkably different. George Whitefield, a young Anglican priest, had been preaching to crowds of many thousands outdoors in England during the spring and summer of 1739, and Whitefield was thoroughly Reformed. Field preaching itself was revolutionary in an Anglican setting. Whitefield was defying the tightly organized and decorous Anglican parish system and appealing to the laity over the heads of their priests. That his doctrines were Reformed was an equally extraordinary reversal of a long trend in Anglicanism away from the teachings of the sixteenth-century Reformers.

And Whitefield was coming to New England! He had already been in the new colony of Georgia in 1738, organizing in Savannah a mission and an orphanage inspired by the Francke model. The vigorous young itinerant, unlike Edwards, seemed not at all inhibited by two-month ocean voyages and had returned to America in fall 1739, landing in Philadelphia. Whitefield was a master at publicity and his fame had preceded him. His Philadelphia reception was a fitting sequel to his triumph in London. Several of the enthusiastic crowds to which he preached numbered about 8,000, or close to two-thirds of the city's population. After preaching a month in the Philadelphia area and New Jersey, he worked his way south to Savannah. He promised a tour to the north and New England the next year.

In Northampton, Edwards eagerly followed the news of the evangelist's triumphs. Whitefield's feats were well reported in the Boston newspapers, which he received periodically, and through the networks of correspondents who made Reformed pietism a vital international movement. Benjamin Colman was corresponding with Whitefield and forwarding intelligence to his Hampshire County allies. Even Benjamin Franklin, despite profound theo-

George Whitefield (1714–70) and admirers. The scene is probably in England.

logical differences with the evangelist, saw the enterprising Whitefield as a kindred spirit and published some of his writings.[4]

Learning of Whitefield's plans to come to New England, Edwards excitedly wrote to him in February 1740. He wanted the itinerant to include Northampton in his plans. If one traveled from New York to Boston, Edwards pointed out, Northampton was only slightly farther than the shortest route and took one through one of the most populous parts of the country. Edwards warned the young evangelist not to expect too much: "Indeed I am fearful whether you will not be disappointed in New England, and will have less success here than in other places: we who have dwelt in a land that has been distinguished with light, and have long enjoyed the gospel, and have been glutted with it, and have despised it, are I fear more hardened than most of those places where you have preached hitherto." Nonetheless Edwards had seen enough success to remain optimistic. "I hope, if God preserves my life, to see something of that salvation of God in New England which he has now begun, in a benighted, wicked, and miserable world and age and in the most guilty of all nations."

Mention of "the most guilty of all nations," referring to Britain of which New England was a part, led Edwards to an assessment of Whitefield's ministry that grew directly out of his recent assessment of the state of the world in the *History of Redemption* sermons. First he rejoiced to Whitefield that God had used such an unlikely vessel as the Church of England. "It has been with refreshment of soul that I have heard of one raised up in the Church of England to revive the mysterious, spiritual, despised, and exploded doctrines of the gospel, and full of a spirit of zeal for the promotion of real vital piety." Edwards saw Whitefield's success as fulfillment of the prophecy. God "will not suffer the smoking flax to be quenched, even when the floods seem to be overwhelming it; but will revive the flame again, even in the darkest times." If apostate England might begin to be revived, who could say that they were not seeing the dramatic early signs of the coming of the kingdom? "I hope," Edwards continued, "this is the dawning of a day of God's mighty power and glorious grace to the world of mankind." He prayed that God would raise up a host of preachers like Whitefield who would be blessed against all opposition "until the kingdom of Satan shall shake, and his proud empire fall throughout the earth and the kingdom of Christ, that glorious kingdom of light, holiness, peace and love, shall be established from one end of the earth unto the other!"[5] Whitefield and by implication Edwards himself stood near the epicenter of current history.

Whitefield had, of course, heard of Edwards and Northampton. Not only had he read the celebrated *Faithful Narrative,* he had also profited from the revival handbook of "the great Stoddard," *A Guide to Christ,* and from his *Safety of Appearing in Christ's Righteousness.* In July Whitefield wrote to Colman of his intention to visit New England that fall and asked the Boston patriarch to pass copies to various clergy, including Edwards, to be read from their pulpits. Using the same image that Edwards used in his letter, he affirmed that "surely our Lord intends to put the whole world in a flame."[6] Whitefield would come to Northampton, but a better tactician than Edwards, he first mounted a major campaign in the sophisticated capital city of Boston, turning to the New England hinterlands on his way back to New York.

Edwards need not have worried that the New Englanders would harden their hearts toward Whitefield, at least not the masses of the laity. Just the opposite. The populace of New England, attuned as they were to religious themes, embraced him, often with abandon. Whitefield was, as Harry Stout has observed, the first American "star." He was only twenty-five, and his tour demonstrated for the first time that in America, where established institutions were weak, popular opinion could counter any authority. Whitefield was also revolutionary in being the first to apply modern commercial technique to religious ends.[7] The advance publicity, aided by the clergy of Benjamin Colman's circle, was tremendous. Everyone had heard of the phenomenal crowds. Boston would be no exception. Staying in the Boston vicinity four weeks, Whitefield repeatedly drew huge audiences, often numbering from five to eight thousand. Soon after his arrival in mid-September, one Boston church was so crowded that the gallery began to give way. The crowd, having heard of such disasters, panicked. Some jumped from the windows onto the main floor, where others were rushing to escape. Five people were killed and more were gravely injured. Whitefield, arriving in the midst of the catastrophe, was undeterred. Even though the weather was wet, "God was pleased to give me presence of mind." He moved the meeting to the common, where a stunned crowd of several thousand heard him "improve" the Lord's awful judgment. After that he preached mainly out-of-doors.[8]

No one was a greater supporter of Whitefield in Boston than Governor Jonathan Belcher. The governor, a member of Thomas Prince's pro-revivalist Third Church (Old South), dined with the evangelist on several occasions, escorted him in his coach, attended many of his services, and tearfully met with him in private for prayers. Whitefield, who could be critical, judged Belcher's affections as clearly sincere. On Whitefield's final Sabbath in Boston, the governor dined with him, prayed privately with him, and then escorted him in his coach to the common for a late afternoon gathering of nearly 20,000, probably the largest audience ever gathered in the colonies. Two days later, at Marlborough, thirty miles from Boston, Whitefield was surprised to find the governor again in the crowd. "Though it rained, and he was much advanced in years" (the governor was fifty-eight), Belcher accompanied him fifteen miles farther to Worcester.[9]

When Whitefield met Edwards in Northampton on Friday (October 17) of that week, the two evangelists must have made a striking pair. Whitefield was "a young, slim, slender, youth," energetic and driven by his mission. The tall Edwards, twelve years his senior, was equally driven, but as so often, he was "at present, weak in body" and a little too thin.[10] Each was personally somewhat reticent, but Whitefield was cheerful and an indefatigable activist entrepreneur who could always seize the moment with little preparation or thought. Edwards was just the opposite. Though quick and resourceful in argument, he was always serious and meticulously careful to make distinctions and not to move beyond the implications of his premises.

In public, Whitefield was a born actor. He preached without notes, had a splendid voice that Benjamin Franklin calculated could readily be heard by 25,000, and was a master of painting vivid pictures that would draw an audience emotionally into the theme of the text. He often portrayed the feelings of biblical characters or lost sinners, but his own personality was never far from center stage. "My Master. My Lord," he would cry out.[11] Seldom did he preach a sermon in which he did not weep and reduce multitudes to tears. Edwards, despite his efforts to emulate his grandfather, had still not learned to preach with notes only, let alone extempore without them. He could depict some powerful images, but he seldom sustained them. The power of his preaching came from his relentless systematic delineation of all the implications of his theme. Although his personal intensity could hold audiences spellbound, his voice was weak. He almost never referred to himself or his own experiences.

Despite their differences, the two men admired each other and had much in common. They were both deeply passionate, and they were passionate about the same concern: true Gospel preaching that God would use to save souls and to bring in his kingdom. Both were ardently spiritual and almost Spartan in their zeal for the higher cause and their aspirations to throw off every worldly concern. Each had been both humbled and gratified by the marvels of God they had seen through their preaching.

In a weekend of constant activity, Whitefield triumphed in Northampton as he did everywhere else. After preaching at Hadley Friday morning, October 17, he crossed the ferry to Northampton and preached at Edwards' church in the afternoon and to a gathering in the Edwardses' home in the evening. Saturday morning he rode the five miles to Hatfield to preach there and to pay respects to the aged patriarch, William Williams. Returning to North-ampton, he preached again in the afternoon and twice on Sunday. When he reminded the Northampton people of their former awakening, "it caused many to weep sorely." During the Sabbath morning service, he reported, "good Mr. Edwards wept during the whole time of exercises. The people were equally affected; and, in the afternoon, the power increased yet more."[12]

Edwards' uncontrollable tears came from seeing what he had prayed for so desperately for the past five years: that the intensity of the revival of 1734–35 would be renewed. In the weeks and months that followed he was not dis-appointed as the flame that Whitefield had reignited spread once again throughout the town, often more intensely than before. By December he could report to Whitefield the "joyful tidings" that it had spread to many of the young people and children, including some of his own, whom he believed "savingly brought home to Christ." A father's joy could not be greater. In a retrospective account, written in 1743, he described the fervor in the town as having gone beyond the first awakening and continuing for many for two years.[13]

Whitefield in the meantime was much impressed by the Edwardses. He had stayed in their home and on the Saturday morning not only joined them in their usual family devotions but, at Jonathan's request, spoke to his little children. Sally (Sarah Jr.) was twelve, Jerusha was ten, Esther was eight, and Mary was six. Four-year-old Lucy probably was included as well (the others were two-year-old Timmy and Susannah, born that summer). The young evangelist's visit with the girls, Edwards rejoiced, bore much fruit. Edwards showed his love for his daughters by putting concern for their salvation above all else.

Whitefield was particularly impressed that the Edwards children "were not dressed in silks and satins, but plain, as become the children of those who, in all things, ought to be examples of Christian simplicity."[14] In Boston, Whitefield had complained that the population was "very wealthy" and much "conformed to the world" and to "the pride of life." Women often wore jewels, face patches, and gay apparel at meetings. "The little infants who were brought to baptism, were wrapped up in such fine things, and so much pains taken to dress them, that one would think they were brought thither to be initiated into, rather than to renounce, the pomps and vanities of this wicked world."[15] Whitefield likely made the same remark to the Edwardses, who would have appreciated such sanctified irony.

Whitefield was also charmed by Sarah. Doubtless keeping her own modest interest in Boston fashions to herself, she could talk of spiritual things as well as show off the cottage industries that she managed. "A sweeter couple I have not yet seen," Whitefield wrote of Sarah and Jonathan. "Mrs. Edwards," he added, "is adorned with a meek and quiet spirit; she talked solidly of the things of God, and seemed to be such a helpmeet for her husband, that she caused me to renew those prayers, which for some months, I have put up to God, that He would be pleased to send me a daughter of Abraham to be my wife."[16]

This was no offhand remark, but the desperate plea of a twenty-five-year-old in the throes of agonizing passions and dilemmas. Whitefield was part of the "methodist" movement, in fact its most prominent spokesman (though in England it was being taken over by his friends the Wesleys, with whom there would soon be a break over Whitefield's Calvinism). Behaviorally, methodism demanded sacrifice of all worldly pleasures in order to serve Christ. Whitefield had at first attempted to follow the example of the Apostle Paul, conducting his itinerancy as a celibate, free from encumbrance. Soon after his rise to fame, even while he seemed circumspect in his dealing with his female admirers and converts, he concluded that the correct Pauline admonishment for him was that "it is better to marry than to burn."

Although methodists' emphasis on the affections paralleled some ideals of romantic love emerging in the eighteenth century, methodists deplored earthly loves if they distracted from single-minded service to Christ. Whitefield's problem, however, was that in England in 1739 he had fallen in love with a well-to-do convert, Elizabeth Delemotte. Explicitly attempting to suppress any romantic or passionate aspects of his longings, in May 1740 he had at last proposed, emphasizing in his letter that nothing could hold the marriage together but the mutual love of Christ, and that Elizabeth should expect hardship and suffering. Elsewhere he had remarked that a wife should not cause him to preach one less sermon. Elizabeth turned him down.

On the weekend he visited the Edwardses, Whitefield had only recently heard this demoralizing news. He had not given up on Elizabeth, but by the time he returned to England the following spring he found he would have to look elsewhere. Almost desperate to settle the matter, he seems to have married the first eligible saint willing to put up with his conditions. That turned out to be Elizabeth James, a rather plain widow ten years his senior, who mostly remained at home while he traveled and to whom he seems to have had a minimal emotional attachment.[17] He had married but the itinerant had hardly begun to duplicate the much-admired settled relationship of

the Edwardses, who apparently had managed to both subordinate and enhance their relationship by constant prayerful reminders that it was a type of
Christ's love for his church.

It was customary for hosts to accompany honored guests to set them on
their way on the first stage of a journey, but Edwards did much more. Although it was cold and snow threatened, he left with Whitefield on the
Sabbath evening and rode with him by horseback two more days, guiding
him to East Windsor, where they visited with Edwards' aged parents. Once
again, Whitefield was impressed as much by Esther Stoddard Edwards as by
Timothy; he remarked, "I fancied that I was sitting in the house of Zacharias
and Elizabeth."[18]

In the meantime Jonathan got to hear Whitefield preach out-of-doors to
audiences of several thousand. Monday of their journey had been blustery, so
that most of the ferries across the Connecticut stopped running, which kept
the crowds down. Tuesday was a better day. Wherever they went messengers
rode ahead heralding the exciting news that Whitefield was about to preach
at a nearby town. As the news spread, virtually everyone who could get away
rushed to hear the great itinerant. As the time approached the country roads
would, as one farmer described it later that week, reverberate "like a low
rumbling thunder" and be engulfed by clouds of dust as throngs pressed
toward the place, as though fleeing for their lives. "Every horse seemed to go
with all his might to carry his rider to hear the news from heaven for the
saving of their souls. It made me tremble to see the sight how the world was in
a struggle."[19]

Whitefield's visit changed Edwards' life, as it changed New England and
the American colonies generally. As Edwards watched Whitefield preach to a
crowd of several thousand at Suffield on Tuesday morning, October 21, he was
witnessing the dawn of a new age—the age of the people. Awakenings were
familiar in the Connecticut Valley, and Edwards played a key role in one that
touched as many people there as did Whitefield. Yet there were some notable
differences. Whitefield's tour was a truly international phenomenon. It was
also the first intercolonial cultural event, the beginning of a common American cultural identity. Moreover, like most everything else that succeeded in
America, it was founded not so much on what was imposed from above as by
the popular response generated from below.[20]

All previous revivals in western New England had been generated and
controlled by local pastors. The awakenings were, in fact, as in Edwards' case,
notable means of gaining control over parishioners. They were first of all

about salvation, but also about authority—ultimately God's authority but also the authority of his spokesmen. Edwards' experience, all he had learned from his father and his grandfather, fit this traditional model of authority from the top down.

Whitefield, by contrast, was a new modern type, the young rebel against authority. An Anglican, he had made his name by defying Anglican parish authority. Opposing the pretensions of the hierarchy and dismissing the weight of social tradition, he had gone to the people for his authority. He was, as Edwards was not, an eighteenth-century revolutionary.

Whitefield raised the crucial issue dramatically at Suffield. Earlier on that Tuesday morning, on their way from Springfield, the crowd traveling with him was joined by a minister who insisted that it was "not absolutely necessary for a Gospel minister, that he should be converted." The minister (it could have been Robert Breck, now a well-settled pastor in Springfield, or one of his allies) apparently appealed to the authority of Solomon Stoddard, a point perhaps designed to put Edwards in an awkward position. Whitefield replied that he much admired Stoddard but felt he had done great damage in "endeavouring to prove that unconverted men may be admitted to the ministry." Whitefield also observed that he fully agreed with a recent sermon, preached that spring in Pennsylvania by Gilbert Tennent, on "the Danger of an Unconverted Ministry." Tennent, a fiery young Presbyterian, had been Whitefield's principal local associate and guide in his recent visit to Pennsylvania and New Jersey. His sermon had been directed against some of the more staid ("Old Side") of his fellow Presbyterian clergy who took a dim view of Whitefield's revival methods. Tennent's implicit accusation that his opponents were unconverted created a furor in the Presbyterian churches. The controversy, which soon led to a Presbyterian schism, and the sermon were being much discussed by the New Englanders. In Boston Whitefield himself had preached on the theme of unconverted ministers.

Fresh from the horseback debate on the topic, Whitefield saw that there were many ministers in the throng that gathered at Suffield, so he decided to preach again on the dangers of the unconverted ministry. "I insisted much in my discourse," he wrote in his daily journal, "upon the doctrine of the new birth, and also the necessity of a minister being converted, before he could preach Christ aright. The Word came with great power, and a strong impression was made upon the people in all parts of the assembly. Many ministers were present. I did not spare them."[21]

Whitefield's revolutionary message has been well characterized as an "inverted jeremiad."[22] Up to this point in New England it had been the clergy who, lamenting decline in the mode of the prophet Jeremiah, railed against their unconverted parishioners. Whitefield was suggesting that the tables might be turned. A spiritual people should challenge the authority of insufficiently spiritual clergy. The office by itself carried no authority. Although these revolutionary implications would become apparent within the year, the controversy that swirled out of Whitefield's sermon had most immediately to do with his having called some of the local clergy "unconverted." Most of the ministers, he said, thanked him for his frankness, but one took great offense, and Whitefield was sure there were more like him in New England.

The discussions continued as Whitefield and his entourage made their way to Windsor ("where," Whitefield recorded, "a converted man is minister") and East Windsor.[23] Sometime during the day Edwards offered some friendly criticism. He told Whitefield and others present that while he agreed heartily with Whitefield's preaching that clergy must be converted, he thought the young man was ill-advised to be jumping to conclusions as to whether particular clergy were converted or not. Edwards knew from his own agonizing years of uncertainty as well as from his difficulties in gauging the genuineness of his parishioners' professions that many cases were too difficult to judge.[24]

Edwards made clear that, despite Whitefield's occasional indiscretions, he was wholeheartedly on the young itinerant's side. He saw Whitefield's visit and the revival not only as an answer to prayer but also as potentially the glimmerings of a new age, perhaps even the millennial dawn. Edwards was convinced, as he wrote for publication the next year, that "we have reason from Scripture prophecy to suppose, that at the commencement of that last and greatest outpouring of the Spirit of God . . . the manner of the work will be very extraordinary, and such as never has yet been seen; so that there shall be occasion then to say, as in Isa. 66:8, 'Who hath heard such a thing.' "[25]

At the same time Edwards was concerned to "try the spirits" (I John 4:1), testing new phenomena against Scripture. He had no objection to new practices or extraordinary spiritual manifestations not directly found in Scripture, just so long as they did not contradict Scripture.[26] So, while he rejoiced in much good that seemed to come from Whitefield's new methods and the overwhelming emotional and sometimes spiritual effects they produced, he was not so taken by the young evangelist as to be without criticism.

Never one to put politeness above principle, Edwards had already taken the young man aside and spoken to him privately about the danger of relying on "impulses." Whitefield and many of his fellow awakeners were following what they took to be direct leadings from God's Spirit. They would, after intense prayer about a decision, become convinced that God was directly telling them what they should do. Edwards believed such "impressions" were often products of the imagination rather than "impulses from above." He strongly favored prayerful spiritual intensity accompanied by wonderful images of God's grace, and so forth. But for Edwards these ecstatic experiences had to be disciplined by the rational mind, informed by Scripture. The point was crucial. If everyone who had intense spiritual experiences could claim special messages from God, there would be no way of checking all sorts of errors and delusions.

Almost as soon as the itinerant left the region, Edwards delivered a series of sermons warning his congregation against being deceived by the enthusiasm that Whitefield so facilely generated. Preaching on the parable of the sower (Matthew 13:3–8), Edwards concentrated several sermons on the seed that fell on the "stony places" and sprang up quickly, only to die in the heat of the sun from lack of deep roots. Reminding the congregation that many of them had lapsed from their fervor of five or six years earlier, Edwards was determined not to have the same thing happen again. Clearly he was uneasy with some of Whitefield's style and cautioned against being distracted by mere "eloquence," "aptness of expression," and "beautiful gestures." Edwards was delighted that Whitefield had been used of God to spark a new awakening among his congregation, but he was determined to cultivate it carefully by his own methods.[27]

When Edwards had frankly chided Whitefield for following spiritual "impulses," the itinerant seemed not at all convinced and rather coolly let the subject drop. Whitefield may have sensed that Edwards had other reservations as well. The two evangelists remained firm allies, but were too different in style to work together closely. Edwards, in a rare personal remark, later noted that "I thought Mr. Whitefield liked me not so well, for my opposing these things: and though he treated me with great kindness, yet he never made so much of an intimate of me, as of some others."[28]

One of the striking paradoxes of American history is that among the three most famous men in the colonies before the Revolutionary era, Whitefield and Franklin became closer personal friends than did Whitefield and Edwards. Edwards was always one of Whitefield's chief defenders, and when the itinerant and his wife visited Northampton in 1745, Edwards was pleased that Whitefield had matured in his opinions and become more prudent in his conduct, so that "he endeared himself much to me."[29] Yet it was with Franklin that Whitefield developed an intimate friendship; he stayed in Franklin's home whenever he visited Philadelphia and corresponded frequently with the Pennsylvania entrepreneur. Though Franklin remained far from evangelical in his religious views, the two men had much in common. Each was a born innovator who knew how to exploit the possibilities of the emerging commercial age. Rebellious against old hierarchical authorities, each was a founder of societies and charities that would mobilize public interests. In 1756 Franklin, always thinking big and looking for something to crown his career, even proposed to Whitefield that the two friends might found a colony in Ohio that would be a better example of Christianity for the Indians than was seen among the traders.[30]

Edwards, for all his openness to the new age and his ardent support for Whitefield's work, was in some respects a person of another era. Much ink has been spilled on whether Edwards was essentially a medieval or a modern. The answer is that he was both. Like Whitefield and Franklin he was looking for a revolution, but he was thoroughly committed to the age of Constantine in a way that they were not. Caught between two eras and determinedly and sometimes brilliantly trying to reconcile the two, he spent the rest of his life in an agonizing struggle to fully affirm the new without giving up anything of the old. He would be trying to pour new wine into old wine skins.

## CHAPTER 13

# The Hands of God and the Hand of Christ

As the snows deepened in the hard winter of 1740–41, the joys within the Edwards household seemed only to increase. In mid-December Edwards wrote to Whitefield with "joyful tidings" of the spiritual blessings since his visit, especially among young people of the town, including his own children. "I hope salvation has come to this house since you was in it, with respect to one, if not more, of my children." Probably he was referring to ten-year-old Jerusha, who like the lost sister for whom she was named, was becoming a spiritual gem. By March, he could write to Colman that "this winter has been a time of the most remarkable and visible blessing of heaven upon my family that ever was" and that he believed that "my four eldest children (the youngest of them between six and seven years of age) have been savingly wrought upon, the eldest some years ago."[1]

Twelve-year-old Sarah, the eldest, tended to be sickly. In the summer she went to visit her uncle and aunt William and Abigail Edwards Metcalf in Lebanon, Connecticut. When Jonathan wrote to her he characteristically reminded her first that because she had "a very weak and infirm body," she may "not . . . be long-lived," and in the meantime she would probably have to live without many comforts other than "the presence of Christ and communion with him." (As it turned out, she lived to be seventy-six.) Then he asked that her aunt give her a little work, even if she could not do much. His only news was that religion was flourishing even more in the town and the region than when she left.[2]

By this time Jonathan was thoroughly preoccupied by an awakening greater than any before and one in which Northampton had only a supporting role. This awakening differed from the Connecticut Valley awakening of six years earlier in three striking ways. First, it seemed to radiate out from Boston to include the entire region. The earlier awakening (and its smaller New England predecessors) had arisen in the hinterlands and never penetrated the cultural capital. Second, Whitefield's itinerancy connected the New England events directly to both an intercolonial awakening and an international movement. Third, Whitefield's spectacular successes suggested that awakenings were more likely to be generated by itinerants or visiting preachers than under the strict guidance of local clergy. This weakening of the role of local pastoral authority would soon have more revolutionary implications.

Whitefield's tour had been more a catalyst than a full revival. At least it did not have much immediate impact on New England's church membership roles.[3] Nonetheless, Whitefield, who was suspicious of the spirituality of the majority of the New England clergy, made sure there was a follow-up. In December 1740 Gilbert Tennent arrived in Boston to continue Whitefield's work. Tennent had been a close supporter of Whitefield during his triumph in the Middle Colonies. The same age as Edwards, Tennent was a Scotch-Irish Presbyterian and the son the Reverend William Tennent Sr., a well-educated Scotsman. In 1735 Tennent Sr. established in Neshaminy, Pennsylvania, northeast of Philadelphia, a "log college" for training Presbyterian pastors, including his sons. The school was the earliest root of what became the College of New Jersey (later Princeton University). New England clergy had close contact with their Presbyterian counterparts in the Middle Colonies. Jonathan Dickinson, the principal leader of the pro-awakening wing of the Presbyterians (and first president of the College of New Jersey at its founding in 1746) had been born in Hatfield, Massachusetts, and was an early Yale graduate. When Edwards visited New Jersey in 1735, Dickinson must have been one of his contacts. As recently as 1738 Dickinson had preached in Stephen Williams' church and brought intelligence to Williams and so to the whole clan of ongoing minor awakenings in New Jersey.[4]

Gilbert Tennent's itinerancy in Boston was both controversial and remarkably successful. Thomas Prince Sr., one of Boston's most ardent proponents of revival, at first found Tennent a little disappointing after Whitefield. The Presbyterian had the extemporaneous style and often terrifying content, but not the dramatic presentation. Nonetheless, he who was known for having condemned the "unconverted ministry" among the Presbyterians was transparently spiritual himself, and Prince thought he challenged waverers to search their hearts.[5] Rector Timothy Cutler was utterly appalled. Employing stylish eighteenth-century wit, Boston's leading Anglican characterized Tennent as "a monster" who told his hearers "that they were *damned! damned!*

*damned!* This charmed them; and, in the most dreadful winter I ever saw, people wallowed in snow, night and day, for the benefit of his beastly brayings." Charles Chauncy, one of the few Congregationalist Boston preachers to oppose the awakening, depicted Tennent as "an awkward imitator of Mr. Whitefield, and too often turned off his hearers with meer stuff, which he uttered with a spirit more bitter and uncharitable than you easily imagine."[6]

Yet not long after Tennent left in early March there was no denying that an awakening was sweeping Boston in a way that might not have been thought possible a year earlier. By the end of April thousands of people were crowding to Tuesday and Friday "lecture" sermons, so that the three largest churches had to be opened to accommodate the throngs. William Cooper of Brattle Street Church said more parishioners sought counseling about the state of their souls in one week than in the previous twenty-four years. Another pastor said he counseled a thousand inquiring souls. Many hundreds, from all classes in society, joined the roles of the full communicants in Boston's churches. Many hundreds of others, though under deep religious conviction, stopped short of full communion, having been warned by Tennent of the damnation that they would face if they partook of the Lord's Supper while still not truly converted.[7]

As revival fires were sweeping from Boston throughout New England during the spring, Edwards was enjoying a relatively modest though gratifying awakening among the young people in Northampton, but he was also ready for outside help. Much of the recent awakening was spread by young New England pastors who, following the example of Whitefield and Tennent, were itinerating across the region, preaching extemporaneously.

In June Edwards wrote to one of the most effective New England preachers, Eleazar Wheelock (Yale 1733). Jonathan's immediate concern was for his father's parish, which because of a protracted dispute concerning pastoral authority was one of the few places experiencing no revival at all.[8] Jonathan's plan, which succeeded, was to have Wheelock visit there and preach however long it took to generate a revival, whereupon he believed the deadlock might be broken.[9]

Jonathan added in his letter to Wheelock that there "has been a reviving of religion amongst us of late," but he wished Wheelock and fellow preacher and classmate, Benjamin Pomeroy (related to a prominent Northampton family) to "come up hither and help us" since "your labors have been much more remarkably blessed than mine."[10] By the time he wrote this, the Northampton young people's revival was taking some remarkable turns of its own.

"In the month of May 1741," Edwards later recorded, "a sermon was preached to a company at a private house. Near the conclusion of the exercise one or two persons that were professors were so greatly affected with a sense of the greatness and glory of divine things, and the infinite importance of the things of eternity, that they were not able to conceal it; the affection of their minds overcoming their strength, and having a very visible effect on their bodies." The group adjourned to another room "for religious conference" where the affected young people told of their experiences. "The affection . . . was quickly propagated through the room: many of the young people and children that were professors appeared to be overcome with a sense of the greatness and glory of divine things, and with admiration, love, joy and praise, and compassion to others that looked upon themselves as in a state of nature; and many others at the same time were overcome with distress about their sinful and miserable state and condition; so that the whole room was full of nothing but outcries, faintings and such like."

The meeting had been for one district of the town, but the word spread. Edwards continued: "Others soon heard of it, in several parts of the town, and came to them; and what they saw and heard there was greatly affecting to them; so that many of them were overpowered in like manner: and it continued thus for some hours; the time being spent in prayer, singing, counseling and conferring."

Several similar meetings followed. Then after one Sabbath service Edwards met with all the children under sixteen at a neighboring house, to speak to them more directly about the sermon. "The children were there very generally and greatly affected with the warnings and counsels that were given them, and many exceedingly overcome; and the room was filled with cries: and when they were dismissed, they, almost all of them, went home crying aloud through the streets, to all parts of the town." Some of these displays at this and subsequent occasions were clearly childish and disappeared in a couple of days. But in other cases, as he reported over two years later, "their affections became durable."

About midsummer Edwards called the young people from sixteen to twenty-six to his house for a meeting that was blessed with extraordinary affections so intense that many were overcome. "Many seemed to be very greatly and most agreeably affected with those views which excited humility, self-condemnation, self-abhorrence, love and joy: many fainted under these affections." Ecstatic experiences soon spread from such meetings to the Sabbath services themselves. Outcries sometimes filled the assembly. Several times many of the congregation stayed after the services to meet with those who were overcome, praying and singing as the wondrous contagion spread. "The months of August and September [1741] were the most remarkable of any this year, for appearances of conviction and conversion of sinners, and great revivings, quickenings, and comforts of professors, and for extraordinary external effects of these things." Smaller gatherings at homes were most intense. "It was a very frequent thing to see an house full of outcries, faintings, convulsions and such like, both with distress, and also with admiration and joy." Northampton did not normally hold late night or all-night meetings as did some other towns where the awakening was most intense, yet "it was pretty often, so that there were some that were so affected, and their bodies so overcome, that they could not go home, but were obliged to stay all night at the house where they were."[11]

These overwhelming ecstatic manifestations that seized the normally staid citizenry of New England provide the context for the most famous episode in Edwards' career. In many towns physical effects of terrors and ecstasies equaled or surpassed those in Northampton. For instance, the Reverend Jonathan Parsons, one of the pastors who turned itinerant during the awakening, reported that on election day, May 14, 1741, when the young people of his parish normally would have been reveling, they instead attended his preaching. "Under this sermon, many had their countenances changed; their thoughts seemed to trouble them, so that the joints of their loins were loosed, and their knees smote one against another. Great numbers cried out aloud in the anguish of their souls. Several stout men fell as though a cannon had been discharged; and a ball had made its way through their hearts. Some young women were thrown into hysteric fits."[12] As local itinerants, such as Parsons, Wheelock, Pomeroy, and at least a dozen others, criss-crossed the colonies during the summer, similar sensational phenomena spread from parish to parish. Revival sermons now were typically punctuated by outcries of anguish or of joy, or by convulsions, rages, seizures, and faintings. Sometimes preachers could not continue until the ecstatic were carried off. For a time during this great awakening, unprecedented in its scope and intensity, it seemed as though all New England were seized with spiritual hysteria. Often it was wonderful, often terrifying. Whatever it was, for proponents of revival, there was no denying that many persons' lives were being changed in ways that—the rapturous seizures aside—seemed to meet sober tests for spiritual transformation. In many towns, even those with rigorous rules for communicant status, full memberships were rising at phenomenal rates.[13] For Edwards, who was looking for a spiritual awakening of monumental proportions but who also knew that Satan would try to counter it with excesses and self-delusions, there was nothing to do but to seize the hour.

Whitefield changed Edwards' conceptions of how that was best to be done. We do not know exactly how much Edwards himself itinerated during the extraordinary summer of 1741. At the end of the summer he referred to his "prodigious fullness of business and great infirmity of body."[14] In the meantime he seems to have been using every bit of strength both to tend the renewed revival fires at home and to inflame some abroad as much as his strength allowed.

We find him at Enfield, near the Massachusetts-Connecticut border, on Wednesday, July 8, in a setting that suggests what was going on throughout the New England. The neighboring town of Suffield (where Edwards had heard Whitefield preach) was undergoing a tremendous revival; an amazing ninety-five persons had been added to the communicant roles the previous Sunday. A team of clergymen had gathered to fan the revival fires, minister to the many inquirers, and help spread the spiritual flame from town to town. Stephen Williams was there from nearby Longmeadow and recorded some of the details. Playing the leading role in the efforts was Joseph Meacham, pastor at Coventry, Connecticut.

Meacham's presence is another reminder of who were Edwards' closest associates. As usual it was a Williams family affair. Meacham, a strictly orthodox Calvinist, now in his mid-fifties, was married to Stephen Williams's older sister, Esther. Esther was another of the "redeemed captives" and as a teenager had spent time among the Indians in Canada. The dream of extending the revival internationally, including the Indians, was still high in the family priorities. In what they thought might be a divine sign of hope on that front, the previous summer their lost sister, Eunice, thirty-six years after her captivity, remarkably had returned with her Indian husband to visit Stephen. Jonathan Edwards had traveled to Longmeadow to visit his much-lamented Catholic cousin and had preached a sermon on the occasion. Stephen had high hopes that his sister might return this summer of 1741. He and the rest of the family prayed most of all that she might be touched by the revival "in a saving manner."[15]

Joseph Meacham was from Enfield and so was especially distressed that the village was not sharing in the wondrous revival joys seen in Suffield. To remedy this disparity the campaigners instituted a series of weekday services where they would travel back and forth between pious Suffield and impious Enfield, hoping to spread the infection of revival. On Tuesday morning Meacham preached in Enfield and later the same day Wheelock preached outside at Suffield, followed by another sermon at the meeting-house from Meacham. This last, Williams recorded, produced "considerable crying among the people . . . yea and a screaching in the streets." The next morning Meacham and Wheelock preached again at Suffield, "and the congregation [was] considerably affected—and many cried out."[16]

The team then traveled to Enfield where "Dear Mr. Edwards" preached. According to Wheelock's later recollection, when the ministers entered the meetinghouse the assembly was "thoughtless and vain" and "hardly conducted themselves with common decency."[17] That quickly changed. When Edwards started to preach, they fell under the gaunt pastor's almost hypnotic spell. Although Edwards had none of the dramatic gestures of a Whitefield or a Tennent and was said to preach as though he were staring at the bell-rope in the back of the meetinghouse, he could be remarkably compelling. An admirer described his delivery as "easy, natural and very solemn. He had not a strong, loud voice; but appeared with such gravity and solemnity, and spake with such distinctness, clearness and precision; his words were so full of ideas, set in such a plain and striking light, that few speakers have been so able to demand the attention of an audience as he." Through sheer intensity he generated emotion. "His words often discovered a great degree of inward fervor, without much noise or external emotion, and fell with great weight on the minds of his hearers. He made but little motion of his head or hands in the desk, but spake so as to discover the motion of his own heart, which tended in the most natural and effectual manner to move and affect others."[18] The combination of controlled but transparent emotion, heartfelt sincerity both in admonition and compassion, inexorable logic, and biblical themes could draw people into sensing the reality of ideas long familiar.

Yet this sermon on Deuteronomy 32:35, "Their foot shall slip in due time," went beyond anything Edwards had ever preached. The impact on the recently lighthearted congregation was as though they suddenly realized they were horribly doomed. "Before the sermon was done," as Stephen Williams recorded, "there was a great moaning and crying out throughout the whole house. What shall I do to be saved. Oh I am going to Hell. Oh what shall I do for Christ."

Edwards, who had been building the intensity of the sermon, had to stop and ask for silence so that he could be heard. The tumult only increased as the "shrieks and cries were piercing and amazing." As Edwards waited, the wails continued, so there was no way that he might be heard. He never finished the sermon. Wheelock offered a closing prayer, and the clergy went down among the people to minister among them individually. "Several souls were hopefully wrought upon that night," Stephen Williams recorded, "and oh the cheerfulness and pleasantness of their countenances." Finally the congregation was enough under control to sing an affecting hymn, hear a prayer, and be dispersed.

In its subject, *Sinners in the Hands of an Angry God* was not unusual either for Edwards or for New England preaching. Preaching on hell was a routine part of covering the full range of Gospel topics, and other sermons were more lurid in depicting hell's agonies.[19] In *Sinners* Edwards took hell and its agonies for granted as realities proven by Scripture and confirmed by reason. To be sure, some eighteenth-century people did doubt traditional views of hell, even in New England. Yet Edwards spoke to his audience as though such a denial were not an intellectual option. That he could do so is itself revealing. It suggests how immense the gulf of assumptions is that separates most modern readers from the world of the original auditors. Few today, including many who affirm traditional Christian doctrines, have the sympathies to take seriously some of these deepest sensibilities of ordinary eighteenth-century colonials.

*Sinners* is an "awakening sermon." Building on the widely held premise of New Englanders that hell was as genuine a reality as China, Edwards hoped to awaken people to what that awful reality must mean to them here and now. Language, as he saw it, was not used just to create ideas of reality, as Locke might describe it, but preeminently to arouse affections that would excite vital knowledge among the hearers. As he argued in *A Divine and Supernatural Light*, even devils had theoretical knowledge of many spiritual realities. His hearers needed to grasp truths with their affections, with their whole hearts, so that they would be moved by God's Spirit to act on what they now saw vividly to be true. The seemingly inescapable biblical teaching of eternal punishment, as horrible as Edwards himself found it, could be a wonderful gift if people could be brought to stare into the fire. Only then could they begin to feel its meaning for them. Ironically, that terrifying vision could be the means God used to bring the joys of salvation.

The subject of the sermon is that at this very moment God is holding sinners in his hands, delaying the awful destruction that their rebellion deserves. Despite this unfathomable mercy, God is a just judge who must condemn sinners because they are in rebellion against God and hence hate what is truly good. Yet—and this is the point that is often missed—being in the hands of God means for the moment you are being kept from burning in hell as you deserve. God in his amazing long-suffering is still giving you a chance; his hand is keeping you from falling. What is most remarkable about this long-suffering is that God is at the same time extremely angry with you. He is "dreadfully provoked," just as he would be if he were presently allowing you to burn in hell. You are like the rebel who has broken a sacred pact in rebellion against a wonderfully just and good prince and so deserves only vengeance. Yet God is restraining his anger. Edwards, who wants to focus on this theme with an audience familiar with theology, does not stop to explain the trinitarian complexities of God's anger and love. For now one sees only the righteous rage of the just God against injustice.

Another essential point sometimes missed in the logic of *Sinners* is that, strictly speaking, it is the weight of sinners' own sins that is dragging them toward the abyss. Although Edwards does not distract with a theological exposition, his premise is that God does not create evil, but only permits it. Ultimately, God permits hate and injustice to be their own reward. Rancor and malevolence fuel the flames of hell. Sinners relish their rebellion, and their love of evil pulls them inexorably toward its just and awful consequences. The weight of their sins is so great that at any moment it would drag them down to the fury of unending hatred if God released his restraining hands.[20]

What is extraordinary in this sermon is not such doctrines but the sustained imagery Edwards employs to pierce the hearts of the hearers. For this awakening sermon he does not pause to qualify and explain. Rather he focuses everything on the central theme of what it means for guilty sinners to be held in the hands of God. Occasionally in earlier sermons he sustained powerful images.[21] Yet *Sinners* is so remarkable because Edwards employed so many images and addressed them so immediately to his hearers that they were left with no escape. Early in the sermon, still expounding the "doctrine," he depicts how "unconverted men walk over the pit of hell on a rotten covering, and there are innumerable places in this covering so weak that they won't bear their weight, and these places are not seen. The arrows of death fly unseen at noonday; the sharpest sight can't discern them."[22] Even if his audience had not yet contemplated the reality of hell, they had to be sobered by these images of the tenuousness of life. This was something Edwards knew from grim experience. As a teenager, as he had put it in his "Personal Narrative," God had "shook me over the pit of hell." Since then he had experienced many illnesses. He walked with the arrows of death flying around him—as did everyone in the congregation.

And what would the deadly uncertainties of daily life mean for someone who was unconverted and truly realized it was a horrible hell underneath? How would sinners respond if they realized that only the hands of the righteous God kept them from falling into the eternal fires? In image after image Edwards leads his audience to feel the weight of their sins dragging them to destruction and to sense the awful power of the God's judgments, which built to almost unbearable pressure of impending doom. "Your wickedness makes you as it were heavy as lead, and to tend downwards with great weight and pressure toward hell." "All your righteousness" can have no more effect "than a spider's web would have to stop a falling rock." "There are the black clouds of God's wrath now hanging over your heads, full of the dreadful storm, and big with thunder," yet there is still a moment to seek shelter before he will allow the "whirlwind" to destroy you "like the chaff of the summer threshing floor." "The wrath of God is like great waters that are dammed for the present; they increase more and more, and rise higher and higher." "The bow of God's wrath is bent, and the arrow made ready on the string, and justice bends the arrow at your heart, and strains the bow, and it is nothing but the mere pleasure of God, and that of an angry God, without any promise or obligation at all, that keeps the arrow one moment from being made drunk with your blood."

Then comes the infamous passage:

> The God that holds you over the pit of hell, much as one holds a spider, or some loathsome insect, over the fire, abhors you, and is dreadfully provoked; his wrath towards you burns like fire; he looks upon you as worthy of nothing else, but to be cast into the fire; he is of purer eyes than to bear to have you in his sight; you are ten thousand times so abominable in his eyes as the most hateful venomous serpent is in ours. You have offended him infinitely more than ever a stubborn rebel did his prince: and yet 'tis nothing but his hand that holds you from falling into the fire every moment: 'tis to be ascribed to nothing else, that you did not go to hell the last night . . . but that God's hand has held you up: there is no other reason to be given why you han't gone to hell since you have sat here in the house of God, provoking his pure eyes by your sinful wicked manner of attending his solemn worship: yea, there is nothing else that is to be given as a reason why you don't this very moment drop down into hell.
>
> Oh sinner! Consider the fearful danger you are in.

By now the Enfield audience was probably in hysterics, and Edwards may not have gotten much beyond this point. He may not have been able to press on to biblical arguments to remind them of what hell would be like for some who sat there that very evening. He probably did not get to sound the note of hope that was ultimately the point of the sermon: "And now you have an extraordinary opportunity, a day wherein Christ has flung the door of mercy wide open, and stands in the door calling and crying with a loud voice to poor sinners; . . . many that were very lately in the same miserable condition that you are in, are in now an happy state, with their hearts filled with love to him that has loved them and washed them from their sins in his own blood, and rejoicing in hope of the glory of God. How awful is it to be left behind at such a day!"

When Isaac Watts received the printed version of the sermon he wrote on his copy: "A most terrible sermon, which should have had a word of Gospel at the end [of] it, though I think 'tis all true."[23] Edwards had offered this one brief Gospel word, but indeed if one had taken this sermon as characteristic of his preaching, it would have been dreadfully out of balance. Edwards could take for granted, however, that a New England audience knew well that Gospel remedy. The problem was to get them to seek it.

Edwards had preached the sermon at least once before, in June to his Northampton congregation, when the new revival was building. Then he had ended on a more pastoral note. He preached without interruption and ended with an exhortation that if they have been brought to fear for their souls, "this is very needful that you may be made sensible of your need of Christ. If you were brought to this, then you would be sensible of the absolute necessity of a mediator." Other outline notes indicate that he preached the sermon a number of times after its renowned success in Enfield. Apparently it was one of his standards as he visited various towns in this new era of itinerancy. He also appended to the sermon, in different ink, an outline of six practical steps in seeking salvation. These may have become part of the sermon or perhaps were intended for when he met with smaller groups afterwards, as he had with young people in Northampton. They urged seekers to persevere "as resolute soldiers" in spiritual disciplines, such as prayer and fasting, but also reminded them that "God will never bestow mercy on you because you deserve it, but only because you need it." The whole point of a sermon like this one was to reduce sinners to a sense of their utter helplessness. Paradoxically, only when they reached that point would their strenuous spiritual efforts be consistent with throwing themselves entirely on God's grace.[24]

We get another glimpse of how the pastoral Edwards balanced the stern Edwards of *Sinners* from a remarkable letter Edwards wrote that summer to eighteen-year-old Deborah Hatheway. Hatheway was from Suffield, Enfield's pious neighbor, and had been converted during the revivals of the spring. Suffield's pastor died in April, and Edwards had visited there to fill the pulpit. Edwards helped spark the awakening and perhaps Deborah's conversion. In answer to her request, he responded in early June with what became a famous letter. Published and distributed by the hundreds of thousands in the mid-nineteenth century, *Advice to Young Converts* became, next to *Sinners*, Edwards' most printed work.[25]

The tone was gentle and pastoral, reflecting Edwards' own ever-continuing efforts to nourish his own faith. Addressing her as "dear child," he began by suggesting that the way of the kingdom is hard work. Even as "we advise persons under convictions to be earnest and violent for the kingdom of heaven" (this reflects a biblical phrase), so those converted "ought not be the less, watchful, laborious, and earnest." Among the nineteen points of advice, he counseled Deborah to remember that after conversion one has "a thousand times" more reason "to lament and humble yourself for sins" but at the same time "don't be at all discouraged or disheartened by it; for though we are exceeding sinful, yet we have an advocate with the Father, Jesus Christ the righteous, the preciousness of whose blood, and the merit of whose righteousness and the greatness of whose love and faithfulness does infinitely overtop the highest mountains of our sins."

One item of advice to the young woman was surely a commentary on his ongoing battle with the most subtle of his own sins. "Remember" he wrote, "that pride is the worst viper that is in the heart, the greatest disturber of the soul's peace and sweet communion with Christ; it was the first sin that ever was, and lies lowest in the foundation of Satan's whole building." Pride, he continued, was the sin "the most difficultly rooted out, and is the most hidden, secret and deceitful of all lusts, and often creeps in, insensibly, into the midst of religion and sometimes under the disguise of humility."

The pastoral Edwards encouraged the young convert to become a minister to others her own age, setting up private religious meetings for young women. He went on to urge her, "when you are speaking to your equals, let your warnings be intermixed with expressions of your sense of your own unworthiness, and of the sovereign grace that makes you differ; and if you can with a good conscience, say how that you in yourself are more unworthy than they." Edwards well knew the dangers and difficulties of being cast in the role of the converted person whose duty it was always to exhort the unconverted. Those who enjoyed God's free gift of grace must constantly remind themselves that their privilege came not because they were inherently any better than the worst of the unregenerate.

Converts should not dwell on old experiences, but seek new ones. "One new discovery of the glory of Christ's face, and the fountain of his sweet grace and love will do more towards scattering clouds of darkness and doubting in one minute, than examining old experiences by the best mark that can be given, a whole year." Again Edwards spoke from his own knowledge.

Ultimately—and here is the counterbalance to the hands of an angry God—one had to become as a child taking the wounded hand of the gentle Christ: "In all your course, walk with God and follow Christ as a little, poor, helpless child, taking hold of Christ's hand, keeping your eye on the mark of the wounds on his hands and side, whence came the blood that cleanses you from sin and hiding your nakedness under the skirt of the white shining robe of his righteousness."

# CHAPTER 14

## "He That Is Not with Us Is Against Us"

August 31, 1741, marked a turning point in Edwards' life. Until that time, his star was steadily on the rise: he had gained an international reputation as a preacher of awakening, and he had been gradually taking his place in the galaxy of New England's establishment. In the west he was a bright junior member of the Stoddard-Williams aristocracy. Elsewhere he was connected not only to Yale and the Connecticut elite, but also to Benjamin Colman and the circle of Boston's most influential leaders. Through his uncle John Stoddard he had firm connections with Massachusetts' political leaders, including Governor Belcher. The governor, who so admired Whitefield, was a member of Old South Church, pastored by Thomas Prince, an ardent proponent of revival, and a friend and ally of Edwards'. For all these men the spectacular awakening offered hope for their vision of a Reformed evangelical civilization. As the great revival continued to advance in amazing ways, so did Edwards' prominence. Yet for the rest of his career the beacon that he had hoped would point toward a unified advance of true Protestantism was clouded by storms. Edwards was now a leader in his own right, but he was also a lightning rod for controversies, jealousies, and bitter resentments.

On Monday, August 31, Edwards took time out amid "prodigious fullness of business and great infirmity of body" to respond to a former parishioner, Deacon Moses Lyman, concerning "the great stir" over the alleged excesses of the awakening that was by now ripping apart the New England establishment. At the end he appended a portentous postscript: "The Reverend Williams of Hatfield died this morning." William Williams, in his seventy-seventh year, had been failing for some time. Recently he had sent word to a gathering of the Hampshire Association, where he had been the commanding figure since Solomon Stoddard's death, that he did not expect to see them at another meeting. Still, Williams' demise had been more sudden than expected, and his allies among the county clergy were devastated. Amid the acrimony that still plagued their numbers in the wake of the Breck controversy (earlier in the summer the Williams clan had boycotted an ordination that Breck was to attend) and the increasing agitation over the awakening, William Williams was a revered and often beloved pillar of strength who kept the tenuous evangelical establishment from collapsing.[1]

The reason Edwards was writing to Moses Lyman suggests why the loss of the authority of the older generation, which Williams' passing symbolized, had ominous implications. Deacon Lyman, who had moved from Northampton in 1739, was troubled about the extravagant outcries and bodily effects so common in the new awakening and about the widespread itinerancy of pastors whose work was precipitating many of these reactions. Here was a veteran of the astonishing Northampton revival of 1734–35 who viewed the manifestations of the current awakening as extreme by comparison. New England had long been divided by controversies, yet as in the earlier disputes between Solomon Stoddard and the Mathers or the recent Breck case, these were almost always intraestablishment affairs among men who ultimately stood together. The recent rumblings over the awakenings and Whitefield's visit at first seemed another such instance. In spring 1741 the evident spiritual benefits for the church establishment promised to be sufficient to outweigh the grumbling of those whose sense of decorum was offended. But by the end of the summer, the controversy was moving into a new phase. Even former friends of awakening were wondering if evangelical enthusiasm had gotten out of control.

To add to the sense of crisis, Massachusetts was in the midst of an unprecedented popular political uprising. The issues had some striking parallels to the awakening, although few at the time seem to have directly connected the two. In September 1740, the same month that Whitefield arrived, a private Land Bank without government authorization began issuing notes. These notes of credit, secured in land, were intended to serve as paper money. The value of the bills would also float on the market, so they might have an inflationary impact. Their proponents promised that these bills would give ordinary people access to the ever-increasing number of goods available in the trade with England.

Governor Belcher tried to suppress the Land Bank scheme, but it had such strong popular support that the legislature would not cooperate. Belcher moved ahead anyway, heavy-handedly exercising executive powers to suppress the bills. He removed officeholders and even militia men who were known to subscribe to the bank. The popular outcry was so great that Belcher's rivals in England used the disorder against him. At home Belcher feared insurrection. In May 1741 he wrote to his younger friend Thomas Hutchinson (who would become an authority on insurrection as the colonial governor during the American Revolution), "The common people here [have] grown so brassy and hardy, as to be now combining in a body to raise a rebellion."[2]

Belcher himself was brought down without the armed uprising he had feared. Although Whitehall agreed that the Land Bank must be suppressed, Belcher's alienation of the people weakened his standing in England. By the end of June he learned that he had been replaced by a rival, William Shirley. On August 14 the defeated Belcher turned over the governorship. Shirley was, ominously, an Anglican. The moment for a happy alliance between an evangelical governor and the dissenting clergy had passed.

The Land Bank and the awakening were both tumultuous popular movements presaging a new era. Each promised a new definition of the individual. The Land Bank offered common people increased freedom of choice as participants in the international culture of commercial capitalism. The awakening, though preached as God's grace, emphasized individual commitment and connected the people to a new international evangelical culture. The two movements did not seem connected, but they tended to flourish most among the same populations, especially among nonelites in the countryside.

Opponents of each deplored the instability of the new democratic cultures they signaled. The power of popular uprisings was difficult to restrain. Moreover, that which was not controlled by centralized agencies and traditional local elites was subject to counterfeit. Paper money was liable to both counterfeiting and inflation that would cheapen monetary values. So, too, itinerant evangelism was subject to counterfeiting and inflated experiences that cheapened spiritual truths.[3]

One reason contemporaries did not often link the two movements was that they seemed opposite in their immediate messages. The Land Bank appealed to materialistic aspirations while the awakening deplored displays of worldly goods. Governor Belcher, for instance, had hoped that the "heavenly Whitefield" and his allies would help suppress the greed and "wanton use of liberty" he associated with the Land Bank.[4] Conversion demanded asceticism and strict discipline in using material things. Freedom would include freedom from material dependency. Nevertheless the relation between the Land Bank and the awakening was ambiguous. The awakening did appeal to some of the same people and even to some of the same clergy as had the Land Bank, but the overlap of the two movements was not sufficient to suggest clear patterns of cause and effect.[5]

During late 1740 and the first half of 1741, when both the Land Bank agitation and the Great Awakening were at their heights, Edwards and his immediate circle of elite pro-awakening clergy were no friends of the instability that was widely attributed to the Land Bank. For that matter, neither did they see themselves as challenging the old religious order. Edwards and his closest associates were committed to maintaining the religious order in local parishes, first of all their own. Yet by the end of the summer, the question of whether that order could survive amid such enthusiasm was increasingly pressing. The loss of the calming and respected voice of William Williams could not have come at a worse time. In May Stephen Williams had written in his diary, "I am affected to think that such a poor—weak—ignorant creature as I am—should be left the eldest minister of the county at such a time of this."[6]

Most immediately, the loss of Williams would threaten Edwards' tenuous relationship to his powerful Williams cousins, led by William's magistrate son Israel, who was already snubbing Edwards. William Williams apparently had held his brilliant nephew in high esteem. They had always been allies both in doctrinal concerns and in the awakenings.[7] That Edwards (rather than Stephen Williams, for instance) was chosen to preach the funeral sermon for William Williams likely reflected the express wishes of the uncle and signaled his choice for leadership.

If some of the more secular cousins thought Edwards was a harsh extremist, his funeral sermon was designed to undercut that image. Williams, he said, was "eminently an evangelical preacher," and the sermon had a gentle evangelical tone, perhaps reflecting Williams' own.[8] Rather than speaking, as he often did on such occasions, about the lessons of eternity that death should teach, Edward spoke as a tender pastor to an audience he knew to be deeply bereaved. Using the text Matthew 14:12 ("And his disciple came, and took up the body [of John the Baptist] and buried it, and went and told Jesus"), Edwards urged the congregation, the family, and the fellow ministers with the simple refrain, "go and tell Jesus." As he put it to the family, "go and tell Jesus; tell a compassionate Saviour what has befallen you."[9] Whatever some of the cousins thought of Edwards, they were pleased with the sermon as a tribute to their father and acceded to having it published "at the united request of those reverend and honoured gentlemen, the sons of the deceased."

While any potential for conflict within the Williams clan was for the moment under control, the awakening was not, and Edwards was about to step into a cockpit of controversy. The week after the funeral he was slated to deliver the Yale commencement address. As he was well aware, New Haven was becoming a center for some of the hottest agitation over the revival, and some of the students were nearing a state of rebellion. Probably he was working on his Yale address about the same time that he wrote to Deacon Lyman. The letter is a précis of Edwards' view. He conceded that there were "some imprudences and irregularities, as there always was, and always will be in this imperfect state." Yet the awakening as a whole had "clear and incontestable evidences of a true divine work." Edwards allowed no room for doubt. "If this ben't the work of God, I have all my religion to learn over again, and know not what use to make of the Bible." He would publicly proclaim the same at Yale on September 10, 1741.

The agitations at Yale had begun with Whitefield's visit the previous fall. The grand itinerant found the college spiritually torpid. He preached urgently on "the dreadful ill consequences of an unconverted ministry," and his visit precipitated a revival.[10] Whitefield was followed in March by Gilbert Tennent. The Presbyterian evangelist was more rough-hewn and even more ready with his condemnations of unconverted ministry. Preaching in the New Haven area seventeen times within one week, Tennent brought what Whitefield had started to a fever pitch. As in Boston the same spring, Tennent's visit led to more apparent conversions than Whitefield's in the fall. Samuel Hopkins (nephew to Edwards' brother-in-law of the same name), who was a student at the time, later recalled that the people of New Haven were almost universally aroused and estimated that "thousands . . . were awakened."[11]

Yale's new rector, the conservative Thomas Clap, at first welcomed the awakening and allowed the itinerant to preach three times in the college hall. The growing disorder soon changed his mind.[12] Traditionally student conversions had been means to bring students into line with the ideals of the standing order. Now they were subverting that order. The awakened students, following the lead of the itinerants, were attacking their elders. They condemned many of the clergy and declared Yale and its faculty spiritually dead. When Whitefield's published journal appeared in the spring, it made clear that this subversion went all the way back to him. "Many," he had written of the New England clergy "nay most that preach, I fear do not experimentally know Christ." As for the colleges, Harvard and Yale, "their light is become darkness, darkness that can be felt, and is complained of by the most godly ministers."[13] Friends of the colleges were deeply offended and Whitefield's eventual effort at conciliation could only partly paper over the damage.[14]

Meanwhile, a sensational young itinerant, James Davenport, carried the subversive side of the awakening to an extreme. In July, the same month that New England pastors, such as Wheelock, Pomeroy, and Edwards, were evangelizing across the countryside, Davenport arrived in Connecticut as a missionary determined to reclaim his apostate native land. Far from being a lowly upstart, he had the most elite credentials. Grandson of the founder and first pastor of the New Haven colony and son of a respected Connecticut pastor and late Yale trustee, James had been one of Yale's youngest graduates, at age sixteen in 1732. There he had been friends with Pomeroy and Wheelock. He was also connected to the Williams family, as his older sister was married to Stephen Williams.

Shortly after taking a parish in Long Island, the young man was caught up in the Whitefield fervor. During 1740 he had met and traveled with Whitefield in New York and New Jersey. He had also met Gilbert Tennent, and he shared the Presbyterian evangelist's opinion of the unconverted clergy and dim view of New England. In 1741, believing himself directly called by God to neglect his parish for bigger things, he set out as an itinerant to New England.

Working his way along the Connecticut coast, eighty miles from Stonington to New Haven, Davenport openly condemned almost all the ministers in the region, including some renowned for saintliness, as unconverted. Their preaching was "to their souls," he reportedly told the crowds, "as rat bait is to their bodies." He arrived in New Haven for commencement week, and his sensational methods transformed the usual student revels into revels of another sort. Davenport carried every tendency of the awakening to an extreme, and his critics believed him mad. As he marched to his services he sang all the way, "head thrown back, and his eyes staring up to heaven." His meetings during commencement week in New Haven generally lasted until ten or eleven at night and, by establishment standards, lacked all decorum. At one of these late night commencement-week gatherings, as one critic described it, all order had disappeared, "some praying, some exhorting and terrifying, some singing, some screaming, some crying, some laughing and some scolding, made the most amazing confusion that ever was heard."[15]

The most serious of his offenses, so far as the Yale trustees were concerned, was that he encouraged gross insubordination. Davenport made a point of declaring that the Reverend Joseph Noyes, the pastor of New Haven's First Church, was a "wolf in sheep's clothing." Yale boys were required to attend First Church, on the green a stone's throw from the college. Davenport urged Noyes' congregation to forsake their pharisaical pastor and attend pure separate meetings.[16] The alarmed trustees, fearing a rebellion, demanded to meet with Davenport. The missionary put off several messengers with "dilatory answers," kept them waiting for two hours, and then declared he "reckoned it his duty to stay where he was."[17]

Powerless to control an outside source of trouble, Rector Clap cracked down on the students. He issued a ban on attending services of itinerants. He was especially alarmed at the insubordination encouraged by the spirit of the radical preachers. Students imitated the evangelists, setting themselves up as infallible judges of the spiritual condition of each other, the clergy, and even of college officials. One of the most conspicuous offenders was also one of the brightest students—David Brainerd, well known for both his intense spirituality and his judgmentalism. In their meeting during commencement week the trustees, at Clap's insistence, "voted that if any student of this college shall directly or indirectly say, that the rector, either of the trustees or tutors are hypocrites, carnal or unconverted men, he shall for the first offence make public confession in the hall, and for the second offence be expelled."[18]

Edwards arrived in New Haven in the midst of this commotion. His commencement address was the day after the tumultuous board meeting, and he may have witnessed the disorder of Davenport's services. Another visitor to the commencement, who attended two meetings of itinerants, wrote in his diary: "Much confusion this day at New Haven, and at night; the most strange management and a pretence of religion that ever I saw."[19] Perhaps Rector Clap and his allies had hoped that Edwards, as a renowned friend of both true awakening and orthodox order, would warn the students that they must temper their enthusiasm with respect for constituted authority. If so, they were disappointed to hear him provide a ringing endorsement of the awakening—an endorsement all the stronger because he conceded the very facts on which they based their complaints, that there were many strange and unusual phenomena and even excesses.

Edwards did offer some cautions to the friends of the revival. He warned them against spiritual pride and admonished them, as he had Whitefield himself, about the dangers of being led by "impulses and strong impressions" that were supposedly from God. He argued that even though the awakening might signal "the approaching glorious times of the church," he did not believe that would be a time of extraordinary gifts of the spirit, such as direct inspirations or miraculous gifts. I Corinthians 12 and 13, he believed, made clear that the ordinary gifts of the spirit—faith, hope, and charity—were "a more excellent way" (I Corinthians 12:31) than the extraordinary gifts discussed in the same chapters. Further, he warned the students against populist evangelists who were teaching them to despise human learning.

Perhaps most important for those who were alarmed at the awakening's excesses was that Edwards warned strongly against the censorious spirit that was becoming epidemic in the awakening. Following the lead of the itinerants, converts like David Brainerd were judging professing Christians to be hypocrites who know nothing of true religion. Edwards argued with some passion that such judgments were unscriptural and unwarranted. Scripture left the separation of the wheat from the chaff until the last judgment. All the *visible* church could do in the meantime was to judge who were *visibly* saints "to be received as such in the eye of a public charity." Edwards had much experience in this domain from the revival of 1734–35. "I once did not imagine that the heart of man had been so unsearchable as I find it is," he confessed. "I am less charitable, and less uncharitable than I once was." From hard experience of seeing a revival come and go, he now realized that the wicked may appear more godly than he had thought (hence he was less charitable in judging persons converted). And the godly might appear carnal and ungodly (hence he was less uncharitable in judging others unconverted). While he still searched for rules to tell the difference, humility was the best stance.[20]

All this would have been fine for cautious Yale conservatives had it not been placed at the end of a discourse in which Edwards developed a forceful case in defense of the awakening. A prodigy in disputation from his days in that very hall, Edwards knew how to undercut an opponent's strongest argument. One by one he went through the phenomena that were commonly used to discredit the awakening and showed that none was sufficient to judge whether the awakening "be the work of the Spirit of God or no." Some of the phenomena, while indeed strange and unusual, had biblical precedent. So effects like "tears, trembling, groans, loud outcries, agonies of body, or the failing of bodily strength" did not prove anything one way or the other. Nor were "great impressions on their imaginations," such as ravishing visions, proofs or disproofs of a true work of God. Nor was it a valid objection that preachers used "means" to excite religious affections, appealing to the emotions as well as to Scripture and reason. Nor was it wrong to frighten sinners

with the terrors of hell if there really is a hell. The presence of "great imprudences" and "sinful irregularities," or of "many errors in judgment and some
delusions of Satan intermixed with the work," or that many "fall away into
gross errors or scandalous practices"—these were no arguments that a work
was not the work of God. One had only to look at the New Testament age to
see that such works of Satan accompanied even the greatest outpouring of the
Spirit.[21]

Having thus in a tour de force disposed of the supposed negative signs,
Edwards turned briefly to the perennial New England question of what were
sufficient evidences of a work of the Spirit. These were signs such as love to
Jesus, renouncing of worldly lusts and ambitions, a love of Scripture, a spirit
of truth, and true Christian love. These were "certain, distinguishing marks"
of true awakening. Proceeding, then, from these sure "rules of the Word of
God," one had only to examine "the facts" of the recent events to see if they
fit. Such a candid examination, he concluded, established that "that extraordinary influence that has lately appeared on the minds of the people abroad in
this land, causing in them an uncommon concern and engagedness of mind
about the things of religion, is undoubtedly, in the general, from the Spirit of
God."[22]

This confident brief for the awakening might not have caused the stir it
did had not Edwards also attacked those in the New England establishment
who were cool toward the awakening. Their caution, Edwards warned Rector
Clap and the circumspect Yale trustees, could be a damnable vice if they were
opposing a work of God. When all was said, it was apparent that Edwards
was closer to the incautious students of the Brainerd circle than to the Yale
authorities. Despite his warnings about the students' censoriousness and excesses, he stood with them in insisting that the most essential feature of the
awakening was that it was of the Spirit of God.

We do not have the exact sermon Edwards preached at Yale but rather a
version "with great enlargements" published soon after in Boston. Benjamin
Franklin also published an edition in Philadelphia the next year, and Isaac
Watts oversaw a London edition. John Wesley published an abridgment
which, like the original, went through several editions.[23]

No one who picked up the Boston edition could miss its confronta-
tional challenge to those who were cool or only lukewarm to the awakening.
Brattle Street's William Cooper furnished an effusive preface that highlighted the point. The present "evangelical dispensation," he began, inaugurated by Christ's first coming, was "the brightest day that ever shone." In the

Reformation era "Gospel light broke in upon the church." But since then "what a dead and barren time has it now been, for a great while, with all the churches of the Reformation!" *All* the dead and barren churches, he made clear, included (despite brief isolated exceptions) New England's. Until now! "And now, behold! The Lord whom we have sought has suddenly come into his temple [Malachi 3:1]. The dispensation of grace we are now under is certainly such as neither we nor our fathers have seen; and in such circumstances so wonderful, that I believe there has not been the like since the extraordinary pouring out of the spirit immediately after our Lord's ascension."

If this was the greatest moment in history since Pentecost, where did that leave critics of the awakening? Cooper was clear. Such scoffers, "I am ready to think, would have been disbelievers, and opposers of the miracles and mission of our Saviour, had they lived in his days. The malignity which some of them have discovered, to me approaches near to the unpardonable sin."[24] These were strong words. Cooper knew, after all, that some of his ministerial colleagues were among those who were questioning the awakening. New England's clerical establishment had often been divided, and (as in the Breck case) their rhetoric sometimes got out of hand. Nonetheless, they usually granted that their fellow clergy were within the pale. Now Cooper and others, if their statements were to be taken seriously, were suggesting that opponents of the awakening might be hopeless reprobates.

Edwards himself suggested that opposing the awakening might be the "unpardonable sin" or the "sin against the Holy Spirit." In Matthew 12: 22–32 Jesus declared, in reference to those who claimed Jesus healing work was of the devil, that there was a "blasphemy against the Holy Ghost," which "shall not be forgiven unto men." Edwards pointed out that there was to be "another coming of Christ, a spiritual coming, to set up his kingdom in the world," and that when the Holy Spirit would be poured out in these latter days it should be expected that there would be opposition paralleling that of the "Jewish church" to Christ's first coming. The great outpouring of the Spirit in the latter days would once again divide the church.[25]

In the *History of the Work of Redemption* Edwards had worked out what he was sure was the key to history. God worked through periodic awakenings. That seemed demonstrated through biblical history. Further it seemed sure that this evangelical dispensation, begun at Pentecost, would reach its fulfillment with a worldwide outpouring of the Spirit. People today could not be sure exactly where they stood in this scenario. But they could be sure that if there were awakenings that met Gospel standards, they were part of the Holy

Spirit's work in history. It followed that to oppose that work was to oppose the Holy Spirit.

Relying on what seemed a thoroughly sound argument, Edwards in the publication of his Yale address was daring in his condemnations, not only of those who opposed the awakening, but even of those who did not openly support it. When an awakening was so widespread as the present one, manifest "in the most public places of the land, and almost all parts of it," and many ministers did not so much as give a prayer of thanks for it, something was deeply wrong. "A long continued silence in such a case is undoubtedly provoking to God; especially in ministers: it is a secret kind of opposition, that really tends to hinder the work: such silent ministers stand in the way of the work of God; as Christ said of old, 'He that is not with us is against us.'"

After citing various biblical condemnations of those who opposed God's work, Edwards argued that "pretended prudence" of those who say they are waiting to see if the awakening bears consistently good fruit was "like the fool's waiting at the riverside to have the water all run by." When there was already clear evidence of so many true conversions in this mix of the work of the Holy Spirit and the counterattacks of Satan, those who questioned the whole work should "take heed that they ben't guilty of the unpardonable sin against the Holy Ghost."[26]

So in the same sermon—now a short treatise—in which Edwards admonished itinerants and students not to pronounce judgments on the inner states of the souls of others, especially clergy, he proclaimed an alternative that was almost as divisive. Rather than judging the souls of individuals, he was taking his stand on the more acceptable ground of judging the cause. He was sure that the awakening was truly great, extraordinary, and unprecedented. He related it to the outpouring of the Holy Spirit in the latter days. If all the right signs were there, then all true believers had an obligation to acknowledge that the awakening was, at least in part, the work of the Holy Spirit. Although Edwards stopped just short of saying that opponents of the awakening, or even those who remained silent about it, were ipso facto in league with the devil, he was unmistakably suggesting that they might be.[27]

Opponents of the awakening could not miss what was going on. Edwards, Cooper, and their allies were throwing down the gauntlet. They might have said only, as Cooper summarized it concisely, that they believed that some of the opposition "*approaches* near to the unpardonable sin," but the implication was clear. Unless the clergy who now stood on the sidelines questioning and scoffing added their support to the awakening, the New

England establishment would be hopelessly divided. God might curse the land and the great opportunity would be missed. One party, as Edwards believed he had demonstrated, was on the side of the Holy Spirit. What then of the other party?[28]

Until now most of the clergy who had opposed the awakening had done so cautiously, at least in public. In the gossipy town of Boston it was easy to learn of private conversations in which clerical skeptics expressed their derision, but they had mostly confined any public attacks to the safe distance of the anonymity of newspaper letters where the sensational events were being sharply debated. Edwards' challenge, seconded by Boston's evangelical clergy, forced the opposition into the open. For the next several years much of Edwards' energy would be devoted to what amounted to a verbal duel with the Boston pastor Charles Chauncy, the most outspoken champion of the Old Lights whose honor he had impugned. After more than a century of maintaining an essential unity through many controversies, New England's clerical establishment would be permanently divided between "New Light" awakeners and "Old Light" critics.

# CHAPTER 15

# "Heavenly Elysium"

In the meantime the light of the awakening had been brightening in Northampton during August and September 1741, and Edwards was dealing every day with new confirmations that the work was truly of the Holy Spirit. He was also much in demand as the revival fires continued to blaze all over New England. During November and December he made an extensive preaching tour, and in late January he was to leave for another two-week stint that would involve at least eight stops in Massachusetts and Connecticut.[1]

On January 21, 1742, shortly before leaving on this tour, Edwards recounted the state of the awakening to his younger friend, the Reverend Joseph Bellamy. Bellamy had graduated from Yale in 1735 and had come to Northampton in 1736 to study theology with Edwards, probably the first student to do so. Bellamy then became pastor at the new settlement of Bethlehem in western Connecticut. He was a large, impressive, somewhat rough-mannered young man, known for his wit and intellect and as a powerful preacher. He became one of Edwards' most valued friends and allies.[2] Edwards' closest friendships were with such younger protégés, including a number who succeeded Bellamy as students and guests in the Edwards household.

"Religion in this and the neighboring town has now of late been on the decaying hand," Edwards reported to Bellamy, yet "there has been the year past the most wonderful work amongst children here, by far, that ever was." Moreover, on the larger scene "the work of God is greater at this day in the land, than it has been at any time." Edwards was sure that "Neither earth or hell can hinder his work that is going on in the country. Christ gloriously triumphs at this day." He continued, noting that because he was being called away to preach in Leicester, a town about halfway to Boston, where a "great work has lately broke out," he would not be able to join Bellamy in a meeting at Guilford, on the Connecticut coast. Moreover, he mentioned that he had "at this time some extraordinary affairs to attend at home."[3]

The "extraordinary affairs" at home referred to the beginnings of what was among the most revealing episodes in the whole Edwards saga. On Wednesday morning, January 20, 1742, Sarah Edwards was enraptured by spiritual ecstasy that continued for more than two weeks. Repeatedly she was physically overwhelmed by her spiritual raptures, sometimes leaping involuntarily to praise God and more often so overcome by joys and transports that she collapsed physically. Except for the first two days of these wonders, Jonathan was out of town on his scheduled preaching tour. At one point one of the neighbor ladies remarked that she was afraid Sarah "should die before Mr. Edwards' return, and he should think the people had killed his wife." Sarah, who seemed to keep her wits about her even when repeatedly overcome by ecstasies, saw it only as a spiritual lesson. She assured those gathered round "that I chose to die in the way that was most agreeable to God's will, and that I should be willing to die in darkness and horror, if it was most for the glory of God."[4]

On his return, Jonathan was elated to learn of his beloved's transfixing encounters with the divine. They far surpassed his own raptures, yet they fit the same patterns. Always the eighteenth-century philosopher and collector of evidence, he wrote down her account of the entire episode as she dictated it. Her memory was good. She could recall the day and even the hour of most of her experiences and could detail the notions that brought on her ineffable feelings. During the entire time, the house had been filled with guests in addition to her seven children and some servants, for whom she was the principal hostess and caretaker. Yet she kept up with her domestic duties. She often retired by herself to meditate (as she had delighted to do since her childhood), and much of her ecstasy took place in solitude or at night. Yet many other incidents took place when guests were present and were triggered by their remarks. In the best of Calvinist fashion she attended to her "worldly business" with "great alacrity," reporting that "it being done thus, 'tis found to be as good as prayer."[5]

Jonathan was so impressed by Sarah's spiritual example that he incorporated a disguised version of her account into a long treatise he was writing (*Some Thoughts Concerning the Present Revival of Religion* [1742]) as a sequel to *The Distinguishing Marks*. Sarah's experience, he argued, perfectly fit the highest spiritual standards to which the most mature Christian should aspire.

Sarah Pierpont Edwards at age forty-one

Here was conclusive evidence that conspicuous physical effects, which were common in the awakening, could not be taken in themselves as evidence of deplorable "enthusiasm" or of spiritual immaturity. After pages of recounting her experiences and the evidences of her state of true grace, he concluded, rhapsodically: "Now if such things are enthusiasm, and the fruits of a distempered brain, let my brain be evermore possessed of that happy distemper! If this be distraction, I pray God that the world of mankind may be all seized with this benign, meek, beneficent, beatifical, glorious distraction!"

In this concluding fervor Jonathan finally allowed himself a moment to express his own affections in what was a sustained but otherwise entirely disguised love portrait of Sarah. The preceding many pages were a mature sequel to the "Sarah Pierpont" paean he had written concerning her spiritual beauties when she was thirteen. Yet, except in Northampton, few readers would know that. He had carefully excised all references to the particular context or even to the gender of the person he was describing. He reported only that he had been acquainted with this case "where the affections of admiration, love and joy, so far as another could judge, have been raised to a higher pitch than in any other instances I have observed or been informed of."[6] Although he incorporated many phrases from Sarah's own account and added other details, he referred to her seemingly impassively as "the person." Yet, when we realize the subject, there is no mistaking that he was describing someone he deeply loved and admired.

God was the preeminent subject for both Jonathan and Sarah, but these accounts remain our best sources for clues about their relationships and priorities. We learn, for instance, that Jonathan still affirmed his estimate of her youthful spirituality. "The person" he wrote, is not "in the giddy age of youth" but "was converted above twenty-seven years ago." This detail would throw off most readers because it sets the time of Sarah's conversion at age four or five.[7] It also explains, incidentally, why during the earlier revival Jonathan had been willing to credit the genuineness of Phoebe Bartlett's spiritual awakening at age four.

It was here that Jonathan recorded that Sarah, "in lower degrees of grace," had always been prone to "many ups and downs" and "a vapory habit of body, and often subject to melancholy, and at times almost overborne by it." Her ascent to a higher level of grace and the bodily effects of it had begun during the Northampton awakening in 1735. But it reached "a much higher degree, and greater frequency" in 1739, when there was no awakening. This point was important to Jonathan's argument because he could underscore that these agitations "arose from no distemper catched from Mr. Whitefield or Mr. Tennent."[8] Since the onset of these more wonderful and more frequent experiences in 1739, Sarah's depressions had been "overcome and crushed by the power of faith and trust in God, and resignation to him; the person has remained in a constant uninterrupted rest, and humble joy in God, and assurance of his favor, without one hour's melancholy or darkness." This was all the more remarkable because "vapors have had great effects on the body, such as they used to have before, but the soul has been always out of their reach."[9]

At the core of Sarah's new spiritual strength was her attitude of near-total submission to God. Jonathan made a point of mentioning that even "in times of the brightest light and highest flights of love and joy," she had no belief "of being now perfectly free from sin (agreeable to the notion of the Wesleys and their followers, and some other high pretenders to spirituality in these days)." Thinking along this line, Jonathan added an oblique defense of Sarah's belief in dressing well, noting that the person had "a particular dislike of placing religion much in dress, and spending much zeal about those things that in themselves are matters of indifference" and often seemed outward displays of humility. She also did not believe that the pious needed to affect "a demure and melancholy countenance."[10] (He admired that she was more outwardly cheerful than he in social settings.) Yet while she avoided methodist doctrines and forms, her piety was just as intense, seeking to be so absorbed in the wonders of God's sovereign love that she could submit to God every care of the world. The greater the submission, the greater the transport of being filled with spiritual joys.

Sarah's original version of the narrative focused intensely on this theme of submission. For years she had been working hard to be "weaned" from the world. A perpetual mother, "to be weaned" was one of Sarah's favorite terms. It meant to submit entirely to God's will so that she could give up her cares for "all things here below." Yet two things remained that she could not suffer with tranquility. First was "the ill treatment of the town." Being the minister's wife, she was subject to carping criticisms of the town, which she could not bear. She felt that she valued too highly "My own good name and fair reputation among men, and especially the esteem and just treatment of the people of this town." The second, and even more vexing failing, was her inability to stand any "ill will of my husband." Or to put it positively, she valued too highly "the esteem, and live and kind treatment of my husband."

A small incident with Jonathan had triggered the crisis. Jonathan had said that "he thought I had failed in some measure in a point of prudence, in some conversation I had with Mr. Williams of Hadley." Chester Williams, pastor at nearby Hadley, was a distant cousin. Though Chester was a friend of the revival and even did some preaching while Edwards was absent, Jonathan may have been especially sensitive to anything that his colleague might have taken as a slight. In any case, Sarah was mortified by his criticism and took her hurt and resentment as evidence of her lack of sufficient sanctification.

The next day, Wednesday, January 20, still harboring her concerns about her inability to find "sufficient rest in God," she gathered with the family and guests around ten in the morning for prayers. The Reverend Peter Reynolds, pastor at Enfield, offered a prayer during which Sarah found herself wishing he would address God as "father." She greatly desired to be able "without the least misgiving of heart, call God my Father." Retiring to be alone to contemplate this, she was overcome with ecstasy. "God the Father, and the Lord Jesus Christ, seemed as distinct persons, both manifesting their inconceivable loveliness, and mildness, and gentleness, and their great immutable love to me." The peace that followed "was altogether inexpressible." At the same time "I felt compassion and love for all mankind, and a deep abasement of soul, under a sense of my own unworthiness." In the fashion of New England piety, she saw her sense of her own worthlessness as a sign that God was acting in her life.

For the next days, even as Sarah continued "every act of duty," her sensibilities were dominated by these sublime ecstasies. The following Monday evening—after five and a half days—she faced a new challenge to her abilities to submit all her cares to God. She heard that Samuel Buell was coming to town to preach. The twenty-five-year-old Buell had just graduated from Yale. He had originally intended to study with Edwards, but he had proved such an effective preacher of revival that he had turned to being a licensed itinerant. When Sarah heard of his coming she wished him great success in Northampton, yet she was also chagrined to realize that in her heart of hearts she would be jealous if the young man sparked a new revival greater than what her husband had been recently able to foster. In the 1734–35 revival Jonathan's success had outshone all counterparts. Sarah's loyalty to Jonathan was deep. She also felt insecure toward the town. She knew Jonathan had critics who would be glad to undercut his authority as supreme revivalist.

When Buell began his preaching Wednesday afternoon, Sarah not only overcame her jealously, but she became one of the chief instruments of his spectacular success. After the service, seeing that several people were spiritually moved, Sarah was so overcome by a vision of heaven that she lost her bodily strength. She and others stayed in the meetinghouse for three hours, until well after dark, as she felt led "to converse with those who were near me, in a very earnest manner." Likely she was exhorting men as well as women in this group—in such cases of witnessing to an extraordinary experience, Jonathan allowed exceptions to the rule that women should not teach men.[11] When she returned home Buell and six other guests were there, conversing on divine things. Once again she was overcome, alternately losing bodily strength and feeling impelled to leap from her chair, and praising God in words of hymns.

The next morning in a similar setting she was even more overcome, first falling down in a swoon and later "unconsciously" leaping from her chair when especially moved by the words of some of the "melting hymns" of Isaac Watts, which Buell was reading. Buell was a great proponent of the new hymnody, using hymns not only in private meetings, as Edwards had, but also introducing them for the first time into the regular Northampton church services.[12] Even in ordinary times, Sarah was often singing. On this Thursday morning Sarah felt herself "entirely swallowed up in God" and was totally overcome with "a ravishing sense of the unspeakable joys of the upper world." From twelve to four in the afternoon she lay in bed, conversing on these things to the pious women who attended her. That night was "the sweetest night I ever had in my life," as she spent the whole night in a "heavenly elysium" as though "to float or swim, in these bright, sweet beams of the love of Christ." Each minute seemed part of eternity, "worth more than all the outward comfort and pleasure, which I had enjoyed in my whole life."

With these even higher raptures came ever more total submission. On Friday she met a test even greater than overcoming any mixed feelings at the success of Buell. Chester Williams, clearly not Sarah's favorite person, was scheduled to preach in the afternoon. She woke up in the morning wondering "whether I was willing that he, who was a neighboring minister, should be extraordinarily blessed, and made a greater instrument of good in the town, than Mr Edwards." Submitting herself even to that, her ecstasies both in public and in private continued throughout the day and into the next week.

Having submitted her jealousies to God, Sarah considered whether there were any limits to what she might endure for God's glory. She had already cultivated a willingness to die and said that "I often used to feel impatient at the thought of living." Jonathan's account added that she had shown this resignation "when actually under extreme and violent pains, and in times of threatenings of immediate death." Women of Sarah's time, we must not forget, were constantly in danger of death not only from disease but also from childbirth. They also lived with the shadow of the possibility of the sudden deaths of their children in epidemics. Learning to submit, to face death, and to deal with depression were constant demands. Sarah remarked that she was thankful to God, ever since her 1739 experiences, for making her willing to die any death, even as "on the rack or at the stake."

Such attitudes had long been cultivated in Christian spiritual disciplines, as the believers considered whether they could face a martyr's death. Foxe's *Book of Martyrs* was standard reading in New England. Sarah would have been familiar, for instance, with the story of the martyrdom of the fourth-century saint Theodora, well known in English literature via a fictionalized account by Robert Boyle, *The Martyrdom of Theodora and Didymus* (1687). Even in polite England, cultivating such resignation was seen as an admirable ideal, as suggested by the fact that in Handel's *Theodora*, first performed later the same decade, the heroine in contemplating a "fate worse than death" (forced prostitution) cries out "Lead me, ye guards, lead me on to the rack, or to the flames."[13]

Sarah believed she had now attained the grace to face fates even greater than a torturous death. Without specifying details, she now believed that she could endure not only postponing the joys of heaven but enduring "a thousand years in horror, if it be God's will." Even if she suffered "the torment to my body being so great, awful and overwhelming, that none could bear to live in the country where the spectacle was seen and the torment and horror of my mind being vastly greater than the torment of my body," she could bear it if it were for the glory of God. God's grace so "seemed to overcome me and swallow me up."

Closer to home, she could now imagine accepting with tranquility not only mild criticisms from Jonathan, but she could endure it if somehow he were transformed into a monster. Part of what she said was so graphic that Sereno Dwight, Edwards' great-grandson who first published her account, edited it out. In one brief passage that has survived in Jonathan's hand, she reported: "At the same time I thought of my being cast off by my nearest and dearest friends and as I had thought before of Mr. Edwards's kicking me out of the house and finally casting me off, now I put it to myself how I could bear from him the worst treatment of me at home and thought that if he should turn to be most cruel to me and should horsewhip me every day I would so rest [in] God that it would not touch [my heart] or diminish my happiness. I could still go on in the performance of all acts of duty to my husband and my happiness remain whole and undiminished."[14]

In our era, when traditions of martyrdom and submission have been all but lost and traditions of psychologizing are rampant, it is difficult to view such experiences in their own context. The temptation today is to speculate on what the passage about horsewhipping reveals about Sarah's psyche or about the Edwardses' relationship. Before doing that, however, we should be reminded that trained psychologists and psychoanalysts often hear many hours of testimony from patients without being able to diagnosis the roots of their problems. So one should not jump to a conclusion based on a fragment. Nevertheless, if one holds to a realistic view of human nature (as Calvinists themselves do), one should acknowledge that there are dark sides to every human and to every human relationship, even if we lack the evidence for identifying the specifics. The one thing that is clear from this passage is that the Edwardses valued submission far more than it is usually valued today.

The more totally Sarah thought of her submission the freer she felt of earthly cares and the more totally sublime was her experience of God's acceptance. During at least the next week Sarah's visions, overwhelming ecstasies, and testimonies to others were constantly renewed. Buell continued to preach and counsel people every day. Under his leadership the new revival spread to monumental proportions.

As Edwards rode back into town two weeks later, he heard from one person after another of the wonders that took place under Buell's ministry. Arriving at his house, he warmly welcomed Buell and heard reports from Sarah and others. Soon he sat down in silence in a corner, tears in his eyes. When asked, he explained that he had been humbled. "I am not worthy that *my* labors should be attended with such a blessing!"[15]

Edwards rejoiced in what he believed God had done through the younger man, especially in what he learned from Sarah, but he also soon became concerned about the effects on the less mature. Many, especially among those already converted, were following Sarah's example into higher states of religious intensity, staying long after meetings and being overcome with religious visions and delights. Some were in sorts of trances for up to twenty-four hours. Some were led to such heights that, in Edwards' later judgment, "Satan took the advantage."[16]

The next we learn of Sarah—from an era when surviving evidences regarding women's lives are often fragmentary—is from a truly cryptic source. It is a prescription written for her by the local physician, Samuel Mather, sometime before the end of December 1742. She is supposed to take some remedies, Jovial Bezorardick and decoction of mugwort, every morning and evening until the supply is gone and apply another to the forehead regularly with a damp cloth. Another, Mynsichtu's Emplastrum Matricale, Mather thought so effective for "hysterical cases" that it would be worth sending to Boston for. It was to be applied to the navel and worn there for "some weeks or months" and was "an admirable remedy" for "all diseases retaining to an hysterical original."[17]

We know of Dr. Mather's prescription only because the always economizing Jonathan used the paper for a sermon preached in December 1742. Another sheet of paper used for the same sermon contains a prayer bid, one of the written requests for prayer that parishioners would give the pastor. This one is from a daughter of the Lyman family, who thanked God for her preservation in a terrible house fire of December 8 in which two of her sisters died. In Sarah Edwards' earlier narrative she recounted that one of the tests she had long put to herself was whether she could endure—what was apparently one of her worst fears—"if our house and all our property in it should be burnt up, and we should that night be turned out naked." Now she had seen that happen to neighbors, prominent citizens, who also had a family of girls, probably friends of her own.[18]

Whether the fire and the prescription are connected by anything more than being on paper bound into the same sermon is a matter of speculation. The undated prescription could have been written much earlier. Also, we can not be sure of the nature of Sarah's malady. "Hysterical" in the eighteenth century usually referred to nervous disorders that were thought to originate in the womb. Dr. Mather's mention of "diseases retaining to an hysterical original" suggests that diagnosis.[19]

One possibility would be that Sarah, known to be susceptible to ups and downs, was suffering from some mental and physical distress (the concoction on a damp cloth for the head may imply headaches), perhaps exacerbated by being badly shaken by the horror of the Lyman fire. There are, of course, lots of other possibilities. Her difficulties (whenever they occurred) also could have been related to childbearing. In 1742 Sarah had, for the first time since 1728, not had a child on a regular two-year cycle. Some have speculated that her remarkable spiritual experiences early in 1742 were related to a miscarriage. In December 1742, she was pregnant again, probably about four months along (their eighth child, Eunice, was born May 8, 1743).

We are on firmer ground if we view Sarah's euphoric experiences of early 1742 as an accentuation of some characteristic patterns in New England piety. Puritans viewed the submission of wives in marriage as a type of the spiritual submission to Christ to which all should aspire. The church was the bride of Christ. Calvinist theology constantly emphasized that only when the saints completely gave up on their own willfulness would God seal the covenant. Some of the most effective sermons, including some of Jonathan's, urged men as well as women to think of themselves as "virgins" preparing for Christ, "the bridegroom."[20] One might be ravished by the love of Christ and be filled with the Spirit. Accepting this intimate eternal covenant, believers were gladly to submit to the authority of God's laws of love and promise lives of service to God, to the family of God, and to neighbors.

Although Puritans did not think that women should be any more submissive to God than men, women seem more often to have attained the requisite submission. For generations women had outnumbered men as full members of churches, sometimes by large numbers. Recent historians of gender have also seen women's spiritual submission as a way of establishing their spiritual authority. Anne Hutchinson was a striking case, claiming to be more thoroughly submitted to God's grace than the allegedly works-righteous clergy and using that claim to challenge their earthly authority. Far more common were women who became spiritual models by submitting both to God and to properly delegated male authorities. Anne Bradstreet's poetry shows spiritual power through such submission. Mary Rowlandson presented her narrative of captivity during King Philip's War as a type of the redemptive suffering of Israel.[21] Sarah Edwards' raptures likewise had the side effect of establishing her as a spiritual authority—though it may be misleading to put it that way since that was the opposite of her expressed intention. In any case, during Buell's visit she both kept scrupulously to her place (for instance, witnessing for three hours to lingering congregants only after the formal service ended) and rivaled him as a promoter of the revival.[22]

Given the persistence of intense female piety in New England, it is arguable that the Great Awakening of 1740–42 was especially remarkable because comparable numbers of males also were caught up in such raptures. Jonathan was a natural leader in the new style of awakenings because he had long had such spiritual sensibilities. By the early 1740s on both sides of the Atlantic and throughout the colonies, many men were experiencing spiritual ecstasies as well. Still, Jonathan's models of exemplary piety were almost all women. Young Sarah Pierpont and his sister Jerusha were models in his youth, Sarah remained a model, and his daughter Jerusha, now aged twelve, had become another. In his *Faithful Narrative* of the 1734–35 revival, Phoebe Bartlett and a young woman, Abigail Hutchinson, were his principal models. Only in the subsequent years when he came to know the dying David Brainerd did he find a male model of the submissive piety he so loved.

Whatever the intense vicissitudes of Sarah's disposition, by surviving accounts she was greatly admired. The outside observer who has written most about her, Samuel Hopkins, was present in the Edwards household during her weeks of euphoria as well as at some later times. Hopkins had been a senior at Yale College (and a classmate of Buell) during the 1740–41 year of awakenings. Naturally reserved and intellectual, Hopkins had agonized about whether he was converted. Despite his assent to Reformed doctrines and his thorough sympathy for the awakeners, he had not experienced the over-whelming affections that now seemed requisite. During Hopkins' senior year the zealous sophomore David Brainerd visited his college room one day to inquire as to the state of his soul. The taciturn Hopkins was determined that no one should discover his lack of zeal, yet he inwardly believed that Brainerd was right in saying that he should at least sometimes experience overwhelm-ing affections toward Christ. At the same time, Hopkins thought that Gilbert Tennent was the greatest preacher he had ever heard and planned to go study with him in New Jersey. Then in September he heard Edwards' commence-ment sermon. Although he did not speak to his new hero, he knew it was with him that he must study.[23]

After spending most of the fall secluded at home and in a morose search for true piety, the twenty-two-year-old Hopkins arrived in Northampton in December. Edwards was away preaching when he arrived. After a few days Sarah came to his room and, as he recalled, said "As I was now become one of the family for a season, she felt herself interested in my welfare; and [as] she observed that I appeared gloomy and dejected, she hoped I would not think she intruded by desiring to know, and asking me what was the occasion of it." Hopkins opened up to Sarah as he had not been able to do with others. He told her that he feared he was in a "Christless, graceless state." Sarah as-sured him that she had been praying much for him and believed he would "receive light and comfort" and "that God intended yet to do great things by me, etc."[24]

Within a couple of months Hopkins found the spiritual comfort that Sarah had predicted, and he eventually became Edwards' best-known suc-cessor and the leading American theologian of his generation. Sarah Ed-wards' counsel and example in his early spiritual formation had a lasting impact. Hopkins' mid-nineteenth-century biographer, Edwards A. Park, in recounting part of Sarah's ecstatic narrative, remarks that her reflections "would *now* be termed Hopkinsian."[25] Sarah's willingness to spend a thou-sand years of hell on earth if that were for the greater glory of God had a "Hopkinsian" ring to nineteenth-century ears. Hopkins restated Jonathan Edwards' emphasis on "love to Being in general" as simply "disinterested benevolence." Hopkins himself became a leading proponent of antislavery during the Revolutionary era and "disinterested benevolence" became a powerful motto for American reformers. Harriet Beecher Stowe memori-alized Hopkins in *The Minister's Wooing* as the personally and theologically stiff minister who eventually redeems himself by putting "disinterested benevolence" ahead of his romantic interest.

Hopkins, for his part, was the literary executor and first biographer of Edwards. His biographical memoir, published in 1765, included a glowing tribute to Sarah. Admiring her for, among many other virtues, having "the law of kindness on her tongue," Hopkins' portrait follows that same rule. He described her as "a more than ordinary beautiful person; of a pleasant, agreeable countenance." The genuineness of her piety was manifested in her concerns for charity toward the poor and her extraordinary kindness to guests and strangers. Moreover, she "paid proper deference to Mr. Edwards," catered to the peculiarities of his Spartan diet, and was a tender nurse to him in his illnesses. She too frequently "labored under bodily disorders and pains" but cheerfully and without complaint.

Hopkins also admired her "excellent way of governing her children," bringing them to obey cheerfully "without loud, angry words, or heavy blows." Though she was firm, she was mild and always explained her reasons for discipline. As a result, the children were remarkably well-behaved and seldom (Hopkins says "never") quarreled. When there was any special difficulty she would consult with Jonathan, who would treat it with solemn importance. Jonathan was called in particularly to quell any sign of willfulness among their young children. He showed "the greatest calmness" as well as the greatest firmness in his discipline and "as a consequence of this, they reverenced, esteemed and loved him."[26]

Hopkins doubtless had romanticized the Edwards home, which had fostered spiritual warmth at a crucial time and to which he often returned, first as a student and then as a friend. The role of the seven children must have been particularly striking. The older girls had all become very pious. When Hopkins first arrived the frail eldest, Sarah, was thirteen. The next three, Jerusha, Esther, and Mary, ages eleven, nine, and seven, were, as Edwards Park put it, "beautiful and sprightly." At one of his subsequent visits in July 1743, Hopkins recorded in his diary "Made Miss Jerusha a present of a Bible."[27] The spiritual Jerusha was now thirteen and perhaps not too young to be admired.

Sarah Sr. remained the prototype of Hopkins' veneration.[28] He particularly admired her household management, which he portrayed as efficient and frugal. Often she would repeat to the children the words of Jesus in telling the disciples to gather up the fragments from the loaves and fishes, "that nothing be lost." Sarah, says Hopkins, "was better able than most of her sex to take the whole care" of the household in her hands.[29] Partly that was out of necessity, since Jonathan assiduously tried to keep himself free from worldly cares and, according to Hopkins, paid little attention to the house- and farmwork going on around him.[30] Sarah was thus left as the sole manager of a substantial enterprise overseeing children, servants, animals, and what amounted to an active boarding house.

Particularly in the early 1740s we have glimpses of her traveling back and forth to Boston, presumably on family business. In one instance, she and a young man who accompanied her made an overnight stay at the Reverend Ebenezer Parkman's home at Westborough. Later, in 1744, Parkman re- corded, "At my house found Mrs. Edwards of Northampton and her Daugh- ter Jerusha, accompanied by Reverend Mr. Hopkinton [Samuel Hopkins] of Sheffield." Hopkins' journal for the previous day reads, "Set out today from Northampton to Boston, in company of Madam Edwards and her daughter, who rides behind me" (i.e., on the same horse). Whether this arrangement reflected more than disinterested benevolence we cannot tell.[31]

# CHAPTER 16

──────── ◆·◆ ────────

# Conservative Revolutionary

D espite the abundance of Edwards' writing in his notebooks, sermons, publications, and more than two hundred surviving letters, he reveals remarkably little that is personal, excepting as spiritual and intellectual concerns are deeply personal. Most of the detail we know of his daily life and work comes from Samuel Hopkins' admiring biographical memoir. Judging from Hopkins' portrait, Edwards was deeply spiritual, intensely hardworking, intellectual, introspective, and somewhat withdrawn. He regulated his days by the strictest disciplines.[1]

What would it have been like to meet Edwards? Hopkins acknowledged that those who did not know Edwards well found him "*stiff* and *unsociable*," but, the biographer quickly adds, "this was owing to want of better acquaintance." Edwards, Hopkins explains, followed his resolve not to speak evil of others and so did not participate in the usual banter of lively light conversation. He followed the biblical advice to be "slow to speak" and hence spoke only when he had something to say. Edwards also believed it unprofitable to get into verbal disputes with strangers and felt he was at "the best advantage with his pen in his hand." Further, "his animal spirits were low, and he had not strength of lungs to spare, that would be necessary in order to make him what would be called, an affable, facetious gentleman, in all companies."

Yet his friends, Hopkins insisted, knew how "groundless" the accusation was that he was "*stiff* and *unsociable*." They, like his family, knew his warm and affectionate side. Friends "always found him easy of access, kind and condescending; and though not talkative, yet affable and free." His trusted allies liked to talk with him about serious spiritual and intellectual issues. Such intimates felt free to challenge his opinions and to enter into argument with him. On the subjects of his concern, said Hopkins, "his tongue was as the pen of a ready writer," and his intimates found these heartfelt discourses "most entertaining and instructive." Toward Sarah, Hopkins reports, "Much of the tender and kind was expressed in his conversation with her and conduct toward her."[2]

Hopkins' portrait of Edwards as personally warm, despite almost painful reserve and austere public formality, gains credibility if we consider Edwards' successes in the awakenings. No pastor ever held a large congregation more under his spell than he had in 1734–35. At that time and during the sequel in 1741–42 the town's folk lined up at his study to seek his counsel. During those times at the least, and apparently for much of the fifteen years he had been in Northampton, many people—young and old, poor and rich—found him attractive and inspiring. Although in some respects he may have fit the image of the withdrawn intellectual, few scholars have put more emphasis on the primacy of the affections. In his preaching and in earnest personal encounters, that affective side of his personality seems to have shown through.

A key to understanding this spectrum of reaction to Edwards is to recognize that he was single-mindedly dedicated to a cause. Like many such persons, he sought total loyalty. Hopkins notes that he selected his intimate friends carefully and on that basis, and it is only with them that he would truly open up. Not surprisingly, many of his intimate friends were younger, though he could form close ties with anyone who was loyal to the cause. He was close to members of his extended family who, especially during the eras of Solomon Stoddard and William Williams, shared his concerns. With his children he followed the New England practice of breaking any signs of willfulness, and he cultivated intense spirituality at early ages. He treated the people of Northampton almost the same way, maintaining strict discipline, asking heartfelt loyalty, and he was not content when they showed anything else. He saw the loyalty he sought as only secondarily loyalty to himself. It was first of all a heartfelt loyalty to the triune God. That meant renouncing all purely worldly affections and allegiances.

What sort of person Edwards appeared to be depended largely on how fully one shared his vision. Unsympathetic strangers interpreted his reserve as aloofness and his dogmatism as arrogance. As New England divided over the awakening, those who differed with him increasingly saw him as an unbending party partisan. Even aside from the Great Awakening, he had a reputation for insisting that clergy "be very critical in examining candidates for the ministry, with respect to their *principles,* as well as their religious dispositions and morals." For this, says Hopkins, "he met with considerable difficulty and opposition."[3] While opponents found such scrupulousness cold and lacking in charity, those in Edwards' own party saw it as admirable integrity. The arguments that Edwards used in his attempts to demolish opponents' positions might be seen as arrogant sophistry or as brilliant clarity. The passion in his sermonic rhetoric might be seen as ruthless manipulation or as warm, loving spirituality. His reserve in conversation about personalities might be seen as cold disregard of others or as self-renouncing discipline. His single-minded dedication to his work could be seen as self-centered lack of sociability or as selfless dedication to serve God and neighbor with all his heart, soul, strength, and mind.

We must also take into account that Edwards stayed as much as possible in his strict pastoral role because he understood himself to have a high calling in a universe governed by ordered authorities. He saw himself called to lead his congregation as surely as Moses was called to lead Israel. He was to be a father to the town folk, authoritarian yet loving. Like Moses (whom the Bible characterized as meek and slow of speech),[4] he had compassion for his often wayward people. He also knew that, like Moses, he had his weaknesses. Yet he had no doubt that he was ordained to lead his people in God's prescribed way and that they must follow him as God's spokesperson and servant.

## Slavery

We can consider Edwards' attitudes toward slavery in the context of his hierarchical assumptions. Nothing separates the early eighteenth-century world from the twenty-first century more than this issue. Many elite New Englanders owned African slaves, and Edwards and his close relatives seem usually to have had one or two slaves per household. Although the records are incomplete, we know that in 1731 Edwards traveled to Newport, Rhode Island, where he purchased a young slave named Venus. By 1736 another African—named Leah—seems to have replaced Venus (or perhaps the Edwardses gave Venus a biblical name more appropriate for a ministerial family). In 1740 Jonathan and Sarah cosigned to guarantee financial support for "Jethro Negro and his wife Ruth," who were manumitted in the will of Sarah's stepmother. Nonetheless, the Edwardses themselves seem usually to have owned at least one slave.[5]

Although there were scattered protests among European Americans against African slavery before and during Edwards' time, the first widespread revolution in attitudes did not take place until the decades immediately after his death. In the era of the American Revolution, many elite Americans, including such Edwards followers as Samuel Hopkins and Jonathan Edwards Jr., were outspoken opponents of slavery. Before that most British-Americans simply absorbed African slavery into their hierarchical views of society, where it was assumed that the higher orders of society would have servants to perform domestic and farm labor. White servants, most indentured for a period of years, were treated much like slaves. They were thoroughly dependent on the patriarchal authority of their masters. They needed permission to marry, buy or sell property, or leave the premises. They could be bought or sold, seized to pay debts, or willed to heirs. The vast differences, of course, were that African slavery was always involuntary and usually perpetual. Slaveowners were well aware of these anomalies and that Africans were unhappy in their servile condition.[6] Yet before the Revolutionary era British colonials typically rationalized enslavement of Africans as an extension of long-accepted practices of servitude and dependency.[7]

All we know of Edwards' views comes from a fragmentary and recently discovered source. Sometime in summer or fall of 1741, just when the Great Awakening was reaching its peak, Edwards took time to jot down a cryptic list of arguments in response to a controversy over slavery. The dispute that occasioned these observations was highly unusual, with few if any known counterparts in New England near this time. Some parishioners of the church in Northfield (near Deerfield) had denounced their pastor, Benjamin Doolittle, for owning African slaves. The accusation was only one part of larger controversy between Doolittle and part of his congregation, led by a number of the older men in the town. The "disaffected brethren" accused Doolittle, who had been their pastor since 1716, of making exorbitant salary demands—an issue Edwards and many other pastors also were encountering. Some of the discontent arose from suspicions that Doolittle had Arminian leanings and that he was cool toward awakenings. At the moment, however, the controversy over slaveowning had come before the Hampshire Association, and Edwards was chosen to draft a response.[8]

Edwards viewed the accusation regarding slaveholding as insincere and saw his primary job as defending the authority of a fellow minister. That he would do so is especially striking because he probably shared the suspicions that Doolittle had unorthodox and Old Light leanings. Edwards' jottings for his arguments are incomplete and often hard to interpret. Nonetheless he is clear that he believed that the dissidents were raising the slavery question "only to make disturbances and raise uneasiness among people against their minister to the great wounding of religion."

Edwards and his slaveowning colleagues and "river gods" friends and relatives must have been especially eager in 1741 that the status quo regarding slaveholding not be disturbed. That summer New York City had once again experienced what many believed to be a major slave conspiracy to burn down the town. The frenzy of the New Yorkers to suppress the alleged terrorists was well reported in the Boston papers, and fears of slave uprisings had spread to New England.⁹ One feature of the Northfield accusations that Edwards seemed most disturbed about was that Doolittle's accusers had "boasted" that they had "baffled" their pastor with their arguments concerning the immorality of slavery. Though Edwards did not mention the implication, if the word got around that, as was claimed, the minister "could say nothing that was worth a saying" in defense of slaveholding, such talk could inflame the slaves.

Despite his interest in defending ministerial authority and in protecting his fellow slaveholders, Edwards' arguments revealed his deep ambivalence toward the institution of African slavery. His main argument was that using one's "neighbor's work without wages" was not itself sinful, since the Bible expressly allowed slavery and it would not contradict itself. Whereas God had temporarily "winked at" some ancient practices that were later revealed to be objectionable [he was probably thinking of polygamy], slavery was not condemned in the New Testament, and there was "no other sin generally prevalent that is not expressly mentioned and strictly forbidden."

At the same time that he defended slavery as not wrong in itself, Edwards made a point of condemning the African slave trade. Do "other nations" Edwards asked, "have any power or business to disfranchise all the nations of Africa?" Slavery had, of course, long been justified as a more humane alternative to killing captured troops in warfare, but that principle did not apply when Europeans claimed a universal right to enslave any African they could get their hands on. The only plausible justification for that would be that Christian nations somehow had the right to take what they wished from non-Christian nations, as Israel had, for instance, been told they could take property from the Egyptians. It would be absurd, Edwards suggested, to interpret such precedents as a universal rule. Rather, the principle had to be that "all mankind were their neighbors" so that the moral law applies to treatment of all nations. Hence the European nations had no right to steal from the Africans.¹⁰

Even though Edwards regarded African and Native American civilizations as vastly inferior to Christendom, especially since these heathen peoples had suffered so long under Satan's rule, he thought they were equal to

Christian nations both in their rights and in their potentialities. In his sermons on *The History of the Work of Redemption* in 1739 he had assured the
Northamptonites that although these peoples now lived almost like the beasts
in some respects, it would not always be that way. In the millennial era, only a
few hundred years hence, he assured his congregation, "It may be hoped that
then many of the Negroes and Indians will be divines, and that excellent
books will be published in Africa, in Ethiopia, in Turkey—and not only very
learned men, but others that are more ordinary men, shall then be very
knowing in religion."[11]

Edwards explicitly denied that there was any inherent inferiority among
different peoples in God's eye. "We are made of the same human race," he
had written in a note on Job 31:15 in the early 1730s, perhaps soon after he had
first become a slaveowner. "In these two things," he wrote, "are contained the
most forceable reasons against the master's abuse of his servant, viz. That
both have one Maker, and that their Maker made 'em alike with the same
nature."[12]

For the same reason, Edwards regarded Africans and Indians as spiritual
equals. During his ministry, the Northampton church had already admitted
nine Africans into full communicant membership. Six of these, including the
Edwardses' slave Leah, were products of the awakening of 1734–35 and became communicants in 1736. Around this same time, the church admitted two
Indian members, Mary and Phoebe Stockbridge.

True to his hierarchical instincts, Edwards pulled back from any politically disruptive implications of this evangelical Christian egalitarianism. Resourceful in disputation as he was, in his notes regarding the Doolittle case he
used the immorality of the African slave trade as a way of showing that the
arguments of the critics of the ministerial slaveowner proved too much. The
whole economy of New England, he implied, depended on products produced by African slavery (a key part in New England's trade was with the
slave economies of the Caribbean). If it were wrong to partake in this system
immediately, then it would also be wrong to partake in it remotely, as for
instance, in purchasing goods produced by slave labor. If the objectors wished
to claim that it was all right to benefit from slave labor indirectly, "they would
do well to fix the number of steps" that one had to be removed from the
slavery from which one benefited. By this *reductio* Edwards was in effect
saying that in a world filled with sin it was impossible to keep oneself from
benefiting from others' evil. Hence, until the millennial conversions got to the
heart of the problem, one should simply make the best of imperfect social
arrangements.[13]

# Patriarchal Authority

Edwards' views on slavery, like his authoritarian views of his ministerial role, are those of someone who was by instinct a social conservative. He viewed the universe and this world as hierarchical and assumed that social relationships should be governed by respect for divinely instituted authority. He found in Scripture ample justification for that long-standing viewpoint since the Scripture writers also took hierarchy for granted. Edwards was moreover an elite male colonial British citizen in an era when there were strong status distinctions and expectations of deference. He was in many respects a thoroughly eighteenth-century man—an eighteenth-century traditionalist. In American political and social terms, he was pre-Revolutionary.

Paradoxically, nothing was more revolutionary in his own era than the popular spirit of the awakening that he did so much to promote.[14] Further, Edwards' Calvinistic theological heritage included revolutionary potential, as the Puritan revolution of the previous century had demonstrated. As his views on the future equality of the races suggested, conversionist theology had potentially leveling implications. In Edwards' millennial view of history he projected a great worldwide revolution based on the combination of awakenings and Reformed theology. Yet, while he was correct in anticipating a momentous worldwide expansion of evangelical Protestantism, he did not envision its predominantly populist character. Rather, he believed a great international Reformed revolution would help establish properly constituted authority, especially that of the learned clergy who correctly interpreted Scripture.

Edwards' social views, inherited from the conservative Timothy Edwards, reflected seventeenth-century American Puritan ideals of a biblical commonwealth led by authoritarian patriarchs. Edwards was looking forward to a worldwide triumph of Reformed-evangelical culture that would amount to those Puritan ideals writ large. He was a progressive in that he helped adapt the awakenings to that purpose. Yet built within New England civilization were other progressive potentialities—for an increasingly individualistic acquisitive modern culture and for more popular authority—with which he was essentially uncomfortable.

As Edwards faced various challenges in Northampton during the 1740s, his responses were built around an old style of authoritarian paternalism that was under increasing strain.[15] His policies were those of which his father would have approved and which might have worked in a New England village of half a century earlier. Nowhere, in fact, had the strain of holding onto the old assumptions become more apparent than in East Windsor itself. There Timothy Edwards had suspended communion for three years from 1738 to 1741 as a result of a bitter dispute over his efforts to discipline a couple who had married without consent of the young woman's father—an issue of paternal and ministerial authority if ever there was one.[16] Jonathan was solidly on his father's side on such matters. In Northampton he continued to present his congregation with a grand picture of the future, but in the difficult decade of the 1740s he too would find it increasingly difficult to shape the town according to his social and spiritual expectations.

## The Awakening Sealed

In March 1742 Northampton was at another peak of revival fervor. When Edwards had returned from his preaching tour in February he encountered not only Sarah's wonderful ecstasies but also a town that under the preaching of Samuel Buell was nearly out of control. Working together with Buell for the next several weeks, Edwards tried at once to fuel the revival and quell its excesses. "A great deal of caution and pains" he wrote, "were found necessary to keep the people, many of them, from running wild." Parishioners were attempting to outdo each other in enthusiasm, spreading the false impression that the more violent the emotions and the more vehement the expressions of zeal the greater the true piety.[17] Edwards labored vigorously to make the point, as he would throughout the awakenings, that great excitements were not *essential* to true spirituality—even if they were often *compatible* with it.

At the same time, while the revival fires were hot, Edwards initiated a plan to try to consolidate the gains. From hard experience he had learned that revival passions were fleeting. He did not want a repetition of what had happened in the late 1730s. Then, as he later acknowledged, he had been taken in by some superficial enthusiasms and found himself in the embarrassing position of presiding over a spiritually torpid town just as it became internationally renowned as a model of spiritual transformation.

This time Edwards attempted to transform the volatile euphoria of revival into a more stable spirituality that could be controlled in the fixed channels of the covenant. Early in March he drafted an elaborate church covenant, which he presented to some of the leading men of the congregation. He then brought it to the various religious societies that met in the several districts of the town. Winning their approval, he declared a day of fasting, prayer, and of owning the covenant for Tuesday, March 16, 1742. On that day the whole congregation assembled in the meetinghouse, and in a solemn ceremony, all the people over fourteen years of age rose and assented to the document.

Covenant renewal ceremonies were patterned on the Old Testament, and covenants had been a staple of New England since its founding. One of the uses of the law, according to Reformed theology, was as a guide to Christian living in response to grace. So Puritans could both preach salvation by wholly unmerited grace and at the same time guide the church with a legal system of the moral law (but not the ceremonial law) that replicated practices of ancient Israel. In joyous gratitude for their undeserved salvation, true believers would gladly contract to adopt the full moral law as their guide for life, even if they knew they could never keep it perfectly.

Edwards' lengthy covenant is a remarkable constitution for a model town. After acknowledging God's grace and asking forgiveness for earlier backslidings, the people agreed to an elaborate set of promises as to how they should live. By far the largest section dealt with how Christian neighbors should live together. This part could have been called "A Model of Christian Charity," and it is reminiscent of the famous declaration by John Winthrop, Massachusetts' first governor, of how the bonds of charity should unite the Christian commonwealth. Because Edwards' document was a formal contract, he did not speak so much of the principle of charity that summarizes the law (as he had in *Charity and Its Fruit*), but rather spelled out the specific rules for applying that principle. In the process he also catalogued the past failings of the often-contentious Northamptonites and had them promise to renounce all those vices.

Those who had defrauded their neighbor in any way promised not only to change their ways but that "we will not rest till we have made that restitution, or given that satisfaction, which the rules of moral equity require." Further, everyone promised to renounce backbiting, a spirit of revenge, enmity, ill will, and secret grudges. Particularly in public affairs, they agreed to give up their notorious party spirit and "to avoid all unchristian inveighings, reproachings, bitter reflectings, judging and ridiculing others, either in public meetings, or in private conversation."

In a briefer section, but one that would soon have great significance, the young people promised "that we will strictly avoid all freedoms and familiarities in company, so tending either to stir up or gratify a lust of lasciviousness" and any other behavior they would be afraid to engage in if they knew that in a few hours they would have to give account to a holy God.

Finally, everyone promised to "devote our whole lives to be laboriously spent in the business of religion" and to "run with perseverance the race that is set before us." Recognizing these vows might in the future be contrary to their corrupt inclinations, they would "be often strictly examining ourselves by these promises, especially before the sacrament of the Lord's Supper" and praying for grace to "keep us from wickedly dissembling in these our solemn vows."[18]

The most evident aspect of Edwards' outlook revealed in the Northampton Covenant is that he was attempting to institutionalize the spirit of the revival. In this he was following not only the Old Testament covenant model, but also asking the congregation to seal their commitment to specifically New Testament rules for Christian living. Yet the larger practical problem was how to keep the revival light from fading once more. Like the disciple Peter on the mount of transfiguration, Edwards was proposing to build a permanent structure that would conserve so spectacular a spiritual outpouring.

He was also indirectly addressing another matter about which he was increasingly uneasy. Many of the revivalists in the international and intercolonial circles in which he moved were strongly opposed to the Stoddardean practice of open communion. Edwards disagreed with those who claimed that they could reliably tell the converted from the unconverted, but he felt the force of their point that the church should examine candidates for full communicant membership to be sure they showed the visible signs of commitment in their profession and practice. Whitefield admired Solomon Stoddard's evangelistic writings, but he was astonished to learn that his practice of open communion would even allow that ministers might be unconverted. This subject was likely discussed on the day (October 21, 1740) Whitefield and Edwards had visited Jonathan's parents, since that is the date of Whitefield's journal comment on Stoddard.[19] Timothy Edwards, who doubtless retained an emotional hold over Jonathan, had in his 1732 published election-day sermon openly criticized Stoddardean leniency regarding church membership and, by implication, his son's continued complicity in it.[20]

The unease that Jonathan was feeling about this topic could be mitigated if virtually everyone in the church of age to be a communicant (apparently fourteen) showed some evidence of conversion. Edwards seemed to believe the town was approaching that level of nearly universal conversions during the 1734–35 awakening, but the subsequent behavior of some had convinced him otherwise. Once again in winter 1742 the awakening, or at least interest in religious things, was close to universal. Even if he was not sure that everyone was ready to give evidence of conversion, he had persuaded "the people in general that were above fourteen years of age" to solemnly swear to the covenant. Furthermore, he underscored that it would be especially before each celebration of the Lord's Supper that they would "strictly examine ourselves by these promises."[21]

## The Dawning of a Glorious Day?

Whatever Edwards' disillusion about the long-term impact of the 1734–35 awakening, in the winter and spring of 1742 he was still immensely optimistic about the prospects of this much greater awakening. He was giving all his time and energy to it. Not only was he traveling frequently, but when he was at home lines of parishioners waited for his counsel. Further, he was devoting most of his intellectual energies to writing a much longer defense of the revival, to appear the next spring as a 378-page treatise entitled *Some Thoughts Concerning the Present Revival of Religion in New England: And the Way in Which It Ought to Be Acknowledged and Promoted.*[22]

*Some Thoughts* reveals Edwards at the height of his exhilaration over the awakening. True, as he was writing about it in 1742, the revival was becoming increasingly divisive, yet he insisted that such a potential revolution deserved every Christian's wholehearted support. Alluding in his preface to the current conflict between England and Spain, the "War of Jenkins' Ear" to which New England had to send some expeditionary forces, he announced that "We in New England are at this day engaged in a more important war."[23] As in any war there was much confusion, and *Some Thoughts* was designed to be a comprehensive handbook to sort out truth from error. Its essential argument was the same as that of *Distinguishing Marks.* Edwards' first goal was to demonstrate irrefutably that the awakening was essentially a great work of God. At the same time he condemned its excesses, carefully distinguishing among evidences of true spirituality practices that went beyond biblical norms and ecstatic experiences that were neither necessary to spirituality nor necessarily incompatible with it. Although he described the contest as a war, he saw himself as a moderate. He especially deplored censoriousness on each side. He admonished not only those who condemned the whole awakening because of its excesses, but also those awakeners who were too quick to condemn many church members and clergy as unconverted.

In spite of his efforts to carve out this judicious middle ground on which he hoped all right-thinking Christians might stand, his treatise became best known for an unguarded remark that revealed his immense hopes for the New England awakening. Trying to establish the larger point that to oppose the awakening is to oppose a great work of God, he wrote: " 'Tis not unlikely that this work of God's Spirit, that is so extraordinary and wonderful, is the dawning, or at least a prelude, of that glorious work of God, so often foretold in Scripture, which in the progress and issue of it, shall renew the world of mankind."

Further, since these events ushering in the end-times and eventually the millennium, or thousand-year reign of Christ on earth, had been so long expected, he argued, "we can't reasonably think otherwise, than that the beginning of the great work of God must be near." Such predictions would not have been unusual had not Edwards immediately added: "And there are many things that make it probable that this work will begin in America."[24]

He went on with more than eight pages of tortured arguments as to why the patterns of the history of redemption made it probable that the dawn of this work should be first seen in America. It is not surprising that the otherwise sympathetic Isaac Watts would remark, "I think his reasonings about America want force."[25] According to Edwards, the prophecy of Isaiah 60 (which begins "Arise, shine; for thy light is come, and the glory of the Lord is risen upon thee" and ends describing a time when the sun and moon will not set and "the Lord shall be thine everlasting light" and "thy people also shall be all righteous") seemed to fit America because it referred to events in distant isles and the conversion of the gentiles. Edwards also reasoned that there was some symmetry in God's work of redemption. Since the first great work had been done in the old hemisphere, the new work would be done in the new. The last would be made first. God would not build a paradise "where there is some good growth already, but in a wilderness." Contrary to nature, the spiritual sun would now go from west to east. (Edwards' view of geography, like his view of spiritual history, was thoroughly Eurocentric). All these and other biblical types led Edwards to conclude: "And if these things are so, it gives us more abundant reasons to hope that what is now seen in America, and especially in New England, may prove the dawn of that glorious day: and the very uncommon and wonderful circumstances and events of this work, seem to me strongly to argue that God intends it as the beginning or forerunner of something vastly great."[26]

Many friends of the revival were suggesting that it was the beginning of the glorious last days when the gentiles would be gathered in, leading toward the millennium. William Cooper's effusive preface to *The Distinguishing Marks* was only one of many such expressions in which such grand expectations were taken for granted. Deborah Prince, the talented daughter of Edwards' pro-revivalist friend, Boston's Thomas Prince Sr., wrote in 1743 (a year before her untimely death), "It is the opinion of many eminent divines, that it is the dawning of that glorious day, when the whole earth shall be filled with the knowledge of the Lord as the waters cover the sea."[27]

Edwards did not explain his own variation on the current end-time scenarios, which he had preached in the still unpublished *History of Redemption* sermons and worked out in his private notebooks. The basic outline of his interpretation was like that most commonly held among his peers. He did not expect to see the full-blown millennium at any moment soon, but rather he saw the revivals as the beginning of a momentous era of both triumph and strife that would culminate in the millennial peace.[28] The last days would be ushered in by a great series of revivals and the ingathering of the gentiles and extraordinary anticipations of millennial spirituality. Yet these latter days would be days of unprecedented conflict as well.

Because Edwards did not explain the details of his variant of millennial views, he opened himself up to the accusation that he had claimed the millennium was already beginning in America. Two years later, he complained to a Scottish correspondent, that "it has been slanderously reported and printed concerning me, that I have often said that the millennium was already begun, and that it began at Northampton. A doctor of divinity in New England [Charles Chauncy], has ventured to publish this report to the world from a single person, who is concealed and kept behind the curtain; but the report is very diverse from what I have ever said." Edwards went on to explain his actual view, which was that there would "be many sore conflicts and terrible convulsions, and many changes, revivings and intermissions" before the church would rest in millennial peace.[29]

Edwards, in fact, did not believe that he was viewing the start of the millennium itself, but it is understandable that his remarks in *Some Thoughts* have been interpreted, both at the time and since, as suggesting that the millennium might be beginning in America. He certainly did say that what was happening in New England might prove to be "the dawn of that glorious day" and either "the beginning or forerunner of something vastly great." Edwards was thinking of a long set of events of the "glorious day" preliminary to the millennium. Those events would commence with great revivals, go on through great conflicts and even greater revivals, and culminate in an evening of rest and peace.[30] In 1742 he did believe that the Great Awakening in New England was likely the beginning of an era of worldwide revivals that would radiate from America.[31]

Edwards' extravagant estimate of what was happening was a reflection of the intersection of his own experience, his theological vision, and the extraordinary events of the year. We must think of him as someone who was often so overwhelmed with the glory of God that he seemed to sense it directly. His immediate experiences confirmed the spiritual realities of which he spoke. Moreover, at the core of his vision of God was the beauty of God's irrepressible love manifested in Christ. While he also expected continuing evil, or the horrors generated by rebellion against such wonderful good, his theology demanded a culmination of history in the triumph of universal love over hatred. In this end-time victory the Gospel would finally triumph in every nation.

Now he found himself in an extraordinary time when many thousands all over New England were sharing in the immediate experiences of the spiritual realities that he knew so well. He was also surrounded by evidences of answered prayers and genuine spiritual experiences far too numerous to discount. He thrilled at the spiritual ecstasies of his wife and at seeing his daughters transformed into spiritual gems. The cantankerous Northamptonites had promised to translate their revived spirituality into an exemplary community. Even if he was enough a Calvinist to recognize that living according to New Testament principles of mutual love and forbearance would be contrary to residual "corrupt inclinations and carnal desires," his parishioners had agreed to give their all toward pursuing the highest ideal. Although Edwards did not expect to see the millennium, he provided his town with a constitution that was a type of what millennial life would be like.

In such a heady atmosphere, Edwards could hardly conceive of how Christians might dismiss the greatest event that anyone in New England had ever witnessed. Yet there it was. Even some of the clergy were belittling what in all probability was the beginning of the spectacular end-times ingathering of the nations.[32]

Nor was the fault just in the churches. The civil authorities were also to blame. Invoking the traditional language of God's covenant with New England, he challenged the governments: "whether we han't reason to fear that God is provoked with this land, that no more notice has been taken of this glorious work of the Lord that has been lately carried on, by the civil authority." Alluding to the celebrations of the arrival of the Anglican Governor Shirley the previous year, Edwards pointed out that lack of fanfare on such occasions would have been interpreted as an insult. So by analogy, "shall the Head of the angels, the Lord of the universe, come down from heaven in so wonderful a manner into the land, and shall all stand at a distance and be silent and unactive on such an occasion?"[33]

Edwards continued his challenge to those who were cool toward the awakening by once again raising the sensitive question of New England's colleges, Harvard and Yale. Friends of the colleges were still seething from Whitefield's scathing remark that "their light is become darkness." Whitefield's reply to criticisms, though positive in tone, conceded nothing but rather merely rejoiced that Gilbert Tennent's tour had brought more light among the students.[34] Edwards, acknowledging that the colleges were "out of my proper sphere," nonetheless observed that he would "take the liberty of an Englishman (that speaks his mind freely concerning public affairs)" as well as his liberty as a minister to speak on spiritual matters.

Edwards' assessment of the colleges was nearly as scathing as Whitefield's. Particularly, he was appalled at what he regarded as the impiety now permitted at the colleges. Because the colleges were primarily to train clergy, it was "the greatest nonsense and absurdity imaginable" that "instead of being places of the greatest advantages for true piety, one can't send a child thither without great danger of his being infected as to his morals, as it has certainly sometimes been with these societies. 'Tis perfectly intolerable, and anything should be done rather than it should be so."[35]

In retrospect we can see that the Great Awakening was indeed part of the emergence of a transatlantic evangelical movement that would have an immense impact on world history, but in New England it was far from what Edwards hoped for. Rather than being the dawn of an era in which awakened New England would be, in John Wintrhop's famous phrase, a "lighthouse on a hill," the model of a Reformed civilization, the awakening signaled the twilight of the old Puritan version of that ideal. As with most revolutions, the transformation of New England had been taking place gradually, sometimes with little notice. The clergy had already lost much of their authority, and now they could no longer pretend to speak with one voice. Public morals were becoming more like those in England, and even though clergy condemned the laxity, they could not prevent it. Nor was there much hope that the Massachusetts government would support true religion as Edwards understood it. Edwards was correct in recognizing that an unprecedented era was emerging, but his hopes that the new spirit would be contained in the old wineskins of the covenanted Puritan commonwealth led by patriarchs would prove sadly unrealistic.

# CHAPTER 17

# A House Divided

R ather than restoring the dominant place of religion in the colony, the Great Awakening was undermining the already weakened public authority of the old standing clerical order. Not only were laypeople attacking clergy in the name of religion, but any semblance of unity among the congregational clergy was on the brink of collapse. Only gradually was the breach becoming apparent. In Boston, truly New England's hub, a few congregational pastors had been cool to the awakening ever since Whitefield's visit. They were outnumbered, however, nine to three, by proponents of the revival, including all the town's senior pastors.[1] At first, opposition to the revival had been hazardous, as the Reverend Samuel Mather found out in 1741. Mather, son of Cotton Mather, was assistant pastor to pro-revivalist Joshua Gee of Boston's Second Church. Mather had dared to be critical of Whitefield. Friends of the revival said Mather's preaching discouraged "the work of conviction" among parishioners. In summer 1741, a council of local clergy attempted to reconcile the differences between Gee and Mather. The council advised Mather to reform. When soon after they judged he had not, they voted for his dismissal, thus creating bitter dissension and much talk.[2]

Charles Chauncy, junior pastor to Thomas Foxcroft at First Church, was emerging as the spokesman for the minority who were cool to the awakening. Chauncy was respected for his intellect and regarded as essentially orthodox even if he emphasized tolerance and rationality (only later would he emerge as openly liberal). Thirty-six years old in 1741, he was a year younger than Edwards. He was short in stature and assertive in temperament. First Church was known as "Old Brick," and eventually Chauncy picked up the same nickname, perhaps because he resembled a brick both in appearance and in his solid temperament.[3]

During 1741, as tensions over the awakening and the Mather case heightened, Chauncy spoke out cautiously. Some persons were doubtless benefiting from the awakening, he conceded, and regeneration indeed should involve heartfelt experiences. Yet people were easily deceived by uncontrolled emotions. Evangelists who imposed a standardized set of emotional expectations for all the truly regenerate were encouraging a dangerous party spirit. True experience of new birth might take many forms and was often a gradual disciplined process. Similarly, in reference to Mather, Chauncy emphasized that clergy had varieties of gifts and styles and no one pattern should be demanded of all.[4]

By 1742 Chauncy was deeply alarmed at the awakening's excesses. During the visits of Whitefield and even of Tennent there had been few extravagant bodily effects, visions, and trances. Now, especially as a result of the excitements stirred by the itinerants, such as Davenport, Wheelock, Buell, and Pomeroy, such ecstasies were becoming standard, even expected. Judgments against allegedly unconverted persons were commonplace, and congregations were being urged to forsake their pastors. Not only itinerant clergy but now all sorts of laypeople were making unsubstantiated claims to impulses, leadings from the Lord, and visions. Laypeople were exhorting and claiming spiritual authority to which they had no right. Unlike Edwards, who was defending these as peripheral excesses connected with an essentially good work, Chauncy saw the excesses as overwhelming any good that the revival might have done. Such extremes could result only in damage to true religion and irreparable damage to the standing order.[5]

The itinerants, Chauncy now observed, were increasingly preaching in the most extravagant ways, trying to frighten people and otherwise arouse passions. Using vulgar appeals to sentiment, they would generate mass hysteria that they encouraged people to regard as evidence of the work of the Holy Spirit. Scores or even hundreds of people would shriek, swoon, or fall into fits. " 'Tis scarce imaginable" wrote Chauncy, "what excesses and extravagancies people were running into, and even encouraged in. . . . In the same house [of worship], and at the same time, some would be *praying,* some *exhorting,* some *singing,* some *clapping their hands,* some *laughing* some *crying,* some *shrieking and roaring out.*" Often the worst effects, Chauncy observed, would be at night. "It is in the *evening,* or more late in the *night* with

Charles Chauncy (1705–87) in his later years, when he was known as "Old Brick"

only a *few candles* in a *meeting-house*, that there is a *screaming* and *shrieking* to the greatest degree; and the persons thus affected are generally *children, young people*, and *women*." Anyone who dared criticize any of these improprieties would be dismissed as "an *opposer* of the *Spirit*, and a *child of the Devil.*"

To make matters worse, supposed converts might then immediately become exhorters. These might even be women or children, though they were "most commonly raw, illiterate, weak and conceited *young men, or lads*." Such fledgling exhorters would be "generally much better thought of than any ministers, except those in the *New Way.*" Chauncy, a champion of good order and deference, was appalled at these departures from the hard-won traditions of decorum of the New England way.[6]

As itinerants increasingly made ecstatic religion the norm and encouraged disparagement of the authority of any who dared criticize them, Chauncy felt correspondingly bold to speak out. A backlash was developing and he was articulating its sentiments. Friends of the revival sensed the changing atmosphere. Young Samuel Buell, who was preaching in Boston in April 1742 soon after his triumph in Northampton, reported great success but also noted a fast-growing opposition that made one "tremble to think" of the sequel.[7] In mid-May, on a day called by First Church for prayer for the outpouring of the Holy Spirit, Chauncy took off the gloves. While urging that Bostonians should indeed pray for the outpouring of the Spirit, he emphasized that they should also recognize that much that was going on was "a dishounor to God, and may have a tendency greatly to obstruct the progress of real and substantial religion." Bitterness, evil speaking, slander, and lay exhorters showing contempt for pastors were not God's work. Sensationalists were betraying people by overheating their imaginations and calling the result true religion.[8]

During the next two months, Chauncy's case that the awakening was out of control was made for him by James Davenport. The most controversial of the itinerants had returned to Connecticut still in the role of the wild-eyed prophet. The Connecticut General Assembly, meeting in May and alarmed at divisions in its parish churches, was in a strongly anti-revival mood and had just passed a stringent law banning itinerancy except by invitation of the local pastor.[9] Near the end of May citizens of Stratford, Connecticut, brought a complaint that Davenport and Benjamin Pomeroy were agitating for a church schism there. The two were arrested in New Haven (where they were abetting another church separation) and brought before the Assembly in Hartford for a hearing. During much of the two-day proceedings Davenport continued to preach and prophesy whenever he could. The Assembly dismissed the case against Pomeroy, who seemed mild by comparison. Davenport, however, they declared under such "*enthusiastical impressions and impulses, and thereby disturbed in the rational faculties of his mind,* and therefore to be pitied and compassionated, and not to be treated as otherwise he might be."[10] The Assembly ordered to have him transported back to his parish on Long Island.

Neither the Long Island Sound nor the Connecticut Assembly was sufficient to stop a prophet. Davenport heard in the voice of God that his opposition in Connecticut was pointing him toward a greater mission. Before the end of June, there he was in Boston itself. The pro-revivalist clergy were chagrined, alarmed at the damage he might do. The association of local pastors happened to be meeting, and they immediately called Davenport in for an interview. They quickly saw that he was as untamed as ever. The association published a sharp attack on Davenport's excesses and disorderly behavior. Almost all the pastors of Boston signed the document. Conspicuous in its absence, however, was the name of Charles Chauncy, who apparently had been at the discussions. The document, of which Benjamin Colman was the first signatory, concluded with an affirmation of "the great and glorious work of God" in the awakening despite the "devices of Satan against it, of one kind or another," including "the imprudence of its friends, or by the virulent opposition of its enemies."[11]

Chauncy was rapidly moving toward a campaign of all-out opposition to the awakening. The last straw, if one were needed, was that Davenport made a personal call on Chauncy to "inquire into the *reason of the hope that was in me*." Chauncy instead gave him the reasons why he believed Davenport was under "a heated imagination" and deluded. "'Tis too evident to be denied," he told the itinerant, "that you often take the *motions of your own mind for divine communication*."

Chauncy took the occasion of the Sunday after the Harvard commencement in July, while many visiting clergy were in town, to fulminate directly against "enthusiasm." He had the sermon quickly published, prefaced by an open letter to Davenport. Chauncy argued both that the work of the Spirit was more restrained in the current era than it was in New Testament times and that the New Testament expressly forbade many revivalist practices (such as disorderliness and women speaking in the assemblies). "*Enthusiasm,*" he said, "'tis properly a disease, a sort of madness." Almost anyone might be infected by it, but those prone to melancholy were especially susceptible. God was working in New England, but for the Spirit to be effective, religious affections must be strictly restrained by Scripture and by reason. The enthusiasts were defying this fundamental principle.[12]

Chauncy could now speak his mind openly since Davenport's visit had thrown the friends of revival into such disarray. Thomas Prince recorded that a "disputatious spirit most grievously prevailed amongst us" and that "every party" was "sadly guilty" of lamentable acrimony. Davenport stayed in the region inflaming the situation by repeatedly denouncing most of the Boston clergy as unconverted and "leading their people blindfold to hell." He urged the laity to rebel against their lukewarm pastors. "Pull them down; turn them out, and put others in their places." Finally, after nearly two months of notable forbearance, the Boston authorities had heard enough. They collected sufficient evidences of Davenport's incendiary and seditious statements to have him arrested. Still, several of the clergy, led by the venerable Benjamin Colman, petitioned the court for leniency. The court agreed, ruling as in Connecticut that Davenport was under delusions and hence that when he had condemned the ministers he had been non compos mentis.[13]

Edwards remained undeterred in defense of the awakening despite the contentions, the disorders, and the divisions that were dogging it in 1742. Although there is no evidence that he visited Boston during the time of the Davenport fracas, everything that happened in Boston was widely publicized, and he kept closely apprised of such matters. The events of 1735 and since had confirmed his view that the greater the success, the greater would be Satan's counterattacks. So the Northampton pastor persevered, giving almost all his time to tending or defending the awakening. The greater the controversies, the more urgently he worked on *Some Thoughts Concerning the Present Revival of Religion,* which he believed could settle many of the disputed issues.

Chauncy also was turning all his energies toward the awakening, fighting what he saw as mass hysteria that had seized his native land. Like a good eighteenth-century scientist, he sent scores of letters to correspondents throughout New England and collected large files of accounts of abuses. He backed up these accounts with firsthand observations, making a three-month tour of New England, New York, and New Jersey, tracking the steps of the most notorious of the itinerants. By the time Edwards' massive argument was available in March 1743, Chauncy was well armed to focus his projected volume as a refutation of the revivalist champion.

Chauncy's increasingly open anti-awakening campaign contributed to a steadily widening rupture among the Congregational clergy. Even some who had welcomed Whitefield and rejoiced in the numerous conversions were now having second thoughts as they were confronted with the extravagant ecstasies, the disorders, the insubordination, and even schisms encouraged by some of the itinerants. The standing order was falling apart; the only question was, who was responsible, the awakeners or their opponents?

Although Chauncy and some others of the anti-revivalists either were or became mildly liberal in their theologies, the anti-revivalist or Old Light movement, as it was coming to be called, reflected a genuine conservatism about the New England way that might appeal to persons across the theological spectrum. Chauncy himself was deeply loyal to what he considered the essence of the Puritan heritage. Perhaps the best evidence of this conservative impulse was that ever since the Timothy Cutler defection he had been strongly anti-Anglican and had been collecting data for a projected volume on the dangers of episcopacy. On the eve of the American Revolution, in 1771, when fears of an American bishop helped unite New Englanders against England, he finally published *A Compleat View of Episcopacy*. Throughout his career Chauncy was ready to fight for a New England based on true religion and good order.[14] In 1742 orthodox as well as Arminian-leaning clergy might view the disorders of the awakening as a dangerous threat to the standing order. That was especially true in Connecticut where the "Old Light" label seems to have first developed.

Edwards was stung by an ominous defection of one of his former allies from the Williams clan. Late in 1742 Jonathan Ashley, pastor at Deerfield, made a dramatic attack on the revival. Ashley, who had married William Williams' daughter Dorothy, had been a faithful ally in the efforts of the Williams family as long as the patriarch had lived. He had supported the clan in the Breck case and had presided over revivals in Deerfield in both 1735 and 1741. Now with William Williams gone and Edwards taking on the mantel of leadership, family resentments may have begun to play a role. Dorothy Ashley was, after all, the sister of Israel Williams, and her husband was now emerging as part of the younger generation who were cool toward their cousin Edwards, or at least toward his style of religious leadership.

Ashley's public disavowal of the Edwardsean position caused a minor sensation. In November 1742 the Deerfield minister was the guest preacher at Boston's Brattle Street Church, served by Benjamin Colman and William Cooper and a headquarters for the awakening in Boston. Whatever his hosts may have expected, the tone of his sermon was so offensive to some of the congregation that they walked out. Ashley preached that there was a close parallel between the notorious disorders in the New Testament church at Corinth and the present awakening. The church assemblies in both instances had become mad confusion as women as well as men spoke out whenever they felt moved by the Spirit. Insubordination was rife, wives judged their husbands, parishioners condemned the clergy, strife and lack of charity prevailed. The Pauline solution of I Corinthians 13 was that the highest gift of the Spirit was charity.[15]

William Cooper was indignant that a critic of the revival should thus wrap himself in the cloak of charity. Cooper was further incensed that Ashley was so brash as to have his controversial sermon published. In response, Cooper published a letter on the front page of the *Boston Gazette*, and an ugly squabble among the clergy ensued in the newspapers during the winter of 1742–43.[16]

By the time Edwards' *Some Thoughts* was off the Boston press in March 1743, his optimistic intimations that New England might have a glorious role to play in the approach of the millennium already looked dated. Not only were the clergy at each other's throats, James Davenport was back in New England, wilder than ever.

This time Davenport had shown up in New London, Connecticut, on the coast near Rhode Island. New London was one of several coastal towns where the awakening had led to a church separation. It was also a center for revivalist or New Light activities since a local evangelist, Timothy Allen, had organized the "Shepherd's Tent" as a revivalist school that was to rival Yale. About a dozen teenage boys studied there. On the Sabbath of March 6, Davenport led the separatist group, which numbered about a hundred mostly young people, in a ceremonial religious book burning to signal their purity from the corrupt New England establishment. The books included leading Puritan and Congregational works in divinity, such as those by John Flavel, Increase Mather, and Benjamin Colman. The next day, turning to the problem of idolatry, Davenport ordered his people to burn jewelry, wigs, cloaks, night-gowns, and any item of clothes that Davenport said they loved too much. According to a widely circulated story, Davenport, appearing physically ill and crazier than ever, threw his only pair of breeches on to the pile. A more moderate New Light intervened and raised the possibility that Davenport might be possessed by the devil.[17]

A few weeks later Edwards was on a preaching tour in Connecticut. On March 25, he wrote to Sarah from his sister Abigail Metcalf's home in Lebanon that his return would be delayed because a number of clergy had prevailed on him to go to New London to try to calm the storm. He had said he would not go unless some other ministers went with him, and they had now assembled a delegation including his cousin Solomon Williams, Joseph Meacham, and, probably most importantly, Benjamin Pomeroy, Davenport's sometimes associate.[18] By the time they arrived in New London, several others, including Joseph Bellamy and Samuel Buell, had joined the council. Edwards, who led the delegation, preached "a Lecture Sermon . . . very suitable for the times to bear witness against the prevailing disorders and distractions . . . of enthusiasm."[19]

This council of New Lights was a great success and a credit to Edwards' leadership in shaping a major branch of the party that defended the awakening's new practices while shunning its separatism and excesses. Most of the New London separatists went back to their original congregations.

Davenport was apparently chastened and began to listen to the continuing ministrations of his colleagues, especially Solomon Williams and Eleazar Wheelock (who had been preaching in Northampton when Edwards visited New London). The next year Edwards played a direct role in Davenport's rehabilitation. At that time Edwards assured Wheelock that "Mr. Davenport is truly very much altered" and further that "I think he is now fully satisfied in his duty in making a public, humble, and suitable recantation and confession of his great errors." Two weeks later Davenport completed such a letter and gave it to Solomon Williams, who sent it to Thomas Prince for publication. It reads like pages out of *Some Thoughts*. "Several of the appendages to this glorious work," confessed Davenport, "are no essential parts thereof, but of a different and contrary nature and tendency." He retracted his judging people unconverted, separatism, lay preaching, and listening to impulses or supposed messages from God. Now he believed that in his zeal for these errors and other nonessentials he had been led by a "false Spirit," especially in the matter of the book and clothes burnings in New London.[20]

Edwards shared many of the concerns of Chauncy and the Old Lights for good order, but he believed it could be maintained by simply teaching New Lights to follow the old rules of authority and deference. For instance, he deplored lay preaching, a common practice among those who caught the awakening spirit. When he heard that former Northampton resident Deacon Moses Lyman was "exhorting a public congregation," he urged him to desist. Although lay preaching might seem to do good in the short run, God had "appointed a certain particular order of men to that work and office." If everyone were allowed to preach the result would be chaos. Lyman might admonish privately, but not to public congregations or "by set speech to counsel a room full of people, unless it be children, or those that are much your inferior."[21]

Early in 1743 Edwards met with a ministerial council in Westfield, Massachusetts, to deal with the similar but more difficult case of Bathsheba Kingsley, an ardent New Light who was in dispute with her husband. Two years earlier Mrs. Kingsley had confessed before the Westfield congregation that, in her zeal to witness in neighboring towns, she was guilty of "stealing a horse [and] riding away on the Sabbath with[ou]t her husband's consent." Now she was back at it. According to the council, she spent almost all her time in her own and neighboring towns "wandering about from house to house under a notion of doing Christ's work and delivering his messages." Frequently these messages involved denunciations of local ministers. The council, for whom Edwards drafted the response, seemed intent on re-habilitation rather than punishment. They judged her as wanting in self-knowledge, humility, and in discernment of the workings of God's Spirit and not having her "will subdued to God." They observed that she was of a "weak vapory habit of body" and that Satan had taken advantage of that weakness. (Though a "vapory spirit" suggested female flightiness, the diagnosis resembled that of Davenport.) Her soul had been "for some years . . . almost in a continual tumult, like the sea in a storm; being destitute of that peace and rest in God that many other Christians enjoy." Nonetheless, as in the case of Moses Lyman, they advised that she might continue to witness so long as it was proper to "her station." In her case that meant in the home or when privately visiting neighbors. After much effort, the council persuaded her to agree to these limits and to due subordination to her husband. When she criticized him it ought not be with rough and severe language but "privately in an humble submissive loving manner." They advised her husband, in turn, to "treat her in patience and gentleness without hard words or blows."[22]

By spring 1743 it was too late to restrain the New Light movement by counseling proper deference. With Wheelocks and Kingsleys appearing all over the countryside, there were too many fires to be put out one by one. Too many chain reactions had been set in motion. More lay preachers were condemning clergy, fostering separatist groups in which spiritual excitements were normative. Some of the radical separatist congregations would become Baptist, others would be separatist congregational. Even though most of the scores of separations took place in the subsequent years, there were already enough by 1743 to generate a major conservative reaction against the revival. Eventually about one-third of the churches of Connecticut and one-fifth of those in Massachusetts suffered schism.[23] Once schisms became common, accompanied as they always were by bitter accusations and recriminations, peaceful coexistence among the several parties became impossible.

In Connecticut the conservative reaction had the most bite. The anti-itinerancy laws of May 1742 provided a weapon to restrain the more enthusiastic evangelists. Both Benjamin Pomeroy and Eleazar Wheelock lost tax support for their ministries and had to resort to voluntary contributions from their congregations. Samuel Finley (later the president of the College of New Jersey [Princeton]), a visiting Presbyterian, was arrested under the law as a vagrant when he tried to preach in New Haven. In May 1743 the Old Light legislature took a more extreme step to inhibit church separations: it repealed a 1708 statute that recognized the right to religious dissent. Dissenting groups could still appeal to the Assembly for relief from having to support Connecticut's established churches, but they would have to prove that they truly were neither congregationalist nor presbyterian.

Cousin Elisha Williams, formerly Yale rector, now engaged in business and politics, became the principal New Light spokesman against these repressive laws. In 1744 he published a treatise against these statutes. Drawing on the Lockean and dissenting Commonwealth tradition in England, he offered one of the most important statements of the era on religious liberty.[24]

Edwards too found the laws outrageous. In 1742 when he had written in *Some Thoughts* that civil governments should support the awakening, he was aiming a barb at Connecticut's Assembly for doing just the opposite. In 1743, although he was loathe to publicly endorse separatism, he nonetheless could not help sympathizing privately with a New Light separatist group in Milford, Connecticut, who were attempting to join a New York presbytery. "It is manifest," Edwards wrote in December 1743 to the New York Presbyterians, "that there [are] many in that government [Connecticut] under the most terrible oppression both from civil and ecclesiastical authority." In such situations, it is not required "for these people to yield up themselves in matters of infinite consequences into the hands of those who are . . . their embittered enemies . . . even to that degree of prejudice and spirit that appears to me a sort of madness."[25]

Shortly thereafter he wrote to his first cousin Elnathan Whitman (their mothers were Stoddard sisters), pastor of Second Church of Hartford, from which some New Light parishioners had seceded. Edwards had been Whitman's tutor at Yale, and with as much restraint as he could muster, he lectured the younger man on liberty of conscience. Even if, as was likely, the seceders were ignorant common people whose complaints against Whitman were ill-founded, Edwards argued, their scruples were likely honest and conscientious. In that case, it would be a violation of liberty of conscience to use the law to try to coerce them in matters concerning eternal salvation.[26] Edwards' social and ecclesiastical conservatism was here tempered by a long-standing principle of Puritan dissent.

While Old Light versus New Light differences were hardening into political parties that would define Connecticut politics until the Revolutionary era, in Massachusetts the most remarkable public break was between contending factions of the clergy. In May 1743 the anti-awakening clergy, which had been on the defensive until then, managed a small coup. Each year many of the Massachusetts clergy came to Boston in May for the opening of the colonial legislature. Customarily the clergy met in a "General Convention of Congregational Ministers of Massachusetts" to discuss and make advisory pronouncements on matters of current interest. Edwards was apparently at this May 1743 gathering.[27]

The Old Lights, finding themselves with a slight majority, threw the meeting into a turmoil by drafting a *Testimony of the Pastors of the Churches in the Province of Massachusetts Bay* condemning a number of the practices associated with the awakening, including reliance on "impulses" (which they compared to Antinomianism), uninvited itinerancy, lay preaching, separatism, censorious judging of who is "unconverted," and enthusiastic disorders. Almost everyone agreed in renouncing these errors, but the friends of the awakening insisted that these condemnations be balanced by ones condemning Arminianism as well as Antinomianism and especially by praise for the legitimate blessings of the awakening. After heated debate and complicated attempts at redrafting, the Old Lights prevailed.

The New Lights, alarmed that a group of some forty pastors, about one-fifth of those in the whole province, were speaking as though for the whole, immediately organized a counterconvention. Meeting in July in conjunction with the Harvard commencement, this group was headed by the leading Bostonian friends of the awakening, Benjamin Colman, Thomas Prince, Joseph Sewall, William Cooper, Thomas Foxcroft, and Joshua Gee. Their *Testimony and Advice* effusively praised the awakening as the greatest they had seen. They also condemned nearly the same sets of excesses as had the opponents of the awakening, but they essentially took the line that Edwards had so fully developed—that the excesses were peripheral. Sixty-eight of those present signed this testimony, and another forty-five added their names by letter. Edwards, who declined another lengthy journey, sent a letter of support signed by seven pro-awakening pastors from Hampshire County. Ominously, despite vigorous efforts to solicit wide support, these seven represented a minority of the Hampshire clergy.[28]

In Boston the acrimony among the clergy was amplified by the even less polite debates in the public press. On the pro-awakening side, in March 1743 Thomas Prince inaugurated *Christian History*, a weekly periodical edited by his son Tom, a recent Harvard graduate, containing news of the ongoing international revivals.[29] The fifty-six-year-old Prince Sr. was the most learned Boston pastor, an expert in scientific matters and author of a history of New England, who was sometimes compared to the late Cotton Mather. Prince had become Edwards' closest friend in Boston, and the Edwards family enjoyed visiting in the Prince household. Like his other close relation-ships, Edwards' friendship with Prince was based on thorough dedication to a common cause. Edwards' *Faithful Narrative* had been a model of how pub-lication could promote revival, and Edwards shared Prince's enthusiasm for *Christian History*.

Thomas Fleet, publisher of the *Boston Evening Post*, responded by ridi-culing the proposed new publication. By its own admission, *Christian History* planned to publish only positive accounts of the revival. Fleet proposed as an alternative "to publish the *progress of enthusiasm* in all *ages* and *nations*, with the confusions consequent upon it." Jonathan Ashley of Deerfield, relishing the anti-revivalist role he had established in his debate with Cooper, joined the attack. Fleet made anti-revival communications a leading feature of his weekly paper. Both Ashley and Fleet accused Thomas Prince Sr. of disin-genuousness in saying that young Tom Jr. was the editor, when they were sure Thomas Sr. controlled the publication. Fleet also published separately *A Letter from a Gentleman in Scotland, To His Friend in New England*, sneering at recent narratives of a "great awakening" in Scotland. Accounts of recent spectacular revivals said to have transformed whole Scottish towns were one of the inspirations for *Christian History*. When Tom Prince attempted to rebut Fleet, the publisher simply resorted to ridicule. The front page letter of the *Evening Post* for July 4, 1743 (the week of the Harvard Commencement when the New Lights were meeting) was addressed to "Master Tommy." Referring to the younger Prince as "little master" and "child," Fleet con-cluded that "I look upon it as a wonderful thing that one who undertakes to be a writer of *Christian History* especially relating to Scotland, should be so totally ignorant of its affairs."[30]

Less than twenty years earlier the Boston clerical establishment, led by the Mathers, had been able to suppress James Franklin's *New England Cou-rant*, but that time must have seemed light-years away. Now the clergy were so much at each other's throats that laymen on both sides felt free to condemn their ministerial "superiors." The publishers, happy to combine principles with profits, thrived on the debates that the newspapers took into the streets and the taverns. No one any longer could presume to command general respect simply because of his ministerial office.

Chauncy's *Seasonable Thoughts on the State of Religion in New England* appeared in September in this acrimonious context. The volume listed more than five hundred subscribers, not only clergy but also prominent laymen. Perry Miller referred to it aptly as the New England "social register," with

Governor William Shirley heading the list.[31] Though Chauncy had been collecting materials during the previous fall and winter, he had put most of it together after Edwards' volume appeared in March. (In our day of high-speed technology it would have taken the publisher alone at least a year to produce such a theological volume.) Chauncy's title alluded to Edwards' own, and he attacked many of the Northampton pastor's points directly. He also filled most of the volume with quotations from his own collected observations or from respected authorities, so that his volume at 424 pages was even weightier than Edwards' at 378.[32]

Since Edwards had already acknowledged most of the excesses of the awakening, Chauncy's argument did not depend, except for effect, so much on evidences he had collected as on what one saw as central and what as peripheral. Chauncy, who presented his case within an orthodox Calvinist framework, saw Scripture and reason as the normative guides for the New England way. The recent agitations, he argued, were a repetition of the antinomian controversy of the time of Anne Hutchinson. New England's order and unity had been hard won against persistent dangers of uncontrolled emotions.[33] He also compared the excesses of the awakening to other excesses throughout church history, such as the particularly notorious French Prophets who had arisen among Huguenots (another Reformed group) after the revocation of the Edict of Nantes and were known for especially bizarre hyperspiritual behavior. The disorders brought by the recent enthusiasm, far from being peripheral, said Chauncy, were essential distinguishing features of the current revivalism. Although God surely continued to work in New England and some people may have been truly converted, these excesses should be regarded like any other heresy. They were warnings and punishments from God against delusive practices that would lead people away from true faith.[34]

Underlying the differences between Edwards and Chauncy on the awakening was a crucial philosophical issue. "The plain truth is," wrote Chauncy, "an *enlightened mind,* and not *raised affections,* ought always be the guide of those who call themselves men; and this, in the affairs of religion, as well as other things."[35] Chauncy's view of the human psyche, one of the common theories of the time adapted from ancient Greek philosophy, was that the affections were most essentially related to the passions of one's animal nature, which needed to be restrained by the higher faculty of reason.

Edwards explicitly attacked this low view of the affections in *Seasonable Thoughts* as based on "philosophy" rather than Scripture. "Some make philosophy instead of the Holy Scriptures their rule of judging of this work," he chided, "particularly the philosophical notions they entertain of the nature of the soul, its faculties and affections." To be consistent with the biblical viewpoint, he insisted, one had to recognize that "the affections of the soul are not properly distinguished from the will, as though they were two faculties in the soul." By identifying religious affections with the will, Edwards was making them integral to a higher faculty. There were, of course, base passions, arising from one's animal nature, that misled and on which one could not rely. Yet surely the exalted affections arising from a true sensible knowledge of God should not be classed with such lower impulses. Only rigid philosophical categories that ignored biblical accounts of the affecting character of a change of heart would fail to make such a critical distinction.[36]

Edwards applied these principles in a revealing statement on the nature of good preaching. Critics of the awakenings alleged that when people heard many sermons in one week they would not be able to remember much of what they had heard. Edwards countered, "The main benefit that is obtained by preaching is by impression made upon the mind in the time of it, and not by the effect that arises afterwards by a remembrance of what was delivered."[37] Preaching, in other words, must first of all touch the affections.

As any perusal of Edwards' sermons will confirm, Edwards' exaltation of the affections was never at the expense of reason. Even bodily effects, such as crying out or falling down, he said, were legitimate when "excited by preaching the important truths of God's Word, urged and enforced by proper arguments and motives."[38] He insisted that religious sentiments must be tested for their consistency with reason as well as with Scripture. In other contexts, Edwards had referred to reason as the "noblest" or "highest" faculty.[39] Although he repeatedly emphasized the distinction between mere speculative knowledge and the sensible or practical knowledge of the heart, he also consistently maintained, as he had put it in a 1739 sermon, that "a speculative knowledge is also of infinite importance in this respect, that without it we can have no spiritual or practical knowledge."[40] Chauncy admired Edwards' intellect and in fact commented in *Seasonable Thoughts* that it was odd that Edwards questioned the priority of reason when he "made use of more *philosophy* . . . than anyone that I know of."[41]

Chauncy was well aware, of course, that the underlying debate was an old and familiar one even in Puritan circles. Chauncy stood for the "intellectualist" and more Aristotelian (and Thomistic) tradition, which argued that the will should follow the best dictates of reason. Edwards was in the more

Augustinian "voluntarist" camp that viewed the whole person as guided by affections of the will.[42] Both agreed that the spiritual person had to be strictly guided by Scripture and reason. But the voluntarist emphasized that the intellect, without true affections, was insufficient for true religion. The proper affections of the will must reign in tandem with intellectual truth. The intellectualist, by contrast, saw the affections as first of all unruly emotions, which could serve the good only when brought into submission to properly informed reason. The distinctions were subtle but they could be of immense practical consequence in shaping one's style of religious expression.

Such fine distinctions would be lost—at least for the time being—because events had put Edwards at such a disastrous disadvantage in this much-heralded cannonade exchange between the two great champions. The state of New England in the fall of 1743, when Chauncy's volume appeared, was vastly different from its condition in the fall of 1742, when Edwards had completed his volume. Edwards' account with its glowing picture of bright lights of the Holy Spirit far outshining any peripheral excesses was already out of date. The general revival was rapidly diminishing while much of its remaining fervor was turning into censorious separatism. Chauncy's volume, in contrast, proved truly "seasonable." Increasingly, the portrayal of the events as dangerous disorders typical of the recurrence of radical sectarianism gained plausibility. Within the New England clerical establishment a substantial New Light party remained, dedicated to defending and promoting continuing revival. Yet now they could never be more than a party.

Edwards not only recognized this calamity but also acknowledged that it had been brought on by the excesses of the friends of the revival, who thus opened the door for its enemies. In May 1743, at the time the breach among the Massachusetts clergy was becoming open, Edwards described the current state of New England in a letter to the Reverend James Robe of Kilsyth, Scotland. Revival fires had been sweeping Scotland at almost the same time as the Great Awakening in New England, so the connection with their Scottish Presbyterian counterparts was becoming tremendously important to the New England proponents of revival. Robe's revivalist experience closely paralleled those of Edwards. He had recently published his own *Faithful Narrative*, describing an overwhelming revival in Kilsyth, much like the one in Northampton in 1734–35. Edwards, while rejoicing to hear continuing good news from Scotland, lamented, "we have not such joyful news to send you; the clouds have lately thickened." New England was now sadly divided into two parties. "This is," Edwards added, "very much owing to imprudent management in the friends of the work, and a corrupt mixture which Satan has found means to introduce, and our manifold sinful errors, by which we have grieved and quenched the Spirit of God."[43]

That Edwards was, remarkably, blaming the radical New Lights rather than the Old Lights for the breakup of New England into censorious parties, reflected in part his experience in Northampton. Writing to Thomas Prince in December 1743, in a letter for publication in *Christian History* (and hence casting matters in as positive a light as he could), Edwards acknowledged that in 1742 the Northampton awakening had been corrupted by "our people hearing, and some of them seeing the work in other places, where there was a greater visible commotion than here, and the outward appearances were more extraordinary." The Northamptonites "were ready to think that the work in those places far excelled what was amongst us; and their eyes were dazzled with the high profession and great show that some made who came hither from other places." Edwards attributed the decline of the awakening to the corruptions introduced by these excesses. Some people were deluded by apparent raptures of joy and being bodily overcome, and they proved to have less the temperament of "humble, amiable, eminent Christians" than many who were not so overcome.[44]

In his letter to Robe, he provided a concise summary of what he had learned from seeing two revivals come and go. Gentleness and genuinely self-renouncing humility were far better evidences of true saintliness than were merely intense experiences. "Many among us have been ready to think, that all high raptures are divine," Edwards explained, "but experience plainly shows, that it is not the degree of rapture and ecstasy (although it should be to the third heavens), but the nature and kind that must determine us in their favor." Genuine raptures would be accompanied not by a "noisy showy humility," but rather by "deep humiliation, brokenness of heart, poverty of spirit, mourning for sin, solemnity of spirit, a trembling reverence towards God, tenderness of spirit, self-jealousy and fear, and great engagedness of heart, after holiness of life, and a readiness to esteem others better than themselves."[45]

## Religious Affections

Edwards had done his best to make these points to the Northamptonites. As the awakening was receding, defeated by its own excesses, he had preached a series of sermons on the proper place of religious affections in the Christian life.[46] During the next several years he revised and extensively expanded these into his *Treatise on Religious Affections,* which finally appeared in 1746. This careful exposition was immediately reprinted in England and remains the most widely read and admired of his theological works.

If put in the context of Edwards' deeply sobered assessment of the awakening as he viewed it after it exploded into what he saw as delusive enthusiasm in 1742, it is clear that *Religious Affections* was not just another volley in the exchange with Chauncy, as might be supposed. Rather, unlike his earlier two awakening works, which were first of all designed to show critics that ecstatic phenomena did not prove anything one way or the other, *Affections* was directed first of all toward the misguided emphases of the extreme New Lights who had led many people into arrogant self-delusion. Far more damage has been done throughout church history, he emphasized in his preface, by the seeming friends of true religion than by its open enemies. Satan's most effective device was that while believers were fending off open opposition in front of them "the devil comes behind 'em, and give a fatal stab unseen." Satan's essential stratagem in such sneak attacks was to counterfeit true religious experience and thus to fatally corrupt religious movements. Simulated religious experiences could seduce the unregenerate into one of the most pernicious forms of self-aggrandizement. "By this means, he [Satan] brings in, even the friends of religion, insensibly to themselves, to do the work of enemies, by destroying religion, in a far more effectual manner, than open enemies can do."[47]

Secondarily, though not incidentally, Edwards was also providing an answer to Chauncy. The opening section of the treatise was a concise defense of the proposition that "True religion, in great part, consists in holy affections." Rather than thinking of the affections as primarily related to the inferior animal passions, as Chauncy did, "the affections of the soul" were really not distinct from the will which directed the whole person. The will, or one's inclinations or loves, might be called the "heart" of the whole person. Moreover, "The Holy Scriptures do everywhere place religion very much in the affections; such as fear hope, love, hatred, desire, joy, sorrow, gratitude, compassion and zeal."[48]

Yet Edwards' first concern remained with those who already shared his own premises of the centrality of religious affections. For them the crucial question was how to tell true religion from its Satanic counterfeits. Merely raised affections, as he had said in his earlier treatises, were not decisive evidence one way or the other. He reiterated the point here by expounding briefly on twelve signs (essentially various displays of religious fervor) that were "No Certain Signs that Religious Affections Are Truly Gracious, or They Are Not." He followed these with a much longer section, the heart of the treatise, on twelve "Distinguishing Signs of Truly Gracious and Holy Affections."

One might have supposed, from this systematic format, that Edwards was providing definitive tests for distinguishing true believers from self-deluded counterfeits. Instead, he took the greatest care to argue that such a project was impossible. Only God could judge the heart. All one ever encounters is the "outward manifestations and appearances."[49] Judging true affections was like trying to judge objects beyond our clear view. "A fixed star [a true believer] is easily distinguishable from a comet [an enthusiastic hypocrite] in a clear sky; but if we view them through a cloud, it may be impossible to see the difference." From his scientific thinking Edwards was always alert to the problems of perception (such as when we perceive the color green, we encounter only the power of a leaf to make us see green). Though he did not go into that difficult analogy in dealing with the issue of judging spiritual things, he did point out that not only is the object beyond our adequate vision, but also "the prevalence of corruption . . . darkens the sight as to all spiritual objects, of which grace is one." "Sin," he went on to explain, "is like some distempers of the eyes, that make things to appear of different colors from which properly belong to them, and like many other distempers, that put the mouth out of taste."[50]

Even individuals, then, could not rely simply on looking within to their own intense spiritual experiences, however luminous. As he had in *A Divine and Supernatural Light*, Edwards described the "spiritual sense" that he associated with his "First Sign" of genuine affections. This sense, which was a restoration of a love for divine things lost in the Fall, was not a new faculty, but "a new foundation laid in the nature of the soul" for the exercise of the existing faculties. Regeneration, in other words, changed the whole person by changing the love at the heart of the person's being. The resulting spiritual sense was wonderfully different from anything previously experienced. So Edwards, in a celebrated allusion to Locke, compared the new sense to "what some metaphysicians call a new simple idea."[51] Despite all that, however, this direct empirical experience was not sufficient proof that the experience was genuine.

Edwards' "First Sign" was not about individuals' experience (which has been a tendency in American evangelicalism ever since the awakening) but rather about the divine origin of that experience. As he summarized the sign, it was not an empirical test but a tautology: "Affections that are truly spiritual and gracious, do arise from those influences and operations on the heart, which are *spiritual, supernatural* and *divine.*"[52] Genuine experiences of such divine work had certain features that could be identified. Yet, invaluable as such experiences were to the true believer, Edwards as the scientific observer warned that sin could warp the perceptions and Satan could produce counterfeits of these features. So one could never be sure on the basis of seemingly profound experience alone.

In mounting his all-out attack on radical New Lights who relied so readily on subjective feelings, Edwards was drawing on both his own youthful searchings and his disheartening experience of having been misled by some of his parishioners in Northampton. One of the poignant passages in *Religious Affections,* if one realizes the degree of Edwards' disappointment with some of his most promising converts at the time he was writing, is one that begins: "It has been a common thing in the church of God, for such bright professors, that are received as eminent saints, among the saints, to fall away and come to nothing." Edwards went on at length to describe these apparent saints who seemed to go through all the proper preparatory steps, who displayed all the proper depths of contrition and heights of joy, and who seemed to validate their faith with abundance of tears, love for Scripture, praise for God, love for others, and on and on. Finally he almost cried out: "How great therefore may the resemblance be, as to all outward expressions and appearances, between an hypocrite and a true saint!"[53]

The devil often prevailed against awakenings by manufacturing counterfeits, as he had in the apostolic times, during the Reformation, and in New England "about an hundred years ago." Although Edwards avoided using the term "Antinomian," as Chauncy and others derisively did, he clearly had in mind the controversy surrounding Anne Hutchinson. Radical New Lights, as Hutchinson before them, used heightened subjective experiences as a basis for establishing their own authority and then for judging others. "I know of no directions or counsels which Christ ever delivered more plainly," Edwards responded, "than the rules he has given us, to guide us in our judging of others' sincerity; viz. that we should judge the tree chiefly by the fruit; but yet this won't do; but other ways are found out, which are imagined to be more distinguishing and certain."[54]

Edwards' treatise was indeed a powerful defense of the primacy of religious affections, but the bulk of its argument was an attack on the authority

of subjective experience alone. Since the overwhelming danger in any awakening was self-aggrandizing self-deception, Edwards looked for signs that
would be checks against these Satan-inspired vices. Several of his twelve signs
of genuine affections had to do with God being truly both the source and the
object of the affections. Those signs that had a subjective dimension emphasized self-renunciation and gentleness, as in the signs he designated as "evangelical humility," a "lamblike, dovelike spirit," and "tenderness of spirit." True
affections would be manifest in a "beautiful symmetry and proportion" of
virtues, as opposed to the imbalance often seen in the meteoric zeal of the
hypocrites.

One can see autobiographical reflections in these signs of true affections.
For instance, cultivating a "lamblike, dovelike spirit" and "tenderness of
spirit," were goals of his own spiritual discipline, especially difficult to achieve
for someone in authority. He deplored a proud, censorious spirit and worked
hard to suppress it in himself. Likewise, in his account of "evangelical humility" he explored the paradox of how the truly eminent saints would not think
of themselves as eminent as compared with others. Drawing on his aesthetic
understanding of the relation between good and evil, he observed that the
greater one's sense of the glories and perfections of the divine, the greater
one's own sense of deformity. Hence, while acknowledging that genuine
saints might know that they have some true grace, he concluded his exposition of humility with a scathing condemnation of those who set their saintliness on a pedestal or assumed their own spiritual superiority. "And this may
be laid down as an infallible thing: *that the person who is apt to think that he, as
compared with others, is a very eminent saint . . . in whom this is a first thought,
that rises of itself, and naturally offers itself, he is certainly mistaken.*"[55]

The culmination of all the evidences of grace was the twelfth sign, that
"Gracious and holy affections have their exercise and fruit in Christian practice." Edwards gave by far the longest attention to this test. "Religion consists
much in holy affections;" he repeated, "but those exercises of affection which
are most distinguishing of true religion, are these practical exercises."[56] So the
way to gauge the genuineness of one's faith was not to look at one's feelings,
but at one's practice. Edwards spoke as an empirical scientist. "As that is
called experimental philosophy, which brings opinion and notions to the test
of fact; so is that properly called experimental religion, which brings religious
affections and intentions, to the like test."[57]

Edwards was a man of Scripture and a man of rules. He could find no
Scriptural rules for infallibly identifying true religious affections, especially in

others, since only God knew the heart. Yet he found many biblical rules as to what true affections ought to look like and insisted that one could do no better than take these signs as one's guides. Mature true saints who examined themselves by these guidelines could attain a high degree of assurance, even though they would find in themselves many imperfections and increasing knowledge of their own self-deceptions. Weaker or backslidden saints might never be able to be sure of their true estates but still would benefit by holding up their experience to the biblical template.

Edwards concluded *Religious Affections* by answering the objection that this emphasis on practice might seem like a new legalism. To the contrary, he said, it was all carefully premised on standard Calvinist doctrine that a genuine work of grace would lead to keeping God's commandments. Edwards was dedicated to the old New England way that celebrated grace and lived by law. He was not going to let revival enthusiasm displace that balance which was disciplined into the very marrow of his bones.

Especially he feared Satan's ability to subvert the awakening by appealing to human self-centeredness. The inflated human ego was the devil's playground, and in revival times his favorite ploy was to simulate evangelical experience. Edwards refused a blanket condemnation of the reliance on personal testimony that would become normative for evangelicalism, but he had already seen how Satan could use the contagiousness of revival enthusiasm as a means of exploiting human egotism. "True saints," Edwards observed with typical God-centeredness, are "inexpressibly pleased and delighted with . . . the things of God." Hypocrites, by contrast, revel in themselves. "The hypocrite has his mind pleased and delighted, in the first place, with his own privilege, and the happiness which he supposes he has attained, or shall obtain."[58]

The best answer to such superficiality was disciplined Christian action. The community of believers would be far better off, Edwards wrote in his concluding sentences, if "it would become fashionable for men to shew their Christianity, more by an amiable distinguished behavior, than by an abundant and excessive declaring their experiences." Christians would be far more effective in their witness if they, with "becoming Christian humility and modesty," were "lively in the service of God and our generation, than by the liveliness and forwardness of our tongues, and making a business of proclaiming on the house tops, with our mouths, the holy and eminent acts and exercises of our hearts." An awakening of such effects, he concluded, "instead of hardening spectators, and exceedingly promoting infidelity and atheism, would above all things tend to convince men that there is a reality in religion, and greatly awaken them, and win them, by convincing their consciences of the importance and excellency of religion."[59]

Although Edwards still championed the priceless blessings of the awakening and was thoroughly constructive in tone, he could well understand something of the objections of the Chauncys of the world. Even though his whole treatise was a refutation of Chauncy's premise of the priority of reason over the affections, Edwards was nearly as critical of the turn the awakening had taken as was the Boston pastor and often in nearly the same ways. New England was deeply divided and in religious shambles. The over-zealous purveyors of a spiritual religion who ignored biblical rules had not only given comfort to Old Light cynicism but also had unwittingly promoted atheism and infidelity. The revival that Edwards longed for so intently had come, but many of its results were not what he had anticipated.

---

# CHAPTER 18

# A Model Town No More

dwards dismissed from his congregation? At the beginning of 1744, after one of the most remarkable decades in the history of parish ministries, it would have been hard to imagine that by 1750 he would be gone. The admiring Samuel Hopkins, who in 1744 was still a frequent guest in the Edwards household, later wrote that "Mr. Edwards was very happy in the esteem and love of his people for many years, and there was the greatest prospect of his living and dying so." In fact, claimed Hopkins, "he was the last minister almost in New England that would have been pitched upon to be opposed and renounced by his people."[1]

Edwards himself was publicly optimistic, if guardedly so. Writing in December 1743 an account of the past few years of awakening in North-ampton for Thomas Prince's *Christian History*, he put the best construction on things in hopes of edifying an international audience by the experience of his city on a hill. Although the revival fires had cooled during the past year and he feared that "a considerable number" may "have woefully deceived themselves," that was outbalanced by "a great number" among whom "there are amiable appearances of eminent grace." So far as he knew, there were few instances among the professing Christians of "scandalous sin." And the notorious party spirit that had plagued the town for the past thirty years had greatly diminished. The townspeople had recently settled a particularly troubling dispute that pitted the older ideals of common lands against newer emphases on private property. After fifteen years of fighting over the matter, they agreed to allow residents to cut much-needed wood on designated strips of private but unimproved land.[2] This arrangement was limited to ten years but evidenced just the sort of Christian spirit Edwards had hoped to cultivate by instituting the town covenant in 1742.[3]

A twentieth-century artist's conception of late eighteenth-century Northampton, showing the 1737 meetinghouse and the town house of 1739

By March 1744 Edwards' hopes for the long-term effects of the awakening took a severe jolt. Writing to Reverend William McCulloch, a Scottish
correspondent, he acknowledged he had been too optimistic in thinking that
the awakenings might be the dawn of the days preceding the millennium.
McCulloch had enjoyed one of the greatest of the Scottish revivals in his
parish at Cambuslang, near Glasgow. Yet McCulloch was more cautious
about the immediate future than Edwards had been. He agreed with Edwards
that it was remarkable that Isaiah 59:19 predicted God's triumph in a final
worldwide awakening progressing from west to east, but he believed Edwards
had failed to allude to "some dreadful stroke or trial" that must precede those
"glorious times."[4] Edwards, always trying to be alert to the counterattacks of
Satan, was ready to back away from the brighter hopes published in *Some
Thoughts*. He now reported that the present state of New England was "on
many accounts very melancholy."[5]

In Northampton much that Edwards had built up in the past fifteen years
came crashing down in one small-town squabble. Around the time Edwards

wrote to McCulloch, he learned that a number of young men of his congregation, all aged twenty-one to twenty-nine, had been passing around books on
popular medicine and midwifery, quoting from them to each other in a lewd
joking manner and using the information in them to taunt young women
about their menstruation. To make matters worse, the books had been used
for salacious mirth for as much as five years. Three young men—Oliver
Warner, an enterprising apprentice who had offered to show the principal
book to others for ten shillings, and cousins Timothy and Simeon Root—
were the leading offenders, but up to twenty of the mostly unmarried young
men had been peripherally involved. All but three were church members.[6]

Samuel Hopkins, who was in Northampton during at least part of the
episode (it was in May that he escorted Jerusha to Boston), reported that the
turning point in Edwards' standing in Northampton came as a result of a
tactical error in his initial handling of the crisis. According to Hopkins, when
Edwards learned of the lascivious behavior and gathered some preliminary
evidence, he brought the matter to the church. After preaching on Hebrews
12:15–16, "Looking diligently, lest any man fail of the grace of God, lest any
root of bitterness springing up trouble you, and thereby many be defiled: lest
there be any fornicator, or profane person . . . ," Edwards asked "the brethren
of the church" to stay after the Sunday service to hear about the matter. They
readily assented to choose a number of leading men of the community to
assist the pastor in hearing the case. This was all standard procedure for a
matter that had, at least, a semipublic character.

Edwards announced a time when the committee would meet at his house
and, in a fateful mistake, read off a list of people ordered to report there. The
list included some who were accused and some who were witnesses, but
Edwards failed to disclose any such distinction. Some of the young people
named were from, or related to, prominent families. According to Hopkins,
before the townspeople reached their homes some leading citizens were condemning the procedure. By the time the committee met "the town was suddenly all on a blaze."[7]

The case was not simply one of an overzealous pastor trying to stamp out
minor expressions of illicit sexuality when he learned that a few young men
were making erotic use of books on sex and midwifery. Edwards abhorred
sexual indulgence as especially distracting from the vastly higher beauty of
spiritual things, but he knew that young people were always prone to private
sexual sins and that, except perhaps at the height of revivals, there was always
some loose social behavior among the town's youth. He could not have hoped

to suppress every private misdemeanor. Church discipline would normally be reserved for much graver sins, such as fornication, and even that was to be dealt with privately before becoming a matter of church discipline.[8] Edwards knew that lewd uses of sexual information from medical books was hardly the worst of what went on when the barn doors were closed. Yet he was convinced there were factors in this case—and he initially persuaded the leading men of the congregation—that made it more than a matter of ordinary sexual misdemeanors.

With the town in an uproar, Edwards presented a defense of his action. We still have his notes. (Ever frugal, Edwards wrote these notes on three pieces of fan paper, apparently scraps of the material Sarah and her daughters used for making fans.)[9] The pastor, people were saying, should not have taken the initiative in launching such an investigation. "Shall the master of the ship," he retorted, "not inquire when he fears the ship is running on the rocks." All societies, including churches, have the power of self-preservation. It was his duty to be the watchman who sounded the alarm. Even though no one else had filed a formal complaint, if he himself saw a danger he could not responsibly ignore it.

Crucial to his case for bringing the matter to the church was that the offense was a *public* matter. Had it been private, he would have properly followed the biblical injunction of Matthew 18 and dealt with the matter privately, as some were now saying he should have done. He replied that the matter already had become one of some fame, and there was no way to determine the extent of the lascivious behavior without examining witnesses, which would inevitably make it all the more notorious.

Even by today's standards the behavior might have been a public concern. Men were taunting women about sexual matters. Joanna Clark testified, for instance, that about a year before, Oliver Warner had jeered at her and others, "'When does the moon change girls? Come, I'll look at your [face] and see whether there be a blue circle 'round your eyes.'" This was the sort of lore that one could get from any one of a number of a well-known handbooks written by pseudo-Aristotles. One popular version, *Aristotle's Compleat Master Piece in Three Parts: Displaying the Secrets of Nature in the Generation of Man*, featured, as its subtitle suggested, information and lore about men's and women's anatomy and sexual functions, presented in a scientific tone but also designed to titillate with "secret" information.[10] Another book was a more straightforward midwife's manual, *The Midwife Rightly Instructed*, which Elizabeth Pomeroy, from a prominent Northampton family, testified she found hidden—not by her mother—in the chimney of her house.[11] Mary Downing testified that two years earlier Oliver Warner and others had been reading from a book: "They all did so. What they laughed and made sport of was about girls, things concerning girls that is unclean to speak of. They seemed to boast as if they knew about girls, knew what belonged to girls as well as girls themselves." Bathsheba Negro, a slave of Major Seth Pomeroy, added that those who were laughing at the book and at the girls were "Ready to kiss them, and catch hold of the girls and shook 'em. Timothy Root in particular." Mary Downing further testified that as recently as two weeks previously another young man referred to "a granny book" and then laughed and "talked exceeding uncleanly and lasciviously so that I never hear any fellow go so far." After he left all the young women there agreed that "we never heard any such talk come out of any man's mouth whatsoever. It seemed to me to be almost as bad as tongue could express."[12]

By today's standards, this would be a case of sexual harassment. We might add that Edwards was, after all, the father of teenage daughters. So one might understand why he would be outraged by such recurring patterns of behavior. Judging from the witnesses, he had learned about the offenses from a network of women with whom his daughters or other women in his household may have had connections. His action might be seen as taking the side of women who, once encouraged to speak, had real complaints.

To attempt to justify Edwards by our contemporary norms, however, would be at least partly anachronistic because he viewed things through such different lenses. The taunting of the women was indeed a serious public concern.[13] Sensitivities from having lived most of his life in households surrounded by women may have increased Edwards' revulsion against breaking taboos about what men might say to women. Yet the foreground of his thought was very different from most of today's standards. Not only did he approach the matter strictly in his role as pastor, keeping his personal feelings out of sight, he viewed the issues, as he did everything else, through the lens of Scripture. His main point to the Northamptonites was that the offenses were "scandalous." In the biblical sense "scandal" meant a stumbling block or that which injures one spiritually. He quoted numerous biblical texts that made this point, the clearest being Romans 14:13, "that no man put a stumbling-block or an occasion to fall in his brother's way." Other verses, he pointed out, explicitly condemned sexual sins, such as looking on a woman's nakedness, even in imagination. Yet crucial to the matter being a *public* church concern was that the offenders were communicating the practices to others and hence causing them to stumble. Colossians 3:8, "Put away all filthy communication out of your mouth," and other verses made the biblical demand unmistakable.[14]

Edwards framed the question then not as a gender issue, but as contagious public speech that threatened souls. Young men had created a lascivious underground and were corrupting other young people. Most of those involved were church members who had been taking communion. Those who were promoting a profane culture among the young had created stumbling blocks that endangered the eternal destinies of their neighbors.[15]

For Edwards, the most agonizing aspect of the discovery was that most of the young men involved were his spiritual children. He knew that the seductive culture they were promoting in the taverns and behind the barns was a powerful countermovement to the awakening. The reemergence of a profane and irreverent young people's culture could quickly subvert the successes of the internationally renowned revivals. Young people had been at the center of his success as a pastor. He had told the world the story in his celebrated *Faithful Narrative*. When he had inherited the flock from his grandfather, many of the young people had been out of control—disrespectful in the meeting and accustomed to Sunday night frolics, loose speech, and other licentious behavior. His greatest triumph in the awakening of 1734–35 was in vastly reducing the public manifestations of such behavior—not by repressing it, but by organizing young people's religious meetings and by helping foster a contagious spiritual atmosphere so that for a time the young seemed to talk of almost nothing but spiritual matters.

Most of the young men involved with the lascivious use of the books had been in their early teens during that first awakening and had joined the church since.[16] In the hiatus between the two awakenings Edwards felt the spiritual condition of Northampton had fallen low and saw some of the old practices returning. In a 1738 afternoon sermon on a communion Sunday, Edwards preached on how Joseph had fled the seductions of Potiphar's wife. All experience with human nature, he argued, showed that certain practices led toward sin. Tavern-haunting accompanied by excessive drinking and card playing, for instance, had been shown throughout history to lead to much wickedness. Even more alarming was "the custom in particular, of young people of different sexes reclining together—however little is made of it, and however ready persons may be to laugh at it being condemned." Not only bundling, but late night frolicking and dancing were being revived. "When the wise man says, 'there is a time to dance,'" he observed wryly, "that does

not prove that the dead of night is the time for it." Surely nighttime mer-
rymaking led to the "frequent breaking out of gross sins; fornication in particular." Young people who had just partaken of communion, yet were not
fleeing such irresistible temptations, were (as Scripture said) "eating and
drinking judgment to yourselves."[17]

Always uncomfortable with the Stoddardean standards for church membership because they increased the probability that profane persons would
desecrate the most holy worship of God, Edwards had long used communion
services to warn against the terrible dangers of hypocrisy. Eating and drinking
unworthily, he warned his congregation, was to partake of Christ's flesh like
bloodthirsty animals, to eat it in malice like murderers, "guilty of the body
and blood of the Lord." It was like coming into the presence of a great prince
with garments purposefully defiled with excrement.[18] Because Edwards had a
high view of Christ's holy spiritual presence, not just in the bread and the
wine but in all of worship, the warnings extended to any irreverence toward
the "ordinances" for proper worship. To pretend to praise Christ, while living
lives that mocked him, with no intention of reform, was like joining those
who taunted him at his crucifixion and shouted "*Hail, King of the Jews.*"[19]

The hypocrisy of profane persons at communion was especially reprehensible because the ceremony involved the most solemn renewal of the covenant
on which Christ, in the sacrament, put his seal. "What a horrible piece of
mockery is it," Edwards cried in a typical passage, "to engage and promise
themselves explicitly at owning the covenant . . . when they actually . . . do live
allowedly in things directly contrary: contrary to the gospel, contrary to the
holy religion of Christ!" These hypocrites "go on in the indulgences of their
filthy lusts and come away from them, and pretend, like saints, to commemo-
rate Christ's death and to eat his flesh and drink his blood and give up
themselves to Christ, and then go from the table of God to their old courses
again."[20]

In 1744 that was still the heart of the matter. In his notes for his defense he
concluded with, "Why I can't give these persons the ordinance of the Lord's
Supper." In light of what was ahead in his relationship to his congregation,
these words might be seen as the proverbial fire bell ringing in the night. The
scandalous counterspiritual culture he was combating was a matter for church
concern because the church itself was being corrupted. Townspeople, who in
good Stoddardean fashion made little distinction between the church and the
town, saw the young men's behavior as just more of the usual misdemeanors
that it would be unrealistic to try to suppress. Edwards saw it as critical to the

purity of the church and to the health of young parishioners, more and more of whom might be drinking damnation to themselves. Stoddardean practice did provide for barring persons of scandalous behavior from communion. Yet for Edwards, if the town was unwilling to bear the scrutiny that rule properly implied, then it might be time to rethink the whole system that so confused the line between church and town.

Edwards had already attempted to solve the problem through the solemn covenant just two years earlier. While the adults renounced all sorts of contentiousness and promised to live in Christian charity, the young, who had again been at the heart of an awakening, renounced the sins of youth. They had solemnly promised "never to allow ourselves in any youthful diversions and pastimes" that "would sinfully tend to hinder the devoutest, and most engaged spirit in religion." Specifically, they swore "that we will strictly avoid all freedoms and familiarities in company, so tending either to stir up or gratify a lust of lasciviousness."[21] Now Edwards found that some young church members had all along been engaged in the very behavior they had so piously renounced. Although he was always upset about sexual sins, this case was vastly compounded by both covenant breaking and betrayal of the international awakening

Edwards had much invested in the larger issues. He had just published his account of the recent revival in Thomas Prince's *Christian History* where he featured this solemn covenant as a model for all the world to see. Edwards' narrative did note that "some of the young people especially have shamefully lost their liveliness and vigor in religion and much of the seriousness and solemnity of their spirits."[22] Now he gained a new glimpse at the depth of the subversive subculture of some of his young adult church members.

From his preliminary investigations Edwards recognized that the behavior was not only scandalously sexual in nature, but it involved the spread of a young people's underground that was consciously defiant of church authority. Several of the principal witnesses, who told of the most notorious instances of taunting young women, testified that the young men had been reading "a book that they called the Bible in a laughing way." Timothy Root in particular called it "the young folks' Bible."[23] In a Calvinist community where there were few sacred objects and where the Bible was the highest authority, this was serious sacrilege.

Irreverence and disrespect of church authority soon became a much larger issue. During the initial church meeting when Edwards asked the congregation to stay after the regular service so that he could alert them to the situation, Timothy and Simeon Root were seen whispering and laughing. Soon, perhaps emboldened by the complaints from prominent citizens about the procedure, their disrespect turned to open defiance. The accused and witnesses gathered to meet with the committee of the church at the Edwardses' home. The committee was a formidable group, including Colonel John Stoddard, Edwards, and four other leading men. While the committee deliberated and interviewed witnesses, everyone else was asked to wait, probably sitting on hard benches. It was a fine spring day. When the committee-room door was open Simeon Root said loudly, "What do we do here? We won't stay here all day long." Next the two Roots sent someone in to ask if they could go out for refreshment. He came back saying "the committee was very much displeased." Timothy Root declared dramatically, "I won't worship a wig." When others objected that some persons were due respect, Root kept repeating, "I won't worship a wig."

Making good on his defiance, Timothy Root and his cousin Simeon quietly walked out. They were next seen at the tavern with a "company that called for a mug of flip and drank it." Returning to the Edwardses' house, the rebels convinced the other young men to go outside as well. Timothy Root, in a wonderful example of how a Calvinist low view of human nature might make one a revolutionary, declared that the committee "are nothing but men molded up of a little dirt." He added (in less Calvinistic terms), "I don't care a turd" and "I don't care a fart" for any of them. The revolution was limited, however, since the young men went only as far as the back of Edwards' lot where they played leapfrog and other games. Yet they had made their point of defiance. Timothy Root finally left the premises entirely, urging others to do the same. "If they have any business with me," he loudly proclaimed, "they may come to me; I ben't obliged to wait any longer on their arses, as I have done."[24]

Eventually the committee caught up with Root, but the case was not settled until June. In the meantime, the town was seething with resentments as debates dragged on. In the end, the committee required only the ringleaders to make public confessions. That may have reflected the town's resistance to making a public example of every offender, but it was also consistent with Edwards' point that it was the scandalous or stumbling-block character of the offenses with which he was most concerned.

In the end, the confessions of Timothy and Simeon Root do not mention the sexual offenses at all, even though these had been copiously documented in the testimony. Rather, their confessions concern solely their "scandalously contemptuous behavior towards the authority of this church in their late proceeding in the affair."[25] Perhaps town pressures had forced Edwards and the committee to drop any public rebuke for the sexual misdemeanors. Edwards drew up a confession for Oliver Warner dealing solely with sexual behavior, probably with the intent that Warner be made a public example by having to read it before the church. In it Warner would acknowledge "very unclean and lascivious expressions," specifically referring only to the testimony of Joanna Clark and Bathsheba Negro (who had reported his taunting remarks). That language was "unbecoming of a Christian, and of a very scandalous nature." Edwards noted that the confessions of the Roots were "owned June 1744," but there is no such notation for Warner. So possibly Edwards drew up the sample confession as the strongest case of a public sexual offense, but it was never implemented. We cannot be sure.[26]

This episode is now usually called "the bad book case," but that is misleading. That designation fits a stock story of book censorship. Popular nineteenth-century interpreters speculated that Edwards was trying to suppress such novels as *Pamela* (which turns out to be the one novel we now know the Edwardses owned).[27] The alternative, "'young folks' Bible' case" is somewhat better. It suggests that the offense was more in what was said publicly than in what was read privately. It also highlights the issues of sacrilege, hypocrisy, and "scandal" that were so crucial to Edwards' consternation over this lascivious public speech.

One way to read the incident is as one of changing sexual mores and gender relationships. Puritans had long sought to regulate sexual activities and suppress loose sexual speech. The conflicts in Northampton in the 1740s were in essence not so different from those in English towns that were under Puritan rule in the 1610s and 1620s.[28] Any program of sexual repression would involve perennial conflict with the tavern and youth culture. The difference was that in a town like Northampton, which had always had authoritarian ministerial leadership, sexual speech apparently had long been suppressed in the public domain.

The most striking feature of the "young folks' Bible" fiasco was that the offenders were not fourteen-year-old boys, but young men in their twenties acting like fourteen-year-old boys. Their degree of titillation over basic information about female physiology suggests a remarkable level of sexual immaturity. That such subjects could be the source of perennial mirth suggests, in turn, a notable suppression of above-ground sources for that information.

The origins of the extraordinary awakening of 1734–35 were probably related to an unusually large cohort of unmarried young people. Without new lands, young men and women were postponing marriage and continuing to live with their parents.[29] Young adults with this ill-defined status may have been particularly susceptible to revival. In any case, when the fervor of awakenings wore off, young men, who had lived through years of public restraint, were easily amused by the simplest sexual innuendo. Adding to the tensions of their situation, sexual mores and gender relationships were changing in the British world—as they always are. Historian Ava Chamberlain has pointed out that during the 1740s, in addition to the "young folks' Bible" case, Edwards dealt with three contested paternity cases. In each the young men disputed Edwards' and the church's judgments and were additionally charged with contempt for authority or for evading their responsibility and punishment. Chamberlain interprets these as indicating a breakdown of the older communal ideal and the assertion of greater sexual freedom for men than was allowed for women.[30]

If we consider the suppression of public sexual speech for young men in awakened Northampton in the context of the growing assertions in British culture of male rights to sexual freedom, we can imagine the sort of resentments that had been building. Even when Edwards and the awakening seemed to be largely succeeding, the pressures on unmarried young men were immense—all the more so because they were aware of very different standards elsewhere. Once the awakening collapsed, the resulting resentments came out in the open with little to restrain them. Edwards was attributing momentous importance to behavior that looked trivial, even if childish and distasteful, to many other inhabitants of the town. The more he made of it, the more he lost support. Hopkins remarks that as a result of this incident Edwards "greatly lost his influence," especially among the young people, and that "this seemed in a great measure to put an end to Mr. Edwards' usefulness at Northampton."[31] Edwards himself later referred to it as that "which gave so great offense, and by which I became so obnoxious."[32]

Resentments against the Edwardses now came out in other ways.[33] As in many New England towns, tensions had been building regarding the pastor's salary, a tax matter decided at yearly town meetings. In 1744 that issue was smoldering below the surface when the "young folks' Bible" scandal broke into flames.[34] Underlying the salary disputes was inflation. Edwards' salary, while relatively generous, was not keeping up with the combination of rising prices and a growing family. Also, since money was scarce, payments were often slow. In March 1744 Sarah, who managed the family finances, asked the town for past-due salary, stating that "Mr. Edwards in under such obligations that he can't possibly do without it."[35]

By November, with relations between the pastor and the town now damaged by the young folks' controversy, all the pettiness of a small town emerged over the salary issue. Sarah and their daughters felt the brunt of the criticism, so much so that Edwards wrote a formal rejoinder complaining that while the town had generously voted him an addition of fifty pounds in the spring, there had been "many jealousies expressed of me and my family, as though we were lavish." Among some townspeople "much fault was found . . . with our manner of spending, with the clothes that we wore and the like." Because he believed there were some errors in matters of fact, Edwards proposed to provide a strict accounting of some of the matters in question, especially that which had "been laid up for my children."[36]

One clue that the family did occasionally display some aristocratic pretensions is a surviving bill, which Edwards used for sermon notes in March 1743, for £11 (about a week's salary) for "a gold locket and chain" for "Mrs. Edwards."[37] Another is a silver patch box, designed for holding felt "beauty marks," later found on the Edwards' property in Stockbridge. On the other hand, at the time of Jonathan's death in 1758, the inventory of his estate did not reveal many luxury items. The family owned a set of eighteen knives and forks, a nicety of the gentry in a generation that was still undergoing the transition toward modern eating habits. They also owned a couple of teapots, for the enjoyment of a new delicacy of the day, and twelve china tea cups and plates. They had a dozen wine glasses, a small amount of other china, and many pewter dishes.[38] Still, even a few displays of fashion in Northampton were sufficient to generate backbiting.

The ever-resourceful Timothy Root managed to combine the two controversies for his purposes. When the investigating committee asked him about his remark "I won't worship a wig," Root replied that his only concern had been that some of the witnesses would not be at their best because they would be "terrified with the fine clothes of some of the committee." He did not mean "any disdain or contempt." Colonel Stoddard, presumably dressed in his best court clothes and wig, was certainly formidable, as apparently so were some others of the committee. Edwards dressed plainly, except for a wig, but Root, knowing that the question of expensive clothes was a sore point, made the most of it.

Edwards was so frustrated with begging the town for money each year and then enduring resentments if increases were granted that he proposed

Sarah Edwards' silver patch box

that his salary be fixed except for an adjustment for inflation. Even this, he had to reassure, was not "leading you into any snare." The facts were that he had a large and ever-growing family to bring up. Moreover, their house was virtually a hotel, bearing the expense of increasing numbers of visitors. "By the increase of my family's acquaintance . . . my house will probably become still more a place of resort, as it has been more and more so for many years past."[39] Despite the seeming merits of so resolving the dispute, the argument went on for four more years. The town continued to give him salary increases, even surpassing the rate of inflation, but every year was a battle and Edwards did not think his income kept pace with his ever-increasing expenses.[40]

Edwards' increasing tensions with his parishioners had a broader economic and spiritual dimension. He was trying to shepherd a people who were undergoing a "transition from yeoman society to agrarian capitalism."[41] The capitalist market revolution was only in its fledgling stages in growing Northampton, but Edwards was not among its friends. Unlike some of his British contemporaries who had more optimistic views of the self-regulating market, Edwards deplored free enterprise as bringing out the worst in human nature. He had long condemned the self-interested avarice that permeated the society and pointedly identified inflation and price fluctuations as moral issues.

"'Tis certainly no good rule," he declared, "that men may buy as cheap and sell as dear as they can." Rather than condoning a free economy, Edwards believed that the magistrates should regulate prices so that commodities sold at their intrinsic worth. The calamitous price fluctuations, he declared, were the result of "a greedy sp[irit]" in those who would "advance their private interests on the great loss and damage of the public society."[42]

Edwards' view of the just society was not far from that of Massachusetts' first governor, John Winthrop, in the *Model of Christian Charity*, preached on shipboard in 1630. God had ordained hierarchical orders that should be governed as commonwealth, bound together by the law of love. In the Northampton covenant of 1742 Edwards had the townspeople promise to live under the rule of fair business practice and charity. In 1743, after a four-year campaign, Edwards convinced his congregation to institute a collection for the poor at every Sabbath service.[43] In an era before insurance, that was a vital public service. Samuel Hopkins maintained that Edwards had "uncommon regard" for "liberality, and charity to the poor and distressed." Edwards spoke often of the need for every congregation to keep up "a public stock" for its poor and, said Hopkins, he backed up his public advice with private action. Much of his almsgiving was in secret. Hopkins knew of one case firsthand. Edwards had heard of a man, neither acquaintance nor kin, who was in great distress due to an illness and asked Hopkins to deliver "a considerable sum" to him, but to tell no one. Hopkins was sure there were many such instances that would be "unknown till the resurrection."[44] The townspeople, however, were by the 1740s disposed to see Edwards as himself grasping in his salary demands. He, in turn, saw many of them as not only avaricious but as unwilling to recognize a fundamental principle of the model society: that those in authority should receive their due.

For Edwards the return of the town's contentiousness signaled a deeper and more distressing problem. Many communicant church members were not showing proper evidence of a regenerate life. The "young folks' Bible" controversy and the townspeople's indifference to its seriousness may have been the last straw that broke his patience and settled his mind on this issue that had long been gnawing at him. During 1745, when he was writing *Religious Affections*, it was much on his mind as he described the signs that should distinguish true believers from hypocrites. Many of his contentious Northamptonite parishioners seemed ominously lacking in some of those evidences, such as having "the lamblike, dovelike spirit and temper of Jesus Christ" or displaying the twelfth and most essential sign of "Christian practice." He included in *Religious Affections* some oblique references to his change in view, remarking, for instance, that "there ought to be good reason, from the circumstances of the profession [of faith] to think that the professor don't make such a profession out of a mere customary compliance with a prescribed form . . . as confessions of faith are often subscribed."[45] Yet, for the time being, recognizing the potential explosion in the town if he announced his departure from his revered grandfather Stoddard's practice, he revealed the full implications of his thought only to Sarah and some intimate friends.[46]

# CHAPTER 19

## Colonial Wars

One reason for Edwards to keep to himself about his momentous change of mind regarding church membership in 1744–45 was that New England was at war, both literally and figuratively. The literal war was King George's War, or the War of the Austrian Succession (1740–48), which became a major New England concern when France joined in the hostilities against England in spring 1744. Colonel John Stoddard was the chief military commander in western Massachusetts, and in 1745 the townspeople and Edwards would be united by both a dramatic offensive against the French and a defense against the Indians. Through the lens of Edwards' understanding of biblical prophesies, these hostilities were significant primarily as they fit into the larger picture of God's plans for the spread of the Gospel in the latter days. In the meantime Edwards was deeply embroiled in a bitter, if figurative, intercolonial war.

The Old Light versus New Light hostilities, which were already intense by the end of 1743, reached a fever pitch with the news, in 1744, that Whitefield would be returning to New England in the fall. To many, the spread of separatism threatened to bring alarming social disruptions. Anti-revivalists, strengthened by such fears, had already gained the advantage in elite circles. Now they were proclaiming that Whitefield was a dangerous fanatic. "Many ministers," Edwards recounted in a public letter the next year, "were more alarmed at his coming, than they would have been by the arrival of a fleet from France, and they began soon to preach and write against him, to warn people to beware of him, as a most dangerous person." Edwards, an avid reader of Boston newspapers, had seen how in the *Boston Evening Post* and in pamphlets Whitefield's opponents had kept up a merciless barrage of ridicule, satire, and dire warnings. Edwards, given to hyperbole in historical comparisons, wrote: "I question whether history affords any instance paralleled with this, as so much pains taken in writing to blacken a man's character, and render him odious."[1]

Edwards himself was in the middle of one of the less edifying exchanges. During the Harvard commencement season of July 1744, Rector Thomas Clap of Yale told many people that he had it on the word of Edwards himself that Whitefield was engaged in a plot to overthrow the standing order of New England. Clap was a thoroughly conservative Old Light, a strict defender of Puritan orthodoxy, as contrasted with Chauncy, a progressive Old Light or protoliberal anti-revivalist. Clap was also, if his principal biographer and generations of Yale students are to be believed, a difficult authoritarian personality. As Louis Leonard Tucker, the biographer, put it, he ruled Yale College for twenty-five years in the spirit of Louis XIV, "Le collège, c'est moi!"[2]

Clap had been furious with Edwards since September 1741, when Edwards had undercut Clap and the trustees at the Yale commencement by defending all but the extremes of revival enthusiasm in *The Distinguishing Marks*. Clap and Edwards, who were the same age and not entirely unlike in temperament, had been allied champions of orthodoxy in the Breck case. Clap had even cautiously encouraged Whitefield and the awakening at the college until, with the visit of Gilbert Tennent, he saw it turning students toward enthusiasm and separatism. During the school year after Edwards' visit, Clap's iron-hand efforts to suppress these tendencies brought such strong student reaction that in the spring he was forced to suspend classes and send the students home. Clap was also a principal in convincing the Connecticut legislature to attempt to suppress the New Light movement by legal fiat.[3]

In May 1743 Clap and Edwards happened to meet on the road to Boston, where both were headed for the annual election week activities (the occasion when an Old Light majority made the first ministerial declaration against the awakening). Edwards' oldest daughter Sarah was riding on the same horse with her father (Sarah senior was confined at home, having just given birth to a new daughter, Eunice, their eighth child). Clap rode together with the Edwardses for hours, arguing with Jonathan about the events of the time and their differences. Others were in the larger company of pilgrims, including of all people Robert Breck, which perhaps helped throw Edwards and Clap together.

Over a year later, in July 1744, when all the talk in Boston was of Whitefield's return, Clap told numerous people that Edwards had said that Whitefield "told me he designed to turn the generality of ministers in the country out of their places, and bring over ministers from England, Scotland, and Ireland, and place them in their room."[4] Now Edwards was furious. Clap's report put Whitefield at the center of a conspiracy against the ministerial establishment of New England and, if true, would ruin the itinerant's reputation. Edwards (who was still trying to get over the "young folks' Bible" fiasco of the spring) wrote to Clap to set the record straight. After an exchange of several letters, Clap not only would not give in, but went into print, using the letters to vindicate his claim. Edwards replied and each followed with a second pamphlet-letter.

The exchange over who said what was hardly edifying. Edwards pointed out that if he had heard from Whitefield such an astonishing plot as Clap reported, he would hardly have chosen Clap as the person in whom to confide such information. Edwards did acknowledge that he had heard from Whitefield of a desire to bring some clergy from *England* (certainly not from Ireland where there was no revival) to support the efforts of the Tennents in the Middle Colonies. He also had a few criticisms of Whitefield, but he did not recall having discussed Whitefield at all with Clap. Ever the logician, Edwards in one of his private letters nonetheless tried to settle the issue by distinguishing between what it was *conceivable* he had said, but possibly forgotten, and what was *inconceivable*.

Seizing on what Edwards admitted knowing and on some small differences between what Edwards had said was conceivable and what Clap claimed, Clap insisted that his story was correct in substance and upbraided Edwards for being so exasperated over so little. Clap concluded his second published letter by accusing Edwards of treating him in an "unchristian manner," but he also declared sanctimoniously that "Scripture and my own inclination forbid me to render evil for evil" and offered to "freely forgive" him.[5] Edwards had presented Clap's accusations as evidence of the lengths to which people would go to discredit Whitefield. Not entirely in his lamblike mode in the face of what he was sure were false accusations damaging to the Gospel cause, Edwards concluded the exchange by citing Clap's offered absolution and praying that in the future, when his temper has cooled, Clap might "be enabled to look on your own conduct with real seriousness, as in the sight of God."[6] Each of the combatants in this ministerial duel of honor was so arrayed with logic and rhetoric that neither could dent the other's armor, and by the time the last futile shot rumbled off the press in summer 1745, Whitefield and other events had settled the original issue.

Whitefield arrived in New England in fall 1744. Since his last triumphant visit he had enjoyed another spectacular success during the "great awakening" in Scotland which broke loose in 1742. Edwards had played a role in the Scottish revivals as well. The awakenings in several towns, especially in James Robe's parish of Kilsyth and William McCulloch's in Cambuslang, preceded Whitefield's visits and were inspired in part by Edwards' *Faithful Narrative.* These awakenings closely paralleled the New England events of 1741 and 1742 in many ecstatic physical manifestations. The Scottish leaders eagerly welcomed Edwards' *Distinguishing Marks* and soon became his most faithful correspondents and strongest supporters. Edwards was quickly becoming more highly honored in Scotland than he was in his own country.[7] Whitefield's Scottish triumph placed the grand itinerant and Edwards even more closely in the same international evangelical circle.

Whitefield's alliance with these Scottish leaders was especially significant to the American controversy because they were established Presbyterian clergy. In 1741 Whitefield's initial Scottish contacts had been largely with a seceder group, the Associate Presbytery. These separatists had made secession from the established church a test of their faith and soon attacked Whitefield because of his Anglican ordination and willingness to work with those who were less than pure. After that Whitefield viewed separatism with a jaundiced eye and in America could point to his break with the seceders as evidence that he harbored no revolutionary scheme.[8]

Almost as soon as Whitefield arrived in Boston in late November the core group of his former supporters—Colman, Prince, Sewall, and Foxcroft—met with him to learn his true intentions. The accusations of Clap and others had done their work, so these former supporters quizzed Whitefield closely. They asked about his published condemnations of New England clergy and colleges and especially about his views of separatism. When they were soon assured that Whitefield was not part of any conspiracy, they immediately opened their pulpits to him.[9]

The resumption of Whitefield's daily ministry in Boston only increased the barrage of publications from his attackers. Most notable was *The Testimony of the President, Professors, Tutors, and Hebrew Instructor of Harvard College, against George Whitefield,* issued late in 1744. Whitefield replied to this and a number of the other severe condemnations with displays of humility far different from his judgmental tone of 1741. He acknowledged that he had been too much guided by "impressions" and that he had been too quick to make censorious judgments and especially unwise in publishing them. He specifically rejected Clap's accusations. He never contemplated any scheme to replace the New England clergy, and he had no intention of being part of a party that turned people against their ministers. While Whitefield's detractors still considered him an uncharitable enthusiast and a dangerous deluder of the people, his contrite replies helped him to regain much of his former support.[10]

New England's other war provided an additional opportunity for the evangelist to win more popular acclaim and to establish himself in the region's lore. To counter the French threat to the British colony of Nova Scotia and so to New England fisheries, commerce, and coasts, colonial leaders devised an audacious plan to try to capture the formidable French fortress at Louisbourg on Cape Breton Island just north of Nova Scotia. William Pepperrell, a pious admirer of Whitefield, was chosen to lead the expedition. Pepperrell and his wife (later both correspondents of Edwards) consulted with Whitefield before accepting the command and had him preach to the troops before they embarked. Another friend of Whitefield had asked the evangelist to provide the motto for the flag for the expedition. Knowledge of Whitefield's participation, he said, would be an important recruiting tool. Whitefield, after a brief show of reluctance, provided the motto, "*Nil desperandum Christo duce*" (No need to fear with Christ as our leader).[11]

In mid-July 1745 Whitefield and his wife (the widow he had married rather unromantically in 1741) visited the Edwardses in Northampton for nearly a week. The two wars gave them much to talk about. Whitefield noted the parallel between warfare and evangelism. When the expedition to Louisbourg was in its early stages, he observed, many letters came back saying the fortress was greater than they supposed and the situation was desperate. "I smiled, and told my friends," Whitefield recounted, "that I believed now we should have Louisbourg; for all having confessed their helplessness, God would now reveal His arm and make our extremity His opportunity."[12]

Spiritually, New England no longer confessed its helplessness, so even though Whitefield preached to many eager crowds, there was no new awakening. In Edwards' view, the fault was not Whitefield's. He found the thirty-year-old itinerant more "solid and judicious" than five years earlier and was all the more convinced that the continuing savage attacks on him were deeply unjust. Whitefield's latest ministries in New England, he believed, had been helpful, but their impact was limited by alarms sounded by his detractors.[13]

Just about the time of the Whitefield's visit, Northampton was celebrating the news of New England's spectacular triumph at Louisbourg. About twenty of Edwards' parishioners had been part of the expedition that had laid siege to and captured the French fortress. Major Seth Pomeroy, from one of Northampton's first families, led the local regiment, and Joseph Hawley III (Yale 1742), who was considering the ministry, had been the general's chaplain. No one was more enthusiastic than Edwards. When the troops returned, he sought to learn every detail about the victory. He was especially buoyed by what Major Pomeroy described as "a variety of remarkable providences in favour of our great design."[14] Once again, as he had been during the awakenings, Edwards was convinced he had found firm evidence of God's working in history. In his established role as a scientific correspondent regarding God's works in history, he sent a lengthy account of the siege as part of a letter for publication in Scotland in James Robe's *Christian Monthly History*.

Edwards' epistle makes clear that he saw God's providence in New England's military triumph and in the international awakenings as part of a single pattern. He began with a strong endorsement of the Concert of Prayer, a campaign for coordinating international prayer for the outpouring of the Holy Spirit, proposed by his Scottish counterparts. He acknowledged that spiritually "the day is so dark here in New England," yet he rejoiced in the awakenings in Scotland and he could report hopeful signs elsewhere in America. The ministries of the Tennents and their associates had spread to Virginia, and in New Jersey Presbyterian leaders were responding to the scarcity of ministers by proposing to establish their own college (eventually settled in Princeton). Especially notable were the successes of the missionary efforts of David Brainerd among the Indians, another cause close to Edwards' heart. Having just mentioned Brainerd, Edwards made a remarkable transition in his narrative to the military campaign. "While I am speaking of the late wonderful works of God in America," he wrote, "I cannot pass over one, which, though it be of a different kind from those already mentioned; yet is that wherein the Most High has made his hand manifest, in a most apparent and marvelous manner, and may be reckoned among the evidences of its being a day of great things, and of the wonderful works of God in this part of the world."[15]

In Edwards' scheme of things a remarkable victory over the French was a fitting sequel to the awakenings if one were tracking the pattern of God's work in history. For years Edwards had been recording news of Catholic setbacks in his notebooks. Now he had what he considered irrefutable evidence of God's providential interventions in political affairs. Perhaps they were seeing the predawn glimmers of millennial days after all. With his usual thoroughness, he made the most of the evidence.

The people of New England, despite their lamentable divisions over the awakening, had united in "an extraordinary spirit of prayer" greater than for any public affair that Edward could remember. Edwards had often warned his people that their sins could keep God from listening to their prayers. During the "young folks' Bible" scandal in 1744 he had preached a fast day sermon on Psalm 66:18, "If I regard iniquity in my heart, the Lord will not hear me."[16] In June of the same year, for the fast day called in response to the outbreak of war with France, he had preached on Israel's defeat at Ai because of one unrepentant sinner, expounding the doctrine, "Sin above all things weakens a people at war."[17] By contrast, in his sermon of April 1745 on the fast day called to support the dangerous expedition against Cape Breton, Edwards put more emphasis on the positive. Nations might justly be called to fight wars for many reasons and ordinary citizens must serve when called unless "it be notoriously manifest that the war is unjust." Truly repentant prayers of the people, he emphasized, were crucial to success. New England had been so blessed in the past and many examples from Old Testament Israel proved that God would hear such prayers.[18]

The belief of New Englanders that total dependence on God was the key to capturing the great fortress at Louisbourg opened them to ridicule from those who believed the expedition foolhardy. Benjamin Franklin mocked New England's piety. Writing to his brother John in May, the Philadelphian wondered whether it was realistic for an army of amateurs to capture such a fortress. "Some seem to think forts are as easy taken as snuff," he quipped. "You have a fast and prayer day," he continued, "in which I compute five hundred thousand petitions were offered up to the same effect in New England." In addition, if every family in New England had prayed for victory twice a day since January 25 (when the General Court had narrowly approved the military plan), that would amount to "forty-five millions of prayers; which set against the prayers of a few priests in the garrison, to the Virgin Mary, give a vast balance in your favor." Franklin concluded, "If you do not succeed, I fear I shall have but an indifferent opinion of Presbyterian prayers in such cases, as long as I live. Indeed, in attacking strong towns I should have more dependence on *works*, than on *faith.*"[19]

Edwards' account of the victory was a small treatise on evidences for answered prayer and providence, as though to respond directly to scoffers such as Franklin. Had New Englanders been better informed of the strength of the fortress, observed the theologian, they would never have undertaken the venture. More remarkably, the French at Cape Breton had not learned of

New England's design, despite its wide publicity and it being known in Albany, where Indians friendly to the French frequently visited. The winter was uncommonly mild to allow preparations. Repeatedly the weather favored the New England cause. Even a delay by bad weather prevented arrival before the ice had melted. An English man-of-war, on its way to help protect the New England coast, intercepted a fishing boat and learned that the New England forces were on their way north. The commodore took a skilled pilot (a draft dodger) from the boat, changed his own course to Cape Breton, and sent orders that resulted in three other men-of-war aiding the siege. The invasion was such a surprise that the French immediately abandoned their grand battery of cannons to a smaller force. The fleeing French spiked their cannons, but not effectively. Although they took their gunpowder, they left the cannon balls, which were more essential. When the New Englanders' one large mortar broke, it turned out that another had just been sent from Boston. Once, when an immovable rock kept the English from completing a trench, a French cannon bomb fell on the exact spot and blew the rock out of the way. After weeks of seemingly futile siege, the British force decided they would have to assault the walls of the main fortress. Had they attempted it, they would have had no chance; the walls were twice as high as they believed, the lower twelve feet being hidden by a trench. Wonderfully, just before this proposed assault, the French surrendered. By these and many other marvelous ways "God gave into our hands" the greatest French fortress in the New World and the principal staging ground for French harassment of New England shipping and trade. Edwards' account was exaggerated and selective, yet the overall success of the daring expedition was so extraordinary that everything fit as "a dispensation of providence, the most remarkable in its kind, that has been in many ages, and a great evidence of God's being one that hears prayer."[20]

Edwards was far from alone in his providentialist patriotism. Charles Chauncy in a sermon celebrating the victory recounted a similar "train of providences." Invoking the standard New England analogy to Old Testament Israel, Chauncy declared, "I scarce know of a conquest, since the days of Joshua and the Judges, wherein the finger of God is more visible."[21] Thomas Prince, who through *Christian History* had become Edwards' closest associate in Boston, was just as extravagant. He also recited a list of providences and urged New Englanders to rejoice in increased safety for their shores and their commerce. "But let our joy rise higher, that hereby a great support of Antichristian power is taken away and the visible Kingdom of Christ is enlarged."

Much like Edwards, Prince tied the defeat of the Roman Antichrist to the promised spread of the Gospel to all lands. Closing with a rhetorical flourish, Prince suggested that when the southern gates of Louisbourg were lifted to let in the victorious colonists, "the King of Glory went in with them . . . the Lord Mighty in Battle." He prayed that "this happy conquest be the dawning earnest of our divine redeemer's carrying on his triumphs through the Northern Regions; 'till he extends his empire . . . from the river of Canada to the ends of America." Then God's name would truly be praised "from the uttermost parts of the earth."[22]

Before New Englanders could fully absorb the heady meaning of God's blessings, sobering new evidence came from abroad of God's warnings of judgment on their British nation. In July 1745 Prince Charles Edward Stuart entered Scotland and raised an army. The grandson of England's last Catholic king, James II, "the Young Pretender" proposed to place his father "the Old Pretender" on his rightful throne. By September "Bonnie Prince Charlie," supported by a largely Highland Catholic army, had captured Edinburgh and by December threatened London. Failing to gain popular English support, he retreated, was defeated, and in the spring was forced back to France.

Edwards followed these events closely. He sent condolences for the sufferings of his Scottish friends and reminded them that God mingled his mercy with severity. "Great shakings and commotions have commonly preceded glorious changes in the state of the church."[23] Particularly, he saw the setbacks of the papal Antichristian powers as the prophesied "drying up the River Euphrates." Later he reported another manifestation of God's hand in hastening the destruction of the Antichrist. In fall 1746 a French fleet was sent to recapture Louisbourg and harass New England but turned back because of terrible storms and the death of its commander. Providences such as that and the defeat of the Pretender were clear signals to the Protestant British peoples that God was remarkably sparing them, despite their great wickedness in squandering the blessings of the Reformation.[24]

In itself, Edwards' biblicist anti-Catholicism was not out of step with the sentiments of much of the British Protestant world. Particularly since the accession of the Hanoverian Protestant monarchs in 1714, British nationalism had become firmly wedded to the Protestant cause. English and Scottish preachers routinely compared their nation to Israel. When George II succeeded to the Protestant throne in 1727, George Frederick Handel furnished a coronation anthem that specifically elicited the parallel to Zadok the priest and Nathan the prophet anointing Solomon. Anti-Catholicism was routinely part of British Whig politics.

In New England, Edwards' political views were thoroughly conventional. Eighteenth-century New Englanders had shed their Puritan outsider image and identified themselves with the Protestant and British cause. Religious and political interests could be equated because Great Britain under the Hanoverians was the strongest champion of international Protestantism.[25] Old Light and New Light equally shared such views. Charles Chauncy, in a sermon on the rebellion of the Pretender, referred to "the way popish princes, bigotted to the religion of Anti-Christ," and to "the interest of Rome and Hell." He reminded New Englanders of the "popish and despotic principles" that had oppressed them in the 1680s under James II.[26] Thomas Foxcroft, one of Edwards closest New Light allies, on New Year's Day 1747, reminded his Boston congregation that "Never to be forgotten is that glorious year 1714, signalis'd as a *year of the right hand of the most high*, by the happy and most seasonable *accession* of the illustrious House of HANOVER to the *British* throne."[27]

What separated the otherwise conventional religious-political views of Edwards, the New Lights, and their international circle of Reformed evangelicals from those of their British and New England Protestant contemporaries was the way they combined their hopes for the political advance of international Protestantism with millennial expectations for a worldwide awakening. The marriage of these two ideals was not entirely comfortable. Evangelicals were ardent nationalists, at least when the national cause could be seen as antipapist. Yet they also saw the Protestant nations as terribly corrupt. God had chosen them to be the guardians of true religion, new Israels in the modern era; yet they had forsaken him. To whom much was given much would be required. Their wickedness was therefore far more reprehensible than that of nations who never knew true religion. Repentance and awakening were their only hope. Yet as with Old Testament Israel, God was not giving up on them.

In broader historical perspective, exclusivist-conversionist Christianity and inclusivist Protestant nationalism, however unequally yoked, had a future together. During the next centuries they would beget a revolutionary world missionary movement. By the beginning of the twenty-first century, although the movement would not be nearly as universal nor as Reformed as Edwards and his visionary friends imagined, it would, as they did anticipate, bring more people to Christian conversion experiences than in all previous history combined.

Dependent as they were on Protestant civil power for their own safety, and as heirs to a long era when it was hard to imagine evangelical advance without political conquest, they believed that God would use his own nations, however imperfect, for his Gospel purposes. After all, God had blessed the whole world through ancient Israel, a nation that had been far from perfect. Preaching on the August 1746 thanksgiving day for the "victory over the rebels," Edwards reminded the Northamptonites of the disparity between their Protestant British nation's status as blessed by God and its deplorable spiritual condition. "Sometimes God is pleased," he observed, "to go out of his usual way. Sometimes [he] bestows temporal mercies on a very wicked people." This was particularly true in the Gospel age, which was an age of mercy, during which God often withheld his terrible judgments so that people could heed his providential warnings and have time to repent.[28]

Northampton was receiving many warnings. Beginning in the summer of 1745 the town was struck with "a sore sickness and mortality." In the four years from 1745 through 1748, more than one-tenth of the town's population died, or about thirty-five people per year, or almost three funerals per month—a devastating toll for a town of perhaps twelve or thirteen hundred.[29] Such affliction, which the pastor assured them was God's hand warning them to repent, further undercut the town's sagging spirits.

At the same time, the town faced renewed threat of Indian attacks. At first the theaters of this war had been rather distant from Northampton. Still, the town was deeply involved. Colonel Stoddard, working from his home base, had been in charge of building a new line of forts near the New York border to the west. He also made Northampton the headquarters for a planned, but never consummated, invasion of Canada, which was to follow up the Louisbourg victory. Major Seth Pomeroy, the local hero of Louisbourg, was in charge of raising troops for this always popular American enterprise.[30]

By August 1746, about the time the town was celebrating the defeat of the Young Pretender, Massachusetts had been set on the defensive. In the spring Stoddard, exasperated by the difficulties of defending a long wilderness frontier, had written to Connecticut's Governor Wolcott, "I have as many messengers with evil tidings as Job had, though I have not so much patience."[31] On August 19 French and Indians captured one of the new forts, Fort Massachusetts, about thirty miles northwest of Northampton. Small bands of

Indians had been harassing settlements all along the frontier and now had broken through the outer line of defenses. At Deerfield, horrible memories of a generation earlier were revived when Indians killed and scalped several men from two families who were out harvesting hay. On August 25 a small group of Indians threatened Southampton, the newer second precinct of North-ampton, eight miles to its southwest, ransacking the houses of two families who had fled. Northampton went into a high alert.[32]

We get a momentary view of the Edwards family in this tense circum-stance. Edwards often took a late summer trip, and in 1746 he traveled to East Hampton, Long Island, to preach the ordination sermon for Samuel Buell, the young evangelist who had brought the last Northampton awakening to its height. Whether for fear of the Indians, for social reasons, or for their spir-itual edification, Edwards took two of his daughters, Sarah and Esther, aged eighteen and fourteen, with him and left them there. The Edwards girls traveled frequently and often made extended visits with friends or family. In early November Jonathan wrote to Esther (who did have special fears of Indians),[33] describing Northampton in wartime. Northampton was well for-tified, but it was also a military headquarters that might be target for attack. During the fall, a couple of soldiers were billeted at the Edwardses' home. "Our house is now forted in," Edwards reported, "and a watch is kept here every night in the fort." Yet the French and Indian army had not done any real destruction in the vicinity after taking Fort Massachusetts. Edwards believed it had probably moved toward Nova Scotia to meet the French fleet, which God had since so wonderfully confounded. After reminding her of God's presence everywhere, Edwards offered Esther some consolation that may have been only partially reassuring: "Your circumstances at East Hampton are on some accounts much more comfortable than [those] of your sisters at home, for you lie down and arise and have none to make you afraid. Here we have been in much fear of an army suddenly rushing in upon the town in the night to destroy it."[34]

Despite the fortifications and the soldiers, life's ordinary concerns con-tinued. In October Edwards had written to his friend and protégé Joseph Bellamy, pastor at Bethlehem, Connecticut, on an uncharacteristically practi-cal matter (at least in the surviving correspondence). Edwards wanted to purchase twenty sheep if Bellamy could find some at a good price to purchase. Perhaps the Indian threats had driven up the costs of local wool.[35] Usually Sarah seems to have managed household affairs, and wool was essential for spinning and family clothes. Perhaps because he had other reasons to contact

Bellamy, Edwards took over the negotiation. In a second letter, sent in January, he mentioned intriguingly, "it might be perhaps expedient, on some accounts, for the present, not to let it be known who the sheep are for."[36]

This same letter shows that Edwards, as we might expect, had much weightier matters on his mind. Bellamy had asked him to find him some of the classic Reformed works on divinity. Edwards mentioned Francis Turretin, the seventeenth-century Swiss systematizer of Reformed dogma, as excellent on the five points of Calvinism and polemical divinity. Even better, he said, was the Dutch theologian, Peter van Mastricht of the late seventeenth century. "But take Mastricht," Edwards advised, "for divinity in general, doctrine, practice, and controversy; or as an universal system of divinity; and it is much better than Turretin or any other book in the world, excepting the Bible, in my opinion." In the meantime, Edwards said he was reading deeply in the Arminian controversy and writing on it in his notebooks. "I have got so deep into this controversy, that I am not willing to dismiss it, till I know the utmost of their matters."[37]

Indian threats continued through the next two years as the war dragged on. In both 1747 and 1748 Indian bands again got as close as Southampton, and each time they killed a resident. On the second occasion, in spring 1748, the attack caused such a panic that the settlers abandoned Southampton, most of them crowding into Northampton for the summer. Fear of Indians, frustrations from trying to counter guerrilla attacks, casualties among the men who had gone to war, overcrowding from refugees and billeted soldiers, and the continued high natural death rate all depressed Northampton's morale.[38] The official end of the war, primarily a European affair, in the peace of Aix-la-Chapelle, October 18, 1748, was hardly a cause for rejoicing either. England had done the unthinkable. To the colonists' chagrin she traded away the great trophy of the war that Providence had so unmistakably given into the hands of New England. Louisbourg went back to the French. New England was once again judged for her pride, though it probably did not please many to have the minister say so.

Edwards viewed these hard times in the much larger perspective of God's long-term redemptive plan. Promotion of the Concert of Prayer was his principal public contribution to aiding the primary international cause, of which the war was only a tiny part. Closer to home, these years of constant talk of Indian threats and military campaigns only increased his missionary zeal. Always close to his uncle John Stoddard, Edwards kept well informed on military matters and doubtless kept the pious Stoddard appraised of the larger spiritual picture. We do not know exactly how much the uncle and nephew collaborated, but Stoddard had long been a chief negotiator with the Indians and in the current conflict was active in conciliating some of the tribes in nearby New York. In one small glimpse that we have, Stoddard appears as a champion of fair dealings. "The Indians," he wrote to Governor Shirley, in May 1747, "are of such a humor that if we deal justly and kindly by them, they will put their lives into our hands, but if we deal deceitfully with them, that will soon raise an abhorrence of us."[39] Such sage advice, which the British could have used more of, reflected years of experience and military interests. Yet it also reflected the larger concern for Indian missions that the colonel shared with his nephew. Stoddard had helped found the Stockbridge mission near the New York border and likely had been there during his efforts to gain intelligence on the mood of the local Indians. A few weeks after his letter to Governor Shirley, he was vividly reminded of their ultimate goal in Indian affairs: late in May, David Brainerd arrived at the Edwardses' home.

CHAPTER 20

## "Thy Will Be Done"

If Sarah Edwards, renowned as the model wife and caring hostess, ever
felt entirely overwhelmed, the arrival of David Brainerd on Thursday
May 28, 1747, may have been one of those times. Just three weeks earlier
she had given birth to an eighth daughter, Elizabeth. In addition were two
boys, Timothy, nearly nine, and Jonathan Jr., who had just turned two. Remarkably, all ten children had thus far survived. By contrast, in John Stoddard's household, with which the family must have had constant interchange,
only five of the ten children survived to adulthood.[1]

When Brainerd arrived, gaunt with tuberculosis, the Edwardses already
had another gravely ill New Light on their hands. Eleazar Wheelock was
staying with them, and Edwards had written Bellamy that the young evangelist might never preach again.[2] Wheelock did recover (and lived to found both
a charity school for Indians and Dartmouth College). The Edwardses were
surrounded by illness and other troubles. Northampton had become terribly
unhealthy during the war years. The cool attitude of much of the town toward
its pastor did not make matters any easier for the family. The war itself
added to the tensions. The town was still fortified, although soldiers probably
were no longer billeted in the Edwardses' home. Colonel Stoddard was still
hoping to mount an invasion of Canada, but most of the time he was occupied with the frustrating task of overseeing the defense of a sometimes
indefensible frontier.

Despite these burdens, the Edwards family was still flourishing at near its
peak, and we can try to get some sense of what the household was like. The
home was a substantial two-story, eighteenth-century frame structure heated
by a large central fireplace and chimney, to which most of the separate rooms
would be adjacent. The hearth was the center of home life. The interior of the

home probably was not plastered, and the furnishings were modest. Included were the standard carding machines and spinning wheels for the typical home industries of the day. The Edwardses had a garden plot and also the rights to some nearby acreage that they tilled or used for grazing sheep, pigs, and cattle. An African woman slave, who probably had her own children, helped with the household duties.[3]

The first impression a visitor would have upon arriving at the Edwards home was that there were a lot of children. The second impression would be that they were very well disciplined. Jonathan aided Sarah in disciplining the children from an early age. "When they first discovered any considerable degree of will and stubbornness," wrote Samuel Hopkins, "he would attend to them till he had thoroughly subdued them and brought them to submit." Edwards did this "with the greatest calmness, and commonly without striking a blow." Soon he "effectually established his parental authority, and produced a cheerful obedience ever after."

Care for his children's souls was, of course, his preeminent concern. In morning devotions he quizzed them on Scripture with questions appropriate to their ages. On Saturday evening, the beginning of the Sabbath, he taught them the *Westminster Shorter Catechism,* making sure they understood as well as memorized the answers.[4] "As innocent as children seem to be to us," he had recently written in defense of teaching them of hell fire and eternal damnation, "yet if they are out of Christ, they are not so in God's sight, but are young vipers, and are infinitely more hateful than young vipers." At the judgment day unregenerate children would hardly thank their parents for sentimental tenderness that protected them from knowing the true dangers of their estate.[5] Always looking for opportunities to awaken the young to their condition, he had, for instance, taken the children of the town to view the remains of the Lyman house fire that claimed two girls' lives.[6]

By far the greater burden of childrearing fell to Sarah. According to Samuel Hopkins, "she had an excellent way of governing her children: she knew how to make them regard and obey her cheerfully, without loud angry words, or heavy blows." Hopkins reported that it was her manner to reprove her children "in a few words, without heat or noise, with all calmness and gentleness of mind." Usually she had only to speak once and would be "cheerfully obeyed." "Quarreling and contention," the admiring Hopkins claimed, "as it frequently takes place among children, was not known among them."

Sarah began the discipline of her children when they were very young in order to suppress their self-will. "She carefully observed the first appearances

The Edwards parsonage at Northampton, from a nineteenth-century drawing

of resentment and ill will towards any, in her young children," said Hopkins, "and did not connive at it and promote it, as many who have the care of children do, but was careful to shew her displeasure at it, and suppress it to her utmost."[7] Subduing the will was both a necessary step in preparation for grace and a key to domestic tranquility.

The older Edwards daughters must have aided Sarah in the childrearing, but this did not keep them from long visits away from home. Sarah Jr., known as "Sally" (who may have been outshone by her next three brilliant sisters, Jerusha, Esther, and Mary), seems to have spent considerable time in New Haven, where she was in 1744 and in the fall of 1747.[8] Jerusha and Esther were also sometimes included in visits to Boston and may have spent some extended time there. Esther became a close friend of Sarah Prince, daughter of

Thomas Prince Sr. Although Colonel John Stoddard's daughters were said to have been educated in Boston (as were Jonathan's sisters), there is no evidence of such formal schooling for the Edwards girls, although they appear to have been well schooled at home.

Sarah Sr., as mother to this large family, overseer of operations for farming, cooking, clothing, washing, cleaning, admonishing, and much of the educating, was the embodiment of the Puritan ideal of industry. If she truly was, as Samuel Hopkins implies, "a deputy husband" or the de facto manager of the house and farm as well as the mother of eleven children, her accomplishments were monumental.[9] On one occasion, when she was out of town in 1748, Jonathan was soon near his wits' end. The two eldest daughters, he wrote, were both "beat out and having the headache" and were sleeping in. Children of almost every other age, from the one-year-old up, needed to be taken care of. "We have been without you," Jonathan lamented, "almost as long as we know how to be."[10]

In addition to caring for her own family and household, Sarah operated what amounted to a small inn to accommodate travelers (most often unannounced) and various young boarders who came to learn from her husband. As her attentiveness to young Samuel Hopkins when he came first into their home as a student illustrates, she concerned herself with the welfare of her guests. Hopkins later wrote: "She would spare no pains to make them welcome, and provide for their convenience and comfort. And she was peculiarly kind to strangers who came to her house."[11]

So while Sarah may have rejoiced spiritually at the visit of David Brainerd, renowned for his self-sacrifice, her saintliness may have been tested by now having two gravely ill young preachers as part of the household. Sarah was, after all, prone to inner turmoil and low spirits. Fortunately, Eleazar Wheelock soon recovered, and she had daughters, especially Jerusha, to serve as nurse for Brainerd. Just turned seventeen, Jerusha was the most like her parents in spiritual intensity. In a household where the highest goal was to subordinate one's will to God's, selfless sacrifice was the supreme virtue. David Brainerd was already legendary for his willingness to endure any hardship in his efforts to bring the Gospel to the Indians. Jerusha, in turn, was ready to give herself to caring for this physically wrecked embodiment of her spiritual ideals.

Edwards and his circle were keenly aware that one of the great weaknesses of the international Reformed movement was its failure to sustain effective missions to the Indians. Edwards' brother-in-law, Samuel Hopkins the elder, his cousin Stephen Williams, and his uncle John Stoddard had pioneered the reestablishment of a New England mission at Stockbridge a decade earlier. The current war only intensified the sense of urgency for extending such efforts. Winning the hearts of Indians would have incalculable strategic advantage. At the same time the international awakening reinforced concerns for their souls. Evangelical societies in Scotland and England were eager to support missionaries, but the candidates were few.

David Brainerd was a man driven to serve. After an intense conversion experience in 1739, he entered Yale College, at age twenty-one, to prepare for the ministry. His new convert's zeal soon flared among the flames of the awakening as Whitefield, Tennent, and Davenport created sensations in New Haven in 1741. Rector Clap's legislation against student condemnations of the faculty's spiritual authority in September 1741, the week of Edwards' commencement address, may have been directed at Brainerd. The next winter a freshman, passing his room, overheard Brainerd say that Tutor Chauncey Whittelsey "has no more grace than this chair." The freshman reported the remark to a lady of the town, who told President Clap. The imperious Clap, perhaps waiting for his chance, launched an investigation and sought a public confession. Brainerd took exception to having to make a public confession for a private remark. Clap had him expelled for this, for attending one New Light meeting without permission, and for an alleged remark that he thought Clap might "expect to drop down dead" for fining students who went to hear Gilbert Tennent preach.[12]

Excluded from Yale, Brainerd went to study with a local pastor. In the meantime, he worked to get himself reinstated, but even after the intervention of some of Yale's most respected graduates, including Jonathan Dickinson and Aaron Burr, Clap would not budge. In summer 1742 Brainerd was preaching, without proper licensing, with Joseph Bellamy in Bethlehem, Connecticut. Dickinson and Burr then secured for him an appointment as missionary to the Indians under the auspices of the Society in Scotland for Propagating Christian Knowledge, a position he undertook in spring 1743. For about a year he worked in the Mahican village of Kaunameek about twenty miles from Stockbridge under the guidance of Stockbridge missionary John Sergeant.

The attempt to get Brainerd reinstated at Yale had in the meantime become a cause célèbre. Brainerd's final effort was to try to graduate with his class in September 1743 on the basis of his private study. Edwards, in New Haven for the commencement, met Brainerd for the first time, counseled him on this matter, and may have helped him write a contrite confession. Although Yale was now willing to admit him for an additional year of study, it was not ready to grant him a degree, despite the fact, according to Edwards, that he would have stood first in his class.[13]

By this time Brainerd was committed to his missionary work. Despite little success in Kaunameek, he turned down a conventional pastorate in spring 1744 and traveled to the Delaware and Susquehanna rivers in search of Delaware Indians to convert. Already ill, he endured extraordinary hardships but had little to show for it. Finally, in fall 1745, after many discouragements, his world-renouncing efforts began to have visible results. An awakening broke out in the Delaware Indian village at Crossweeksung, south of Trenton, New Jersey. But by fall 1746 Brainerd was too ill to continue his work. In desperation, he set out for his native New England, believing he had "little hope of recovery, unless by much riding." He also thought it his "duty" to "divert myself among my friends whom I had not now seen for a long time."[14] He got only as far as the home of his principal sponsor, Jonathan Dickinson in Elizabeth, New Jersey, where he collapsed. He spent the winter there recovering. In April he felt well enough to resume his therapeutic ride to New England, and in late May he arrived at Stephen Williams' home in Longmeadow, where he stayed five days before riding to Northampton.

When Brainerd arrived, Jonathan found him not as deathly ill or "broken in his understanding" as he had heard. He was impressed that Brainerd had ridden the twenty-five miles from Longmeadow in one day. The young man also appeared "cheerful and free from melancholy." When Dr. Mather examined him, he "gave him over," but the town's other physician, Dr. Pynchon, held out hope, as did Edwards. As usual, Edwards was most impressed by spiritual intensity. He found Brainerd's prayers in the family stunning. Even his prayers returning thanks for food were awe inspiring. Brainerd and the Edwards found much in common in their millennial hopes. "In his prayers, he insisted much on the prosperity of Zion, the advancement of Christ's kingdom in the world, and the flourishing and propagation of religion among the Indians."[15]

The doctors, then as now ready to prescribe what has already worked, decided that horseback riding was good for Brainerd; so after two weeks in Northampton he set off for Boston, accompanied by Jerusha "to be helpful to him in his weak and low state." The trip, usually two and a half days, took four. As usual for the Edwardses, they spent one night at the Reverend Ebenezer Parkman's in Westborough. Less than a week after arriving in

Boston, Brainerd once again fell gravely ill. Jerusha wrote to her father that the doctors said that either he might die any day or he might have another respite for a few months. By late July he had gained the respite and set out with Jerusha and his younger brother Israel, a Yale student, on a slow trip back to Northampton.[16]

Again at the Edwardses, the invalid was well enough to go out for brief daily horseback rides and may have still hoped to return to New Jersey.[17] By early September he was too weak to leave the house. Jerusha, although not especially well herself, cared for him all this time as she had since May. He was still strong enough to continue entries and editing on his diary and to speak with Jerusha, her father, and other family members on serious spiritual matters.

On Sunday, October 4, he was near death. When Jerusha entered the room, as Jonathan recorded it, "he looked on her very pleasantly and said, 'Dear Jerusha, are you willing to part with me? I am quite willing to part with you: I am willing to part with all my friends: I am willing to part with my dear brother John; although I love him the best of any creature living: I have committed him and all my friends to God, and can leave them with God. Though, if I thought I should not see you and be happy with you in another world, I could not bear to part with you. But we shall spend an happy eternity together!'" Three days later, his younger brother John arrived. David loved John "best of any creature living" in part because he was his coworker and successor in his all-important mission work with Indians in New Jersey. Jerusha, who was "of much the same spirit with Mr. Brainerd," would understand such kingdom priorities. Two days later David Brainerd died, attended by those closest to him.

Edwards made a point that the funeral would be simple, not with the "pomp and show" that Brainerd had feared would have attended it had he died in Boston.[18] Edwards preached on "True Saints, When Absent from the Body, are Present with the Lord" in a passionate exultation of the Christ-centered wonders of the heavenly state. The saints, he emphasized—perhaps particularly with Jerusha's grief in mind—were not in a sort of limbo waiting for the Lord's return, but rather were immediately "with Christ." That meant they were in perfect union with Christ. In Christ all darkness of sin was "abolished before the full blaze of the sun's meridian light." Yet this was no blind state of ecstasy. Those who on earth were betrothed to Christ were in heaven married to him and conversed with him as an intimate friend in most perfect mutual love. So "the souls of departed saints with Christ in heaven, shall have Christ as it were unbosomed unto them, manifesting those infinite riches of love toward them, that have been there from eternity." These souls, far better than when they had bodies, "shall eat and drink abundantly, and swim in the ocean of love." Edwards lavished his hearers with biblical images. As the spouse of Christ they were "the king's daughter" and so shared with Christ the "ineffable delights" of the glory of the Father. Yet while "eternally swallowed up on the infinitely bright, and infinitely mild and sweet beams of divine light," they would still follow with keen interest and joy the advance of the Christ's kingdom on earth. They would be eagerly looking forward to the day when they would return with Christ to help judge the world and reign forever with him. David Brainerd could endure his sufferings and impending death with profound tranquility because he so clearly saw reality in this cosmic context. Such a God-centered perspective enabled him to act as one who "had indeed sold all for Christ" and even in death had maintained his preeminent concern for the kingdom arising "from a pure disinterested love to Christ and desire of his glory."[19]

## "Like a Flower That Is Cut Down"

In spite of all his efforts to embrace heavenly loves so fully that even the dearest earthly affections paled in comparison, Edwards was not entirely prepared for the sequel four months later. On February 14, a Sabbath, his beloved Jerusha died of an acute fever. She was, he confided to a correspondent in Scotland, "generally esteemed the flower of the family."[20] Her illness had been less than a week, so there was little time to prepare for the agony— even though he had for a lifetime been preparing for such.

The next Sabbath the grief-stricken Edwards preached Jerusha's eulogy sermon on the poignant theme from Job, "Youth is like a flower that is cut down." He had preached the doctrinal part of the sermon before a youth meeting regarding the death of a young man in 1741 near the beginning of the post-Whitefield awakening. The haunting theme was too appropriate to pass up, and the added portions were the most personal of any of Edwards' sermons. The lost beauty of the flower cut down was a "fit emblem of a young person in the bloom of life, with amiable, pleasant, and promising qualifications, not only with a blooming body but mind also; with desirable natural and moral endowments." Jerusha was a model of one "remarkably weaned" from the world, "very indifferent about all things whatsoever of a worldly nature, setting her heart" on another world. She "declared in words, showed in deeds, [that she was] ever more ready to deny herself, earnestly inquiring in every affair which way she could most glorify God."

Edwards assured the congregation that he was not there to boast of his daughter's saintliness, or of himself, but to use her death for the good of others. Her death had come without warning. "In the very flower of youth, [she] was the sabbath before last here at meeting without any sensible signs of approaching death." Everyone could see her empty place and take warning. This admonition from God did not stand alone. For three years now it had been a "doleful time among us . . . with regard to the state of religion," and God was repeatedly sending warnings in the deaths of "many young people." Yet the behavior of many of those who remained was worse than ever.

Edwards acknowledged the cordial expressions of condolences that Jerusha's death had brought from the townspeople, but he was determined to turn their sentiments to eternal good. So many other young people seemed thoroughly unprepared as they dedicated themselves, not to the company of saints, but to gatherings for mirth and frivolity that only cultivated their sensual natures. Worse was their frolicking "and that shameful lascivious custom of handling women's breasts, and the different sexes lying in beds together." What if such young people were suddenly taken?

The ashen Edwards turned the congregation's attention to his own transparent grief. Even though the one who "died in the bloom of her youth [was] my own dear child," he knew the comfort of a parent who could see every evidence that she had set her love on Christ. What horror it would be to a parent if the evidence were to the contrary? What comfort would it be to the parent to reflect that "This my departed child was an eminent frolicker, much of a gallant, a jolly companion"? Although this providence, Edwards concluded, is "in itself so bitter and afflictive to me," it would be a great comfort to him if it would become "the beginning of a general awakening and reformation among you, the young people of my flock."[21]

Edwards had Jerusha's wilted body buried next to Brainerd's. On his deathbed David had told Jerusha that he would not have been able to bear parting with her if he had not been sure that they would spend eternity together. Edwards was confident that their souls were already blissfully united in Christ, yet in what seems for him an unusual display of earthly sentiment, he placed her remains next to Brainerd's, awaiting the bodily resurrection. Eight months later, referring to Jerusha's passing, Edwards confessed that he was still "the subject of an afflictive dispensation of late." God was teaching him, he believed, "how to sympathize with the afflicted."[22]

The graves of David Brainerd and Jerusha Edwards

The story of David and Jerusha is one of the history's fabled spiritual love tales and has led to much speculation. Edwards' account of Brainerd's parting speech to her suggests that they cared deeply for each other, even if their deepest loves were for things spiritual. Legend has it that they were betrothed, but there is no real evidence for that. Some have even suggested that Brainerd traveled to Northampton in order to see Jerusha, but there is no indication that they previously had met.[23]

Jonathan himself loved Brainerd. Immediately after the young man's death, he set aside some of his own cherished projects to edit Brainerd's diaries, which he would eventually publish as *An Account of the Life of David Brainerd*. As late as summer 1747, he had written to John Erskine, a Scottish correspondent, that he intended to write "something particularly and largely on the Arminian controversy," beginning with "a discourse concerning the Freedom of the Will, and Moral Agency." Providence, he wrote the next year had "unexpectedly laid in my way, and seemed to render unavoidable" the higher priority of publishing the *Life of Brainerd*.[24] The death of Jerusha, who may have been helping with the project, only increased his zeal to see it completed.

Completing the *Life of Brainerd* was of such paramount importance—so

momentous as to postpone his long-planned tour de force against the Arminian menace—because Edwards was convinced that his chief priority was the
international awakening. He had just completed his work promoting the
transatlantic Concert of Prayer for revival, and he saw the memorial to Brainerd as a providentially sanctioned sequel. In his work, as in his life, piety
preceded intellect.

Secondarily, but not incidentally, the *Life of Brainerd* was pivotal in the
intra-Reformed contests to win North America. Within just the past few
years, the Reformed churches (Presbyterians and Congregationalists) had
become badly divided between Old Lights and New Lights. In New England, both Harvard and Yale were firmly under Old Light control. In response, transplanted New Englanders in New Jersey, allied with New Light
("New Side") Presbyterians of the Tennent circle, had just founded their own
college there.

Brainerd stood near the center of the college controversy. His expulsion
from Yale became a test case that symbolized the whole controversy. Who
had the power to educate and hence to control ordination? The spat between
Yale's Rector Thomas Clap and Edwards grew out of Clap's fears that Whitefield and his cohorts would destroy the near-monopoly that Yale and Harvard
had on the supply of clergy. Clap also saw to it that Connecticut banned
ordinations of those, such as Brainerd, who had not graduated from Yale,
Harvard, or a European university. In 1744 New Light Presbyterians ordained
Brainerd in New Jersey.

The leading figure among these New Jersey Presbyterians was Jonathan
Dickinson, at whose home Brainerd nearly died in the winter of 1746–47.
Dickinson, not quite sixty, had been born in Hatfield, Massachusetts, and so
provided a major tie between New Jersey–New York Presbyterianism and
Stoddard country. During the winter of Brainerd's visit Dickinson was organizing the new College of New Jersey, of which he was chosen the first
president. The college at his home in Elizabeth opened its doors for its first
students in May 1747, a few days after Brainerd set out for New England.
When in October 1747 Dickinson died suddenly, the college was moved to the
care of the Reverend Aaron Burr of Newark, a young Edwards protégé, who
became its next president.[25] Burr was later said to have remarked that "if it
had not been for the treatment received by Mr. Brainerd at Yale, New Jersey
College would never have been erected."[26]

After reading through Brainerd's diaries, Edwards wrote to John Brainerd to fill in some details, especially those concerning the expulsion from Yale.

Edwards wanted to be sure that his was an "exact and certain account of that affair, that the Rector may have no cause, nor find any room to complain of the least misrepresentation in any respect."[27] In summarizing the episode (Edwards had honored Brainerd's wish, left via Jerusha, that the diaries for his Yale years be destroyed), Edwards acknowledged Brainerd's "intemperate imprudent zeal." Edwards' only attempt at defending him was to write that he had then been "not only young in years, but very young in religion and experience." The crucial point, one that Edwards repeatedly stressed, was that Brainerd had thoroughly repented of these youthful excesses. Thus while Edwards granted the justice of the Yale officials in disciplining Brainerd, he implied that Clap and company were at fault in 1743 for not fully restoring one who was such a model of repentance.[28] Indeed, in Edwards' account Brainerd had become a paragon of mature, balanced, restrained, nonjudgmental, anti-separatist, intensely spiritual, self-abasing, orthodox Christianity.

Edwards had, of course, a purpose far larger than the college controversies in portraying Brainerd as the exemplary New Light. The missionary, in Edwards' account, had all the traits of the model Christian. The *Life of Brainerd,* seen in this larger framework, is *Religious Affections* in the form of a spiritual biography.

It might also be seen as in part a spiritual autobiography. Although the substance of the volume is edited diaries, it is often difficult to distinguish between author and editor. From a portion of the earliest diary, for which we have the original, we can tell that Edwards, while mostly following Brainerd's words, also took some broad liberties, as editors of the time typically did. Sometimes he merely left out words or phrases because of considerations of length or because they repeated other material or because of imprecise theology. He also tended to moderate and depersonalize some of Brainerd's accounts of his religious experience and to stiffen Brainerd's language—for example, he changed Brainerd's regret at "frolicking" to "frolicking (as it is called)." At other times he altered Brainerd's meaning to fit his own agenda. For instance, he left out an entry in which Brainerd rejoiced at a report of Whitefield's success, an element of possible controversy that Edwards wanted to avoid.[29] We cannot tell, of course, how much of real substance Edwards left out. The reason Brained ordered his Yale diaries destroyed was doubtless because they contained criticisms of people, and we know Edwards excised such passages in what remained, omitting entirely, for instance, a painful face-to-face attempt for restoration at Yale in July 1743 that had left Brainerd bitter. The Brainerd that Edwards wished remembered exemplified (closely paraphrasing the "Eighth Sign" of *Religious Affections)* "the lamb-like, dove-like spirit of Jesus Christ! How full of love, meekness, quietness, forgiveness, and mercy!"[30]

Because Edwards' goal was to present an exemplary spiritual biography, some things were best omitted or corrected. The exemplary narrative of spiritual experience was a well-established Puritan form and fit in with the wider campaign to use the press to promote awakening. *Christian History* and its counterparts abroad were regularly publishing edifying accounts of the revivals, and Boston presses still reprinted Puritan spiritual narratives. Brainerd himself, during his illness in Boston and Northampton, wrote a preface for the *Meditations and Spiritual Experiences of Mr. Thomas Shepard,* the much-revered Puritan divine, published by Thomas Prince in 1747.[31]

Compared to modern biographies, what is most striking about Edwards' *Life of Brainerd* is that it centers on the missionary's internal spiritual life and uses the externals of his missionary travels only as scaffolding on which that real story is built. Edwards was much more interested in the sacrifice involved in Brainerd's mission than in its success. In fact, willingness to persevere even when he had nothing to show for it was what made Brainerd's story so admirable. The missionary had already published the part of his *Journal* dealing with his one external success in New Jersey. While Edwards strongly recommended that readers purchase this published *Journal,* as "the most pleasant part of the whole story," he saw at least as much edification in the spiritual struggles of a suffering saint.

Brainerd was temperamentally a lot like Edwards, given to periods of melancholy and spiritual deadness as well as to intense spiritual ecstasies. Edwards acknowledged that "gloominess of mind," or "dark thoughts" that were the result of "the disease of melancholy," could be of a "very hurtful nature." Early in his spiritual life, Brainerd had attributed such episodes to "spiritual desertion." Later he had learned, as he had discussed most judiciously with Edwards, to recognize his recurrent illness not as spiritual desertion but occasion for true humiliation and godly sorrow. Here we have a valuable clue to how Edwards himself had learned to deal with his own times of gloomy melancholy.

Edwards acknowledged editing out or summarizing some of the darkest reflections recorded in Brainerd's diary. Especially during his lonesome, dangerous, and often fruitless travels on the Susquehanna, the missionary experienced lengthy times in the slough of despondency. Yet for Edwards, renouncing comforts of the world and even being brought to the point, like Christ on the cross, of feeling forsaken by God, was evidence of sainthood.[32]

At the height of his success in Crossweeksung in May 1746, Brainerd expressed the world-renouncing Christlike qualities that Edwards so admired. He was, according to Edwards' rendition of his diary, greatly tempted to settle in the village. "But now," Brainerd wrote, "these thoughts seemed to be wholly dashed to pieces; not by necessity, but of choice: for it appeared to me that God's dealings towards me had fitted me for a life of solitariness and hardship; it appeared to me I had nothing to lose, nothing to do with earth, and consequently nothing to lose by a total renunciation of it: And it appeared just right that I should be destitute of house and home, and many comforts of life which I rejoiced to see others of God's people enjoy."[33]

Edwards' and Brainerd's emphasis on such readiness to renounce the world for the kingdom helps account for the immense impact of *The Life of David Brainerd*, Edwards' most popular work and one of the most influential missionary accounts of all time. John Wesley published an abridgment that went into many printings. During the awakenings of the first half of the nineteenth century *The Life of Brainerd*, republished in various editions, became one of the most popular of American literary works, both at home and abroad. Brainerd's example gave concrete meaning to the influential evangelical ideal of "disinterested benevolence." Many missionaries carried *The Life of Brainerd* with them. Benjamin Franklin's *Autobiography*, the story of the self-made man, eventually became paradigmatic of the American ideal, but at least before the Civil War, Edwards' *Brainerd*, the self-renouncing man, offered a major alternative.[34]

Had Edwards built his account around what would have been a relatively modest missionary success story (Brainerd counted fewer than a hundred converts), his *Brainerd* would never had such lasting effect. Edwards *was* deeply concerned for practical matter of the spread of Indian missions and rejoiced that Brainerd's last stay in Boston had inspired the founding of a new mission society there.[35] Yet the heart of the matter was his example of world-sacrificing piety for a cause of infinite worth.

## "The Advancement of Christ's Kingdom on Earth"

"This morning," David Brainerd wrote in his diary on Lord's Day, August 23, 1747, "I was considerably refreshed with the thought, yea, the hope and expectation of the enlargement of Christ's kingdom; and I could not but hope the time was at hand when Babylon the great would 'fall and rise no more.' "[36] When Brainerd visited the Edwards home, it is important to remember, Northampton was in the midst of a war and the house was fortified. Hostile Indians were rumored to be close at hand. Only four days after Brainerd's diary entry, a band of Indians scalped and killed Elisha Clark, a well-known local farmer, who had been threshing in his barn in Southampton.[37] Despite such painful inversions of his hopes, Brainerd could rejoice with the Edwardses in the long-term prospects.

Brainerd's self-sacrificing missionary zeal and Edwards' wider activism must be understood in the context of their earthly optimism. Edwards' theology was not simply philosophical reflections growing out of his contemplations of God and a heavenly eternity. Rather, since it was always refracted through Scripture, it was grounded in a breathtaking historical perspective that provided incentive for unflagging evangelical action.

While Brainerd was in Northampton, Edwards was completing yet another book on awakening, one that must have provided subjects for many hours of their prayers and conversations. The book, *An Humble Attempt to Promote an Explicit Agreement and Visible Union of God's People thro' the World, in Extraordinary Prayer, for the Revival of Religion, and the Advancement of Christ's Kingdom on Earth, Pursuant to Scripture Promise and Prophecies Concerning the Last Time,* completed by September 1747, had two focal points, as its complicated title suggested. First it was a plea for the international Concert of Prayer. Yet most of the exposition was on the second point, the prospects for the coming millennial kingdom on earth.

Prayer societies, while not new, were essential parts of the evangelical awakenings. Edwards had organized meetings for prayer and praise for various groups and districts of Northampton since before the revival of 1734–35. The Scottish awakenings were similarly sustained by weekly prayer meetings. In 1744 Scottish leaders, including Edwards' correspondent John McLaurin, organized two years of concerted prayer at designated times for international revival. Edwards eagerly promised to help. By this time New England's great awakening (unlike its Scottish counterpart) was in shambles and prayer seemed the only hope. "It is apparent that we can't help ourselves," Edwards wrote to a Scottish correspondent in November 1745, "and have nowhere else to go, but to God."[38] In *An Humble Attempt* Edwards was arguing for a Scottish proposal to formalize and extend the Concert of Prayer, involving international agreements to regularly scheduled extraordinary prayers for awakenings, either in societies or privately, on Saturday evenings or Sabbath mornings and on quarterly days of prayer. Edwards did everything he could to encourage the Concert among prayer societies in Northampton, but the town was in its spiritual doldrums and little came of it.

Edwards' case in *An Humble Attempt* for instituting the Concert of Prayer was built largely around his hopes for the millennium, a subject on which he had been wanting to write. The connection between the two themes was not artificial. After all, at the center of the prototypical Christian prayer was "thy kingdom come; thy will be done in earth as it is in heaven."[39] Edwards, with his usual thoroughness, assembled all the Scriptural data depicting what it would mean for Christ's kingdom to come and his will to be done on earth.

The biblical pictures of the coming kingdom were awe inspiring. Edwards allowed that the millennium might mean either a thousand years or "a very long time" and was critical of those authorities who attempted to set exact dates (although he himself had earlier speculated that it would begin around A.D. 2000). During the long era that would follow, almost everyone would truly follow Christ. As a result, wars would cease, nations would dwell together as brethren, "the wolf should dwell with the lamb." There would be "vast increase of knowledge," and "all heresies and false doctrines shall be exploded." In short, the triumph of Christ's kingdom "is an event unspeakably happy and glorious."[40]

This amazing future had a remarkable theological implication. During the millennium humans would live in harmony with nature as well as with each other. With the resulting combination of "great health and peace," Edwards pointed out, the population would accelerate phenomenally. Even if it doubled only every one hundred years, the world population after a millennium would be a thousand times greater than at the beginning. If it doubled every fifty years (less than the growth rate for New England), the population would increase a millionfold. Virtually everyone in the millennium, furthermore, would be regenerate. Jesus' prophesy that "I, if I be lifted up from the earth, will draw all men unto me" (John 12:32) referred to such a time. So since the overwhelming majority of all humans that ever lived would live during the millennium and virtually all of those would be redeemed, the percentage of humans damned would be tiny.[41]

Edwards did not spell out the point, but he was indirectly commenting on an issue that greatly bothered him and many of his contemporaries. If, as he argued, God was essentially love, how could the Lord condemn some to an eternity of suffering in hell? Edwards' millennial logic did not resolve the fundamental issue, which he addressed in other venues. Still, if God damned far fewer than one person in a thousand God's overall governance of the universe looked far more benevolent than if only a select few people would be saved. A decade later Edwards' close ally, Joseph Bellamy, published a sermon including a chart that used the same statistics to show that the ratio of saved to lost would be more than 17,000 to 1. In a related sermon Bellamy argued that if, as Jesus taught, there is more joy in heaven over one sinner found than in ninety-nine never lost, and that if only two-thirds of all humans were saved, the surplus of joy in the universe created by the permission of evil would be many million times increased.[42] Edwards, who surely later talked long and hard with Bellamy on these points, was in *An Humble Attempt* not addressing the problem of evil. For now he was demonstrating that it was certainly worth much praying to hasten the day when this painful era of rebellion would be succeeded by the reign of righteousness.

The inspiring brightness of this coming Christ-centered utopia contrasted sharply with the dark hues of the present. Especially in New England, religion had hit a low. Fierce contentions divided churches. People held ministers in contempt. Church discipline was lax. Wild delusions inspired by the devil prevailed among enthusiasts. Others despised all vital piety. Vice and immorality of all kinds were "unusually prevailing." In the homelands things were worse. This was all the more ironic because "It is an age, as is supposed, of great light, freedom of thought, and discovery of truth in matters of religion, and detection of the weakness and bigotry of our ancestors." Yet the so-called advances of this supposed "age of great light" were undermining morals. On another front, the forces of Rome were increasing their attacks on Protestantism. France had renewed persecutions of Huguenots, and there were recent efforts "to restore a popish government in Great Britain, the chief bulwark of the Protestant cause."[43]

Despite such machinations of the devil, God was moving history toward the millennium. This was where Edwards marshaled his evidences of God's recent intervention, such as in the defeat of the Pretender, the recent remarkable preservation of New England from the French fleet, and the "almost miraculous" capture of the Louisbourg fortress on Cape Breton. The latter, he believed, was the closest parallel in "these latter ages" to God's wonderful interventions in biblical times. Even small signs might signal a turning point in history. Although it "may seem trivial," he pointed out, the capture of Cape Breton deprived popish countries of much of their fish, "their superstition forbidding them to eat any flesh for near a third part of the year."[44] The world prospects were bright enough, he insisted, that there was good reason to believe that God might be ordaining the Concert of Prayer as part of a dramatic turn for the better.

Some of Edwards' usual supporters thought he was too optimistic. As usual a group of five evangelical Boston clergy, including Thomas Prince, furnished a preface; but their endorsement was tepid. Readers, they said, might best judge for themselves regarding "the author's ingenious observations on the prophecies." Particularly they questioned his interpretation of the "slaying of the witnesses" of Revelation 11. They believed, as did the prevailing interpreters in their circle, that a great persecution was yet to come, whereas the hopeful Edwards said it referred to past sufferings of the saints in the Reformation era. Edwards believed that pessimistic views of the immediate future could dampen zeal for the Concert of Prayer and was attempting to show that there was no necessary reason that the recent awakenings might not still turn out to be early signs of the coming of the kingdom.[45]

As with much of Edwards' work, the best immediate reception for *An Humble Attempt* was in Scotland; yet, as was also generally true, his views—or variations much like them—eventually became a force in nineteenth-century America. Down to the Civil War, millennial optimism became the dominant American Protestant doctrine. Although Edwards is not usually thought of as a progenitor of the American party of hope, one can easily see continuities between *An Humble Attempt* and reforming millennial optimism as late as "The Battle Hymn of the Republic" or even into the progressive era.[46]

In his own day Edwards might have been seen, even by some in his own party, as grasping at straws. Increasingly he became preoccupied with gauging the prospects for the kingdom. Almost immediately after David Brainerd's funeral, he began a new section of his notebook on the "Apocalypse," entitled "An Account of Events Probably Fulfilling the Sixth Vial on the River Euphrates, the News of which was Received since October 16, 1747." Part of his argument in the just-completed *Humble Attempt* was that the rise of the Antichrist (the papacy), from which 1,260 years were to be calculated to its overthrow, need not be one date (such as A.D. 756) but could refer to a series of events. Hence God's work in overthrowing the papacy would also be a series of events already in process and need not be delayed. So even if the millennium itself were not at hand, the dramatic events leading to the *coming* of that kingdom might be.[47] Particularly, if this calculation was correct, it would mean they were currently living in the time of the pouring out of the sixth (of seven) vials of God's wrath, which was to dry up the great river Euphrates

(Rev. 16:12). That, he believed, could be interpreted as the drying up of the *"incomes* and *supplies"* of Babylon, i.e., the Roman papacy.[48]

Edwards accordingly transferred into a notebook detailed reports mostly from Boston newspapers that had to do with defeats of Catholic forces, which might be interpreted as drying up the wealth that supplied Babylon (or Rome). Whenever the British captured French ships—a staple of the early entries—Edwards copied down the number of men and guns captured. No friend of learning for its own sake, Edwards included as one of the first evidences of God's work a report from Vienna of a Jesuit library "one of the best-chosen and most curious in Europe" that was struck by lightning and burned.[49]

The counterpart of God's destruction of the Antichrist was the spread of the Gospel, which Edwards argued could likewise be about to advance dramatically. Accordingly, in spring 1748 Edwards added another section to the "Apocalypse" notebook where he listed newspaper accounts of "Events of an Hopeful Aspect on the State of Religion."[50] In his much discussed comments in *Some Thoughts Concerning the Revival of Religion* (1742), he had suggested that the American awakenings might be glimmers of light that presaged the millennial dawn. Now he said nothing about the priority of America and suggested rather that the lights were going out all over New England. Yet the larger international horizon still revealed numerous glimmers, of which Brainerd's sacrificial work was just one. That gave reason for hope and prayer even in the darkest hours before dawn.

In reckoning the progress toward Christ's kingdom, Edwards did not draw any sharp line between the spiritual and the political. The work of David Brainerd, the Concert of Prayer, and the war with the French and their Indian allies were all of one piece. The spread of the Gospel was the preeminent goal, but he never doubted that one precondition was Protestant military success against "papal" regimes. Protestant countries indeed needed to be reclaimed for true Calvinist piety, but in the meantime God used nominally Protestant British gunboats and profane British soldiers to thwart outright anti-Christian papist designs.

Edwards accordingly searched for political signs to put on the positive side of the ledger, evidencing the advance of the Gospel. He wrote to his Scottish correspondents, with whom he was now exchanging long letters on prophetic interpretations, for confirmation of reports that some minor members of the English government had turned to orthodox Christianity.[51] He also rejoiced that another of his Scottish brethren had referred to the current archbishop of Canterbury as "orthodox" and at reports that Whitefield had confounded scoffing sophisticates by winning respect in high places, "even in Caesar's household" as it were.[52]

Nearer to home, he hoped for the happy convergence of political and evangelical interests. Aside from Colonel Stoddard's local influence, Massachusetts' government was cool to awakening, and Connecticut was in the hands of Old Lights. But prospects had become brighter to the south. In 1747 New Jersey dissenters successfully prevailed on the British government to appoint their old friend Jonathan Belcher governor of New Jersey. Belcher's appointment consolidated the growing power of New Englanders such as Dickinson and Burr. The new governor would also be a friend to the fledgling College of New Jersey.[53]

Edwards was delighted at this new political prospect and wrote to Belcher requesting that he might dedicate his *Life of Brainerd* to the governor. Belcher apparently declined the honor (it might have been impolitic so openly to ally himself with a controversial New Light), but he assured Edwards at some length that he might "be sure of me as a friend and father to the missionaries this way, and of all my weight and encouragement for spreading the everlasting gospel of God our Savior."[54]

Edwards also sent some advice to the governor concerning the conduct of the tiny College of New Jersey, which in the fall of 1747 was shaken by the sudden death of its first president, Jonathan Dickinson, and for which the governor was proposing a new charter. Belcher may have urged Edwards to accept the presidency.[55] In any case he was effusive in assuring Edwards that he had adopted the college "for a daughter" and would do everything to keep it true to the Gospel. "The accounts I receive," said the governor, in unreconstructed Whitefieldian tones that he knew would please Edwards, "give me too much reason to fear Arminianism, Arianism and even Socinianism, in destruction to the doctrines of free grace, are daily propagated in New England Colleges. How horribly and how wickedly are these poisonous notions rooting out those noble pious principles on which our excellent ancestors founded those seminaries!" The governor further praised Edwards' book promoting the Concert of Prayer and promised to help John Brainerd and two new missionaries to the Indians, Elihu Spencer (an Edwards protégé) and Job Strong from Northampton, in every way he could.[56]

The New Light party had remnants of political strength only on the fringes of the British Empire, in parts of Scotland, and in aging magistrates in America, such as John Stoddard and Jonathan Belcher, both in their late sixties. Yet in Edwards' view their cause had bright hope because they were conforming to God's plan. All the pieces of their comprehensive program fit together: awakening, for which they needed the Concert of Prayer; education, for which they needed the new College of New Jersey; missions, for which they needed more David Brainerds; and political influence, which would depend on awakened leaders. Despite some bleak immediate conditions, Edwards was convinced there was much reason to hope for those who would depend on God, pray, and serve.

# CHAPTER 21

## "I Am Born to Be a Man of Strife"

hey have never maintained him in any measure," Sally complained of the town's treatment of her father in the winter of 1747–48, just before Jerusha died. "These things," she went on, after summarizing recent salary disputes, "I am sensible have done much toward making my father willing to leave his [people] if convenient opportunity present." Sally was writing with striking frankness to her missionary friend Elihu Spencer, one of the men Edwards had recommended to Governor Belcher for work with John Brainerd in New Jersey. Spencer, like David Brainerd, had visited the Edwardses' home in summer 1747. Apparently there was more than one romance that summer. Sally justified the candor of her letter by observing, "I have felt the greatest freedom to one whom I esteem so cordial a friend." She also mentioned that Jerusha was recently in much better health than she had been when Spencer visited, though "this day was taken very much out of order but we hope it will prove but a short term"—suggesting the letter may have been written the day Jerusha fell into her final illness. In any case, we know that just before that calamity Edwards' relation to Northampton was still in a dismal state.[1]

Sally's letter reminds us that while he was doing everything else, Edwards was constantly involved in a crowded, thriving, and often demanding home life. Sally reported that he had furnished the town with an account of the family's essential expenses and that these were several hundred pounds more than the town thought it could afford. The letter also reveals that by this time the largely female Edwards household was constantly dealing with suitors for the teenage daughters. From as early as when Samuel Hopkins seemed to have had his eye on Jerusha, ardent young admirers of Jonathan who visited the intensely spiritual Edwards home romanticized the potentialities of the daughters. We have one well-documented case that suggests some of the passions and intrigues that must have often attended daily life in such a prominent home.

In fall 1748, sixteen-year-old Esther, later described as "of great beauty,"[2] attracted a fervent admirer. Joseph Emerson, a young Massachusetts pastor, returning from the Yale commencement met Jonathan on the road. Edwards invited him to travel with him and to come to Northampton. They spent the Sabbath with Timothy and Esther Edwards in East Windsor, where Edwards preached in the morning and Emerson in the afternoon. The next night they stayed with Edwards' sister Esther Edwards Hopkins and her husband, Samuel Hopkins (the elder) of Springfield. Arriving in Northampton Tuesday evening, Emerson was immediately impressed by what he described in his private diary as "the most agreeable family I was ever acquainted with." Doubtless this estimate had something to do with meeting the third very impressive Esther Edwards he had encountered in as many days, but that pleasure was enhanced by "much of the presence of God here." Elihu Spencer was also there, but apparently his major interests were not in Sally. He was about to leave as missionary to the Indians of the powerful "six nations." "The most wonderful instance of self denial I ever met with," wrote Emerson.

Although he stayed only one full day in the Edwards home, Emerson was hopelessly smitten. By the end of the next week he was writing letters both to Jonathan and to Esther, "a very desirable person, to whom I purpose by divine leave to make my addresses." A month later he set out for Northampton "to treat for marriage." After four days in the Edwards home, Emerson left despondently the next Monday. "I could not obtain from the young lady the least encouragement to come again," he wrote in his diary, "the chief objection she makes is her youth, which I hope will be removed in time."

Still holding out a glimmer of hope, Emerson resolved to try again the next spring. In the meantime he was agonizingly distracted by thoughts of Esther, noting in his diary observations like "so discomposed I could not study," or "I read a little but spent the chief part of the day meditating on my troubles," or "I write two letters to Northampton one to dear Mrs. [Miss] Esther Edwards, who I find ingrosseth too many of my thoughts." Finally in March 1749 he heard back, not from Esther, but from Sally, "who entirely discourages me from taking a journey again there to visit her sister, who is so near my heart." Devastatingly disappointed, he concluded: "The Lord teach me to profit. May I be resigned."[3]

# The Patron

By this time Jonathan may have been praying much the same, although he had not yet given up his desperate suit to win back the hearts of his people in Northampton. Many of the townspeople were feuding with him as only former lovers in a long-term relationship could. There had been a brief respite in spring 1748, perhaps because the death of Jerusha in February brought a temporary wave of sympathy for the Edwardses. In any case, the next month, after years of refusing Edwards' persistent requests to stabilize his salary, the town meeting voted "by a great majority" to a generous inflation-proof settlement, which made him one of the highest paid pastors in the region.[4]

Then another blow—once again the death of a patriarch—shook the foundations of Edwards' relationship to the town. On June 19, 1748, Colonel John Stoddard died unexpectedly in Boston. Edwards' world was built on patriarchy, and the major turning points of his life were precipitated by the deaths of his patrons. In the political realm it would be difficult to overestimate the importance of his uncle John Stoddard to Edwards. Probably no eighteenth-century clergyman in America sustained a closer relationship to so powerful a regional magistrate. Edwards' view of history and the millennium projected such close cooperation of Reformed churches and pious magistrates on a large scale. In Northampton John Stoddard was his perennial benefactor. Most recently, "Squire Stoddard" had been the head of the committee that recommended Edwards' stabilized salary. Magistrate and pastor, uncle and nephew, stood shoulder to shoulder as God's representatives for preserving the old order and promoting true religion.

At sixty-six, Colonel Stoddard had been heavily burdened as commanding officer overseeing the western operations during the continuing war. In late May 1748 he made his usual journey to Boston to serve as Northampton's representative to the General Court. The court appointed him to undertake another trip to Albany to pursue once again the arduous task of negotiating with the Iroquois. Before he could leave Boston, he suffered a stroke and died a few days later.[5]

One clue as to the closeness between the Edwardses and the Stoddards was that when the colonel suffered his stroke, it was Sarah Edwards who cared for him. Possibly she was already in Boston and stayed on.[6] The two households had long been intertwined. Until 1736 Edwards' grandmother, Esther Warham Mather Stoddard, had lived in Stoddard's home and Edwards' sister

Mary had cared for her. Colonel Stoddard's wife, Prudence Chester Stoddard, was near in age to the Edwardses, and the Stoddard children each had Edwards cousins their own age.

Edwards valued Stoddard as a firm champion of theological orthodoxy. In the Breck case Stoddard had stretched his authority as the most powerful judge of the region in turning the defense of orthodoxy into a legal issue. During the controversies over the Great Awakening of 1741–42, Stoddard had written a treatise (now lost) defending much the same view as his nephew's. Jonathan found him "no inconsiderable divine," as able as the best divines he knew to give advice in cases of conscience, and able to "discourse of experimental religion" as one "intimately and feelingly acquainted with these things."

Edwards' eulogy for Stoddard, preached in Northampton the Sabbath after the squire's death and soon published, spared nothing in praise of his patron. Stoddard was among the very wisest of politicians; the best judges of people and of circumstances; the shrewdest and most foresighted of counselors; the most reliable of friends; the most honest, the most public-spirited, and the most knowledgeable of the affairs of New England, Canada, and of all the Indian nations. He had truly cared for his people like a father for his children. "Perhaps never was there a man that appeared in New England," Edwards declared, "to whom the denomination *great man* did more properly belong."

Never given to excessive tact, Edwards could not resist the opportunity to contrast his uncle's virtues with the vices of the many of the men who had surrounded the magistrate, some of whom were in the audience. Hampshire County's leaders, including some of his Williams cousins, might swell with pride as Edwards lauded the fallen patriarch, but the awakener also turned that admiration into a challenge: "How far [was Stoddard] from any sly and clandestine management to fill his pockets with what was fraudulently withheld, or violently squeezed, for the laborer, soldier, or inferior officer. How far was he from taking advantage from his commission or authority." "How far was he from secretly taking bribes." By contrast were men of "a narrow private spirit" who used "little tricks" to gain a few pounds and were "not ashamed to grind the faces of the poor, and screw their neighbors." So Edwards went on, describing practices that had become notorious during the war.[7] The Williams family, some of whom were scrupulous and some of whom were not, controlled the wartime commissary business and related patronage in Hampshire County. It was no coincidence, for instance, that the major staging areas for the regiment headed by a brother-in-law were three centers of Williams influence: Deerfield, Hatfield, and Stockbridge.[8]

Edwards' relationship with the surviving Hampshire elite was precarious since the heir-apparent to much of Stoddard's power was cousin Israel Williams. The young "river god" was married to Sarah Chester, sister to Prudence Chester Stoddard, but he had long snubbed the Edwardses on his frequent visits to the Stoddards. Israel had sided with Jonathan Ashley of Deerfield (married to Israel's sister) in openly breaking with Edwards over the awakening, and Edwards suspected his religious principles. John Stoddard, he pointed out to his captive audience, was not only a friend of the revival but of the "religious principles and doctrines of the first fathers of New England, usually called *the doctrines of grace* and he had a great detestation of the opposite errors of fashionable divinity."

While he was at it, Edwards used Stoddard's virtues to take a swipe at some more widespread vices. "Who," he asked, "ever saw him irreverently and indecently lolling, and laying down his head to sleep, or gazing about the meeting house in time of divine worship?" And Stoddard was "an enemy of vain or profane conversation," said Edwards, alluding to the sore point of his alliance with his uncle in attempting to suppress vice in the "young folks' Bible" case. Stoddard's death was another "testimony of the divine displeasure, added to all the other dark clouds God has lately brought upon us, and his awful frowns upon us." One of the frowns was the alarming death rate—in 1748 alone the toll was forty-three, over 3 percent of Northampton's population.[9]

## The Revolution

Edwards could hardly have picked a worse time to launch his conservative revolution. The dispirited town had lost its leading citizen—the last great Stoddard—and Edwards had lost his strongest ally. Almost immediately the pastor began a campaign that seemed to betray Stoddard's name and memory. With John Stoddard out of the way, or so it seemed to Edwards' opponents, he attempted a coup that would abolish Solomon Stoddard's practices concerning church membership and the sacraments.

His first step, or misstep, was to propose an antidemocratic revision of the congregation's government. In a four-part sermon preached in June 1748 Edwards argued that: "'Tis the mind of God that not a mixed multitude but only select persons of distinguishing ability and integrity are fit for the business of judging causes." Edwards had inherited from Solomon Stoddard the practice of having cases of church discipline brought before the entire congregation of male communicants. The purpose of discipline, Edwards pointed out, was to "heal the wounds" of the church, but long experience had proven that the customary practice did just the opposite. It was the occasion of "many great wounds [and] contention, quarreling with the minister, quarreling with one another." Often the dissensions resulting from the cure were worse than the original disease and lasted "till death puts an end" to them.

Edwards proposed having a council of elders, such as was the practice in Holland, Geneva, Scotland, the Presbyterian churches of the Middle Colonies, and almost all Calvinistic churches. He assured his church that he did not want to revert to the older New England and Northampton practice of having just one or two lay elders with powers equal to the minister, including powers to ordain ministers. Rather he believed it more consistent with Scripture to have a representative judicial board that would aid the minister in governing the church.

Edwards' principal arguments came from Scripture, but he also pointed out that in civil government and the military it was common sense that the multitudes should not judge every case or enter equally into every decision. In a revealing line of thought, he argued that men could not use "the rights of human nature" as "ground of the power of judgment in a church." Such claims—increasingly popular among eighteenth-century men—would prove too much. If human nature were the ground of such rights, then women would have the same rights because "they have the human nature entire, all its faculties if the human nature only be the ground of the claim." Many women in Christian churches," he went on, "are much more capable than some of the men." For instance, "it will be found difficult to say what there is in nature that shows that a wise woman ought not to have as much power in the church as a male servant that hasn't a tenth part of the understanding." Scripture must be the preeminent guide, even when if it seems to go against the dictates of nature.[10]

Edwards' reasons for proposing this governmental revision, which predictably did not go anywhere, are not clear,[11] but within a few months he was proposing the far more radical surgery of repudiating his grandfather Stoddard's views on the terms of admission to communion. People immediately raised the issue of the timing, so soon after John Stoddard's death. Edwards responded that he just had been waiting for the right occasion. As it happened, no one had joined the congregation for several years—a commentary in itself. He was waiting for someone to seek membership who showed sufficient signs of piety to meet his new stricter standards. Edwards was not demanding step-by-step conversion narratives, as his father still required, but he did want something more than the rather formal assent that had satisfied his grandfather Stoddard. He was asking for a "credible profession"—which he would judge—of a *heartfelt* faith and dedication to serve God.[12]

Finally, in December 1748, not long after the news of the war's end had arrived, an apparently pious young man about to be married sought church membership. This was just the sort of case Edwards wanted because he did not want to mark the institution of his new standards with the exclusion of an applicant, which would make the move look petty and personal. In addition to examining the young man on the usual Stoddardean standards of orthodoxy, moral sincerity, and lack of scandal, Edwards gave the young man some samples of brief professions of heartfelt faith that he might affirm and told him he might draw up something similar in his own words. The applicant said that he thought he could affirm such a statement and would consider the matter. As soon as word got out as to what was afoot, the lid blew off the town. The young man, not wanting to be a party to the unpopular innovation, returned and told Edwards he did not want to join the church under the new conditions.

The following February Edwards explained his views to the committee of the church and asked if he might preach on the subject. The animosity against his views was so strong that the great majority of the committee refused to let him preach about the matter. As an alternative, they allowed, he was free to publish his views. He immediately set himself to writing a treatise.

Soon after, a young woman came to him to join the church, willing to affirm a profession according to Edwards' standards. In April 1749, Edwards brought her application to the committee and asked that she be accepted under these terms. He assured them that he would not use the case as a precedent. Dramatically underscoring that point—and how tense things had gotten—he offered them a signed statement promising to resign if they still rejected his views after reading the treatise he was preparing. Despite this conditional promise of resignation, the committee rejected the young woman's application for membership by a vote of fifteen to three.[13] The controversy would drag on for more than another year, but the townspeople had made up their minds.

Their outrage was fueled not only by their long-standing resentments and vehement disagreements with what Edwards was proposing, but also by their belief that he was being devious, even duplicitous. Why had he waited until he had attained a fixed salary to announce his new views? Why had he not disclosed them while Colonel Stoddard was living? Was it that he knew that Solomon Stoddard's son, who had so long protected him, would be the most formidable opponent of a repudiation of his father's heritage?

Edwards answered that he had long had scruples about his grandfather's view and that a number of years ago, around the time he wrote *Religious Affections,* he had settled on his current conviction. Knowing how difficult it would be for the townspeople to accept a repudiation of the revered Solomon Stoddard's policies, he had decided that it would be best to gradually let his opinion be known so as to let them get used to the idea. He had publicly (though obscurely) alluded to his position in *Religious Affections* and had discussed his views openly with friends and with a number of townspeople. He had intended to fully discuss his views with Colonel Stoddard, who he knew would oppose him, but had been waiting for the occasion of a suitable applicant for church membership.[14]

In the poisoned atmosphere, many of the people were not convinced. Rather than engage the real issues, they complained to each other about how Edwards had not been open and honest with them. Eventually, as the contentions dragged on, Edwards secured a number of depositions from people confirming that he had indeed spoken openly of his views before his salary was settled or Stoddard's death. These testimonies provide some rare glimpses of Edwards in conversation.

The most vivid was a conversation with Sarah, probably early in 1746, when they were out riding together because she was ill and was riding for her health. As Sarah recounted it, Jonathan took the opportunity to tell her at length of his qualms about the Stoddardean practice of admitting to membership those who make "no credible profession of Godliness." He had already told her that he had inserted the passage in the forthcoming *Religious Affections* revealing his position, but when she asked him if he might write more on the subject, he replied that he was reluctant to publicly oppose his grandfather and was still not absolutely sure of his opinion.

Soon afterwards, Sarah continued, he became sure and on a number of occasions expressed his determination not to admit anyone without a credible heartfelt profession. Still, he felt that until the occasion arose, it would be best to let the word get out gradually. During the next two years, she testified, Edwards openly expressed his view to various well-known persons, such as Samuel Buell, John Brainerd, and Aaron Burr. When townspeople were also present or came in on the conversation, he made no effort to conceal his opinions. To Burr he suggested that his parishioners might well throw him out and bring his family to poverty. Burr replied that then he had might as well immediately accept the presidency of the College of New Jersey.

Before Colonel Stoddard died, Sarah had heard open talk of Edwards' views in New Haven and Hartford, and she herself had talked of it with one of the prominent townsmen, Elisha Pomeroy, on the road to Boston before Colonel Stoddard's death. Though Sarah surely highlighted the facts to Edwards' advantage, other witnesses corroborated that he had not entirely hidden his views from the townspeople.[15] In an especially memorable conversation from early 1747 recalled by John Searle, a former Northampton resident, the pastor had spoken of his previous controversies and of what he knew lay ahead. Then he said with great emotion, "It seems I am born to be a man of strife." To Sarah he lamented that the prospect ahead appeared to him "like a bottomless ocean."[16]

That Edwards was willing to sail the foundering ship of his pastorate into the teeth of the storm, knowing well that he and his family were likely to go down, tells us much about his character. First, he was irremediably a man of principle. Once he arrived at a conclusion, he was not ready to give in. Like many eighteenth-century people, he believed that through observation and logic one should be able to settle almost any question. His own logical powers increased his sense that he could settle an issue by argument. Even after he had faced the force of his people's animosities, he still remained hopeful that he might convince them if only they would read his treatise.[17] Edwards' reverence for Scripture enhanced his sense of the authority of whatever beliefs he derived from it. His conviction that the life or death of eternal souls was at stake made him willing to risk his own welfare.

That he was willing to risk comfort and status for high principle does not mean he was without fault. For one thing, his brittle, unsociable personality contributed to the breakdown of the once-warm relationship with the townspeople. Try as he might to temper his natural propensities by cultivating Christian virtues of gentleness, charity, and avoiding evil-speaking, he still seemed aloof. He was not able to build up the reserve of personal goodwill that more pastoral ministers enjoyed. Edwards was keenly aware of these failings, and as the disaster developed he suggested a number of times that he might not be suited for anything but writing.[18]

Added to that, Edwards was not a keen judge of the full range of human behavior. The point has to be stated carefully because he was a master at

judging the deceitfulness of the human heart and at analyzing religious affections. Yet the very intensity with which he viewed such things, always
through the lenses of Scripture and strictly Reformed tradition, kept him
from ordinary shrewdness about what was possible. Although he was a Calvinist in theology, he was a perfectionist by nature. He asked more than could
be hoped for from a people, applying to a town the disciplined standards he
held for himself. The Northampton covenant of 1742 was probably the clearest instance of overreaching. It was like asking the whole town to live according to his personal resolutions writ large. Or it was like asking a town of the
1740s to become like a Puritan village of the 1640s. When the town reverted to
its eighteenth-century ways, after making promises it could not keep, both
sides were disheartened and embittered.

Edwards was impaled on the horns of a dilemma inherited from his
tradition. Puritanism and its Reformed-pietist successors constantly vacil-
lated between whether they were rebuilding Christendom by making towns
and eventually nations into virtually Christian societies, or whether they were
advocating a pure, called-out church. Edwards had strong commitments to
both ideals. Heir to the Puritan establishment and part of a powerful ruling
clan, he was jealous of the privileges of ministerial prestige in town and
province. He looked forward to a worldwide Reformed Christendom as the
millennium approached.

Yet he was also a luminary among the international awakeners whose
insistence on conversionism could—like earlier Puritanism—be disruptive of
the standing order. The awakeners worked on the premise that many church
members, including many clergy, were unconverted. The implication seemed
to be that true churches should be made up of true believers only. Edwards
had spoken out against New Lights who were quick to judge others' spiritual
states and had emphasized how difficult it was to identify who was truly
converted. Yet scores of New Light congregations in New England had separated from what they considered to be the impurities of the established
churches of their towns.[19] Some had become Baptists, applying the logic of
converts-only purity to both sacraments. It is easy to see why Edwards' opponents would accuse him of moving toward separatism.

Edwards wanted rather to resolve the old conundrum without resorting
to separatism.[20] He would show how to maintain both the purity of the
church and the establishment. As in so much of his thought, he seemed
determined to demonstrate how the Puritan tradition he had grown up with
could work in eighteenth-century settings. Not that he followed his pre-

decessors in any exact ways. Rather, based on his own reexamination of Scripture, he reformulated their essential ideals on what he regarded as a firmer foundation.[21]

The great problem was how to reconcile the Old and New Testaments. According to Puritan teaching, the church, being the "new Israel," was successor to the covenant with the Old Testament nation. This point was crucial for infant baptism because the main justification for children receiving the New Testament sign and seal of the covenant was that God had included children in the promises of the covenant to Israel, ratified by the sign of circumcision.

Solomon Stoddard had attempted to resolve this dilemma by highlighting the Old Testament model. Developing his views at a time when it was becoming clear that Puritans could no longer be assured of control over colonial governments, he emphasized the side of the heritage that said there should be a national (or territorial) church. Anyone who was upright and would affirm Christian principles should be a full member of the church. Conversion could come later. That was what the church ordinances, the Lord's Supper as well as Gospel preaching, were designed to promote.[22] Combined with the half-way covenant, this policy meant that almost every child—as in the old European establishments—would be a baptized member of the church. Most adults would become communicants, even if some stayed away because of moral failings, scruples, or mere indifference. Clergy would thus retain moral authority over almost the whole community.[23] The nation would be, like Israel of old, standing before God as a people who observed his ordinances.[24]

Yet the effect of Stoddardeanism was that church and town were more or less coextensive. The Stoddard family (and their clerical and magisterial allies and kin in neighboring towns) could preside over something like an Old Testament tribe. The New Testament agenda of fostering conversions remained a leading goal, but it was pursued in this Old Testament framework.

Edwards, while wanting to balance the two testaments, can be understood as insisting that the New Testament should have priority if one was attempting to find the model for the church. Whereas God did indeed show favor to the whole nation of Israel, even though not all its people were regenerate—as he still might favor whole nations even though they were very imperfectly Protestant—God did so "according to the flesh." The church, by contrast, was constituted by the Holy Spirit. That meant that its *truly* full members were those whose hearts were changed by regeneration. True, no one but God could reliably judge the heart, yet those admitted as *visible* full members should at the least be able to produce the outward signs of regeneration, including a heartfelt profession.[25]

Convinced that he had found the true middle way between the separatists' attempt at a pure church and the more open practices of birthright membership, Edwards would brook no contradictions to his view once he went public. Writing almost nonstop during early spring of 1748, he produced the treatise *An Humble Inquiry into the Rules of the Word of God, Concerning . . . Full Communion in the Visible Christian Church,* which he hoped would persuade the townspeople.

He had, he wrote, once held his grandfather's views and had "conformed to his practice," yet he had never been comfortable with them. Now, after years of wrestling, he was willing to undertake the unseemly task of opposing such a venerable ancestor. Stoddard himself, he emphasized at the outset, had said, "It may possibly be a fault to depart from the ways of our fathers: but it may also be a virtue, and an eminent act of obedience, to depart from them in *some* things."[26]

Looked at one way, Jonathan's problem was that he was Timothy Edwards' son more than he was Solomon Stoddard's grandson. Timothy, who had never approved of Stoddardeanism, was still a force in his life, and the son regularly visited his aged but still active parents. Jonathan had always been ready to depart from his father "in *some* things," but it had never been easy. Not willing to give up an argument, in *Religious Affections* he had settled to his own satisfaction the dispute with his parents regarding exact preparatory steps as evidences of conversion. Once he had removed that obstacle—which had been such a sore point with him personally—he could focus on the essence of the question that separated his father from his grandfather. His father's demand that prospective members recount the proper steps of a conversion experience was indeed too much to ask, yet his grandfather had gone too far to the other extreme. Jonathan's solution of asking for a heartfelt profession yet following no set formula preserved the essential virtue of his father's view while avoiding its excess.

## A High View of the Sacraments—Low Church Style

Whatever its psychological roots, Jonathan's insistence that professions of faith must show evidence of being heartfelt grew out of the core of his theology. True religion, he had long held, must involve the affections. The will must be radically transformed from its natural self-love to love to God. The great divide among people was between those whose hearts were enraptured by this love and beauty and those whose self-indulgent hearts rejected it. Whatever their relatively good intentions, persons who could not show heartfelt evidence of regeneration must be judged to be on the wrong side of this divide.[27]

In order to appreciate his change of mind one must imagine the grandeur of Edwards' vision of the "divine and supernatural light"—enough to send him into ineffable bliss—in contrast to his disappointments with the town. Having once thought that most of his parishioners shared the life-changing encounter with blazing beauty, it was all the harder for him to see them day after day preoccupied with petty jealousies, avarice, and lusts, and to endure their sullen expressions and bored irreverence as they went through the forms of weekly worship. If Edwards' attitude toward the town seemed like that of a betrayed husband, it was because that was just the sort of issue he thought was at stake. Edwards viewed the Lord's Supper as most essentially a sign and a seal "renewing and confirming of the covenant." It was, he said, "at least as a woman's taking a ring of the bridegroom in her marriage is a profession and seal of her taking him for her husband." To make such vows lightly and to break them repeatedly would be terrible crimes. No wonder I Corinthians II described it as to eat and drink judgment to oneself.[28]

The emphasis on the covenant or solemn promise in his argument on the Lord's Supper is illuminating. In expounding the gravity of the sacrament he explained that "the established signs in the Lord's Supper are fully equivalent to words."[29] He then proceeded to the analogy of the ring to the wedding promises. Edwards indeed had a high view of sacrament, but he understood it in a thoroughly low church framework. His universe was filled with signs and types. *Everything* pointed to the real presence of Christ. Every part of the worship service, including most solemnly the Supper, was designed to elicit a sense of that ineffable spiritual presence. Yet—biblicist Protestant that he was—he saw *words* as the most essential symbols guiding hearts to God's communication of the love of Christ. Words provided the key to all the other rich symbols with which one was surrounded. God's revelation in Scripture was an elaborate promise to humankind, an offer of marriage. Christ would take his people as a spouse. The sacramental signs confirmed the promise that Christ had sealed with his own blood.

Even if words were the keys to all the symbols of the divine mysteries, the symbols themselves pointed to the reality of Christ in communion. "There is a presence of Christ," Edwards proclaimed in a communion sermon, "by special manifestation of himself and tokens of his presence whereby Christ may be said to be present with Christians and not all others." So beneficial was the communion as a symbol eliciting a sense of Christ's communal presence with believers that Edwards agreed with his Scottish correspondents who were advocating weekly communion.[30]

Since Christ was truly present in communion with his people, it was a mockery for those who betrayed him to renew their vows, as though in a marriage to which they had never been faithful. It was like those who witnessed Christ's crucifixion, he told his people in communion sermon in 1745 near the time he began intimating his new views. Those who gathered around the dying Christ were either his "disciples" or "his murderers." So with communion, there were only two possibilities. People could partake the "body and blood" either "as friends and disciples," or "as blood thirsty cannibals." The solemn covenant ceremony would seal either "communion with Christ" or "damnation."[31]

This radical view of the Lord's Supper, the townspeople soon found out to their bewilderment, was not all—Edwards was extending his either-or logic to the rite of baptism. He was repudiating the half-way covenant. The hypocritical betrayers of Christ, he reasoned, did not deserve to have their children baptized. So he was proposing, much to the consternation of the Northamptonites, that parents seeking baptism for their children would have to be full professing members. When this news broke, the uproar in the town became, if possible, more heated. "I am not sure," the disheartened Edwards wrote to his Boston friend and literary agent, the Reverend Thomas Foxcroft, in May 1749, "but that my people, in length of time and with great difficulty, might be brought to yield the point as to the qualifications for the Lord's Supper, though that is very uncertain. But with respect to the other sacrament [baptism], there is scarce any hope of it. And this will be very likely to overthrow me, not only with regard to my usefulness in the work of the ministry here, but everywhere."[32]

We can well understand why such proposed restrictions on baptism would infuriate the townspeople even more. Edwards was not only repudiating the revered Stoddard, he was rejecting the long-standing practice of most of Christendom, the prerogative of upright Christian citizens to have their children baptized. Even many New Lights, such as the New Jersey Presbyterians, did not go that far—that may be why he feared he was ending his ministerial usefulness "everywhere."

In Northampton, one of the practices he was attacking was the custom that when young people married at least one would become a communicant member so that their children might be baptized. Not only was Edwards ending that practice, but in addition he was proposing to remove the half-way covenant (which provided a way for the children of baptized noncommunicants to be baptized) as a backup to accomplish the same thing. Although infant baptism was not as much a matter of course in New England as in Anglican England, it was by now regarded virtually as a right. For a respectable family to have unbaptized children or grandchildren would be a stigma.

Edwards believed that attitude savored of "stupidity." How was it, he asked, that parents could be so upset that their children lacked the "honorable badge of Christianity" when they seemed blithely unconcerned that in reality they were "children of the devil, and condemned to eternal burnings"? What was the sign without the substance? It was like parents of a child dreadfully swollen from a snake bite being indignant that the child's clothes were dirty. By withholding baptism he hoped to jolt parents into being first concerned about what was truly important.[33]

Edwards treated his own children by just that standard. He always kept their eternal destinies in the forefront, even if it went against natural sentiments. In late July 1749, in the midst of the Northampton controversy, he wrote to his fifteen-year-old daughter, Mary, who was visiting in Portsmouth, New Hampshire. Edwards began by saying that it was "natural for a parent to be concerned for a child at so great distance" since she might well die before they even heard she was ill. "But," he immediately added, "my greatest concern is for your soul's good." Mary, who had been only eight at the time of the last awakening, was not yet considered to be in a state of grace. So, her loving father exhorted her, "if the next news we should hear of you should be of your death (though that would be very melancholy)," yet it would be a greater comfort to hear that there were "great grounds to hope that you died in the Lord" than to have been with her and to know she died out of grace. Midsummer, he went on to remind her, had been in recent years a great "dying time" in Northampton, and already one family had lost their only remaining son. Only after these sobering warnings did he turn to some instructions for Mary's coming trip to Boston and news that the family was tolerably healthy despite the ongoing controversy.[34]

Mary, who lived to be the matriarch of one of America's most distinguished evangelical families, had a sense of humor, even if her father suppressed his. She later told the story of Edwards' visit to Portsmouth that spring. Mary had preceded him there, where he was to preach the sermon for the ordination of one of his protégés, Job Strong. Drought conditions had slowed Edwards' journey, so he had not arrived when the service was to begin. The aging Reverend Joseph Moody of York, "perfectly unique in his manners" agreed to take over. During the prayer before the sermon, Edwards arrived. "Being remarkably still in all his movements," he ascended the pulpit while the unaware Moody continued praying. Perhaps still stalling for time, Moody extravagantly and at great length told God and the congregation of Edwards' many virtues, finally concluding with a prayer for Mary, whom he pointed out was in an unconverted state. When Moody finished and turned around, he was startled to see Edwards directly behind him. "Brother Edwards," he declared, "we are all of us much rejoiced to see you here to-day, and nobody, probably as much as myself; but I wish that you might have got in a little sooner, or a little later." "I didn't intend to flatter you to your face," he blustered on, "but there's one thing I'll tell you: They say that your wife is a going to heaven, by a shorter road than yourself." Edwards, never quick on his feet, had no comeback. He simply bowed, read his text, and preached on what was much on his mind, that ministers must be imitators of Christ. That meant not only having gentle Christ-like virtues, but also seeking first the salvation and happiness of eternal souls.[35]

# CHAPTER 22

# The Crucible

The tumult is vastly greater than when you were here," Edwards wrote to his friend Joseph Bellamy in December 1749, "and is rising higher and higher continually." The personable Bellamy had tried to intercede in Northampton in the late spring and even had believed that some of the key townspeople could be brought around once Edwards' book came out.[1] Now, Edwards told him, their opponents had roused such resentments against Bellamy that "you are spoken of by 'em with great indignation and contempt." Since Bellamy's visit townspeople and church committees had held countless meetings. Few people had read Edwards' book and few intended to. Further, they would not allow Edwards to hold a public debate on the subject nor to preach on it. Rather, they were seeking simply to neutralize the book by getting someone, preferably Edwards' most distinguished cousin, former Yale rector Elisha Williams, to write a reply. Not only had they not allowed any new members to join the church, they had now resorted to the extreme measure of suspending the sacraments.[2]

During the next months matters only got worse as the town and church majority pushed relentlessly for Edwards' removal. Time-consuming wrangles regarding procedural matters kept fanning the flames of controversy. Church government in Massachusetts had evolved in such a haphazard way that it seldom was entirely clear who had charge over what. By the time Edwards was writing to Bellamy, the "Precinct" (town) meeting had already asked the governing committee of the church to explore a separation. Edwards had objected that the town should not be doing church business, but since the same leaders were involved, he did not have much prospect of sympathy in either venue.

Leading the effort to oust him were the eighty-year-old town patriarch

Deacon Ebenezer Pomeroy and his son Major Seth Pomeroy, the local hero of Louisbourg. The Pomeroys had built a monopoly in the blacksmith trade. Joining them was Edwards' cousin, the ambitious young Joseph Hawley III, a lawyer and son of the man whose suicide had put a damper on the 1735 awakening.

Young Hawley's defection was a blow. A few years earlier Edwards had spoken highly of his cousin Hawley as a "worthy pious" man when the young man had been serving as chaplain to the army at Louisbourg.[3] Edwards had probably acted as something of a guardian and mentor to the boy, who had been only eleven at the time of his father's death. Young Joseph had duly gone off to Yale ('42) and returned to study theology with his distinguished older cousin.[4] Now Hawley and Edwards had a falling out on two counts. First, as with much of the recent resentment in the town against Edwards, there was an underlying dispute about changing mores regarding sexual liberties for males. Joseph Hawley had taken the side of his younger brother, Lieutenant Elisha Hawley, in a paternity case brought by Martha Root, who claimed the soldier was the father of her twins (one surviving). Edwards had refused to accede to the plan of the two families, who were from differing social classes, for a cash settlement. The pastor argued that, based on Old Testament law, the couple should marry. "'Tis utterly unfit," he insisted, that "men should think to put away at their pleasure, those whom they have seen cause for their pleasure, thus to unite themselves to." The case, which began in 1747, dragged into the summer of 1749, when an ad hoc council of local clergy ruled against Edwards, saying that Hawley needed only to confess to the sin of fornication. Two years later Elisha Hawley married a Pomeroy.[5]

Joseph Hawley's break with Edwards was also theological. By the time he returned from his military chaplaincy late in 1748, the young man was openly proclaiming, much to his former mentor's chagrin, some fashionable liberal or Arminian views. As he wrote to his brother Elisha early in 1749, he believed that true religion consisted "in that which the unprejudiced reason and sense of all mankind says is right." Edwards said he was "very open and bold" in expressing his new beliefs. Perhaps related to his change in theology, Hawley had given up any plans for the ministry and had settled in Northampton as a lawyer.[6]

Edwards did have a couple of prominent allies, including Dr. Samuel Mather and, most notably, Colonel Timothy Dwight, one of the leading merchants and gentry of the region. Although Dwight was a man of "a rough way of talking," he was pious, public spirited, and a rival to Israel Williams as a successor to John Stoddard's power.[7] Edwards' supporters, however, were a small minority.

In order for a church to sever its relationship with a pastor it needed the approval of an ad hoc committee of neighboring churches. Through the winter and spring of 1749–50 much of the ever-increasing turmoil centered on how to constitute that committee. The two parties were to be given an equal say in naming which churches should send delegates, but Edwards insisted that he did not have a chance at a fair hearing unless he were allowed to go outside of Hampshire County in selecting at least some of the churches. As his critics noticed, he was now taking the opposite position from the one he had defended fifteen years earlier in the Robert Breck case. Yet he felt he had no choice because almost the whole Hampshire Association was against him. Breck and his friends were still there, and the Williams clan and other Stoddardeans controlled most of the rest of the churches.

Edwards was painfully exasperated that he could not get the townspeople even to listen to his views. Finally in February he took matters into his own hands and announced a series of five Thursday lectures on the topic. Predictably, few of his congregation attended, although people from neighboring communities filled up the audience. Edwards scheduled the first lecture for February 15, the day the county courts were meeting in the town. His cousin Israel Williams was particularly furious at this maneuver and at the Court of Common Pleas for adjourning to hear the lectures. The Court of General Session of the Peace, on which Colonel Williams himself sat, refused to adjourn, and Williams made several vehement speeches against his cousin, calling him a "tyrant" who was "unsufferable" in "lording it over [his] people."[8]

Such revolutionary language alarmed even some of Edwards' opponents among the Hampshire clergy. Unbridled zeal of laypeople to overthrow a ministerial tyrant, they feared, would set a bad precedent. Chester Williams of nearby Hadley, Sarah Edwards' sometimes nemesis, who was now leading ministerial efforts to oust Edwards, sounded the alert to his fellow Hampshire Association clergy. "Unless we do concert some measures," he warned, "we are in danger of being overrun, and Northampton will proceed to extreme measures, being conducted by some gentlemen not over-tender of ministers of the churches."[9]

The clergy managed to keep the revolutionary sentiments in Northampton under their oversight, perhaps because most of the local clergy were on the side of the aroused townspeople. They had reason to fear because the people of many New England towns in 1750 were in a rebellious mood.

Revolution against ecclesiastical and civil tyrants was part of their heritage. In Boston, the liberal clergyman Jonathan Mayhew had just preached, on January 30, 1750, *A Discourse Concerning Unlimited Submission,* commemorating the execution of Charles I (now often taken as an early statement of American revolutionary ideology). Few at the time would have connected Mayhew's sentiments with unrest against the clergy in the hinterlands. Yet the recent rash of New Light schisms was also a legacy from the Puritans. Laymen as well as clergy such as Mayhew were talking more and more about their "rights." At the beginning of 1750 there was no predicting in what direction revolutionary sentiments would carry.[10]

Throughout the spring the Northampton agitation swelled from crisis to crisis and from one to another emergency meeting of town, church, local clergy, or countless caucuses. Yet, in spite of the overheated rhetoric and procedural muddles that were as irritating as the New England roads during a spring thaw, everyone seemed determined to play by some sort of rules. At length, as a concession to Edwards or to his adamancy, he was allowed to go outside the county for two of the five churches that he was allowed to choose to send representatives to a ten-church council. Unfortunately for him, one of the out-of-county churches, Cold Spring, was almost as much at odds with its pastor, Edward Billing (whom they would oust two years later), as North-ampton was at odds with Edwards. Billing, a good friend of Edwards, sat on the council anyway, but the church refused to send an additional lay delegate as each church was invited to do.

That meant that when the crucial council finally met in Northampton from June 19 to 22, Edwards was one vote short in a party-line division. The minority argued for slowing down the process so as to be able to seek reconciliation. The vocal townspeople would hear nothing of delay. Only immediate separation would do.

Leading the charge to deliver the Northamptonite coup de grace was Joseph Hawley, who had insinuated himself as the church's chief spokesman before the council. Hawley, volatile but persuasive, would countenance no delay or mediation. The vast majority of the congregation was behind him. When the council asked the church to express its views on whether to continue the pastoral relationship, only 23 of the 230 male members voted on Edwards' side. Some others stayed away and Edwards felt he probably had additional support among some women who could not vote and did not dare speak out, but still the opposition was overwhelming. The church council, which included some of his long-standing antagonists, such as Robert Breck and Jonathan Ashley, voted for his immediate dismissal.[11]

The council, however, did exonerate Edwards personally from widely circulated accusations of his lack of sincerity and integrity in the matter. They concluded that he was "uprightly following the dictates of his own conscience" and commended him for his "christian spirit and temper." He was, they declared, "eminently qualified for the work of the Gospel ministry" in any church that shared his views.[12]

Edwards' demeanor during these proceedings apparently was remarkably calm and helped earn him this affirmation even from his opponents. His supporters viewed him as simply saintly. One of those, the Reverend David Hall, recorded in his diary: "I never saw the least symptoms of displeasure in his countenance the whole week, but he appeared like a man of God, whose happiness was out of the reach of his enemies, and whose treasure was not only a future but a present good, overbalancing all imaginable ills of life, even to the astonishment of many, who could not be at rest without his dismission."[13]

In his farewell sermon, preached July 1, 1750, Edwards firmly reminded his congregation of such an eternal perspective, which had been the central motif of his ministry. With the intensity and unrelenting logic to which they were so accustomed, he depicted a compelling scene of how they would meet again before the great throne of God on the judgment day. At that meeting they would have to give an accounting of how they had treated each other as spiritual father and children these twenty-three years. The rejected pastor kept the tone compassionate, yet he did not let anyone miss the point that *his* conscience was clear and that he was confident of vindication in the final reckoning. He mentioned in passing that they would find out whether his stance concerning admission to the sacraments was "Christ's own doctrine," but the real issue would be his ministry as a whole. He could point to his tireless care for their souls. He had not acted out of any temporal concerns of self-interest for himself or his family. If that had ever been obscured during the salary disputes, he had in the communion controversy proved that he did not put temporal concerns first. He had chosen a course that was "plunging me into an abyss of trouble and sorrow."

On the judgment day his congregation would have to give an accounting as well. Their eternal souls were are stake. That—as they would find it difficult to deny—had always been Edwards overarching concern. In point after point, Edwards expressed his reasons to fear that they might not measure up. If in the last judgment he should "be acquitted and shall ascend with Christ," he prayed that would not be his former congregation's final and most melancholy parting from him.

Edwards closed by reiterating advice he had often given the town. To the young people he said that he knew his efforts to suppress vice had made him become "so obnoxious," but it was a thing "exceedingly beautiful" when young people truly loved and followed God. To parents he emphasized that "family order" was another essential. "Every Christian family ought to be as it were a little church." The people of the town needed to avoid their perennial contentions, not just with him but with each other. They furthermore had to be especially wary of Arminianism, which was growing in their midst. It would be a great calamity, he said, "if these principles should greatly prevail in this town, as they very lately have done in another large town I could name, formerly greatly noted for religion." Northampton must find a new pastor with these orthodox concerns, especially for their souls. Edwards promised to continue to pray that they might have "truly a burning and shining light set up in this candlestick."[14]

Much of the congregation must have sat in sullen indignation as Edwards implied that he would be exonerated while many of them would be found irredeemably guilty on the last day. Still, Edwards had displayed his transparently genuine concern for the state of their souls, and he believed the sermon was effective. "Many in the congregation seemed to be much affected and some are exceedingly grieved." Although a few might have relented, the vast majority never would.[15]

Edwards was suffering deeply, even if he controlled his outward demeanor. There are, he wrote, "but few that know the heart of a minister under my circumstances."[16] He believed that God had permitted these afflictions as a means of humbling him, and he had come to doubt whether he had the personal skills to be a pastor. He worried what would happen to his "numerous and chargeable family" now that his salary was cut off and they were "thrown upon the wide ocean of the world." To John Erskine, his most supportive Scottish correspondent, he wrote, "I am fitted for no other business but study."[17]

Erskine and other of Edwards' Scottish friends were attempting to step into the breach and inquired whether Edwards might accept a pastorate in Scotland. Edwards replied in July 1750 that he would have no difficulty accepting "the substance of the Westminster Confession" and that he had long admired the Church of Scotland's Presbyterian form of government, especially in the light of the chaos of New England's polity. But he shrank from the prospect of moving so large a family across the ocean, especially at his advanced age of forty-six. More important, he worried whether his "gifts and administration" would suit any congregation that accepted him without trial. Nonetheless, despite these expressed misgivings, he definitely left the door open and assured that "I think my wife is fully of this disposition."[18]

Edwards was duly humbled regarding his personal skills, but he had not the least doubt that he was fully in the right in the controversy and that he had been maligned with great injustice by the townspeople. It should have been obvious to them, he believed, that he was acting on principle since he was acting so much against the worldly interests of himself and his family. Instead the townspeople had circulated numerous false rumors, such as that he was trying to "ensnare the church" and acting out of "sinister views, from stiffness of spirit, and from pride, and an arbitrary and tyrannical spirit, and a design and vain expectation of forcing all to comply with my opinion."[19]

Despite their painful relations with most of their neighbors, Edwards' "large and chargeable family" had a life of its own with its own dramas in 1750. In April Sarah bore their eleventh child (tenth surviving) and third son, Pierpont. The next youngest son, Jonathan Jr., was sickly and dangerously ill during the spring and summer but would live to follow his father's footsteps as a pastor (even to be dismissed from his church), theologian, and college president.

On Wednesday, June 11, 1750, just eight days before the fateful council, twenty-one-year-old Sally married Elihu Parsons, a prospering local young man. In November, Mary, only sixteen but sparkling and intelligent, married twenty-four-year-old Timothy Dwight Jr., a neighbor and son of the one local aristocrat who supported Edwards. The younger Dwights would reside in Northampton, though Mary's relation to the local congregation always remained strained, and she traveled to another town on communion Sundays.

The immediate problem after his dismissal was that he and his family had nowhere else to go, and so they remained awkwardly in Northampton for a year. Their relations with the town were filled with tensions. For instance, about a month after the dismissal the townspeople voted not to allow Edwards to continue to use the pastureland that was usually granted to him. Edwards, deeply worried about his family's finances, protested (to no avail) that he had been granted use of the pasture for the year.[20]

The relationship to the church, where the Edwards family still wor-
shipped, was particularly strange. The church could not always find visiting
preachers and so resorted to the clumsy expedient of asking Edwards to
preach on a week-to-week basis. Edwards remarked that, while they asked
him to preach frequently, they always did so as a last resort and with great
reluctance. Finally by November, the outcry was so great from some parishioners, unhappy to continue to endure their ousted pastor, that at a public
meeting they voted that he should no longer be asked, even if it sometimes
meant going without preaching.[21] A smaller group of Edwards' supporters
were urging him to begin a separate congregation.

He had, in the meantime, been scouting prospects for a move elsewhere
in New England, and in December he received an opportunity to which he
was much attracted. He had in October traveled to Stockbridge, Massachusetts, forty miles over the mountains to the west, partly to care for some land
he owned there but also to explore an opening. Now he had an invitation to
consider the possibility of settling there as the pastor of the English congregation and missionary to the Indians. Despite his interest, Edwards moved
cautiously, perhaps because of his doubts concerning his pastoral gifts. To
test the situation, he left for Stockbridge in January and stayed until early
spring, preaching to both whites and Indians and securing formal invitations
to settle there.[22]

Despite this prospect, soon after he returned to Northampton in spring
1751 the town was once again in an uproar. Friends of Edwards were mounting
a campaign to start a local church with Edwards as pastor. All over New
England, church division had recently become the common way to resolve
the problems of irreconcilable differences within congregations. At the core
of the group pressing for this solution was Colonel Timothy Dwight, whose
son had just married Mary Edwards. In the winter Colonel Dwight had been
making efforts to reconcile members of the congregation to Edwards. That
proved a thankless task. In the absence of Edwards himself, his enemies had
displaced their anger to Dwight and "now threaten to dismiss me from my
office."[23] By spring the Dwights were ready to break with their old congregation. They and other Edwards supporters argued that they had scruples about
taking communion where the majority held looser (Stoddardean) views about
the ordinance. They gained assurances from a number of like-minded persons from neighboring towns that they would join an Edwardsean Northampton church.[24]

Edwards said later that he never had any intention of becoming pastor of a new church in Northampton and that he tried to discourage that campaign. Nonetheless, since his few loyal friends and probably both his married daughters were so strongly pleading with him to stay, he left the possibility open.[25] Perhaps there was some trepidation in his family concerning a move to a potentially dangerous frontier town. Rather than personally quash the warm entreaties to stay, Edwards followed what he believed the proper procedure whenever contemplating a move: he agreed to convene an ad hoc council of clergy that would meet in May to advise him what to do.[26]

Edwards' enemies in the town were once again up in arms. They were sure that his calling of a council proved that he was behind the conspiracy to found a rival church. Led once again by the Pomeroys and Joseph Hawley, they replayed the acrimony of the previous summer. This latest move, they told their supporters, confirmed their earlier claims that Edwards' motives from the start had been to enhance his own power. Although they refused to recognize the council as a proper ecclesiastical body, they nonetheless presented it with a strongly worded "Remonstrance." Edwards in turn advised the council that he much preferred Stockbridge to presiding over a remnant in Northampton. Not surprisingly the council concurred and advised that he accept the Stockbridge calls.[27]

## "Misrepresentations Corrected"

At nearly the same time Edwards was trying to stamp out the renewed fires of false accusations, he was exasperated to see new fuel provided to feed those fires. A shipment of copies of a book written by his cousin Solomon Williams and printed at the townspeople's expense arrived in town. In this work, entitled *The True State of the Question Concerning the Qualifications Necessary to Lawful Communion in the Christian Sacraments*, Williams defended the views of his grandfather Solomon Stoddard against Edwards' criticisms. Edwards believed his cousin had grossly misrepresented his views and felt it necessary to reply—at length.[28] In early summer he went by himself to assume his duties in Stockbridge, where he was installed in August. He had much to do in preparation for his family's move, but as soon as he could, he began devoting his spare hours to the engrossing process of setting the record straight. He had his reply ready by the following spring.

From the beginning, the Northampton majority, though their own minds were made up, had sought an intellectual champion to formally respond to Edwards. Like many eighteenth-century people, they believed it important to have reason and principle on their side. At first the most likely candidate seemed to be Elisha Williams. When Edwards got wind of this, he was alarmed that his formidable cousin might enter the fray and wrote to Thomas Foxcroft in Boston in May 1749 to see if Foxcroft could dissuade Williams.[29]

After leaving his post at Yale, Rector Williams had pursued a career as a merchant and politician. Deeply involved in the political conflicts in Connecticut, in 1744 he had published anonymously an important volume defending New Light freedom of conscience—a work Edwards apparently admired.[30] During the war Elisha had served as a chaplain at Louisbourg and then was appointed as commander of the Connecticut regiment that was supposed to invade Quebec. In fact, his soldiers spent most of their time on furlough. Elisha headed a group of speculators who nonetheless paid them immediately in expectation of greater reimbursement from England. When, after the war, England balked at paying the salaries of soldiers who had mostly stayed at home, the Connecticut government dispatched Williams to England in late 1749 to recover their claims.

In England, Williams divided his time among political, economic, spiritual, and romantic interests. He gained partial reimbursement for the soldiers' salaries and transformed his business into an international enterprise. At the same time he retained his zeal as a New Light Calvinist, associating with notable English evangelicals, such as George Whitefield, the Countess of Huntington, and Dr. Philip Doddridge (a biblical commentator whom Edwards also admired). While Williams was in England he received news that his wife had died. Doddridge soon introduced him to one of the most remarkable women in the evangelical circle, Elizabeth Scott, known for her hymn writing. Since the Williams family is typically vilified by evangelical writers for its role in opposing the pious Edwards, it is worth quoting Philip Doddridge's estimate of Elisha: "I look upon Col. Williams to be one of the valuable men upon earth; he has joined to an ardent sense of religion, solid learning, consummate prudence, great candor and sweetness of temper and a certain nobleness of soul."[31]

It is easy to understand why Edwards feared published opposition from his highly regarded cousin, and he must have been relieved that Elisha Williams abandoned his plan to reply, most likely because of the upcoming trip to England. Elisha apparently turned over his notes to his brother Solomon, pastor at Lebanon, Connecticut, who completed the project.[32]

Edwards' principal opposition outside of Northampton was coming from one unmistakable major source, the children of his onetime patron, the late

Elisha Williams (1694–1755), former rector of Yale College and leading Williams family spokesman

William Williams. Some of them, like the ambitious young magistrate Israel Williams, had long-standing antagonisms towards Edwards. The Reverend Jonathan Ashley of Deerfield (married to William Williams' daughter Dorothy) also had fallen out with Edwards earlier (over the awakening) and aided the Northamptonites in the dismissal.[33] The two most influential sons, Solomon and Elisha, had long been close allies of Edwards and were, understandably, especially indignant that Edwards had betrayed the family cause.[34]

Solomon Williams in his answer to Edwards made the mistake of overstating his case, thus setting himself up for his logician cousin, who proceeded to chop his arguments into splinters. Williams represented Edwards as demanding that the church require "the highest evidence a man can give of sincerity." Edwards' view, as Williams characterized it, amounted to the old practice of requiring "an account of their experience of the sanctifying work of God's Spirit on their hearts."[35]

In *Misrepresentations Corrected, and Truth Vindicated* . . . , published in 1752, Edwards truly had some misrepresentations to correct. He had, he insisted, not required the "highest evidence a man can give of sincerity" but was asking only for credible evidence of *real godliness* as opposed to credible evidence of *moral sincerity*, which had been sufficient for Solomon Stoddard. Edwards showed that he had repeatedly said it was impossible to judge people's hearts and that the church could deal only in probabilities in evaluating visible sainthood. Furthermore, he had explicitly said that some charity must be granted to people who had scruples about the evidence of their own godliness. So he was not requiring the *highest* evidence of godliness; all he was demanding was *some* believable evidence that a candidate was truly godly.[36]

Edwards might have said all this and further clarified his differences with Stoddard in a few pages, but he was convinced that Williams' volume was so confused and self-contradictory as to conflict with Stoddard as much as with Edwards himself. So in a long final section he presented numerous examples of Williams' logical fallacies and inconsistencies. He concluded with a letter to his former congregation in Northampton, warning them to be aware of dangers lurking in Williams' book that went beyond the immediate controversy. Williams, he conceded, was himself orthodox, but in trying to defend his position he had unwittingly introduced confused and faulty arguments that, if followed to their conclusions, would lead to Arminianism. As in his farewell sermon, Edwards concluded by warning against tendencies "which have lately appeared in Northampton" that "tend to lead the young people among you apace into a liking to the new, fashionable, lax schemes of divinity, which have so greatly prevailed in New England as of late."[37]

Edwards' repeated admonitions to the people of Northampton did eventually bring a small bit of vindication. Joseph Hawley later repudiated his own role in the affair. Hawley, who like his father could be overwhelmed by guilt and melancholy, wrote a letter of apology to Edwards in 1754. Edwards replied gratefully but coolly that since Hawley's offense had helped lead the town in public sin, he should now lead them in public repentance. After Edwards died, Hawley did publish a letter in which he repented in the strongest terms, declaring himself equivalent to Judas and other biblical traitors. He and others, he confessed, had rashly promoted "severe, uncharitable, and if I remember right, groundless and slanderous imputations on Mr. Edwards, expressed in bitter language."[38]

## The Tragedy of Jonathan Edwards?

The scene of America's greatest theologian and colonial America's most powerful thinker being run out of town and forced into exile in a frontier village has intrigued observers ever since. Is it the tragedy of the great man being crushed by following his own high principles? Or is it the pathos of a brilliant but impractical intellectual whose prudery and zeal for control brought out the latent pettiness of a small town? As in most of real life that rises beyond the ordinary, it was a mixture of both the exalted and the pathetic.

Biographers and historians have struggled to make sense of this drama by searching for one or two essential underlying causes. Ola Winslow, writing in the heyday of mid-twentieth-century American democracy, found the essential theme in the nascent spirit of the American Revolution. As she put it, "The church member of 1750 was a democrat, although as yet he did not know it; and a good many of the 'Boys of '76' were already born." Adding plausibility to her explanation is the fact that Joseph Hawley became a patriot leader in the Stamp Act crisis and a representative in a revolutionary Massachusetts government, and Major Seth Pomeroy died as a general in the American Revolution. Colonel John Stoddard, by contrast, was considered a "Tory" in his time, and Edwards' son-in-law Timothy Dwight Jr. was a Tory during the Revolution.[39]

Patricia Tracy offered a more nuanced analysis. Writing in the 1970s, when social history was in vogue, she carefully examined the social and economic forces involved in the controversy. Edwards' strained relation with the changing mores of young people, she pointed out, was related to relative scarcity of new land and hence rising average age of first marriages. Tracy did not find, however, any clear economic or social explanation of Edwards' ouster. Timothy Dwight Sr. and Israel Williams, for instance, were rivals in the same elite magistrate social class, and during the American Revolution Israel Williams turned out to be a Tory.[40] The vast majority of Edwards' family and supporters, it might be added, supported the Revolution.

Tracy should be credited with developing the point that a major source of the breakdown in Edwards' rapport with the townspeople was his old-fashioned view of ministerial patriarchy. Edwards was attempting to perpetuate the role of authoritarian father and moral arbiter that Solomon Stoddard had exercised for sixty years. That ideal, she correctly observed, had been characteristic of the seventeenth century but was breaking down by the mid-eighteenth century. Tracy also points out the irony that Edwards was both an authoritarian conservative and a revolutionary. Her concluding sentence is that "perhaps, like all good fathers, Edwards gave his children the inner resources to rebel when it came to be time for them to be men."[41]

Edwards had some tragic flaws that contributed to his undoing in Northampton, so that the issues can not be reduced to inevitable social tensions or to his being out of step with the times, even if these were factors. Edwards was a perfectionist who had insufficient ways of coping with imperfections in others. That trait, combined with his authoritarian assumptions and conservative views of sexuality, created some tensions in the community, notably in the "young folk's Bible" episode. Yet the real tensions with the town came not so much from his defending old ways as from relying on something relatively new, the nearly universal awakening. After the awakening of 1734–35, he came to realize that he had raised his hopes too high. Still, he could not get over holding his church members to the promises that they made at the height of the awakenings. Part of Edwards' problem was that he was building his nearly perfectionist hopes for the long-term spiritual strength of the town on the inherently unstable sands of revival.

Further, we must be reminded that Edwards' conflict with Northampton was not primarily about his efforts to suppress vice, but over the terms of admission to the sacraments. Without his clumsily managed reversal of direction on that subject, he would have remained pastor in Northampton. True, there were pent-up resentments that came pouring out when the occasion arose.[42] Nonetheless, the question of admission to the sacraments was in itself a momentous issue, with potential to disrupt even a harmonious relationship between a pastor and a town.

Perhaps the greatest tragedy for Edwards was that his pastorate was undone by his commitment to principle. As he pointed out to his congregation, he had much to lose by attempting to reverse the policies of his grandfather. He was willing to give up his own and his family's worldly security for the cause of protecting eternal souls. He pursued that personally disastrous course because he was convinced that the logic of his conversionist theology demanded it.

It should also be noted that to the extent that the issue of suppression of vice was involved, which it surely was, Edwards was in one respect moving away from the Stoddardean version of patriarchy in which the minister had moral oversight of most of the town. One of his deep concerns in the "young folks' Bible" case was that communicant church members were indulging in vulgar parodies of holy speech. Accordingly, his radical reform was directed toward standards for church membership. He thus was moving toward what would become the more typically modern evangelical attitude in which clergy would have moral oversight over only those set aside by the sacraments as members of their congregations. Evangelical preachers would challenge male machismo (among other things), but the evangelical society would be a people set apart in a church called out from the dominant standards of the culture.[43]

## Edwards' Own Analysis

On July 1, 1751, after he had arrived in Stockbridge, Edwards sat down to write his own analysis of the town dynamics in a letter to Thomas Gillespie of Scotland.[44] Usually Edwards wrote history in purely theological terms, of God's or Satan's actions, and he has been criticized for not understanding history in the modern sense of analysis of temporal causes.[45] Yet his examination of the underlying factors in the Northampton controversy, though written from a deeply interested perspective, showed that he could deal with history in that mundane sense when the occasion arose.

He observed, as American colonial historians later discovered, that just as nations and individuals differ in natural temperament, so do towns. Northampton had long been "famed for a high-spirited people, and close [i. e., stingy], and of a difficult, turbulent temper." It was in this letter that he recorded that for the past forty or fifty years (or since the rise of John Stoddard), there had been "something like the Court and Country Party in England." Some men had great wealth and power and influence in the town and the church, and others had always been jealous of them, leading to "innumerable contentions." Edwards was thus suggesting that there was a social-economic base for the town's contentiousness. He was not suggesting, though, that his dismissal had such a base; his repudiation of the Stoddards' view of communion alienated people from both the usual camps.

Town pride, inflated by its spiritual reputation, was a related problem. Not only had Northampton prospered, but it had become famous. "There is this inconvenience," Edwards confessed, that "attends the publishing of narratives of a work of God among a people: such is the corruption that is in the hearts of men, and even of good men, that there is a great danger of their making it an occasion of spiritual pride."

Added to that was that "Mr Stoddard, though an eminently holy man, was naturally of a dogmatical temper." So people brought up under him, especially their leaders, "seemed to think it an excellency to be like him in this respect." Furthermore, since Stoddard had presided over the community for sixty years, many of the older generation "looked on him almost as a sort of deity," so opposing Stoddard's teachings "appears to 'em a sort of horrid profaneness."

Despite his respect for his grandfather, Edwards believed that the Northamptonites "had got so established in certain wrong notions and ways in religion, which I found them in and never could beat them out of." Particularly, they were too ready to stress the "impressions on the imagination" that they took to be their conversion experiences and too unwilling to see "the abiding sense and temper of their hearts" and the "exercises and fruits of grace" as the true evidences of regeneration. Edwards acknowledged that, being young, "I was not thoroughly aware of the ill consequences of such a custom" and as much as admitted that he was taken in by the town's emphasis on the excitements of supposed conversions. Had he been more mature at the time of the awakening of 1734–35, he would have insisted on testing the spirits more carefully. Although "there were numerous instances of saving conversions" he confessed, "the number of true converts was not so great as was then imagined."

Having helped cultivate the Northamptonites' spiritual pride, Edwards eventually reaped the consequences. It was a great advantage to his opponents, especially in stirring up the common people, "that the controversy was a religious controversy." Because "a precious and important doctrine of the Word of God" was said to be at stake, the people could "look on their zeal against me as a virtue." They could "christen even their passions and bitterness in such a cause with sanctified names, and to let 'em loose and prosecute the views of their bitterness and violence without check of conscience." Only after suggesting these and other factors in the controversy did Edwards conclude with a theological analysis that confirmed his own adamant stand. "I believe the devil is greatly alarmed," he wrote, "by the opposition made to Mr. Stoddard's doctrine, and the agreeable practice, which had been so long established in Northampton, and so extensively in the country." God had permitted Satan "to exert himself in an extraordinary manner in opposition, as God ordinarily does when truth is in the birth."

Though more convinced than ever that his analysis of the town's disparity between profession and action confirmed his own principles, Edwards acknowledged in a general way that he too was at fault. In what must have been a refrain in his prayers during these painful years, he wrote: "God knows the wickedness of my heart and the great and sinful deficiencies and offenses which I have been guilty of in the course of my ministry at Northampton. I desire that God would discover them to me more and more, and that now he would effectually humble me and mortify my pride and self-confidence, and empty me entirely of myself, and make me to know how that I deserve to be cast away as an abominable branch, and as a vessel wherein is no pleasure."[46] In classic Puritan fashion, he saw his humiliation as a reminder of his utter unworthiness and prayed that God might use it like a refiner's fire suiting him for more adequate service.

Edwards knew from decades of self-examination that his "pride and self-confidence" were the traits for which he most needed to be humbled. Perhaps again recognizing these propensities, he acted with the disciplines of restraint he had so long cultivated. Although Edwards believed his opponents were being used by the devil, he seems to have made a mighty effort to manifest a personal demeanor of the gentleness that he espoused. He also kept in the foreground the constructive purposes of his pastoral role and frequently reminded the Northampton congregation that it was care for their eternal souls that was his preeminent concern.

Yet while his personal and pastoral disciplines may have tempered manifestations of his pride and self-confidence in personal relationships, he drew a sharp line between pride and self-confidence as personal vices and the confidence one should have in standing for God's truth. If one was sure of God's revealed truth, then confidence was a Holy Spirit–inspired virtue. Edwards believed he had learned something and grown through his years of struggling with the high-spirited Northamptonites, but that lesson had a paradoxical relation to his perennial struggles with his pride and self-confidence. He thought the best lesson he had learned was that he should have been firmer in his convictions from the start. He should earlier have settled his mind on what God's Word demanded and then forgone all personal concerns. The paradox between this lesson and his critique in the same letter of his grandfather Stoddard for being of "a dogmatical temper" seems to have escaped him.

Edwards could justify his behavior, which others saw as unbending and dogmatical, because he saw himself as a reformer who was part of a cosmic struggle. The devil's ragings were the pangs to be expected "when truth is in the birth." Like Luther, he believed that the surrounding churches were falling into complacency and corruption and giving their blessings to worldliness. If the churches of the Reformation were to lead the way to the promised glorious new day, then they must themselves be once again purified. Scripture and his pastoral duties to watch over eternal souls, he was convinced, compelled him to take his stand no matter what the cost.

For someone who is known for his analysis of the centrality of affections in religion, Edwards retained remarkably high confidence in the power of well-argued principle to prevail. As he observed in retrospect, because it was a religious controversy, his opponents took their stand on the high ground of principle and saw supreme spiritual concerns at stake. Once the bonds of affection were broken, each side, as in any controversy, soon saw the other as unreasonable and even perverse. In the Northampton case, the intensity of the feelings was heightened by the fact that the two parties had once been great lovers, each of whom now viewed themselves as betrayed.

# CHAPTER 23

# The Mission

When Edwards moved to Stockbridge, in June 1751, he had reason for renewed hopes. He could see the beauties of the setting on the Housatonic River in the Berkshires as communications of Christ's redemptive love. The village itself could inspire high expectations. It was designed to be a model community, a prototype for future missions where English and Indians would live side by side in peace. In Edwards' view this product of Gospel zeal was a glimmer anticipating the dawn of the millennium, when every tribe and nation would see the light of God's righteousness and dwell together in harmony (cf. Isaiah 60). Yet he also knew that the village's short history had sometimes been stormy. When the Gospel light was spreading, as his experience in Northampton had confirmed, Satan was sure to counterattack by exploiting human self-interest. Though hopeful, Edwards also expected to have a struggle on his hands.

The Stockbridge experiment centered around a couple of hundred Mahican Indians (also known as Mohican, Muhhakaneok, Stockbridge, Housatonic, or Housatunnuck),[1] the largest single part of the remnant of the once-great Mahican confederacy, now struggling for survival and willing to be under English protection. In 1730 Governor Belcher proposed the establishment of a missionary village for Indians. Four years later a group of Mahicans living on the Housatonic expressed interest to Edwards' brother-in-law Samuel Hopkins (the elder) of West Springfield in having a Christian missionary sent to them. The Massachusetts Commissioners for the Propagation of the Gospel among the Indians in New England chose a recent Yale graduate, John Sergeant, to be the first missionary. Sergeant was soon joined by Timothy Woodbridge, a schoolmaster from Springfield. Between 1736 and 1739 they established Stockbridge, a town for the Mahicans that also included four

English (New Englander) families.[2] The idea was that Indians might be more effectively evangelized if they learned to live with the English and according to English principles. Civilizing, it was believed, should go hand in hand with evangelizing. The government granted the Indians lots from some of the best land by the river, and the English families land in the hills above the meadows. Although several of his close relatives and associates, including Colonel John Stoddard and Stephen Williams, helped lead the effort, Edwards' only direct involvement seems to have been that he was one of several clergy who helped buy some outlying land owned by an earlier Dutch settler.[3]

Almost everyone directly involved in the project had some connection to the Williams-Stoddard Calvinist-evangelical clan, headed at that time by William Williams of Hatfield. Ephraim Williams, the patriarch's younger brother, moved to Stockbridge in 1737, and by the time the town was incorporated in 1739 had assumed the role of English squire of the village. Two of the Indians, Captain John Kunkapaut and Lieutenant Paul Umpeecheanah were elected as selectmen in the town. Ephraim Williams was chosen moderator.[4] (For Edwards' Williams relatives, see charts of Edwards' Extended Family in Appendix A of this volume.)

True love helped seal the family connection to the mission. Sergeant, the missionary pastor, had been willing enough to take on a life of self-sacrifice, but he preferred not to do it alone. When he was first embarking on the mission he had unsuccessfully courted Edwards' sister Hannah. The arrival of the Ephraim Williams family after he had been in Stockbridge for some time on his own seemed a Godsend. Sergeant was soon smitten by Ephraim's brilliant and charming daughter, Abigail, and the two married in 1739 when she was just seventeen. "You will forgive me Sir," Sergeant wrote to Benjamin Colman, one of his Boston sponsors, "if I think that most ingenious woman is not the smallest gift of divine bounty that I have received since I undertook a life thought to be so self-denying. The more tenderly I love her the more thankful I am to heaven, who has formed her as if on purpose for me, and given her to me as if (like the father of mankind) he thought it not good for me to be here alone."[5]

Abigail was ready to play Eve to Sergeant's Adam. Although she was pious enough to be happy to marry a missionary-saint, she also had the English tastes of New England's eighteenth-century elite and saw to it that they lived according to the style to which she had become accustomed. Sergeant had built a modest house on the plain near the Indians. Abigail, one of the more remarkable women of the time, convinced him that they must live in

The Mission House, Stockbridge, Massachusetts. Home of Edwards' rival Abigail Williams Sergeant Dwight, it originally sat on a hillside overlooking the plain where the Edwardses lived, closer to the Indians.

a home of the highest quality, on the hill overlooking the town. The Mission House (which has been preserved), hauled by ox team from Connecticut and decorated with tasteful paneling and an elegant carving above the front door, is a tribute to Abigail's good taste.[6] It is also a monument to one of the classic tensions long found in elite American missions.

Sergeant had moderate success in working with the essentially friendly Indians. His efforts were supported both by the Massachusetts Commissioners made up of the Colman circle in Boston and, more substantially, by the London-based Company for the Propagation of the Gospel in New England. The Reverend Isaac Hollis, a wealthy English dissenting pastor, was the principal benefactor. As historian Edmund S. Morgan observed, the Stockbridge experiment "became more appealing to those who heard of it in direct proportion to their distance from the scene."[7] In 1743 Benjamin Colman published a letter "Containing Mr. Sergeant's Proposal of a more effectual Method for the Education of Indian children: to raise 'em if possible into a civil and industrious People, by Introducing the English Language Among them." The gist of Sergeant's argument was that, in order to overcome what seemed to be destructive habits of Indian lifestyles, it was essential to put more emphasis on teaching them the habits of English industry and husbandry. Specifically, Sergeant proposed a boarding school for Indian children of various tribes, which would provide opportunity to train a new generation in more thoroughly Christian and European ways.[8]

Sergeant's plans for a boarding school were delayed by King George's War. Isaac Hollis, however, sent enough money to begin a school in 1748 for twelve Indian boys in a place safer than Stockbridge. Sergeant secured the aid of Captain Martin Kellogg of Newington, Connecticut, to instruct them there "in learning and hard labour." The school emphasized the disciplines of agricultural life, the lack of which the English viewed as one of the greatest failings of Indian men. Typically, Indian men relegated most agricultural activities to their women, and by strict Yankee standards the men seemed conspicuously undisciplined.[9] Captain Kellogg, rough-hewn in his sixties, had been educated by hard experience on the frontier. As a boy, he had been one of the Deerfield captives and so had learned some Indian languages. That valuable skill had put him in the middle of New England Indian affairs as an interpreter ever since. Early in 1749, soon after the end of King George's War, Sergeant had Kellogg move his school to Stockbridge, where it occupied a partially constructed building on an attractive piece of land donated by the Mahicans. Then calamity struck. Just as the school was getting settled in Stockbridge, Sergeant was stricken with a fever and a throat canker and died in mid-1749. He was only thirty-nine.

At the time of Sergeant's death, 218 Indians were living in Stockbridge, of whom 125 had been baptized and 42 were communicants in the church. In addition to Captain Kellogg's fledgling boarding school was Timothy Woodbridge's day school with 55 students. The town in 1749, much as Edwards would have found it when he visited the next year, had a single rambling main street with fifty-three Indian dwellings, twenty of which were English-style homes. The number of English families in the surrounding area had grown from the original four to around ten.[10]

The death of Sergeant threw the model village into a crisis. Already tensions had been mounting. The issue was the classic one that would plague every mission to the natives during the era of English and American expansion. Closely following the missionaries were settlers who, even if sympathetic to the mission, had stronger interests in their own lands, their economic opportunities, and the security of their expanding families. Though Stock-bridge was still predominantly a town for Indians, it was nonetheless an English town. The Indians were used to a more communal system of owner-ship and reluctant to adopt the more individualized English model; yet they also knew they had to play by the English rules if their claims were to continue to be recognized. The New Englanders, familiar with their own system, kept outmaneuvering them. No one had told them, the Indians com-plained to a government committee late in 1749, that the number of English families would be expanded from four to the current ten. The New En-glanders were also buying up some of the best land or not mentioning that in measuring some of the acreage they traded they were including ponds and swamps. Most irritating to the Indians were the land maneuvers of Squire Ephraim Williams and his adult sons, who were building the family fortune by consolidating claims to choice real estate.[11] John Sergeant, Ephraim Williams' son-in-law, had served as a sort of buffer between the Indians and the Williamses, but with their pastor removed, the Indians' distrust of the Williams clan increased.

By spring 1750 the Williams faction, led by Abigail and her father, had found their candidate for a replacement for Sergeant. Abigail, still only twenty-seven, was thinking of a replacement in more ways than one.[12] In April, Ezra Stiles, an urbane twenty-three-year-old Yale graduate, had come to preach on successive Sabbaths and had stayed the week at the widow's home. Stiles (later to be a distinguished president of Yale) matched Abigail in brilliance, and the two spent time talking of the meaning of life during, as he put it, "the pleasant week I spent at your house; when sorrow itself appears beautiful."

Stiles was going through a stage when he had deep doubts about his faith, even venturing beyond the fashionable Arminianism toward Deism. As he confided to Abigail, he believed in "no other religion but that of *Nature* and the *Bible*," and in fact he had his doubts about the Bible. From his week with her, Stiles had learned that Abigail too was of a liberal spirit, probably more so than most of her family. John Sergeant after marrying her had changed in his outlook (Edwards later said his effectiveness as a missionary suffered after the marriage).[13] Sergeant became an Old Light during the awakening, one of the subscribers to Charles Chauncy's *Seasonable Thoughts*, and he had shocked some of his Williams relatives by questioning some traditional Cal-vinist doctrines.[14]

Meanwhile Timothy Woodbridge led a firmly New Light Calvinistic

majority of the English in the mission town who soon became suspicious of
Stiles. The schoolteacher was popular with the Indians and could enlist their
support.

We can imagine the consternation of the Williams faction when in the
fall Jonathan Edwards suddenly replaced Ezra Stiles as the leading candidate
to fill the vacancy. Abigail could not understand why Stiles, after the assurances of the spring, had not pursued his candidacy. She wrote to admonish
him for backing out, confessing meaningfully in the process, "I find I am a
great deal too much disappointed." Stiles explained that he was caught in an
impossible bind. His father, the Reverend Isaac Stiles (Edwards' older protégé in college and later an Old Light pastor), had advised him to withdraw.
To receive the position Ezra would have to be examined by the Commissioners in Boston. Their antennae for sensing heterodoxy were acute; they
would surely discover his unacceptable views and his reputation would be
ruined.

When Edwards visited Stockbridge in the winter of 1750–51, the Williams family at first strongly opposed him, but by late February when the
town invited their cousin to settle as minister, Abigail and her father appeared
to have relented somewhat. Edwards later viewed their acquiescence as pure
disingenuousness, arising only when they knew they did not have the votes to
defeat him.[15] In fact, however, Abigail had been genuinely well impressed.
"Mr. Edwards is now with us," she wrote to Stiles in February. "He has
conducted [himself] with wisdom and prudence. . . . He is learned, polite,
and free in conversation, and more catholic than I had supposed."[16] Abigail
may have enjoyed anyone who could intelligently converse on deeper issues.
In any case, this was high praise from someone who had been ready to vilify
her notorious relative.

Abigail's half-brother, Captain Ephraim Williams Jr., a young man of
action, persisted in his misgivings. Ephraim Jr. had made a name for himself
in the recent King George's War and was still stationed as commander at Fort
Massachusetts. In May 1751 he wrote to his cousin by marriage, the Reverend
Jonathan Ashley of Deerfield, enumerating the reasons he had opposed Edwards. First, "he was not sociable" and so (quoting Scripture) "not apt to
teach." Second, "he was a very great bigot, for he would not admit any person
into heaven, but those that agreed fully to his sentiments, a doctrine deeply
tinged with that of the Romish church." (Ephraim Jr. shared his sister's
preference for a generically Protestant "catholicity" or openness.) Third, he
was too old to learn the Indians' tongue. Fourth, the military man could

neither understand nor agree to Edwards' principles on the sacraments and, he wrote, "that I had heard almost every gentleman in the country say the same." Though Ephraim Jr., "like an honest fellow," had communicated these views to Edwards himself, he had eventually relented in his open opposition to the Stockbridge majority, "since they are so set for him." Still, he did not think Edwards would do any good for the town except (in a telling admission) "raise the price of my land." Edwards, he believed, was thoroughly impractical. "I am sorry," he summarized in what must have been the prevailing view among the "gentlemen" of his acquaintance, "that a head so full of divinity should be so empty of politics."[17]

The Stockbridge Williamses were not, as has sometimes been suggested, simply Old Lights dead set against Edwards and his New Light advocates. The family itself was divided, ambivalent, and in transition in its views. In May 1748 Ephraim Jr., shortly after Colonel John Stoddard had appointed him to command Fort Massachusetts, had drawn up a will in which he named Edwards as one of three ministerial overseers, "being of the Calvinistical persuasion and principles," to administer a small fund left for educating Indians in Stockbridge. Further, the squire, Ephraim Sr., was, like most of his clan, New Light and Calvinist. In 1749 he sent his youngest son, Elijah, to study with Aaron Burr at the College of New Jersey. He kept the young man supplied with a steady stream of letters urging him to care for the state of his soul.[18] He was perhaps worried—probably with good reason—that his children were turning away from strict Calvinism. Yet the family had a New Light orthodox reputation.

The Williams family also had some genuine commitment to the Indian mission. This is important to point out because much of the story of Edwards' relation to them involves his opposition to what he regarded as their efforts to exploit the mission for their own advantage. Just about every interpreter takes Edwards' side in these controversies. As Ephraim Jr.'s offhand remark that Edwards' coming would raise the price of his land suggests, financial matters were seldom far from the family's concerns. The acquisition of land in the Stockbridge area was crucial for the economic advance of an expanding elite family, yet they did not see that interest as conflicting with their support for the mission. The Williamses had taken a risk to move to such an experimental frontier village and, especially through Abigail's connection with Sergeant, had become intimately involved with the mission.

If we put the story of the Williamses at Stockbridge in its larger historical context, we can view the family's experience as prototypical of that of many

European-American Christians who were displacing the Indians. By the time of the American Revolution, Elijah Williams, the younger son who had studied at Princeton, had succeeded his father as the wealthiest man in the region and had bought up much of the Indian land. As Stockbridge became increasingly a white village, its attractiveness declined for the Indians, even those who were Christianized. The Williamses' road to success in fostering this transition was paved with good intentions, some genuine piety, and a desire to benefit both Indians and whites. Yet leading them down that road and eventually obscuring their original purposes were motives of self-interest and enterprise, which led the family to take for granted that they should exploit their economic opportunities. By the time Edwards arrived in Stockbridge in the 1750s, the forces of economic self-interest were, as he was especially alert to see, in control. Yet strains of piety and interest in the mission were still there as well, so that the Williamses could show some authentic righteous indignation in their efforts to keep it under their guidance.

As for the Indians, the larger perspective on Stockbridge has a tie to the saga of "the last of the Mohicans." James Fenimore Cooper's novel is set in New England in 1757 during the French and Indian War and was based very loosely on the model of some Stockbridge Mahicans in Robert Rogers' rangers. Edwards would have known the original men involved. The actual Stockbridge Mahicans faithfully served the English against the French and the Americans against the English, but after the Revolution there was little in Stockbridge to keep them there. They moved to New York State where Cooper, growing up in the early 1800s, may have encountered a remnant of the once great tribe.[19]

When Edwards arrived to settle in Stockbridge summer 1751, the potential for the mission's success—despite the disruption from the loss of Sergeant—was still near its peak. The prospects were exciting because the new boarding school, under Captain Kellogg, had attracted the attention of tribes beyond the Mahicans. The Mahicans were much diminished in numbers and could benefit from English protection. At the same time the English desperately needed the goodwill of the powerful Six Nations of the Iroquois Confederacy, which occupied territory in New York, from just across the Hudson to Lake Ontario and the headwaters of the Susquehanna. Closest of these nations were the Mohawks, whose leaders had already shown interest in the Stockbridge boarding school. In August 1751, in connection with other negotiations with the English at Albany (only thirty miles west of Stockbridge), the Mohawk leaders agreed to come to Stockbridge to consider a treaty that would involve bringing Mohawk children and possibly those of other nations to the boarding school.

Such a prospect had immense strategic importance to the English, who expected renewal of war with the French and urgently needed to do better in winning Indian allegiance. Enthusiasm for such practical benefits of the mission was often wed to zeal for its spiritual benefits, though we should not suppose that the union necessarily made either sort of motive the less genuine. Few eighteenth-century Christians would have thought of the two interests as separable. Especially in England, the happy coincidence of temporal and eternal interests as represented at the boarding school had attracted wide attention, and the Reverend Hollis' mission society contributors had included the Prince of Wales.[20]

Stockbridge, after two years of struggle, seemed to be coming to life as the potential hub of New England missions. Since his arrival, Edwards was preaching and overseeing a major expansion of John Sergeant's original house in the village in preparation for occupancy in the fall by the Edwards household.

On Saturday, August 10, 1751, a committee of western Massachusetts notables headed by Brigadier General Joseph Dwight, an Edwards admirer from Brookfield (near Worcester), arrived in town. The next Tuesday almost all the Mohawk chiefs "came with a great train," some ninety-two in their entire company. The English proposed that the Mohawks settle in New England and send their children to the boarding school at Stockbridge. The chiefs responded by reminding the English of their many broken promises and that the same must not happen again. Nonetheless, they were favorable to the proposal "and gave a belt of wampum in consideration of it." As Edwards summarized it, they indicated that this "not only was done on their own behalf, [but] for all nations of Indians [presumably all nations of the Iroquois]; that by this they opened the door for all nations, that they might come and bring their children hither to be instructed, and as a confirmation that they would do what they could to persuade other nations to send their children hither."[21]

On Friday, August 16, in a solemn gathering in the Puritan style, Edwards preached to the Mohawks. A violent storm the night before had broken the heat, though Edwards presumably would have appeared in wig and robe no matter what the temperature. The Indians probably knew of the tall Englishman by reputation as a great holy man. The Mohawks were on friendly terms with the local Mahicans (though their dialects differed), and the Mahicans

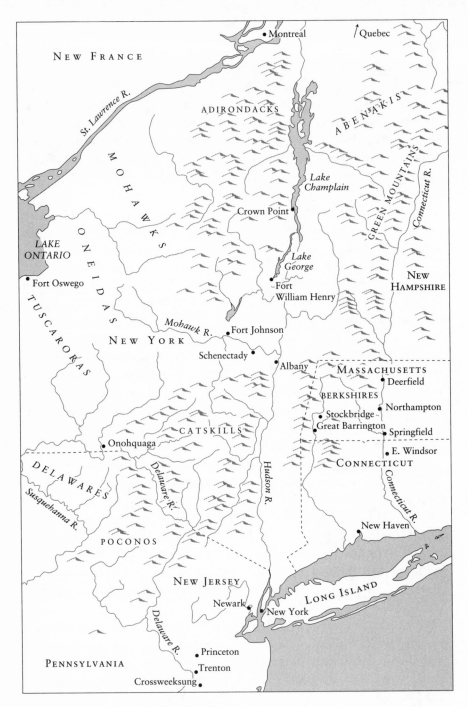

Edwards' world as the embattled American west

had learned of Edwards as a friend of the saintly David Brainerd who had worked nearby with some of them. Edwards had also met with the venerable Chief Hendrick. Known as a great orator, Hendrick was a Christian, had visited England, and was celebrated as one of the most loyal Indian allies of the British. Edwards was also impressed by Hendrick's elder brother, Abraham Conaughstansey, also a dedicated Christian and the strongest proponent of the boarding school, "who," Edwards said, "I can't but look upon as a remarkable man."[22]

Edwards' sermon, a straightforward summary of the Gospel, also encapsulated his view of the Indians. Although Edwards in many respects viewed the natives through typically English categories, he also refracted his vision through the lenses of Scripture and his theology, which made his evaluations considerably different from those of the English who had other priorities. For Edwards, people were not to be judged first of all by nationality, although nation was for him an important category. He did believe God dealt with nations, as the Old Testament indicated. Yet even more important was his New Testament and New Light view that distinguished the regenerate from the unregenerate within every nation. As Edwards was more acutely aware than ever by 1751, many of the English, even in New England, belonged to the tribe of Satan. So while Edwards believed God was highly displeased with the degenerate state of most of Indian culture, he believed most of the Europeans in North American were equally degenerate, but worse for having rejected so many opportunities to hear the Gospel.

Building his message around the image of light and darkness, Edwards described how the Gospel potentially put all peoples on equal footing. "It was once with our forefathers as 'tis with you," he assured them. "They formerly were in great darkness." In Edwards' view of history all peoples had common ancestors in Adam and Eve less than six thousand years ago and all had equally fallen into darkness. All need the same gift of God's light. "We are no better than you in no respect," he explained, "only as God has made us to differ and has been pleased to give us more light. And now we are willing to give it to you."

Most of the Europeans had failed them; "they have not done their duty toward you." "The French, they pretend to teach the Indians religion, but they won't teach 'em to read. They won't let 'em read the Word of God." Most others are no better. "And many of the English and the Dutch are against your being instructed. They choose to keep you in the dark for the sake of making a gain of you." Edwards kept the tie close between the light of the Gospel

Chief Hendrick (Theyanoguin, ca. 1680–1755), a Mohawk leader much celebrated by the English as one of their most faithful allies, was a friend of the Stockbridge mission

education and the Indians' practical interests. "For as long as they keep you in ignorance," he continued, "'tis more easy to cheat you in trading with you."

Nothing, however, was nearly as important as the Gospel itself. "The temporal concerns that they treat with you about at Albany from year to year are mere childish trifles in comparison with this." The devil kept people blind and ignorant of the Gospel so he could destroy them and their children. "I have read of some nations," he told the Indians, "that when they take children captives in war, they keep 'em well for a while and feed 'em with the best till they are fat, and then kill 'em and eat 'em. So the devil does by wicked men." Edwards knew that the Indians loved children. So if the Indians wanted to protect their children from such deceptive slavery, they should consider that education is the best means to bring them to the light of God's Word through which they could see their true interests.[23]

Edwards, who characteristically saw himself as involved in grand historical moments, reported to Thomas Hubbard, the speaker of the Massachusetts House of Representatives, that the Stockbridge treaty with the Mohawks was possibly "God in his providence . . . opening the door for . . . the gospel among these nations, more than ever [he] has done before." The new missionary's enthusiasm, however, was tempered by a cool assessment of many practical problems. The French, he told Hubbard, were making extraordinary efforts to win the Indians. The Church of England was discouraging Abraham Conaughstansey from moving his people under dissenter auspices. Other Indians mocked Abraham for his Christian interests and trust in English education. The English typically gave the Indians so much rum that constructive living together became impossible. Much was needed to improve the "miserable state" of the facilities of the boarding school under Captain Kellogg. A "young gentleman" was needed as a teacher who could learn the Mohawk tongue. Also there was need for a distinguished gentleman or gentlemen to be appointed in residence to oversee the enterprise. Brigadier General Joseph Dwight was his first choice of several candidates to counter the Williamses' de facto control.

The time to act on all this, Edwards emphasized in this lengthy report, was "*now* or *never*." Aside from spiritual concerns, educating the Mohawks and instructing them in the Protestant religion would greatly aid the British cause. "The only remaining means that divine providence hath left us to repair and secure these Indians in the British interest," he wrote, "is this very thing . . . of instructing them thoroughly in the Protestant religion, and educating their children." One of the British officers had assured Edwards that the plan deserved to be promoted simply on those grounds. It was crucial for the Massachusetts government to give the mission its full support.[24]

The more he learned, the more Edwards was appalled by the English policies toward the Indians. As he put it in an extensive letter the next winter to Joseph Paice, an English Presbyterian merchant and prospective supporter for the mission, British negligence had "brought the whole British America into very difficult and dangerous circumstances." The French were much wiser by comparison. For generations their missionaries had faithfully lived among the Indians. It was in Edwards' self-interest, of course, to represent missions as crucial to British survival in North America, yet he claimed this was confirmed by the Indians themselves. In his first year in Stockbridge, wrote Edwards, "I have had much acquaintance with many of the Iroquois or Six Nations (as we call them); and have had frequent conversation with some of their chiefs." English traders typically defrauded the Indians. Most of the king's annual present of £500 sterling to the Iroquois was embezzled before it ever got there, and the Indians were induced to spend the rest on rum. The Iroquois so mistrusted their English allies that many said that if they sent their children to English schools, the English would enslave them. The French had been awake to the strategic importance of the Indians while the English had been asleep. Edwards' Indian informants told him of how the French laughed about the English ineptness. "Indeed," Edwards warned, "there is a great prospect of the French king's having the greatest part of North America in his possession; though the king of Great Britain has much the greatest number of subjects here." Joseph Paice was so impressed by Edwards' analysis that he forwarded a copy to the Archbishop of Canterbury—despite having to apologize for a passage in which Edwards excoriated the Anglican missionaries as "great bigots" who would root out all dissenters and "build up themselves here on the ruins of Protestant and British interest."[25]

In these letters on Indian affairs and continuing through his Stockbridge years we see a new Edwards, or at least a new side of Edwards. If all we had were Edwards' letters from Stockbridge (more than four hundred large pages as published in the Yale edition), we would know him as a missionary deeply involved in the practical affairs of his day. His letters provide detailed accounts of subjects ranging from the personal dynamics of a biracial village to strategies for empire. It is almost as though he had heard Ephraim Williams Jr.'s remark about "a head so full of divinity should be so empty of politics" and resolved to show them otherwise.

Perhaps, as he contemplated the wreck of Northampton, Edwards simply resolved to stay more on top of practical affairs. Or perhaps the situation demanded attention to a wider range of issues. In Stockbridge there were far fewer precedents for how things should be done and no John Stoddard whom he could rely on to take charge. In Stockbridge Edwards was forced to manage more himself. It is possible, of course, that he always displayed the wider practical interests and that we simply know more about them in the Stockbridge years because he was forced to write letters about them. If so, our image of him in Northampton should be revised to see him as more like other notable eighteenth-century men who had an informed interest in everything. Nevertheless, we know that when he left Northampton he had a reputation for having his head in the clouds, while in his six and a half years at Stock-bridge he not only contended with some formidable adversaries over practical matters but often prevailed.

Such practical concerns, it must be noted, hardly took most of his time or kept him from divinity. In Stockbridge, in addition to his preaching and pastoral duties, he produced four major treatises, two of which are often regarded as classics in the history of Christianity and in the history of American intellectual life. The Edwards who emerged at Stockbridge after passing through the fires of Northampton, while hardly without his flaws, was truly an extraordinary figure.

One subject he immediately took an interest in was the methods of teaching the Indians. As his sermon to the Mohawks suggested, he believed that literacy was a key to effective missions, since the Indians needed to be able to read and understand God's Word. Because no Scriptures existed in the local Indians' tongue, Edwards believed that they must become proficient in English if real progress were to be made. In fact, he believed, "Indian languages are extremely barbarous and barren, and very ill-fitted for communicating things moral and divine, or even things speculative and abstract. In short, they are wholly unfit for a people possessed of civilization, knowledge and refinement."[26] Edwards had low regard for Indian culture but high trust in Indian potential.

Edwards was dismayed at the method of teaching English to Indians employed at Stockbridge and among the English generally. As far as he could see, what almost always happened was that "the children learn to read, to make such sounds on the sight of such marks; but know nothing what they say, and have neither profit nor entertainment by what they read, they neglect it when they leave school, and quickly lose [it]."

Edwards had some remedies for this colossal waste of time. Most basically, "the child should be taught to understand *things,* as well as *words.*" This observation, aside from being common sense, grew from Edwards' deeper reflections that words were symbols to excite vital encounters with realities. Ever since he was a child he had been against rote learning of languages. His solution was not only that the meanings of the words needed to be explained, but also that the teacher "should enter into conversation with the child about them." The teacher should ask questions on the lesson and the child should be encouraged "to speak freely and in his turn also to ask questions." This he believed would "accustom the child, from its infancy, to think and reflect, and to beget in it an early taste for knowledge, and a regularly increasing appetite for it." Drawing on his own work with children, Edwards believed that Scripture stories were the best means of so engaging the children. They could eventually learn the fascinating intricacies of the whole saga of the biblical history of redemption.

Edwards recommended that girls be educated as well as boys and that they all be taught not only reading, but spelling and the basics of arithmetic. Those with the best genius should be encouraged to go on. Periodically the schools should also hold public assemblies to which families and all the chief persons would be invited. Children would recite their lessons in competitions and prizes would be awarded.

He also believed that it would be unusually popular with the Indians to teach singing, which he thought would have a powerful effect in leading them to civilized attitudes. "Music, especially sacred music, has a powerful efficacy to soften the heart into tenderness, to harmonize the affections, and to give the mind a relish for objects of a superior character."

These innovations, aimed at making school engaging and entertaining, would best be supplemented by some stronger methods to bridge the cultural gap. Some English children should be integrated into the Indian schools, thereby reinforcing the idea of English as a living language. More radically, Indian children should be encouraged to live a year with the best English families. The Edwardses eventually took at least one Indian boy into their home and perhaps others.[27]

Edwards had confidence in the Indians' abilities if they could be properly educated. In his letter to Joseph Paice he remarked, "they are a *discerning people*." That, he believed, gave the English an advantage over the French. The French, he said, forbade them to read the Bible and did not teach them to read and write. The English (at least the English dissenters), by contrast, had the truth on their side and so nothing to hide. "And we have also this advantage, that our religion would recommend itself more to their reason and to the light of nature in 'em than the religion of the French." As always, convinced of the power of reason, Edwards was sure that a combination of education and the Gospel would be the key to enlightening the native peoples.[28]

In addition to trying to determine how to turn Stockbridge into an effective center for Indian schooling, Edwards had plenty of practical concerns with relocating his family. Edwards' search for quiet in the modest John Sergeant mission house was interrupted daily by workmen building a much larger addition suitable for a large family.[29] Meanwhile, their Northampton home had not sold. Although they received some funds from collections made by friends, especially from Scotland, their immediate financial situation was disheartening.[30]

In October 1751 Edwards returned to Northampton to move his family. It was October 16 (October 27 by our calendars), about as late as one could wait before truly cold weather might set in. Amid much anxiety and sadness, the family left their home and friends. Seventeen-year-old Mary and her husband Timothy Dwight remained in Northampton. Sally and her husband Elihu Parsons planned to move to Stockbridge but remained temporarily in Northampton, probably in the unsold family home. As the rest of the family departed with carts stacked high with worldly possessions, a sense of defeat and banishment heightened the inevitable sense of loss.

Despite the hardships, Stockbridge proved a welcome respite. Even though Jonathan was already doing his best to correct what he considered mismanagement of the mission school by the Williamses and their ally Captain Kellogg, personal relations with his relatives may have still been cordial. If not, the tension in Stockbridge seemed to the Edwards family like child's play after years of feeling ostracized by the majority of former friends in Northampton. By January 1752 Edwards could write reassuringly to his aging parents that his family was very pleased with Stockbridge: "They like the place far better than they expected. Here, at present, we live in peace; which has of long time been an unusual thing with us. The Indians seem much pleased with my family, especially my wife."[31]

Esther, just turning twenty, was especially delighted with Stockbridge in the winter. There was skating on the river and excitement in sledding. "My sister and I had two Indian boys to pull our sleds for us," she wrote, "and to guide them over the crust . . . we speed from one descent to another until we finally reach the level of our quiet street."[32] Her second brother, six-year-old Jonathan Jr., soon had Indian playmates and seldom heard English outside the home. "I knew the names of some things in Indian," he later recalled, "which I did not know in English; even all my thoughts ran in Indian."[33]

Although family morale was high, their financial straits were severe. Edwards told his father he was "about 2,000 pounds in debt, in this province's money," and could not come to the aid of his widowed and destitute sister Eunice, who had just suffered the ordeal of the deaths of two "likely promising children."[34] In Stockbridge the family thanked God for their health, but family finances were at an all-time low. Sarah and the girls helped support the family by making decorated fans out of silk paper. Jonathan was reduced to writing on the margins of useless pamphlets, on the covers of letters, and on the scraps of paper from the fans.[35]

The great excitement of the spring was the arrival of Aaron Burr, a New Light admirer of Edwards who was pastor in Newark, New Jersey, and president of the College of New Jersey there. Though Stockbridge was isolated, it was relatively accessible to the New York City–New Jersey area via Albany and the Hudson. The thirty-six-year-old Burr's intentions were to ask for the hand of Esther. His rapid success caused much comment. "He made a visit of but three days to the Rev. Mr. Edwards' daughter at Stockbridge," recounted Joseph Shippen, one of the students at the New Jersey College, "in which short time, though he had not . . . seen the lady these six years, I suppose he accomplished his whole design." When he saw her in Newark, Shippen judged the twenty-year-old Esther "a person of great beauty" but "rather too young for the president."[36]

Sarah accompanied Esther to Newark where the wedding took place on June 29, 1752. The Edwardses' oldest son, Timothy, just turning fourteen, went along to enroll at the college and to live with the Burrs. Jonathan remained behind, perhaps because of pressing matters in Stockbridge or because he was already committed to travel to New Jersey in the fall. He did visit the newlyweds in September, at the time of the college commencement. He was especially pleased to meet there the Reverend Samuel Davies, chief architect of the late revival in the Virginia backcountry. Edwards was also several times at the home of his old friend Governor Jonathan Belcher. On the same trip he met with correspondents of the Society for Propagating Christian Knowledge and preached before the Presbyterian Synod of New York a sermon published as *True Grace Distinguished from the Experience of Devils.*[37]

In Stockbridge during his first full year Edwards had established an apparently effective ministry as preacher to both the English and the Indians. Although the church included both English and Indians, Edwards preached separately to the two groups, addressing the Indians through an interpreter, usually John Wauwaumpequunnaunt, whom Edwards described as "an extraordinary man on some accounts." Edwards thought him an excellent interpreter and was impressed by his abilities to read and write English. He especially honored Wauwaumpequunnaunt for his understanding of Scripture and theology, which he thought might exceed that of any Indian in America. Even though Wauwaumpequunnaunt had a weakness for alcohol,

Edwards valued him both as his interpreter and as an assistant at Timothy Woodbridge's school and urged that he be better paid for his diligent labors.[38]

Edwards' sermons to the Indians reflect a good sense of his audience. For one thing, he did not just preach simpler versions of his sermons to the English, which were almost all old Northampton sermons. Rather, consistent with his advice regarding Indian education, he picked themes that involved narratives and plain vivid metaphors. He wrote out his sermons in outlines in such tiny hand that it would have required his spectacles to read. Probably he more-or-less memorized these but had them available to glance at as the interpreter was speaking. His outlines confirm the recollection of a fellow missionary that, "to the Indians he was a plain and practical preacher; upon no occasion did he display any metaphysical knowledge in the pulpit. His sentences were concise and full of meaning; and his delivery, grave and natural."[39]

Seeking to explain the Gospel to those who knew little about it, Edwards preached predominantly on New Testament texts, especially from Matthew and Luke. Some of his most effective sermon series were from the parables. Early in his preaching to the Indians, Edwards emphasized, as he always had in Northampton, their sins and vices. After the first year, though, he seldom provided catalogues of Indians' sins. This may have reflected in part the logic of Calvinist evangelism or a conscious shift in preaching strategy. It may be that Edwards' experience confirmed what he had learned from David Brainerd who had written, "the more I discour'ed of the love and compassion of God in sending his Son to suffer for the sins of men; and the more I invited them to come and partake of his love, the more their distress was aggravated, because they felt themselves unable to come. It was surprising to me to see how their hearts seem'd to be pierc'd with the tender and melting invitations of the Gospel, when there was not a word of terror spoken to them."[40]

Edwards did not shrink from preaching terror to the Indians or from explaining in narrative terms some hard points of Calvinism, such as original sin and the reasons for God's wrath and judgment, but he tempered these points with God's mercy as much as he could. Judgment and loving mercy were intertwined in all of Edwards' preaching and theology. He presented God as loving but righteously indignant at those who reject love and live under the rule of the devil. God was also marvelously forgiving in suffering to provide salvation for many. While not altering his theology, Edwards dwelt especially on the mercy and compassion of God in allowing his own son to suffer and die. In a moving sermon on Revelation 3:20, Edwards pictured a bleeding Christ standing at the door and knocking. "Let him in," Edwards pled. "Will you shut him out of doors when he comes to you and knocks at your door with his wounded, bleeding hands?"[41]

Although Edwards seems to have kept the respect of his Stockbridge Indian congregation, there was no revival there and he made no reports of remarkable conversions. Many of the adult Indians in his congregation were already communicant members. We do not know how many more became communicants, but we do have several Indian professions of faith, written in Edwards' hand, following the standards of the sample professions he had composed for Northamptonites during the controversy.[42]

Edwards apparently kept good relations with the Indians through both his ministry to them and his even-handed ways of judging all people by the same spiritual standards. Once a week he took the time to teach their children the essentials of Christianity through Bible stories. He and his family also lived among them, so that there must have been daily contact as Sarah and the Edwardses' daughters shared everyday concerns with Indian families and dealt with sicknesses, births, deaths, marriages, and care of children. Jonathan may have seemed an imposing, aloof figure, closed off in his study most of the day, and doubtless he and his family let Indians know of behaviors of which they disapproved, much as they had among the English in Northampton. They also shared many of the English prejudices of their time, assuming the inferiority of almost everything in Indian culture. Yet it also must have been apparent that regarding matters spiritual, which the Edwardses insisted were most important, they could be genuinely more approving of a spiritual Indian woman or child than of a profane English gentleman.

# CHAPTER 24

# Frontier Struggles

While the Edwardses seemed to live in peace with their Indian neighbors, by spring 1752 relations with the most powerful of their English neighbors, the Williams family, took a sharp turn for the worse. Almost the first thing Edwards had done to secure his position against the Williamses was to convince the authorities to appoint his friend Brigadier General Joseph Dwight of Brookfield to be resident overseer of the schools and to convince the brigadier to settle in Stockbridge. Edwards' first instinct, in other words, was to find a pious magistrate-aristocrat to play the role of patron to the pastor as John Stoddard had so long done in Northampton. The Mohawks had liked Dwight during the negotiations, and the brigadier had been one of Edwards' great supporters during the communion controversy. Dwight's rather grand military title came from having been commander of the artillery in the famed campaign at Louisbourg, and he had also served as second in command of western forces under John Stoddard during the recent war. The brigadier, the same age as Edwards, was originally from Hatfield and was a grandson of the first Joseph Hawley of Northampton (who had established that family's fortune in the late seventeenth century). He was a typical western Massachusetts politician, merchant, and aristocrat.[1]

Dwight seemed to Edwards to be the ideal magistrate-patron. The brigadier had been Edwards' great friend, confidant, and adviser during the Indian negotiations in summer 1751 and had told Edwards that he had always wanted to sit under preaching such as his. Edwards, in turn, needed Dwight to wrest control of the Hollis-funded schools from the Williams family. In particular, he was alarmed that a proposed school for Mohawk girls was to be run by Abigail. The alliance between Edwards and Dwight seemed made in heaven—except for one thing.

Dwight's wife, Mary, had died in the spring of 1751, and although that made him more movable, Edwards had not calculated the whole equation. Edwardsean preaching and Indian missions were not the only things the widower found charming about Stockbridge. There was also Abigail. Almost before Edwards knew it, the brilliant young woman and the impressive brigadier, nearly twenty years her senior, had won each other's hearts. By February 1752, soon after Dwight's arrival, they were engaged to be married.[2]

Edwards was aghast. In February, less than a month after he had written to his parents that for the first time in years "we live in peace," he was writing to Andrew Oliver, secretary of the Commissioners in Boston, that Brigadier Dwight had turned out to be "the furthest of any gentleman whatsoever from having the most necessary qualification" to oversee the mission.[3] Rather than helping Edwards lay siege to the corrupt Williams fortress on the hill, the brigadier was about to move in with the enemy. Suddenly Dwight had reversed his opinions concerning the very problems that Edwards had hoped he would correct: the influence of Colonel Ephraim Williams Sr.; Captain Kellogg's leadership of the boys boarding school; and, most decisively, Abigail's suitability to run the girls school.

Three factors were entwined in Edwards' opposition to the Williams faction in Stockbridge and to Abigail in particular. First, although he never mentioned it directly in his correspondence, he must have had some suspicions about Abigail's theology. He surely knew that Abigail opposed his own strictest principles, and he did report that the Indians said John Sergeant had changed for the worse after his marriage. Second, Edwards viewed the opposition of Colonel Ephraim Williams Sr. (who was orthodox) as part of the larger Williams family opposition to him over the communion controversy. Ephraim Sr. was the younger brother of the late patriarch William Williams of Hatfield and so uncle to Edwards' principal opponents. Fueling Edwards' fears in that regard was news that the formidable Elisha Williams, while in England, had been appointed a commissioner of Isaac Hollis' London society that supported the mission schools.

The third factor, underlying all of Edwards' complaints, were intimations of financial improprieties. At the root were the machinations of Ephraim Williams Sr. "The Indians," Edwards reported to the Commissioners in Boston, "have a very ill opinion of Colonel Williams and the deepest prejudice against him, he having often molested 'em with respect to their lands and other affairs." The Indians, "without anybody saying anything to lead 'em in

Brigadier General Joseph Dwight (1703–65)

it," had at Edwards' house expressed a similarly negative view of Abigail as thoroughly in league with her father in these matters.[4]

The Edwardses' relationship with Abigail was complicated by another factor: she was a friend of Aaron Burr. Abigail admired intelligence and perhaps had cultivated the friendship with the eminently eligible bachelor (her younger brother was a student at the College of New Jersey). Just before his marriage, Burr, probably trying to patch up relationships among his various friends, wrote a letter of congratulation to Brigadier Dwight on his engagement to "so excellent a person so well qualified to communicate and have the joys of a refined and virtuous friendship" as Abigail. "She is high in my esteem and has long been among the number of my particular friends." Something Burr had said to Abigail led to a misunderstanding for which Burr apologized to Edwards, but the issue is obscure.[5]

Edwards professed that his disposition was "entirely to have suppressed what I know that would be to the disadvantage of any of the people here," but that the more he learned about the management of the finances of Stockbridge, the more astonished he was. He was especially alarmed about what had been happening since the death of John Sergeant to the monies donated by Isaac Hollis to the mission. Under Abigail's and her father's control, the funds were either being wasted or were going for "selfish designs and intrigues for private interest." The Hollis money was going into Captain Kellogg's school, and Kellogg, in Edwards' view, was entirely incompetent as a schoolmaster. The Williams faction recognized his insufficiencies, but they kept him on because he was a firm ally—and, Edwards believed, Brigadier Dwight hoped to replace him with his own son.

The selfish designs consuming much of the rest of the Hollis contributions related to Abigail's appointment as mistress of the proposed girls school for the Mohawks. Abigail was drawing a salary and was having the schoolhouse built on the Williamses' private land, which Edwards (correctly) suspected would then be turned to the Williamses' profit. Abigail also had put her servants under salary from the public funds. Dwight, who was first of all a merchant, was the steward of the boarding schools and was selling them all their supplies from his own shop for a profit. Edwards, first writing about all this in February just after learning of Abigail's engagement to Dwight, had lost all his inhibitions about exposing the sorry mess. With the impending marriage, "things are like to [be] situated more preposterously still" as the brigadier would become, in effect, the sole overseer, commissioned by the General Assembly, to watch over what would now be his own wife's financial affairs.[6]

On the other side of the ledger, Edwards had the support of the schoolmaster, Timothy Woodbridge, most of the other white settlers, and most of the Indians. Woodbridge, who had worked with the Stockbridge Mahican Indians since the town's beginning, was Edwards' most valuable ally. "By his long-proved justice and integrity," wrote Edwards, "he has gained a vast esteem with the Indians, who are a people peculiar in that respect, if once they find a man is mean, [and] deceitful, never will trust him again; but their friendship is mightily gained by upright dealing." By contrast, Edwards repeatedly emphasized that the Indians distrusted his English antagonists.[7] Edwards' own transparent integrity seems to have won him the confidence of the Indians.

Edwards procured his own candidate, Gideon Hawley, a recent Harvard graduate, to teach the Mohawk boys at the boarding school. Hawley arrived in early February 1752, and Edwards reported that the Indians were very pleased with him. In addition to about thirty-six Indians, including Mohawks and other Iroquois, Hawley's school included "a couple of English" (likely including six-year-old Jonathan Jr.), so that they might eventually learn to be missionaries or Indian teachers.[8] Predictably, conflict soon broke out between Captain Kellogg and Hawley. Kellogg refused to yield to Hawley and continued to claim partial authority over the school. Sometimes he would call the boys out of the school for his own purposes or to teach them himself, causing huge confusion in the school and dissatisfaction among the Mohawks. Kellogg thus kept up some pretense that he continued to conduct what he called the "Hollisian School," drawing a substantial salary from Hollis but actually teaching only a few boys erratically for several weeks.[9] Edwards countered by calling a meeting of the Stockbridge Mahican Indians in April at which Timothy Woodbridge and others of Edwards' allies convinced them to withdraw the few children who were still under the tutelage of Captain Kellogg at the so-called Hollisian School.[10]

In May the conflict reached a crisis that threatened to destroy the entire Mohawk mission. Jonathan Hubbard, "a great friend of Captain Kellogg," was at the boarding school and struck the child of one of the chief Indians. The Indians were enraged. Gideon Hawley came to Edwards for advice, but Edwards declined to intervene because Brigadier Dwight had told him in no uncertain terms to stay out of the Mohawk affairs. The brigadier, on hearing of the blow-up, went to the school while it was in session and "for three hours together by the watch" loudly berated the young schoolmaster, Hawley. The Mohawk children were alarmed and said, according to Edwards, "they did not know but that great man would kill their schoolmaster, and were very much afraid Mr. Hawley would go away."[11] In the wake of this conflict, about half the Mohawks left.

By now the gloves were entirely off in the battle to control Stockbridge. Edwards was reporting that "the Brigadier has plainly discovered many designs tending to bring money into his own pocket" and that the Williamses were building the girls school on their own land so that they could sell it to the state for a profit.[12] The Williamses countered that Edwards was attempting much the same thing. Desperate for cash, Edwards had petitioned, via his ally Timothy Woodbridge, to the Massachusetts General Assembly that they purchase his Stockbridge house and house lot from him to be a parsonage. The popular Woodbridge had just been elected as Stockbridge's representative to the lower house, thus providing Edwards with political support. The Assembly, meeting in June, turned down Edwards' request, and word got back to Edwards that the culprit was Captain Ephraim Williams Jr., who was there "the whole time of the sitting of the Assembly, constantly busy with the representatives, with his lime-juice punch and wine." The objections offered against the petitions, Edwards concluded, could only have come from the captain.[13]

Despite the concerted attacks against him, Edwards still hoped to prevail. With half the Mohawks having left Stockbridge and almost all of the town, both English and Indians, on the side of Woodbridge and Edwards, the Williamses were having second thoughts about Stockbridge. The health of Ephraim Sr. was failing, and he was becoming increasingly irascible and erratic. He was thinking of returning to Deerfield, where another son lived. Captain Kellogg, having little to do but still drawing support from the Hollis funds, spoke of perhaps leaving as well. Joseph Dwight and Abigail, who were to be married August 12, 1752, were not certain they would stay in Stockbridge either.[14]

The balance of power swung dramatically back in the Williamses' direction, however, with the arrival of the clan's most distinguished member, Colonel Elisha Williams, and his renowned new wife, Elizabeth Scott Williams, just in time for the Dwight-Williams wedding. As a commissioner of Isaac Hollis' missionary society, Elisha claimed authority to adjudicate the Stockbridge dispute. Personal relations between the Williamses, who lived on the hill, and the rest of the village were already strained. The Edwardses were not invited to the wedding, a snub the pastor alluded to in his correspondence, reporting that the wedding had taken place, "as we have been informed."[15]

Elisha Williams and his new wife did make a call on the Edwardses, but it did not go well. Jonathan was not at home, so Sarah received the distinguished couple. Sarah, likely wanting to explain the embarrassing Northampton situation to the pious Elizabeth Scott, brought up the topic, re-marking that it had been Solomon Stoddard's practice "to admit all sorts of persons" to communion. The imperious Elisha cut her off. "Madam, you must know better," as though she were telling an untruth. "Mr. Stoddard has plainly declared in his book on that subject his sentiments were that none but visible saints ought to be admitted." Sarah confessed that she had not read Stoddard's book. Elisha retorted with another put-down: "Then Madam I ask beg your pardon. I took it for granted you had read it when you used those words." Sarah expressed some resentment, whereupon "another person" (as Elisha reported it) remarked that "it was natural to suppose you had read Mr. Stoddard's book as the controversy was on foot in that place."[16]

Elisha Williams' larger errand was, as agent for the London society, to inquire why the mission had been brought to such an impasse and, if possible, to reconcile the contending parties. Particularly he wanted to know the true reasons for Edwards' adamant opposition to Abigail as head of the girls school. So far Edwards had offered as his reason (to Abigail directly and publicly) only that Abigail, now with two families to care for, would not have the time personally to conduct the school. He had not gone into the delicate subject of his belief that she, as Colonel Ephraim's daughter, was distrusted by the Indians. Nor had he raised the question of the impropriety of the financial benefits she would gain by merging the school's and her family's finances.[17]

In Edwards' view, Elisha Williams was one of the last people who could impartially adjudicate the contentions, so he refused to meet with his former teacher or recognize his authority. Edwards was convinced that the opposition to him in Stockbridge was closely related to the Northampton contro-versy, in which Elisha was deeply involved.[18] Rather than meeting with Elisha, Edwards corresponded with him while both were in Stockbridge. Edwards agreed that a commission should review the mission controversy, but Elisha's view of the matter had already been too distorted by his friends and family for him to serve in that role. The insult to Sarah, which Sarah had interpreted as being accused of lying, was just one evidence. To the larger point Williams responded, not unreasonably, that as a commissioner it was his duty to hear all parties and to seek some Christian reconciliation. Edwards would hear none of it.[19]

Now it was all-out war for control of Stockbridge. Rather than pulling out, the Williams-Dwight-Kellogg faction, bolstered by Elisha's assurances of Isaac Hollis' continued support, stepped up their campaign to rid the town

of Edwards. Ephraim Williams Jr. had returned in July from Fort Massachusetts to take over family affairs from his failing father. The sociable soldier was
telling people he would gladly spend £500 to rid the town of its minister.

Ephraim Sr., who was simultaneously losing his senses and becoming
obsessed with righting his family's position, woke up one morning in September with another plan. (September 1752 was the shortest month in Anglo-
American history, eleven days being removed to reform the calendar). Rising
before dawn, the old squire went from house to house of most of the dozen or
so English families, attempting to buy them all out. Rousing some out of bed,
he offered them very high prices waving cash in hand and demanding that
papers be drawn immediately, but in utter secrecy. Then the word got out and
the scheme fell apart. His family and all involved wrote it off to "distraction"
but worried about what other damage the old man might do.[20]

Edwards was more concerned about Brigadier Dwight, who went to
Boston in November to report on the mission.[21] Edwards especially feared
that Dwight might turn his former commander, Sir William Pepperrell, the
colony's most famous New Light layman, against him and that Pepperrell
would convince the London society to help oust him.[22] Edwards countered by
providing Pepperrell with his fullest account of the Williams family's opposition to him (including the now-influential Israel Williams' long-standing
coolness) and answered Dwight's charges one by one. Particularly, he demonstrated that he had authority from the Commissioners to preach to the
Mohawks and to introduce Gideon Hawley as the schoolmaster.

Edwards was especially eager to refute decisively the accusation, now
dogging him, that he was of an "exceeding stiff, inflexible temper." Because
the contentions in Stockbridge followed hard on the heels of those in Northampton, Dwight had made a case that it was Edwards' "stiffness and willfulness" that was at the heart of the troubles. "It has been represented," Edwards
remarked, using an uncharacteristically worldly image "that I had rather undo
myself and my family than yield an ace." Edwards responded that his inflexibility had only to do with religious principles and that it was always the case
that people who stood on conscience for a religious truth were accused of
inflexibility. "You must, Sir," he wrote, pulling out all the stops, "be so well
acquainted with the history of the martyrs as to be sensible that this has ever
been the cry against the sufferers for religion, that they were stiff, willful,
perverse, and inflexible."[23]

Edwards believed he could speak with such assurance because he often
agonized over whether he might in fact be at fault. As he later wrote to one of

his critics, if his actions arose "from private resentment, from implacableness of spirit, or stiffness and willfulness of temper . . . [etc.]," he would "never . . . expect to be justified before my great Master and judge." With stakes so high, he constantly examined himself and was confident that "if I have acted from such unchristian principles, and without an hatred of all remains of 'em in myself . . . it must be because I have been extremely and totally blinded concerning myself."[24]

Edwards' friends in Boston could see that he had too much support in Stockbridge for the troubles to have arisen primarily from his failings, as Dwight alleged. Josiah Willard, secretary of the province, wrote to Sir William Pepperrell in February 1753 to say that the Commissioners for Indian Affairs had carefully examined Dwight's charges and were "well satisfied as to the general conduct of Mr. Edwards." Moreover, they affirmed, "he has acquired the general affections of the Indians, and influence over them, which he constantly employs for the best purposes, and the success thereof will doubtless be more evident, were it not for the unwearied opposition of some people from personal prejudices." Pepperrell wrote back assuring Willard that "I never thought of writing a syllable against [Edwards] in my life."[25] Pepperrell was not going to intervene with London on Dwight's behalf. Still, any decisive action on the mission school would have to come from Isaac Hollis, who supplied most of the funds. Given the pace of transatlantic communication, that was not likely to happen soon.

Meanwhile, the situation at the school went from terrible to worse. In February 1753, Gideon Hawley's boarding school, including all his books and possessions, went up in flames. Rumors circulated that it may have been arson by the Williams clan.[26] The few Mohawks that remained were fed up with what they had seen of English tribalism and announced their intention to leave. Chief Hendrick, who had been the most influential promoter of the boarding school plan, told Edwards that his people were thoroughly disgusted with Kellogg and Dwight.[27]

Gideon Hawley, disillusioned with trying to conduct an Indian mission in a settlement of feuding English, decided he would do better carrying his missionary work into Iroquois' own towns. In Stockbridge he had developed good relations with a number of Oneida from the village of Onohquaga at the headwaters of the Susquehanna in New York, about two hundred miles away. The Onohquagas (Oneida) had earlier heard of the boarding school, and a number had lived for a time in Stockbridge so their children could be educated.[28] Hawley now planned to take his mission to Onohquaga itself.

Edwards enthusiastically endorsed this plan and hoped that the Scottish Presbyterian missionary society and the Massachusetts Commissioners would be able to coordinate sending at least three missionaries to settle among the Iroquois. As it turned out, only Hawley went, accompanied on his initial journey by Timothy Woodbridge and taking along one of Stockbridge's most valued interpreters, Rebecca Kellogg Ashley (younger sister of Martin), her husband Benjamin, an ardent New Light, "and three or four blacks."[29]

Jonathan, Sarah, and others accompanied the entourage a considerable distance on "our departure upon so great an errand as the planting of Christianity in the wilderness," until the road to Albany turned into an Indian track. The journey to the headwaters of the Susquehanna itself proved harrowing—it could be straight out of James Fenimore Cooper or, more likely, something Cooper read. More than once the party feared for their lives. Near Lake Ostego they made the mistake of joining up with a rum trader. The result in the Indian village where they stayed was disastrous. Hawley wrote: "We soon saw the Indian women and their children skulking in the adjacent bushes, for fear of the intoxicated Indians, who were drinking deeper. The women were secreting guns, hatchets, and every deadly or dangerous weapon, that murder or harm might not be the consequence. Poor unhappy mortals! Without law, religion, or government; and therefore without restraint." The next morning in a canoe, only a fortuitous shift of his head saved Hawley from having his head blown off by the hunting gun of a still drunken and disgruntled Indian guide in what Hawley suspected may have been an assassination attempt. Despite all that, the group arrived safely and Hawley's mission at Onohquaga met with some initial success.[30] The depth of the Edwardses' commitment is suggested by their willingness in 1755, knowing full well the dangers, to send ten-year-old Jonathan Jr. with Hawley to prepare for a possible missionary career.

Meanwhile, as hopes shifted toward this "errand in the wilderness," the grand ideal of the Stockbridge boarding school for the Mohawks was virtually ruined, but the competing English factions were too locked in a their death-grips to give up their struggle over it. Control of the town and the Williams family fortunes were also at stake. So was the church. Since there was no hope of dislodging Edwards in that domain, the Dwights and Williams had simply stopped going. Joseph Dwight did not officially belong to the local congregation, but Abigail and Captain Ephraim Jr. did, so Edwards made their absence a matter of church discipline.[31]

By fall 1753 Edwards' hopes that he might prevail were growing. Ephraim Sr. was fast failing and had left town to live out his few remaining days in

Deerfield, turning his lands over to his son Elijah, who was about to graduate from the College of New Jersey. Captain Martin Kellogg returned to Newington where he died in the fall. Brigadier Dwight personally took over a small remnant of the Hollis School until he could find another teacher. He waited for instructions from Isaac Hollis that he hoped would confirm his control. Edwards, in the meantime, had his own hopes buoyed by strong encouragement from the Commission for Indian Affairs in Boston and from interventions by New Jersey's Governor Belcher.[32]

On February 25, 1754, Edwards finally received the vindication he had so long awaited. Isaac Hollis had appointed *him* to be the overseer of the boarding school. Edwards immediately informed Brigadier Dwight and went to the boarding school to inform Dwight's recently hired teacher, Cotton Mather Smith, who was teaching six remaining students.

Edwards now faced the sobering prospect that his victory might be empty. Since the fall, the Mohawks had expressed their intention to leave Stockbridge in the spring. Hollis' support was specifically directed toward the internationally significant Mohawks, who might provide a mission entry into the Iroquois Confederacy. Now the Mohawks were about to leave for the spring sugaring season, and had announced their intention not to return. Edwards at once conferred with the Mohawk men, women, and children at his house, asking if they would stay under a new administration. Despite his entreaties, they persisted in their plans, which they said had been determined by a council in the fall. Nevertheless, in the next few days a few of the parents came to Edwards asking him to take their children in the school after they returned from sugaring. That was enough encouragement to try to keep the school alive.[33]

Brigadier Dwight retreated, but not before firing one more salvo. Noting that the Mohawks had definitively left Stockbridge immediately after Edwards took control of the school, Dwight blamed the exodus on dissatisfaction with Edwards. Edwards responded with indignation, documenting that the Mohawks' oft-announced intentions to leave antedated the takeover and that they had often expressed their dissatisfaction with the broken promises of Kellogg and Dwight. "They have been this several years," wrote Edwards bitterly, "murdering the Mohawk affair themselves with cruel hands; and now just as it is expiring, they lay to me the mischief which they have most apparently done themselves."[34]

By the late spring, Edwards had six students in the school, five Stockbridge Indians and one Mohawk. He boarded the Mohawk boy in his own home, and the Stockbridge students lived with another English family. They all attended school with Timothy Woodbridge, who was to give them special attention until they could find a regular teacher. Edwards believed that the only hope for the Mohawks to return in numbers would be if they saw that there was a well-regulated school, firmly established.[35]

## Missions, Settlers, and Empire

By now, though, the darkest of clouds were overhanging the entire Stockbridge enterprise. Rumors of a renewed French and English conflict, and hence of Indian wars, were flying. Worse, some Stockbridge Mahicans had become thoroughly disillusioned with English rule. Some even had threatened an uprising.[36]

The incident that aroused the Stockbridge Mahicans had taken place the year before and was a version of what was becoming the classic story of how the best efforts of British Americans and Native Americas to live together seemed always to collapse. In April 1753 the son and grandson of the leading Stockbridge Mahican, Solomon Waunaupaugus, were out sugaring. They saw two Englishmen whom they believed were stealing horses. When the Indians tried to stop them, the English shot and killed Solomon's son. The Indians were furious. To Edwards' chagrin, since Solomon and many other Stockbridge Mahicans were his parishioners, the Indians buried the young man according to their own rituals. The village sheriff captured the two men and promised they would be tried in Springfield, but some Indians spoke of taking justice into their own hands.

The Indians were further outraged when, at the trial in September, the English court acquitted one man and convicted the other only of manslaughter. Resentments continued to grow, especially among some of the younger Mahicans. The English heard that the Mohawks and other Indians were upset about the incident. It was around this time that the local Mohawk council decided to leave Stockbridge definitively the next spring. Meantime the English, so sharply divided among themselves, were united in their desire to appease the Indians. Timothy Woodbridge wrote to Governor Shirley urging the General Court to send some money to "wipe away the tears" of Solomon Waunaupaugus.

In the winter the General Court voted to send six pounds sterling. Then, hearing that the situation in Stockbridge was deteriorating and at the urging of both Woodbridge and Joseph Dwight, it increased the sum to twenty pounds. By late May 1754 the money had not yet arrived. Deeply alarmed,

Edwards wrote to Secretary Josiah Willard, pleading that the money be sent before it was too late.

Some of the younger Mahicans, the dismayed Edwards reported, in league with some disaffected Mohawks, had been found to be planning to massacre the English inhabitants of Stockbridge. The Indians were said to have attempted to draw the African slaves into the plot, but the slaves apparently reported it to their masters. Edwards believed the accusations, though he hastened to add, "I am far from supposing that the generality of the Indians were in the conspiracy." One of the friendly Indians, who wanted his name withheld, had told Edwards that the Stockbridge killing was widely discussed among the Iroquois nations, and some were saying, encouraged by the French, that the English were planning to drive out all the Indians in the area. The young Stockbridge Indians who designed the conspiracy had been told that their people were fools for being taken in by pretended shows of English kindness and instruction when the English "were only opening a wide mouth to swallow 'em up, when they should see a convenient time."[37]

The events that led to the disaffection of many of the Indians who had spent time at Stockbridge illustrate the great defect in English missions to the Native Americans and why they were so much less successful than their French counterparts. The English were almost always trying to settle the territories where they evangelized. Heroic French Jesuit missionaries who went to live among the Indians presented little immediate threat to the natives' territories or interests. The French population of New France was tiny and spread out compared to the situation in New England. Edwards and other English missionaries faced a situation where colonization was steadily advancing by way of settlement of land-holding families. Inexorably the Indians were being displaced. Even in a settlement like Stockbridge, where genuine efforts were made to balance the interests of the two peoples, the ever-expanding English population inevitably tipped the balance in their own favor. When the French and their native allies said the English "were only opening a wide mouth to swallow 'em up," it was difficult to demonstrate otherwise.[38] Gideon Hawley's efforts to carry his mission into the native territories seems to have been a response to these problem, as perhaps were David Brainerd's forays before him. British settlements were advancing so rapidly, however, that it was already too late.

Although an uneasy calm was reestablished in Stockbridge by summer 1754, the international situation became increasingly unstable. In June, representatives from seven colonies, led by Benjamin Franklin, met nearby in the

Albany Congress with representatives of the Iroquois Confederacy to discuss the renewed French threats. The English proposed among themselves a colonial federation to help coordinate defense and regulate the frontiers. Elisha Williams was one of the Connecticut representatives and Oliver Partridge of Hatfield, a Williams relative who had some involvement in Stockbridge affairs, was in the Massachusetts delegation. Joseph Kellogg, Martin's brother, now of Stockbridge, served as translator for the Indians.

Behind the scenes at the Albany Congress, Timothy Woodbridge turned his goodwill among the Indians into an advantage for white New Englanders. Connecticut, which claimed a border on the Pacific, was in competition with Pennsylvania for millions of acres of land in the upper Susquehanna Valley that the Iroquois appeared ready to sell. Woodbridge had learned of this land while accompanying Gideon Hawley on a preliminary mission tour. Acting as chief agent of the Susquehanna Company of Connecticut and working with a disreputable Indian trader, John Henry Lydius, Woodbridge completed a treaty with some Indian leaders for the land. Woodbridge and company claimed Chief Hendrick's endorsement of their purchase. Unfortunately, Hendrick was not happy with the arrangement, and Pennsylvania's respected negotiator, Conrad Weiser, convinced him to cede much of the same land to that colony—thus leading to a half century of disputes between Connecticut and Pennsylvania. Hendrick was disillusioned with what he considered Woodbridge's underhanded methods, further damaging the Mohawks' view of the Stockbridge mission.[39]

The incident once again illustrates the flaw in even the best-intended government-supported mission. This was not the first time that Woodbridge, though a genuine friend to the Stockbridge Mahicans, had used his growing political influence for white advantage and his own profit.[40] He was, after all, emerging as a leading magistrate in Stockbridge and was doing what almost every magistrate of western New England did—invest in land to secure his family's position. At the same time, he did enough for the Indians to keep their trust. In expanding his interests to the Susquehanna Company, although he may have been overtaken by Yankee avarice, he also doubtless saw himself as performing a public service. In his view, Indians' true interests were spiritual, so that the advance of Protestant New England went hand in hand with Indian welfare.

Edwards, without being involved in the details of the land deals,[41] shared the essential conceptual framework in which Woodbridge, his closest Stockbridge ally, operated. For Edwards the preeminent goal was to reach the

Indians with the Gospel. Working from a Constantinian perspective, he never questioned the premise that God used Christian empires to bring his message to unevangelized peoples. In his view the crucial concern was that as the British advanced they not neglect to teach the Indians Reformed Christianity. That was first a spiritual duty, but it also had a humane cultural program. Once Christianized and taught European ways, Indians could live at peace with their new neighbors, benefiting from a civilization that had much to offer. In the meantime, Christians like Woodbridge, who were true fathers to the Indians, might properly turn a profit fitting their own position, so long as they did so honestly.

One major practical flaw in this outlook was that few European settlers had nearly as much concern for Indian welfare as did Timothy Woodbridge—who, imperfect though he was, spent his career working with the natives. Most settlers were overwhelmingly concerned with protecting their own interests and were quick to blame the nearest available Indians when something went wrong. The European governments and their militaries who supported colonization were driven primarily by distant affairs of state in which Indians served largely as dispensable pawns. Furthermore, the benefits of British imperialism were lost on most of the Indians, who understandably were ready to fight for their homelands. Adding to the difficulties, the various Indians were divided among themselves and on the whole were no more virtuous than Europeans.

By summer 1754 too many such forces were at work for there to be much hope that a peaceful kingdom, such as Stockbridge was supposed to exemplify, would soon be realized. Even before the delegates assembled at the Albany Congress, they had heard of bloody encounters between the French and Virginians under the leadership of a young colonel named George Washington. By the time the congress was over in July, reports had arrived of Washington's surrender. The proposals of the Albany Congress for intercolonial unity and mutual protection would come to nothing. Warfare among the British, French, and Indians had resumed. Once again any settlement on the frontier, including Stockbridge, was vulnerable to attack.[42]

In mid-summer 1754, likely in part from strain, exhaustion, disappointments, and anxieties, Edwards fell into his most protracted illness since his student days. For the better part of seven months, between July 1754 and February 1755, he suffered first "under extreme weakness," then, after some respite in September, under "fits of the augue" or fever, so that he "became like a skeleton" and was so weak that he feared he was "going into a dropsy."[43]

If his long illness involved despondency, there was much to be despondent about. The mission school was in pathetic condition, war seemed inevitable, and the survival of any English in Stockbridge was an open question. In addition, the onset of illness interrupted the most ambitious writing program of his career. In Stockbridge, amid everything else, he had already completed his lengthy reply to Solomon Williams and a treatise on *Freedom of the Will*, and he dearly hoped to finish a shelf of other treatises before he died.

On Sunday, September 1, the first Sunday Edwards was back in the pulpit after the first round of his illness, the town was suddenly overtaken by terror and panic. Between the meetings, a man came rushing into town to report that he had just come upon a Canadian Indian who was abducting an English child from an outlying home. The Indian, seeing that he was pursued, tomahawked the child and escaped. The horrified Englishman returned to the house to find a servant and an infant dead, while the father and two other children were cowering before another Indian, who promptly fled. An hour later the Indians killed another man on the outskirts of the town.

Predictably, in the midst of the pent-up fears, the Europeans in the area panicked. Terrified settlers fled south from one town to the next. People from the north were clamoring into Stockbridge, and Stockbridge residents were fleeing south. Abigail Dwight left so quickly that she had to leave charge to a servant to bring her infant daughter. Edwards' friend Samuel Hopkins the younger, pastor in nearby Great Barrington to the south, described the scene two days later in a letter to Joseph Bellamy. When the news arrived during his afternoon service, the town went into a frenzy, some people fleeing. Before long "women, children and squaws presently flocked in upon us from Stockbridge, half naked and frightened to death." Wild rumors circulated that the enemy was amassed on the other side of Stockbridge and about to attack.

During the following days, armed English and Dutch men from the region flooded into the town. The men built a stockade around the Edwardses' house at the center of the town, and the Edwardses had to help accommodate them. Some of the town's new protectors, inflamed by the earlier rumors of a Mahican uprising, accused the Stockbridge Indians of encouraging the attacks and threatened to kill them. In fact, the attack had come from Abenaki Indians, long since displaced to northern New England and Canada by King Philip's War and now encouraged by the French. One gentleman of the town, suspecting that source, offered a reward for the scalp of a "Canadian" Indian. A couple of visiting English scoundrels dug up one of the local Indians who had recently died and trying to claim the reward.

Although the men were apprehended and punished, the Stockbridge Indians were again thoroughly outraged at English barbarism.[44]

"Two Indians," an exasperated Samuel Hopkins remarked, "may put New England to a hundred thousand pounds charge, and never expose themselves." The troops that had flooded in and were now leaving had done no good: "They have seen Stockbridge and eaten up all their provisions, and fatigued themselves, and that's all; and now we are left as much exposed as ever."[45]

The Edwardses bore the brunt of the care of the town's would-be protectors, who had trampled down most everything in sight. When things had settled, by October, Edwards signed a report to the General Court, asking for reimbursement for serving "800 meals of victuals, pasturing 150 horses, and 7 gal. of good West Indian rum" as well as food for "all poor people driven from their homes above thro fear." In addition, they had served another 180 meals to the workers building the fort and supplied some of the lumber.[46]

The Edwardses now lived in constant fear. In November, Esther, safe in New Jersey, was "almost out of my wits" at a report from a man from Albany that all but two or three Stockbridge Mahican families had left the village in great disgust with the English and that they had even spoken of sending a neighboring tribe to wipe out the town. Jonathan and Sarah were taking precautions and had sent at least several of their children to live with relatives. Esther wrote to eighteen-year-old Lucy, who had gone to live with her sister Mary in Northampton, that she was glad that "Pinty" (four-year-old Pierpont) and "Betty" (seven-year-old Elizabeth) were also in Northampton and hoped "they will not go to Stockbridge till the danger is quite over."[47] We can only try to imagine the distresses of such times when rumors flew and reliable news traveled slowly and one lived weeks or months in dread of disasters that may have already happened. Esther prayed desperately that she could "commit them to God who orders all things in mercy, and doesn't willfully afflict nor grieve any of his children." Yet she could hardly bring herself to such acceptance of God's will as she had been trained. "Why is it," she sighed. "Why does God suffer his own most dear children to be hunted about in this manner! But this is a very wrong temper of mind. I hope I may be able to crush it by divine assistance."[48]

By late fall the Stockbridge situation had stabilized, but now the town was an armed camp, with the large Edwards home one of several fortresses.[49] In February 1755 Edwards wrote a note to Brigadier Dwight saying that they could not board and lodge more than four soldiers in their home and pleading his continuing ill health (hence "under much greater disadvantage than others to get provisions").[50]

By spring, while Edwards' health was only slowly returning, his discouragements were greater than ever.[51] He was nearly ready to give up on the Hollis Indian school altogether "in this time of war and confusion." In addition to the new external threats, the "difficulties from within," from the Dwight-Williams faction, "don't diminish, but increase."[52] Brigadier Dwight was using all his influence in Boston to recover control of the school. Edwards' prospects in Stockbridge had fallen so low that in Northampton the other Dwights renewed their hopes he might return there. Colonel Timothy Dwight Sr. (father of the Edwards' son-in-law) wrote to Thomas Foxcroft that, especially because of "the difficulties that arise from the Indians being made so dependent on Brigadier Dwight," Edwards in Stockbridge was "like a candle set under a bushel."[53]

Timothy Woodbridge countered Brigadier Dwight's effort to recapture the school by leading a delegation of Indians to Boston to testify to their affection for Edwards and the schoolmaster and against their opponents. The brigadier fought back by lobbying his friend Governor William Shirley. He also enlisted Edwards' old nemesis Colonel Israel Williams of Hatfield, now one of the most powerful men in the province, as his "chosen representative." In June Edwards heard that "they have lately conceived new hopes of accomplishing their designs."[54]

The only bright spot was Gideon Hawley's mission to Onohquaga. Even though a war was going on, it was at this time (April 1755) that the Edwardses packed Jonathan Jr. away to ride with the missionary on another dangerous two-hundred-mile trip to the Indian settlement. In the distant village the English boy's skill with Indian dialects proved a great hit. "It is also pleasing to the Indians, that Mr. Edwards' little son was with me," wrote Hawley. "The Indians love him and make much the more so as he makes proficiency in their language."[55]

In May, a day after young Jonathan's tenth birthday, Edwards wrote to him, in a typical epistle to his children. He was much thinking about the boy, he said, but glad that he was always in God. The one thing for the lad to remember was that he might die at any time. Recently David, an Indian boy who had lived at the Edwards home and been a playmate of young Jonathan's, had died. "This is a loud call of God to you to prepare for death." "Never give yourself any rest," the loving father pleaded, "unless you have good evidence that you are converted and become a new creature."

Curiously and revealingly, Edwards included almost no family news. He closed only mentioning that he had heard that the boy's sister and brother in Newark "are well" and bringing salutations from "your aged grandfather and grandmother," whom Jonathan Sr. had visited in Windsor. Yet, revealing of his priorities, he did not mention (as he did to a friend a few days later) "a great hurt I received in a late journey to Windsor by a dangerous fall from my horse, the horse pitching heels over head with his whole weight upon me."[56] Most parents would think such a harrowing experience at least of interest to a ten-year-old or even a lesson to be careful—as Edwards' own father would have made it. Yet the theologian had one concern and was not going to dilute it with personal trivia any more than one would expect such distractions in a Pauline epistle.

Death was indeed a prominent presence in eighteenth-century lives and aided by its ally, warfare, was rapidly changing the nature of the contest over the Stockbridge mission. Ephraim Williams Sr. and Captain Kellogg were already gone. In July Colonel Elisha Williams, the former Yale rector and one of Edwards' most influential opponents, died. Before the summer was out the war itself would take others. For the next several years, news of the war, in which so many Stockbridge families, both Indian and English, had a personal stake, would submerge other temporal concerns.

The war also made the main purpose of the school—educating the Iroquois—something of a moot point. In September Edwards received a letter from Isaac Hollis, providing funds to continue the school and to increase its enrollment to sixteen. The funds once again confirmed Edwards' control. He gathered eleven boys, apparently all Stockbridge Mahicans, and kept up a semblance of a school, though apparently with Timothy Woodbridge still as their teacher. Edwards told Thomas Prince that he had "reserved room for four or five Mohawk boys" but realized that finding them was unlikely so long as the war continued.[57]

# CHAPTER 25

# Wartime

O the dreadful, awful news! General Braddock is killed and his army defeated," cried Esther Edwards Burr in Newark. "Oh my dear what will, what must become of us! O our *sins*, our *sins*—they are grown up to the very heavens, and call aloud for vengeance, the vengeance that the Lord has sent—'Tis just, 'tis right."[1]

The overwhelming destruction of General Edward Braddock's proud army of redcoats as they approached Fort Duquesne on July 9, 1755, sent shock waves through the colonies. From Virginia to northern New England, British settlers on the frontier were thrown into a panic. Braddock had confidently expected to capture the strategic French fort (now Pittsburgh) as part of a multipronged British effort to use superior military force to dislodge the French from their frontier strongholds. Instead, the British failure to enlist much Indian support proved disastrous in the bloody forest encounter. The French had demonstrated their ability to marshal Indian allies, and the victory on the Monongahela immediately drew more tribes to the French side and others away from the British into neutrality. Of the major tribes, only the Mohawks in the east under old Chief Hendrick remained willing to join with British forces.[2] The less numerous Mahicans were among the few other Native Americans willing to lend support.

Nothing struck more terror into the hearts of colonists than the threat of a general Indian uprising—another King Philip's War, more Deerfields! Esther agonized over the dangers for her family in Stockbridge. Even in New Jersey she did not feel safe. Later in the fall she heard a report from Madam Belcher, the governor's wife, that fifteen hundred French and Indians were amassed on the borders of New Jersey. Even before that Esther was expecting the worst. "You can't conceive my dear friend," she wrote to her beloved Boston correspondent, Sally Prince, daughter of Thomas Prince Sr., "what a tender mother undergoes for her children at such a day as this, to think of bring[ing] up children to be *dashed against the stones by our barbarous enemies*—or which is worse, to be enslaved by them, and obliged to turn Papist."[3]

Esther's fears were grounded in Aaron Burr's millennial theology, which was much like her father's but more immediately pessimistic. On New Year's Day of that same year (1755) President Burr had preached a fast-day sermon of lament in light of the renewed French and Indian threats. Unlike Edwards, who believed the church had already suffered its worst persecutions, Burr believed that the most horrible birth pangs preceding the millennium were still to come. Ministering in the Middle Colonies during these rapidly changing times, when vice seemed rampant and awakenings rare, may have disposed Burr to view the current state of Protestantism as bleak. In his sermon he painted in lurid terms how God might use the French and Indians to bring judgment. "Our men slaughtered!—Our *wives* and *daughters* delivered to the lusts and fury of a lawless soldiery!—Our helpless *babes* dashed against the stones." Esther, whose daughter Sally was less than one, came away terrified. She wrote that same day to Sally Prince: "'Tis very probable *you* and I may live to see persecution, and may be called to give up every thing for the cause of God and a good conscience—even to burn at the stake." The next day she added that she was grateful to see people shaken from their spiritual lethargy by "the danger of being swallowed up by our popish enemies."[4]

Back in Stockbridge, Jonathan was, to all appearances, decidedly more tranquil. While duly concerned that disaster could strike Stockbridge at any moment, and always prone to melancholy, he was also steeled by years of discipline to be prepared for whatever God might will—an attitude that his daughter, as a young mother, worried she could not emulate. He even urged Esther to visit when Timmy returned from the college before commencement in September.

Preaching on a fast day called in response to General Braddock's defeat, Edwards assured his anxious English congregation that "we haven't reason at all to despair" even though "God hath awfully rebuked us in this defeat." Edwards' long-range confidence was built on his optimistic eschatology. His text, Psalm 60: 9–12, was a prayer for Israel's victory over Edom—an ancient nation that was a type of the Antichrist. Despite British setbacks, there was great reason to hope for victory when the enemy was the Antichrist, "the greatest enemy of God's church that ever was on earth."

Edwards was still tracking the decline of the papacy in his notebook "An

Account of Events Probably Fulfilling the Sixth Vial," which had to do with the drying up of the Rivers of Babylon (i.e., Rome). In it he was meticulously recording items from newspapers that dealt with any adverse financial news about the pope and his minions. (A recent entry: "*Boston Evening Post*, July 21, 1755, the clergy . . . [of France] will be required to make a free gift suitable to the exigencies of the state," followed by details of various accounts of the amount.)[5] Given this trajectory, Edwards had high hopes for eventual British victory in the New World.

Yet in the short run there would be defeats and disasters that were both Satan's counterattacks and God's loud calls for repentance. Braddock's defeat was particularly a judgment on British pride and self-confidence. That divine message was evident in that God had so humiliated the British in the eyes of the Indians. "The killing of so great a number of the chief officers [two-thirds had died]," Edwards lamented in the sermon, "whose clothing, armor, treasure, and scalps are fallen into the hand of the enemy to be carried in triumph through the French settlements of America, 'tis an awful rebuke of the most high for our pride and vain confidence."[6] For the near future Edwards saw the defection of the Indians as the greatest danger. Although the British had a twenty-to-one population advantage over the French, he explained to Scotland's William McCulloch, the British colonies were in real danger because of the French ability to enlist the Indians.[7]

Most immediately Edwards and other English townspeople pled strongly with Edwards' politically influential cousin Colonel Israel Williams in early September 1755 for adequate troops to protect Stockbridge. Thirty of the Indian men of Stockbridge had gone off to war under Governor William Shirley only on the condition that troops be sent to defend the town. Their enemies, argued Edwards, would glory in destroying Stockbridge and its several forts "and so breaking the union between the English and Indians, and drawing off this tribe, among the many others that are forsaking the English interest and joining with the French since the Ohio defeat."[8]

A few days later, Stockbridge was shaken to the core by news of a fierce battle near Lake George, about fifty miles north of Albany near the south end of Lake Champlain. A regiment of about a thousand colonial troops under the command of Stockbridge's own Colonel Ephraim Williams Jr. and accompanied by Ephraim's friend, the seventy-five-year-old Chief Hendrick, and two hundred Mohawks marched into an ambush of Canadian Indians and elite French troops under the command of the French general Baron Jean-Armand de Dieskau. Chief Hendrick and Ephraim Jr. both died in the initial fighting. Unlike the similar encounter with Braddock's troops, the remaining colonials had enough savvy to break ranks and regroup so that they could help counter the French and Indian assault. Reinforced with troops under General William Johnson, the colonials eventually repulsed the enemy advance and captured the wounded Dieskau on the battlefield.[9]

Edwards thought it a Pyrrhic victory. "The army under General Johnson had a kind of victory over the French," he wrote, "yet we suffered very greatly in the battle." Aside from Hendrick and Ephraim Williams Jr., the Edwardses knew at least five young men (including their cousin Captain Elisha Hawley, Joseph's sometimes wayward brother) from Northampton who died in the conflict.[10]

Whatever the mixed feelings of the Edwardses, Abigail was devastated by the death of her brother. "There was not a gentleman in the army," she lamented, "who could have been less easily spared." Abigail and Brigadier Dwight were again talking of leaving Stockbridge. Abigail wrote to a friend in New York City, "I long to be with you eating lobsters, crabs, and oysters, and drink[ing] lemons: but must content myself with small beer and country fires and yet is too good for me since I am suffered to live when so many of my dearest friends are gone to the dead."[11] The Dwights did stay. By spring the brigadier had secured some Connecticut troops to help protect the town. Though Ephraim Jr. was gone, two younger sons of Ephraim Williams Sr. also remained. (Ephraim Jr. left a lasting legacy. In July 1755, the day after he heard of General Braddock's defeat, he revised his will. He removed an earlier small benefaction for the Stockbridge Indian school but left a substantial sum to found a school in nearby Williamstown. In 1785 the money was used to endow Williams College.)[12]

Aside from the cost in lives, Edwards saw Lake George as only a "kind of victory" because the original purpose of the English expedition had been to drive the French from their fortress at Crown Point (near Ticonderoga) at the base of Lake Champlain, the route to Montreal. The battle had instead led to a standoff. Having an English army stationed north of them provided some protection from the ravages of the sorts of Indian attacks that were now common on the Virginia and Pennsylvania frontiers. Altogether, though, 1755 was a year of "great frowns of providence on British America." Only in Nova Scotia did the British arms succeed. On the mainland the French held their ground and, having consolidated their Indian alliances, appeared stronger than ever.[13]

Shortly after hearing the news from Lake George, Edwards left for

Death of Colonel Ephraim Williams Jr. at the Battle of Lake George, 1755

Newark, where he arrived in time for the college commencement in late September 1755. Aside from the pleasure of seeing his daughter and toddler granddaughter, Edwards found himself in the vortex of alarmed colonial wartime politics. Immediately after the commencement he and Aaron Burr set out for Philadelphia for a meeting of the Synod of New York and New Jersey.[14] Burr was an outspoken proponent of intercolonial unity.[15] If ever Edwards met Benjamin Franklin, it would have been on this visit to Philadelphia. Franklin had published and even read some of Edwards' works, and the circles of elite men in Philadelphia were not large. If they did meet, their conversation may have included talk of their mutual friendship with Whitefield and shared intelligence about the military situation since the battle of Lake George.

We can imagine another sort of conversation with Esther and her circle when Edwards was back in Newark. The subject there may have turned to Samuel Richardson's *Pamela, or Virtue Rewarded.* Esther had read the novel in the spring. Her father, if he had not read it himself, had certainly heard a lot about it from his family in Stockbridge. Gideon Hawley noted in his diary that when he had visited the Edwardses in summer 1754, he had found a copy of *Pamela* there, which he read and enjoyed.[16] That was at the time when Jonathan was ill, so it is possible that the theologian read it during his convalescence. As Esther was reading this moral tale of a lowly maid who, after refusing to be seduced by her master, married him, she believed the author was setting up "riches and honor as the great essentials of happiness." When Pamela's husband proved unfaithful, Esther was disgusted and believed the title should be "virtue tried." Nonetheless, Esther admired the pious Pamela's angelic character and her exemplary views of her marital duties and was relieved to learn that her long-suffering virtue finally won faithfulness from her husband.[17] Esther's father would have had some theological reflections on all this. He had been working on a treatise on "The Nature of True Virtue," which would refine evangelical thinking about the much-discussed eighteenth-century topic of "virtue."

Edwards could be talkative in the right circles of friends and family, so long as the conversation stayed on serious edifying themes. Esther, a year earlier, painted our most vivid picture of a typical gathering. Writing to Sally Prince when Aaron Burr was away in Boston and her father was supposed to be there also, Esther visualized the scene at the home of Sally's father, Thomas Prince. "I imagine now this eve Mr. Burr is at your house. *Father* is there and some others. You all set in the Middleroom, *Father* has the *talk,* and Mr. Burr has the *Laugh,* Mr. Prince gets room to stick in a word once in a while. The rest of you set and see, and hear, and make observations to yourselves . . . and when you get up stairs you tell what you think, and wish I was there too."[18]

In this portrait the women are deeply involved with the intellectual-spiritual fare, but in their subordinate position. They are making mental notes and then debating the issues once alone in their bedroom. Esther, though not questioning her social subordination, was used to women being taken seriously as spiritual and intellectual (even if not educational) equals of men. Hardly able to abide "trifling women" who "talk about fashions and dress," she deplored one group of "young women from Trenton" as "poor vain young creatures as stupid as horses." Yet Esther was not shy about putting men in their place if they denigrated women's capacities. On one occasion a male guest made the mistake of saying that he believed women did not know what true friendship was since *they were hardly capable of anything so cool and rational as friendship.* Esther, whose extraordinary friendships were with other women of high intelligence, let him have it. "(My tongue you know, hangs pretty loose, thoughts crowded in—so I sputtered for dear life)," she wrote to Sally Prince. "You may guess what a large field this speech opened for me. I retorted several severe things upon him before he had time to speak again. He blushed and seemed confused." They argued for an hour, until the guest finally retreated. "He got up and said your servant and went off." "I talked him quite silent."[19]

When Edwards left Newark and his formidable daughter in October 1755, he sailed from New York City, where he was delayed some days by contrary winds. There he spent his time among Presbyterians almost as divided as they had been more than three decades earlier when he had been a young intern. Currently they were in a fracas concerning choosing a new pastor, complicated by the insistence of a Scottish party that they sing only psalms.[20] Edwards still had friends in New York, and we can imagine that, even as they argued church politics, they may have served him lobsters, crabs, oysters, and lemon drinks. Presumably his appreciation of all of creation would have allowed him to relish these, though always in strictly disciplined quantities. In any case, we can be almost sure that he brought home a supply of chocolate, which had become a favorite family indulgence.[21]

Back in Stockbridge, the winter of 1756 was relatively free of alarms, but the war was taking a distressing toll on Indian missions. Especially painful to Edwards was that Gideon Hawley's mission to Onohquaga, in which they had placed such high hopes, was in danger of being "entirely broke up." The

Esther Edwards Burr, ca. 1750–60

French had aroused the Delawares who now controlled much of the upper Susquehanna. In mid-December, the village became a place of constant dread after Onohquaga received news that the Delawares had declared war on all English, accompanying their message with a couple English scalps. The Indian villagers feared for their lives so long as any English were there, so in early January Hawley and Jonathan Jr. left through the snows on a trek back to safety. They spent most of the winter northwest of Albany at the fortress-mansion of Sir William Johnson, recently commanding general at the costly victory at Lake George. The powerful Sir William, who had been a close friend of Chief Hendrick and was the English's best link to the Indians, used

Indian conference at Johnson Hall. The conference depicted here took place the decade after the one in which Gideon Hawley served as interpreter. When Hawley and Jonathan Edwards Jr. visited in 1756, during wartime, Johnson lived in an older, fortress-like mansion, Fort Johnson.

Hawley as an informant and interpreter for an Indian congress designed to shore up deteriorating relationships.[22]

Although young Jonathan returned home safely in late winter from his precarious adventures, the Edwardses worried that Stockbridge would soon become as dangerous as Onohquaga. Massachusetts and Connecticut were recruiting new volunteer armies for another strike against Crown Point, but this plan involved a risk for the frontier settlements. The colonial army would be largely amateur, and Edwards and his friends feared a defeat would unleash French and Indian forces against weakly fortified frontier towns. Conducting an Indian school under such wartime circumstances was unrealistic. As an expedient to preserve a remnant of the Indian school, Edwards sent the Stockbridge boys to study with Joseph Bellamy in Bethlehem, Connecticut.

Bellamy believed Edwards should care more for his personal safety. "I am in pain," Bellamy pleaded in late May, "fearing our army against Crown Point will be defeated. God only knows how it will be." Bellamy offered "all the comforts our house affords," if Edwards would bring his family to Bethlehem.[23] Edwards, whose spiritual disciplines were a lifelong preparation for calamity, remained a pillar of resolution. All things were in God's hands and he was determined to do what he had been called to do. If it all ended in a horrible Indian attack, so be it. Death always stalked family and friends in any case. Edwards would remain at his post and accept whatever God willed.

We have one vivid picture of the terror Stockbridge could inspire during the darkest days of the war. Somehow Jonathan and Sarah persuaded their daughter Esther to make her postponed visit from New Jersey in late summer of 1756, now bringing with her the latest grandchild, six-month-old Aaron Burr Jr. The young mother was filled with trepidation, but, as she said, "I have endeavored to know duty and think I am doing of it." Esther kept a candid daily record of her sojourn, written for Sally Prince in Boston.[24]

After a five-day journey by sail and wagon, Esther arrived on August 30, 1756, drenched from a rainstorm, surprising her family "almost out of their wits." Her sisters Lucy (aged twenty) and Sueky (Susannah, aged sixteen) were "almost overcome" with joy. But then "the melancholy news that I brought them filled the house with gloom." The news was of the capture of Fort Oswego in New York by the French and Indians. The French general, Montcalm, had obtained the Anglo-American surrender after a brief resistance, promising safe treatment of the prisoners. While Montcalm acted in good faith according to European conventions, he did not fully appreciate his Indian allies' rules of war, which demanded trophies of scalps, prisoners, and booty. The Indians accordingly fell upon and killed scores of captives and carried off others before Montcalm could stop them.[25] The colonials were convinced the fort was taken, as Esther said, "by treachery."

Esther spent most of her three weeks in Stockbridge "scared out of my wits about the enemy." Two days after her arrival there was "an alarm." The townspeople set up a watch at the fort that surrounded the house, and for two nights "most of the Indians came to lodge here." Some reported they had seen the enemy at night. "This place is in a very defenseless condition—not a soldier in it," she wrote a few days later. Almost all the fighting Indians had gone into the army, as were many of the white men. Esther lamented, "10 Indians might with all ease destroy us entirely." Enemy Indians, she now heard, had been sighted within thirty miles. "I want to be made willing to die in any way God pleases," wrote the distraught Esther after many fitful nights, "but I am not willing to be butchered by a barbarous enemy nor can't make myself willing."

To make matters worse, after about a week of Esther's stay, her mother announced that she was going to Northampton, where the next daughter, Mary Dwight, was soon expecting her third child. Clearly Sarah was the person who did most to keep family spirits up. "My mother gone!" Esther moaned. "It adds double gloom to everything." A few days later seventeen soldiers arrived to help protect the town. Esther believed them still too few to defend the three small local forts. Some were staying with the Edwardses, which created more work, especially for Lucy who was in charge in Sarah's absence.

On the Sabbath Jonathan preached on Amos 8:11, "Behold I send a famine in the land, not a famine of bread nor a thirst for water, but of hearing of the words of the Lord." Esther concluded, as apparently her father had warned, "that God is about to deprive this land of his word and ordinances for their shameful abuse of them, and just and right will he be in so doing." At night she comforted herself with the assurance that still "God would be glorified—and oh my dear this is refreshing that the ever blessed God will lose none of his glory, let men or devils do their worst."

God would be just as much glorified, she reasoned, if she and her son were not butchered in Stockbridge. So the next day she proposed to her father that she go home early. He would hear none of it. "If the Indians get me," she grimly resigned herself, "they get me, that is all I can say, but 'tis my duty to make my self as easy as I can." Finally, on the eve of the last Sabbath, Esther had a candid talk with her father: "Last eve I had some free discourse with my

father on the great things that concern my best interest—I opened my difficulties to him very freely and he as freely advised and directed. The conversation has removed some distressing doubts that discouraged me much in my
Christian warfare—He gave me some excellent directions to be observed in
secret that tend to keep the soul near to God, as well as others to be observed
in a more public way—What a mercy that I have such a Father! Such a guide!"

Edwards himself, despite knowing how to find spiritual solace, was far
from confident concerning matters temporal. "What will become of us, God
only knows," he wrote to Gideon Hawley in early October, a few weeks after
Esther left. The war had displaced Hawley from his Onohquaga Indian
mission, and the missionary was now serving, apparently with Edwards'
urging, with the large colonial expedition that was supposed to move against
Crown Point. Now in the wake of the disastrous loss of Fort Oswego, the
colonists had abandoned that offensive against Lake Champlain, disbanded
much of the volunteer army, and built defensive positions. A recent letter
from Hawley included some "very affecting accounts" of the expedition.
Edwards responded that, indeed, God seemed to be "remarkably frowning on
us everywhere" and the English were rapidly losing credibility in Indian eyes.
"It looks as if something great, and perhaps almost decisive, were to happen
before winter." The war might be nearly over and the worst to come soon.
The only hope was prayer, "humble cries to the God of armies."[26]

Gideon Hawley's time with the army had given him a new view of how
the British and American military were using missions to the Indians. Hawley saw that his expected function in the army was to try to keep the loyalty of
the few remaining Indian allies. He also witnessed the dissipation among
New England soldiers and some of the brutality of warfare. Having lived
among the Iroquois, Hawley appreciated better than did most of his European contemporaries some of the ambiguities and paradoxes in the warfare
with the Indians.[27] He recorded in his diary, for instance, the swiftness with
which the English beheaded a passing Indian who was foolish enough to
boast of taking British scalps in Ohio.

Hawley's experiences with actual warfare were leading him to disagree
with his mentor Edwards, who tended to view warfare through the lenses of
his millennialist categories and Constantinian assumptions. In fall 1756 Hawley returned briefly to Stockbridge, where he may also have had an unrequited
interest in Lucy Edwards, "a charming girl," as he later put it. Hawley then
attempted to return to Onohquaga but was turned back by early winter and
ended up spending the winter studying with Samuel Hopkins in nearby

Sheffield. By now he was bitter and disillusioned with the role he was put in as a missionary in wartime. Edwards was among those who had celebrated the dual role of the missionary as minister of the Gospel and agent for winning Indian alliances. "I won't go among the Indians in the character of a Christian missionary, except I can go upon Christian principles," Hawley wrote bitterly in his private journal. "But why do I talk of *Christian* zeal in this case 'tis a *political* affair." "Those who talk about the propagation of Christianity among the Indians, don't care much whether any of them go to heaven," he wrote, referring apparently to many of the provincial officials and army officers. Even Edwards, Hawley was convinced, was not exempt from allowing his political interests to interfere with his higher goal. "Mr. Edwards . . . has blind notions about things and no wonder seeing he knows nothing but by hearsay and the half has never been told him. If he would endeavour to excite me to engage in my mission and use only the motives which are suggested in Christianity I should like it better. Mr. Edwards is a very good man but capable of being biased."[28]

Hawley's dose of realism in the army helped him recognize the essential defect in the Anglo-American missions to the Indians, as Edwards did not. The sheer numbers of Anglo settlers meant that, whatever the announced intentions, almost all the British interest in the Indians was with the ultimate aim of displacing them. Many of the less religious British and Americans acknowledged that explicitly. Others, such as Edwards, who wed the political to the religious, were in Hawley's view naïve if they thought that the Gospel was not undermined when it was used for military recruitment.

In summer 1757 Hawley was again frustrated in an attempt to return to Onohquaga, this time by a smallpox epidemic in the region. He again returned to Stockbridge and accompanied Edwards to Boston. Presumably he expressed some of his misgivings to Edwards, and the outcome of the visit was that the Commissioners for Indian Affairs assigned Hawley to inspect the old Indian churches at the isolated settlement at Mashpee, on Cape Cod. Hawley soon made Mashpee the base for what turned out to be a long and fruitful life's work, far from the wars and political upheavals that would disrupt Indian missions almost anywhere to the west, including Stockbridge.[29]

During winter 1756–57 Stockbridge remained distressingly vulnerable. In November, Edwards, Woodbridge, and other townspeople sent a petition to the Massachusetts General Court begging for protecting troops. Because the Stockbridge Indians were among the few natives who had fought as allies of the British the previous year, the people feared reprisals against the town. The next spring the still defenseless townspeople sent two more petitions, the latter written by Brigadier Dwight and signed not only by him and the two remaining sons of Ephraim Williams Sr., but also by Edwards. Common danger had brought a rare show of cooperation. Both Massachusetts and Connecticut finally sent some troops for the summer when most of the Indian men would again be gone.[30]

While the military situation remained precarious, the Edwardses celebrated one bright victory in the larger spiritual warfare for the soul of North America. A revival—of late a rarity in their circles, except in Virginia—broke out at the College of New Jersey. Just a few months earlier, in November 1756, the college had moved from Newark to its new site at Princeton. There they had constructed an impressive new building, described as "the most spacious on the continent." Burr and the trustees named it Belcher Hall in honor of the old governor, their greatest benefactor. Belcher saved generations of students from bad jokes by modestly suggesting that it instead be named Nassau Hall in memory of King William III, thus dedicating it to the Protestant political-religious cause. The Burrs settled into a tastefully elegant president's house on the property.[31]

The remarkable revival that broke out among the students at Nassau Hall in February 1757 seemed a most wonderful inaugural of the school's history at Princeton. Both Aaron Burr and Esther took time to write excitedly to Edwards. One veteran of the Great Awakening of 1740–42, Esther reported, said "he never saw anything more remarkable in the late revival than what he saw last night." "Religious concern has been universal," added Aaron Burr, "not one student excepted." Though only time would tell how many would be permanently changed, Burr believed that many showed the most promising signs. Immediately this auspicious new beginning for the relocated college revived hopes for the reformation North America desperately needed.[32]

Edwards too had his hopes slightly raised. He reported to John Erskine that, amid the "great darkness," was the "truly joyful" news of the Princeton revival and that of a few other scattered revivals.[33] Though he had no local revival to recount, he was at least heartened that "we have had less drunkenness of late among the Indians than for many years."[34] Esther continued to rejoice throughout the spring at the ongoing work among the Princeton students and hoped that as they returned to their homes in May, they would carry the revival fervor with them. As always, she also feared that Satan would counter the revival's progress.[35]

In August, Aaron Burr (who was racing from one task to another) made a

quick trip to Stockbridge to see Edwards. His stay coincided with another
military disaster, the worst yet for the New Englanders. The French under
Montcalm, aided by an unprecedented number of Indians from as far away
as the shores of Lake Michigan, besieged and captured the new Anglo-
American fort on Lake George, Fort William Henry. This time after the
surrender the Indians, in quest of what they saw as the just fruits of victory,
went on a much larger rampage than they had at Fort Oswego, killing nearly
two hundred soldiers, mostly of the wounded, and taking hundreds more
captive. When Burr returned home he told Esther "they heard the firing at
the fort very plain," referring to the fierce bombardment with heavy French
canons during the siege, seventy miles away. The family, he said was "under
dreadful apprehensions of the enemy." Edwards was almost ready to give in.
He added a postscript to a letter to Bellamy, written the day they first heard
the distant thunder of the relentless cannonade, "I don't know but we must
soon flee to Bethlehem."[36]

## A New Beginning?

The attacks that would decimate the family in the next year came from a
different direction and an older enemy. No sooner had Aaron Burr reached
Princeton on September 1 than he received word that Governor Belcher had
died the day before and that Burr was wanted to preach the funeral sermon in
Elizabethtown. Though Belcher was seventy-five, his death was a great blow
to the Burrs. "This is such a loss that we can't expect to have made up in a
governor," wrote Esther. When Aaron heard the news, he became too melancholy to think of much else. The next day, as he was writing the sermon, he
was seized by "a fit of the intermitting fever on him and the whole night after
was irrational." Still he managed to get to Elizabethtown to deliver the eulogy
on September 4. Three weeks later Burr was dead. He was forty-one.[37]

Esther was devastated but also transformed. She had been deeply attached to her energetic husband. Esther's letters to Sally Prince had alluded to
countless occasions when she and Burr enjoyed discussing common concerns
and acquaintances. Now she was left suddenly lonely with two small children.
Yet, when almost the worst imaginable had happened, she had also found
spiritual resources that she had not realized she had. To her mother, she wrote
in early October, not long after the funeral, that "God has seemed sensibly
near. . . . I think God has given me such a sense of the vanity of the world, and
uncertainty of all sublunary enjoyments, as I never had before. The world

vanishes out of my sight! Heavenly and eternal things appear much more real and important, than ever before."

The next month she wrote to her father, "such a near and dear affectionate father and guide," whom she longed to see. Her young son, Aaron, had contracted a fever and been near the grave. Yet even then she found that she could cry, "O how good is God." God had given her the child and God could "recall what he had lent." So she found herself willing "to offer up the child by faith," knowing of Christ's "willingness to accept of such as were offered to him." Esther herself was transformed. A year earlier in Stockbridge she had been unable to find resignation. Now she could say with Job, "although thou slay me yet will I trust thee."

One evening, a few days after finding strength for this submission, when she was "talking of the glorious state my dear departed husband must be in," Esther experienced quintessentially Edwardsean ecstasy with which both her parents could resonate. "My soul was carried out in such longing desires after this glorious state," she told her father, "that I was forced to retire from the family to conceal my joy. When alone I was so transported and my soul carried out in such eager desires after perfection and the full enjoyment of God and to serve him uninterruptedly that I think my nature could not have borne much more—I think dear sir I had that night a foretaste of Heaven."

Edwards, ever the wise counselor, wrote back immediately rejoicing in God's blessing and reminding Esther that true faith was not found in perpetual ecstasy, but in God's covenant faithfulness. "How do the bowels of his tender love and compassion appear, while he is correcting you by so great a shake of his head! Indeed, he is a faithful God; he will remember his covenant forever; and never will fail them that trust in him. But don't be surprised, or think some strange thing has happened to you, if after this light, clouds of darkness should return."[38]

While Esther was finding spiritual comforts, the College of New Jersey, at its new location in Princeton, was reeling from the dual blows of the losses of Governor Belcher, its patron, and Aaron Burr, its president. In spring 1757, the new Nassau Hall, spiritually aflame with revival, had shone as the brightest light for the Protestant cause on the continent. How could it now recover? The solution was not hard to think of, and the college trustees lost no time in finding it. On September 29, five days after Burr's death, the clerk of the trustees, Richard Stockton (later a signer of the Declaration of Independence), wrote to Edwards of the board's choice of him to succeed his son-in-law. They hoped he and his family could be there within six weeks.[39]

In a long and revealing letter of October 19, Edwards equivocated. Moving so precipitously, he began, without time to dispose of their property, would be a financial disaster. They had only just begun to recover from the calamitous move from Northampton. But, having made his characteristic point that his large family would need better compensation, he moved to his two main objections. The first was the matter of his physical health. He described his "peculiar unhappy" constitution in a way that suggests chronic poor digestion resulting in low spirits, "childish weakness and contemptibleness of speech, presence, and demeanor; with a disagreeable dullness and stiffness, much unfitting me for conversation, but more especially for the government of a college."[40]

His second objection, which he expounded at length, seemed the primary one. He had spent his entire career using every spare moment to write on innumerable subjects in what was now an immense collection of notebooks. He was nearing completion of a set of works in which he purported to consider "all the . . . controverted points" in the disputes between Arminianism and Calvinism. As soon as those were completed, he had in mind to write two major lifeworks and many smaller ones. The largest was to be "a great work, which I call *A History of the Work of Redemption*, a body of divinity in an entire new method, being thrown into the form of an history, considering the affair of Christian theology, as the whole of it, in each part, stands in reference to the great work of redemption by Jesus Christ." The second, on which he had also done much work, was "*The Harmony of the Old and New Testament*, in three parts," which would be, part 1, a comprehensive compendium of all the prophecies of Scripture and their fulfillment, part 2, all the types of the Old Testament point toward their fulfillment in Christ, and part 3, an exposition, of "the harmony of the Old and New Testament, as to doctrine and precept."

"My heart is so much in these studies," Edwards continued, "that I cannot find it in my heart to be willing to put myself into an incapacity to pursue them any more." In part this was a negotiating point. Were he to be president, he would not do nearly the teaching that Burr had done. Burr had taught all the languages and also the entire instruction of the senior class. Edwards was willing only to serve as professor of divinity and to assist in some instruction in arts and sciences to the seniors. He would teach no languages, except perhaps Hebrew, which might help his biblical study.[41]

Even gaining all these concessions, to which the trustees promptly acceded, Edwards followed his practice of putting such a move in the hands of a council of local ministers. "What the council will do, I can't tell," he wrote to Esther in November. "Deacon Woodbridge is a cunning man, and an eloquent speaker," he warned, and he knew that Woodbridge would make a powerful case for him to stay and might persuade the Indians to do the same.[42]

When the council, delayed by snow, finally met at Stockbridge on January 4, 1758, it heard both sides and quickly decided that Edwards should accept the Princeton offer. His close friend Samuel Hopkins, who served on the council, wrote: "When they published their judgment and advice to Mr. Edwards and his people, he appeared uncommonly moved and affected with it, and fell into tears on the occasion; which was very unusual for him, in the presence of others: and soon after said to the gentlemen, who had given their advice, that it was a matter of wonder to him, that they could so easily, as they appeared to do, get over the objections he had made against his removal, to be the head of a college; which appeared great and weighty to him."[43]

Why did Edwards weep? Perhaps it was the show of affection of his congregation, in such dramatic contrast to the council at Northampton. Perhaps it was at the sorry state in which he was leaving the Indian mission and school. That he should stay to serve the Indians, however, seems not one of his major concerns. On that issue, he believed the local prospects might be improved, since both the English and Indians had agreed to attempt to bring John Brainerd from New Jersey to be missionary to the Indians.[44] Perhaps he wept at the prospect of going back to a college setting, a position for which he was not sure he was suited. Or, more likely, he was overwhelmed by the sense of loss at maybe never getting to his projected great works. In his letter to the Princeton trustees he mentioned several times how deeply "my heart is . . . in these studies."

As soon as he composed himself after hearing the council's decision, he said he would cheerfully follow what he saw as God's will and his duty. Within weeks he would leave for Princeton, planning to move his family from the dangers of Stockbridge in May.[45]

# CHAPTER 26

## Against an "Almost Inconceivably Pernicious" Doctrine

E dwards' life did not lack for drama. He played major roles in the awakenings, some of the most momentous events of his day. He long served as a pastor who agonizingly cared for immortal souls. He spent much time in his relationships with a large immediate family of siblings, wife, and children. He took leading parts in the affairs of his extended family and local communities. He was enmeshed in partisan international politics and the violent clashes of nations and religions.

Yet his heart was most often in his work as a writer. If one can judge true affections by how one's time is spent, the center of Edwards' life was his devotion to God expressed with pen and ink. That devotion was not divorced from the many hours he also spent weekly in formal worship. Rather, his studying was another kind of worship. Much of it was directed toward the immediately practical goal of sermon preparation, closely tied with his passion for souls. Nor should we see his work on his beloved notebooks and treatises as a retreat from the world. He was just as engaged in combat as any New England colonel who might lead an assault on the French and their Indian allies. He had certainly done his share of preaching and teaching, but he believed his scholarship to be an even more important ministry. "So far as I myself am able to judge of what talents I have," he wrote to the Princeton trustees, "for benefiting my fellow creatures by word, I think I can write better than I can speak."[1] So great was his passion for writing that, had his ministerial peers agreed to it, he would have been willing to forgo accepting the presidency of the most pivotal training center for his cause in North America. He did not let even the prospect of moving his family to safety be decisive in determining how best to serve God and his fellow creatures.

Edwards turned fifty-four in October 1757, and as he grew older his calling to complete the intellectual tasks seemed increasingly urgent. He knew that his physical constitution was not strong, yet even more the sense of urgency reflected the crisis of the times. By the 1750s what we call "the Enlightenment" and what Edwards called sardonically "this age of light and inquiry," was waxing toward its meridian.[2] Edwards was determined to demonstrate, as only a true philosopher of the age could, that what most of its proponents took to be the sun was only dimly reflected light.

Most alarming was how popular the deceptive doctrines had suddenly become in New England. Since his youth, Edwards had been well aware of advanced opinions in England, which had brought into the churches there, both Anglican and dissenter, an array of Arminian, Socinian (rationalist anti-Calvinist and unitarian), and even Deist doctrines that threatened to destroy the Protestant kingdom from within. As early as the 1730s, he had campaigned to suppress even the mildest expressions of such views before they infected the countryside. Now, since the later 1740s, views that Robert Breck would not admit to in the 1730s and that Charles Chauncy would not broach during the Great Awakening were suddenly being widely and openly expressed.

Even in western Massachusetts Edwards had been encountering boldly open expressions of what he sometimes loosely lumped together as "Arminian" (i.e., anti-Calvinistic) views. During his ouster from Northampton, his outspoken cousin, Joseph Hawley III, proved to have been infected with liberal opinions. Though young Hawley had been a ward and protégé of Edwards, he had picked up the advanced ideas in eastern Massachusetts or else while serving at Louisbourg. True religion, he affirmed, echoing the commonplaces of advanced British thought, "is the most reasonable of all things," consisting "in that which the unprejudiced reason and sense of all mankind says is right."[3] In Stockbridge in 1750 Ezra Stiles and Abigail Williams Sergeant had shared similar views. Stiles, following the advice of his father, feared his views were so liberal that if subjected to theological examination by the orthodox commissioners for the Indian mission, they might permanently ruin his reputation, especially in his native Connecticut.

Edwards, who had long kept his ear to the ground for any Arminian rumblings, was keenly aware of how rapidly the fashionable opinions were spreading not only among laity, but also among clergy. Boston turned a corner in 1747 when the well-to-do and relatively new West Church, already known for progressive views, ordained young Jonathan Mayhew (Harvard 1744) as its pastor. Mayhew's rationalist and moralist, or "Arminian," leanings were already well known and his ordination took place conspicuously without the presence of the town's orthodox New Light clergy, such as Thomas Prince, Benjamin Colman, Joseph Sewall, and Thomas Foxcroft. Two years later, Lemuel Briant (Harvard 1739), a friend of Mayhew, preached a guest sermon in Mayhew's church, published under the provocative title, *The Absurdity and Blasphemy of Depretiating Moral Virtue* (Boston, 1749), attacking the Calvinist teaching of salvation by grace alone. A pamphlet barrage ensued, followed by the ecclesiastical equivalent of hand-to-hand combat in Briant's congregation in Braintree, just south of Boston. In 1753 a council of local pastors condemned Briant for a number of offenses, including his celebrated sermon. One of their specifications was that he had recommended to a parishioner "Mr. *John Taylor's* book (which we esteem very erroneous)," referring to a well-known English dissenting theologian's attack on Calvinism in *The Scripture-Doctrine of Original Sin, Proposed to Free and Candid Examination* (1740). The majority of Briant's congregation nonetheless supported him and refused his dismissal. Soon after he was forced to resign owing to ill health and he died in 1754. John Adams, who had been a teenager in Braintree during the controversy, recalled in 1815 that Briant was one of the first New Englanders to promote unitarianism. More precisely, Briant was an early proponent of the rational Christianity that during Adams' lifetime virtually displaced Calvinism in and around Boston. In 1751 Edwards' friend Thomas Foxcroft described Briant's views as not strictly Arminian but more "Socinian," referring to a more thoroughly rationalist movement, which included denial of traditional notions of the Trinity and of most distinctive Calvinist doctrines. Foxcroft was particularly alarmed at Briant's claim that "Christ's Sermon on the Mount contains his whole doctrine" and his apparent denial of Christ's substitutionary atonement.[4]

More important than the labels was the overarching principle that guided the proponents of the advanced views: that universal truths of reason and morality should be the standards by which to interpret Scripture. Mayhew himself made this point in a series of sermons published in 1749. Reason was a gift of God, and it would be wrong not to use it. The "doctrine of a total ignorance, and incapacity to judge of moral and religious truth, brought upon mankind by the apostacy of our first parents, is without foundation." Human freedom to choose the good followed from the gift of reason. "Exercise your reason, and the liberty you enjoy, in learning the truth and your deity from it," Mayhew proclaimed in another set of sermons. While still using much of the old language of grace in ambiguous ways, Mayhew and the many other New

England Christian rationalists of the 1750s had set up a standard that, if allowed to stand, would surely undermine not only Calvinism but Nicene trinitarian orthodoxy.[5]

By 1757 Edwards was so distressed by what was going on in Boston that he took the extraordinary expedient of writing to Edward Wigglesworth, Hollis Professor of Divinity at Harvard, asking him to intervene. Wigglesworth was an Old Light to whom Edwards was not close, but he knew Wigglesworth to be an orthodox Calvinist. Edwards' alarm was over one of Jonathan Mayhew's published sermons that contained a marginal note where, in Edwards' words, "he ridicules the doctrine of the Trinity." Edwards urged Wigglesworth to answer Mayhew. Wigglesworth politely declined, pleading that other Boston pastors had already lectured in opposition to Mayhew and that he himself had been defending the more basic doctrine of biblical inspiration.[6]

The same day he wrote to Wigglesworth, Edwards penned a letter to his friend and chief Boston publicist, the Reverend Thomas Foxcroft, explaining his concern for doctrinal laxity, especially at a time when the war was going badly. "I cannot in the least doubt," he declared, "but that the guilt of the land (which already is great, and awfully testified against by heaven at this day) will be greatly increased by the neglect, if none should now appear to attempt a full vindication of the doctrine of Christ's divinity."[7]

Crucial to the outlook of the fashionable new theologians and essential to their appeal in New England was that they claimed to be more true to Scripture than were their Calvinist opponents. They were, they believed, applying new superior standards of reason to clarifying the old texts. As in much of advanced eighteenth-century thought, they believed that a thorough application of reason, based on unimpeachable foundations of common sense, would put to rest the interpretive controversies that had torn apart the Christian world.

In England various anti-Calvinist theologians had been judging biblical texts according to the current standards of reason. John Taylor's *Scripture-Doctrine of Original Sin* (1740) and *A Key to the Apostolic Writings* (1745) were especially influential in popularizing such rationalist ideas among New Englanders. An ex-Calvinist himself, Taylor clarified how one might turn the old technique of "comparing Scripture with Scripture" to subvert Calvinist biblicism. When one assembled biblical statements on a disputed doctrine, one could use those that seemed most consistent with universal principles of reason and morality as lenses through which to interpret more mysterious passages that by themselves might seem to contradict these universal sensibilities. Charles Chauncy, for one, was inspired by Taylor's volumes to spend seven years after the awakening revising his doctrines away from his earlier Calvinism. In young Jonathan Mayhew, who was less hesitant in proclaiming his new views, Chauncy had found a valuable ally.[8]

As in Chauncy's case, reactions to the Great Awakening had opened the floodgates for anti-Calvinist doctrines, already far advanced in Great Britain, to surge into New England. The awakening, like all radical renewal movements, created a liberal backlash among those whom it had judged spiritually cold. Not all of anti-awakeners became liberal. Some "Old Calvinists" used strictly Reformed arguments to oppose the awakeners' allegedly excessive emotionalism. Nonetheless, a considerable number, of whom Chauncy was prototypical, reacted against what they saw as New Light "enthusiasm" and triumphalism by jettisoning Calvinism in favor of doctrines more consistent with the preeminence of reason.

The Calvinist awakening thus had the ironic consequence of undermining the structures of Calvinist orthodoxy, especially around Boston. The very divisions of the Boston clergy as well as strong insistence on Congregational government in eastern Massachusetts made it difficult to enforce strict doctrinal standards. By 1750 Boston was a vastly different place than it had been in 1740. Theologically, no one was in charge. And once the dikes of orthodoxy were breached in Boston it seemed as though there might be no stopping the flood of anti-Calvinism in the countryside.

## Freedom of the Will

Ever since his college days Edwards had thrilled to the intellectual challenges of his era. Calvinism had been dismissed by the greatest minds in this so-called age of light. It was ridiculed among the learned and in polite circles. Since the beginning of his ministry, Edwards had been warning against the almost inevitable inroads of such fashionable beliefs in New England. Having wrestled with the new views as a youth, he knew their power. For years he had been caught up in the practical response of promoting the great local and international revivals. Yet all that time he had been mapping his grand design to reestablish Calvinism's international intellectual respectability. Just when he was completing the several revival treatises, the death and *Life* of David Brainerd intervened. Still, by 1747 and 1748 he had been well under way in sketching a treatise on the freedom of the will and had told friends he would soon be writing it for publication. Then he was interrupted once again, this time by the communion controversy, which preoccupied him for the next four years. Finally, by mid-1752, he got back to his anti-Arminian project.

In July 1752 Edwards explained to the Reverend John Erskine, a young ally who would be his chief publicist in Scotland, why he was commencing with a treatise on free will and moral agency. One of the objections most widely used to dismiss Calvinism as an "absurdity" was that its view of God's sovereignty and consequent human moral inability without divine grace undermined common sense notions of moral responsibility. Particularly, Edwards designed to answer "that grand objection, in which the modern writers have so much gloried, and so long triumphed, with so great a degree of insult towards the most excellent divines and, in effect, against the gospel of Jesus Christ, viz. that the Calvinistic notions of God's moral government are contrary to the common sense of mankind."⁹

This single sentence epitomizes Edwards' view of his intellectual calling. He was an apologist for "Calvinistic" theology versus "the modern writers." Specifically, he was determined to answer objections to Calvinism based on appeals to the great touchstone of so much of eighteenth-century thought, "the common sense of mankind." Edwards was determined to show that reason, even "common sense" itself, was more consistent with "the gospel of Jesus Christ," as "the most excellent divines" of the Reformation had understood it.

Edwards had his argument for this long-planned volume well worked out in his notebooks. He began writing in August 1752 but was soon distracted by the struggle to control Stockbridge following the marriage of Abigail Williams Sergeant to Brigadier Joseph Dwight, the visit of Elisha Williams in August, and by his trip to New Jersey. Even though he did not get back to *Freedom of the Will* until the winter, he had it finished in 1753, ready for publication the next year.¹⁰

Edwards' full title summarizes the position he was refuting as a keystone of modern thought: *A Careful and Strict Enquiry into the Modern Prevailing Notions of That Freedom of Will, Which Is Supposed to be Essential to Moral Agency, Virtue and Vice, Reward and Punishment, Praise and Blame*. Everything else in the current assault on Calvinism, he was convinced, depended on that "modern prevailing notion." His estimate of its importance knew almost no bounds. "I think the notion of liberty, consisting in a contingent self-determination of the will, as necessary to the morality of men's dispositions and actions," he wrote to John Erskine in 1757, "almost inconceivably pernicious." "The contrary truth," however, was "one of the most important truths of moral philosophy that was ever discussed." If modern notions prevailed on this matter, then the game was up for Calvinism. "For allow these adversaries what they maintain in this point, and I think they have strict demonstration against us."

The past fifteen lean years of Edwards' ministry, moreover, had convinced him of the destructive practical effects of the spread of the modern views. "Notions of this sort," he told Erskine, "are one of the main hindrances of the success of the preaching of the Word, and other means of grace, in the conversion of sinners." People needed to be "properly convinced of their real guilt and sinfulness, in the sight of God, and their deserving of his wrath." Increasingly, however, people were "excusing themselves with their own inability." If their hearts were "as cold as a stone" in rejecting Christ's infinite love, they blamed their wicked disposition on God and said they could do nothing about it. While they might feel occasional guilt for particular sins, such as lewd behavior, lying, or intemperance, they felt no guilt for their rebellious hearts that spurned God's love.[11]

From our vantage point of two and a half centuries later, regardless of whether one shares Edwards' theological assessments, we can see prescience in Edwards' sense of the direction that Western thought, culture, and religion were heading. Culturally, the emphasis on the individual's wholly unfettered free will was part of what is sometimes characterized as the invention of the modern self. Contemporaneous with the scientific revolution of the seventeenth century is a tendency to objectify the self. The philosophy of Descartes (isolating the self as a philosophical certainty) is the best-known intellectual illustration of a much wider cultural trend. John Locke likewise posited rules by which individuals could step back and rationally evaluate their beliefs and commitments, thus fostering an ideal of self-responsible independence.[12] By the time Edwards was writing his treatises, many British colonials were already beginning to think of themselves as having individual rights that were self-evidently endowments of nature.[13] Two generations earlier virtually everyone's position in society had been (at least in principle) defined by status in community. In Edwards' day many social relations (subject, wife, child, apprentice, servant, slave, etc.) were still so defined. Yet a political and social revolution was nearly at hand. One harbinger of that revolution was the transformation in belief that was already sweeping through even the New England countryside. Individuals, especially adult men, were beginning to think of themselves as self-defined. Essential to self-definition was unfettered choice. The individual man might submit to government, for instance, but only by his own free and sovereign consent.

The Protestant Reformation, ironically, was a principal contributor to this revolution. Christ, as the only mediator between God and humans, could free people from the claims of human institutions. No Protestants were more insistent than were the Puritans on self-examination of one's standing before God or on relationships defined by covenants demanding assent. Further, Calvinist revivalists, such as Edwards himself, were part of the eighteenth-century revolution that accentuated individual choice and subverted the authority even of many Reformed churches and clergy. Yet rigorous Calvinists, such as Edwards and his Puritan forebears, kept such modern individualizing tendencies in severe check, balanced against their even greater insistence that one's status was defined only in relation to the absolutely sovereign God and to the communities that God ordained. Remove divine sovereignty from the emphasis on individual choice and the whole system would collapse.

Edwards had glimpsed something of the future of American religion as well. Self-controlled individuals, as he had observed in his parishes for the past fifteen years, would acknowledge guilt for particular sins, but not guilt for their fundamentally rebellious hearts. Guided by conscience, they saw particular sins as failures of will power, which might be overcome by exercising greater self-control.[14] The liberal Christianity of the new republic would be built around such moral principles. Even the most popular evangelicalism of the next two centuries tended to emphasize guilt for and victory over known sins. Although the submission of one's will to God and a subsequent infilling or baptism of the Holy Spirit typically would be urged as necessary to achieve moral purity, God's power was most often seen as cooperating with or working through the native powers of the sovereign individual will. While American Christianity in general and evangelicalism in particular came in too many varieties to allow easy generalization, we can at least say that Edwards was correct in identifying a trend toward what he called "Arminianism" in what would become "the land of the free."[15]

Edwards' consternation over modern views of individual autonomy and moral agency led him to frame an old debate in a new context. Debates over freedom and determinism were as old as philosophy and familiar to the history of Christianity. Augustine had famously attacked Pelagius on the subject and Luther had taken on Erasmus. Yet Edwards had reason to see the stakes as higher in the mid-eighteenth century. As always, his first concern was theological—to demonstrate the implications of God's sovereignty. Now, however, the alternative individualistic moralism, spreading like a flood through formally Calvinistic lands, threatened to undermine the achievements of the Reformation itself.

Not only was Edwards distressed by the emergent modern individualism, he was also well aware of a modern threat on the opposite flank, that of mechanistic determinism. A Newtonian universe of the mechanics of matter in motion could be seen as entailing ultimately materialistic causes for every effect, including acts of will. Already before Newton, Thomas Hobbes, the notorious English skeptic of the mid-seventeenth century, had propounded such determinism. Arguably, the zeal of subsequent philosophers to defend free will was designed to counter such threats posed by a Newtonian universe.[16] Eighteenth-century philosophers typically argued that the Creator had instituted *moral* law as much as mechanical law and that the moral law, as reason and a trustworthy human intuition confirmed, simply entailed true free will.

The heart of Edwards' treatise, as its full title announced, was that moral agency, virtue and vice, reward and punishment, and praise or blame did not depend on the sort of freedom that Arminians and others asserted. His opponents—representing a broad spectrum of theological opinion from Deist to evangelical—claimed as necessary to freedom that the will must be self-determining or sovereign over itself so that the will could freely choose between alternatives "as opposed to all necessity, or any fixed and certain connection with some previous ground or reason of its existence."[17]

Edwards responded that the idea that such freedom was necessary for praise or blame was, quite literally, nonsense. For one thing, it posited a "free will" as though the will could produce effects without any prior cause, other than itself. It was as though the proponents of such an uncaused free will imagined that the faculty of the will were an agent independent of the person in whom it resided. The "will," said Edwards, is simply a term for a person's power of choosing. As such, the will does not itself have some sort of hidden power of free choice. "For the will itself is not an agent that has a will: the power of choosing, itself, has not a power of choosing." Rather, said Edwards, it is the *person* who has a will or the power of choosing. So it did not make sense to talk as though in order to be free the will must be free from the controlling dispositions of the person who is doing the willing.

In Edwards' view the only sensible way to talk of the free will was that one is free to do what one wants to do. That was also, he said, the common sense meaning of freedom. "Let the person come by his volition or choice how he will, yet, if he is able, and there is nothing in the way to hinder his pursuing and executing his will, the man is fully and perfectly free, according to the primary and common notion of freedom."[18] If having free will, then, meant being free to do what one wanted to do, that was another way of saying that one was free to follow one's own strongest motive. Choosing and acting freely could not mean anything other than that one was free to follow one's own strongest inclinations.

The alternative, said Edwards, that there was an agent called the "will" inside us that was free not to follow our own strongest inclination, is absurd. One might respond that our inclinations themselves are determined by our own choices of the will that were free in some other sense. But any such previous free choice would be subject to exactly the same constraints as any other choice. It would have to be itself caused by the person's own strongest inclination. Each inclination, in turn, has to be caused by something prior to itself in the disposition of the person, ad infinitum.[19]

Although Edwards deplored those who substituted ridicule for argument, he was willing to supplement hundreds of pages of careful arguments with a rare touch of levity. His opponents' views that acts of will, in order to be truly free, must be caused by themselves led to an absurd picture of human volition. Similarly, "if some learned philosopher . . . should say, he 'had been in Tierra del Fuego, and there had seen an animal . . . that begat and brought forth itself, and yet had a sire and a dam distinct from itself; that it had an appetite, and was hungry before it had being; that his master, who led him, and governed him at his pleasure, was always governed by him, and driven by him as he pleased; that when he moved, he always took a step before the first step . . .': it would be no impudence at all, to tell such a traveler, though a learned man, that he himself had no notion or idea of such an animal as he gave an account of, and never had, nor ever would have."[20]

Edwards' alternative to what he saw as an equally absurd notion of a will that caused itself, was his definition of what it must mean to have free will. Our acts of will can still be "free" in the only coherent meaning of that term if all that determines our choices is what we ourselves want to do, that is, something in our own moral character, as opposed to some external constraint.

Edwards here developed a crucial distinction between *natural necessity* and *moral necessity*. By natural necessity Edwards meant constraints of natural causes that can be distinguished from "moral causes, such as habits and dispositions of the heart." For instance, when persons are wounded there is a natural necessity that they feel pain—and no one would hold them morally responsible for that feeling. Moral necessity is also part of the nature of things, but it is the constraint we experience when our motives or inclinations are so strong that we can not resist them. Even those who might deny that the will is always controlled by one's strongest motive would have to concede, said Edwards, that *sometimes* a motive may be so strong that a person can not overcome it. So, at the very least, sometimes the will is inexorably determined by a person's own moral inclinations.[21]

One can think of many such instances, said Edwards, where people's moral character make them unable to choose other than they do: "A woman of great honor and chastity may have a moral inability to prostitute herself to her slave. A child of great love and duty to his parents, may be unable to be willing to kill his father. A very lascivious man, in case of certain opportunities and temptations, and in the absence of such and such restraints, may be unable to forbear gratifying his lust. . . . A very malicious man may be unable to exert benevolent acts to an enemy, or to desire his prosperity: yea, some may be so under the power of a vile disposition, that they may be unable to love those who are most worthy of their esteem and affection."[22]

Now, said Edwards, what indeed does common sense tell us about praise and blame in such cases? Clearly we praise the virtuous woman whose character made her unable even to think of prostituting herself more highly than the woman who chose correctly but could hardly make up her mind. Or common sense does not excuse a man of a very haughty and vicious disposition because of his character. Proponents of the modern concept of free will spoke as though for an act to be a virtue or vice the will has to act from a sort of equilibrium, selecting among options without any decisive constraints. In fact, however, common sense rightly assigns virtue or vice to a virtuous or vicious *character* as well as to the acts that inevitably arise from that character. The theological counterpart was that God and Jesus were praiseworthy even though their characters were such that they could do only what was best.[23]

As always, Edwards' philosophy started with his theology. While his opponents were starting with principles of human morality and psychology and from those inferring what God's moral government of the universe must be like, Edwards was starting with what God must be like and then examining the human condition in that light. If God is absolutely sovereign, as Scripture claimed and Calvinists emphasized, and if God is eternal, omniscient, and omnipotent, how can there be meaningful freedom and moral agency?

If God is the omnipotent creator and sustainer of the universe, then everything that happened must be the result of God's will. There is no escaping this conclusion. God wills to govern creation in a variety of ways. Everything that happens according to the sequences of nature, for instance, must happen because of the original design of nature. God, of course, is not bound by nature and can will to interpose. Yet whether God wills to interpose or wills not to interpose, whatever happens is still just as certainly dependent on God's will. It does not make sense to suppose that at every moment in the universe there are millions of *uncaused* free acts of will that are not the subject of God's will, either positive or negative.

Such a universe is further unintelligible if we consider that God is eternal. An eternal God cannot be waiting for uncaused and hence unpredictable acts to happen. Rather, God sees all events simultaneously and so sees the sequences of events as they are determined by their antecedents. God's omniscience, or knowledge of these sequences, entails that they cannot be other than what they are, or in human terms, what they will be. In short, there is no escaping that all that happens does so under the control of God's will.[24]

Such a rigorous Calvinistic view of a God-controlled universe might seem fatalistic and demoralizing if God were not supremely good and loving. It is at this point that Edwards' grand theological vision as articulated briefly in *A Divine and Supernatural Light* becomes most important for understanding his enthrallment with God-willed reality. All created reality is like a quintessential explosion of light from the sun of God's intertrinitarian love. Though creatures experience this light in time, God sees it from beginning to end, from the perspective of eternity. Unlike humans, God sees the ultimate consequences of everything. So God wills to *permit* evil but only because that permission grows out of the ultimately loving and just will of God who can do no other than create what is ultimately the greatest good.[25]

Opponents of Calvinism derided it as fatalism. They equated it with " 'Hobbes' necessity,' or 'making men mere machines.' " Edwards responded that the resemblances were superficial. It was true that some of his arguments regarding the will being necessarily caused by the person's dispositions could be found in Hobbes. Anticipating this objection, Edwards remarked that "it happens I never read Mr. Hobbes" and that there was no rule that one needs to "reject all truth which is demonstrated by clear evidence, merely because it was once held by some bad man."[26]

The crucial point for Edwards was *how* God governs the universe. Far from creating a purely mechanistic universe and then letting it run by some inexorable natural laws, as some Deists might posit, in Edwards' conception God governs by multiple means. For inanimate things God normally governs by natural laws, so in the Newtonian universe every motion is related by natural laws to every other motion, except when God occasionally intervenes miraculously. With persons, who are higher on the scale of being, however, God governs increasingly through moral necessity. God allows them choices that are *their own* choices.[27] Ultimately, of course, their wills, like everything else in the universe, are subject to God's will and design—Edwards saw no escape from that if God is eternal, omniscient, and all powerful. Yet the crucial point was that God exercised that sovereignty in a variety of ways. So he created intelligent beings who were free to choose what they wanted in the most significant ways possible in a God-governed universe. Their choices were fully their own, and they were morally responsible for their choices. Only in a universe of personal relationships, in fact, would there be room for moral responsibility. In an impersonal universe persons' choices would still necessarily be caused by antecedent circumstances, but there would be no basis for assigning moral responsibility to such choices.[28]

The prototype for the meaning of freedom in the universe, for Edwards, was God's freedom. God acted out of moral necessity to do good, but God was perfectly free in the sense of not being bound by any necessity outside of himself. Human's choices were, of course, in an ultimate sense dependent on an omnipotent, omniscient God, like everything else in the universe that God created and governed. Yet in the choices for which they were held morally responsible, they were free in the highest possible meaning of that term in a universe of causes and effects. Their choices were thoroughly their own, not bound except by their *own* moral natures and inclinations.[29]

Edwards concluded triumphantly against the cultured despisers of Calvinism. Modern writers had spoken with magisterial condescension of "the first Reformers," whom they said "taught the most absurd, silly and monstrous opinions, worthy of the greatest contempt of gentlemen possessed of that noble and generous freedom of thought, which happily prevails in this age of light and inquiry." Arminians and others arrogantly trumpeted the triumph of common sense. Yet Edwards challenged them "to produce any doctrine ever embraced by the blindest bigot of the church of Rome, or the most ignorant Mussulman, or extravagant enthusiast, that might be reduced to more, and more demonstrable inconsistencies, and repugnancies to common sense" than the moderns' own views. True, the modern inconsistencies might be more subtle, having been propounded by some "men of great abilities," some of whom had done great service to the church. Yet, Edwards believed, he had decisively demonstrated their own absurdities.

Modern thinkers, rather than celebrating the widespread disparagement of Calvinism "as an instance of the great increase of light in the Christian Church," ought to listen with "truer modesty and humility" to "God's wisdom and discerning." Some contemporaries were so vain as to proclaim that if Scripture taught the doctrines Calvinists found in it, then God "is unjust and cruel, and guilty of manifest deceit and double-dealing, and the like" and that no book that so teaches against reason is worthy to be regarded as "the Word of God."

The facts of the matter, Edwards concluded with his characteristic hyperbole, were just the opposite. If Scripture taught "the Arminian doctrine of free will" that "would be the greatest of all difficulties that attend the Scriptures, incomparably greater than its containing any, even the most mysterious of the those doctrines of the first Reformers, which our late free thinkers have so superciliously exploded." So confident was Edwards that he had produced a strict demonstration against the Arminians that he could proclaim with what his opponents must have seen as bravado: "Indeed it is a glorious argument of the divinity of holy Scriptures, that they teach such doctrines, which in one age and another, through the blindness of men's minds, and strong prejudices of their hearts, are rejected, as most absurd and unreasonable, by the wise and great men of the world; which yet, when they are most carefully and strictly examined, appear to be exactly agreeable to the most demonstrable, certain, and natural dictates of reason."30

Edwards lived just long enough to see the first glimmers of the impact of the most influential of his philosophical works. In 1757 John Erskine wrote to him that *Freedom of the Will* was being used to support some of the views of the noted Scottish philosopher Henry Home, Lord Kames. Edwards responded in a letter carefully prepared for publication, pointing out his difference with Kames. Kames had said that the necessity that controls people's actions was inconsistent with liberty. Edwards, by contrast, wanted to make clear his most fundamental point: that he was not *denying* free will but *defending* it in the highest intelligible meaning of the term. His opponent's view of an uncaused free will was a logical absurdity—which therefore could not possibly be a condition for moral responsibility. "I have abundantly expressed it as my mind," he reiterated, "that man, in his moral actions, has true liberty; and that the moral necessity which universally takes place, is not in the least inconsistent with anything that is properly called liberty, and with the utmost liberty that can be desired, or that can possibly exist or be conceived of."31

Even though Edwards did not settle the perennial conundrum of free will and determinism to everyone's satisfaction, *Freedom of the Will* had an immense influence for at least a century, especially in Scotland and America. Although it was not as widely read as *David Brainerd* and not appealing to as broad a range of evangelicals as *Religious Affections*, "Edwards on the Will" became a staple of Calvinist theology. In the United States prior to the Civil War most educated Protestants had to make peace with its arguments. Its power, it can be argued, was a significant factor in the intellectual resilience and influence of Calvinism in America well into the nineteenth century.[32]

Before the Civil War, America produced many impressive theologians, but none as philosophically powerful as Edwards. Since the Civil War, America has had many great philosophers, but none who was, like Edwards, primarily a theologian. To fully appreciate *Freedom of the Will* one needs to view it not just as another piece of modern philosophy. More fundamentally, it is a philosophical tour de force by someone who was first of all a theologian.[33] Edwards' unrelenting commitment to the sovereignty of God led him to marshal his formidable dialectical skills in an assault on one of the seemingly impregnable fortresses of modern thought.

# CHAPTER 27

# Original Sin "in This Happy Age of Light and Liberty"

The crucial strategic question was what to write on after *Freedom of the Will*. By 1752, when Edwards was beginning that work, he was already sketching a larger master plan. Between 1742 and 1752 he had completed six treatises. In Stockbridge, where he saw his vocation more as a writer than as a speaker, he had every prospect of increasing that pace, so long as his health held up. Although he had local duties and encountered real distractions, the frontier village, surrounded by hills in the corner of the colony, had the advantages of isolation. Unlike Northampton, it was not on the way to anywhere. Unexpected guests were far less likely to appear at the door. He was not nearly so often called away for church councils or to fill neighboring pulpits.[1] What to do with this grand opportunity?

His answer was that he must devote the next years, if God willed, to a series of defenses of the faith that would continue what he had begun in *Freedom of the Will*. This set of works would include not only some more specific focus on the Arminian challenge in New England, but also continued attention to some of the broadest philosophical trends of the day. In preparation for this defense of the faith, he was developing a set of notebooks, titled "Book of Controversies," in which he included sections covering most of the controversial Calvinistic teachings: "Original Sin," "Perseverance," "Regeneration," "Universal and Particular Redemption," "Justification," "Saving and Foreknowledge of God," "Efficacious Grace," "Nature of True Virtue," "Importance of Doctrine and Mysteries," "Future Punishment," and "Predestination."[2]

Of these, defense of the Reformed doctrine of "original sin," and a number of other issues that clustered around it, was his most urgent concern. At least by the time he had completed his reply to Solomon Williams in summer

Jonathan Edwards' desk. Edwards increased its size to include separate spaces for his notebooks and papers on a wide variety of topics.

1752, Edwards had determined that as soon as he had completed the long-delayed *Freedom of the Will*, he should move in that direction.

In his letter to John Erskine of July 1752, Edwards revealed that his distress about rising apostasy had turned into alarm. As long as he could remember, England had been the source of a barrage of attacks on Calvinism, ranging from Arminianism, to Latitudinarianism, to Socinianism, and Deism. Now he saw the Calvinist defenses, both in Great Britain and America, collapsing. John Erskine had related a disturbing account of the inroads in Scotland of the anti-Calvinistic teaching of the notorious John Taylor of Norwich. Edwards connected that to his own observations of what he saw as a virtual revolution of thought in New England to conclude, in hyperbolic terms, that the world might be seeing "a remarkable time, perhaps such an one as never has been before." Edwards could hardly have been more gloomy. "Things are going downhill so fast," he lamented to Erskine, "truth and religion, both of heart and practice, are departing by such swift steps that I think it must needs be, that a crisis is not very far off. And what will then appear, I will not pretend to determine."[3]

Edwards' anguish about the encroachments of Taylorite views was tied not only to his dismay at the international and New England trends but also to his personal preoccupation with vindication in the communion contro-versy. The Northamptonites' lax views, he had concluded, were connected to the spread of anti-Calvinist doctrines. Not that he thought any but a tiny minority of his parishioners were anything but Calvinists in their profession. Yet he saw their willingness to accept naturally virtuous "Christian" citizens as communicants as smacking of the delusive optimism regarding human nature that was sweeping the British world.

Edwards dwelt on this danger in his open letter to his former North-ampton congregation, appended to the end of *Misrepresentations Corrected,* his reply to Solomon Williams, completed in June 1752. No less than three times he made the point that Solomon Williams' views of the virtue and sincerity of some unregenerate persons would inevitably lead—despite Wil-liams' own intentions—to the views of "Mr. Taylor of Norwich in England, that author who has so corrupted multitudes in New England." Such "new, fashionable, lax schemes of divinity, which have so greatly prevailed in New England of late," he warned, were likely to corrupt Northampton's young people and to "utterly explode" the Calvinism of Solomon Stoddard that the Northamptonites professed to revere.[4]

Edwards conceived of his counter to the Taylorite tide in New England as part of a three-pronged assault that would undermine the international trends at their source. The broader counterpart to the question of original sin was "the nature of true virtue." "Virtue" was becoming the watchword of eighteenth-century thought. Modern thinkers characteristically saw virtue as a universal natural human trait that might be employed as the basis for society and cultivated as both the source and object of religion. The Northamp-tonites' perplexities at excluding good citizens from the church were a reflec-tion of such trends. The theological implications of such sentiments were far larger. If modern ideas of virtue became the standards by which to judge the-ology, as they already were in most of the British domain, Calvinism would soon disappear. In eastern New England, Lemuel Briant's proclamation of

*The Absurdity and Blasphemy of Depretiating Moral Virtue* in his published 1749 sermon was just one indication of how rapidly such new views were being accepted. Edwards, by contrast, insisted that one must start with theology, or the revealed character of God, in thinking about true virtue. To make that point explicit, he designed the third (logically the first) part of his attack. He would precede his dissertation on true virtue with a companion piece that would "treat God's end in creating the world."

After completing *Freedom of the Will,* Edwards worked on these three related topics at more or less the same time. At one point he thought he might produce a work in three volumes, one on original sin, one on true virtue, and one on God's end or purpose in creating the world.[5] Eventually he decided, instead, that *Original Sin* should stand on its own as a purely defensive work and that the other two dissertations (*End for Which God Created the World* and *True Virtue*) should be complementary parts of a separate volume. Before his long illness in 1754, he had preliminary drafts of much of what became the *Two Dissertations.*

By February 1756, he was ready to present a nearly completed draft of *End for Which God Created the World* to some colleagues. Samuel Hopkins recorded in his diary for February 12, "Mr. Bellamy came to my house last Tuesday, with whom I went to Stockbridge and stayed there two nights and one day, to hear Mr. Edwards read a treatise on 'The Last End of God in the Creation of the World.'"[6] We can imagine the three theologians gathered around a fireplace as Edwards read all through a winter's day, perhaps with Sarah, Lucy, and others sometimes sitting on the periphery.

This scene underscores that Edwards was not working alone. He was not only benefiting from his friends' criticisms, but also promoting a school of thought. Bellamy had published a major defense of Calvinistic doctrines, *True Religion Delineated* (1750), "versus the principal errors of the Arminians and Antinomians," for which Edwards had furnished a laudatory preface. The younger Hopkins, who would be Edwards' most influential disciple, was now trying his hand at a major treatise. Very shortly before Edwards left Stockbridge in 1758, Hopkins had Edwards review his efforts. "Mentor has heard them," he wrote happily to Bellamy, "and commended them and offered to be the first subscriber if I would draw up proposals for printing them."[7]

The three apparently had agreed that, in the light of the controversy raging in New England over the origins of human sin, they should first of all offer concerted defenses of Reformed teachings on the topic. Hopkins' volume would be titled *Sin, Thro' Divine Interposition, an Advantage to the Universe* (1759). Bellamy issued *Four Sermons on the Wisdom of God in the Permission of Sin* in 1758. Edwards had put aside his other treatises in spring 1756 and turned to *Original Sin,* which by May 1757 he had ready to send to the publisher. It would appear shortly after his death.

Edwards focused *Original Sin* very specifically on John Taylor's recent attack on Calvinism. He justified his attention to the English writer's popular volume by observing that "no one book has done so much towards rooting out of these western parts of New England, the principles and scheme of religion maintained by our pious and excellent forefathers." Nonetheless, he assured his readers that his response to Taylor would also be "a *general defense* of that great important doctrine."[8]

The doctrine of original sin—that all humans inherited both the guilt of Adam's sin and a corrupt nature—was one of the chief points on which eighteenth-century Calvinists were at odds with their optimistic era. The emphasis on human freedom and innate capacities for virtue reflected growing modern tendencies toward views that men, or at least gentlemen, could control their own destinies. Further, as ideas spread that even kings and queens must be bound by higher rational principles of morality and justice, the Calvinist system—which asserted that God's sovereign government was by definition good, even when humans could not fully understand God's ways—seemed increasingly out of step.

Edwards viewed his task as the vindication of some of Scripture's difficult teachings which, as he declared in his full title, *The Great Christian Doctrine of Original Sin,* he believed to be the doctrine long held by the true church. The Bible made many direct claims about the fall of the human race into sin, the race's universal wickedness, and the helplessness of humans to save themselves—all views that offended fashionable eighteenth-century standards of morality and justice. Taylor and his kind avoided these doctrines by starting with the modern standards and then selectively appropriating Scripture as it suited their purposes. Especially, Edwards claimed, they ignored some plain statements of the Apostle Paul, who in many places directly affirmed the basics of the doctrine. Edwards cited Romans 3:10: "As it is written, There is none righteous, no, not one" and Romans 5:12: "Wherefore, as by one man sin entered into the world, and death by sin; and so death passed upon all men, for that all have sinned." And so forth. The Stockbridge theologian devoted the largest part of his long treatise to demonstrating that there was no way to make such statements fit the modern views.

Although his rigorously Calvinistic biblical expositions made up the bulk of the dissertation, Edwards began and ended, as he characteristically did, with appeals to reason and observation. The biblical positions, he was determined to show, were at least as consistent with experience and reason as were any of the alternatives. Every natural born human who ever lived and who became a moral agent, he argued, had sinned against God. This universal propensity to sin was evidence of an *inclination* to sin or of a sinful nature. Even on this point he relied substantially on Scripture declarations as well as on other history. To clinch the argument Edwards pointed out that the most essential commandments were to worship the one true God and that the heathen nations did not come close to doing that naturally. Further, even when people had the Gospel presented to them, they were inclined to ignore it for lesser pleasures. On this latter point, Edwards enlisted a lengthy quotation from John Locke to the effect that if people were totally rational, they would immediately forsake all earthly concerns in favor of eternal heavenly rewards. What else could account for such well-known "stupidity" with regard to religion, said Edwards, but a depraved disposition?[9]

Edwards could draw on his firsthand knowledge of the American Indians to reinforce his point that the human race was not naturally inclined to do its duty. "What appearance was there," he asked, "when the Europeans first came hither, of their being recovered, or recovering, in any degree from the grossest ignorance, delusions, and most stupid paganism?" Yet if Edwards had a dim view of the natives' culture, he believed their faults arose not out of any inherent inferiority, but from being part of the human race. Furthermore, by the standards that counted, European culture was in many respects far worse because of the lengths to which many people had gone in rejecting the light of the Gospel. "To what a pass are things come in Protestant countries at this day, and in our nation in particular," Edwards exclaimed. "To what a prodigious height has a deluge of infidelity, profaneness, luxury, debauchery and wickedness of every kind, arisen! The poor savage Americans are mere babes and fools (if I may so speak) as to proficiency in wickedness, in comparison of multitudes that the Christian world throngs with."[10]

Taylor, said Edwards, ignored all this evidence of universal declension and argued that, on balance, most people were more often virtuous than not. Nonsense, Edwards retorted. First of all, that was not true with respect to religious duties. Further, even if it were true, it would be like arguing that a ship setting out for an Atlantic crossing yet sure to sink would nonetheless "sail above water more hours than it will be sinking."

The Genesis history and other biblical passages taught that God demanded perfect righteousness from Adam and Eve and condemned them and their posterity for one failure. Humans might think that unfair, but experience taught that one mistake often led to disproportionately dire consequences. A young man, for instance, might be induced by his friends to take a drink. He might, rather innocently consent to do so (as Adam and Eve were deceived by the serpent in the garden), but then he might soon become addicted. So it was not contrary to reason that a relatively innocuous first action could lead to a life of ruin.

The much harder question was whether this doctrine of original sin did not make God the author of sin. Edwards responded that every version of Christianity had the same problem. All Christians taught that there *is* sin in the world and that God created the world. Much as he had argued in *Freedom of the Will*, Edwards pointed out that the claim that free will makes sin unpredictable does not solve the problem. God would still be allowing sin. Since God could intervene, God would have no less culpability for *continuing* to allow the sinful acts than he would for allowing humans to be born with depraved natures that inevitably inclined them to sin.[11]

Edwards had a relatively simple explanation of how God could *permit* people to sin without being the author of their sin. Arminians and many other Christian traditions made this same distinction, but Edwards was showing how it fit well into a Calvinistic framework. God created the first humans with two principles within them, Edwards explained. First, was a lower principle that "may be called *natural,* being the principles of mere human nature; such as self-love, with those natural appetites and passions, which belong to the nature of man, in which his love to his own liberty, honor and pleasure, were exercised." In addition God implanted in humans higher *supernatural* principles "that were spiritual, holy and divine, summarily comprehended in divine love."

So long as the higher principle of love to God reigned supreme, Adam and Eve had been perfectly happy, in communion with God. Yet they also had the ability to choose evil. When they did, spurning God's love, God withdrew the higher spiritual principle from them, leaving the lower nature to rule. God thus allowed their sin but did so only by withdrawing the supernatural gift and allowing humans to act according to their own dispositions. The setting of the sun might permit frost, but strictly speaking it did not cause it except in a negative sense. So God by withdrawing the higher spiritual gift permitted his creatures to choose evil.

The lower nature that God created for humans, furthermore, was not bad in itself. It was good so long as it remained, as originally created, a servant to the higher spiritual principle. When humans freely chose to sin, however, a revolution took place. "The immediate consequence . . . was a *fatal catastrophe*, a turning of all things upside down, and the succession of a state of the most odious and dreadful confusion." Humans set themselves up as supreme, displacing God. Their "inferior principles," Edwards explained, "are like fire in an house; which, we say, is a good servant, but a bad master; very useful while kept in its place, but if left to take possession of the whole house, soon brings all to destruction."[12]

Once the supernatural principle was withdrawn, humans naturally bequeathed only their lower nature from generation to generation. That was no more difficult to understand, said Edwards, than that acorns will always produce oaks. Righteousness, in contrast, is not something that can be naturally inherited or acquired; rather it comes to each redeemed person according to a much higher spiritual principle, the gift of God of being engrafted into the tree of which Christ is the root.[13]

Edwards' commonsensical account of how corrupt human nature might be inherited was leading toward his explication of the more difficult biblical teaching, that all humans inherited the *guilt* of Adam's sin. It was one thing to show how human nature based on self-love, unchecked by a higher love to God, might be passed from one generation to the next, so that each person who became a moral agent would inevitably sin. But Scripture, especially Paul in Romans 5, spoke of *all* Adam's posterity as sinners and all in need of Christ's righteousness.[14] Calvinists, following older Christian traditions, spoke of the *imputation* of the guilt of Adam's sin to all Adam's natural descendants as a way of explaining such teaching. How could one convince enlightened eighteenth-century readers that there could be justice in holding the whole race, including infants, guilty for sins they did not personally commit?

Edwards answered first by clarifying that the source of the guilt was that every human had a disposition dominated by an inclination to sin. Sin, as Edwards had insisted in *Freedom of the Will,* involved a person's inclinations, not just isolated acts. So Adam was guilty for his dominant inclination to commit the first sin as well as for the act itself. Similarly, people were culpable for their corrupt natures that inclined them to sin even before they might actually act on those inclinations.[15]

The imputation of the *guilt* of Adam's sin could thus be understood according to the acorn-and-oak analogy that Edwards used to explain the universally inherited *propensity* to sin. The corrupt propensity was itself a fault, even before a sinful act. Every new branch and leaf of a tree would partake of its disease, even before the blight became apparent. One might think of it, Edwards suggested in a long note, as though "Adam and all his posterity had *coexisted*" and had been constituted by God as one complex person, as a tree is connected to its root or as the members of the body are connected to the head. Then one might imagine all taking part in a common disposition, and "the hearts of all the branches of mankind, by the constitution of nature and the law of union, would have been affected just as the heart of Adam, their common root, was affected." In something of this same way the whole race concurs in Adam's sin.[16]

Edwards still had to answer the objection that there seems something unreasonable in God treating the human race collectively, rather than as individuals. Yet, said Edwards, we accept such continuities in nature all the time. Once again think of the acorn and the oak or that a whole species of trees might be blighted. Moreover, we think of a man of forty as the same person he was as a child, even though almost everything about him is different. The same principle extends to questions of guilt. We hold people responsible for crimes they committed many years earlier. There is nothing contrary to the nature of things if God should extend these same principles to the whole race.

To bolster this difficult point—that the problem of the identity of the race was analogous to personal identity—Edwards unveiled his most complex metaphysics. If God sustained the universe, then the universe depended on God for each moment of existence. If God withdrew his energy the universe would dissolve into nothing. So, as he had observed in his early notebooks, it was as though the universe was recreated at every moment. That made God's will the cause of everything, even if God exercised that will through significantly varied methods of causation, such as constituting what we perceive as laws of nature or permitting people to make their own choices. So personal identity, like laws of cause and effect, and everything else are dependent on God's will and wisdom because if God suddenly withdrew the power that governs the universe, nothing in the universe would happen in the next moment.

A helpful analogy, Edwards explained in another long note, is to think of the continuing light of the moon, to which we assign a single identity. In fact, there is nothing in the moon itself that causes it to shine from one moment to the next. Similarly, if we view an object in a mirror, we assign a continuing identity to the object, but in fact it has no more real continuity than if it were a series of images flashed on the mirror. Edwards was here speculating, somewhat as David Hume did, on the implications of Lockean empiricism for causation. If what we know about reality is nothing but a series of experiences or impressions on our mind (like the images in a mirror), how do we know that phenomena we *experience* as cause and effect are actually so connected? Edwards, unlike Hume, resolved the problem by observing that the divine will constituted the system of cause and effects and kept it going.[17] Hence one can count on particular effects consistently following certain causes because God's will continues to constitute such sequences. So God's will continues to constitute all identities, whether of natural objects, of persons, or of the race. Some readers, Edwards acknowledged, would not be able to follow such "metaphysics." For them, it should be sufficient that the Bible plainly teaches that God *does* deal with the race as a whole and that we must accept "the sovereign constitutions of the supreme Author and Lord of all, 'who gives none account of any of his matters, and whose ways are past finding out.'"[18]

While Edwards was defending traditional doctrines, he was doing so in some distinctly modern ways. Throughout his treatises he argued that various Reformed teachings were in fact consistent with the highest standards of reason and common sense. Such defenses of the faith by contemporary standards of reason could make one vulnerable to attack by the same standards. Nonetheless, as Edwards made especially clear in *The Great Christian Doctrine of Original Sin,* he was not resting his case on reason alone. At the end of the day he was ready to acknowledge that some of the plain teachings of Scripture must remain mysteries to feeble human intelligence.

Edwards had once used a story to illustrate the limits of human understanding. "I once told a boy of about thirteen years of age," he recounted, "that a piece of any matter of two inches square was eight times so big as one of but one inch square, or that it might be cut into eight pieces, all of them as big as that of but an inch square." The boy (apparently not the brightest of thirteen-year-olds) thought the idea absurd, and nothing Edwards did could convince him otherwise. Finally Edwards got a saw and cut a two-inch cube that he then cut into eight one-inch cubes. The boy still could not believe it and kept counting the cubes. "He seemed to [be] astonished as though there were some witchcraft in the case and hardly to believe it after all, for he did not yet at all see the reason for it." So, said Edwards, it was as difficult a mystery for the boy as is the doctrine of the Trinity to a Socinian or Deist.

"And why should we," he reflected, "not suppose that there may be some things that are true, that may be as much above our understandings and as difficult to them, as this truth was to this boy. Doubtless, there is a vastly greater distance between our understanding and God's, than between this boy's and that of the greatest philosopher or mathematician."[19]

Consistent with such a recognition of the limits of his understanding, in *Original Sin* Edwards was considerably more modest than he had been in *Freedom of the Will,* as a comparison of the conclusions of the two treatises nicely reveals. At the end of *Freedom of the Will* he proclaimed that he had so conclusively demonstrated his view that it would have cast doubt on Scripture if it had taught otherwise. In *Original Sin,* by contrast, he claimed only that his combination of common sense and metaphysics had clearly demonstrated that the Scripture doctrines were not *unreasonable.* In the last analysis the argument came down to what Scripture said—and the plain meanings of Scripture were sometimes philosophically difficult.

So this time he turned his irony not against the supposedly enlightened philosophers of the age, but rather against the new biblical interpreters. How wonderful is it, he mocked, that these "*new writers*" have discovered in the Apostle Paul meanings so deep that they escaped the view of all previous interpreters for fifteen or sixteen hundred years. "No wonder then, if the superficial discerning and observation of vulgar Christians, or indeed of the herd of common divines, such as the Westminster Assembly, etc. falls vastly short of the Apostles reach." We have to realize, Edwards continued his irony, that the Reformers and all interpreters before and since "dwelt in a cave of *bigotry* and *superstition,* too gloomy to allow 'em to use their own understandings with freedom, in reading the Scripture." Now, though, moderns have left the cave and ascended to the light. "It must be understood, that there is risen up, now at length in this happy age of light and liberty, a set of men, of a more free and generous turn of mind, a more inquisitive genius, and better discernment."

Yet while Edwards was supremely confident that he had defeated those who read modern meanings into Paul, he closed on a humble note, as though he recognized that the Scripture doctrine left mysteries that even the best metaphysics might not penetrate. "The candid reader" could judge the success of his arguments, but "the success of the whole must now be left with God, who knows what is agreeable to his own mind, and is able to make his own truths prevail; however mysterious they may seem to the poor, partial, narrow and extremely imperfect views of mortals, while looking through a cloudy and delusory medium." However imperfectly humans might understand, God had promised that "the Gospel of Christ . . . shall finally be victorious" and that God's Word "'shall not return to him void.'" "Let God arise, and plead his own cause, and glorify his own great name. AMEN."[20]

Edwards' defense of original sin bears on the perennial debate concerning his modernity and fits into a general pattern that we have already seen, that he was simultaneously a strict conservative and an innovator. Almost all of his views were scrupulously consistent with those that had prevailed in New England a century earlier. Yet he was not, as Peter Gay suggested, a tragic anachronism fighting for outdated opinions long after they were defensible.[21] Edwards' genius was to show how his core theological views were intellectually viable in the Enlightenment era. Of course, not everyone in the eighteenth century accepted his New Light Calvinism, but then neither did everyone, or even all well-educated men, accept the fashionable liberal divinity and mores. In fact, in the "century of lights" it was sharply contested as to what counted as true "light." The histories written by Gay and other twentieth-century "winners," or the liberal heirs to the Enlightenment, have not taken that aspect of the past seriously enough. John Wesley had more impact on the eighteenth-century English-speaking world than did David Hume. Edwards not only posed conservative challenges to the fashionable ideas and mores of his era, but he showed the way for New Light Calvinism to flourish in subsequent generations. He was not just a latter-day Puritan, although puritan he was, but also the fountainhead for a vital movement that played a leading role in American religious and intellectual life for the next century.[22]

More to the point than the definitional debate over what in the eighteenth century we should call "modern" is the larger issue of whether it is not liberal modernity that is tragically flawed, and precisely at the point that Edwards and his tradition said it was, in its optimism regarding human nature. As has often been observed, no Christian teaching has had more empirical verification during the past century than the doctrine of innate human depravity. Champions of modernity or postmodernity may not agree with Edwards' way of accounting for the defects of the human race, but they may have more difficulty in arguing that Edwards was wrong to be challenging the emerging optimism of the "age of light."

# CHAPTER 28

# Challenging the Presumptions of the Age

A t the same time Edwards was focusing narrowly on defending the Calvinist doctrine of original sin, he was designing a broader counterattack against some of the most prevalent assumptions of modern thought. Apparently because he perceived a theological crisis in New England, he regarded the publication of *Original Sin* as a priority. He may also have thought it prudent to secure one's defenses before venturing on an offensive.

As soon as he sent *Original Sin* to the press in May 1757, he turned back to the largely completed drafts of the *Two Dissertations*. These were virtually complete before his death, although not transcribed into his legible public hand for the press. Hopkins and Bellamy became his literary executors, but it took until 1765 for them to see these works through to publication.

In February 1757 Edwards described these two treatises to Thomas Foxcroft, his Boston literary agent, as answering "the modern opinions which prevail concerning these two things, [which] stand very much as foundations of that fashionable scheme of divinity, which seems to have become almost universal."[1] These paired works would be less directly polemical than *Freedom of the Will* and *Original Sin*. Rather than defending particular doctrines, he would be attempting to undermine the *foundations* of what had gone wrong in modern thought. The first dissertation would lay out the fundamental premises for understanding human relationships by considering the question "What is the purpose for which God created the universe?" Only then, with a correct understanding of God's intention for human existence, would one be in a position to approach the subject of the second dissertation—one of the great topics of his day—"the nature of true virtue."

# Why Would God Create a Universe?

The key to Edwards' thought is that everything is related because everything is related to God. Truth, a dimension of God's love and beauty, is part of that quintessentially bright light that pours forth from the throne of God. Every other pretended light, or source of truth, is as darkness if it keeps God's creatures from seeing the great sun of God's light. The created universe itself is a dynamic expression of that light, yet sin blinds humans from acknowledging the source of the light that surrounds them. Having turned away from the true light of God's love, they now grope in darkness, inordinately loving themselves and their immediate surroundings, or chasing after false lights of their own imaginings. Only the undeserved gift of redemption, bought with Christ's blood, can open their eyes and change their hearts so that they see and love the triune God and the created universe as wholly an expression of God's creative and redemptive will. Only through the prism of the revelation recorded in Scripture can they discover the nature of God's creative and redemptive purposes. Once sinners experience God's love, they begin to love what he loves.

If we recognize this essentially Augustinian framework that shapes all of Edwards' thought, it becomes apparent that the *Dissertation Concerning the End for Which God Created the World* was a sort of prolegomenon to all his work. Although he paired it specifically with *The Nature of True Virtue*, the most philosophical of his writings, to which its theology is the necessary premise, the *End for Which God Created the World* might be seen as the logical starting point for all of his thinking.[2] Had he lived to work on his great projected "History of the Work of Redemption," the dissertation would have surely been a point of departure for that "body of divinity in an entire new method."

*The End for Which God Created the World*, though often highly acclaimed, is one of the less read (and less easy to read) of Edwards' treatises because it focuses on the narrow starting point for this larger theological vision. Nevertheless, this theological and Scriptural prolegomenon is essential for understanding how Edwards positioned himself in relation to the prevailing philosophies of the era. Eighteenth-century moral philosophers and moral popularizers were increasingly speaking of the deity as a benevolent governor whose ultimate interest must be to maximize human happiness. Alexander Pope's *Essay on Man* is the best-known popular expression:

Edwards' library table

> All Chance, Direction, which thou canst not see:
> All Discord, Harmony not understood;
> All partial Evil, universal Good:
> And, spite of Pride, in erring Reason's spite,
> One truth is clear, "WHATEVER IS, IS RIGHT."

Edwards himself might have assented to these few lines, justifying the ways of God to man. He and his friends were deeply engaged in a similar enterprise.[3] But in Pope's version the natural order was essentially benevolent.

> God in nature of each being, founds
> Its proper bliss, and sets its proper bounds:
> But as he fram'd the Whole, the Whole to bless,
> On mutual Wants built mutual Happiness:
> So from the first, eternal ORDER ran,
> And creature link'd to creature, man to man.[4]

Voltaire's *Candide* (1759), a bitter satire on the idea of the "best of all possible worlds" written in the aftermath of the Lisbon earthquake of 1755 and at nearly the same time Edwards was finishing his dissertation, represents another well-known pole in this same debate concerning God's purposes. Whether the "best of all possible worlds" was celebrated by a popularizer like Pope or a sophisticate like the German Leibniz (who was in some ways like Edwards without the Calvinism), the French philosophe thought it demonstrably nonsense.[5] Yet like other moralists of his day, Voltaire believed that following the light of nature would lead toward human self-improvement.

*The End for Which God Created the World,* in the meantime, sidestepped all secondary questions, such as the problem of evil or of eternal punishment, and concentrated on a crucial prior issue. If "our modern freethinkers" were determining God's character by gauging what sort of universe would maximize human happiness, they were starting at the wrong end by looking first at humans' interests rather than at God's.[6] In effect, they were setting up principles regarding human happiness as higher than God because they were insisting God must conform to these principles. Or, to put it in the framework in which Edwards addressed the issue, they were setting up their own perceptions of what constituted the greatest human happiness as the ultimate (or highest) end or reason that God created the universe.

Edwards insisted that any inquiry into the ultimate end for which God created the universe must be derived from knowledge of the revealed character of God. The heart of Edwards' exposition was his analysis of the many Scriptural references that the highest end of creation is "the glory of God." As in all of Edwards' thought, his premise was that God is infinitely above all his creatures and is infinitely good. While it would be inappropriate for an inferior being to be ultimately motivated by self-love, preeminent love to self is not inappropriate to a being who is infinitely good because in that case self-love is simply to love what is infinitely good.

Yet why would such an infinitely good, perfect, and eternal being create? How could creation of the time-bound and less than perfect be anything but a diminishment of God? Here Edwards drew on the Christian trinitarian conception of God as essentially interpersonal. Although Edwards did not emphasize the trinitarian basis of the argument (as with most topics, he had expounded that subject in another manuscript),[7] he did allude to it to make the point that God's infinite goodness is essentially the goodness of love, expressed first in intertrinitarian love such as between the Father and the Son.

The ultimate reason that God creates, said Edwards, is not to remedy some lack in God, but to extend that perfect internal communication of the triune God's goodness and love. It is an extension of the glory of a perfectly good and loving being to communicate that love to other intelligent beings.

God's joy and happiness and delight in divine perfections is expressed externally by communicating that happiness and delight to created beings. God's internal perfection or glory radiates externally like the light that radiates from the sun. The glory of God "is fitly compared to an effulgence or emanation of light from a luminary, by which this glory of God is abundantly represented in Scripture. Light is the external expression, exhibition and manifestation of the excellency of the luminary, of the sun for instance: it is the abundant, extensive emanation and communication of the fullness of the sun to innumerable beings that partake of it."[8]

The happiness of humans, then, when rightly understood, is not an ultimate end of creation in any way apart from God and God's glory. "The beams of glory come from God, and are something of God, and are refunded back again to their original. So that the whole is *of* God, and *in* God, and *to* God; and God is the beginning, middle and end in this affair."[9]

That last sentence encapsulated the central premise of his entire thought. It is as though the universe is an explosion of God's glory. Perfect goodness, beauty, and love radiate from God and draw creatures to ever increasingly share in the Godhead's joy and delight. "God's respect to the creature's good, and his respect to himself," Edwards explained, "is not a divided respect; but both are united in one, as the happiness of the creature aimed at is happiness in union with himself. . . . The more happiness the greater union: when the happiness is perfect, the union is perfect. And as the happiness will be increasing to eternity, the union will become more and more strict and perfect; nearer and more like to that between the Father and the Son." The ultimate end of creation, then, is union in love between God and loving creatures. Because eternity is infinite, this union between God and the saints can be ever increasing, like a line ascending toward an infinite height but never reaching it. So the saints' happiness will continually increase as they are drawn ever closer toward perfect union with the Godhead.[10]

This conception of an exploding God-centered universe in which God creates in order ever increasingly to share divine happiness with his creatures had countless theological implications that Edwards had long been working on in his publications and notebooks. He looked forward to his magnum opus, "The History of Redemption," where he would treat all of these and many other theological issues in their place. First, however, he was determined to show how a consistent theology that recognized a loving and dynamic creator God would undercut the most influential philosophy of the era.

# "True Virtue" in an Age of "Virtue"

Edwards addressed *The Nature of True Virtue* to the eighteenth-century philosophers. Although he paired it with a theological treatise, he kept the
theology of *Concerning the End for Which God Created the World* as broadly
Christian as he could, so as to establish a wide foundation for his philosophical analysis of virtue. Unlike his other works, in *The Nature of True Virtue*
Edwards did not quote Scripture, although he did appeal to its authority for
the theistic basis of his ethics. His object was to establish an analysis in which,
if one granted merely a few essential principles of Christian theology, one
would be forced to reconsider the whole direction of eighteenth-century
moral philosophy.

To feel the force of this challenge, we must view Edwards and *True Virtue*
in their international context.[11] In broadest terms, the British moralists since
the time of John Locke were attempting to establish a new moral philosophy
as a science equivalent to the new natural philosophy, or natural science. True
to the spirit of the age, modern thinkers were striving to establish firm foundations for knowledge that would be universally valid for all humans. Christendom, ever since the Reformation, had been torn by the absolutist dogmas
of warring religious authorities. The grand hope of the modern moral philosophers was that they could discover universally valid moral standards with
which they could adjudicate competing absolute claims and in effect stand
above them.

In the English-speaking world, the overwhelming consensus was that the
foundations for a universal morality must have an empirical as well as a
rational base. Just as the natural laws of the physical world could be established on the foundations of universal principles of perception, so the philosophers of the day believed that moral principles could be based on similarly
firm foundations that no reasonable person could doubt. John Locke was the
best-known progenitor of this project. Not only did he develop an empirical
philosophy that explained perceptions of the physical world, he also established a political philosophy based on "self-evident" first principles of morality, most notably the rights to life, liberty, and property. Since Locke's time
the discussions had advanced on many fronts among British moralists. Most
were attempting to show that normal human beings were endowed with
powers to know and to obey the moral laws that were built into the scheme of
things, just like other natural laws.

The new moral philosophy was part of the modern project that made

nature normative for understanding the self and self-understanding normative for morality. The Reformation challenged the mediatorial role of the
church but asserted the authority of Scripture as the preeminent source for
theology and ethics. It also encouraged, as was notable among Puritans,
examination of one's own experience to determine whether one was truly a
recipient of God's redeeming grace. In England after the Puritan era, the
immediate sequel was Cambridge Platonism, which deemphasized dogma
and asserted human abilities to be attuned to the divine. The next step,
suggested especially by Anthony Ashley Cooper, third earl of Shaftesbury
(1671–1713), was to posit a natural moral sense that was a reliable guide to the
moral principles a benevolent Creator had built into the natural order.[12]

Francis Hutcheson (1694–1746), a Scottish ex-Calvinist, best developed
Shaftesbury's views. His *Inquiry Concerning Beauty, Order, Harmony, Design*
(1725) established him as the most influential moral philosopher of the era and
the one whom Edwards was most eager to counter. Moralists since Locke
were agreed that humans must be endowed by the Creator with a natural
faculty with which to make reliable moral judgments. They were divided,
however, between those who insisted that this moral faculty was dependent
on the right judgment of intellect and those who, like Shaftesbury and
Hutcheson, viewed it as a "moral sense." All agreed that the moral faculty led
people to approve of benevolence and that benevolence could be perceived as
a type of beauty, since benevolence promoted harmony versus disharmony.
Hutcheson argued that the moral sense, also called *conscience*, was closely
analogous to a *sense* of beauty. "What is approved by this sense we count as
*right* and *beautiful*, and call it *virtue;* what is condemned, we count as *base* and
*deformed* and vicious."[13]

Edwards' language and categories sounded a lot like Hutcheson's because
the two had worked within the same wider eighteenth-century discourse.
Edwards had long since expounded on a spiritual sense analogous to a sense
of beauty and had made that familiar principle the bedrock of his analysis in
*Religious Affections.* For Edwards a *truly spiritual* sense of beauty was what
distinguished the regenerate from the unregenerate. Hutcheson, by contrast,
had been arguing that *all* humankind were endowed by their Creator with a
sense of moral beauty sufficient to lead them, if they followed its dictates, to a
life of virtue for which they were also promised eternal rewards.

Although Hutcheson and Edwards worked in the same universe of discourse, their views were poles apart because the Scottish philosopher, like
most of his contemporaries, was assuming that nature and human nature

provided normative guides to human life. In the view of Hutcheson and his peers, God must be a benevolent deity who created a universe designed for moral harmony. Humans needed only to discover and follow the inbuilt natural laws.

Such assumptions about the sources of morality had immense implications for shaping the modern world. They were crucial for teaching people that they could free themselves from external authorities and at the same time internalize moral principles that would make them useful citizens. Attitudes of self-discipline were socially useful in helping to produce free individuals who could compete in the new commercial culture. Another common view of the era was that even private vices, growing out of self-interest, could result in public virtue.[14] A generation later Hutcheson's countryman Adam Smith (1723–90) most famously applied such assumption regarding benevolent natural laws explicitly in defense of a free market economy. Hutcheson's emphasis on sentiment anticipated the romantic views of the self, reliant on the guidance of nature from within, so important to the emergence of the nineteenth-century middle classes.[15]

Much of American thought from the Revolution to the Civil War was shaped by the immensely impressive Scottish Enlightenment. It is illuminating to think of Edwards in that Scottish context. American colonists in the 1750s thought of themselves as British provincials and increasingly looked to Scotland, the preeminent British province, for intellectual guidance.[16] Edwards was no exception. He depended on his Scottish correspondents for the latest intelligence and to supply many of the books he needed to participate in the international conversation.

Just as Edwards was writing his great treatises in the 1750s, Scotland was emerging as the brightest intellectual center in the Western world. In addition to Hutcheson there was Henry Home, Lord Kames, whose views on the will Edwards contrasted with his own in 1757, and David Hume, whose *A Treatise on Human Nature* (1739–40) Edwards read with great interest. Edwards did not live quite long enough to learn of the work of the two other Scottish philosophers who had the most influence in America, Thomas Reid (1710–1796), the most famous articulator of "common sense" philosophy, and Adam Smith.

Nonetheless, Edwards thought of himself first of all as a British citizen and was especially in touch with the Scottish Enlightenment. Late in 1755 Edwards wrote to John Erskine that he had read Lord Kames' *Essay on the Principles of Morality* (1751) "and also that book of Mr. David Hume's which you speak of. I am glad of an opportunity to read such corrupt books; especially when written by men of considerable genius; that I may have an idea of the notions that prevail in our nation."[17] Edwards' use of "our nation" is one of those inconspicuous clues that reveals how he thought of his national identity. Great Britain was crucial to him because it was a Protestant nation. Now even Presbyterian Scotland, where he found his strongest allies, was in danger of being destroyed by the new corrupt thought.

As he was finishing *The Nature of True Virtue* in 1757 Edwards could for the first time begin to see some fulfillment of his lifelong ambition to lend his own considerable genius to the great philosophical debates of the day. *Freedom of the Will* had put him on the intellectual map, a position he hoped his letter contrasting his views to those of Lord Kames would help underscore. *The Nature of True Virtue* had the potential to extend the challenge.

In the very first sentence Edwards signaled both that he was entering into this international conversation on moral philosophy and that he was at home with its fundamental terms. "Whatever controversies and variety of opinions there are about the nature of virtue," he began, "yet all (excepting some skeptics who deny any real difference between virtue and vice) mean by it something *beautiful,* or rather some kind of *beauty* or excellency." Further, this same sentence indicated that he was not here particularly concerned to sort out all the "controversies and variety of opinions there are about the nature of virtue." Unlike most of his other treatises, this one did not mount polemics against the statements of particular authors, Hutcheson or anyone else. Rather, he was laying gunpowder at the foundations of the entire project of all the celebrated moral philosophers of the day.

Edwards' basic point was as simple as it was characteristic of all his thought. "Nothing is of the nature of true virtue," he explained, "in which God is not the *first* and the *last*." God is love and the source of all love. True love, true benevolence, is love that resonates with God's love and is in harmony with it. This conclusion, Edwards pointed out, is a necessary implication of "the preceding discourse of *God's End in Creating the World*." God's very being is "love and friendship which subsists eternally and necessarily between the several persons in the Godhead." The ultimate end or purpose of creation is as an expression of that love. Intelligent beings are created with the very purpose to be united in love with the Godhead. And to be united in love with the Godhead means to love what God loves, or all being. God is "the foundation and fountain of all being and all beauty; from whom all is perfectly derived, and on whom all is most absolutely and perfectly dependent; *of whom,* and *through whom,* and *to whom,* is all being and all perfection; and whose being and beauty is as it were the sum and comprehension of all existence and excellence: much more than the sun is the fountain and summary comprehension of all the light and brightness of the day."[18]

Because Edwards was writing primarily for moral philosophers, he subordinated such theological language to more abstract arguments—the sorts of arguments that only philosophers might love. "True virtue," he said in his primary statement of his thesis, "most essentially consists in benevolence to Being in general." "Or perhaps to speak more accurately," he continued, "it is that consent, propensity and union of heart to Being in general, that is immediately exercised in a general good will."[19] These statements become clearer if seen in their theological framework. True virtue, or universal benevolence, is possible only if one's heart is united to God, who is love and beauty and the source of all love and beauty. Any other loves, absent from this properly highest love, will be love for much less than all that one ought to be loving, and hence contrary to the very purpose for which one was created.

Edwards' central argument to this conclusion was simply an expansion of a distinction, common to the modern moralists, between private interests and benevolence. Hutcheson, for instance, argued "That we have a *moral sense* or determination of our mind, to *approve* every *kind affection* either in our selves or others and all publicly useful actions which we imagined do flow from such affection without our having a view to our *private happiness,* in our appropriation of these actions." So, for instance, all people will instinctively approve when they hear of someone who found a treasure and used it for benevolent purposes. Even people who themselves would use the treasure only for private self-indulgence will share this sentiment of approval of those who use it in the public interest.[20] All Edwards was doing was taking this distinction between private interests and public benevolence and pressing it to its conclusion if one considered the entire universe.

Much of what was lauded as true virtue, Edwards pointed out, was no more than private interests writ large. People universally admired, for instance, familial love. Yet love for one's family, however admirable in itself, was still quite evidently an expression of private rather than public benevolence. Families often are very selfish with respect to other families. Other wider loves, such as for community or nation, were only larger illustrations of the same principle. Such loves were indeed admirable within their limited contexts, but not ultimately virtuous in the sense of promoting universal benevolence. "Hence," wrote Edwards, "among the Romans love to their country was the highest virtue: though this affection of theirs, so much extolled among them, was employed as it were for the destruction of the rest of the world of mankind." The general principle that followed was simple: "The larger the number is that private affection extends to, the more apt men are, through the narrowness of their sight, to mistake it for true virtue; because then the private system appears to have more of the image of the universal system."[21]

Benevolence within such private systems is so widely admired, said Edwards, because it partakes of "secondary beauty." "As a few notes in a tune," he explained, "taken only by themselves, and in their relation to one another, may be harmonious; which, when considered with respect to all the notes in the tune, or the entire series of sounds they are connected with, many be very discordant and disagreeable."[22] Humans naturally admire the harmonies of benevolence on a purely human scale. The more complete the harmonies, the more they admire them. Yet if such benevolences, however attractive in themselves, are out of tune with the great symphony of God's love that animates the universe, they are ultimately discordant, rather than truly beautiful.

Like the other moral philosophers, Edwards believed that humans had an inbuilt moral faculty. Yet he saw it not as a reliable subjective sensibility so much as a rational ability to approve of proportion and harmony, as one might appreciate the proportions of a triangle or the harmonies of a melody. For instance, natural conscience most characteristically involves a sense of justice, or an appreciation of the harmony of acts and their appropriate consequences. All normal people have a sense of desert with respect to themselves, and they can develop a sense of justice for others by imagining themselves in other's places. Conscience tells people when they are out of harmony with their own best judgments or acting inconsistently with what they would approve in others.[23]

This natural moral faculty is in fact, said Edwards, of great value for regulating society. Although the ultimately limited expressions of natural benevolence or its approval of acts of justice are not *true* virtue, they have "a true *negative* moral goodness in them." "By 'negative' moral goodness," Edwards explained, "I mean the negation or absence of true moral evil."[24] So Edwards could heartily endorse all acts of benevolence, compassion, justice, and the like, whether by individuals or governments, which limited vice. These were expressions of "common grace," or gifts that God bestowed on all humanity. It was consistent with this view, for instance, that Edwards strongly supported the British military, even though he was appalled by the impiety and lax morals of most of its members. They were being used by God to restrain evil.

At the same time that Edwards granted the value of "true *negative* moral goodness," or of the "virtues" of a limited purely human system of morality, he also insisted that nothing can be *true* virtue when the benevolence is not first of all benevolence to God or to most of the being in the universe. "Such a private affection, detached from general benevolence and independent on it, as the case may be, will be *against* general benevolence, or of a contrary tendency; and will set a person *against* general existence, and make him the enemy to it." The reason for this sharp dichotomy is that one's private affections, apart from God, no matter how much extended to family, community, or nation, will inevitably be one's highest loyalty, above loyalty to God or to Being in general. "For he that is influenced by private affection, not subordinate to regard to Being in general, sets up its particular or limited object *above* Being in general; and this most naturally tends to enmity against the latter. . . . Even as the setting up another prince as supreme in any kingdom, distinct from the lawful sovereign, naturally tends to enmity against the lawful sovereign."[25]

True love, Edwards pointed out, is to identify our interest with that of others.[26] What makes others happy makes us happy. In an essentially interpersonal universe persons are either united to or divided from each other by their affections. One's love can either be confined to some limited set of created persons and things, or it can be first of all love to the Creator which will entail love to all being. Characteristically, Edwards was insisting that the only important question in life is whether one is united to God or in rebellion against God. If united with God (which for Edwards was always an ongoing process), then one will learn to love all that God loves—which includes benevolence and justice toward others. God's happiness will be our happiness.

True virtue is ultimately distinguished from its imitators by motive or disposition. This crucial point needs to be underscored because it reflects Edwards' overall vision of a personal universe and affective religion. True virtue grows out of a disposition to true love. True love is the widest possible affection for persons and all that is good (being) in the universe. It is doing good for its own sake—for its beauty. Merely natural "virtue," which superficially may look very similar, is ultimately motivated by humans' natural inclinations to love themselves and their own kind.[27]

In *The Nature of True Virtue*—an intellectual gem by any standard—

Edwards was challenging the project that dominated Western thought, and eventually much of world thought, for the next two centuries. The grand ideal of that hopeful era was that humans would find it possible to establish on scientific principles a universal system of morality that would bring to an end the destructive conflicts that had plagued human history. Only after the first half of the twentieth century, when the clashes of such ideals had led to the bloodiest era in history and threatened to annihilate humanity, did much of the faith in that project collapse, even though there were no clear alternatives to put in its place.

Edwards' recognition of the vast importance of the assumptions that lay behind such efforts and his insight into their faults arose not because he was so far ahead of his time, but rather because his rigorous Calvinism—and his position in a distant province—put him in a position to critically scrutinize his own era. His theological commitments alerted him to the momentous implications of trends that were already formidable in Britain when he first came onto the intellectual scene and which during his lifetime advanced rapidly even in New England. Edwards was a thoroughly eighteenth-century figure who used many of the categories and assumptions of his era to criticize its trends. Although he may have underestimated the short-term benefits of the emerging culture, he had genuine insight into the emptiness of its highest hopes.

# CHAPTER 29

# The Unfinished Masterworks

As Edwards set off for Princeton in January 1758 he had to resign himself to the reality that it might be God's will that he not finish the two "great works" he had described in his letters to the college trustees. But at only fifty-four years old, he was certainly going to try. There was much to make him believe that these works were within God's purposes. Such comprehensive treatises, he was convinced, could be bulwarks in the battles against fashionable infidelity.

Much of the work was already done. The wagon that carried his essentials to Princeton probably contained boxes in which his massive notebooks were carefully wrapped—notes on Scripture, typology, miscellanies, sermons, and much that he could hardly do without. These notebooks would fill many thousands of pages when published (a process that has taken two and a half centuries). Some of the "Miscellanies" were small treatises in themselves and were sufficiently complete to be published in nineteenth-century collections of his works under such topics as "Evidences of Christianity" (with subtopics on prophesies, miracles, the future state, Scripture, faith and reason, moral government, "Mahometanism," "the Jewish Nation," "Mysteries of Scripture, "Deity of Christ," "God's Moral Government," "Endless Punishment," "Divine Decrees," "Satisfaction for Sin," "Faith," "Perseverance of the Saints," "Angels," "the Devil," and "Heaven"). Doubtless he was referring to some of these items when he told the Princeton trustees, "I have also many other things in hand, in some of which I have made great progress."[1]

The mystery, however, to which we do not have a complete answer, is what the two other masterworks would have looked like. He referred to each as a "great work" and surely thought of these complementary volumes as the capstone of his career, works that would tie together in a comprehensive way some of the most important themes in his thought.

## The Other "Great Work": The Harmony of the Old and New Testaments

In Edwards' account of these works, by far the most attention is given to his "History of the Work of Redemption," which he described so intriguingly as something that would have been revolutionary, "a body of divinity in an entire new method." Nevertheless, Edwards told the Princeton trustees that his heart was also set on another "great work," "The Harmony of the Old and New Testaments." He had "done much toward" this work and may have intended to publish it first. He had at least five hundred pages of it already drafted and a lifetime of daily biblical study to provide a ready base for the rest.[2]

We might think of Edwards' unfinished works as analogous to the two great works that J. S. Bach did live long enough to finish in the 1740s, the *B-Minor Mass* and the *Art of the Fugue*. In each of these works Bach drew on a lifetime of achievement for one great summation. The subject of the *B-Minor Mass* is, of course, the same as that of "The History of Redemption," although Bach was following a conventional mass format. In Bach's music one can readily find sensibilities regarding the glory of God, Christ's death and resurrection, the work of the Holy Spirit, and much else in Christian doctrine that would have resonated with the affections of the American theologian. The *Art of the Fugue*, in contrast, represents the Baroque scientist at work, attempting "an exploration in depth of the contrapuntal possibilities inherent in a single musical subject."[3] Edwards' "Harmony" may be seen as a similar sort of technical work of a Baroque scientist, attempting the most elaborate explorations of the variations on a theme essential to the theologian's art.

Edwards may have wanted to complete the "Harmony" first because of the paramount importance of Scripture for everything else in his thought. In his daily life and work, biblical study had a priority for Edwards that is difficult for a biographer to convey. It was an activity, like prayer or family interactions, that was so habitual that it gets obscured in accounts of more unique events and works that frame the narrative from day to day and year to year. Yet all these are constantly present.

The difference between Edwards' biblical study and most of his other daily routines is the immense record he left of his work on Scripture. "I had, then, and at other times," he wrote in his "Personal Narrative" of his maturing as a Christian, "the greatest delight in the holy Scriptures, of any book whatever." Throughout his life, he combined that delight with discipline.[4] Much of his work is found in entries in four large notebooks called "Notes on Scripture," kept throughout his career and now published in well over five hundred pages. Another very large collection of commentaries is found in his "Blank Bible," or "Miscellaneous Observations on Scripture," which was a small printed Bible with interleaved pages for notes. From 1730 to 1758 Edwards made perhaps ten thousand entries, or an average of more than one entry for every weekday, in this collection alone. Meanwhile he produced well over a thousand sermons, all of which contained at least some brief exegetical work. Further, in most of his published works, he included exegetical sections, and some of these were extensive. Over half of *The End for Which God Created the World* and more than a third of *Original Sin*, for instance, consisted of expositions of Scripture. In addition was all that he had "done much toward" in drafting his proposed great "Harmony of the Old and New Testaments."[5] Everything else rested on Scripture, which was one of his great passions.

When Edwards studied Scripture, he did not simply sit in his study with the Bible and try to discern its meanings. Rather, he worked directly within a tradition of interpretation. He surrounded himself with standard commentaries, such as those of Matthew Poole (1624–79), Matthew Henry (1662–1714), Moses Lowman (1680–1752), Philip Doddridge (1702–51), and others, and he was always on the lookout for more. When he declared a teaching to be "biblical," he was doing so within the frameworks provided not only by earlier Reformed theologians but also by this commentarial tradition. For instance, the typological interpretations that were so central to his reading of Scripture reflected a long heritage. And one can find many of his prophetic and millennial interpretations anticipated in Lowman and other works. At the same time, Edwards regarded Scripture alone as truly authoritative, so earlier interpreters could be revised. The project of understanding Scripture's true meanings was an ongoing progressive enterprise to which Edwards hoped to contribute.[6]

Edwards explained to the Nassau Hall trustees that his "Harmony" would be "in three parts." The first would be a comprehensive compilation of the prophecies of the Messiah and of their fulfillment. This would demonstrate "the universal, precise, and admirable correspondence between predictions and events." On this topic he had nearly three hundred neatly written notebook folio pages, complete with tables and indexes.[7] The second part of the three-part harmony was to be on "the types of the Messiah." This would display evidences of Old Testament persons and events as "being intended as representations of the great things of the gospel of Christ." Edwards had also already drafted this part of the work in a notebook during the 1740s and had revised it, probably late in his Stockbridge years.[8] His great-grandson Sereno Dwight first published the "Types of the Messiah" among Edwards' *Works,* and it is some one hundred thirty pages as published in the Yale edition. The "third and great part" of the intended work apparently was mostly yet to come. It was to demonstrate "the harmony of the Old and New Testament, as to doctrine and practice." If Edwards had more than one notebook on this topic, it has not survived.[9]

The surviving parts of Edwards' "Harmony" tell us much about his view of Scripture in addition to pointing to the centrality it had for his thought and life. Most prominently, they reveal how acutely concerned he was to defend traditional views of the Bible from attack. Since the late seventeenth century modern biblical criticism had been emerging as an important means for progressive intellectuals to free themselves from Protestant dogmatism. In an era of ecclesiastical establishments, when much of intellectual and political life was tied to the church, questions of biblical authority had immense implications for other areas of thought and society. Many of the secular dimensions of the Enlightenment depended on displacing biblical accounts of history and human nature. It is not surprising, then, that Edwards spent vast amounts of time preparing to answer biblical critics.

The attacks, which were already common when Edwards came on the scene, arose along several fronts. John Locke, for instance, who had written extensive biblical commentaries himself, had argued that reason should stand as a judge of what to believe in Scripture. Various late seventeenth- and early eighteenth-century writers likewise asserted the priority of reason in questioning biblical accounts of the miracles and Christian claims concerning the fulfillment of Old Testament prophecies. Others, following the lead of Thomas Hobbes, questioned the Mosaic authorship of the Pentateuch and the historical accuracy of other biblical accounts. Much of this skepticism was canonized in Pierre Bayle's massive *Dictionaire historique et critique* (1697–1702), the product of the son of a French Reformed pastor. The influential *Dictionary,* which included much ridicule of biblical claims, was updated and published in an English edition (1734–41). Many British writers entered the debates over the Bible's reliability, and Edwards addressed much of his biblical study to those disputes. He read everything he could get his hands on and cited scores of such sources in his notebooks.[10]

The crucial issue was the widely popular idea that reason should be the judge of revelation. "Multitudes of free thinkers," he argued in his "Controversies" notebook, "deceive themselves through the ambiguous or equivocal use of the word REASON." Their "blunder" was in not making a proper distinction between two uses of "reason." "Sometimes by the word *reason,*" he observed, "is intended the same as *argument* or evidence . . . as when we say we should believe nothing without reason or contrary to reason . . . or against evidence." That legitimate use of reason as an essential tool should be distinguished from making the unjustified claim that reason should be the "highest rule" in judging Scripture. The latter would be to speak as though "evidence and divine revelation [were] entirely distinct, implying that divine revelation is not of the nature of evidence or argument." It would illegitimately enthrone "reasonable opinions" that humans arrived at on their own as necessarily higher than what they could learn from special revelation. That would be like jumping from the fact that the eye is a necessary tool for seeing to claiming that it is the "highest rule" for seeing and then refusing to believe the novelties that one sees in the best microscope or telescope.

Those who set up reason as the "highest rule" often disparaged biblical accounts of miracles as being contrary to reason. In such cases they were improperly excluding one important type of evidence: reliable testimony. To illustrate, said Edwards, suppose you have long known a man of "the soundest judgement and the highest integrity" who brings back from a trip eyewitness accounts of "some strange phenomena or occurrences" that you would not have believed otherwise. It would be unreasonable to reject his accounts as "not agreeable to REASON." That would be judging his claims by making one's previous "reasonable opinions" one's highest rule but not taking into account the reasonableness of believing such a man's testimony.[11]

It was "contrary to all rules of common sense," Edwards argued in a late "Miscellany," to reject specific teachings of Scripture as "unreasonable" while ignoring its overall character. Referring specifically to the Deist Matthew Tindal's notorious *Christianity as Old as Creation* (1730), which attacked many biblical claims as contrary to teachings of nature and reason, Edwards pointed out that people commonly accepted many seemingly unreasonable propositions because they followed from some larger rational principle. Drawing on the principles of "common sense" philosophy, Edwards noted that "numberless truths are known only by consequence from the general proposition that the testimony of our senses may be depended on." Or the same could be said of reliable knowledge that depended on memory or the testimony of others. "Thus," said Edwards, "there are many things that I am told concerning the effects of electricity, magnetism etc. and many things that are recorded in the Philosophical Transactions of the Royal Society, which I have never seen, and are very mysterious." If such things were well attested, their mysteriousness "is no manner of objection against my belief of the accounts, because from what I have observed and do know, such a mysteriousness is no other than is to be expected in a particular and exact observation of nature."

As in nature, so even more in Scripture, one should expect mysteries that by themselves would seem contrary to reason. Here Edwards was following the line of argument best known in Bishop Joseph Butler's *Analogy of Religion* (1736), which maintained that the difficulties and mysteries attending acceptance of Scripture are no greater than those attending acceptance of well-accredited laws of nature. "Difficulties and incomprehensible mysteries," wrote Edwards, "are reasonably to be expected in a declaration from God, of the precise truth as he knows it, in matters of a spiritual nature."

Inevitably God would have to deal in mysteries in a revelation that concerned matters beyond human comprehension, such as the nature of human souls, the relation of time to eternity, how a perfect God might permit evil, and much else. Equally complex were the mysteries of God's grand moral system, particularly in dealing with evil and "the most extreme calamities, in which it had been involved by the malice and subtly of the chief and most crafty of all God enemies." God in his "unsearchable and absolutely infinite wisdom" pursued "his deepest scheme, by which mainly the grand design of the universal, incomprehensibly complicated system of all his operations, and the infinite series of his administrations, is most happily completely and gloriously attained." Surely in revealing this humanly incomprehensible scheme in a "large book, consisting of a vast variety of parts" and genres, "all connected together; all united in one grand drift & design," we should expect many particulars that we do not understand.

A premise of all Edwards' theology—that humans must face the stark implications of the infinite differences between a perfectly good eternal God who governs the immense universe and his finite imperfect creatures—led him to his firm conviction that special revelation provided the only hope to know God's ways. Further, it led him to expect that such a revelation must involve mysteries beyond human comprehension. Some subjects, such as eternity, or the soul surviving without the body, or many other aspects of spiritual reality, were so much beyond human experience as to be like colors to a blind person. One might accept explanations about such things on the basis of good testimony and consistency with other experience, yet ultimately they would remain mysteries.[12]

All the controversial doctrines that he defended were teachings he held simply because he was sure they were taught in Scripture. God's sovereignty in choosing those whom to save, the imputation of Adam's sin to the whole race, the unacceptability in God's eyes of even the best natural virtue, the chasm between the regenerate and the unregenerate, the eternity of punishment for sin, and much else were biblical teachings one might not dare ignore, however mysterious or unreasonable they might seem. Edwards spent much intellectual energy arguing that these revealed doctrines were reasonable, or at least not *necessarily* unreasonable, and that therefore they could be consistent with the moral government of a benevolent deity.

In that concern—to justify the ways of God to man—Edwards was akin to the progressive philosopher-theologians of his age, yet he radically differed from most of his contemporaries in that he was not willing to judge God by eighteenth-century standards of moral law. God, for Edwards, was not to be understood as something like the most virtuous of all humans. Rather, because Edwards took so seriously the immensity of the gap between the ways of the infinite and eternal God and the limits of human understanding, he was willing to make the best of the biblical accounts, as counterintuitive as they might sometimes seem. Upon rigorous examination, he consistently claimed, those accounts could be proved more consistent with reason and experience than any alternatives, even if deep mysteries remained.

Edwards regarded Scripture as like God's works in creation. Each was "a system" and "the voice of God to intelligent creatures." Each pointed to the mysteries of God's "unsearchable wisdom." Yet each was also intended to be a guide to rational creatures.[13]

Viewing Scripture as designed by God to reveal, Edwards dismissed objections from modern critics who questioned Calvinist interpretations on the grounds that ancient meanings might be different from modern readings. "They say the ancient figures of speech are exceeding diverse from ours, and that we in this distant age can't judge at all of the true force of expressions used so long ago but by skill in antiquity, and being versed in ancient history, and critically skilled in ancient languages." Nonsense, said Edwards. Such critics fail to consider "that the Scriptures are written for us in these ages, on whom the ends of the world are come, yea were designed chiefly for the latter age of the world, in which they shall have their chief and, comparatively, almost all their effect." So God could not have been planning that one had to be an expert in ancient languages and history in order to understand the essential meaning of the Scriptures. Rather "they were written for God's people in these ages, when at least ninety-nine out of an hundred must be supposed incapable of such [expert] knowledge."[14]

Nonetheless Edwards studied ancient languages and history as avidly as he studied everything else. He kept a notebook titled "Hebrew Idiom," in which he made lists of Hebrew words as he studied Scripture in the original. He offered Hebrew as the one language he might teach at Nassau Hall as a way of honing his own skills. He copied passages from authorities on ancient history into his notebooks. Further, he would have yielded to no one in his conviction that common people should be guided by a learned clergy. Yet he could not believe that God would have revealed Scripture in a manner that it could be interpreted by scholars only. "It is to be considered that this [Scripture] is given for the rule of all ages; and not only of the most learned, and accurate, and penetrating critics, and men of vast inquiry and skill in antiquity." If the essentials of Scripture were that difficult to understand, "how unequal and unfit is the provision that is made! How improper to answer the end designed!" Almost as though he anticipated the age of hermeneutics he continued: "If men will take subterfuge in pretences of a vast alteration of phrase, through diversity of ages and nations, what may not men hide themselves from under such a pretence! No words will hold and secure them. It is not in the nature of words to do it."[15]

Edwards tried to view Scripture from God's perspective, as intricately designed luminously to reveal the great end of creation, God's redemptive love. God had built into Scripture, as he had into nature and the rest of history, elaborate harmonies all resolved in the grand theme of Christ's love. Hence at the center of the three-part "Harmony of the Old and New Testaments" were Edwards' typological studies of how numerous Old Testament people and events pointed to Christ. All reality was of one Christological piece. "I am not ashamed to own," Edwards wrote in his "Types Notebook," "that I believe that the whole universe, heaven and earth, air and seas, and the divine constitution and history of the holy Scriptures, be full of images of divine things, as full as a language is of words; and that the multitudes of those things that I have mentioned are but a very small part of what is really intended to be signified and typified by these things."[16]

By amassing the evidence for the typological and Christological harmonies of Scripture, Edwards was countering the skeptical critics by fighting the battle on a higher ground. Edwards was simply not allowing the premise of the critics that Scripture was to be interpreted like other books. If Scripture were in some sense a revelation of God—as most of the critics still allowed—then its design must contain excellencies that far transcended the vicissitudes of the historical circumstances or the limits of the language in which it happened to be revealed. Understanding the ancient language and history would be a valuable enterprise, just as the natural philosophers should profitably study natural phenomena. Yet to regard such historical study as the key to understanding the meaning of Scripture would be as great a mistake as to regard the laws of physics as the key to understanding the meaning of creation.

Scripture could not be defended, in Edwards' view, if one conceded the critics' claim that it was most essentially a product of human history and then tried to fend off this or that claim about its accuracy. Edwards *was* concerned to answer particular criticisms. For instance, his longest entry (nearly fifty pages in the Yale edition) in his "Notes on Scripture" was on "Whether Moses wrote the Pentateuch," a topic on which he had written well over a hundred pages in an additional notebook. Yet he kept the argument on his own ground. The Mosaic authorship fit with all the other evidence within Scripture itself. Essentially he argued in numerous ways for the internal consistency of Scripture. In the same vein, he showed how one could reconcile the four seemingly disparate Gospel accounts of the events surrounding Christ's resurrection.[17]

Much of his proposed "Harmony" would likewise demonstrate internal biblical consistency. He would assemble overwhelming evidence of prophecies that had been fulfilled, of types that pointed to Christ, and of doctrines that agreed in the two testaments. Edwards assumed that if the Bible was a special revelation of God, it must have a consistent design. Once one recognized Scripture's Christocentric redemptive purpose, then all the evidence could be decisively shown to be part of a harmonious whole.[18]

The question of biblical authority, Edwards was convinced, could not be entirely settled apart from the work of the Holy Spirit, who would give people the spiritual sense intuitively to see the beauty of the truths it contained. Scripture had excellencies that were there for anyone to see. Yet sin could "blind the mind," just as "natural temper oftentimes very much blinds us in secular affairs; as when our natural temper is melancholy or jealous, cowardly, and the like."[19] Only if the Holy Spirit removed the blinders of sin would one immediately see the luminous truths of Scripture and it superiority to all other books.

Arguments might occasionally convince someone of the high probability of historical claims, but seldom to the extent that one would stake one's life on them alone. Any historical claim could be questioned. As he had written in *Religious Affections:* "How do I know when these histories were written? Learned men tell me these histories were so and so attested in the day of them; but how do I know that there were such attestations then?" Although external evidences of the truths of Scripture were important, they were not sufficient without the internal evidence of "a sight of its glory." Only with the spiritual sense that provided direct experience of the divine excellencies revealed in Scripture would one "run the venture of the loss of all things, and of enduring the most exquisite and long-continued torments, and to trample the world under foot, and count all things but dung, for Christ." If Christians had to wait until scholars answered all the objections to the truth of Scripture, "miserable is the condition of the Houssatunnuck Indians, and others, who have lately manifested a desire to be instructed in Christianity; if they can come at no evidence of the truth of Christianity, sufficient to induce 'em to sell all for Christ, in no other way but this."[20]

Edwards' eagerness to complete his *Harmony* reveals the urgency he felt in demonstrating how the Bible was a unique God-given book. He had spent a lifetime collecting arguments on that topic and seems to have spent increasing time in his later years answering specific critical challenges to biblical history. At the same time, characteristically, he did not see the question of biblical authority as settled simply by arguments. Ultimately, the truth of Scripture, like God's redemptive work itself, would be recognized only through the illumination of the Holy Spirit. A scholar could show the way especially by pointing out the Bible's marvelous harmonies and also by clearing the path of some critical obstacles. Nonetheless, seeing the perfections of God's revelation was of one piece with being given the eyes to see God's redemptive work in Christ.

## "A Body of Divinity in an Entire New Method"

As Edwards traveled to Princeton, he especially hoped that his presidency would not too long delay his projected "History of the Work of Redemption." He envisioned it as the culmination of his life's work, a universal extension of the themes to be explored in "The Harmony of the Old and New Testament." All history, prophecy, types, and doctrine would center in Christ's redemptive work. Clearly the "History of the Work of Redemption" would contain some basic material from the 1739 sermon series of the same title. Yet, just as certainly, it would have been far more ambitious than that largely narrative work. What did Edwards have in mind when he described this magnum opus in such revolutionary terms?

We must begin with a close look at his account in his letter to the Princeton trustees. "I have had on my mind and heart," he wrote, "(which I long ago began, not with any view to publication) a great work, which I call *A History of the Work of Redemption,* a body of divinity in an entire new method, being thrown into the form of an history, considering the affair of Christian theology, as the whole of it, in each part, stands in reference to the great work of redemption by Jesus Christ; which I suppose is to be the grand design of all God's designs, and the *summum* and *ultimum* of all the divine operations and decrees; particularly considering all parts in the grand scheme in their historical order."

After summarizing the events of the history of redemption, he described his approach. "This history will be carried on," he proposed, "with regard to all three worlds, heaven, earth and hell: considering the connected, successive events and alterations, in each so far as the Scriptures give any light; introducing all parts of divinity in that order which is most scriptural and most natural: which is a method which appears to me the most beautiful and entertaining, wherein every divine doctrine, will appear to greatest advantage in the brightest light, in the most striking manner showing the admirable contexture and harmony of the whole."[21]

Throughout his career Edwards had aspired to write some great masterwork that would vindicate the faith against its detractors. In 1729 or 1730 he outlined "A Rational Account of the Main Doctrines of the Christian Religion Attempted." That design had been conventionally systematic.[22] Sometime after preaching the *History of Redemption* sermons in 1739, however, Edwards abandoned this earlier plan and conceived of his revolutionary "entire new method."

What would this comprehensive theology "thrown into form of an history" have looked like? What was the significance he saw in this "entire new method"? The completed masterwork would have included much of the straightforward historical narrative from the *History of Redemption* sermons, but that core narrative would have been surrounded and interspersed with theological discourses on every subject "in that order which is most scriptural and natural." In effect, Edwards would have been attempting to combine the "History of Redemption" with the "Rational Account," except that on a number of polemical topics he could refer readers to his more extended theological arguments in other published treatises and dissertations.

We can get some glimpses of what Edwards had in mind from three notebooks on the "History of Redemption," which he began in Stockbridge around 1755 and were among the things he was working on when he received the call from Princeton. The extraordinary physical quality of the first of these notebooks is worth pausing to notice. It is 123 numbered pages of all sorts of scraps of paper of various shapes and sizes, sewn with a cover. Early pages are printer's proof from Joseph Bellamy's *True Religion Delineated*. Edwards then seems to have rummaged for any other paper he could get his hands on. A number of pages are copies of the official proclamation in Northampton of the marriage of Sarah Jr. and Elihu Parsons. One page is a draft of a prayer for ailing Deacon Clark. Others are from drafts of letters or a title page from his farewell sermon. Many of the irregularly shaped pages seem to be trimmings from the fans that his family was producing for sale in Boston.[23]

This first notebook contains a number of outlines that Edwards was sketching out. One of the last entries reads: "Title. The Nature and History of Redemption," a title that better suggested the work's dual character. He also indicated how he hoped to handle the awkward task of interspersing the historical narrative with theological expositions. "Let there be large MAR-GINAL NOTES at the bottom of the page," he wrote, "and the reflections and doctrinal observations and disputations [?] be in them as I go along. Let rational proofs be offered of such things wherein this scheme differs from that of the Arminians."

The cosmic history would begin with a substantial theological prologue. One note says, "FIRST PART concerning THE CAUSE of the work of Redemption and of the TRINITY. That the holiness of God consists in love to himself." This exposition would have again rung the changes on the great theme he had sounded in *The End for Which God Created the World* but would have added some of the trinitarian motifs that he omitted from the earlier work.[24] After that topic and perhaps some reflections on the decrees of God, he would have presented an account of the rebellion and fall of the angels and then the fall of the human race. "One general observation at the beginning" he reminded himself, was that "this affair was always carried on between Christ and Satan."

As to the history of earth, which was still to be the centerpiece of the

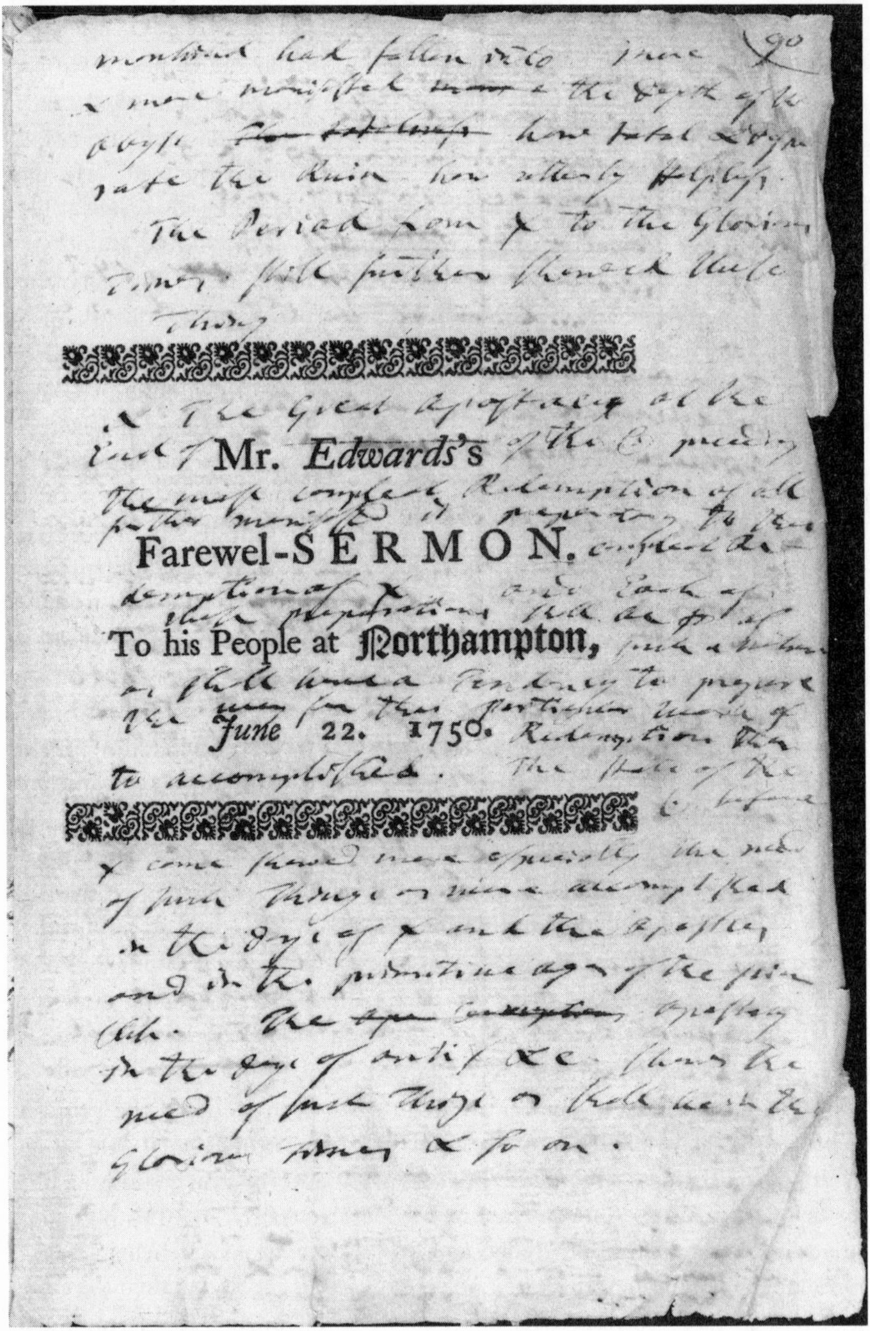
Mr. Edwards's
Farewel-SERMON.
To his People at Northampton,
June 22. 1750.

From Edwards' "History of Redemption" notebook, which reused his Farewell Sermon for paper work, there were three great periods, with Christ at the center. First was the creation to the birth of Christ. The second was Christ's life and death. The third extended from Christ's death to the end and consummation of all things. Each of these periods would be "preparation for the next." He also planned to divide Christian history into seven periods. These were: "1. The work begun at pentecost. 2. Destruction of Jerusalem. 3. Destruction of heathenish empire in Constantine's time. 4. The Reformation. 5. The fall of the Antichrist. 6. The overthrow of Judaism, Mahometanism, and heathenism through the world. 7. The consummation at the end of the world." In the final era, the millennium, all people "shall be brought into the church of Christ and it looks as if they would generally be true Christians. There will be a new world. The multitude of people will be such then that all the number [of] the preceding world of inhabitants are nothing to it."

Although this scenario was optimistic in the long run, Edwards now had projected two major eras that yet had to come prior to the millennium, indicating that he expected some hard times in the future. "'Tis reasonable to suppose," he wrote, "that just BEFORE THE END OF THE WORLD the wickedness of the world should be at its greatest height." He also noted a number of biblical images he should use in explaining how God acted in history: "1. the revolutions of the wheels of a chariot, 2. the erecting a great building, 3. the growing of a tree, 4. the flowing of a great river in its innumerable branches, 5. carrying on a war." These images depicted different dimensions of history. The chariot wheels suggested cycles but also progress. The building was more progressive, one era built on the next. The tree was organic. The great river suggested an immense pattern that could be seen as connected only from a great height. The warfare indicated the central theme of conflict. Taken together, the picture is of history as organically related progressive cycles, in which God's method of effecting redemptive progress is, as at the cross, through conflict and suffering.[25]

A major feature of his history would have been to detail the primary conflict of the present era, that with the Antichrist of Rome. One of his "History of Redemption" notebooks included information mainly on the history of the papacy—a topic he found endlessly engrossing. His notebook on setbacks to papal power, or the "drying up of the rivers of Babylon," might have supplemented such accounts.

In the seven eras into which Edwards divided history since the coming of Christ, the next to last (the one following the defeat of Antichrist) was "the overthrow of Judaism, Mahometanism, and heathenism through the world."

Edwards had an intense interest in other religions, gathered all the information he could about them, and made numerous entries on them in his various notebooks. His time in Stockbridge, when he was daily confronted with Indian culture, only increased his interest in the topic. Much of his concern was to answer the Deist challenge to the particularity of Christianity. Was there not some truth in all religions drawn from the universal light of nature? For his answer Edwards drew on a tradition of *prisca theological*, that whatever elements of truth were found in other religions were remnants of earlier revelations to the ancestors of all people, as indicated in Genesis. Although reason could provide some limited knowledge of the truth, true religion could only be based on the revelation that pointed to Christ. Moreover, while other religions, such as those of the ancient Greeks or the Chinese, might produce some relatively good people, true virtue arose only from true religion. Most fundamentally, he viewed other religions, such as Islam, as false and pernicious.[26]

Each era of history ended with the triumph of Christ over Satan, so Edwards would have included the hopeful dimensions of the present era as well. Presumably he still would have emphasized the theme of periodic awakenings, so prominent in the Northampton sermons. In the notes though, drafted when he had turned his ministry so largely to writing, it is his hopes for intellectual triumph that are most striking. "The true philosophy of Isaac Newton," he wrote, is "one thing to make way for the universal setting up of Christ's kingdom." He also noted "THE SETTLEMENT OF NEW-ENGLAND as one great thing done to prepare the way for the introducing of the Gospel light into the American world—being a colony chiefly enlightened etc. where colleges are erected, etc." He added: "The erecting New Jersey college"—a revealing comment that suggests his estimate of the practical relationship between his grand historical vision and his subsequent call to Princeton. Learning, specifically the true philosophy of Isaac Newton as refracted through the theology of early New England, was not only the source of true "enlightenment," it was a key to the kingdom.

Yet the particulars of what Edwards was projecting were not as important as the firmness with which he was challenging another of the most formidable trends of the age. Most broadly put, leading eighteenth-century thinkers were severing history from divinity. Throughout the ages peoples of most cultures had seen divine agency as the main force in shaping historical events. In Christendom, as in the biblical world, history had always been a source of revelation and a locus of divine action. Even Protestants, who demystified the world in some ways, understood history as first of all a providential order in which God was the primary actor.

By Edwards' time Western thinkers were increasingly looking on history as driven by self-actuating powers. The study of history might yield some moral principles, many leading thinkers assumed, and these principles in turn might be ascribed to a distant "Creator" or to "Providence." Such terms allowed for equivocation on the divine role or at least its separation from specific biblical precedents. A few brave skeptics even dared to drop the divine from the equation altogether. It was not simply coincidence, therefore, that in the very decades Edwards was determining that history must provide the framework for his theology, both Voltaire and Hume turned to historical studies. Even though Edwards never saw *Siècle de Louis XIV* (1751) or the *History of England* (1754–1762), he shared with the two greatest skeptics of his age the conviction that many of the questions of modernity would be settled on the battlefields of historical understanding.[27]

At the same time, the great challenge of the era to traditional Christian faith was the assertion that historical claims were insufficient to establish universal religious truths. That was one of the grand arguments of the Deists. The accidental truths of history, they said, could yield only partial knowledge from local perspectives. Only reason could yield universal truths on which the whole race could rely.

When Edwards answered Matthew Tindal's *Christianity as Old as Creation* (1730) by pointing out that there were many truths in electricity, magnetism, and the like that were well attested and accepted as "reasonable" even though their first principles were not understood, he was defending history, when it is a well-attested experience, as a source of truth. Deists were operating with too narrow a definition of reason if they excluded historical knowledge from rational sources of religious truth. As he put the matter more bluntly to his Northampton congregation, "To object against a book's being divine merely because it is historical is a silly objection."[28]

It would be another generation until such objections were canonized in Western thought in Gotthold Ephraim Lessing's famous aphorism, "Accidental truths of history can never become the proof of necessary truths of reason," but that fateful handwriting was already on the wall.[29] Edwards recognized that if history were allowed to stand as an autonomous authority, then Christian revelation would be dissolved into cultural relativism. Deism would be the only reasonable option. If one allowed the undemonstrated premise that history was essentially accidental, then there would be no way to get from the historical claims of Scripture, across what became known as "Lessing's ditch," to essential theological truths. The new history started out with human experience, on the wrong side of the ditch. For Edwards the only place to start in trying to understand history was—as for everything else— with the triune God. History, like nature, was the language of God's redemptive love.

Edwards was so enamored with seeing the eternal significance of human history that his "entire new method" not only ran counter to the Deist trends of the age but also departed from the traditional deductive-logical method that had long shaped Christian theology itself. Although Edwards yielded to no one in utilizing rational deductive arguments, he was determined that a true view of universal reason must include *historical* knowledge as well as deductive. Hence his grand comprehensive theology would not imitate the forms used by Thomas Aquinas or even the Reformed systematizers such as Francis Turretin or Peter van Mastricht, but rather it would imitate Scripture itself, by being "thrown into the form of a history."[30] History, instead of being an encumbrance to the logic of theology, was of the essence for understanding God's ways.

Edwards was also addressing the ancient theological conundrum: How could God be perfect and complete in himself and yet be involved in history? Would not creation and involvement with its imperfections necessarily be a diminishment of God's perfections? Drawing on his Augustinian heritage, much of Edwards' deepest theological insight involved explaining how history was an extension of the intertrinitarian love. For Edwards, history was an expression of the "external existence" of divine glory. Like language, history was of God, but not identical to God. The triune God had an essential disposition to communicate his love to other persons, so he created creatures whose purpose was to return his love yet who had the power to resist.[31] That rebellious resistance led to even higher expression of God's love as God the Son took on the guilt of sin and God's wrath and died for absolutely undeserving human rebels.[32] In Edwards' favorite image, Christ is the bridegroom who is bringing his bride, the church, into a creature's fullest possible experience of trinitarian love.

History, according to Edwards, was in essence the communication of God's redemptive love in Christ. The history of redemption was the very purpose of creation.[33] Nothing in human history had significance on its own, any more than created nature had significance on its own. Christ's saving love was the center of all history and defined its meaning. Human events took on significance only as they related to God's redemptive action in bringing increasing numbers of humans into the light of that love or as they illustrated human blindness in joining Satan's warfare against all that was good.

CHAPTER 30

## The Transitory and the Enduring

Edwards spent his whole life preparing to die. As he often reminded his congregations, those who were sitting comfortably one Sabbath might be in the grave by the next. For those who spurned God's Spirit, life was like walking on a rotten canvas, and at any moment they might suddenly find themselves plunged simply by the weight of their sins into everlasting hell. By contrast, if one had experienced God's transforming work, then death would be a release in which one was borne upward to see Christ's glory. Holding to that hope, Edwards worked constantly to cultivate gratitude, praise, worship, and dependence on his Savior. Whatever his failings, he attempted every day to see Christ's love in all things, to walk according to God's precepts, and to give up attachments to worldly pleasures in anticipation of that closer spiritual union that death would bring.

In an era when life was precarious and when on every return home one had to hope one would not be greeted by a new grave, the Edwards family had been remarkably free from such sorrows. At the beginning of 1758, when Edwards accepted the position at Princeton, both his parents were still living. His father, though failing, was in his eighty-ninth year. His mother was in fine health and would live until 1771, dying at age ninety-eight. Jonathan's own health was seldom robust, but it may have been better than usual. His memorialist in the *New York Mercury* remarked that "in middle life he appeared emaciated (I had almost said mortified) by intense study and hard labour," implying perhaps that he had appeared less so in his later years.[1] At age fifty-four, still hoping to complete his massive writing projects, Edwards could easily imagine the possibility of living into the 1770s or 1780s, even if he was always prepared for less.

In January 1758, soon after the council in Stockbridge confirmed that he should accept the call to Nassau Hall, Edwards set out for Princeton. He left Sarah and his children in Stockbridge, as seventeen-year-old Susannah later reported, "as affectionately, as if he should not come again." When he was outside the house, he turned and declared, "I commit you to God."[2] He arrived in Princeton amid some fanfare. Not long afterward, he received the news that his father had died, on January 27. A great force in his life was finally gone, though the power of the personality had faded some years earlier.

In Princeton, Jonathan immediately assumed his duties. He preached several Sundays in the college chapel. The trustees met on February 16 and officially installed him as president. Since Nassau Hall had three tutors under Edwards, his immediate tasks were light. The one thing he did was to set some questions in divinity for the senior class. When he met with them, according to Samuel Hopkins, "they found so much entertainment and profit by it, especially by the light and instruction Mr. Edwards communicated . . . that they spoke of it with the greatest satisfaction and wonder."[3]

Just one year earlier Nassau Hall had been inaugurated by the remarkable awakening that had lasted until the boys went home in the spring. The death of President Burr just before the fall commencement of the school year must have been a great sobering event for the returning boys, and likely many of them were still in a reverential mood as they welcomed their renowned new president. Ezra Stiles later remarked of Edwards' presidency, "The volatility of 100 youth would have disturbed his calm quiet and made him unhappy."[4] Stiles, who presided over Yale College during the Revolutionary era, was probably right. But in the brief time Edwards was at Princeton, he likely saw little of such volatility. Edwards himself, by Hopkins' account, "seemed to enjoy an uncommon degree of the presence of God." He remarked to his daughters that, although he had experienced great apprehensions about taking on the position, he now saw it as a calling he could cheerfully pursue.[5]

Edwards came alone to Princeton but was comfortably situated in the handsome president's home next to the college hall. Sarah was still in Stockbridge, preparing to move the household in the spring, but two daughters were already in Princeton to meet their father and to care for him. Esther was there with her two children, and Lucy had been there since at least the previous spring. Esther presumably still enjoyed some of the glow of her heightened spirituality in the otherwise agonizing months after Aaron Burr's death. Her deepened piety was a source of the greatest satisfaction to her father, and their mutual joy and comfort in their shared devotion may have increased the sense of the presence of God for each.

A North-West Prospect of Nassau-Hall, with a Front View of the President's House, in New-Jersey.

Nassau Hall and the president's house, where the Burrs and Edwards lived and where Aaron Burr and Edwards died

Jonathan also got to spend some time with his Burr grandchildren. Sally, aged four, could recite prayers and some of Isaac Watts' verses. Aaron Jr. was just turning two. In her final entry of her surviving diary or letters to Sarah Prince, dated September 2, 1757, when Aaron Jr. was just nineteen months, Esther Burr described the future vice president and duelist who killed Alexander Hamilton in terms that sound almost prophetic. "Aaron is a little dirty noisy boy," she wrote, "very different from Sally almost in every respect. He begins to talk a little, is very sly and mischevious. He has more spri[ghtliness] than Sally and most say he is handsomer, but not so good tempered. He is very resolute and requires a good governor to bring him to terms."[6] One might picture the encounters between the strict grandfather and the rambunctious grandson. Edwards may have felt confirmed in his views on original sin.

## Submission

Edwards was concerned for his family's health in Princeton. Smallpox was rampant in the area, and Edwards himself had been closely exposed to it on his trip. Always the scientist, Edwards was a champion of inoculation, one of the few eighteenth-century medical practices proven beneficial. Although inoculation with a mild case of the disease involved some risk, in times of epidemic the procedure substantially improved chances of survival. In 1752 Edwards had urged Aaron Burr, when Burr was contemplating a trip to England and Scotland, "If you can find a skillful, prudent physician, under whose care you can put yourself, you would take the smallpox by inoculation before you go, after properly preparing your body for it, by physic and diet."[7] Burr had not gone abroad nor had he been inoculated. In spring 1757 Esther had received a deep scare when Lucy contracted smallpox and she feared, incorrectly, that Aaron Sr. might have too.[8] Still, Lucy had survived, and none of the family had taken the precaution of inoculation until Jonathan, after much consultation and advice, decided on it. William Shippen, an excellent Philadelphia doctor and a close friend of Nassau Hall, agreed to inoculate the whole family on February 23 and to oversee their recoveries.[9]

At first everything went fine. Some days after the inoculation Edwards was "quite easy and cheerful" about his decision to undergo the inconvenience. Then, while Esther and the children were recovering normally, Edwards contracted smallpox on the roof of his mouth and throat. It soon became impossible for him to swallow the liquids that were considered necessary to prevent a secondary fever. After weeks of fever and starvation ravishing his "feeble frame" he died peacefully on the afternoon of March 22.

When he realized that he would not survive, he called his daughter Lucy, who was attending him, and said (in words she almost immediately wrote down): "Dear Lucy, it seems to me to be the will of God that I must shortly leave you; therefore give my kindest love to my dear wife, and tell her, that the uncommon union, which has so long subsisted between us, has been of such a nature, as I trust is spiritual, and therefore will continue forever: and I hope she will be supported under so great a trial, and submit cheerfully to the will of God. And as to my children, you are now like to be left fatherless, which I hope will be an inducement to you all to seek a Father, who will never fail you. And as to my funeral, I would have it be like Mr. Burr's; and any additional sum of money that might be expected to be laid out that way, I would have it disposed of to charitable uses."[10]

Edwards always chose his words carefully, and "uncommon union" was an expression of the deepest affection, coming from someone for whom the highest relations in the universe were unions of affections among persons. Most important for Jonathan, the union was spiritual and hence eternal. As to the funeral, Samuel Hopkins explained that Burr and Edwards had opposed the custom of "modish funerals" for the famous, "attended with that pomp and cost, by procuring and giving away a great number of costly mourning-scarfs, etc. and the consumption of a great quantity of spirituous liquors." Edwards asked that equivalent sums be instead donated from his estate for care of the poor.[11]

Dr. William Shippen immediately wrote to Sarah assuring her of the peacefulness of his passing. "And never did any mortal man," the doctor consoled, "more fully and clearly evidence the sincerity of all his professions, by one continued, universal, calm, cheerful resignation, and patient submission to the divine will, through every stage of his disease, than he; not so much as one discontented expression, nor the least appearance of murmuring through the whole. And never did any person expire with more perfect freedom from pain;—not so much as one distorted hair—but in the most proper sense of the words, he really fell asleep. Death had certainly lost its sting, as to him."[12]

Although this account was written by a devotee to a bereaved widow in an era when it was conventional to give embellished accounts of how the saintly had "died well," it is also consistent with everything else we know about Edwards.[13] Edwards, despite some evident shortcomings, was a saint according to the highest Reformed spiritual standards to which he aspired. Opponents, of course, viewed him as sanctimonious. Yet all would admit that few people have been so thoroughly disciplined. Far fewer have left so much written evidence that is so thoroughly consistent with a desire to know and to submit to the will of God.[14]

Sarah was ill at the time she received the news in Stockbridge and was able to write only a few lines in comfort to Esther:

O My Very Dear Child,
    What shall I say? A holy and good God has covered us with a dark cloud. Oh that we may kiss the rod [of reproof], and lay our hands on our mouths! The Lord has done it. He has made me adore his goodness, that we had him so long. But my God lives; and he has my heart. Oh what a legacy my husband, and your father, has left us! We are all given to God: and there I am, and love to be.
    Sarah Edwards.[15]

Esther never saw this letter. Less than two weeks after her father's death she was seized with a fever that soon turned severe, produced a violent headache, and then delirium. She died a few days later, on April 7. Apparently the fever was not from the smallpox. Her sister Sally believed it was much like the sudden fever from which Jerusha had died.[16]

Despite knowing that such chastisements were to teach them to depend more on God, family and friends were suffering grievously. The oldest daughter, Sally (Sarah Edwards Parsons), wrote from Stockbridge to her sister Mary Dwight in Northampton, "Sister I hope you are in a much better [way] under these trials than I am." She agonized for Lucy in Princeton and especially for the two orphaned children. Still she hoped that "God's dealings might be sanctified" and that "God grant these corrections may be in covenant love and faithfulness."[17]

What could be the meaning of such chastisements? Back in Northampton, Mary's husband, Timothy Dwight Jr., had been already reflecting on that before learning of the family's second loss. His perspective, shaped by the same conventions as Solomon Stoddard had propounded fifty or seventy-five years earlier, looked most at the public implications. The College of New Jersey had lost as presidents three of the most distinguished leaders on the continent, Jonathan Dickinson, Aaron Burr, and now Jonathan Edwards. The prospects in the war with France still looked bleak. "God seems to have a controversy with this land in general with the College of New Jersey and with us of the bereaved family in particular," wrote young Dwight. "'Tis God's strange works as to us, his calling so many faithful servants from his service here, the pillars of our sinking land seems to portend some strange grievous and heavy judgments to be brought upon us which are only to be prevented by repentance and turning to God which I pray God we may all do and the tokens of his displeasure be averted."[18]

The family members were supposed to fit their personal agonies into the conventions of greater submission to God but, as Esther's sisters knew, that was far easier said than done. One close friend of the family, Sarah Prince of Boston, best expressed the struggle involved. Upon learning that Esther Burr, her most deeply beloved friend, was suddenly taken, she wrote a private lament. It is one of the most poignant reflections in all of colonial literature on the anguish that many must have experienced in trying to place the deepest earthly loves in the expected spiritual context.

Sarah Prince began with a properly pious quotation: "God will have no rival in the heart which he sanctifies for himself." Yet for her, she soon made clear, Esther's love was a rival. "My whole dependence for comfort in this world gone: she was as dear to me as the apple of my eye—she knew and felt all my griefs." This was theological language, usually reserved for Christ. Celebrating Esther's friendship, she went on, "How faithful? How sincere? How open hearted? How Tender how careful how disinterested—And *she was mine.*" Her friend had exemplary virtues. "The mortified humble self-denied lively Christian—generous affable courteous and kind to all—But— she is gone! Fled this world forever. Tired, she longed for rest—dead to this world, she prayed and panted and agonized for a better and with her went almost *the all* in which I had summed up my earthly good."

Where was the spiritual comfort? The emptiness reached to the bottom of Sarah's soul. "My earthly joy is gone! Not only so but my God hides his face! Can't see love in this dispensation! All seems anger yea wrath to me. . . . God points his arrows at me. . . . My judgement is passed over from my God and that he has set me as a mark for his arrows!"

Despite her agonizing doubts, she worked her way to the proper evangelical conclusion. She would be glad to die herself, but even that was not an option since she was not sure of her spiritual state. "O! were I ready," she lamented, "I would gladly welcome the kind summons to follow my dear beloved into the valley of DEATH. Had I the evidence I want of a title to glory, joyfully wou'd quit earth and all that earthly minds admire." She closed with a prayer of desolate resignation. "I want to lay low at the foot of God and resign to him. I choose to live at loose from the world, and live only on him and have done with idols and get prepared. . . . Acquaintance with him, the all *in all*. Lord grant these mercies for thy Son's sake. AMEN."[19]

Had Esther, her sisters, her mother, even Jonathan himself, been able to see Sarah Prince's elegy they would have readily understood and sympathized. They had all been through the same. All had experienced the absence of God in the face of deep sorrow. Some had found wonderful release, even ecstasy, as Esther had after Aaron's death, but even that, as Jonathan warned her, would be followed by "clouds of darkness."[20] All who viewed the world through this lens had often confessed, as Sarah Prince did, that their earthly loves were more powerful than their love to God. Even as they resolved to put away every idol, to subordinate every good love to perfect love, they would find themselves loving the lesser more than the greater.

In the Edwardses' world, the meaning of life was found in intense loves, including earthly loves. Yet as overwhelming as earthly affections might be, they were supposed to have their true value only when subordinated to heavenly and eternal loves. In that proper relationship even the most humble lives and loves radiated with eternal significance. In such eternal perspective death lost its power to take meaning from life. In the face of a devastating loss, however, temporal loves often overwhelmed that perspective. Submission was the only proper response, the great lesson being taught, and ultimately the path to immense comfort. Yet for almost everyone in the Edwards circle, such submission involved heart-wrenching struggles.

Sarah Edwards is remembered as an exemplar of how the saints were to cope with their calamities and was a model her daughters and friends found difficult to emulate. For Sarah the expected attitudes had not come easily either. Her great spiritual ecstasy of the 1740s had grown precisely out of a terrible internal struggle as to whether she was ready to accept God's will. Would she submit to God, she asked herself, even if it would mean losing her children, Jonathan, or even her own life? According to Samuel Hopkins, who long had admired Sarah, "She had long told her intimate friends, that she had, after long struggles and exercises, obtained, by God's grace, an habitual willingness to die herself, or part with any of her most near relatives." Though she grieved deeply at her terrible double loss, still, says Hopkins, "she was quiet and resigned, and had those invisible supports, which enabled her to trust in God with quietness, hope, and humble joy."[21]

We cannot know how much emotional turmoil may have lain beneath Sarah's discipline and exterior calm in accepting such devastation, but it soon took its toll. She also faced immense responsibilities. She determined that she

should take care of her two orphaned grandchildren herself. In September she
traveled to Princeton and then to Philadelphia to pick up the children who
had been staying there. Soon after arriving, she was seized with dysentery.
She died October 2, 1758, aged forty-eight. She was buried next to Jonathan in
Princeton.[22] The family had lost another tower of strength, their fourth sudden loss in a year.[23]

## The Edwards Legacy

It is tempting to speculate what would have happened had Edwards lived as
long as his contemporary Benjamin Franklin, through the Revolutionary era.
How would he have viewed the Revolution? How would he have coped with
such a hotbed of rebellion as Princeton during those heady years, adverse as
he always had been to insubordination to authority? As it happened, one of
his successors as president of Nassau Hall, the Scotsman John Witherspoon,
was the only clergyman to sign the Declaration of Independence. Edwards
surely would not have played that role, but he probably would have found a
religious rationale, as almost all his disciples did, for supporting the Revolutionary cause. Still he would not have been happy to see spiritual concerns
submerged amid the political ardor. In the same vein, we might wonder
whether James Madison, just one of many statesmen trained by Witherspoon
at Princeton, would have been any different with Edwardsean training.
Would Edwards have spoken out against slavery as Samuel Hopkins and
Jonathan Edwards Jr. did? Would Aaron Burr Jr., had he been reared in his
grandparents' household, persevered in his plans to go into the ministry?
Would the Edwardsean spiritual-theological movement, with its mentor
firmly entrenched near the center of the continental culture, have flourished
as a national movement in the Revolutionary era? Would it have changed the
new nation or perhaps even divided the Revolutionaries?

As it turned out, Edwards' death, especially since it was followed so soon
by the onset of the American Revolution, diminished his immediate influence. He did, of course, have a loyal following. Hopkins and Bellamy eventually saw to the publication of *Two Dissertations* and a few of his other
writings. John Erskine oversaw the publication of a number of his works in
Scotland, where Edwards' reputation remained strong. In America, however,
Edwards' impact waned until after the Revolutionary era. President Ezra
Stiles of Yale predicted in 1787 that Edwards' works "in another generation
will pass into as transient notice perhaps scarce above oblivion, and when

posterity occasionally comes across them in the rubbish of libraries, the rare characters who may read and be pleased with them will be looked upon as singular and whimsical."[24]

Stiles, whose own work is dusty on library shelves, underestimated the resiliency and popular support of strict Calvinism. Even in the era of Revolutionary politics, Edwards had a following, especially in Connecticut, and a good reputation among heirs to the New Lights elsewhere. John Adams in his retirement correspondence with Thomas Jefferson claimed that Aaron Burr Jr. "from the single circumstance of his descent" was always ensured of one hundred thousand votes.[25] Though Adams likely exaggerated in order to help explain his own defeat in 1800, he correctly recognized that Edwardseans were a cultural force.

After the French Revolution, when many New Englanders were seeking to recover a distinctive heritage, Edwards' reputation began to soar in some circles. His grandson Timothy Dwight (1752–1817) became president of Yale in 1795 and from there helped spark a long era of zeal for revival and reform that New Englanders eventually called "the Second Great Awakening." Timothy Dwight's protégés, such as Lyman Beecher (1775–1863), the progenitor of the most influential evangelical family of the era, helped expand the Edwardsean heritage from theology and revival into a program for national transformation. Connecticut Yankees, their offspring, and their allies took the lead in settling much of New York State and the upper Midwest. In this new era, Edwards' reputation was a force to be reckoned with. Many of his admirers—the famed revivalist Charles Finney (1792–1875) is the best-known example—modified significant details of his thought. Yet for about half a century from 1800 to 1850, Edwards was the polestar of the most formidable and influential American theology.[26]

Through the Civil War era, Edwards' spiritual offspring infused some significant aspects of American culture with Reformed and evangelical concerns. Much of antebellum collegiate education was shaped by New Englanders with an Edwardsean heritage. "Disinterested benevolence," popularized by Samuel Hopkins as the practical meaning of Edwards' "benevolence to being in general," became a slogan for many evangelists and social reformers. Not only did *The Life of David Brainerd* inspire countless missionaries to lives of self-denial, a similar Edwardsean ideal of sacrificial service was institutionalized in the path-breaking women's school Mount Holyoke Seminary, founded by Mary Lyon in 1837. Mount Holyoke is best remembered for providing one of the first opportunities for American women to achieve educational parity with men, yet at the time it was equally renowned for the number of its graduates who served as foreign missionaries, described by one historian as "nineteenth-century versions of Jerusha Edwards."[27]

By the late nineteenth century, however, rigorous Calvinist theology was in full retreat in most American cultural centers, and Edwards' reputation suffered accordingly. All but a dwindling group of ardent followers jettisoned the particulars of his Calvinist teachings. Oliver Wendell Holmes Sr. entertained his contemporaries with "The Deacon's Masterpiece, or The Wonderful 'One-Hoss Shay'" (1858), which lampooned the dramatic collapse of New England Calvinism. The heirs of Charles Chauncy had finally won a long-standing battle for cultural supremacy. Still, Edwards remained, as Joseph Conforti has put it, "a kind of white whale of American religious history."[28] The relentless rigor of his Calvinism long hovered as a force that could obsess even its enemies. As late as the early twentieth century, Mark Twain was worrying about Edwards. "A resplendent intellect gone mad," he wrote in 1902. In *The Mysterious Stranger* and *Letters from Earth*, Twain was still contending with versions of Edwardsean theology he had first encountered on the Missouri frontier.

Even as specific Calvinist beliefs were being discredited in the cultural mainstream, New Englanders of the later nineteenth century increasingly celebrated Puritanism in American hagiography and iconography as they constructed a heroic heritage that had endowed them with moral fortitude.[29] Anglo-Protestants still hoped to define America's heritage as essentially Protestant, but in an era of growing diversity they substituted morality for theology as the essence of that heritage. Edwards, who had opposed earlier versions of such moralistic trends, might seem difficult to fit into that mold. Nonetheless, he could be presented as someone who exemplified the ruggedness of earlier days and who left a laudable legacy of moral discipline. One famous study, for instance, celebrated Edwards' contribution to the moral character of America through his descendants. The work, published in 1900, contrasted the character and intelligence of 1,200 descendants of one of his most dissolute contemporaries to those of 1,400 of Edwards' heirs. The descendants of Max Jukes, a New York Dutchman whose name the researchers changed to protect the guilty, left a legacy that included more than three hundred "professional paupers," fifty women of ill repute, seven murderers, sixty habitual thieves, and one hundred and thirty other convicted criminals. The Edwards family, by contrast, produced scores of clergymen, thirteen presidents of institutions of higher learning, sixty-five professors, and many other persons of notable achievements.[30]

By the early decades of the twentieth century, however, Puritan bashing had become widely acceptable as a way for progressive Americans to free themselves from Victorian moralism. Edwards was an easy target. This was the era of the invention of American literature as a field of study and the canonization of Holmes' "One-Hoss Shay" and of *Sinners in the Hands of an Angry God.* The latter fixed Edwards in the public mind as simply a hell-fire preacher. Edwards' biographer of this era, Henry Bamford Parkes, writing in the 1920s, was explicit in blaming Edwards and his disciples for much of what was wrong with America. "It is hardly a hyperbole to say," wrote Parkes, "that, if Edwards had never lived, there would be to-day no blue laws, no societies for the suppression of vice, no Volstead act." Parkes found some things to admire in Edwards, but he viewed him mostly as a tragic figure who poured his youthful "pantheistic" insights into the rigid mold of John Calvin's theology. Calvinism, according to Parkes, was based on a "cosmic despot, God," and was "an amazing travesty of . . . Christianity." "If he had thought about it more deeply, he might have become the greatest figure in the history of American thought; he might have altered the whole of the future history of America."[31] Even Ola Winslow's largely sympathetic biography, published in 1940, reflected this progressive tone, regretting that Edwards spoke "through an outworn, dogmatic system" that "needed to be demolished."[32]

Already by the time Winslow was writing, however, the theological and cultural climate was changing and a new Edwards—best characterized as the neo-orthodox Edwards—was emerging. This new trend was signaled in 1932 by the publication of theologian A. C. McGiffert's sympathetic biography and the more explicitly neo-orthodox Joseph Haroutunian's *Piety versus Moralism: The Passing of the New England Theology,* which characterized everything after Edwards as a decline into moralism.[33] H. Richard Niebuhr in a number of influential publications from the 1930s through the 1950s also celebrated what he saw as the essence of Edwards' theology, even while moving far from most of its particulars.[34]

At the same time, and closely related, was the emergence of the scholar's Edwards. Perry Miller contributed immeasurably to this trend with the publication of his intellectual biography in 1949, characterizing Edwards as America's greatest genius and as a profound modern philosopher who happened to use Calvinist categories. Miller thereby created the possibility of "atheists for Edwards." At the same time he enlisted scholars from a wide spectrum of theological or nontheological views to launch the Yale publication of Edwards' *Works*. Since Miller's time Edwards has been a major scholarly industry.[35] Many of the scholars who have worked on Edwards in the recent decades have sympathies to some aspects of his thought, and some have been theologians who have appropriated many aspects of his outlook.[36] Others are scholars simply intrigued by his intellectual power, his cultural influence, or his interconnections with the social and cultural forces of his day.

One of my hopes is that this book may help bridge the gap between the Edwards of the students of American culture and the Edwards of the theologians. Historians of American culture, thought, and literature are primarily concerned to understand Edwards in relation to his time or perhaps to understand his influence in relation to subsequent times. Theologians are concerned to appropriate aspects of Edwards' thought for their own times. As a biographer attempting to understand Edwards first as an eighteenth-century figure, I have been working most directly as a cultural historian. Yet I have been doing this always with an eye on the theological question, taking his thought seriously as part of the larger Christian tradition.

If one has, as I do, theological mentors from across the ages, then it is valuable to realize that their insights on spiritual matters come framed by their particular personal and cultural circumstances. My belief is that one of the uses of being an historian, particularly if one is part of a community of faith, is to help persons of such communities better understand what they and their community might appropriate from the great mentors of the past and what is extraneous and nonessential. Everything is, of course, time-bound and there is a danger for us who are so shaped by historical consciousness to dismiss every authority from the past once we have understood the peculiarities of the historical, personal, or theoretical factors that shaped its outlook. A far more profitable approach is to employ historical consciousness for developing more *discriminating* assessments of the wisdom of the past. The point of historical scholarship should not be, as it so often is today, simply to take things apart, to destroy myths, or to say that what looks simple is really quite complex. It should also be to help people see how to put things back together again. We need to use history for the guidance it offers, learning from great figures in the past—both in their brilliance and in their shortcomings. Otherwise we are stuck with only the wisdom of the present.

My hope, then, is that this account will be helpful to others, as it has been to myself, in thinking about what might be best appropriated from Edwards.

I realize, of course, that the criteria various readers employ in making such judgments will vary hugely according to points of view. So I can not speak as though my judgments should represent the consensus of what all right-thinking people should think about Edwards. What I can do, however, is attempt to provide as full an account as is feasible of Edwards' own theological and spiritual concerns, including both his most profound insights and his peculiarities. By attempting first to understand these in terms of his own eighteenth-century outlook, we can better see the assumptions and characteristic patterns of his thought. Once we have identified such assumptions and patterns and see how they differ from our own, we are in a better position to respond to the particulars of his thought.

How Edwards may be appropriated, then, should not be an all-or-nothing question. Almost everyone will find in Edwards some theological views, biblical interpretations, or eighteenth-century social attitudes that were based on assumptions that seem antiquated beyond recovery. Some readers' lists of these will be long, others short. In either case, such views need not distract us from whatever else might be of merit in his outlook.

At the least, we should be open to regarding other dimensions of Edwards' thought that grow out of assumptions different from our own as challenging our own assumptions and conclusions. We will never learn anything from sages of the past unless we get over our naive assumption that the most recently popular modes of thought are the best. Edwards had a wonderful ability to carry the implications of widely held Christian assumptions to their logical conclusions, sometimes with unnerving results. Not everyone will agree with all his premises and so will not be compelled by all his conclusions. Nevertheless, anyone might do well to contemplate Edwards' view of reality and its awesome implications.

Among other things, Edwards challenges the commonsense view of our culture that the material world is the "real" world. Edwards' universe is essentially a universe of personal relationships. Reality is a communication of affections, ultimately of God's love and creatures' responses. Material things are transitory and ephemeral. Their meanings are found in their relation to the loves at the center of reality. Although they are transitory, they can have great eternal significance if they are recognized for what they are, signs or expressions of God's love.

Our culture's intellectual life is largely preoccupied with observing material and social forces that lead to change. Typically we think we have found the best explanation of an event when we can see some of the cultural or psychological dynamics that contribute to its development. This biography itself reflects some of those characteristic concerns. Edwards, while not indifferent to such matters, would challenge us to see the universe as most essentially God's unceasing action.

Living as he did at a time and in a place when there was a substantial cultural overlap between the late medieval–Reformation outlook, preserved largely intact in Edwards' Puritan heritage, and the world of the scientific revolution and the Enlightenment, Edwards saw the immense challenges to a rigorous God-centeredness in the modern era. Sharing with his theological predecessors the premise that God was the creator and sustainer of reality, Edwards applied that premise to a vastly expanded Newtonian universe. The theological tradition that Edwards inherited included the belief that God must be eternal and unchanging—a doctrine that led some toward a view of the deity as static and impassive in his perfections. Edwards instead emphasized all those dimensions of his trinitarian heritage that helped to understand God as the active creator and sustainer of an inconceivably immense universe. The universe of Newton was one of constant action and changing relationships, and Edwards' conception of God was matched to that dynamic universe. Lockean and early modern idealist philosophies, as Edwards appropriated them, added the notion that created reality was not independent of the minds that engage it. That reinforced the point that the universe most essentially consisted of personal relationships. All of creation was a system of powers to communicate. Creation was most essentially a means by which the creator-sustainer communicated his holiness, beauty, and redemptive love to other persons.

Edwards thus addressed one of the greatest mysteries facing traditional theism in the post-Newtonian universe: how can the creator of such an unimaginably vast universe be in intimate communication with creatures so infinitely inferior to himself? How can it be that God hears their prayers and responds by caring not only about their eternal souls but even about the details of their temporal lives? To answer such questions one would have to face more starkly than is usually done the immensity of the distance between God and humans and between God's ways and our understandings. At the same time, Edwards insisted, if God is meaningfully related to us, God must be intimately involved with the governance of all the universe in its detail. Further, God must be governing it in some way that also grants the maximum possible autonomy to created beings. Whether Edwards, or anyone else, adequately explains how this mystery may be resolved is a matter of some debate.

Yet Edwards' solution—a post-Newtonian statement of classic Augustinian themes—can be breathtaking. God's trinitarian essence is love. God's purpose in creating a universe in which sin is permitted must be to communicate that love to creatures. The highest or most beautiful love is sacrificial love for the undeserving. Those—ultimately the vast majority of humans—who are given eyes to see that ineffable beauty will be enthralled by it. They will see the beauty of a universe in which unsentimental love triumphs over real evil. They will not be able to view Christ's love dispassionately but rather will respond to it with their deepest affections. Truly seeing such good, they will have no choice but to love it. Glimpsing such love, they will be drawn away from their preoccupations with the gratifications of their most immediate sensations. They will be drawn from their self-centered universes. Seeing the beauty of the redemptive love of Christ as the true center of reality, they will love God and all that he has created.

# Genealogical Table of Edwards' Relatives

## Edwards' Extended Family

(Selected members who played important roles in his kinship connections. Many siblings of these figures are omitted.)

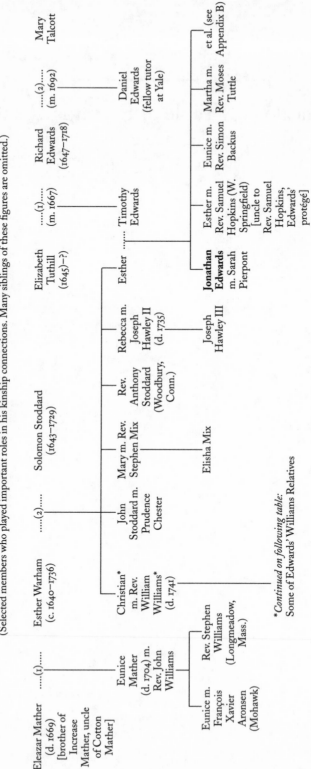

*Continued on following table:
Some of Edwards' Williams Relatives

## Some of Edwards' Williams Relatives
*(Continued from previous table)*

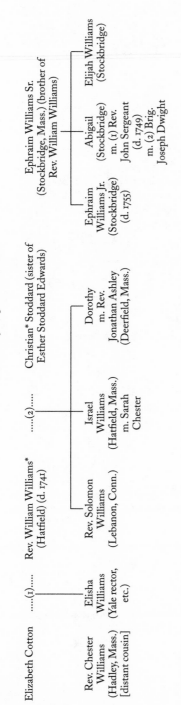

Elizabeth Cotton .....(1)..... Rev. William Williams* (Hatfield) (d. 1741) .....(2)..... Christian* Stoddard (sister of Esther Stoddard Edwards)

Ephraim Williams Sr. (Stockbridge, Mass.) (brother of Rev. William Williams)

Elisha Williams (Yale rector, etc.)

Rev. Chester Williams (Hadley, Mass.) [distant cousin]

Rev. Solomon Williams (Lebanon, Conn.)

Israel Williams (Hatfield, Mass.) m. Sarah Chester

Dorothy m. Rev. Jonathan Ashley (Deerfield, Mass.)

Ephraim Williams Jr. (Stockbridge) (d. 1755)

Abigail (Stockbridge) m. (1) Rev. John Sergeant (d. 1749) m. (2) Brig. Joseph Dwight

Elijah Williams (Stockbridge)

The Williams-Stoddard clan intermarried with other influential Connecticut River Valley families, including the Chesters, Ashleys, and Partridges. See Kevin Michael Sweeney, "River Gods and Related Minor Deities: The Williams Family and the Connecticut River Valley, 1637–1790" (Ph.D. diss., Yale University, 1986), 733–55.

# Edwards' Sisters

The following is from Kenneth P. Minkema, "Hannah and Her Sisters: Sisterhood, Courtship, and Marriage in the Edwards Family in the Early Eighteenth Century" *New England Historical Register* 146 (January 1992): 35.

Children of TIMOTHY EDWARDS (1669–1758) and ESTHER STODDARD EDWARDS (1672–1770)

ESTHER, 1695–1766, m. Rev. Samuel Hopkins of West Springfield, Mass., 1727

ELIZABETH, 1697–1733, m. Jabez Huntington of Windham, Conn., 1724

ANNE, 1699–1790, m. John Ellsworth of East Windsor, Conn., 1734

MARY, 1701–76, cared for aged Stoddard grandparents in Northampton and parents in East Windsor

*JONATHAN, 1703–58, m. SARAH PIERPONT, 1727*

EUNICE, 1705–88, m. Rev. Simon Backus of Newington, Conn., 1729

ABIGAIL, 1707–64, m. Rev. William Metcalf of Lebanon, Conn., 1737

JERUSHA, 1710–29

HANNAH, 1713–73, m. Seth Wetmore of Middletown, Conn., 1746

LUCY, 1715–36

MARTHA, 1718–94, m. Rev. Moses Tuttle of Granville, Mass., 1746

# Edwards' Immediate Family, from His Family Bible

The following is a transcription from Edwards' entries, in his own hand, in his family Bible, from *Works of Jonathan Edwards*, ed. Hickman, cclxxiv.

Jonathan Edwards, son of Timothy and Esther Edwards of Windsor in Connecticut. I was born October 5, 1703.

I was ordained at Northampton, Feb. 15, 1727.

I was married to Miss Sarah Pierrepont, July 28, 1727.

My wife was born Jan. 9, 1710.

My daughter Sarah was born on a sabbath day, between 2 and 3 o'clock in the afternoon, Aug. 25, 1728.

My daughter Jerusha was born on a sabbath day, towards the conclusion of the afternoon exercise, April 26, 1730.

My daughter Esther was born on a sabbath day, between 9 and 10 o'clock in the forenoon, Feb. 13, 1732.

My daughter Mary was born April 7th, 1734, being sabbath day, the sun being about an hour and a half high, in the morning.

My daughter Lucy was born on Tuesday, the last day of Aug. 1736, between 2 and 3 o'clock in the morning.

My son Timothy was born on Tuesday, July 25, 1738, between 6 and 7 o'clock in the morning.

My daughter Susannah was born on Friday, June 20, 1740, at about 3 in the morning.

All the family above named had the measles, at the latter end of the year 1740.

My daughter Eunice was born on Monday morning, May 9 1743, about half an hour after midnight, and was baptized the sabbath following.

My son Jonathan was born on a sabbath-day night, May 26, 1745, between 9 and 10 o'clock, and was baptized the sabbath following.

My daughter Jerusha died on a sabbath day, Feb. 14, 1747, about 5 o'clock in the morning, aged 17.

My daughter Elizabeth was born on Wednesday, May 6, 1747, between 10 and 11 o'clock at night, and was baptized the sabbath following.

My son Pierrepont was born on a sabbath-day night, April 8, 1750, between 8 and 9 o'clock; and was baptized the sabbath following.

I was dismissed from my pastoral relation to the first church in Northampton, June 22d, 1750.

My daughter Sarah was married to Mr. Elihu Parsons, June 11, 1750

My daughter Mary was married to Timothy Dwight, Esq. of Northampton, Nov. 8, 1750.

My daughter Esther was married to the Rev. Aaron Burr of Newark, June 29, 1752.

Mr. Burr aforesaid, President of the New Jersey college, died at Princeton, Sept. 24, 1757, of the nervous fever. Mr. Burr was born Jan. 4, 1715.

I was properly initiated President of New Jersey college, by taking the previous oaths, Feb. 16, 1758.

# Notes

## Note on Sources

*Works* refers to *The Works of Jonathan Edwards*, 22 volumes to date (New Haven: Yale University Press, 1957–), Perry Miller, John E. Smith, Harry S. Stout, general editors, and will be cited simply by volume number (e.g., *Works*, 18) and page.

The short form Diary refers to Edwards' diary, which can be found in *Works*, 16: 759–89, and in other editions, cited by dates of entries only.

Dwight, *Life*, refers to Sereno Dwight's *Life of President Edwards*, vol. 1 of *The Works of President Edwards, with a Memoir of His Life*, 10 vols., ed. Sereno Dwight (New York, 1829).

Hopkins, *Life*, refers to Samuel Hopkins, *The Life and Character of the Late Reverend Mr. Jonathan Edwards* (Boston, 1765). Page numbers will be cited from the more accessible reprint in David Levin, ed., *Jonathan Edwards: A Profile* (New York: Hill and Wang, 1969), except for Hopkins' appendices on Esther Edwards Burr and Sarah Pierpont Edwards, which are available only in the original.

*Reader* refers to *A Jonathan Edwards Reader*, ed., John E. Smith, Harry S. Stout, and Kenneth P. Minkema (New Haven: Yale University Press, 1995).

Citations for works found in the various two-volume editions of Edwards' works are from *The Works of Jonathan Edwards*, ed. Edward Hickman, 2 vols. (London, 1865) and are cited as *Works of Jonathan Edwards*, ed. Hickman.

Unpublished sermons are from The Works of Jonathan Edwards transcriptions and will be cited by Scripture text and date. The originals are found in the Beinecke Rare Book and Manuscript Library, Yale University.

*Sibley's Harvard Graduates* is used as the short citation for *Biographical Sketches of Those Who Attended Harvard College*, ed. Clifford K. Shipton, 14 vols., vols. 4–17 (Boston: Massachusetts Historical Society, 1933–75), successor to *Biographical Sketches of Graduates of Harvard College*, ed. John Langdon Sibley, 3 vols., vols. 1–3 (Boston, 1873–85). It will be cited by volume number and name of biographical subject.

Beinecke is the Beinecke Rare Book and Manuscript Library, Yale University, New Haven, Connecticut.

ANTS is the Franklin Trask Library, Andover Newton Theological School, Newton Centre, Massachusetts.

# Introduction

1. On Edwards' *Life of Brainerd,* see Joseph A. Conforti, *Jonathan Edwards, Religious Tradition, and American Culture* (Chapel Hill: University of North Carolina Press, 1995), 62–86. On recent scholarly and popular interest in Edwards, see Leigh E. Schmidt, "The Edwards Revival: Or, The Public Consequences of Exceedingly Careful Scholarship," review essay, *William and Mary Quarterly* 58, no. 2 (April 2001): 480–86. Schmidt refers to the work of a Baptist pastor, John Piper, *God's Passion for His Glory: Living the Vision of Jonathan Edwards* (Wheaton, Ill.: Crossway Books, 1998), as a "Wheaton bestseller." *God's Passion for His Glory* includes the entire text of Edwards' formidable *The End for Which God Created the World.* In February 2002, Amazon.com listed *God's Passion for His Glory* as its bestselling book by or about Edwards, followed by another book by Piper and *Life of Brainerd.*

2. Gordon S. Wood provides a wonderful sense of the implications of the hierarchism of pre-Revolutionary eighteenth-century America in *The Radicalism of the American Revolution* (New York: Knopf, 1992), 11–92. This paragraph is mostly a summary of some of his points. Jon Butler, *Becoming America: The Revolution before 1776* (Cambridge: Harvard University Press, 2000), argues to the contrary that colonial America was already modern.

3. Edwards occasionally used "Calvinistic" as a description of his theology, but he seldom cited or mentioned John Calvin by name. Edwards' theology was refracted mostly through Reformed, or Calvinistic, writers of the seventeenth or early eighteenth centuries, especially Puritan and Scottish Presbyterian writers from Great Britain and Reformed theologians from the continent. The entire movement is frequently referred to as "Reformed," and I often use that term because it more clearly suggests that the movement had evolved beyond direct dependence on Calvin himself and was diverse and changing in many ways, even while it had various creeds that defined widely used standards of Reformed "orthodoxy."

4. Edwards, like his Reformed and Puritan predecessors was "biblicist" in the sense of rigorously attempting to follow the Reformation principle of "the Bible alone" as an authority, particularly in matters pertaining to theology and the church. Many of their beliefs and practices were determined because, according to their scholarship, such were taught in Scripture. At the same time, every biblicist interprets the Bible through a tradition of interpretation, and Edwards' biblicism was refracted through the scholarship of his Calvinistic heritage. When I refer to his views as being "biblical" or being "refracted through the lens of Scripture," etc., I am, of course, taking into account that his understandings were shaped largely by traditions of Reformed interpretations.

5. Thomas J. Haskell, *Objectivity Is Not Neutrality: Explanatory Schemes in History* (Baltimore: Johns Hopkins University Press, 1998).

6. Harriet Beecher Stowe, *The Minister's Wooing* (1859). Cf. her *Oldtown Folks* (1869) for similar themes.

7. See Barbara B. Oberg and Harry S. Stout, eds., *Benjamin Franklin, Jonathan Edwards, and the Representation of American Culture* (New York: Oxford University Press, 1993).

## CHAPTER 1. A Time to Be Born

1. James R. Trumbull, *History of Northampton, Massachusetts, from Its Settlement in 1654,* 2 vols. (Northampton, Mass., 1898, 1902), 1: 559 and passim. This account is heavily

indebted to the much more nuanced account in Paul Lucas, "'The Death of the Prophet Lamented': The Legacy of Solomon Stoddard," in *Jonathan Edwards's Writings: Text, Context, Interpretation,* ed. Stephen J. Stein (Bloomington: Indiana University Press, 1996), 69–84.

2. Lucas, "Death of a Prophet," 261, notes, "the notion of the 'pope' of the Connecticut Valley is a myth." Lucas shows that Stoddard at least did not succeed in controlling the valley or even all of Northampton. That is contrary to Perry Miller's depiction, *Jonathan Edwards* (New York: Meridan, 1959 [1949]), 9, Nonetheless, there were at least intimations that aspects of Stoddard's proposals to strengthen of the role of the clergy in church government smacked of popery. [Cotton and Increase Mather] in "A Defense of the Evangelical Churches," published as an introduction to John Quick, *The Young Man's Claim Unto the Sacrament of the Lord's Supper* (Boston, 1700), 28–29, in a general reference to Stoddard's views, quote an English source that says that for the minister to assume the sole power of admitting to the sacrament "'is to make himself a *Congregational* POPE.'"

3. Coffman, *Stoddard,* 7. Coffman, whose work has to be taken with caution, cites no source, but his observation is consistent with what else we know of Stoddard. Cf. Perry Miller, "Solomon Stoddard, 1643–1729," *Harvard Theological Review* 34 (1941): 277–320, esp. 281–82, although Miller's accounts also must be taken with caution.

4. From a letter of July 29, 1701, published in Solomon Stoddard, *An Answer to Some Cases of Conscience Respecting the Country* (Boston, 1722), 7.

5. Westminster Assembly, *The Confession of Faith; the Larger and Shorter Catechisms* (London, 1860), 207–15, 302–3.

6. Cf. James Axtell, *The Invasion Within: The Contest of Cultures in Colonial North America* (New York: Oxford University Press, 1985).

7. Solomon Stoddard, *The Way for a People to Live Long in the Land That God Hath Given Them* (Boston, 1703), 15–16, 17, 19.

8. John Demos, *The Unredeemed Captive: A Family Story from Early America* (New York: Knopf, 1994), 11–12.

9. Letter from Solomon Stoddard to Governor Joseph Dudley, October 22, 1703, *New England Historical and Genealogical Register* (1870), 269–70. Given the cruelty of warfare on both sides since King Philip's War, what seems more remarkable than that Stoddard was asking for dogs was that he, or the people to whom he was writing, felt the need to justify his request in terms of criteria for just warfare. After all, they were already hunting Indians with guns and had offered bounties for scalps. Stoddard wrote: "If the Indians were as other people are, and did manage their war fairly after the manner of other nations, it might be looked upon as inhumane to pursue them in such a manner. But they are to be looked upon as thieves and murderers, they do acts of hostility, without proclaiming war. They don't appear openly in the field to bid us battle, they use those cruelly that fall into their hands. They act like wolves and are to be dealt with all as wolves."

The Massachusetts General Court authorized money for the training and use of dogs in 1708. After that they were regularly used, especially when Solomon's son, Colonel John Stoddard was in command of western Massachusetts. In 1747, for instance, Gideon Lyman, one of Jonathan Edwards' parishioners, received the large sum of £250 for purchasing dogs. Trumbull, *Northampton,* 1: 477n. The Stoddards were also leading advocates of Indian missions which, whatever else they may have been, were affirmations of Indians' essential humanity and of a desire to live at peace.

10. Eleazar Mather (1637–69) was a brother of Increase Mather (1639–1723), the most influential Boston pastor of his era.

11. Trumbull, *Northampton*, 1: 479–80.

12. John Williams, *The Redeemed Captive, Returning to Zion* (Boston, 1707), 3–24. Demos, *Unredeemed Captive*, 12–39.

13. Demos, *Unredeemed Captive*, draws on a large literature in providing helpful perspectives on the Indians' views of the episode.

14. Esther Stoddard to Esther Edwards, ca. 1705, from *Proceedings of the Dedication of the Memorial Gateway to Jonathan Edwards at the Burying Ground South Windsor, 25 June, 1929* (New Haven: privately printed, 1929), 18–20. This letter is described as "preserved" by "a descendant of the family." It is dated "Dec. 7, 1703." Many of the details in the letter indicate that it is authentic. However, the date can not be correct because it is before the attack on Deerfield. Esther Stoddard begins by thanking God for her daughter's "safe delivery," which whoever supplied or misread the date took to refer to Jonathan's birth. I am dating it from Esther Stoddard's report of "the news of my grandson, Stephen Williams, arriving safe with some other captives in Boston." Stephen arrived in Boston on November 2, 1705. Likely the letter was dated Dec. 7, 1705 and was misread as 1703. Jonathan's next sister, appropriately named Eunice, was born August 20, 1705.

15. Williams, *Redeemed Captive*, passim. Demos, *Unredeemed Captive*, 46–51, 95.

16. Kenneth Pieter Minkema, "The Edwardses: A Ministerial Family in Eighteenth-Century New England" (Ph.D. diss., University of Connecticut, 1988), 59–63, based on Timothy Edwards, diary, Beinecke.

17. Timothy to Esther Edwards, August 7, 1711, ANTS, as transcribed in Ola Winslow, *Jonathan Edwards, 1703–1758: A Biography* (New York: Macmillan, 1940), 40–41. Dwight, *Life*, 17, that all the daughters learned Latin but seems to base that on Timothy's letter.

18. Kenneth P. Minkema, "The Authorship of 'The Soul,'" *Yale University Library Gazette* 65 (October 1990): 26–32, attributes it to the eldest sister, Esther, who apparently wrote it shortly before her marriage to the Reverend Samuel Hopkins of Hartford in 1727.

19. Minkema, "Edwardses," 155–57.

20. Kenneth P. Minkema, "Hannah and Her Sisters: Sisterhood, Courtship, and Marriage in the Edwards Family in the Early Eighteenth Century," *New England Historical and Genealogical Register* 146 (January 1992): 46, re Hannah, from Hannah Edwards, Journal, Beinecke, and 47, re Martha, quoted from John Stoughton, *Windsor Farmes: A Glimpse of an Old Parish* (Hartford, Conn., 1883), 67–68. Timothy's remark regarding Martha is often attributed to Jonathan, concerning one of his daughters, Sarah. Minkema's article is the best resource on the Edwards sisters, concerning whom he also lists basic biographical information, 35.

21. Dwight, *Life*, 16, 18.

22. Timothy Edwards to Esther Edwards, August 7, 1711, as transcribed in Dwight, *Life*, 14.

23. Samuel Sewall, *The Selling of Joseph: A Memorial* [Boston, 1700], Sidney Kaplan, ed. (Amherst: University Massachusetts Press, 1969). Kaplan's notes, 27–67, provide a summary of the early debates. Lorenzo Johnston Greene, *The Negro in Colonial New England, 1620–1776* (New York: Columbia University Press, 1942), is still a valuable overview. On Cotton Mather's views, see his *The Negro Christianized* (Boston, 1706), and

Kenneth Silverman, *The Life and Times of Cotton Mather* (New York: Columbia University Press, 1985), 263–65. When Timothy Edwards was at Harvard he sat under the preaching of Increase and Cotton Mather, was later educated by their protégé, Peletiah Glover, had many of Cotton Mather's books in his library, and seems to have shared many of the Mathers' views. In 1717 he applied to Cotton Mather, distantly related through the Stoddard-Mather connection, for a loan. Minkema, "Edwardses," 26–29, 124, 645–65.

24. John Wesley, "On Obedience to Parents," in *The Works of the Rev. John Wesley*, 16 vols. (London, 1809–12), 7: 103, quoted in Philip Greven, *The Protestant Temperament: Patterns of Child-Rearing, Religious Experience, and the Self in Early America* (New York: Knopf, 1977), 35. Greven, 31–36, uses the Wesleys and Jonathan and Sarah Edwards and their daughter Esther as principal eighteenth-century examples of "breaking the will." Greven is often criticized for generalizing too broadly about "evangelical," including Puritan, childrearing practices and for depicting them as harsher than they usually were. Nonetheless, since the next two generations of Edwardses subscribed to "breaking the will," it seem probable that so did Jonathan's parents. All three generations, however, tempered strict disciplines with warm loving affection. For one example of "moderate" childrearing practices among evangelical Puritan contemporary of the elder Edwards, see Judith S. Graham, *Puritan Family Life: The Diary of Samuel Sewall* (Boston: Northeastern University Press, 2000).

25. Timothy Edwards to Esther Edwards, August 7, 1711, Winslow, *Edwards*, 41–42.

26. Timothy Edwards to Esther Edwards, August 11, 1711, in Dwight, *Life*, 14. Timothy's letters to his family are strikingly more filled with open expressions of familial affections than are Jonathan's, who was personally more reserved.

27. Timothy Edwards, sermon on Isaiah 54:5, June 28, 1730, pp. 1 and 3, Connecticut Historical Society, Hartford, Conn., quoted in Minkema, "Edwardses," 153–54.

28. Timothy Edwards, "Some Things Written for My Own Use and Comfort," 1, 45–60, ANTS, quoted in Minkema, "Edwardses," 22, 144–45. Cf. Greven, *Protestant Temperament*, 53.

29. This estimate and what follows is indebted to Minkema's very valuable account of Timothy in "Edwardses."

30. Divorce proceedings quoted in Winslow, *Edwards*, 18, and see 18–20. Winslow speculates that the "erratic strain" persisted in some of the later Edwards family, including Aaron Burr Jr. See also Minkema, "Edwardses," 25.

31. Richard Edwards, Connecticut Archives, "Crimes, Misdemeanors, and Divorces," vol. 3, item 235, Connecticut State Library, quoted in Minkema, "Edwardses," 27.

32. Minkema, "Edwardses," 23, 28.

33. Ibid., 26–30 has the best account of this.

34. Ibid., 148.

CHAPTER 2. The Overwhelming Question

1. *Faithful Narrative of the Surprising Work of God, Works*, 4: 154.

2. "Personal Narrative" (ca. 1740), *Works*, 16: 790–91. Edwards' narrative was apparently written for the edification of one of his protégés, perhaps his future son-in-law Aaron Burr. See George S. Claghorn, "Introduction" to "Personal Writings," *Works*, 16: 747.

3. Timothy Edwards, sermon on Acts 16:29–30, pp. 11–12, 1695, Washington University Library, quoted in Kenneth Minkema, "The Edwardses: A Ministerial Family in Eighteenth-Century New England" (Ph.D. diss., University of Connecticut, 1988), 82. See 80–95, re Timothy Edwards' views on steps toward salvation. Other information on Timothy Edwards is drawn from Minkema, passim.

4. Charles Hambrick-Stowe, *The Practice of Piety: Puritan Devotional Disciplines in Seventeenth-Century New England* (Chapel Hill: University of North Carolina Press, 1982), 219–21. See ibid., 219–41, on Puritan preparation for death.

5. Exercises on endpapers of Timothy Edwards, sermon on I Kings 2:2, February 7, 1744/45, Connecticut Historical Society, Hartford, quoted in Minkema, "Edwardses," 155. Cf. ibid., 153–55 re the Edwardses' home life.

6. Hambrick-Stowe, *Practice of Piety*, 219. Erik R. Seeman, *Pious Persuasions: Laity and Clergy in Eighteenth-Century New England* (Baltimore: Johns Hopkins University Press, 1999), 52–53, finds that eighteenth-century New England laypeople almost always believed their own dead children were in heaven. Seeman understates, however, the degree to which the clergy, specifically Jonathan Edwards himself, allowed room for salvation of infants. As Gerald McDermott, *Jonathan Edwards Confronts the Gods: Christian Theology, Enlightenment Religion, and Non-Christian Faiths* (New York: Oxford University Press, 2000), 137, points out, Edwards says in his Miscellany no. 78 that infants may be regenerate already at birth.

7. Kenneth P. Minkema, "The East Windsor Conversion Relations, 1700–1725," *Connecticut Historical Society Bulletin* 51 (winter 1986): 30.

8. Timothy Edwards, sermon on Acts 16:29–30, p. 5, quoted in Minkema, "Edwardses," 83. The influential Puritan writer William Perkins (1558–1602) referred to this stage as "legal terrors" brought on by a sense of total unworthiness to keep God's law. See Norman Pettit, *The Heart Prepared: Grace and Conversion in Puritan Spiritual Life* (New Haven: Yale University Press, 1966), esp. 65; Edmund S. Morgan, *Visible Saints: The History of a Puritan Idea* (New York: New York University Press, 1963), esp. 68; and Janice Knight, *Orthodoxies in Massachusetts: Rereading American Puritanism* (Cambridge: Harvard University Press, 1994). These accounts deal with the varieties of Puritan opinions, a point Knight emphasizes. On Timothy Edwards' insistence on this step, see chapter 3.

9. Minkema, "East Windsor Relations," 13, summarizes the usual paradigm as involving four steps. I have compressed the second, "realization of God's anger against sin" (when one backslid into sin) and "a recognition that God has every right to condemn sinners to hell." The steps were not exact. Cf. idem, 3–66. "Light" and "glorious change" are from Timothy Edwards' Theological Notebook, reflections on Richard Baxter, Connecticut Historical Society, as quoted in Minkema, "Edwardses," 83. The rest is from New England's most often used authoritative creed, the *Westminster Confession of Faith*, chaps. 12–15. The confession can be found, among other places, in *Creeds of the Churches*, 3d ed., ed., John Leith (Atlanta: John Knox, 1982).

10. William K. B. Stoever, *"A Faire and Easie Way to Heaven": Covenant Theology and Antinomianism in Early Massachusetts* (Middletown, Conn.: Wesleyan University Press, 1978), 63–67 and passim, provides a lucid account of the subtleties of the New England debates. Opinions varied, of course, as in the Antinomian controversy, over the subtleties of the relation between law and grace. The Edwardses' views followed the dominant opinions of New England clergy, here summarized.

11. Regeneration is the act of God in transforming a heart through the new birth. Conversion is the individual's experience of that change, usually a gradual process. Often the two are and were conflated.

12. Minkema, "Edwardses," 81. Hambrick-Stowe, *Practice of Piety*, 197–241.

13. *Westminster Confession of Faith*, chap. 19. Cf. Stoever, *"A Faire and Easie Way to Heaven,"* 81–118.

14. *Westminster Confession of Faith*, chap. 27:1.

15. Williams is usually credited with founding the first Baptist church in America in 1639, but after a few months he decided that even that practice was not pure enough and abandoned institutional churches entirely.

16. Robert G. Pope, *The Half-Way Covenant: Church Membership in Puritan New England* (Princeton: Princeton University Press, 1969). E. Brooks Holifield, *The Covenant Sealed: The Development of Puritan Sacramental Theology in Old and New England, 1570–1720* (New Haven: Yale University Press, 1974).

17. James F. Cooper Jr., *Tenacious of Their Liberties: The Congregationalists in Colonial Massachusetts* (New York: Oxford University Press, 1999), provides a rich account of relations between clergy and laity in church government. On ruling elders, see esp. 130–31, where Cooper observes that some eighteenth-century churches retained ruling elders and even those who did not gave a prominent role to "worthy laymen" (as was the case in Edwards' Northampton).

18. Solomon Stoddard, *The Doctrine of Instituted Churches Explained and Proved from the Word of God* (London, 1700), 8. On Stoddard's views, see Thomas A. Schafer, "Solomon Stoddard and the Theology of the Revival," in Stuart Henry, ed., *A Miscellany of American Christianity; Essays in Honor of H. Shelton Smith* (Durham: Duke University Press, 1963), 328–61, and Holifield, *Covenant Sealed*, 208–20. Stoddard also practiced the half-way covenant. His more lenient standard for communicant membership, however, made the half-way covenant less of an issue because more townspeople would be communicants and he stopped making the distinction between half-way and full members in 1679. Ralph J. Coffman, *Solomon Stoddard* (Boston: Twayne, 1978), 81.

Regarding ruling elders, Stoddard said, "It is not the work either of the Brethren or Ruling Elders anyways to intermeddle . . . or limit him [the pastor]." *Instituted Churches*, 12, quoted in Perry Miller, "Solomon Stoddard, 1643–1720," *Harvard Theological Review* 34 (1941): 311.

19. Holifield, *Covenant Sealed*, 200–206.

20. Thomas Johnson, ed., *The Poetical Works of Edward Taylor* (Princeton: Princeton University Press, 1943), 123.

21. Seeman, *Pious Persuasions*, 15–25. Holifield, *Covenant Sealed*, 197–224.

22. Taylor to Stoddard, February 13, 1687/88, Taylor Notebook, quoted in Paul Lucas, *Valley of Discord: Church and Society along the Connecticut River, 1636–1725* (Hanover, N.H.: University Press of New England, 1976), 161. See also Thomas and Virginia Davis, eds., *Edward Taylor vs. Solomon Stoddard: the Nature of the Lord's Supper* (Boston: Twayne, 1981).

23. Edward Taylor elegy on the death of Samuel Hooker, as quoted by Perry Miller, "Solomon Stoddard," 302.

24. See note 2, chapter 1, above.

25. Minkema, "Edwardses," 34–38, 54–64. Davis, ed., *Taylor vs. Stoddard* (Boston, 1981). Lucas, *Valley of Discord*, 159. Lucas, "'An Appeal to the Learned': The Mind of

Solomon Stoddard," *William and Mary Quarterly,* 3d ser., 30 (1973): 269. See Miller, "Solomon Stoddard," 303–4n, for a list of the principal titles in the controversy.

26. In 1710 some townspeople had complained that his standards for admission to communion were too strict, a charge that he dismissed. Minkema, "Edwardses," 36–37.

27. Edwards to Mary Edwards, May 10, 1716, *Works,* 16: 29.

28. Stephen Williams, diary, February 22, 1715/16, 1: 6 (typescript), Storrs Library, Longmeadow, Mass., quoted in Minkema, "Edwardses," 75.

29. Edwards to Mary Edwards, May 10, 1716, *Works,* 16: 29. Dwight, *Life,* 17, notes that family letters indicate that Jonathan's mother as well as two sisters "made profession of their christian faith" during this revival. Minkema, "Edwardses," 199n26, finds that Timothy Edwards' diary, p. 110 (Beinecke), lists "A[nne] and Eun[ice] their relations" but does not mention his wife. It would be remarkable if Solomon Stoddard's daughter would have ceased to be a communicant when she married Timothy and not met her husband's higher standards until after twenty-two years of marriage.

30. Minkema, "Edwardses," 80–82.

31. Dwight, *Life,* 17. The above account is closely dependent on Minkema.

32. Ibid., 16.

33. Ibid.

34. Minkema, "Edwardses," 116–17.

35. Like Jonathan, Timothy had lengthy salary disputes with his congregation, as he argued that his payments should keep up with inflation. He also showed his meticulousness in such matters by keeping accounts on what was owed him, almost literally to the last grain of corn. He had two severe disputes over his opposition to marriages to which parents had not given consent (his care on such issues may have been related to the memory of his own parents' tumultuous marriage). Minkema, "Edwardses," 103n8, 114–15, 120–36.

36. Edwards to Mary Edwards, March 26, 1719, *Works,* 16: 31.

37. Edwards to Timothy Edwards, July 24, 1719, *Works,* 16: 33. Cutler also approved of Jonathan, congratulating Timothy Edwards on his son's "promising abilities and advances in learning." Timothy Cutler to Timothy Edwards, June 30, 1719 (ANTS), quoted in Ola Winslow, *Jonathan Edwards, 1703–1758: A Biography* (New York: Macmillan, 1940), 60.

38. "Personal Narrative," *Works,* 16: 791.

39. In his first "Miscellanies" entry on the beauty of holiness he wrote, "We drink in strange notions of holiness from our childhood, as if it were a melancholy, morose, sour, and unpleasant thing." *Works,* 13: 163.

40. All these points can be inferred from his later diary when he is trying to strictly reform his habits and cultivate a more positive disposition.

41. "Personal Narrative," *Works,* 16: 791.

42. Edwards, draft to Stephen Mix, ca. November 1, 1720, *Works,* 16: 35–36.

43. Undated fragment of letter from Timothy Edwards to Stephen Mix, folder 1720–29 A, item 6, ANTS, quoted in Minkema, "Edwardses," 171.

44. Edwards to Timothy Edwards, March 1, 1721, *Works,* 16: 37–38. Cf. Richard Warch, *School of the Prophets: Yale College, 1701–1740* (New Haven: Yale University Press, 1973), 259–60.

45. In his "Personal Narrative," *Works,* 16: 795, he writes that his intense experiences began about a year and a half before he left for New York, which was on August 10, 1722.

46. "Personal Narrative," *Works*, 16: 791–92.

47. Edwards, *The Value of Salvation*, sermon, Matthew 16:26 (1722), *Works*, 10: 311–36, reflects on these themes.

48. "Personal Narrative," *Works*, 16: 792.

49. See, e.g., Westminster Assembly, *Shorter Catechism*, questions 1 and 4.

50. "Personal Narrative," *Works*, 16: 793.

51. Richard Bushman's insightful but highly speculative, "Jonathan Edwards as a Great Man: Identity, Conversion, and Leadership in the Great Awakening," *Soundings, An Interdisciplinary Journal*, 52, no. 1 (spring 1969): 15–45, suggests something akin to this, although principally in Freudian terms that Edwards's conversion was a psychological resolution of conflict with his father arising out of competition for the love of his mother.

52. Jonathan, of course, used biblical images to describe God's love, including that God "will be a tender father to us," a phrase from his first extant sermon, perhaps written before the dramatic experiences of his conversion. *Christian Happiness* (ca. 1720–21), *Works*, 10: 304. Nonetheless, even in the early development of his theology, his primary emphasis is on the infinite attributes of God, which make his condescending love all the more remarkable.

## CHAPTER 3. The Pilgrim's Progress

1. "Personal Narrative," *Works*, 16: 793–94, 801.

2. George S. Claghorn, "Introduction" to "Personal Narrative," *Works*, 16: 747.

3. "Personal Narrative," *Works*, 16: 802–3.

4. Ibid., 803.

5. Sermon, *The Value of Salvation*, Matthew 16:26 (spring or summer 1722), *Works*, 10: 319. Sermon, *Glorious Grace*, Zechariah 4:7 (1722), *Works*, 10: 388–99. This sermon, proba- bly written in summer 1722 when he was candidating for a church, also expresses distinctly anti-Arminian themes, suggesting that Edwards was already distancing himself from any trace of the fashionable divinity that was already a matter of controversy in New England. Most of the themes in Edwards' later thought and preaching can be found in these early sermons. See Wilson Kimnach's excellent introduction, *Works*, 10: 3–293.

6. Iain H. Murray, *Jonathan Edwards: A New Biography* (Edinburgh: Banner of Truth Trust, 1987), 52–53. Wilson H. Kimnach, "Preface to the New York Period," *Works*, 10: 261–93.

7. "William Smith," Franklin Bowditch Dexter, *Biographical Sketches of the Graduates of Yale College, October 1701–May 1745* (New York: Henry Holt, 1885), 207–13. Cf. "John Smith," 359–60.

8. *Religious Affections*, *Works*, 2: 165.

9. "Personal Narrative," *Works*, 16: 797. On the origin of his notebook, "Notes on the Apocalypse," see Stephen J. Stein, "Editor's Introduction," *Works*, 5: 8–15.

10. *Works*, 16: 795.

11. All references to the "Resolutions" and Diary, below, are from *Works*, 16: 753–89.

12. *Poverty of Spirit* (1722–23), *Works*, 10: 497–99. Edwards repreached this sermon on several occasions.

13. Arthur Cushman McGiffert Jr., *Jonathan Edwards* (New York: Harper and Brothers, 1932), 12.

14. Renewals of baptismal covenants were normally church ceremonies where those

who had come of age could "own the covenant" by renewing the promises made for them at baptism. In churches such as Timothy Edwards' such a renewal was an affirmation of a baptized person's status as a half-way member and did not entail that person's becoming a full member who could participate in the Lord's Supper. We do not have any record of when or where Jonathan became a full church member. So being "received into the communion of the church" does not necessarily imply anything more than an earlier "owning of the covenant"—though we can not be sure. In any case, Jonathan was reappropriating these most solemn vows. I am indebted to Kenneth Minkema for this interpretation. On baptismal renewals see, for instance, his "The Lynn End 'Earthquake' Relations of 1727," *New England Quarterly* 69 (1996): 473–99. On "owning the covenant," see Robert G. Pope, *The Half-Way Covenant: Church Membership in Puritan New England* (Princeton: Princeton University Press, 1969), 38–39; 206–38.

15. "Personal Narrative," *Works*, 16: 795.

16. This observation is based on the perceptive comments of Conrad Cherry, *The Theology of Jonathan Edwards* (Garden City: Doubleday, 1966), 38. The quotations from the *Life of David Brainerd, Works*, 7: 91, 93.

17. *Dedication to God* (ca. 1723), *Works*, 10: 553. This sermon seems closely related to his reflections on renewing his baptismal vows on January 12, 1723.

18. *Christ the Light of the World* (ca. 1723), *Works*, 10: 540–41. Cf. Kimnach's commentary on this sermon, pp. 247–50, 533–34. Cf. sermon fragment "Application on Love to Christ" for impressive imagery, pp., 608–17.

19. Edwards to the Committee of Bolton, Connecticut, December 10, 1722, *Works*, 16: 41.

20. "Personal Narrative," *Works*, 16: 797–98. Diary, May 1, 1723, *Works*, 16: 768.

21. We also do not have the originals of the Diary but only versions copied by his admiring editors. See George S. Claghorn, "Editing the Texts," *Works*, 16: 750–52.

22. This interpretation essentially follows that of Kimnach, *Works*, 10: 169–76. However, I do not think Kimnach has sufficient grounds to read the dispute back into the first accounting of Edwards' experience to his father in spring 1721. Edwards says in the "Personal Narrative" that he was "pretty much affected" by this conversation after which he had one of his most extraordinary experiences of the divine. An upsetting dispute seems an unlikely prelude to such a positive experience, although that is possible.

23. Timothy Edwards, sermon on Acts 16: 29–30 (1695), p. 5, Washington University Library, quoted in Kenneth Minkema, "The Edwardses: A Ministerial Family in Eighteenth-Century New England" (Ph.D. diss., University of Connecticut, 1988), 83. "Personal Narrative," *Works*, 16: 791.

24. Diary, August 12, 1723. In "Miscellanies" notebooks from the 1720s Edwards continued to affirm the view that humiliation accompanied by fears of hell was a normal preparatory step, even though he saw his experience as an exception to the rule. For a summary of these views, see Thomas A. Schafer, "Introduction," *Works*, 13: 22–24.

## CHAPTER 4. The Harmony of All Knowledge

1. For chronology, see Wallace E. Anderson, "Editor's Introduction," *Works*, 6: 8–9, 29. For dating of "Notes on the Apocalypse," see the remarkable reconstruction by

Thomas A. Schafer, described in Stephen J. Stein, "Editor's Introduction," *Works*, 5: 74–77. All dating is based on Schafer's monumental efforts.

2. From cover of "Notes on Natural Philosophy," *Works*, 10: 181. See also 181n concerning the date.

3. Ibid., 185.

4. Communication from Kenneth Minkema, April 23, 1997.

5. Norman Fiering, *Jonathan Edwards's Moral Thought and Its British Context* (Chapel Hill: University of North Carolina Press, 1981), 16–17.

6. Perry Miller, *Jonathan Edwards* (New York: William Sloane, 1949), 52–53, 74, 72, 77–78. Norman Fiering says that "Miller's discussion of Locke and Edwards on 52–68 is probably the worst piece of writing he ever did, judged in terms of substance and interpretive accuracy." Fiering, *Edwards's Moral Thought*, 36n. Nonetheless, Miller's enthusiasm mixed with some brilliant insights was of immense value in promoting appreciation and study of Edwards.

7. Thanks to the prodigious research of Norman Fiering, *Edwards's Moral Thought* and *Moral Philosophy at Seventeenth-Century Harvard: A Discipline in Transition* (Chapel Hill: University of North Carolina Press, 1981). Also, William S. Morris, *The Young Jonathan Edwards: A Reconstruction* (Brooklyn, N.Y.: Carlson, 1991).

8. Fiering, *Edwards's Moral Thought*, 17–23, 109. On the general intellectual climate in New England see also John Corrigan, *The Prism of Piety: Catholick Congregational Clergy at the Beginning of the Enlightenment* (New York: Oxford University Press, 1991).

9. Edwards' obituary, *New York Mercury*, April 10, 1758, p. 1. The author may have been William Smith, a New York lawyer and trustee of the College of New Jersey who was the older brother of John Smith, Jonathan's New York friend. William graduated from Yale in 1719 and was a tutor there from 1722 to 1724. Although his time at Yale did not overlap much with the years Edwards was there, they would have been well acquainted. See "William Smith," in Franklin Bowditch Dexter, *Biographical Sketches of the Graduates of Yale College, October 1701–May 1745* (New York: Henry Holt, 1885), 207–13.

10. Hopkins, *Life*, 5–6.

11. Anderson, "Editor's Introduction," *Works*, 6: 15–27, does the remarkable detective work on this issue, concluding that Hopkins' story is unlikely. I am convinced, however, by the counterargument of George Claghorn, personal correspondence, September 2001, that Hopkins' account is still plausible, especially since Anderson's is only negative evidence. It is also possible, of course, that Edwards had been referring to his second year at Yale College in New Haven, and Hopkins interpreted it as his second year in college (when Edwards would have been only fourteen, by the way).

12. We have some correspondence between Elisha Williams, begun when he was just graduated from Harvard in 1711 at age seventeen, and his cousin Stephen (the redeemed captive) still at Harvard, in which they are dealing with heady and relatively current philosophical issues. See Fiering, *Edwards's Moral Thought*, 25–27.

13. Perry Miller, *The New England Mind: The Seventeenth Century* (Cambridge: Harvard University Press, 1939), 111–53.

14. Our knowledge of the updating of the curriculum in 1718–19 is based on the later recollections of Samuel Johnson, the tutor whom the Wethersfield boys had been unhappy with and who was dismissed in spring 1719 to make way for Cutler. Johnson claimed credit

for the modernizing. Elisha Williams may have been ahead of the New Haven tutors in introducing modern authors. Anderson, "Editor's Introduction," *Works*, 6: 13–15.

15. He remarks on his distinct memory of this change and of not understanding it at the time in "Personal Narrative," *Works*, 16: 792. See, above, chapter 2, where this passage is quoted.

16. Fiering, *Edwards's Moral Thought*, 33–40. See also Anderson, "Editor's Introduction," in *Works*, 6: passim; and Morris, *Young Jonathan Edwards*, 164.

17. Conrad Cherry, *The Theology of Jonathan Edwards: A Reappraisal* (Garden City: Doubleday Anchor, 1966), 15, citing a similar comment by Leon Howard.

18. These are the best surmises concerning the dating based on careful detective work by Thomas A. Schafer and by Anderson, "Editor's Introduction," *Works*, 6: 147–53.

19. "Of Insects," *Works*, 6: 154–62.

20. The literature on this topic is immense. John Hedley Brooke, *Science and Religion: Some Historical Perspectives* (Cambridge: Cambridge University Press, 1991), and Margaret C. Jacob, *The Newtonians and the English Revolution, 1689–1720* (Ithaca: Cornell University Press, 1976), both put such arguments in their social contexts.

21. Anderson, "Editor's Introduction," *Works*, 6: 147–50.

22. Anderson, "Note on the 'Spider' Papers," *Works*, 6: 152–53, 163n. Edwards has usually been credited with some originality in his observations, although Lister anticipated some of them. See Anderson, "Editor's Introduction," *Works*, 6: 39–40n.

23. "Things To Be Considered an[d] Written Fully About," *Works*, 6: 219–95.

24. Ibid., 221; and "Of the Rainbow," *Works*, 6: 298–304.

25. Hopkins, *Life*, 6.

26. Kenneth Silverman, *The Life and Times of Cotton Mather* (New York: Harper and Row, 1984), 336–63.

27. Ibid., 41.

28. David D. Hall, *Worlds of Wonder, Days of Judgment: Popular Religious Belief in Early New England* (New York: Knopf, 1989), 71, and 71–116 for best account of this.

29. Michael G. Hall, *The Last American Puritan: The Life of Increase Mather, 1639–1723* (Middletown, Conn.: Wesleyan University Press, 1988), 81–89, 158–61, 165–66. Cf. Michael Winship, *Seers of God: Puritan Providentialism in the Restoration and Early Enlightenment* (Baltimore: Johns Hopkins University Press, 1996), 26.

30. Winship, *Seers of God*, 93–105.

31. Diary, January 2, 1723. Edwards retained this skepticism as exemplified when he criticized George Whitefield and others for being guided by "impulses" (see chapter 14, below) or edited out such leadings from David Brainerd's diary. Cf. Winship, *Seers of God*, 151.

32. "Things To Be Considered," in *Works*, 6: 231.

33. On deists, see, for instance, Gordon Rupp, *Religion in England, 1688–1791* (Oxford: Oxford University Press, Clarendon Press, 1986), 257–77.

34. Richard Westfall, *Never at Rest: A Biography of Isaac Newton* (Cambridge: Cambridge University Press, 1980), 302. Descartes would have denied this implication of his philosophy, maintaining that God was necessary to sustain the material world from moment to moment. Anderson, "Editor's Introduction," in *Works*, 6: 57.

35. Westfall, *Never at Rest*, 303.

36. Anderson, "Editor's Introduction," in *Works*, 6: 58n. Cf. Westfall, *Never at Rest*, 505, 509–10, 647. My account of Newton is based on Westfall's, passim.

37. Westfall, *Never at Rest*, 301–5, and Anderson, "Editor's Introduction," in *Works*, 6: 57–61.

38. Fiering, *Edwards's Moral Thought*, 16; Norman Fiering, "The Rationalist Foundations of Jonathan Edwards's Metaphysics," in Nathan O. Hatch and Harry S. Stout, eds., *Jonathan Edwards and the American Experience* (New York: Oxford University Press, 1988), 84.

39. Anderson, "Editor's Introduction," *Works*, 6: 23–24, 98, 111–12. Avihu Zale, in his valuable overivew "Jonathan Edwards and the Language of Nature: The Re-enchantment of the World in the Age of Scientific Reasoning," *Journal of Religious History* 26, no. 1 (February 2002): 15–41, suggests some of the other sources of Edwards' scientific thinking.

40. Louis E. Loeb, *From Descartes to Hume: Continental Metaphysics and the Development of Modern Philosophy* (Ithaca: Cornell University Press, 1981), 29–30, cited in Fiering, "Jonathan Edwards's Metaphysics," 77.

41. It is not clear when the young Edwards read Malebranche or even if the Frenchman was a direct influence, yet there is enough resemblance to make it seem that Malebranche's formulations may have helped him consolidate his views. Fiering, "Jonathan Edwards's Metaphysics," 84–88, and see also Fiering, *Edwards's Moral Thought*, 40–45. Mason I. Lowance Jr., "Jonathan Edwards and the Platonists: Edwardsean Epistemology and the Influence of Malebranche and Norris," *Studies in American Puritan Spirituality* 2 (1991): 129–52. Anderson, "Editor's Introduction," *Works*, 6: 72–73, 86–87.

42. Anderson, "Editor's Introduction," *Works*, 6: 36, and ibid., 102–3, 123–24, for comparison of the two.

43. On Berkeley's work in America, see Edwin S. Gaustad, *George Berkeley in America* (New Haven: Yale University Press, 1979). On Edwards' trip see, Kenneth Minkema, "Jonathan Edwards's Defense of Slavery," *Massachusetts Historical Review* 2 (2002).

44. "Things To Be Considered," *Works*, 6: 235, and Anderson, "Editor's Introduction," *Works*, 6: 53–57.

45. Anderson, "Editor's Introduction," *Works*, 6: 66.

46. "Of Atoms," *Works*, 6: 216.

47. "Things To Be Considered," *Works*, 6: 241–42. This view of continuous creation is consistent with teachings of Augustine and Scripture, as in Hebrews 1:3 and Colossians, 1:16–17. I'm grateful to George Claghorn for pointing this out.

48. "Of Atoms," *Works*, 6: 216.

49. "Things To Be Considered," *Works*, 6: 234–35. Cf. Sang Hyun Lee, *The Philosophical Theology of Jonathan Edwards* (Princeton: Princeton University Press, 1988), 10–14, on the implications of this relational-dispositional view of reality.

50. "Of Being," *Works*, 6: 203–6.

51. "I used to be mightily pleased with the study of the old logic, . . . because it was very pleasant to see my thoughts . . . ranged into order and distributed into classes and subdivisions." "The Mind," *Works*, 6: 345. Cf. Stephen H. Daniel, *The Philosophy of Jonathan Edwards: A Study in Divine Semiotics* (Bloomington: Indiana University Press, 1994), 68–83.

52. William Ames, *Technometry*, trans. and with introduction and commentary by Lee W. Gibbs (Philadelphia: University of Pennsylvania Press, 1979), 93.

53. See, e.g., the account of Samuel Johnson's learning of these ideas as a student at the Connecticut Collegiate school, just a few years before Edwards, in Joseph Ellis, *The New*

*England Mind in Transition: Samuel Johnson of Connecticut* (New Haven: Yale University Press, 1973), 30–31.

54. For clarifying the strong impulse in New England to maintain the unity of all knowledge, I am indebted to David Hill Scott, "The 'Circle of Knowledge' and Jonathan Edwards' Integration of Reason and Revelation" (M.Div. thesis, Gordon-Conwell Theological Seminary, 1997). Scott traces this impulse through such major seventeenth-century Calvinist thinkers as Alexander Richardson, William Ames, John Alsted, John Comenius, and Adrian Heereboord.

Stephen R. Yarborough and John C. Adams, *Delightful Convictions: Jonathan Edwards and the Rhetoric of Conversion* (Westport, Conn.: Greenwood Press, 1993), esp. 69–77, emphasize the direct influence on Edwards of Alexander Richardson's encyclopedic philosophy of art found in the preface to his *Logicians School-Master* (1629; 1657). See also Fiering, *Edwards's Moral Thought*, and Morris, *Young Jonathan Edwards*, concerning such influences. On Edwards' theological relationship to Calvinism see Conrad Cherry, *The Theology of Jonathan Edwards: A Reappraisal* (Garden City: Doubleday, 1966).

55. Miscellany no. 92, *Works*, 13: 256. The first long entry directly on the Trinity is no. 94, pp. 256–63, which Thomas Schafer dates around the end of 1723. Cf. Amy Plantinga Pauw, *"The Supreme Harmony of All": The Trinitarian Theology of Jonathan Edwards* (Grand Rapids, Mich.: Eerdmans, 2002).

56. "Personal Narrative," *Works*, 16: 794.

57. Ibid., 82.

58. "The Mind," *Works*, 6: 332–36. See also Roland A. Delattre, *Beauty and Sensibility in the Thought of Jonathan Edwards* (New Haven: Yale University Press, 1968).

59. Ibid., 336–38.

60. Christoph Wolf, *Johann Sebastian Bach: The Learned Musician* (New York: W. W. Norton, 2000). Richard A. Spurgeon Hall, "Bach and Edwards on the Religious Affections," in Seymour L. Benstock, ed., *Johann Sebastian: A Tercentenary Celebration* (Westport, Conn.: Greenwood Press, 1992), 69–81.

61. Diary, January 10, 1724. This entry written at Bolton, Connecticut, when he was pastoring and also probably working on some of the abstract ideas contained in "The Mind."

62. "The Mind," *Works*, 6: 353.

63. "Of the Prejudices of Imagination," *Works*, 6: 196–97.

64. Diary, September 23, 1723.

65. "Of the Prejudices of Imagination," *Works*, 6: 197.

## CHAPTER 5. Anxieties

1. Diary, August 9. Cf. July 29 and August 24, *Works*, 16: 777–80.

2. This account is based on the introduction to Edwards' *Quaestio*, by George G. Levesque, *Works*, 14: 47–53.

3. This is the term used in Proceedings of the Trustees, October 16, 1723, in Franklin Bowditch Dexter, ed., *Documentary History of Yale University: Under the Original Charter of the Collegiate School of Connecticut, 1701–1745* (New Haven: Yale University Press, 1916), 246.

4. Samuel Sewall to Yale Rector Elisha Williams, August 22, 1729, "Am glad to see you

have so large and fair a harvest to reap next September, exhibited in the public theses" and goes on the criticize one of the Latin terms used. "Letterbook of Samuel Sewall," *Collections of the Massachusetts Historical Society*, 6th ser., 2 (Boston, 1888), 272–74.

5. The "amens" are conjecture but seem likely, especially since they all met with the trustees the next day. Three of these were dissuaded, the others went to England for Anglican ordination. This account is based on Richard Warch, *School of the Prophets: Yale College, 1701–1740* (New Haven: Yale University Press, 1973), 96–125.

6. Samuel Sewall, "To Governor Saltonstall at New Haven," October 15, 1722, "Letter-book of Samuel Sewall," 144.

7. Samuel Sewall, "Diary of Samuel Sewall," September 25, 1722, *Collections of the Massachusetts Historical Society*, 5th ser., 7 (Boston, 1882), 309. Sewall reports that Increase attempted another prayer, but he could not hear it, "was spent." Ibid., 310. Two days later, Increase blacked out and although he lived another year, he never went out in public again. Michael G. Hall, *The Last American Puritan: The Life of Increase Mather, 1639–1723* (Middletown, Conn.: Wesleyan University Press, 1988): 361.

8. John Davenport and Stephen Buckingham to Cotton Mather, September 25, 1722, in Dexter, ed., *Documentary History*, 226. See related documents, pp. 226–34. See Warch, *School of the Prophets*, 110–11.

9. Quoted in Warch, *School of the Prophets*, 111, from *Collections of the Massachusetts Historical Society*, 2d ser., 2 (Boston, 1814), 133–36.

10. Kenneth Silverman, *The Life and Times of Cotton Mather* (New York: Columbia University Press, 1985): 359.

11. *New England Courant*, October 1–8, 1722, p. 1 (Standfast and Dogood); October 22–29 (Nausawlander); and October 29–November 5.

12. I am indebted to R. Bryan Bademan for his graduate paper "'A Little Sorry, Scandalous Drove': The Congregational Reaction to Anglicanism in Boston, 1719–1725" (University of Notre Dame, 1998). On Shute, see, Michael C. Batinski, *Jonathan Belcher: Colonial Governor* (Lexington: University of Kentucky Press, 1996), 40–42. J. C. D. Clark, *The Language of Liberty, 1660–1832: Political Discourse and Social Dynamics in the Anglo-American World* (Cambridge: Cambridge University Press, 1994), 29, argues that "Americans derived their perceptions of England's corruption far less from any free-standing Commonwealth tradition than from denominational sources." Cf. Carl Bridenbaugh, *Mitre and Sceptre: Transatlantic Faiths, Ideas, Personalities, and Politics, 1689–1775* (New York: Oxford University Press, 1962).

13. The classic "Reformed" doctrines as were contrasted with alternatives attributed to Arminius were defined at the international Reformed Synod of Dordrecht (or Dort) of 1618–19 and are sometimes referred to as "the five points of Calvinism," summarized in English by the acronym TULIP: (1) total depravity, (2) unconditional election, (3) limited atonement, (4) irresistible grace, and (5) perseverance of the saints. New England's orthodox party would have subscribed to these teachings but seldom used the precise formulations of Dordrecht, and they had come to think of "Arminianism" as a broad set of alternatives to these doctrines. Usually New England orthodox looked to the Westminster Confession of Faith in defining orthodoxy, as their actions regarding Yale, see below, illustrate. Westminster, though consistent with Dordrecht's anti-Arminianism, was a comprehensive confession of faith.

14. On Harvard, see John Corrigan, *The Prism of Piety: Catholick Congregational*

*Clergy at the Beginning of the Enlightenment* (New York: Oxford University Press, 1991), 19–21. For Harvard background, see Norman Fiering, *Moral Philosophy at Seventeenth-Century Harvard* (Chapel Hill: University of North Carolina Press, 1981). On the prevailing Calvinism of New England clergy, see Corrigan, *Prism of Piety,* and Harry S. Stout, *The New England Soul: Preaching and Religious Culture in Colonial New England* (New York: Oxford University Press, 1986), 127–81.

15. Proceedings of the Trustees, October 17–22, 1722, in Dexter, ed., *Documentary History,* 233.

16. "Apocalypse Series," *Works,* 5: 129. Unlike Samuel Sewall, he did not give the Church of England a prominent place in the predicted scenario. He did think that the warnings in Revelation 2 to the church at Pergamos, described as both steadfast and infected with heresy, "suit the case of the Church of England; and where thou dwellest, even where Satan's seat is." Still, he believed that the fifth vial of God's wrath was being poured out especially on Rome, Italy, and Spain. "Exposition on the Apocalypse," *Works,* 5: 99, 116. See, Stephen J. Stein's introduction to this volume, and James West Davidson, *The Logic of Millennial Thought: Eighteenth-Century New England* (New Haven: Yale University Press, 1977), for valuable expositions of these themes. Edwards' millennial views are discussed in more detail below, especially in chapters 11 and 19.

17. Richard Westfall, *Never at Rest: A Biography of Isaac Newton* (New York: Cambridge University Press, 1980), 321.

18. Nathan O. Hatch, *The Sacred Cause of Liberty: Republican Thought and the Millennium in Revolutionary New England* (New Haven: Yale University Press, 1977).

19. "Personal Narrative," *Works,* 16: 797. Edwards was not so unusual in this respect. Thomas S. Kidd, "From Puritan to Evangelical: Changing Culture in New England, 1689–1740" (Ph.D. diss., University of Notre Dame, 2001), documents the wide concerns for "the Protestant interest" in the New England press of this era. Anti-Catholicism was basic to popular expressions of cultural identity and was often associated with millennial speculations.

20. "Exposition on the Apocalypse," *Works,* 5: 114.

21. Ibid., 117–18.

22. Cf. The passage from ibid., 118, quoted more fully above as the epigram to chapter 4.

23. *Questio, Works,* 14: 60–64.

24. "Appendix to *Quæstio:* Syllogistic Notes," *Works,* 14: 64–66. Miscellanies nos. 12 and 13, pp. 206–7.

25. James Pierpont to Timothy Woodbridge, November 5, 1723, *Publications of the Colonial Society of Massachusetts,* 6, "Transactions," 1899, 1900 (Boston, 1904), 200.

26. George S. Claghorn, introduction to "On Sarah Pierpont," *Works,* 16: 745–47. See Claghorn's notes for literature on this piece.

27. "On Sarah Pierpont", *Works,* 16: 789–90.

28. Diary, September 22, 1723.

29. Ibid. This comment was preceded by the observation to remain open to new discoveries as an old man, quoted in chapter 4.

30. Wallace E. Anderson, "Note on 'The Mind,'" *Works,* 6: 326. Thomas A. Schafer dates this entry as probably just before the "Spider" letter, dated October 31.

31. Kenneth P. Minkema, "Preface to the Period," *Works,* 14: 5.

32. The last quotation is from Resolution 57, *Works,* 16: 757.

33. James Pierpont attempted to remove this obstacle in his November 5 letter to Timothy Woodbridge. Pierpont reported that a delegation that the Yale trustees had recently sent to New York to try to heal the breach between the Scottish and the English congregations had failed because of "the Scotch parties extravagant terms." That meant that "this affair . . . is so circumscribed that Mr. Edwards will not any more engage in it" thus freeing him for the North Haven post, which "is a much better place than where he is now." By this time Edwards himself must have recently received the confirmation that there was no hope to return to New York and may have already moved to Bolton.

34. Cf. Diary, February 23, 1724: "When I am at a feast, or a meal, that very well pleases my appetite, I must not merely take care to leave off with as much of an appetite as at ordinary meals; for when there is a great variety of dishes, I may do that, after I have eaten twice as much as at other meals, is sufficient."

35. *The Pleasantness of Religion* (ca. late 1723), *Works*, 14: 102, 107.

36. *A Spiritual Understanding of Divine Things Denied to the Unregenerate* (ca. late 1723), *Works*, 14: 75, 79, 90.

37. *Living Peaceably One with Another* (ca. December 1723), *Works*, 14: 132, 129, 121–22, 128. On the "catholick" spirit of the Boston clergy, see Corrigan, *Prism of Piety*.

38. *Nothing upon Earth Can Represent the Glories of Heaven* (ca. early 1724), *Works*, 14: 137–60, quotations pp. 145–46, 146, 157.

39. Miscellany no. 108, *Works*, 13: 278–80. Schafer dates this as February or March 1724.

## CHAPTER 6. "A Low, Sunk Estate and Condition"

1. *Works*, 16: 786.

2. Cf. Proceedings of the Trustees, November 21, 1722, in Franklin Bowditch Dexter, ed., *Documentary History of Yale University: Under the Original Charter of the Collegiate School of Connecticut, 1701–1745* (New Haven: Yale University Press, 1916), 235–36.

3. Thomas Clap, *The Annals or History of Yale College* (New Haven, Conn., 1766), 35–36, quoted in Richard Warch, *School of the Prophets: Yale College, 1701–1740* (New Haven: Yale University Press, 1973), 134. President Clap, who resented Edwards' later rivalry at Princeton, may not be wholly reliable on this point.

4. Diary, February 16 and May 22, 1725.

5. Warch, *School of the Prophets*, 191.

6. Thomas A. Schafer, "Editor's Introduction," *Works*, 13: 7, 15–19; Kenneth P. Minkema, "Preface to the Period," *Works*, 14: 8; Wallace E. Anderson, "Editor's Introduction," *Works*, 6: 32–34; Warch, *School of the Prophets*, 206–7. On Deism, see Gerald McDermott, *Jonathan Edwards Confronts the Gods: Christian Theology, Enlightenment Religion, and Non-Christian Faiths* (New York: Oxford University Press, 2000), 34–51.

7. Trustees, October 16, 1723, in Dexter, ed., *Documentary History*, 246.

8. Diary, September 30, 1724, note, re: "vacancy" as vacation. Trustees, September 9, 1724, in Dexter, ed., *Documentary History*, 255–56, on offering the rectorship to William Russel. The fact that the crisis began before the commencement might suggest that the issue of the rectorship was a concern.

9. This remark could, of course, be the sort of thing one might say after seeing an acquaintance renounce Calvinism without such consultation.

10. Schafer, "Editor's Introduction," *Works*, 13: 17.

11. The average age for women to marry was about twenty-three and for men twenty-six. David Hackett Fischer, *Albion's Seed: Four British Folkways in America* (New York: Oxford University Press, 1989), 76.

12. James Pierpont apparently was not still a full-time tutor, but he was paid by the college for his services until March 20, 1725. Proceedings of the Trustees, April 20, 1725, in Dexter, ed., *Documentary History*, 258.

13. Miscellany no. 193, *Works*, 13: 334, dated July or August 1725.

14. Miscellanies nos. 188 and 182, *Works*, 13: 331, 329, cf. 328 re "ravishing," above. Cf. "The Beauty of the World," *Reader*, 14–15, written around this time, which is similar to Miscellany no. 108, quoted at the end of the previous chapter. On the Edwardses and singing in four-part harmonies, see chapter 8, below.

15. Miscellany no. 189, *Works*, 13: 331–32. In an earlier miscellany, no. 37, 220, written in East Windsor in summer 1723, Jonathan expressed very conventional views of proper gender roles. Men had "more wisdom strength and courage, fit to protect and defend; but he [God] has made woman weaker, more soft and tender, more fearful, and more affectionate, as a fit object of generous protection and defense." These reflections were on the nature of Christ's love for the church.

16. *A Spiritual Understanding* (1723–24), *Works*, 14: 87.

17. Diary, November 16, 1725. Cf. July 27, 1723, October 5, 1724. Since the diaries were published and probably edited by Edwards' admirers, we may not have a complete record of his struggles with these matters.

18. Diary, September 2, 1724. Cf. September 30, where he indicates that he gave up the diet for a time but resolved to resume it.

19. Jonathan's account of the experiences of Sarah, whose anonymity he guards, is in *Some Thoughts Concerning the Present Revival of Religion in New England* (1742), *Works*, 4, quotations from p. 333. See also chapter 15, below.

20. Diary, November 16, 1725.

21. Timothy Edwards to Esther Edwards, November 10, 1725, ANTS, quoted in Kenneth Minkema, "The Edwardses: A Ministerial Family in Eighteenth-Century New England" (Ph.D. diss., University of Connecticut, 1988), 186–87. Timothy Edwards to Esther Edwards, October 11, 1725 and October 20, 1725, ANTS, confirm the seriousness of the concern, especially by mid-October. I am grateful to George Claghorn for his transcriptions of these letters.

22. Miscellany no. 198, *Works*, 13: 336–37.

23. "Personal Narrative," *Works*, 16: 789. Trustees, September 13, 1726, in Dexter, ed., *Documentary History*, 267, indicates a vote to pay his back salary, not an ordinary piece of business. Later Edwards had perennial salary disputes in Northampton.

24. Schafer, "Editor's Introduction," *Works*, 13: 18n.

25. James R. Trumbull, *History of Northampton, Massachusetts, from Its Settlement in 1654*, 2 vols. (Northampton, Mass., 1898, 1902), 2: 43–45. Schafer, "Editor's Introduction," *Works*, 13: 18–19. Schafer writes he arrived in October, though Trumbull says that he was already voted a month's salary in August. Perhaps the salary was an advance, if indeed he had not yet been paid at Yale for the year (see above).

26. I am indebted to George Claghorn for this information and his interpretation, based on his examination of a sermon fragment at Beinecke from a Stockbridge Indian sermon *Seeking the Heavenly Canaan*.

27. Miscellany no. 294, *Works*, 13: 385. I am indebted for this observation to Ava Chamberlain, "The Immaculate Ovum: Jonathan Edwards and the Construction of the Female Body," *William and Mary Quarterly*, 3d ser., 57, no. 2 (April 2000): 289–322.

28. That is especially so since the dating of this diary entry is not absolutely firm. The diary entry is dated "Sept. 26, 1726," but that seems to be a mistake, most likely from a transcriber or typesetter doubling the 26s (the original is lost). This is the only diary entry between November 1725 and January 1728. The correct year, it seems, has to be 1727. Nothing in his diary or the record at Bolton would suggest that his spiritual crisis began in 1723. In his "Personal Narrative" he explicitly says, "Continued much in the same frame in the general, that I had been in at New York, till I went to New Haven, to live there as Tutor of the College; having one special season of uncommon sweetness: particularly once at Bolton. . . . After I went to New Haven, I sunk in religion." Further in his diary of September 1724, he twice notes the spiritual calamity that began just before commencement. In his "Personal Narrative," he writes, "since I came to this town [Northampton], I have often had sweet complacency in God." Apparently he did not move to Northampton until October 1726. Schafer, "Editor's Introduction," *Works*, 13: 19. So every other piece of evidence but the printed text is consistent with a date of September 26, 1727.

29. "Images of Divine Things," no. 57, *Works*, 11: 67. One of the subtitles which he added was "The Language and Lessons of Nature," p. 50. Richard Godbeer, *Sexual Revolution in Early America* (Baltimore: Johns Hopkins University Press, 2002), 71–83, shows how widely used in New England was the imagery of the church (or believers) as the bride of Christ, but he misses the role of typology for explaining its significance.

30. Miscellany no. 362, *Works*, 13: 435. Before his first entry of "Shadows" he wrote, "Under the Head of Creation, vid." Miscellany no. 362. *Works*, 11: 51.

31. "Images of Divine Things," nos. 5 and 12, *Works*, 11: 52, 54.

32. "Images of Divine Things," no. 18 (probably written about January 1729), *Works*, 11: 54.

CHAPTER 7. On Solomon Stoddard's Stage

1. To Thomas Gillespie, July 1, 1751, *Works*, 16: 385.

2. Kevin Michael Sweeney, "River Gods and Related Minor Deities: The Williams Family and the Connecticut River Valley, 1637–1790" (Ph.D. diss., Yale University, 1986), 2, cites some period uses of "river gods." Sweeney's outstanding dissertation is a very valuable source on the intermarried families (especially the Williamses, Stoddards, Porters, Partridges, and Dwights) who governed the Connecticut River Valley.

3. The elegant late colonial home now at the location is the result of an addition by one of John's sons in the Revolutionary era. The home in Edwards' time was probably more on the scale of Abigail Williams' Mission House, which can still be seen in Stockbridge. I am grateful to the current owner for showing us through her home and for uncovering its architectural history. Laurel Thatcher Ulrich, *The Age of Homespun: Objects and Stories in the Creation of an American Myth* (New York: Knopf, 2001), 115–16, pictures a fine linen towel featuring the image of George I, probably imported from Germany, that belonged to Prudence Chester, who married John Stoddard in 1731.

4. Gregory H. Nobles, *Divisions Throughout the Whole: Politics and Society in Hampshire County, Massachusetts, 1740–1775* (New York: Cambridge University Press, 1983), 30.

Patricia J. Tracy, *Jonathan Edwards, Pastor: Religion and Society in Eighteenth-Century Northampton* (New York: Hill and Wang, 1979), 149–52, has a good summary of biographical information on John Stoddard. See also James R. Trumbull, *History of Northampton, Massachusetts, from Its Settlement in 1654*, 2 vols. (Northampton, Mass., 1898, 1902), 2: 165–78 and passim. Also *Sibley's Harvard Graduates*, 5: 96–119.

5. Trumbull, *History of Northampton*, 2: 15–42. Colin Calloway, *The Western Abenakis of Vermont, 1600–1800*, (Norman: University of Oklahoma Press, 1990), 113–31. I have also been helped by the chapter on Father Râle's War in Thomas Saunders Kidd, "From Puritan to Evangelical: Changing Culture in New England, 1689–1740" (Ph.D. diss., University of Notre Dame, 2001). Sometimes a distinction is made between Grey Lock's War and Father Râle's War, although the colonists conflated them.

6. Diary, January 10, 1723, *Works*, 16: 761. Tracy, *Jonathan Edwards, Pastor*, 53, summarizes the evidence. In December 1721 Jonathan wrote to his sister Mary, then in Hatfield, inquiring if Solomon was to be settled. Early in 1723 Timothy incorrectly recorded in his account book that Solomon had been chosen.

7. Philip F. Gura, "Sowing for the Harvest: William Williams and the Great Awakening," *Journal of Presbyterian History* 56, no. 4 (winter 1978): 330–31, may overstate the degree of their difference regarding the Lord's Supper. Gura's "Going Mr. Stoddard's Way: William Williams on Church Privileges, 1693," *William and Mary Quarterly*, 3d ser., 45, no. 3 (July 1988): 489–98, shows that Stoddard and Williams agreed more closely on church membership than was previously thought.

8. Ted Campbell, *The Religion of the Heart: A Study of European Religious Life in the Seventeenth and Eighteenth Centuries* (Columbia: University of South Carolina Press, 1991).

9. Paul Lucas, *Valley of Discord: Church and Society along the Connecticut River, 1636–1725* (Hanover, N.H.: University Press of New England, 1976), 159.

10. Williams' principal publications are summarized in Gura, "Sowing for the Harvest," 326–27. His concern for orthodoxy is indicated in his *The Great Concern for Christians* (Boston, 1723). On Stoddard see, Thomas Schafer, "Solomon Stoddard and the Theology of the Revival," in Stuart Henry, ed., *A Miscellany of American Christianity; Essays in Honor of H. Shelton Smith* (Durham: Duke University Press, 1963), 328–61.

11. Solomon Stoddard, *Question Whether God Is Not Angry with the Country for Doing So Little Towards the Conversion of the Indians?* (Boston, 1723), 6, 8–11. For a modern analysis of Jesuit and English attitudes, see James Axtell, *The Invasion Within: The Contest of Cultures in Colonial America* (New York: Oxford University Press, 1985).

12. William Williams to Samuel Sewall, January 22, 1728, "Letterbook of Samuel Sewall," *Collections of the Massachusetts Historical Society*, 6th ser., 2 (Boston, 1888), 250. He closed, p. 253, indicating that Stoddard is "comfortable" and "still useful to others."

13. Solomon Stoddard, *A Treatise Concerning Conversion* (Boston 1719), 57, 34.

14. To Thomas Gillespie, July 1, 1751, *Works*, 16: 381.

15. Miscellany no. 301, *Works*, 13: 387.

16. From Solomon Treat's account of Stoddard's views in his preface to Solomon Stoddard, *The Defects of Preachers Reproved* (Boston, 1724), iv–v.

17. Ibid., 10

18. Ibid., 13

19. Solomon Stoddard, *The Efficacy of the Fear of Hell, to Restrain Men from Sin* (Boston, 1713), A1, 25–27.

20. Ibid., 14.

21. Stoddard, *Question Whether God Is Not Angry,* 8.

22. See, for instance, *Wicked Men's Slavery to Sin* (summer 1721–summer 1722), *Works,* 10: 339–50, and other references to hell, see index, Ibid., 653.

23. *Warnings of Future Punishment Don't Seem Real to the Wicked* (1727), *Works,* 14: 200–212. Another hellfire sermon, *The Torments of Hell Are Exceeding Great,* from late 1728 or early 1729, *Works,* 14: 301–28, is one of Edwards' most effective attempts prior to *Sinners in the Hands of an Angry God* (1741) to excite a vivid sense of the torments of hell.

24. *Faithful Narrative, Works,* 4: 146. This account closely follows Kenneth P. Minkema, "Preface to the Period," *Works,* 14: 32–34, and Harry S. Stout, *The New England Soul: Preaching and Religious Culture in Colonial New England* (New York: Oxford University Press, 1986), 177–79. See also Erik R. Seeman, *Pious Persuasions: Laity and Clergy in Eighteenth-Century New England* (Baltimore: Johns Hopkins University Press, 1999), 149–54, who finds no mention of fear of the judgment day among the laity, although they did say they feared going to hell, which would seem to amount to the same thing.

25. *Faithful Narrative, Works,* 4: 146.

26. *Impending Judgements* (1727), *Works,* 14: 216–27. Conceivably Edwards attributed the "opinion" to "some" because of his reservations regarding reading the exact meanings of special providences, as expressed earlier in his Diary. In his later Northampton ministry, however, he regularly interpreted the special meanings of calamities for his people.

27. He was also wrestling with Stoddard's teachings on the "utter despair" of humiliation that must precede conversion, part of his ongoing problem with this part of the Puritan heritage. See esp. Miscellanies nos. 317, 325, 335, 338, and 345 (all written probably in late 1727 or 1728), *Works,* 13.

28. "The Spiritual Blessings of the Gospel Represented as a Feast" (August 1728–February 1729), *Works,* 14: 290.

29. Timothy Edwards, *All the Living Must Surely Die* (New London, Conn., 1732), 23. Jonathan's earlier views seem to have been those of his father. In New York he wrote in a Miscellany no. qq, *Works,* 13: 189, that "'tis their [ministers'] business to instruct who are worthy of the name of Christians among them and who not. . . . If Christ has given to him the administration of the sacraments, he has given to him the administration of them to them that he thinks Christ would have him." Cf. Miscellany no. 40 (ca. summer 1723), 222.

30. Trumbull, *History of Northampton,* 2: 45, 47–48. Trumbull is quoting from town records.

31. Sewall to Stoddard December 10, 1723, in "Letterbook of Samuel Sewall," 259–60.

32. *Faithful Narrative, Works,* 4: 146. Obituary, *Weekly Newsletter* (Boston), no. 112, February 13/20, 1729, p. 2.

33. William Williams, *The Death of a Prophet Lamented and Improved* (Boston, 1729), 23; Benjamin Colman, *The Faithful Ministers of Christ Mindful of Their Own Death . . .* (Boston, 1729), 2.

34. Obituary, *Weekly Newsletter,* no. 112, p. 2.

35. Ibid. Cf. the helpful account in Tracy, *Jonathan Edwards, Pastor,* 13–20.

36. To Thomas Gillespie, July 1, 1751, *Works,* 16: 381–83. That this was not just sour grapes is indicated by the fact that Edwards deplored the contentions of these two parties also in *Faithful Narrative, Works,* 4: 146. On court and country parties as well as views of the monarchy, see Benjamin Lewis Price, *Nursing Fathers: American Colonists' Conception of English Protestant Kingship, 1688–1776* (Lanham, Md.: Lexington Books, 1999).

37. Minkema, "Preface to the Period," *Works,* 14: 36–38. Tracy, *Jonathan Edwards, Pastor,* 91–98.

38. *Faithful Narrative, Works,* 4: 146.

39. *Signs of God's Displeasure in the Removal of Useful People.* Sermon no. 119, Isaiah 3:1–2, Works of Edwards transcription (probably preached in summer 1729).

40. *Living Unconverted Under an Eminent Means of Grace* (probably preached in spring 1729), *Works,* 14: 365–67, 370.

41. Minkema, "Preface to the Period," *Works,* 14: 13.

42. Edwards indicated that there were about 200 families in Northampton in the 1730s. Iain Murray, *Jonathan Edwards: A New Biography* (Carlisle, Pa.: Banner of Truth Trust, 1987), 89, estimates the population as between 1,250 and 1,400 based on a similar ratio of population to families thirty-five years later. Cf. chapter 21, note 24, below.

43. To the Trustees of the College of New Jersey, October 19, 1757, *Works,* 16: 726.

44. Timothy Edwards to Anne Edwards, September 12, 1729, as quoted in Minkema, "Preface to the Period," *Works,* 14: 13. Minkema notes that whereas Dwight, *Life,* 115, says Edwards was incapacitated through the entire summer, Thomas Schafer has demonstrated that Edwards wrote too many sermons during this period for that to be the case. He also was actively working on his notebooks when he was not preaching, suggesting stability in state of mind. Dwight says that his health failed, "in consequence of too close application," p. 115.

45. *New England Weekly Journal,* February 2, 1730.

46. Dwight, *Life,* 116–18. Kenneth Minkema, "The Edwardses: A Ministerial Family in Eighteenth-Century New England" (Ph.D. diss., University of Connecticut, 1988), 155–57, 199, quotation p. 157 from Timothy Edwards, "An Account of the Last Sickness of My Dear Daughter, Jerusha," n.d., Timothy Edwards Papers, ANTS.

47. See *Works,* 14: 548–50, for a summary of themes of sermons for late 1729.

48. Edward H. Davidson, *Jonathan Edwards: The Narrative of a Puritan Mind* (Boston: Houghton Mifflin, 1966), 34.

49. Miscellany no. 462, *Works,* 13: 505. Jonathan's greater willingness to criticize Stoddard is indicated also in Miscellany no. 411, written shortly after Stoddard's death, where he spelled out his differences with Stoddard's view that the humiliation that precedes conversion is not a manifestation of genuine faith. Cf. Schafer, "Editor's Introduction," *Works,* 13: 28

50. Sermon, Luke 22:48 (ca. 1729). Cf. sermon, *The Threefold Work of the Holy Ghost* (1729), *Works,* 14: 429–30.

51. Tracy, *Jonathan Edwards, Pastor,* 238n29. Tracy cites Tiziana Rota, "Marriage and Family Life in Northampton, Massachusetts: A Demographic Study, 1690–1750" (M.A. thesis, Mount Holyoke College, 1975), who found that from 1691 to 1710 the figure was 6 percent and from 1711 to 1730 it was 10 percent. From 1731 to 1750 the figure dropped to 4.7 percent, which suggests that Edwards' revivals and strictures did have some impact on behavior. The Northampton Church Records record only one case of someone (a man) being disciplined for fornication (in 1743) during Edwards' era. On the large patterns, see Daniel Scott Smith and Michael S. Hindus, "Premarital Pregnancy in American, 1640–1971: An Overview and Interpretation," *Journal of Interdisciplinary History* 5 (1975): 537–70. Their figures, based on studies mostly in New England, suggest that the percentage of premarital pregnancies rose steadily in the colonies during the period from 1700 to 1750,

reaching over 20 percent by 1750, which would make the Northampton case more exceptional. Cf. John Demos, "Families in Colonial Bristol, Rhode Island: An Exercise in Historical Demography," *William and Mary Quarterly,* 3d ser., 25, no. 1 (1968): 56, which finds that the percentage of couples with a first child born within eight and a half months of marriage jumps from 10 percent from 1720 to 1740 to 49 percent from 1740 to 1760. See Cornelia Hughes Dayton, *Women Before the Bar: Gender, Law, and Society in Connecticut, 1639–1789* (Chapel Hill: University of North Carolina Press, 1995), for helpful insights on the trends. On bundling, see Richard Godbeer, *Sexual Revolution in Early America* (Baltimore: John Hopkins University Press, 2002), 246–55.

52. *Sin and Wickedness Bring Calamity and Misery on a People, Works,* 14: 500–503.

53. David Hall, "Narrating Puritanism," in Harry S. Stout and D. G. Hart, eds., *New Directions in American Religious History* (New York: Oxford University Press, 1997), 62–64, makes this point.

54. See David W. Conroy, *In Public Houses: Drink and the Revolution of Authority in Colonial Massachusetts* (Chapel Hill: University of North Carolina Press, 1995), esp. 189–240, on Northampton, 226.

55. Helen Westra, *The Minister's Task and Calling in the Sermons of Jonathan Edwards* (Lewiston, N.Y.: Edwin Mellen, 1986), 7. Cf. pp. 11–12 for other images. Westra provides a valuable account of Edwards' understanding of his ministerial authority.

56. Miscellany no. 40, *Works,* 13: 222.

57. Timothy Edwards to Anne Edwards, September 12, 1729, quoted in Minkema, "Preface to the Period," *Works,* 14: 13–14. Another evidence of the town's goodwill was the unusual practice of paying expenses for one or two members of the congregation to accompany him and be "waiting on Mr. Edwards" when he went on trips to New Haven or Boston. After 1733 the practice was discontinued. Trumbull, *History of Northampton,* 2: 48–49.

58. An incident early in 1734 illustrated the same point. On Saturday morning, January 19, fire destroyed the shop of Deacon Ebenezer Hunt, a "felt-maker" from an old Northampton family. Friends and neighbors immediately went into action raising money to compensate his losses. Nearly every family contributed. Before the embers had cooled townsmen were gathering lumber for the rebuilding, and the deacon was back in business within a week. Trumbull, *History of Northampton,* 2: 39–40.

## CHAPTER 8. And on a Wider Stage

1. Hopkins, *Life,* 39–40. Hopkins' information is based on later years, beginning when Hopkins was a divinity student studying in Edwards' home in the early 1740s, though presumably Edwards already had established comparable habits. Other details of his personal routines and character are from Hopkins.

2. Daniel Walker Howe, *The Making of the American Self: Jonathan Edwards to Abraham Lincoln* (Cambridge: Harvard University Press, 1997), 38.

3. See Stephen J. Stein, "Introduction," *Works,* 15: 1–46. Cf. Iain Murray, *Jonathan Edwards: A New Biography* (Carlisle, Pa.: Banner of Truth Trust, 1987), 138–39.

4. "Outline of 'A Rational Account,'" *Works,* 6: 396–97.

5. Ola Elizabeth Winslow, *Jonathan Edwards, 1703–1758: A Biography* (New York: Macmillan, 1940), 122–23.

6. Hopkins, *Life*, 49–50.

7. Diary, January 22, 1734.

8. Kenneth P. Minkema, "Jonathan Edwards' Defense of Slavery," *Massachusetts Historical Review* 2 (2002). On Edwards' views of slavery, see chapter 16.

9. Hopkins, *Life*, 49.

10. "Images [originally "Shadows"] of Divine Things," no. 29, *Works*, 11: 58.

11. Dwight, *Life*, 111. This is, at least, the family lore as Dwight reports it.

12. "Images of Divine Things," no. 1, *Works*, 11:51.

13. Account and memoranda book, Beinecke, Works of Edwards transcription, notes dated May 5 and May 14, 1736, and May 7, 1737. He may also have been noting that 1736 was a particularly late spring, May 25, by our calendars. "Images of Divine Things," no. 60, *Works*, 11: 70.

14. *God Makes Men Sensible of Their Misery before He Reveals His Mercy and Love* (1730), *Works*, 17: 142–72, quotation, p. 143.

15. In one of his more controversial observations, Edwards argued that the saints in heaven would rejoice in knowing of the punishment of the wicked. Although most people today instinctively find such views repelling, that may be largely because most people today do not take seriously the doctrine of hell as eternal punishment. If one accepts that premise, then it is helpful in terms of understanding Edwards' observations to be reminded that even today we rejoice when we see the Evil One and his minions destroyed in one of our moral tales.

In a sermon on Revelation 18:20, preached in March 1733 and published in nineteenth-century editions of his Works, such as *Works of Jonathan Edwards*, ed. Hickman, 2: 207–12, Edwards dealt with the problem of why the torments of hell will not be an occasion of grief to the saints in heaven. As with most subjects, he followed a long tradition of Christian interpretations in saying that the saints' happiness will be derived from being conformed to God whose glory is manifested when justice is done. Love and sorrow for the fate of the wicked, which is demanded in this life, will be supplanted by conformity to God's perspective regarding evil.

In his "Miscellanies" notebooks Edwards often came back to the problem, often raised by eighteenth-century humanitarian critics, of reconciling God's love with the eternal torments described in Scripture. Late in life, for instance, he wrote some long entries (nos. 1348 and 1356) on why the punishments of hell were not *purifying* and hence ultimately redemptive, arguing essentially that Scripture did not indicate such and then arguing how that could be consistent with God's love and justice. These are published in *Works of Jonathan Edwards*, ed. Hickman, 2: 515–25. See Norman Fiering, *Jonathan Edwards's Moral Though and Its British Context* (Chapel Hill: University of North Carolina Press, 1981), chap. 5, "Hell and the Humanitarians," 200–260. Also note his discussions of problems of free will and permission of sin, the purpose of creation and the nature of the truly good as discussed in chapters 26–28, below.

16. "Images of Divine Things," no. 3, *Works*, 11: 52

17. Cf. Gordon Rupp, *Religion in England, 1688–1791* (Oxford: Oxford University Press, Clarendon Press, 1986) for an overview.

18. Rupp, *Religion in England*, 249–56.

19. Arthur Paul Davis, *Isaac Watts: His Life and Works* (London: Independent Press, 1946), 40, writes, "Of thirty-nine Presbyterian churches surveyed in 1731, eleven were

Arminian, twelve were unwilling to declare themselves, and only sixteen were orthodox Calvinist." Independents were not as heterodox.

20. Dummer to Timothy Woodbridge, June 3, 1723, Franklin Bowditch Dexter, ed., *Documentary History of Yale University: Under the Original Charter of the Collegiate School of Connecticut, 1701–1745* (New Haven: Yale University Press, 1916), 241.

21. Richard Warch, *School of the Prophets: Yale College, 1701–1740* (New Haven: Yale University Press, 1973), 172–75. Former Rector Cutler wrote to an Anglican friend in England that Johnson had assured him that more Yale students would soon defect "and nothing keeps the brightest of our youth from coming into the Church." Cutler to the Rev. Dr. Zachary Grey of Cambridge, England, September 4, 1732. Dexter, ed., *Documentary History of Yale*, 195.

22. Warch, *School of the Prophets*, 115.

23. Perhaps alluding to Colman's reputation of being "catholick" in the sense of not sectarian, Williams added that he was assured that the gift had been made in "a true catholick spirit, as much (if I mistake not) as Mr. Hollis's to Harvard College." Williams to [Colman], January 11, 1733, Harvard College Library, quoted in Warch, *School of the Prophets*, 175. Cf. Perry Miller, *Jonathan Edwards* (New York: William Sloane, 1949), 8.

24. Colman to Eliphalet Adams, December 2, 1732, Dexter, ed., *Documentary History of Yale*, 298.

25. Cotton Mather, *Ratio Disciplinae Fratrum Non-Anglorum. A Faithful Account of the Discipline Professed and Practiced: In the Churches of New England* (Boston, 1726), 5, quoted in Gerald J. Goodwin, "The Myth of 'Arminian-Calvinism' in Eighteenth-Century New England," *New England Quarterly* 41 (June 1968): 225.

26. Goodwin, "Myth," 215–37. Goodwin also argues (versus Perry Miller and others) that what the orthodox, including Edwards, meant by "Arminianism" included precisely the doctrines condemned at the Synod of Dort and by Westminster, not (à la Anne Hutchison) a crypto-Arminianism implicit in New England Calvinists' emphases on good works. Against Arminian alternatives Dort affirmed: total depravity, unconditional election, limited atonement, irresistible grace, and perseverance of the saints.

27. Cf. this and the subsequent account to Perry Miller's *Jonathan Edwards*, 3–34, where he elegantly and for the most part accurately paints the picture of the tensions surrounding the occasion.

28. *God Glorified in the Work of Redemption by the Greatness of Man's Dependence in the Whole of It* (Boston, 1731), *Works*, 17: 205, 212, 213–14.

29. Thomas Prince, William Cooper, "Advertisement," August 17, 1733, *Works*, 17: 215.

30. On this theme, see Thomas S. Kidd, "From Puritan to Evangelical: Changing Culture in New England, 1689–1740" (Ph.D. diss., University of Notre Dame, 2001).

31. "Thomas Prince," *Sibley's Harvard Graduates*, 5: 341–68. "William Cooper," ibid., 626–27. Cf. "Diary of Samuel Sewall, 1674–1729," in *Collections of the Massachusetts Historical Society*, 5th ser., 7 (Boston, 1878–79), 235 (November 27, 1719), when Cooper and the Princes visit the judge, and 235–36 (December 1, 1719), when Cooper is courting Judith.

32. Michael J. Crawford, *Seasons of Grace: Colonial New England's Revival Tradition in Its British Context* (New York: Oxford University Press, 1991), 70.

33. John Corrigan, *The Prism of Piety: Catholick Congregational Clergy at the Beginning of the Enlightenment* (New York: Oxford University Press, 1991), 131–34 and passim.

34. "Diary of Sewall," 6, p. 391 (July 5, 1713), 7, p. 164 (February 2, 1718), cf. p. 171

(February 23, 1718). I am indebted to Aaron Sprague for his graduate paper "From Psalmody to Hymnody in Congregational Massachusetts: The Issue of Extra-Biblical Song in Public Worship" (University of Notre Dame, 1996), for information on this topic. See also Robert Stevenson, *Protestant Church Music in America: A Short Survey of Men and Movements from 1564 to the Present* (New York: Norton, 1966), 1–31; Bruce C. Daniels, *Puritans at Play: Leisure and Recreation in Colonial New England* (New York: St. Martin's Press, 1995), 52–66.

35. Both quoted in Daniels, *Puritans at Play,* 54.

36. Cotton Mather was recommending them in the 1710s, "Diary of Cotton Mather, 1709–1724," *Collections of the Massachusetts Historical Society,* 7th ser., 8 (Boston, 1912), 142, 169, as cited by Sprague, "From Psalmody to Hymnody."

37. Cynthia Adams Hoover, "Epilogue to Secular Music in Early Massachusetts," in *Music in Colonial Massachusetts, 1630–1820: Music in Homes and Churches* (Boston: Colonial Society of Massachusetts, 1985), vol. 2, 734–53. At Harvard in 1717 a student defended the school's first thesis on music, including the proposition "Harmony is the symmetry of well proportioned sounds." Edward T. Dunn, "Musical Theses at Colonial Harvard," in *Music in Colonial Massachusetts,* vol. 2, 1162. Cf. Daniels, *Puritans at Play,* 60–61.

38. As early as March 1721, Samuel Sewall recorded in his diary that Mather preached on a Thursday night to "the young musicians" and that "the singing extraordinarily excellent, such as has hardly been heard before in Boston." "Diary of Sewall," 7, p. 285 (March 16, 1721).

39. Laura L. Becker, "Ministers vs. Laymen: The Singing Controversy in Puritan New England, 1720–1740," *New England Quarterly* 55, no. 1 (March 1982): 79–96. Daniels, *Puritans at Play,* 55.

40. "Diary of Cotton Mather," 606 (March 1721), quotation p. 626 (June 1721).

41. Henry Wilder Foote, *Three Centuries of American Hymnody* (Hamden, Conn.: Shoe String Press, 1961), 105–6.

42. Daniel, *Puritans at Play,* 61.

43. Crawford, *Seasons of Grace,* 68. Davis, *Watts,* passim. On Singer, see Davis, *Watts,* 55–56, and "Benjamin Colman," *Sibley's Harvard Graduates,* 4: 122.

44. Williams diary (typescript), April 19, 1730, Storrs Library, Longmeadow, Mass., quoted in Mark Valeri, "Preface to the Period," *Works,* 17: 19, cf. 17–28, on political context. See also Kenneth Minkema, "Preface to the Period," *Works,* 14: 36–38.

45. Michael C. Batinski, *Jonathan Belcher: Colonial Governor* (Lexington: University of Kentucky Press, 1996), passim. "Jonathan Belcher," *Sibley's Harvard Graduates,* 4: 434–39.

46. This is the thesis of Batinski, *Jonathan Belcher.*

47. "Belcher," *Sibley's Harvard Graduates,* 4: 443–44.

48. Batinski, *Jonathan Belcher,* 86, 88.

49. Belcher to Watts, October 30, 1732, "The Belcher Papers," *Collections of the Massachusetts Historical Society,* 6th ser., 6 (Boston, 1893), 205–6.

50. Batinski, *Jonathan Belcher,* emphasizes this theme.

51. David W. Conroy, *In Public Houses: Drink and the Revolution of Authority in Colonial Massachusetts* (Chapel Hill: University of North Carolina Press, 1995), 203. "Vice and wickedness" is from a proclamation by Belcher in 1730 and "gaming and excessive drinking" from proposed legislation in 1736.

52. "John Stoddard," *Sibley's Harvard Graduates,* 5: 106–7, 111–12. Cf. Batinski, *Jonathan Belcher,* 98, 100, 103.

53. *Envious Men* (August 1731), *Works,* 17: 101–20.

54. *The State of Public Affairs* (between August 1731 and December 1732), *Works,* 17: 355, 354.

55. "Christ's Kingdom Among the Gentiles," Isaac Watts, *Psalms of David, Imitated in the Language of the New Testament and Applied to the Christian State and Worship* (London, 1719), 186. I am grateful to Richard Stanislaw for this information.

## CHAPTER 9. The Mighty Works of God and of Satan

1. *Faithful Narrative, Works,* 4, 146–47.

2. Patricia J. Tracy, *Jonathan Edwards, Pastor: Religion and Society in Eighteenth-Century Northampton* (New York: Hill and Wang, 1980), 237. These figures do not indicate survival rates.

3. This analysis is based largely on the remarkable work of Patricia Tracy in *Jonathan Edwards, Pastor.* See esp., 38–50, 91–108.

4. Sermon, Isaiah 5:4 (March 1734). Edwards repreached this sermon in Stockbridge, August 1757, at another relatively unfruitful time in his ministry.

5. Edwards to Benjamin Colman, May 30, 1735, *Works,* 16: 49. This letter was Edwards' first major report of the awakening. It was later expanded and published as *A Faithful Narrative.*

6. *Faithful Narrative, Works,* 4: 147.

7. Sermon, Psalm 90:5–6 (April 1734).

8. Sermon, Canticles 6:1 (May 1734).

9. Edwards, *Faithful Narrative, Works,* 4: 148.

10. Sermon, Ecclesiastes 7:1 (June 1734). Whether this was for the young woman or another saintly person is not clear.

11. *Faithful Narrative, Works,* 4: 148, 209. In his July 1735 sermon, on Ezekiel 39:28ff., he urges prayer as especially important if the awakening is to survive and advises that more of the private meetings be separated by age and gender. The young men were already holding their own meetings, and he urges the young women to do so also. He mentions that there were groups for all ages and genders, which the women would be attending, so their reluctance to organize separately may not indicate any lack of spirituality.

12. Charles Hambrick-Stowe, *The Practice of Piety: Puritan Devotional Disciplines in Seventeenth-Century New England* (Chapel Hill: University of North Carolina Press, 1982), 137–43. The women in East Windsor recalled Esther Stoddard Edwards teaching a neighborhood women's gathering, see above chapter 2.

13. Watts' *Guide* was one of many popular devotional works. Thomas S. Kidd, "From Puritan to Evangelical: Changing Culture in New England, 1689–1740" (Ph.D. diss., University of Notre Dame, 2001), 211–32, provides a valuable account of the role of prayer in early eighteenth-century New England. Susan O'Brien, "Eighteenth-Century Publishing Networks in the First Years of Transatlantic Evangelicalism," in Mark Noll, et al., eds., *Evangelicalism: Comparative Studies of Popular Protestantism in North America, the British Isles, and Beyond, 1700–1900* (New York: Oxford University Press, 1994), 38–57, documents the role of devotional literature in shaping transatlantic evangelicalism.

14. *Faithful Narrative, Works,* 4: 151.

15. Edwards expounds his views most fully in a sermon on Colossians 3:16, preached at "a singing meeting" on June 17, 1736. He mentions in passing that some may wonder why he does not sing in public services and explains that he needs to save his voice for preaching, which is of greater interest to the congregation than would be his joining the singing. Colossians 3:16 (June 17, 1736).

16. *A Divine and Supernatural Light* (first preached August 1733, printed Boston, 1734), preface. Reprinted as appendix to sermon, *Works,* 17: 425–26.

17. *Divine and Supernatural Light, Works,* 17: 408–25.

18. Timothy Cutler to Bishop Edmund Gibson, May 28, 1739, in Douglas C. Stenerson, "An Anglican Critique of the Early Phase of the Great Awakening in New England: A Letter by Timothy Cutler," *William and Mary Quarterly,* 3d ser., 30 (July 1973): 487. The credibility of Cutler's story must be evaluated in the context of his telling it four years later at a time when he was depicting the awakening as negatively as possible.

19. *Faithful Narrative, Works,* 4: 149.

20. "Resolutions," no. 34, *Works,* 16: 755. *Faithful Narrative, Works,* 4: 149.

21. *Faithful Narrative, Works,* 4: 149–50.

22. Ibid., 205. He mentioned it in the context of Satan being loosed beginning with Joseph Hawley's suicide. See below.

23. Ibid., 157–59. He reports these professions in the context of noting the extraordinary number on whom "this dispensation" "has had a saving effect," suggesting that there were not simply renewed professions of the previously converted.

Under Stoddard and under Edwards before the awakening many Northamptonites, although baptized church members, declined to become communicant members. Edwards himself preached in 1733 that some of his parishioners were overly scrupulous in not partaking of communion. See David D. Hall, "Editor's Introduction," *Works,* 12: 35–51, esp. 44.

24. On enthusiasm and Puritan radicalism, see among others Ronald Knox, *Enthusiasm: A Chapter in the History of Religion* (New York: Oxford University Press, 1950); David Lovejoy, *Religious Enthusiasm in the New World* (Cambridge: Harvard University Press, 1985); Philip Gura, *A Glimpse of Sion's Glory: Puritan Radicalism in New England, 1620–1660* (Middletown, Conn.: Wesleyan University Press, 1984).

25. Letter from Timothy Cutler to Zachary Grey, June 5, 1735, in John Nichols, ed., *Illustrations of the Literary History of the Eighteenth Century,* vol. 4 (London, 1822), 298.

26. *Faithful Narrative, Works,* 4: 152, 188. For examples of these images, see such sermons as Revelation 19:15 (April 1734), on hell, and Isaiah 53:7 (February 1734), a communion sermon on the sufferings of Christ.

27. *Faithful Narrative, Works,* 4: 188–89, on the subject of "vain imaginations."

28. Ibid., 152

29. Ibid., 152–56. See C. C. Goen, "Introduction," *Works,* 4: 21–25, for other evidence confirming Edwards' account.

30. *Faithful Narrative, Works,* 4: 206.

31. James R. Trumbull, *History of Northampton, Massachusetts, from Its Settlement in 1654,* 2 vols. (Northampton, Mass., 1898, 1902), 2: 79–81.

32. Term used by Deacon Ebenezer Hunt in *Works,* 4: 46.

33. Edwards to Colman, May 30, 1735, postscript of June 3, 1735, *Works*, 16: 58. Details are from *Faithful Narrative, Works*, 4: 206.

34. *Faithful Narrative, Works*, 4 : 205–06. See also Goen, "Introduction," *Works*, 4: 46.

35. *Faithful Narrative, Works*, 4: 206.

36. Sermon, Ephesians 5:25–27 (May 1735). Cf. similar themes in sermon on Ezekiel 47:11 (May 1735),.

37. Sermon, I Thessalonians 2:16 (May 1735). This sermon, which is quoted here from the Works of Edwards' transcription, was published as *When the Wicked Shall Have Filled up Themselves in Their Sin, Wrath Will Come upon Them to the Uttermost*, in some early editions of Edwards' sermons or works. See, *Works*, 19: 802, for references.

38. Edwards may have learned something from the disaster of the Hawley case. Later in response to an inquiry from the Reverend Thomas Gillespie of Scotland on how to deal with "a person incessantly harassed by Satan . . . with those strange, horrid injections, that melancholic persons are often subject to" Edwards wrote, "I should by no means advise a person to resist the devil by entering the lists with him, and vehemently engaging their mind in an earnest dispute and violent struggle with the grand adversary; but rather by diverting the mind from his frightful suggestions, by going on steadfastly and diligently in the ordinary course of duty, without allowing themselves time and leisure to attend to the devil's sophistry, or view his frightful representations, committing themselves to God by prayer in this way, without anxiety about what had been suggested. That is the best way of resisting the devil, that crosses his design most; and he more effectually disappoints him in such cases, that treats him with neglect, than he that attends so much to him, as to engage in a direct conflict, and goes about to try his strength and skill with him, in a violent dispute or combat. The latter course rather gives him advantage, than anything else. 'Tis what he would; if he can get persons thus engaged in a violent struggle, he gains a great point. He knows that melancholic persons are not fit for it. By this he gains that point, of diverting and taking off the person from the ordinary course of duty, which is one great thing he aims at." Edwards to Thomas Gillespie, September 4, 1747, *Works*, 16: 228–29.

Edwards had suffered his own mild melancholy, or depressions, over the state of his soul and seemed characteristically to work his way out of them through a rational program of keeping to his religious and working routine. Cf. Gail Thain Parker, "Jonathan Edwards and Melancholy," *New England Quarterly* 41 (June 1968): 193–212.

39. Sermon, I Thessalonians 2:16. The comment re Hawley is from *Faithful Narrative, Works*, 4: 206.

40. Sermon, Romans 5:6, "prepared for the fast appointed on occasion of uncle Hawley's death" (June 1735), *Works*, 19: 385, 383.

41. *Faithful Narrative, Works*, 4: 205–7. Stephen Williams quoted in Goen, "Introduction," *Works*, 4: 47n. *God's Continuing Presence*, sermon, Ezekiel 39:28–29 (July 1735), *Works*, 19: 392–417, addresses the question of the apparent end of the awakening, alludes to the suicide craze, and dwells on the questions of God forsaking them, possible causes, backsliding, etc.

In a "lecture" sermon, Psalm 66:3 (August 1735), apparently preached on a public occasion, Edwards stated, "If were not for fear of future punishment, men's consciences would be no restraint to them and then there would be no dependence on any natural man but that he would be a cut throat or [illegible word]." In light of the impulse to suicide by throat-cutting of that summer, this is an intriguing choice of words.

## CHAPTER 10. The Politics of the Kingdom

1. Jonathan Edwards to Benjamin Colman, May 30, 1735, *Works,* 4: 99–110.

2. Almost every biography has followed Dwight in saying that Colman published this first letter. C. C. Goen shows that he almost certainly did not. See "Editor's Introduction," *Works,* 4: 32–33n.

3. Sermon, Romans 5:6, "prepared for the fast appointed on occasion of uncle Hawley's death" (June 1735). He also dwelled on this point at some length in a July sermon, Ezekiel 39:28ff, Works of Edwards transcription, concerning the apparent passing of the awakening.

4. *Works,* 4: 32–34. The "awful distemper" and the heat are from Stephen Williams' diary, transcription, Storrs Library, Longmeadow, Mass., August 18, 1736. Cf. August 21.

5. Isaac Watts to Benjamin Colman, February 28, 1737, quoted *Works,* 4: 36. This account is drawn primarily from Goen's introduction, *Works,* 4: 32–46.

6. The full title is *A Faithful Narrative of the Surprising Work of God in the Conversion of Many Hundred Souls in Northampton, and the Neighbouring Towns and Villages of New Hampshire in New England.* Watts later apologized for his geography, explaining that his map had "NEW HAMPSHIRE" on it but no Hampshire County. The editors changed a few things to suit their theological tastes and also apologized, much more than the meticulous Edwards liked, for possible "defects" or "imperfections" in the account.

7. Michael J. Crawford, *Seasons of Grace: Colonial New England's Revival Tradition in its British Context* (New York: Oxford University Press, 1991), 147, 149, and 290n25.

8. Samuel Hopkins, *Historical Memoirs Relating to the Housatonic Indians* (Boston, 1753; repr. New York: Johnson Reprint Corp., 1972), 14–81; Patrick Frazier, *The Mohicans of Stockbridge* (Lincoln: University of Nebraska Press, 1992), 13–49.

9. *Faithful Narrative, Works,* 4: 208. Edwards appears to have been away from Northampton from at least early September to about mid-October. Cf. Hall, "Introduction," *Works,* 12: 5n.

10. *Works,* 4: 211.

11. The account of the Breck case that follows is drawn from a number of works that recount its details. These include Clifford Shipton's account in *Sibley's Harvard Graduates,* 8: 661–80; Charles Edwin Jones, "The Impolitic Mr. Edwards: The Personal Dimensions of the Robert Breck Affair," *New England Quarterly* 51 (1978): 64–79; Louis Leonard Tucker, *Puritan Protagonist; President Thomas Clap of Yale College* (Chapel Hill: University of North Carolina Press, 1962), 47–58; Kevin Sweeney, "River Gods and Related Minor Deities: The Williams Family and the Connecticut River Valley, 1637–1790" (Ph.D. diss., Yale University, 1986), 226–51; and *Works,* 12: 4–17. Cf. four letters on the case, *Works,* 16: 58–64.

12. Sweeney, "River Gods," 229–34. Quotation on p. 230, from William Williams to Jonathan Wells, Hatfield, March 12, 1730.

13. Jones, "Impolitic Mr. Edwards," 67n.

14. William Rand, *Ministers Must Preach Christ LORD, and Themselves Servants* (Boston, 1736), 10, cited in Hall, "Introduction," *Works,* 12: 15. This sermon was preached in

late 1735, but Rand was expressing such views in 1734. A few years later he also questioned whether teaching the catechism interfered with children's ability to "judge for themselves." See Sweeney, "River Gods," 236.

Rand and a few others were, by Edwards' standards, lax on other matters. Rand and an ally, Isaac Chauncy, had offered their judgment that "in case a married couple has a child born at seven months after marriage and there be no other evidence against them, this is not alone a sufficient evidence to convict them before a church of the sin of fornication." Quoted in Valeri, introduction to sermon, *Christians a Chosen Generation* (May 1731), *Works,* 17: 274. Edwards used the declaration for sermon paper. Valeri infers that the case was from Northampton and that Edwards' condemnation in the sermon of "lascivious impurities" was a response to it.

15. Shipton, *Sibley's Harvard Graduates,* 8: 661, shows that Breck was in fact dismissed for stealing more than only books. His father had requested that he leave under his care.

16. Edwards, letter, *Works,* 12: 157–59, cites by name about ten witnesses who attested to hearing Breck express these views.

17. Edwards, *Faithful Narrative, Works,* 4: 148–49. See also Edwards' first letter to Benjamin Colman, *Works,* 4: 100–101. On the people's renewed zeal for Calvinism, see Edwards' preface "Justification by Faith Alone" in his *Discourses on Various Important Subjects* (Boston, 1738), which also underscores the role of this sermon in the awakening, repr. in *Works of Jonathan Edwards,* ed., Hickman, 2: 620–21.

18. Benjamin Colman to Stephen Williams, August 19, 1735, quoted in *Sibley's Harvard Graduates,* 8: 668. Cf. p. 667.

19. Hall, "Introduction," *Works,* 12: 4–17, provides a reliable interpretation.

20. Ibid., 146n. Cf. Tucker, *Puritan Protagonist,* 55, from whom I borrowed the saddlebags.

21. *A Narrative of the Proceedings of Those Ministers of the County of Hampshire etc. That Have Disapproved of the Late Measures Taken in Order to the Settlement of Mr. Robert Breck . . . With a Defence of Their Conduct in That Affair. Written by Themselves* (Boston, 1736), 65–66. Jones, "Impolitic Mr. Edwards," 73, ascribes the remark to Edwards, but that is incorrect. See note 23, below.

22. The council, on which John Stoddard probably had some influence, did not concur in bringing the Hampshire justices in for a hearing, cf. *Sibley's Harvard Graduates,* 8: 672.

23. In a letter to William Pynchon, Esq., December 20, 1735, Connecticut Valley Historical Museum, Springfield, Mass., Samuel Hopkins said that he wrote the first part and Edwards the second, but that he (Hopkins) was in such a hurry that he had no time to compare them. The second part, by Edwards, starts on a new page (67) and is titled in bold letters: *The Defence.* Hopkins' longer *Narrative* concludes with the witticism about Balaam's ass, which he attributed to a "young gentleman" who had been present. I am grateful to George Claghorn for a copy of the Hopkins letter. On authorship, see Claghorn's comments, *Works,* 16: 63–64.

24. [Edwards], *The Defence,* 67–93. On authorship, see note 23, above. [William Cooper], *An Examination of and Some Answer to a Pamphlet, Entitled, A Narrative and Defence . . .* (Boston 1736).

25. The reference to "country" clergy is quoted from a anonymous letter to the *Boston Gazette,* October 10, 1735, quoted in Hall, "Introduction," *Works,* 12: 10.

26. Jonathan Edwards, *A Letter to the Author of the Pamphlet Called An Answer to the*

*Hampshire Narrative* (Boston, 1737), 94, 161, 163. On the role of ridicule in the era, see John Redwood, *Reason, Ridicule and Religion: The Age of Enlightenment in England, 1660–1750* (Cambridge: Harvard University Press, 1960).

27. Jonathan Edwards to Sir William Pepperrell, January 30, 1753, *Works,* 16: 554. Edwards' account is the only nearly contemporary record of the origins of the dispute, and he does not detail its causes, which have been the subject of much speculation. Jonathan Ashley, pastor of Deerfield, who was married to Israel's sister, Dorothy, also shunned the Edwards home. Edwards dates the beginning of the opposition to the "great awakening" eighteen years earlier.

28. Perry Miller, *Jonathan Edwards* (New York: William Sloane, 1949), 104–5. Cf. Dwight, *Life,* 122n, and 434–35. Dwight bases this interpretation on Edwards' mention of opposition to his sermons on justification in 1734 but has no evidence that the Williamses were the source of this opposition.

29. Perhaps Israel Williams and a few other younger lay members of the clan were unhappy with aspects of the awakening itself. The Joseph Hawley incident could also have been a factor. Israel Williams, like Edwards, was a nephew of Hawley and may have laid some of the blame for the suicide at Edwards' door, but we have no direct evidence of that.

30. Elisha Williams to Isaac Watts, May 24, 1736, quoted in Anne Stokely Pratt, *Isaac Watts and His Gift Books to Yale College* (New Haven: Yale University Press, 1938), 30–31.

31. Timothy Cutler to Bishop Edmund Gibson, May 28, 1739, quoted in Douglas C. Stenerson, "An Anglican Critique of the Early Phase of the Great Awakening in New England: A Letter by Timothy Cutler," *William and Mary Quarterly,* 3d ser., 30 (1973): 486. Cutler is reporting on a Hatfield resident who said Williams "Wishes Mr. Edwards had not been so full and forward in the matter."

32. Jonathan Edwards to Benjamin Colman, May 19, 1737, *Works,* 16: 67.

33. Dwight, *Life,* 434, hypothesizes that Edwards refused a demand by Israel Williams to desist from preaching on justification versus Arminianism. This seems unlikely in view of William Williams' leadership in the anti-Arminian crusade.

34. In 1741, when Edwards wrote his first treatise on distinguishing the truly awakened, Cooper wrote the preface.

### CHAPTER 11. "A City Set on a Hill"

1. *Faithful Narrative, Works,* 4: 209.

2. Edwards to Benjamin Colman, May 19, 1737, *Works,* 16: 67. In order to impede a return to the lewd practices of tavern culture, the town in 1736 revived the office of tithingmen, eight of whom were elected to oversee their neighborhoods to prevent public disorderliness, such as drunkenness. See Patricia J. Tracy, *Jonathan Edwards, Pastor: Religion and Society in Eighteenth-Century Northampton* (New York: Hill and Wang, 1980), 124–25. Another example of political control, as well as of dissent, is that in late 1735, a Northampton husbandman was arrested for proclaiming, "Mr. Edwards was as great an instrument as the Devil had on this side Hell to bring souls to Hell." Case of Barnard Bartlett, General Sessions of the Peace, Hampshire County, January 17, 1736, manuscript collection, Connecticut State Library, Hartford, Conn., Works of Edwards transcription.

3. Edwards to Benjamin Colman, March 19, 1737, *Works,* 16: 65–66.

4. Ibid., 66; Edwards to Benjamin Colman, May 19, 1737, *Works,* 16: 68.

5. Jonathan Edwards, "Personal Narrative," *Reader*, 293.

6. Edwards mentioned the "backwardness of the spring" in his letter to Colman, May 19, 1737. He noted in his account book that the first blossoms appeared on the cherry trees in front of his window on May 7 (May 18 by our calendar).

7. *Peaceful and Faithful Amid Division and Strife*, sermon, II Samuel 20:19 (May 1737), *Works*, 19: 674. For his other uses of this image see index, *Works*, 19: 815.

8. James R. Trumbull, *History of Northampton, Massachusetts, from Its Settlement in 1654*, 2 vols. (Northampton, Mass., 1898, 1902), 2: 73–75. Tracy, *Jonathan Edwards, Pastor*, 125–29, and 245n12.

9. *The Many Mansions*, sermon, John 14:2 (December 25, 1737), *Works*, 19: 734–36.

10. Massachusetts' first governor, John Winthrop, in his "Model of Christian Charity," which famously referred to "a city on a hill," began by describing God's ordination of "some high and eminent in power and dignity, others mean and in subjection." Perry Miller, ed., *The American Puritans: Their Prose and Poetry* (New York: Columbia University Press, 1956), 83, 79.

11. Tracy, *Jonathan Edwards, Pastor*, 245n13, summarizing Hampshire Association Records, 22–27.

12. Cf. Tracy, *Jonathan Edwards, Pastor*, 130, regarding the empty pulpit.

13. Sermon, Matthew 25: 1–12 (February or March 1738), "g" in Works of Edwards transcriptions.

14. Ava Chamberlain, "Brides of Christ and Signs of Grace: Edwards' Sermon Series on the Parable of the Wise and Foolish Virgins," in Stephen J. Stein, ed., *Jonathan Edwards's Writings: Text, Context, Interpretation* (Bloomington: Indiana University Press, 1996), 10, quoting from sermons on Matthew 25:1–12, booklet 7. I am indebted to Chamberlain for pointing out the significance of this series.

15. *Charity and Its Fruits* (1738), sermon 1 of the series, *Works*, 8: 145.

16. *Charity*, sermon 15, *Works*, 8: 371, 375, 379.

17. Ibid., 370.

18. Charles Wesley, "And Can It Be That I Should Gain?" (1738), *The Works of John Wesley*, vol. 7, *A Collection of Hymns for the Use of the People Called Methodists*, Franz Hildebrandt, et al., eds. (Nashville: Abingdon, 1983), 322.

19. Sermon, I Timothy 2:5 (May 24, 1739), based on précis furnished to the author by Kenneth Minkema. We know of Edwards' preaching on this text and occasion only because the Reverend Ebenezer Parkman recorded this information in his diary. Parkman, pastor at Westborough, where the Edwardses would sometimes stop for one of the two nights on trips to or from Boston, also noted that on Friday, May 25, he dined with Edwards at the home of the Reverend Joshua Gee, and that Edwards preached that evening, probably to a private assembly at "Elder Lymans." Ebenezer Parkman, *The Diary of Ebenezer Parkman, 1703–1782* (Worcester, Mass.: American Antiquarian Society, 1974), 63 (May 24 and May 25, 1739).

20. Timothy Cutler to Bishop Edmund Gibson, May 28, 1739, in Douglas C. Stenerson, "An Anglican Critique of the Early Phase of the Great Awakening in New England: A Letter by Timothy Cutler," *William and Mary Quarterly*, 3d ser., 30 (1973): 482–83.

21. Jonathan Edwards to the Trustees of the College of New Jersey, October 19, 1757, *Works*, 16: 727. See John F. Wilson, "Introduction," *Works*, 9: 14–17, for a summary of the "Miscellanies" notes on this theme. Miscellanies nos. 702 and 710, from 1736 or 1737, *Works*,

18: 283–309, 335–39, are especially important and encapsulate his theology of redemption. On the theology of Edwards' projected work see chapter 29, below.

22. *A History of the Work of Redemption*, sermon 5, *Works*, 9: 176–77. Though few of the sermons have a formal "application," Edwards does interrupt his exposition once in a while for an "improvement." He also preached some other sermons during this same period.

23. Sermon 1, *Works*, 9: 113.

24. Sermon 24, *Works*, 9: 436.

25. Sermon 29, *Works*, 9: 520.

26. Timothy Dwight, *Travels in New England and New York*, ed. Barbara Miller Solomon, 4 vols. (Cambridge: Harvard University Press, 1969), 4: 230–31, quoted in Wilson, "Introduction," *Works*, 9: 8–9.

27. Theodore Dwight Bozeman, *To Live Ancient Lives: The Primitivist Dimensions of Puritanism* (Chapel Hill: University of North Carolina Press, 1988), emphasizes the theme of such "primitivism" (or attempts to live as though in biblical times) regarding seventeenth-century American Puritans, relating it to anthropological categories of myth, "Great Time," etc. See esp. 13–19. Jan Shipps, *Mormonism: The Story of a New Religious Tradition* (Urbana: University of Illinois Press, 1985), suggests how early Mormons quite literally saw themselves as restoring continuity with biblical time. See Richard T. Hughes, ed., *The American Quest for the Primitive Church* (Urbana: University of Illinois Press, 1988), for essays by these and other authors relating such themes to many American religious traditions.

28. Sermon 18, *Works*, 9: 351. Edwards believed Constantine's work was prophesied in Revelation 6, which speaks of the opening of the six seals and a cosmic judgment avenging the blood of the martyrs, also typical of the final judgment.

29. Moses Lowman's *Paraphrase and Notes on the Revelation of St. John* (London, 1737), which Edwards was reading in 1738 or 1739 and was a principal stimulant to his thinking, identified Constantine as one of the heads of the beast (Rev. 12:3), thus as an agent of Satan against the church. See Stephen J. Stein, "Introduction," *Works*, 5: 45–46. Cf. Stein's summary of Lowman, 55–61.

30. I am indebted on these and related points to the insights of Avihu Zakai as presented in an early draft of his forthcoming book *Jonathan Edwards's Philosophy of History: The Re-Enchantment of the World in the Age of Enlightenment* (Princeton: Princeton University Press, 2003), which he was kind enough to let me see.

31. *Works*, 9: 291. "Shall we prize a history that gives us a clear account of some great earthly prince or mighty warrior, as of Alexander the Great or Julius Caesar, or the Duke of Marlborough, and shall we not prize the history that God has given us of the glorious kingdom of his son, Jesus Christ, the prince and savior of the world, and the wars and other great transactions of that king of kings and lord of armies, the lord mighty in battle, the history of the things he has wrought for the redemption of his chosen people."

32. See above, chapter 5.

33. Sermon 18, *Works*, 9: 351–52.

34. Sermon 33, *Works*, 9: 411.

35. Sermon 24, *Works*, 9: 434.

36. Ibid., 434–35.

37. Sermon 22, *Works*, 9: 412.

38. See Stein, "Introduction," *Works,* 5: 18.

39. E.g., see Sermon 22, *Works,* 9: 413n.

40. Sermon 24, *Works,* 9: 437–38.

41. Ibid., 431–38, quotations p. 438.

Interestingly, Edwards' account of the Reformation mentions Calvin only in passing as "one of the eminent of the reformers" (Sermon 23, *Works,* 9: 422). Also of note is that he mentions St. Augustine only as the principal opponent of Pelagius (Sermon 22, *Works,* 9: 406). Edwards does not allude to *The City of God,* and there seems to be no evidence that Edwards used the fifth-century classic as a model.

42. Sermon 24, *Works,* 9: 439–41. Edwards does say that "the increase of learning is in itself a thing to be rejoiced in because in itself it is good" (p. 440), but he also emphasizes that its greatest use is in demonstrating human folly unless it is made the handmaid of true religion.

43. Sermon 26, *Works,* 9: 461.

## CHAPTER 12. God "Will Revive the Flame Again"

1. *A History of the Work of Redemption, Works,* 9: 435–36. In his letter to Josiah Willard, June 1, 1740, *Works,* 16: 83–84, he asked for more information on these and other awakenings.

For the wider context, see W. R. Ward, *The Protestant Evangelical Awakening* (Cambridge: Cambridge University Press, 1992), and Ted A. Campbell, *The Religion of the Heart: A Study of European Religious Life in the Seventeenth and Eighteenth Centuries* (Columbia: University of South Carolina Press, 1991).

2. Isaac Watts and John Guyse, preface to *A Faithful Narrative of the Surprising Work of God, Works,* 4: 132.

3. Edwards to Benjamin Colman, May 27, 1738, *Works,* 16: 78.

4. Michael J. Crawford, *Seasons of Grace: Colonial New England's Revival Tradition in Its British Context* (New York: Oxford University Press, 1991), 151–56, has a valuable summary of advance publicity.

5. Edwards to George Whitefield, February 12, 1740, *Works,* 16: 80–81.

6. Whitefield, "Letter to Benjamin Colman," July 4, 1740, pasted inside the cover of a copy of Benjamin Dorr's *History of Christ Church in Philadelphia* (Philadelphia, 1881) in Huntington Library, quoted in Harry S. Stout, *The Divine Dramatist: George Whitefield and the Rise of Modern Evangelicalism* (Grand Rapids, Mich.: Eerdmans, 1991), 117. On Stoddard, see George Whitefield, *George Whitefield's Journals* (Edinburgh: Banner of Truth Trust, 1960), October 17, 1740, p. 476.

7. See Frank Lambert, "'Pedlar in Divinity': George Whitefield and the Great Awakening, 1737–1745," *Journal of American History* 77 (December 1990): 812–37; Lambert, *"Pedlar in Divinity": George Whitefield and the Transatlantic Revivals, 1737–1770* (Princeton: Princeton University Press, 1994), chap. 2; Lambert, *Inventing the "Great Awakening"* (Princeton: Princeton University Press, 1999).

8. Whitefield, *Journals,* September 22, 1740, p. 461, and pp. 457–74, passim.

9. Ibid., October 12 and 14, pp. 472–74. Cf. Mark A. Peterson, *The Price of Redemption: The Spiritual Economy of Puritan New England* (Stanford: Stanford University Press, 1997), 225–26.

10. On Whitefield, see Nathan Cole, "The Spiritual Trials of Nathan Cole," ed. Michael Crawford, *William and Mary Quarterly*, 3d ser., 33 (1976): 93. On Edwards, Whitefield, *Journals*, October 17, 1740, p. 476.

11. Cf. anonymous contemporary description of Whitefield, from the *New England Journal*, quoted in Arnold A. Dallimore, *George Whitefield: The Life and Times of the Great Evangelist of the Eighteenth-Century Revival*, vol. 1 (London: Banner of Truth Trust, 1970), 435–36.

12. Whitefield, *Journals*, October 17–19, 1740, pp. 475–77. Another often quoted letter, supposedly from Sarah Edwards to James Pierpont, October 24, 1740, describing Whitefield's preaching on this occasion, is an apocryphal nineteenth-century invention.

13. Edwards to Whitefield, December 14, 1740, *Works*, 16: 87. Edwards to Thomas Prince, December 12, 1743, *Works*, 16: 115–27.

14. Whitefield, *Journals*, October 19, 1740, p. 477.

15. Ibid., October 12, 1740, p. 473.

16. Ibid., October 19, 1740, p. 476–77.

17. This interpretation essentially follows that of Stout, *Divine Dramatist*, 156–73. See Dallimore, *Whitefield*, 1: 465–76, for documentation and other information.

18. Whitefield, *Journals*, October 21, 1740, p. 479. Parkman's diary, October 20, 1740, mentions it being very cold with light snow on the ground Monday morning, further east in Westborough. Ebenezer Parkman, *The Diary of Ebenezer Parkman, 1703–1782* (Worcester, Mass.: American Antiquarian Society, 1974), 85.

19. Cole, "Spiritual Trials," 93. Cole's famous account was of Whitefield's appearance in Middletown, Connecticut, two days after Whitefield left Edwards, an appearance which drew no special comment in Whitefield's journal other than that about four thousand were present, not an unusual crowd. Whitefield, *Journals*, October 23, 1740, p. 479.

20. On the awakening as an unprecedented intracolonial popular event, see Stout, *Divine Dramatist*, and Stout, *New England Soul*, chap. 10. On the awakening as an international phenomenon, see esp. Susan O'Brien, "A Transatlantic Community of Saints: The Great Awakening and the First Evangelical Network, 1735–1755," *American Historical Review* 91 (1986): 811–32; and W. R. Ward, *The Protestant Evangelical Awakening* (Cambridge: Cambridge University Press, 1992).

21. Whitefield, *Journals*, October 21, 1740, p. 478.

22. Harry S. Stout, *The New England Soul: Preaching and Religious Culture in Colonial New England* (New York: Oxford University Press, 1986), 194–95.

23. Whitefield, *Journals*, October 21, 1740, p. 479.

24. Edwards to Thomas Clap, October 29, 1744, *Works*, 16: 157.

25. *The Distinguishing Marks of a Work of the Spirit of God, Works*, 4: 230.

26. Ibid., 226, 229

27. This account is based on Ava Chamberlain, "The Grand Sower of the Seed: Jonathan Edwards's Critique of George Whitefield," *New England Quarterly* 70, no. 3 (September 1997): 368–85.

28. Edwards to Thomas Clap, October 29, 1744, *Works*, 16: 157. Edwards elaborates his views most fully in *Religious Affections, Works*, 2: 432–58.

29. Edwards to "Friends in Scotland," after September 16, 1745, *Works*, 16: 178.

30. Stout, *Divine Dramatist*, 220–33.

CHAPTER 13. The Hands of God and the Hand of Christ

1. Edwards to George Whitefield, December 14, 1740, *Works*, 16: 87. Edwards to Benjamin Colman, March 9, 1741, ibid., 88. Ebenezer Parkman, *The Diary of Ebenezer Parkman, 1703–1782* (Worcester, Mass.: American Antiquarian Society, 1974), December 1740, p. 87, refers to the heavy snows.

2. Edwards to Sarah Edwards, June 25, 1741, *Works*, 16: 95–96.

3. Kevin Sweeney, "River Gods and Related Minor Deities: The Williams Family and the Connecticut River Valley, 1637–1790" (Ph.D. diss., Yale University, 1986), 173.

4. Ibid., 269.

5. Thomas Prince, account of the awakening in Boston as quoted in Joseph Tracy, *The Great Awakening: A History of the Revival of Religion in the Time of Edwards and Whitefield*, repr. of 1841 ed. (New York: Arno Press, 1969), 115–16.

6. Edwin Scott Gaustad, *The Great Awakening in New England* (New York: Harper and Brothers, 1957), 33–34.

7. Prince's account as quoted in Tracy, *Great Awakening*, 117–20

8. Edwards to Eleazar Wheelock, June 9, 1741, *Works*, 16: 90.

9. Kenneth Minkema, "The Edwardses: A Ministerial Family in Eighteenth-Century New England" (Ph.D. diss., University of Connecticut, 1988), 126–36. See chapter 16, below, for more detail.

10. Edwards to Eleazar Wheelock, June 9, 1741, *Works*, 16: 89–90.

11. Edwards to Thomas Prince, December 12, 1743, *Works*, 16: 117–18.

12. Jonathan Parsons, account dated April 14, 1744, regarding Lyme, Connecticut, as quoted from *Christian History* 2: 136, in Tracy, *Great Awakening*, 138.

13. Tracy, *Great Awakening*, 120–212, gives quotations from mostly contemporary sources, especially Prince's *Christian History*, and provides accounts of such phenomena in many places. Harry S. Stout, *The New England Soul: Preaching and Religious Culture in Colonial New England* (New York: Oxford University Press, 1986), 200, lists a dozen native "young itinerants," and there were doubtless many more, including Parsons and Edwards. The term "great awakening," by which the larger set of events of the era eventually came to be known, was not the standard designation at the time, though contemporaries certainly would have recognized its meaning.

14. Edwards to Deacon Moses Lyman, August 31, 1741, *Works*, 16: 97.

15. Stephen Williams, diary, September 3, 1740, July 20, 1741 (typescript), Storrs Memorial Library, Longmeadow, Mass. Cf. John Demos, *The Unredeemed Captive: A Family Story from Early America* (New York: Knopf, 1994), 193–201, for detailed account. Edwards' sermon was on Psalm 119:56, September 1740. Its theme was that people are often blessed for doing their duty, even when the immediate cost is great. On Joseph Meacham, see *Sibley's Harvard Graduates*, 5: 533–36.

16. This and the following account of the events surrounding the sermon is from Stephen Williams' diary, July 8, 1741, unless otherwise noted.

17. Eleazar Wheelock's account comes from much later and is in Benjamin Trumbull, *A Complete History of Connecticut*, 2 vols. (New Haven, 1818), 2: 145. Trumbull's note says, "Mr. Wheelock went from Connecticut, who gave me information of the whole affair."

18. Hopkins, *Life*, 47–48.

19. Wilson Kimnach provides an excellent account of the sermon's context and precedents. He makes the point that, strictly speaking, *Sinners* is not a hell-fire sermon. See *Works*, 10: 168–79. Even Edwards' later opponent, Charles Chauncy, used an image similar to Edwards' dangling spider in June 1741. See C. C. Goen, "Introduction," *Works*, 4: 56n.

20. Christopher Lukasik, "Feeling the Force of Certainty: The Divine Science, Newtonianism, and Jonathan Edwards's 'Sinners in the Hands of an Angry God,'" *William and Mary Quarterly* 73 (June 2000): 222–45, makes some astute observations connecting this point to Edwards' interest in Newtonian science of universal gravitation, which in turn can be related to Edwards' dispositional view of reality.

21. For instance, in summer 1739, he interrupted his often matter-of-fact series on the history of redemption to preach a stunning sermon around the image of the sun. Christ's coming for the wicked "will be a scorching sun to them. Yea, it shall set them a-fire as stubble, as dry and dead plants, and shall utterly burn them up and leave neither root nor branch. . . . But with respect to them that fear God's name, his beams shall not be scorching but healing, of a benign, pleasant, healthful nature. His light will be joyfull to them; it will be a glorious morning to them when this Sun arises after such a long night, and their souls shall grow and flourish under the influences of that Sun, as living plants and animals grow and thrive under the warm beams of the sun, so that they shall grow up as calves of the stall."

So on an early summer's day he went on through the entire sermon reiterating with vivid images all the terrible and beneficial qualities of the same sun, which is Christ, whose coming is like a refiner's fire: "Christ will then appear an infinitely holy, just judge. The sight of this holiness and justice will be joyful to the saints; it will appear as a ravishing beauty in their eyes. But the ungodly will hate the sight of it. Christ's pure eyes will pierce their souls with torment, like piercing flames of fire that they cannot endure." Sermon, Malachi 4:1–2 (May 1739).

22. The text of *Sinners in the Hands of an Angry God*, Deuteronomy 32:35 (1741) can be found in many editions. The quotations here are from *Reader*, ed. Smith, Stout, and Minkema, 89–105.

23. Quoted from Ola Winslow, *Jonathan Edwards, 1703–1758* (New York: Macmillan, 1940), 192, from Watts' handwritten comment on title page of volume, owned by Forbes Library, Northampton.

24. Sermon, Deuteronomy 32:35 (June 1741; original version of *Sinners*), edited for Yale edition. I am indebted to the editor's introduction.

25. George S. Claghorn, Introduction to Edwards to Deborah Hatheway, June 3, 1741, *Works*, 16: 90–91. Quotations that follow are from the letter, pp. 91–95.

### CHAPTER 14. "He That Is Not with Us Is Against Us"

1. Edwards to Deacon Moses Lyman, August 31 1741, *Works*, 16: 97–98. Kevin Sweeney, "River Gods and Related Minor Deities: The Williams Family and the Connecticut River Valley, 1637–1790" (Ph.D. diss., Yale University, 1986), 298–300. Edwards' funeral sermon *The Resort and Remedy of Those That Are Bereaved by the Death of an Eminent Minister* (Boston, 1741).

2. Jonathan Belcher to Thomas Hutchinson, May 11, 1741 (Belcher Papers, Massachusetts Historical Society), quoted in Michael Batinski, *Jonathan Belcher, Colonial*

*Governor* (Lexington: University Press of Kentucky, 1996), 144. This account is from ibid., 139–48, and T. H. Breen and Timothy Hall, "Structuring Provincial Imagination: The Rhetoric and Experience of Social Change in Eighteenth-Century New England," *American Historical Review* 103, no. 5 (1998): 1411–39.

3. These last two paragraphs are based largely on Breen and Hall, "Structuring Provincial Imagination," passim. See also Rosalyn Remer, "Old Lights and New Money: A Note on Religion, Economics, and the Social Order in 1740 Boston," *William and Mary Quarterly*, 3d ser., 47 (October 1990): 566–73; and Frank Lambert, *Inventing the "Great Awakening"* (Princeton: Princeton University Press, 1999), 134–36. Land Bank proponents tended to be from New Light churches, even if there was seldom a direct connection.

4. Batinski, *Belcher*, 146.

5. New Light clergy were considerably more likely to have subscribed to the Land Bank than were their Old Light counterparts, but still a large majority of New Light clergy were not subscribers. See Harry S. Stout, "The Great Awakening in New England Reconsidered: The New England Clergy," *Journal of Social History*, 8 (1974): 26. John L. Brooke, *The Heart of the Commonwealth: Society and Political Culture in Worcester County, Massachusetts, 1713–1861* (Cambridge: Cambridge University Press, 1989), explores the complexities of the relation between the constituencies of the two movements and suggests that some former Land Bank constituents were drawn to the awakening as a reaction to the "covetousness" of the preceding era, p. 70 and passim. According to the survey of the literature in Breen and Hall, "Structuring Provincial Imagination," 141, no causal link has been established between the two movements.

6. Stephen Williams' diary, May 16, 1741, quoted in Sweeney, "River Gods," 300. Jonathan Edwards in his funeral sermon for Williams, *The Resort and Remedy of Those That Are Bereaved by the Death of an Eminent Minister* (Boston, 1741), remarked, "It was not many years ago that the country was filled with aged ministers that were our fathers, but our fathers, where are they?" (p. 22).

7. Philip F. Gura, "Sowing for the Harvest: William Williams and the Great Awakening," *Journal of Presbyterian History* 56, no. 4 (winter 1978): 338, points out that Williams protected Edwards from Williams' sons.

8. Edwards, *Resort and Remedy*, 14. Williams' last message to the Hampshire Association, quoted in a note, p. 21n, ended with the advice: "love your master, love your work, and love one another." The note added: "How very expressive of his own spirit? Like John the beloved disciple."

9. Ibid., 19. This version of the theme was addressed specifically to the children.

10. George Whitefield, *George Whitefield's Journals* (Edinburgh: Banner of Truth Trust, 1960), October 25, 1740, p. 480. Whitefield was hosted by "Mr. Pierpont," one of Sarah's brothers.

11. Samuel Hopkins, "Autobiography," in Edwards A. Park, "Memoir," in *The Works of Samuel Hopkins*, 3 vols. (Boston, 1852), 1: 16. Norman Pettit, "Introduction," *Works*, 7: 38–39.

12. Louis L. Tucker, *Puritan Protagonist: President Thomas Clap of Yale College* (Chapel Hill: University of North Carolina Press, 1962), 124–25. Elisha Williams resigned as rector in 1739, citing health reasons. Proceedings of the Trustees, October 30–31, 1739, in Franklin Bowditch Dexter, ed., *Documentary History of Yale University: Under the Original Charter of the Collegiate School of Connecticut, 1701–1745* (New Haven: Yale University Press, 1916), 337.

13. George Whitefield, *A Continuation of the Reverend Mr. Whitefield's Journal: The Seventh Journal* (London, 1741), 54–55, as quoted in Edwin Gaustad, *The Great Awakening in New England* (New York: Harper and Brothers, 1957), 30. The entry is for October 19, 1740.

14. Gaustad, *Great Awakening*, 32.

15. Anonymous letter from Stonington, Connecticut, *Boston Weekly Post-Boy*, July 29, 1741, p. 1; anonymous letter, *Boston Weekly Post-Boy*, September 28, 1741, p. 3. Gaustad, *Great Awakening*, 36–41. "James Davenport," Franklin Bowditch Dexter, *Biographical Sketches of the Graduates of Yale College*, vol. 1 (New York: Henry Holt, 1885), 447–50. "Head thrown back" quote comes from *Boston Evening Post*, July 5, 1742, quoted in Gaustad, *Great Awakening*, 39, but is consistent with 1741 accounts.

16. *Boston Weekly Post-Boy*, September 28, 1741, p. 2. Tucker, *Puritan Protagonist*, 137.

17. *Boston Weekly Post-Boy*, September 28, 1741, p. 3. This same letter (p. 2) describing itinerants generally, remarks how they tell people "that they are now hanging over the pit of eternal damnation."

18. Proceeding of the Trustees, September 9, 1741, in Dexter, ed. *Documentary History*, 351, cf. p. 350 re Brainerd.

19. Daniel Wadsworth of Hartford as quoted in Tucker, *Puritan Protagonist*, 122.

20. *The Distinguishing Marks of a Work of the Spirit of God, Works*, 4: 276–87. Cf. Ava Chamberlain's valuable observations as to what he learned from first revival, "Self-Deception as a Theological Problem in Jonathan Edwards's 'Treatise Concerning Religious Affections,'" *Church History* 63, no. 4 (1994): 541–56.

21. *Distinguishing Marks, Works*, 4: 228–48, quotes from pp. 228, 230, 235, 243, 244. Cf. pp. 273–74. "'Tis probable that the stumbling blocks that now attend this work will in some respects be increased, and not diminished."

22. Ibid., 248–60. Quote from p. 260.

23. *Works*, 4: 53n.

24. William Cooper, Preface, *Distinguishing Marks, Works*, 4: 215–23. Quotes from pp. 215, 216, 217, 223.

25. *Distinguishing Marks, Works*, 4: 271–73. As early as April 1741 the Hampshire Association had as its question for debate, "What is the sin that is commonly called the sin against the Holy Ghost?" "Introduction," *Works*, 4: 55n.

26. *Distinguishing Marks, Works*, 4: 272–76. In quoting Jesus from Matthew 12:30, Edwards changed "me" to "us."

27. His major qualification, ibid., 275–76, was cryptic: "Those that maliciously oppose and reproach this work, and call it the work of the Devil, want but one thing of the unpardonable sin, and that is doing it against inward conviction."

28. Ibid., 276.

CHAPTER 15. "Heavenly Elysium"

1. *Works*, 16: 98n.

2. Mark Valeri, *Law and Providence in Joseph Bellamy's New England: The Origins of the New Divinity in Revolutionary America* (New York: Oxford University Press, 1994), 14. Edwards later characterized Bellamy as "a little unpolished" but of enormous gifts, Edwards to Thomas Foxcroft, February 5, 1754, *Works*, 16: 619.

3. Edwards to Joseph Bellamy, January 21, 1742, *Works*, 16: 98–100.

4. Sarah Edwards, "Narrative" (1742), reprinted in Dwight, *Life*, 171–86, quotation p. 181.

5. *Some Thoughts Concerning the Present Revival of Religion, Works*, 4: 340.

6. Ibid., 331.

7. Ibid., 334. Sarah was born January 9, 1710.

8. Ibid., 333–34

9. Ibid., 334–35.

10. Ibid., 341. John Wesley defined sin as a willful choice and so believed in "Christian perfection" in the sense of the ability of a person to be free from willful transgression of known law. Edwards believed in the inward corruption of human nature that was not entirely eradicated among the regenerate. Cf. C. C. Goen's note, *Works*, 4: 341n.

11. Probably they would have mentioned it if the group were women only. Jonathan wrote, "Indeed, modesty might in ordinary cases, restrain some persons, as women, and those that are young, from so much as speaking when a great number are present; at least, when some of those present are much their superiors, unless they are spoken to: and yet the case may be so extraordinary as fully to warrant it. . . . [For instance, if they are struck by lightening] . . . I have seen some women and children in such circumstances, on religious accounts, that it has appeared to me no more a transgressing the laws of humility and modesty for them to speak freely, let who will be present, than if they were dying." *Some Thoughts, Works*, 4: 486.

12. Jonathan readily adopted this innovation. Later that year he wrote, "'tis unreasonable to suppose that the Christian church should forever, and even in times of her greatest light in her praises of God and the Lamb, be confined only to the words of the Old Testament, wherein all the greatest and most glorious things of the Gospel, that are infinitely the greatest subjects of her praise, are spoken of under a veil." Ibid., 407.

13. Handel, *Theodora* (1749), Aria, act 1.

14. Fragment (in Edwards' hand) of Sarah Edwards' Narrative, Edwards Collections, ANTS, Works of Edwards transcription. The much more vague corresponding passage is in Dwight, *Life*, 183. This fragment is all we have of the original, and we do not know what else Dwight edited out. Sarah's account, on which the present summation is based, is in Dwight, *Life*, 171–83. Jonathan's version in *Some Thoughts, Works*, 4: 331–41.

15. William Patten, *Reminiscences of the Late Rev. Samuel Hopkins, D.D.* (Boston, 1843), 26. Although this late source may be questionable, Hopkins was present at the event. Patten was later for twenty-one years a confidant of Hopkins (1721–1803) and had written down this version of Hopkins' probably often-repeated recollection.

16. Edwards' account is in a letter from Edwards to Thomas Prince, December 12, 1743, *Works*, 16: 120–21.

17. Samuel Mather to Edwards, n.d., in sermon, Luke 12:35–36 (December 1742), Edwards Collection, Beinecke, Works of Edwards transcription.

18. Stephen J. Stein, "'For Their Spiritual Good': The Northampton, Massachusetts, Prayer Bids of the 1730s and 1740s," *William and Mary Quarterly*, 3d ser., 37, no. 2 (April 1980): 273. The two Lyman girls died December 8, 1742. Edwards' sermon was on Luke 12:35–36, which urges people to always be prepared for the immediate coming of the Lord. He also preached a sermon on the occasion of the fire, on Micah 6:9, the first point of which was "God's voice sometimes cries to a city or town in the awful rebukes of his

providence." In the 1749 tax list, Capt. John Lyman is listed as one of the wealthier citizens of the town. James R. Trumbull, *History of Northampton, Massachusetts, from Its Settlement in 1654,* 2 vols. (Northampton, Mass., 1898, 1902), 2: 185.

19. The Works of Edwards furnish the following draft note with their transcription: "In pre-modern medical diagnosis, hysteria was defined as a morbidly excited condition caused by a disturbance of the nervous system due to a disruption in uterine functions. See George Hartmann, *The Family Physician* (London, 1696); William Salmon, *Medicine Practica: or, Practical Physick* (London, 1692); and John Harris, *The Divine Physician* (London, 1767)." Standard histories of hysteria agree that it was regarded as a nervous disorder in the eighteenth century, although by that time some were questioning its uterine origins. See Ilza Veith, *Hysteria: The History of a Disease* (Chicago: University of Chicago Press, 1965), esp. 120–98. For a survey of historians' interpretations see Mark S. Micale, *Approaching Hysteria: Disease and Its Interpretations* (Princeton: Princeton University Press, 1995), 33–107. (I am also grateful to my colleague David Hartley for some comments on this topic.) Supporting the supposition that Sarah's difficulties may have been related to a pregnancy is a notation in Edwards' account book, Beinecke, Works of Edwards transcription, that he sent for "hysterick drops and powders" in January 1745, which is about four to five months before the birth of Jonathan Edwards Jr. on May 28, 1745. That might also support the supposition that Dr. Mather wrote his prescription in December 1742, also four to five months before a birth.

20. Cf. Catherine Brekus, *Strangers and Pilgrims: Female Preaching in America, 1740–1845* (Chapel Hill: University of North Carolina Press, 1998), 38. Ava Chamberlain, "Brides of Christ and Signs of Grace: Edwards' Sermon Series on the Parable of the Wise and Foolish Virgins," in Stephen J. Stein, ed., *Jonathan Edwards's Writings: Text, Context, Interpretation* (Bloomington: Indiana University Press, 1996), 3–18.

21. Amanda Porterfield, *Female Piety in Puritan New England: The Emergence of Religious Humanism* (New York: Oxford University Press, 1992), esp. chaps. 7–8. Cf. Porterfield, *Feminine Spirituality in America: From Sarah Edwards to Martha Graham* (Philadelphia: Temple University Press, 1980). My interpretations in this section have been helped by suggestions from Porterfield and other historians of gender cited.

22. Cf. Sandra M. Gustafson, *Eloquence Is Power: Oratory and Performance in Early America,* (Chapel Hill: University of North Carolina Press, 2000), 51–74. Julie Ellison, "The Sociology of 'Holy Indifference': Sarah Edwards' Narrative," *American Literature* 56, no. 4 (December 1984): 479–95; and Porterfield, *Feminine Spirituality.*

23. Samuel Hopkins, "Autobiography," in Edwards A. Park, "Memoir," in *The Works of Samuel Hopkins,* 3 vols., ed. Edwards A. Park (Boston, 1852), 1: 16–18.

24. Ibid., 19.

25. Ibid., 22.

26. Samuel Hopkins, *The Life and Character of the Late Reverend Mr. Jonathan Edwards* (Boston, 1765), appendix 2, "containing a Short Sketch of Mrs. Edwards's Life and Character," 92–98. Levin's reprint does not contain the appendices. On Edwards' discipline, see Hopkins, *Life,* 43.

27. Samuel Hopkins, "Journal," July 23, 1743, in Park, "Memoir," *Works of Samuel Hopkins,* 1: 49.

28. He also wrote a tribute to Esther after her untimely death, remarking on both her great beauty and intellect. Hopkins, *Life,* appendix 1, pp. 88–92.

29. Ibid., "Sarah Edwards," 95.

30. Hopkins, *Life*, 49, cf. quotation in chapter 8, above.

31. Ebenezer Parkman, *The Diary of Ebenezer Parkman, 1703–1782* (Worcester, Mass.: American Antiquarian Society, 1974), April 1 and 2, 1740, p. 76, and May 25, 1744, p. 97. Samuel Hopkins, "Journal," May 24, 1744, in Park, "Memoir," *Works of Samuel Hopkins*, 1: 49. In December 1743 Hopkins had settled as minister in a tiny frontier church at Housatonock (Great Barrington), near Stockbridge. Some time after that, we are told, he was courting a Northampton young woman who was "rather a belle of the place." She broke off their engagement when a former suitor returned. Hopkins finally married in 1748. From William Patten, *Samuel Hopkins*, 31.

## CHAPTER 16. Conservative Revolutionary

1. Hopkins, *Life*, 39–51. For more detail of Hopkins' portrait see the beginning of chapter 8, above.

2. Hopkins, *Life*, 41–42.

3. Ibid., 53.

4. Numbers 12:3. Exodus 4:10.

5. Kenneth P. Minkema, "Jonathan Edwards' Defense of Slavery," *Massachusetts Historical Review* 2 (2002). I am grateful to Kristin Kobes DuMez regarding the possible name change. When the Edwardses moved to Stockbridge they took a slave named Rose with them. Rose was not mentioned in the inventory of the Edwards estate in 1758, but her son, a boy named Titus, was. Rose was free and a full member of the Stockbridge church by 1771, raising the possibility that the Edwardses had manumitted her or allowed her husband to purchase her freedom before 1758. Alternatively, the Edwardses may have sold her to someone else who later granted her her freedom. During the 1750s, Sarah Edwards was actively seeking to purchase a slave and had Jonathan ask both Joseph Bellamy, February 28, 1754, *Works*, 16: 622, and their daughter Esther Edwards Burr, November 20, 1757, *Works*, 16: 731, about the availability of one of theirs.

6. Samuel Sewall, *The Selling of Joseph: A Memorial* [Boston, 1700], ed. Sidney Kaplan (Amherst: University Massachusetts Press, 1969), 10, takes for granted the knowledge that "their forbidden liberty, renders them unwilling servants."

7. Gordon S. Wood, *The Radicalism of the American Revolution* (New York: Knopf, 1991), 52–55. On the dynamics of the relation between indentured servitude and chattel slavery in colonial Virginia, see Edmund S. Morgan, *American Slavery, American Freedom: The Ordeal of Colonial Virginia* (New York: Norton, 1975).

8. This account of the controversy with Doolittle is based on the remarkably detailed reconstruction the episode in Minkema, "Edwards' Defense."

9. Minkema, "Edwards' Defense," Wintthrop D. Jordan, *White over Black: American Attitudes Toward the Negro 1550–1812* (Baltimore: Penguin, 1969 [1968]), 116–21.

10. "Draft Letter on Slavery," 1741, *Works*, 16: 72–76. Edwards drew a vertical line through the section regarding the Egyptians, but sometimes he did that to indicate he had used that part of a draft. My interpretation of this letter is indebted to that of Kenneth P. Minkema, "Jonathan Edwards on Slavery and the Slave Trade," *William and Mary Quarterly* 3d ser., 54, no. 4 (October 1997): 823–30. Minkema's article includes the text of the letter, 831–34. His notes also list the bibliography relevant to this issue.

11. *A History of the Work of Redemption,* Sermon 27, *Works,* 9: 472, 480. The quotation continues with Isaiah 32: 3–4, "The eyes of them that see shall not be dim and the ears [of them that hear shall hearken]. The heart of the rash shall understand knowledge."

12. MS "Miscellaneous Observations on the Holy Scriptures" ("Interleaved Bible"), Beinecke, as quoted in Minkema, "Edwards' Defense," n68.

13. "Draft Letter on Slavery," *Works,* 16: 72–76.

14. Many commentators have remarked on the parallels between the popular religion of the Great Awakening and the popular political culture of the American Revolution. Alan Heimert, *Religion and the American Mind: From the Great Awakening to the Revolution* (Cambridge: Harvard University Press, 1966), and Harry S. Stout, "The Ideological Origins of the American Revolution," *William and Mary Quarterly,* 3d ser., 34 (1977): 519–41, have argued for the importance of some direct causal connections. John M. Murrin, "No Awakening, No Revolution? More Counterfactual Speculations," *Reviews in American History* 11 (1983): 161–71, provides a helpful overview of the debates, concluding (p. 169), "Without the Great Awakening and its successors, there would have been a revolution in 1775, but in all probability, no Civil War in 1861."

15. This theme and the paradox with Edwards' revolutionary agenda is well developed in Patricia J. Tracy, *Jonathan Edwards, Pastor: Religion and Society in Eighteenth-Century Northampton* (New York: Hill and Wang, 1980), esp. 188–194. Cf. chapter 22, below.

16. Kenneth Minkema, "The Edwardses: A Ministerial Family in Eighteenth-Century New England" (Ph.D. diss., University of Connecticut, 1988), 126–36. Jonathan helped resolve the dispute by encouraging Eleazar Wheelock and Benjamin Pomeroy to preach in East Windsor in 1741, Edwards to Wheelock, June 9, 1741, *Works,* 16: 89–90, the parties being reconciled during the ensuing awakening.

17. Edwards to Thomas Prince, December 12, 1743, *Works,* 16: 121, 125–26.

18. "A Copy of a Covenant Entered into and Subscribed by the People of God at Northampton . . . March 16, 1741/42," in ibid., 121–25. The covenant also contains a short paragraph promising to "perform relative duties, required by Christian rules" in families "towards parents and children, husbands and wives, brothers and sisters, masters or mistresses and servants."

19. George Whitefield, *George Whitefield's Journals* (Edinburgh: Banner of Truth Trust, 1960), October 21, 1740, pp. 478–79.

20. See chapter 7, above.

21. Edwards to Prince, December 12, 1743, *Works,* 16: 121, 124–25.

22. *Some Thoughts Concerning the Present Revival of Religion, Works,* 4. Though it bore a 1742 date, it did not appear until March 1743. Goen, *Works,* 4: 65n.

23. *Some Thoughts, Works,* 4: 291.

24. *Some Thoughts, Works,* 4: 353.

25. Isaac Watts to Benjamin Colman, September 14, 1743, quoted in *Works,* 4: 71.

26. *Some Thoughts, Works,* 4: 353–58.

27. Quoted in Stephen Foster, *The Long Argument: English Puritanism and the Shaping of New England Culture, 1570–1700* (Chapel Hill: University of North Carolina Press, 1991), 298.

28. James Davidson, *The Logic of Millennial Thought: Eighteenth-Century New England* (New Haven: Yale University Press, 1977), 122–75; Gerald McDermott, *One Holy and*

*Happy Society: The Public Theology of Jonathan Edwards* (University Park: Pennsylvania State University Press, 1992), 56.

29. Edwards to Reverend William McCulloch, March 5, 1743/44, *Works*, 16: 135–36.

30. The discussion in McDermott, *One Holy and Happy Society*, 50–92, is very helpful in pointing out that Edwards did not think the millennium was beginning in America, contrary to what most interpreters say, but he tends to play down the extent to which Edwards did say that a last great glorious era of revival was commencing and that it was apparently beginning in America. Edwards also seemed to imply that the millennium itself would center in America, as when he spoke of God hewing out a "paradise" in a wilderness.

31. Although the term "the Great Awakening" was not yet the standard one for the great revival, the high estimate of its eschatological significance by Edwards and many others should put to rest any suggestion that the greatness of the revival was an invention of the nineteenth century. Cf. Frank Lambert, *Inventing the "Great Awakening"* (Princeton: Princeton University Press, 1999).

32. *Some Thoughts, Works*, 4: 497.

33. *Some Thoughts, Works*, 4: 372–73. Charles Chauncy, *Seasonable Thoughts on the State of Religion in New England* . . . (Boston, 1743), from excerpt in *The Great Awakening: Documents Illustrating the Crisis and Its Consequences*, ed. Alan Heimert and Perry Miller (Indianapolis: Bobbs-Merrill, 1967), 299–300, replied that when a people is so divided on a religious question it was quite proper that the civil authorities not take one side or the other.

34. Though Whitefield's letter, from outgoing shipboard, was dated July 25, 1741, it was not published in the *Boston Gazette* until March 16, 1742. See Richard Bushman, ed., *The Great Awakening: Documents on the Revival of Religion, 1740–1745* (New York: Atheneum, 1970), 38, for Whitefield's letter, and pp. 35–38 for a reply to Whitefield's original remarks, *Boston Gazette*, April 20, 1741.

35. *Some Thoughts, Works*, 4: 510–11.

## CHAPTER 17. A House Divided

1. Edwin Gaustad, *The Great Awakening in New England* (New York: Harper and Brothers, 1957), 55.

2. Making his position more tenuous was that the previous year Mather had been one of the few local pastors to oppose the dismissal of the Reverend Samuel Osborn, whom the majority judged to have liberal theological views, tending toward Arminianism. Edward Griffin, *Old Brick: Charles Chauncy of Boston, 1705–1787* (Minneapolis: University of Minnesota Press, 1980), 48–59.

3. Ibid., 6. In his picture (see p. 270 of this book), from age eighty-one, one can see how his square face might suggest a brick, and he is holding a volume at an angle so that it too resembles a brick.

4. Ibid., 59–63.

5. Cf. Ibid., 63.

6. Charles Chauncy, *A Letter from a Gentleman in Boston, to Mr. George Wishart, One of the Ministers of Edinburgh, Concerning the State of Religion in New England* (Edinburgh,

1742), reprinted in Richard L. Bushman, ed., *The Great Awakening: Documents on the Revival of Religion, 1740–1745* (New York: Atheneum, 1970), 117–19. The letter was dated August 4, 1742.

7. Samuel Buell to Eleazar Wheelock, April 20, 1742, reprinted in Bushman, *Great Awakening*, 44.

8. Charles Chauncy, *The Outpouring of the Holy Ghost*, preached May 13, 1742 (Boston, 1742), 43–44, quoted in Griffin, *Old Brick*, 65.

9. "An Act for Regulating Abuses and Correcting Disorders in Ecclesiastical Affairs," reprinted in Bushman, *Great Awakening*, 58–60.

10. "Extract of a Letter from Hartford, June 15th, 1742," *Boston Weekly News-Letter*, July 1, 1742, reprinted in Bushman, *Great Awakening*, 45–49. Quotation is from the Assembly's proceedings.

11. "Declaration with Regard to the Rev. Mr. James Davenport and his Conduct," by the associated pastors of Boston and Charlestown, July 1, 1742, reprinted in Joseph Tracy, *The Great Awakening*, repr. of 1841 ed. (New York: Arno Press, 1969), 242–43.

12. Charles Chauncy, *Enthusiasm Described and Cautioned Against: A Sermon Preached . . . the Lord's Day after the Commencement . . .* (Boston, 1742). Available in Alan Heimert and Perry Miller, eds., *The Great Awakening: Documents Illustrating the Crisis and Its Consequences* (Indianapolis: Bobbs-Merrill, 1967), 228–56, quotation from p. 231. Quotations regarding Davenport are from "A Letter to the Reverend Mr. James Davenport" (prefaced to the original), xi.

13. This follows Tracy's well-documented account, *Great Awakening*, 243–48. Tracy's quotation from Prince (p. 244) is from *Christian History*, vol. 2, around p. 408. The quotations attributed to Davenport are from Grand Jury testimony, August 19–20, 1742.

14. Griffin, *Old Brick*, 29–31, 71–89, 127–38. Griffin suggests the phrase "mass hysteria," p. 71.

15. Jonathan Ashley, *The Great Gift of Charity Considered and Applied . . .* (Boston 1742), passim. For context, see Gregory Nobles, *Divisions throughout the Whole: Politics and Society in Hampshire County, Massachusetts, 1740–1775* (New York: Cambridge University Press, 1983), 50–52.

16. Jonathan Ashley, *A Letter from the Reverend Mr. Jonathan Ashley, to the Reverend Mr. William Cooper, . . .* (Boston, 1743), 3. Cooper, letter in *Boston Gazette*, January 11, 1743. Other comments are in *Boston Gazette*, February 1, 1743; *Boston Evening-Post*, January 17, 24, and February 7, 1743; and J. F., *Remarks on the Rev. Mr. Cooper's Objections to the Rev. Mr. Ashley's Sermon* (Boston, 1743). For biographical information on Cooper, who died December 1743, see *Sibley's Harvard Graduates*, 5: 624–34.

17. *Boston Weekly Post-Boy*, March 28, 1743, reprinted in Bushman, *Great Awakening*, 51–53, provides a very biased and no doubt exaggerated account. It seems confirmed, however, by Davenport's later retraction to the extent that Davenport at least *later* believed he had been possessed of an evil spirit and that he was physically ill. Cf. the accounts in Tracy, *Great Awakening*, 248–49, C. C. Goen, *Revivalism and Separatism in New England, 1740–1800* (New Haven: Yale University Press, 1962), 68–70, and Peter S. Onuf, "New Lights in New London: A Group Portrait of the Separatists," *William and Mary Quarterly*, 3d ser., 37, no. 4 (October 1980): 627–43, for context.

18. Edwards to Sarah Edwards, March 25, 1743, *Works*, 16: 104–5.

19. Goen, *Revivalism and Separatism*, 70, quotation is from *Diary of Joshua Hempsted* (New London, 1901), 407.

20. "The Rev. Mr. Davenport's Retraction," July 28, 1744, is republished, along with information on its context, in Tracy, *Great Awakening*, 249–55. Tracy points out that a debilitating physical condition accompanied Davenport's mental agitations and speculates that a recovery from the former may help explain his retraction. Edwards' direct role, while not stated directly, is implied by what seems to be a firsthand report in his letter to Wheelock, July 13, 1744, from which the quotation is taken.

21. Edwards to Moses Lyman, May 10, 1742, *Works*, 16: 102–3.

22. "Fair copy of Kingsley Case, Congregational Library, London, MS II c 1/59," typescript furnished by Works of Edwards project. On Kingsley's earlier confession, see Catherine A. Brekus, *Female Preaching in America: Strangers and Pilgrims, 1740–1845* (Chapel Hill: University of North Carolina Press, 1988), 23. Cf. Brekus' helpful account of the episode, ibid., 23–26, and her larger account of New Light women preachers.

23. Stephen Foster, *The Long Argument: English Puritanism and the Shaping of New England Culture, 1570–1700* (Chapel Hill: University of North Carolina Press, 1991), 291. Foster offers helpful insights on the long-range dynamics of the divisions.

24. Goen, *Revivalism and Separatism*, 58–64; Gaustad, *Great Awakening*, 74–76. Elisha Williams, *The Essential Rights and Liberties of Protestants: A Seasonable Plea for the Liberty of Conscience and the Right of Private Judgment* (Boston, 1744). An excerpt of this is found in Heimert, *Great Awakening*, 323–39.

25. Edwards to the Reverend Ebenezer Pemberton, December 2, 1743, *Works*, 16: 113–14. Edwards here addressed specifically the question of whether the Milford New Lights must submit themselves to the ecclesiastical rule of the majority of the colony. Despite these strong statements, Edwards stopped short of judging the specific case, saying that he had not been able to hear both sides.

26. Jonathan Edwards to Elnathan Whitman, February 9, 1744, *Works*, 16: 128–33. Biography of Elnathan Whitman in Franklin Bowditch Dexter, *Biographical Sketches of the Graduates of Yale College*, vol. 1 (New York: Henry Holt, 1885), 343–44.

27. In May 1743 Edwards, accompanied by his daughter Sarah, rode to Boston, part way in the company of Thomas Clap, see *Works*, 16: 153–72.

28. Tracy, *Great Awakening*, 286–302, provides the most complete account of these conventions, including reprints of the two testimonies and information from related documents. The Hampshire County letter, June 30, 1743, of which Stephen Williams is the first signatory, is in *Works*, 16: 111–12.

29. For a helpful overview, see John E. Van de Wetering, "The *Christian History* of the Great Awakening," *Journal of Presbyterian History*, 44, no. 2 (1966): 122–29.

30. *Boston Evening Post*, July 4, 1743. Cf. March 14, May 30, and June 13. Cf. account in Frank Lambert, *Inventing the "Great Awakening"* (Princeton: Princeton University Press, 1999), 193, 201–3; and "Thomas Prince," *Sibley's Harvard Graduates*, 5: 356.

31. Perry Miller, *Jonathan Edwards* (New York: William Sloane, 1949), 175. The two sides were playing a numbers game in their futile struggles to vest their rival pronouncements with the authority that clerical assemblies were supposed to have. Even though the *Testimony and Advice* had far more clerical signatories than had the earlier Old Light *Testimony*, the *Boston Evening Post*, August 25, 1743, pointed out that its 111 clergy were still

far short of a majority of the some 400 established clergy in New England. See Lambert, *Great Awakening*, 203–4, for summary of figures. The New Lights had enlisted 90 of the 250 ministers in Massachusetts, which was their primary focus.

32. Griffin, *Old Brick*, 73–79.

33. C. C. Goen, "Introduction," *Works*, 4: 82n–83n, provides a table of parallel arguments and counterarguments in the two volumes.

34. Charles Chauncy, *Seasonable Thoughts on the State of Religion in New-England* (Boston, 1743), vi–xxx, 329–30, and passim. Cf. Griffin's excellent discussion, *Old Brick*, 81–88. Goen, "Introduction," *Works*, 4: 89–97, also provides a useful summary of the exchange. Chauncy also aided in the anonymous publication of *The Wonderful Narrative; Or, A faithful Account of the French Prophets . . . To Which Are Added, Several Other Remarkable Instances of Persons Under the Influence of Like Spirit . . . Particularly in New England* (Boston, 1742), Gaustad, *Great Awakening*, 89n. About the same time he published *A Letter from a Gentleman in Boston*, quoted from above.

35. Chauncy, *Seasonable Thoughts*, 327.

36. *Some Thoughts Concerning the Present Revival of Religion in New England, Works*, 4: 296–97.

37. Ibid., 397. I am indebted to Timothy Keller for pointing out this passage.

38. *Some Thoughts, Works*, 4: 399.

39. As in the sermons, *The Pure of Heart Blessed* (1730), *Works*, 17: 67; *Charity Contrary to an Angry Spirit* (1738), *Works*, 8: 277.

40. *Christian Knowledge: Or, the Importance and Advantage of a Thorough Knowledge of Divine Truth* (1739) in *Works of Jonathan Edwards*, ed. Hickman, 2: 158.

41. Chauncy, *Seasonable Thoughts*, 327, 384. Cf. Griffin, *Old Brick*, 85–87. See *Old Brick*, p. 197n74, for Chauncy's later high estimate, in replying to Ezra Stiles' inquiry about greatest Americans, that, in comparison to Stoddard, "MR. EDWARDS, his grandson was much the greatest man."

42. Norman Fiering, *Moral Philosophy at Seventeenth-Century Harvard: A Discipline in Transition* (Chapel Hill: University of North Carolina Press, 1981), and Norman Fiering, *Jonathan Edwards's Moral Thought and Its British Context* (Chapel Hill: University of North Carolina Press, 1981), provide the best exposition of this.

43. Edwards to James Robe, May 12, 1743, *Works*, 16: 108–9.

44. Edwards to Thomas Prince, December 12, 1743, *Works*, 16: 125–26. In Edwards' letter to William McCulloch, March 5, 1744, *Works*, 16: 134, he dates the beginning of the decline of the New England awakening from two years previously. This coincides with excesses that attended the aftermath of Buell's ministry in Northampton, described in Edwards to Prince, *Works*, 16: 120–21.

45. Edwards to James Robe, May 12, 1743, *Works*, 16: 109.

46. Dwight, *Life*, 223, says the sermons were probably preached at this time.

47. *Religious Affections, Works*, 2: 86–89. Cf. the passage from Leviticus 9 and 10, quoted on the title page, which describes how after the people bowed down to a fire that the Lord brought to the altar, the sons of Aaron, "Nadab and Abihu—offered strange fire before the Lord, which he commanded them not" so that the Lord destroyed them.

48. Ibid., 95, 96–97, 102.

49. Ibid., 181.

50. Ibid., 194–95.

51. Ibid., 205. On Edwards' scientific thinking and his differences from Locke, see chapter 4, above.

52. Ibid., 197.

53. Ibid., 182–83. See Ava Chamberlain, "Self-Deception as a Theological Problem in Jonathan Edwards's 'Treatise Concerning Religious Affections,'" *Church History* 63, no. 4 (1994): 541–56, which is an important basis for some of the present analysis. Edwards explicitly acknowledged his overestimate in a letter to Thomas Gillespie, July 1, 1751, *Works*, 16: 380–87.

54. *Religious Affections*, 87, 185.

55. Ibid., 329.

56. Ibid., 453.

57. Ibid., 452.

58. Ibid., 249–50. John Piper, *God's Passion for His Glory* (Wheaton, Ill.: Crossway Books, 1998), 35, remarks on the "stunning modern relevance" of these observations.

59. *Religious Affections*, 461.

## CHAPTER 18. A Model Town No More

1. Hopkins, *Life*, 53. Hopkins likely overstated the case, since we do know of perennial salary disputes and of Sarah's allusions to tensions with townspeople in her account of her spiritual experiences.

2. Patricia J. Tracy, *Jonathan Edwards, Pastor: Religion and Society in Eighteenth-Century Northampton* (New York: Hill and Wang, 1980), 148.

3. Edwards to Thomas Prince, December 12, 1742, *Works*, 16, 115–27.

4. William McCulloch to Edwards, August 13, 1743, reprinted in Dwight, *Life*, 198–200. See Arthur Fawcett, *The Chambulang Revival* (London: Banner of Truth Trust, 1971).

5. Edwards to William McCulloch, March 5, 1744, *Works*, 16: 134–42. Edwards now admitted that the revivals may have been a false spring. Drawing on one of his favorite analogies, he wrote, "I have known instances wherein, by the heat's coming on suddenly in the spring without intermissions of cold to check the growth, the branches, many of them, by a too hasty growth have afterwards died. And perhaps God may bring on a spiritual spring as he does the natural, with now and then a pleasant sun-shiny season, and then an interruption by clouds and stormy winds, till at length the sun, by more and more approaching and the light increasing, the strength of the winter is broken."

6. Thomas H. Johnson, "Jonathan Edwards and the 'Young Folks' Bible,'" *New England Quarterly* 5 (1932): 37–54, remains a most valuable source because it includes transcriptions of the relevant documents. Patricia Tracy's careful research in *Jonathan Edwards, Pastor*, 160–64, adds valuable information on the demographics of the group. Tracy's note, p. 257, documents that all but three of the twenty-one were church members. The most outspoken of the ringleaders, Timothy Root, was a church member. See note 25, below. Hopkins, *Life*, 53 describes them as church members. Ava Chamberlain, "Bad Books and Bad Boys: The Transformation of Gender in Eighteenth-Century Northampton, Massachusetts," *New England Quarterly* 75: 2 (June 2002): 179–203, adds important insight on the changing gender relationships the case reveals.

7. Hopkins, *Life*, 53–54. The sermon is apparently lost. Tracy, *Jonathan Edwards*,

*Pastor,* 161, refers to "the tradition originated by Samuel Hopkins' biography . . . in 1765" and suggests that Hopkins' account is unreliable. Only one or two of the accused, she finds, were from "leading families" (though Hopkins adds "or were nearly related"), and she thinks the townspeople should have been able to distinguish the accused men on the list from the women witnesses. We have what appears to be the list in Edwards' writing, including ten young men, then the two town doctors, and finally ten women and one man, Johnson, " 'Young Folks' Bible,' " 42–43. Yet even if this is the exact list Edwards read from, there is nothing in it to contradict Hopkins' story. Hopkins knew of the incident either as an eyewitness or from hearing extensive town talk while the controversy was going on, and the incident was likely to remain vividly in his memory.

Sylvester Judd, 1789–1860, in a manuscript history of the region, Forbes Library, Northampton, Mass., reports that Sarah Clark was one of the accused who testified before the committee, Johnson, " 'Young Folks' Bible,' " 43. Her name, however, does not appear on Edwards' list nor in the testimony he preserved, transcribed in Johnson.

8. Tracy, *Jonathan Edwards, Pastor,* 256n36, citing a 1731 decision of the Hampshire Association.

9. Notes titled "Defense of Actions," ANTS, Works of Edwards transcription. We do not know precisely when in the controversy he presented this defense. Probably it was early because it does not deal with some of the issues that arose in the full investigation.

10. This is from "the Twenty-sixth Edition" of this work, "printed and sold by the booksellers" [London?], 1755. Presumably earlier editions of this or similar works were available in New England by this time. One English edition, known to be in America as early as 1685, was *The Problems of Aristotle with Other Philosophers and Physicians: Wherein Are Contained Divers Questions, with Their Answers, Touching the Estate of Man's Body,* printed in 1679 for J. Wright. Johnson, " 'Young Folks' Bible,' " 52–53.

11. This volume was Thomas Dawkes, *The Midwife Rightly Instructed: or the Way, Which All Women Desirous to Learn, Should Take, to Acquire the True Knowledge and Be Successful in the Practices of the Art of Midwifery. With a Prefatory Address to the Married Part of British Ladies, etc.* (London: J. Oswald, 1736). Its unremarkable contents are described in Chamberlain, "Bad Books."

12. Edwards' notes on the testimony, ANTS, Works of Edwards transcription. Most of this testimony is also transcribed, with slight differences, in Johnson, " 'Young Folks' Bible,' " 43–51.

13. See below concerning the confession of Oliver Warner, where his fault lies in the language he allegedly used when taunting two women.

14. "Defense of Actions," ANTS, Works of Edwards transcription. There is also a briefer "List of Questions," which Edwards drew up for reviewing the matter. Ola Winslow suggests that this list may have been intended for a discussion with his (surely sympathetic) father since it is written on a back of a list of items to take or to bring back (such as chocolate) from "Down Country." Ola Winslow, *Jonathan Edwards, 1703–1758: A Biography* (New York: Macmillan, 1940), 225.

15. "The Confession of Oliver Warner," describes the speech as "of a very scandalous nature." Works of Edwards transcription from Edwards' hand, ANTS document. On the importance of the regulation of speech in New England see Jane Kamensky, *Governing the Tongue: The Politics of Speech in Early New England* (New York: Oxford University Press, 1997).

16. Tracy, *Jonathan Edwards, Pastor,* 257n38, says that all but two of the church members had joined after 1736. Under the Stoddardean system one cannot tell how many seemed to be converts.

17. *Temptation and Deliverance: Joseph's Great Temptation and Gracious Deliverance* (1738), in *Works of Jonathan Edwards,* ed. Hickman, 2: 230–33.

18. *Self-Examination and the Lord's Supper* (March 21, 1731), *Works,* 17: 270–71.

19. *A Warning to Professors, or the Great Guilt of Those Who Attend on the Ordinance of Divine Worship and yet Allow Themselves in Any Known Wickedness* (before 1733), in *Works of Jonathan Edwards,* ed. Hickman, 2: 187.

20. *Self-Examination,* 271.

21. Edwards to Thomas Prince, December 12, 1743, *Works,* 16: 123–24.

22. Ibid., 125. His account was published in *Christian History* 1 (1743) and James Robe's *Christian Monthly History* 4 (1745).

23. Edwards' notes of testimony of Rachel Clap, in Johnson, "'Young Folks' Bible,'" 45. Cf. Rebekah Strong's testimony, 44. Cf. Bathsheba's testimony, Works of Edwards transcription.

24. Edwards' notes, Johnson, "'Young Folks' Bible,'" 48–51. Also from Edwards' "Fair copies of foregoing testimonies," which reports the testimony in a slightly different form, transcribed by the Works of Edwards project.

25. "Confession of Timothy and Simeon Root," "owned June 1744." Works of Edwards transcription, ANTS manuscript. Edwards, who wrote out the confession, noted that the following portion in brackets was included for Timothy, a church member, but not for Simeon: "[and violated the obligations I am under as a member of this church, engaged by solemn covenant to be subject to the authority of this church.]"

26. "Confession of Oliver Warner," Works of Edwards transcription, ANTS document. The confessions are in Edwards' hand. Mentioning the testimony, Warner confessed that he may well have used such language, although he claimed not to remember the specifics. Hopkins, *Life,* 54, notes that once the dissent became general, "little or nothing could be done further in the affair," suggesting that Warner may have escaped this public confession.

27. See Johnson, "'Young Folks' Bible,'" 38. Also see below regarding *Pamela.*

28. See, for instance, David Underdown, *Fire from Heaven: Life in an English Town in the Seventeenth Century* (New Haven: Yale University Press, 1992), a study of Dorchester, England. Dorchester was one of the most Puritan towns in England. Dorchester emigrants were among the earliest settlers of Windsor, Connecticut.

29. Tracy, *Jonathan Edwards, Pastor,* 38–50, 91–108. See also chapter 9, above.

30. Chamberlain, "Bad Books." On differing standards regarding men and women and the changing patterns Cornelia Hughes Dayton, *Women Before the Bar: Gender, Law, and Society in Connecticut, 1639–1789* (Chapel Hill: University of North Carolina Press, 1995), is especially valuable. Lisa Wilson, *The Domestic Life of Men in Colonial New England* (New Haven: Yale University Press, 1999), provides illustrations of men's views of their roles, including in courtship.

31. Hopkins, *Life,* 54.

32. *A Farewell Sermon Preached at the First Precinct in Northampton, After the People's Public Rejection of Their Minister . . . on June 22, 1750* (Boston, 1751), in *Reader,* 234.

33. Sarah Edwards, "Narrative" (1742), reprinted in Dwight, *Life,* remarks that one

thing she was worried she was not sufficiently resigned to God to bear was "the ill treatment of the town," p. 174, cf. p. 172. Whether she felt there was already ill treatment is not clear. She parallels the worry with that of not being able to accept "the ill will of my husband."

34. In early March the town refused Edwards' request to pay the expense for the return of his daughter Sarah from Brookfield. It is not clear why the Edwards would think this might be a town expense. Perhaps she had accompanied her father on a trip and had been stranded there by illness. James R. Trumbull, *History of Northampton, Massachusetts, from Its Settlement in 1654*, 2 vols. (Northampton, Mass., 1898, 1902), 2: 99.

35. Tracy, *Jonathan Edwards, Pastor*, 158. Tracy has the best discussion of the salary question. The previous year, in a sermon preached for the installation of Jonathan Judd of the new town of Southampton, an outgrowth of Northampton and including many of Edwards' former parishioners, Edwards made a point of admonishing the new congregation to pay their minister adequately. He also had the sermon published, *The Great Concern of the Watchman of Souls* . . . (Boston, 1743). For summary, see Tracy, *Jonathan Edwards, Pastor*, 155–56.

36. Edwards to "Gentlemen" [Committee of the Precinct], [November 1744], draft, fragment, *Works*, 16: 148–49. Any details that he may have furnished have been lost.

37. Tracy, *Jonathan Edwards, Pastor*, 157.

38. "Jonathan Edwards' Last Will, and the Inventory of His Estate," taken from *Bibliotheca Sacra* 33 (1876): 438–46; the original is at the Hampshire County Courthouse, Northampton, and a MS copy is at the Beinecke. Works of Edwards transcription.

39. Edwards to the First Precinct, Northampton, November 8, 1744, *Works*, 16: 150–51.

40. Edwards noted in 1749 that he had one of the highest ministerial salaries in the area, but also the most expensive family. Edwards to James Foxcroft, May 24, 1749, *Works*, 16: 284.

41. Mark Valeri, "The Economic Thought of Jonathan Edwards," *Church History* 60, no. 1 (March 1991): 53. Valeri summarizes a formulation by Allan Kulikoff. The section that follows is largely from Valeri, 37–54.

42. Sermon on Exodus 22:12, as quoted in Valeri, "Economic Thought," 50.

43. Valeri, "Economic Thought," 46. John Winthrop, "A Model of Christian Charity," is often reprinted, as in Perry Miller, ed., *The American Puritans: Their Prose and Poetry* (New York: Columbia University Press, 1956), 79–84.

44. Hopkins, *Life*, 45–46.

45. Edwards, *Religious Affections, Works*, 2: 417. Cf. 413–20. He later said that in *Religious Affections* he had made "some intimations" of his new views. "Narrative of Communion Controversy," *Works*, 12: 508.

46. See chapter 21 below.

CHAPTER 19. Colonial Wars

1. Edwards to "Friends in Scotland," [after September 16, 1745], *Works*, 16: 175–76, originally published in *Christian Monthly History* 9 (December 1745): 259–63. On the Boston newspapers, see the letter fragment asking for back numbers that he had missed to be sent "by some Northampton man, that you see yourselves." Edwards to "An Unknown Recipient," June 4, 1745, *Works*, 16: 172.

2. "The college, it is I," Louis Tucker, *Puritan Protagonist: President Thomas Clap of Yale College* (Chapel Hill: University of North Carolina Press, 1962), 267.

3. Ibid., 114–35. The intensity of the conflict was heightened in May 1742 when separatists left Joseph Noyes' First Church on the New Haven green next to Yale College.

4. Thomas Clap, *A Letter from the Rev. Mr. Thomas Clap . . . to the Rev. Mr. Edwards of North-Hampton* (Boston 1745), 4; quoted in Edwards to the Reverend Thomas Clap, May 20, 1745, *Works*, 16: 164.

5. Clap, *A Letter from . . . Clap . . . Edwards*, 11.

6. Edwards, *An Expostulary Letter from the Reverend Mr. Edwards* (Boston, 1745), *Works*, 16: 163–72, quotation, p. 172. See also Edwards, *Copies of Two Letters Cited by the Reverend Mr. Clap* (Boston, 1745), *Works*, 16: 153–62.

7. See Christopher W. Mitchell, "Jonathan Edwards's Scottish Connection and the Eighteenth-Century Scottish Revival, 1735–1750" (Ph.D. diss., St. Mary's College, University of St. Andrews, Scotland), 1997.

8. Harry S. Stout, *The Divine Dramatist: George Whitefield and the Rise of Modern Evangelicalism* (Grand Rapids, Mich.: Eerdmans, 1991), 133–55; Arnold Dallimore, *George Whitefield: The Life and Times of the Great Evangelist of the Eighteenth-Century Revival*, 2 vols. (Westchester, Ill.: Banner of Truth Trust, 1970), 2: 83–98.

9. George Whitefield, Tuesday, November 27, 1744 in *George Whitefield's Journals* (Edinburgh, 1960), 528–29.

10. Luke Tyerman, *The Life of the Rev. George Whitefield*, 2 vols. (London, 1876), 2: 129–42, summarizes ten attacks and three replies by Whitefield.

11. This is based on Whitefield's account in a private letter (recipient unspecified) from Boston, July 29, 1745, reproduced in Tyerman, *Rev. George Whitefield*, 2: 150–51.

12. Ibid. I am presuming that Whitefield would have said much the same to Edwards a couple of weeks earlier as he said in this letter.

13. Edwards to "Friends in Scotland," *Works*, 16: 175–79.

14. Seth Pomeroy to his wife, July 30, 1745, in James R. Trumbull, *History of Northampton, Massachusetts, from Its Settlement in 1654*, 2 vols. (Northampton, Mass., 1898, 1902), 2: 119.

15. Edwards to "A Correspondent in Scotland," *Works*, 16: 180–97, quotations, pp. 180, 185.

16. Sermon, Psalm 66:18, part 2 (April 12, 1744). Earlier, March 29, 1739, his sermon on the same text had been on the theme, "It is in vain for any to expect to have their prayers heard as long as they continue in the allowance of sin" (Works of Edwards summaries).

17. Sermon, Joshua 7:12, "Fast for the Occasion of War with France" (June 28, 1744).

18. Sermon, I King 8:44–45, "Fast for Success in Expedition against Cape Breton" (April 4, 1745). On the widespread millennial interpretations of the Louisbourg victory in New England, see Nathan Hatch, *The Sacred Cause of Liberty: Republican Thought and the Millennium in Revolutionary New England* (New Haven: Yale University Press, 1977), esp. 36–51.

19. He continued, "for, like the kingdom of heaven, they are to be taken by force and violence; and in a French garrison I suppose there are devils of that kind, that they are not to be cast out by prayers and fasting, unless it be by their own fasting for want of provisions." Benjamin Franklin to John Franklin, [ca. May] 1745, in *The Papers of Benjamin Franklin*, vol. 3, ed. Leonard W. Labaree (New Haven: Yale University Press, 1961), 26–27.

20. Edwards to "A Correspondent in Scotland," *Works,* 16: 185–97. Cf. Ian Marshall, "Taking Louisbourg by Prayer: Responses of Jonathan Edwards and Benjamin Franklin to a Military Episode in Colonial American History," *University of Dayton Review* 20, no. 1 (summer 1989): 3–19, who observes that Edwards was incorrect that the attack was a complete surprise and was very selective in his account, for instance, omitting many of the British casualties, p. 9. See G. A. Rawlyk, *Yankees at Louisbourg* (Orono: University of Maine Press, 1967), for a modern account.

21. Charles Chauncy, *Marvellous Things Done by the Right Hand and Holy Arm of God in Getting Him the Victory* (Boston, 1745), 12. Cf. pp. 12–19.

22. Thomas Prince, *Extraordinary Events the Doings of God, and Marvellous in Pious Eyes* (Boston, 1745), 34. Cf. p. 35. The "King of Glory," etc. is from Psalm 24. Chauncy, *Marvellous Things* also ended his sermon referring to a coming reign of Christ and age of peace, but in much more general terms.

23. Edwards to the Reverend John MacLaurin, May 12, 1746, *Works,* 16: 204; and Edwards to the Reverend William McCulloch, May 12, 1746, *Works,* 16: 209 (quotation). Gerald McDermott, *One Holy and Happy Society: The Public Theology of Jonathan Edwards* (University Park: Pennsylvania State University Press, 1992), 32, summarizes Edwards' sermons through fall 1745, warning of God's judgments, despite his temporary mercies.

24. Edwards to the Reverend William McCulloch, January 21, 1747, *Works,* 16: 219–20. On October 16, 1746, Edwards preached a fast day sermon, Isaiah 33:19–24, on the occasion of the arrival of the French fleet. On November 27, he preached a thanksgiving sermon, Isaiah 37:27–29, celebrating its "confusion."

25. Particularly useful among the large literature on such themes is Linda Colley, *Britons: Forging the Nation, 1707–1837* (New Haven: Yale University Press, 1992). On the anti-Catholic rhetoric in England in the 1740s, see esp. pp. 30–33, and Paul Langford, *A Polite and Commercial People: England, 1727–1783* (New York: Oxford University Press, 1992), 202. On Edwards' admiration of the Hanoverians, see McDermott, *Holy and Happy Society,* 76, 127, and passim on Edwards' political views. Also see Harry S. Stout, "The Puritans and Edwards," in Nathan O. Hatch and Harry S. Stout, eds., *Jonathan Edwards and the American Experience* (New York: Oxford University Press, 1988), 142–57, on Edwards' continued use of the Puritan view of the national covenant. On New England's changing political-religious identity, I have been helped by Thomas S. Kidd, "From Puritan to Evangelical: Changing Culture in New England, 1689–1740" (Ph.D. diss., University of Notre Dame, 2001).

26. Charles Chauncy, *The Counsel of the Two Confederate Kings . . . A Sermon Occasion'd by the Present Rebellion in Favour of the Pretender. February 6th, 1746* (Boston, 1746), 24, 25, and 27.

27. Thomas Foxcroft, *A Seasonable Memento for New Year's Day* (Boston, 1747), quoted in Hatch, *Sacred Cause of Liberty,* 50. Hatch provides valuable expositions of such themes. (As it happens, Foxcroft was senior pastor of Boston's First Church, and Chauncy was his junior associate.)

28. Sermon, Exodus 33:19, "Thanksgiving for Victory over the Rebels" (August 1746).

29. According to Trumbull, *History of Northampton,* 2: 101n, in 1745 thirty-nine deaths were registered, thirty-two in 1746, twenty-seven in 1747, and forty-three in 1748.

30. Ibid., 149–50; and Kevin Sweeney, "River Gods and Minor Related Deities: The

Williams Family and the Connecticut River Valley, 1637–1790" (Ph.D. diss., Yale University, 1986), 374–75.

31. Quoted in *Sibley's Harvard Graduates*, 5: 115.

32. Trumbull, *History of Northampton*, 2: 147–52.

33. At least she did as an adult. See *The Journal of Esther Edwards Burr, 1754–1757*, ed. Carol Karlsen and Laurie Crumpacker (New Haven: Yale University Press, 1984), e.g., 60–61 and 142. See below, chapter 25.

34. Edwards to Esther Edwards, November 3, 1746, *Works*, 16: 214–15. The war had touched the Edwards family most directly with the death of Jonathan's brother-in-law, the Reverend Simon Backus, husband of his sister Eunice. Backus had been a chaplain to the troops at Louisbourg and died there in February 1746. Edwards to MacLaurin, May 12, 1746, *Works*, 16: 205.

35. Edwards' account book, Beinecke, Works of Edwards transcription, indicates he sent to Rhode Island for wool and molasses in May 1745 (before the local Indian threat) and May 1746.

36. Edwards to the Reverend Joseph Bellamy, October 3, 1746, *Works*, 16: 211; and Edwards to the Reverend Joseph Bellamy, January 15, 1747, *Works*, 16: 217.

37. Edwards to the Reverend Joseph Bellamy, January 15, 1747, *Works*, 16: 217.

38. Trumbull, *History of Northampton*, 2: 153–64.

39. John Stoddard to Governor William Shirley, May 13, 1747, quoted in Trumbull, *History of Northampton*, 2: 169.

CHAPTER 20. "Thy Will Be Done"

1. James R. Trumbull, *History of Northampton, Massachusetts, from Its Settlement in 1654*, 2 vols. (Northampton, Mass., 1898, 1902), 2: 177–78. How many were living in 1747 is not clear.

2. Edwards to Joseph Bellamy, June 11, 1747, *Works*, 14: 223.

3. At the time of Jonathan's death eleven years later, the family owned one armchair and twenty chairs, presumably straight. They owned one table, plus a writing table, a book table, and Edwards' elaborate, many-compartmented desk. The family also owned two foot wheels, a great wheel, a carding machine, a substantial store of cloth, and some unwrought leather and rawhide, all evidence of the typical family industries of the day. Jonathan's possessions left in Stockbridge included two pairs of spectacles, one gun, and two powder horns. In Stockbridge, where they did not keep their own sheep, they owned a yoke of oxen, a yoke of steer, nine cattle, six pigs, and all the standard farm equipment. As would have been true in Northampton, in addition to their house lot, they owned a number of other tracts of land for farming or grazing. "Jonathan Edwards' Last Will, and the Inventory of His Estate," is printed in *Bibliotheca Sacra* 33 (1876): 438–46. The original is at the Hampshire County Courthouse, Northampton, and a MS copy is at the Beinecke, Works of Edwards transcription. Most of their assets in 1758 were in some hundreds of acres of land they owned in and around Stockbridge, presumably more than they had in Northampton. The inventory of "quick stock" included "a negro boy named Titus." See chapter 16, note 5, above.

4. Hopkins, *Life*, 43.

5. *Some Thoughts Concerning the Revival, Works,* 4: 394. My thanks to Kenneth Minkema for this information. Edwards also catechized the children of the town and set for them research questions from the Bible (e.g.: "What was his name that was David's ancestor that we read of as being in the wilderness with Moses. [for] Ezra Clark"). "Questions for Young People," MS, Beinecke, Works of Edwards transcription.

7. Hopkins, *Life,* appendix 2, "Containing a Short Sketch of Mrs. Edwards's Life and Character," 95–96. On breaking the will, see chapter 1, note 24, above.

8. Edwards to Thomas Clap, May 20, 1745, *Works,* 16: 164. Sally stayed at the home of Old Light pastor Joseph Noyes and was friends with the daughters of Rector Clap, indicating that, despite sharp disputes, leading ministerial families might remain on good terms.

9. See Laurel Thatcher Ulrich, *Good Wives: Image and Reality in the Lives of Women in Northern New England, 1650–1750* (New York: Vintage, 1980), 35–50.

10. Edwards to Sarah Edwards, June 22, 1748, *Works,* 16: 247.

11. Hopkins, "Mrs. Edwards's Life and Character," 97.

12. *Life of David Brainerd, Works,* 7: 155, 219.

13. Norman Pettit, "Introduction," *Works,* 7: 51–54; *Life of David Brainerd, Works,* 7: 218–20.

14. *Life of David Brainerd, Works,* 7: 436.

15. Edwards to Joseph Bellamy, June 11, 1747, *Works,* 16: 223; *Life of David Brainerd, Works,* 7: 445–46.

16. *Life of David Brainerd, Works,* 7: 445–57. Ebenezer Parkman was reading a portion of the missionary's published journal when he was amazed to see the returning travelers at his door. He had visited Brainerd in Boston and had not expected to see him again. Ebenezer Parkman, *The Diary of Ebenezer Parkman, 1703–1782* (Worcester, Mass.: American Antiquarian Society, 1974), 156–58.

17. His brother John said that he was "on his return from Boston to New Jersey, detained by the increase in his disorder." Thomas Brainerd, *The Life of John Brainerd* (Philadelphia, 1865), 107, quoted in Pettit, "Introduction," *Works,* 7: 68.

18. *Life of David Brainerd, Works,* 7: 474, 475, 474n, and 472n.

19. *True Saints, When Absent from the Body, Are Present with the Lord,* sermon, II Corinthians 5:8 (October 9, 1747), in *Works of Jonathan Edwards,* ed. Hickman, 2: 26–36.

20. Edwards to John Erskine, August 31, 1748, *Works,* 16: 249. Sarah Edwards Parsons to Mary Edwards Dwight, April 18, 1758, in Esther Edwards Burr, *The Journal of Esther Edwards Burr, 1754–1757,* ed. Carol Karlsen and Laurie Crumpacker (New Haven: Yale University Press, 1984), 303, refers to Jerusha's death as "of an acute fevor."

21. Sermon, Job 14:2 (February 1741 and February 21, 1748).

22. Edwards to John Erskine, October 14, 1748, *Works,* 16: 265.

23. Pettit, "Introduction," *Works,* 7: 68–71. That Jerusha accompanied Brainerd to Boston does not indicate any more than that she was caring for him. Brainerd's stay for several days with Stephen Williams in Longmeadow suggests that he was not rushing to Northampton.

The best possibility for when they might have met earlier is when Edwards had counseled Brainerd at the time of the Yale commencement in 1743, if Jerusha, then fourteen, had accompanied her father to New Haven. That is possible, but pure speculation. Driven as he was by spiritual concerns and desire to promote the mission, Brainerd would have had sufficient reason to seek out the renowned Edwards, who had befriended him in New Haven four years earlier.

Pettit suggests that Jerusha had contracted Brainerd's disease. However, the suddenness of her demise and the number of other Northampton deaths at that time make this unlikely. That they were buried side by side may have had significance, but there is no way to be sure.

24. Summer 1747 letter quoted in Dwight, *Life,* 250. The original is apparently lost and so does not appear in the collected letters. Edwards to John Erskine, August 31, 1748, *Works,* 16: 249.

25. This account is drawn from Pettit, "Introduction," *Works,* 7: 54–56; Mark Noll, "Jonathan Dickinson," in *American National Biography,* ed. John Garraty and Mark Carnes (New York: Oxford University Press, 1999), vol. 6, 571–72; Leonard J. Trinterud, *The Forming of an American Tradition: A Re-examination of Colonial Presbyterianism* (Philadelphia: Westminster Press, 1949), 53–134; and Thomas Jefferson Wertenbaker, *Princeton: 1746–1896* (Princeton: Princeton University Press, 1946), 1–26.

26. The Burr quotation, in Pettit, "Introduction," *Works,* 7: 56, is from Archibald Alexander, *Biographical Sketches of the Founder and Principal Alumni of the Log College* (Philadelphia: Presbyterian Board of Publication, 1851), 77–78. The quotation, which is based on the memory of a woman who said she heard the remark in her father's house when she was a girl, is at least an accurate representation of Princeton lore and is in substance plausible.

27. Edwards to John Brainerd, December 14, 1747, *Works,* 16: 242.

28. *Life of David Brainerd, Works,* 7: 153–55; 219–20.

29. Ibid., 102, 149. (*Works,* 7, prints the original and Edwards' versions in parallel columns.) I am indebted to Pettit, "Introduction," *Works,* 7: 80–83, for his analysis of these and other passages. Edwards, for instance, leaves out a Bunyanesque vision ("Methought I saw a stately house . . . [etc.]"), which Brainerd uses as an extended metaphor for the worthlessness of his preconversion efforts, perhaps, as Pettit suggests (p. 81), because he did not want to appear to condone what might be taken to be an actual vision.

30. *Life of David Brainerd, Works,* 7: 507. Cf. *Religious Affections, Works,* 2: 344–45. On the omission of the July 1743 incident, see Pettit, "Introduction," *Life of David Brainerd, Works,* 7: 45, though the attribution of Edwards' motive is mine.

31. Charles Hambrick-Stowe, "The Spirit of the Old Writers: The Great Awakening and the Persistence of Puritan Piety," in Francis Bremer, ed., *Puritanism: Transatlantic Perspectives on a Seventeenth-Century Anglo-American Faith* (Boston: Massachusetts Historical Society, 1993), 277–91.

32. *Life of David Brainerd, Works,* 7: 299, 91–93. Edwards' recognition of melancholy as a "disease" that could be mistaken for "desertion by God" doubtless would have applied to his reflections back on his own early diary.

33. Ibid., 400–401. This passage runs counter to any suggestion that Brainerd had a romantic interest in Jerusha when he left for Northampton later that year.

34. Joseph A. Conforti, *Jonathan Edwards, Religious Tradition, and American Culture* (Chapel Hill: University of North Carolina Press, 1995), 62–86. On the contrasting ideals of Edwards and Franklin, see Barbara B. Oberg and Harry S. Stout, eds., *Benjamin Franklin, Jonathan Edwards, and the Representation of American Culture* (New York: Oxford University Press, 1993), esp. Daniel Walker Howe, "Franklin, Edwards, and the

Problem of Human Nature," 75–97. Lewis O. Saum, *The Popular Mood of Civil War America* (Westport, Conn.: Greenwood, 1980), xxiii, 27, 56, and passim, documents how in antebellum America the self was often popularly viewed as something to be overcome and controlled rather than celebrated.

35. Edwards to John Erskine, October 14, 1748, *Works,* 16: 265.

36. *Life of David Brainerd, Works,* 7: 461.

37. Trumbull, *History of Northampton,* 2: 155. Cf. Edwards, sermon, Isaiah 9:13–14, *After Elisha Clark Was Killed* (August 1747).

38. Edwards to "A Correspondent in Scotland," November 1745, *Works,* 16: 181. My summary regarding the Concert of Prayer follows closely that of Stephen J. Stein, "Editor's Introduction," *Works,* 5: 37–38. On the role of prayer and prayer societies in New England and the awakenings, see Thomas Kidd, "From Puritan to Evangelical: Changing Culture in New England, 1689–1740" (Ph.D. dissertation, University of Notre Dame, 2001), 222–44, 292–94.

39. Cf. *An Humble Attempt to Promote Explicit Agreement and Visible Union of God's People, Works,* 5: 349, where he quotes a Scottish pastor who said of the Lord's Prayer, that "three petitions in six, and these the first prescribed, do all relate to this case."

40. *Humble Attempt, Works,* 5: 333–40, 396–97.

41. Ibid., 342–43, quotation p. 342.

42. See Joseph Bellamy, "The Millennium" (1758), excerpted in Alan Heimert and Perry Miller, eds., *The Great Awakening: Documents Illustrating the Crisis and Its Consequences* (Indianapolis: Bobbs-Merrill, 1967), 609–35; and Joseph Bellamy, *Four Sermons on the Wisdom of God in the Permission of Sin* (1758), excerpt in H. Shelton Smith, ed., *American Christianity: An Historical Interpretation with Representative Documents,* vol. 1 (New York: Scribner, 1960), 350–54.

43. *Humble Attempt, Works,* 5: 358–59.

44. Ibid., 361–62, 424.

45. Ibid., 310, 378–94, and Stein, "Introduction," *Works,* 5: 43. As in all of his writings, Edwards worked within a well-developed tradition of interpretation. See ibid., 1–74.

46. On the latter, see James H. Moorhead, *World without End: Mainstream American Protestant Visions of the Last Things, 1880–1925* (Bloomington: Indiana University Press, 1999).

47. *Humble Attempt, Works,* 5: 394–427. See p. 399 on Edwards' disagreement with Moses Lowman, an influential recent interpreter who argued that the rise of the papacy should be calculated from A.D. 756. Cf. Stein, "Introduction," 44–45.

48. Ibid., 414.

49. "An Account of Events Probably Fulfilling the Sixth Vial on the River Euphrates, the News of Which Was Received since October 16, 1747" (notebook), *Works,* 5: 253–84, with quotation on p. 253.

50. "Events of an Hopeful Aspect on the State of Religion" (notebook), *Works,* 5: 285–97.

51. See Edwards to John Erskine, August 31, 1748, *Works,* 16: 249, and Edwards to William McCulloch, October 7, 1748, *Works,* 16: 255–56.

52. "Events of an Hopeful Aspect," *Works,* 5: 285–91 (entries in 1747–48).

53. Wertenbaker, *Princeton,* 25–26.

54. Edwards to John Erskine, October 14, 1748, *Works,* 16: 261, quoting part (appar-

ently) of a letter from Jonathan Belcher to Jonathan Edwards, February 5, 1748, in reply to a lost letter of Jonathan Edwards to Jonathan Belcher, "desiring his leave to dedicate the book to him," which Edwards asked John Brainerd to deliver, December 14, 1747, *Works,* 16: 241–42. Belcher says "You are sensible, my good friend, that governors stand in a glaring light."

55. Ola Winslow, *Jonathan Edwards, 1703–1758: A Biography* (New York: Macmillan, 1940), 218, citing *Extracts from the Itineraries and Other Miscellanies of Ezra Stiles,* ed. Franklin B. Dexter (New Haven, 1916), 246.

56. Edwards to John Erskine, October 14, 1748, quoting Jonathan Belcher to Jonathan Edwards, May 31, 1748, *Works,* 16: 262–63.

## CHAPTER 21. "I Am Born to Be a Man of Strife"

1. Sarah Edwards Jr. to Elihu Spencer, n.d., George Claghorn transcription, from pages from MS sermon notes on Job 36: 26–27 and Hosea 3: 1–3, Beinecke. The date is in the winter 1747–48, shortly before the death of Jerusha on February 14, 1748. As Jerusha was very ill for five days previous, the letter was likely written February 10. It is late winter (the "forepart" of the winter is past and her youngest sister [Elizabeth] has been dangerously sick "all winter"). This draft is the only known copy, and we do not know if the letter was sent. Sarah Jr. married Elihu Parsons in 1750.

2. Thomas Jefferson Wertenbaker, *Princeton: 1746–1896* (Princeton: Princeton University Press, 1946), 29, quoting a student of the College of New Jersey in 1752.

3. "Joseph Emerson's Diary, 1748–1749," *Proceedings of the Massachusetts Historical Society* 44 (1911): 267–80, entries from September 17, 1748, to March 11, 1749. A further index of the activity of the Edwards household: while Emerson was there for four days, November 9–14, 1748, he went to hear "Mr. Searle" preach at a house on Wednesday evening and heard Joshua Eaton of Leicester, preach the A.M. Sunday sermon, Emerson himself preaching in the evening.

4. James R. Trumbull, *History of Northampton, Massachusetts, from Its Settlement in 1654,* 2 vols. (Northampton, Mass., 1898, 1902), 2: 196–97.

5. *Sibley's Harvard Graduates,* 5: 113–18. Cf. Trumbull, *History of Northampton,* 2: 165–77.

6. This was the occasion when Jonathan wrote, "we have been without you almost as long as we know how to be." Edwards to Sarah Edwards, June 22, 1748, *Works,* 16: 247.

7. Stoddard eulogy quotations here and below are from *God's Awful Judgment in Breaking and Withering of the Strong Rods of a Community,* June 26, 1748 (Boston, 1748), from *Works of Jonathan Edwards,* ed. Hickman, 2: 37–40.

8. Kevin Sweeney, "River Gods and Minor Related Deities: The Williams Family and the Connecticut River Valley, 1637–1790" (Ph.D. diss., Yale University, 1986), 393–401. Stoddard, despite his own apparent integrity, also seems to have protected his family members, ibid., 399. The businesses of Elisha Williams, the former rector and now a merchant and politician, also profited after he became commander-in-chief of the Connecticut forces. Elisha, though ambitious and dispensing patronage, remained pious and presumably honest. Going to England in 1749, he married into the Whitefield circle. Ibid., 385–92.

9. Trumbull, *History of Northampton,* 2: 101.

10. Sermon, Deuteronomy 1:13–18 (June 1748), parts 1, 2, and 4. The reference to "servant" seems to suggest that male African slaves who were full members of the church were voting members.

11. At the time he was dealing with a difficult paternity case involving his young cousin Lieutenant Elisha Hawley (see chapter 22, below), or he may still have been still reacting to frustrations regarding the "young folks' Bible" case, or he may have seen a board of elders as a first step toward reforming the sacraments.

12. Cf. David D. Hall, "Introduction," and Edwards, *Misrepresentations Corrected* (1752), *Works*, 12: 61–62; 361, for samples of the sort of brief profession he was requesting.

13. "Narrative of the Communion Controversy," *Works*, 12: 507–11.

14. Ibid., 507–8. Testimony of Sarah Edwards, June 17, 1750, from *The Congregationalist and Christian World*, October 3, 1903, reprinted in Iain Murray, *Jonathan Edwards: A New Biography* (Carlisle, Pa.: Banner of Truth Trust, 1988), 485–87.

15. Testimony of Sarah Edwards, 485–87. John Searle to Edwards, June 4, 1750, Hartford Seminary Foundation, as transcribed by George Claghorn, recounted that in winter 1746–47 he had stayed at the home of Deacon Ebenezer Pomeroy Jr., a member of the most powerful family working for Edwards' removal. During that winter he heard Edwards discuss his views with several townspeople, and Searle himself discussed it with Deacon Pomeroy and read him the passage from *Religious Affections*. He knew that others must have talked about it among themselves as well. Searle wondered how so many people in Northampton could have become so forgetful. Searle was a former Northampton resident who had returned to study with Edwards. Other testimonies are from Noah Parsons, Joseph Bellamy, and James Pierpont; see Hall, "Introduction," *Works*, 12: 53n.

16. Searle to Edwards, June 4, 1750. Testimony of Sarah Edwards, 487.

17. Joseph Bellamy thought the same. In a letter to Thomas Foxcroft (Harvard, Houghton Library, MS Am 1427.1 [1]), May 6, 1749, transcribed by George Claghorn, Bellamy reports that after visiting the town for several days, "I am of the opinion that when the book comes out, the *people will generally be brought over.*"

18. E.g., Edwards to John Erskine, July 5, 1750, *Works*, 16: 355.

19. About one in five in Massachusetts and one in three in Connecticut experienced schism by 1750, totaling eighty congregations. Stephen Foster, *The Long Argument: English Puritanism and the Shaping of New England Culture* (Chapel Hill: University of North Carolina Press, 1991), 291, 370n. Foster's work is valuable in exploring the dilemma.

20. Although not a separatist in the New England context, Edwards argued that the Church of England was apostate in response to a suggestion that a Connecticut congregation get relief from an unacceptable pastor by affiliating with the Church of England. Edwards to Deacon Moses Lyman, September 30, 1748, *Works*, 16: 251–52.

21. As David Hall points out, "Introduction," *Works*, 12: 67–68, although Edwards included in *An Humble Inquiry into the Rules of the Word of God, Concerning the Qualifications Requisite to a Complete Standing and Full Communion in the Visible Christian Church*, an appendix, drafted by Thomas Foxcroft, recounting the views of earlier Puritan authors, Edwards himself argues on the basis of Scripture, with little direct appeal to his predecessors or concern for exact consistency with them.

22. Despite his advocacy of a national church, more or less on an Old Testament model, Stoddard denied that the Old Testament practices regarding Passover provided an exact guide for the Lord's Supper, since his opponents, such as Increase Mather and

Edward Taylor, argued that the Old Testament ceremonial restrictions were types of restrictions for admission to the Lord's Supper. E. Brooks Holifield, *The Covenant Sealed: The Development of Puritan Sacramental Theology in Old and New England, 1570–1720* (New Haven: Yale University Press, 1974), 217–19.

23. Northampton's expectation that most adults would become communicant members made the half-way covenant less important than elsewhere, since it applied only to the baptized who did not become commuicants. Paul R. Lucas, *Valley of Discord: Church and Society along the Connecticut River, 1636–1725* (Hanover, N.H.: University Press of New England, 1976), 136. Stoddard did not persuade Northampton to accept all his views and only in 1714 gained consent for all the baptized in the town to be under church discipline, regardless of whether they owned the covenant. Ibid. 157–58.

24. In *Faithful Narrative, Works,* 4: 157, Edwards says "We have about six hundred and twenty communicants, which include almost all our adult persons." Kenneth Minkema in "Old Age and Religion in the Writings and Life of Jonathan Edwards," *Church History* 70 (December 2001): 674–704, indicates (p. 699) a decline in the total of church members (including baptized) from 823 in 1735 to 747 in 1750. Meanwhile, the estimated population rose from 1,100 in 1735 to 1,355 in 1750. The records, however, are not complete. The church membership figures, for instance, are *minimum* numbers. Minkema also shows that not only did Edwards alienate some of the young in the "young folk's Bible" scandal, but that a core of an alienated older generation, reared under Stoddard, were instrumental in his removal.

25. Edwards, *An Humble Inquiry, Works,* 12: 266–83. In reply to the objection that the Israelites, when they left Egypt, all partook of the Passover, with no profession required, Edwards pointed out that the objection would prove too much because all the present parties thought that *some* profession should be prerequisite, p. 274. Also, Edwards said that the Old Testament precedents were hardly relevant when the New Testament was clear, p. 279. Christopher Grasso, *A Speaking Aristocracy: Transforming Public Discourse in Eighteenth-Century Connecticut* (Chapel Hill: University of North Carolina Press, 1999), 131–36, has some helpful discussion of this point.

26. "Author's Preface," in *An Humble Inquiry, Works,* 12: 167–70.

27. Ibid., 174–262.

28. Ibid., 257–62, quotation p. 257. Concerning himself as agent, he uses the analogy of an ambassador to a prince who asks a lady for a tangible sign that she accepts the prince's suit, p. 258. Edwards translates I Corinthians, 11:29, as "eateth and drinketh judgement to himself" (p. 260) rather than "damnation to himself" as the King James Version puts it and as he himself sometimes put it in sermons, see below. Perhaps he did not want to rest his argument on a disputed translation.

29. Ibid., 257.

30. Sermon on Matthew 9:15 (date uncertain), quoted in William J. Danaher Jr., "By Sensible Signs Represent: Jonathan Edwards' Sermons on the Lord's Supper," *Pro Ecclesia* 7, no. 3 (summer 1998): 269. Edwards to John Erskine, November 17, 1750, *Works,* 16: 366.

31. Sermon on I Corinthians 10:16 (August 1745; August and October 1755), as quoted in Danaher, "By Sensible Signs," 283. I am much indebted to Danaher's analysis of the communion sermons, although, as these quotations suggest, I do not think that Edwards elevated communion over covenant, as Danaher argues, p. 287, but saw them as two ways of talking about the same thing.

32. Edwards to Thomas Foxcroft, May 24, 1749, *Works*, 16: 283–84.

33. *An Humble Inquiry, Works*, 12: 315–17, cf. p. 213.

34. Edwards to Mary Edwards, July 26, 1749, *Works*, 16: 288–90. In 1741 Edwards had written "my four eldest children (the youngest between six and seven years of age) have been savingly wrought upon, the eldest some years ago," Edwards to Benjamin Colman, March 9, 1741, *Works*, 16: 88, but apparently he had changed his mind about Mary.

35. Dwight, *Life*, 284–85. (Mary became the matriarch of the Dwight family.) Cf. Edwards to Ebenezer Parkman, September 11, 1749, *Works*, 16: 291–92, detailing the difficulties of his journey and why he did not stop at Parkman's. *Christ the Example of Ministers*, preached at Portsmouth, at the ordination of the Rev. Mr. Job Strong, June 28, 1749 (Boston, 1750) in *Works of Jonathan Edwards*, ed. Hickman, 2: 960–65.

## CHAPTER 22. The Crucible

1. Joseph Bellamy to Thomas Foxcroft, May 6, 1749 (Harvard, Houghton Library, MS Am 1427.1 [1]), transcribed by George Claghorn.

2. Edwards to Joseph Bellamy, December 6, 1749, *Works*, 16: 308–9. (I have changed "was" to "were" in the first quotation to fit modern usage.) Cf. Edwards' detailed account of these events is found in "Narrative of the Communion Controversy," *Works*, 12: 507–619.

3. Edwards to "A Correspondent in Scotland," November 1745, *Works*, 16: 185, refers to Seth Pomeroy and Joseph Hawley as "both worthy pious men."

4. "Joseph Hawley," in Franklin Bowditch Dexter, *Biographical Sketches of the Graduates of Yale College*, vol. 1 (New York: Henry Holt, 1885), 709. Iain Murray, *Jonathan Edwards: A New Biography* (Carlisle, Pa.: Banner of Truth Trust, 1988): 148, says Edwards aided in the education of at least one of his Hawley cousins.

5. Patricia J. Tracy, *Jonathan Edwards, Pastor: Religion and Society in Eighteenth-Century Northampton* (New York: Hill and Wang, 1980), 164–66, 257n, and Kathryn Kish Sklar, "Culture versus Economics: A Case of Fornication in Northampton in the 1740s," *University of Michigan Papers in Women's Studies* (May 1978), 35–56, provide helpful accounts of this episode. On the growing importance of issues of male sexuality, see Ava Chamberlain, "The Immaculate Ovum: Jonathan Edwards and the Construction of the Female Body," *William and Mary Quarterly*, 3d ser., 57, no. 2 (April 2000): 289–322, and Cornelia Hughes Dayton, *Women Before the Bar: Gender, Law, and Society in Connecticut, 1639–1789* (Chapel Hill: University of North Carolina Press, 1995).

The quotation from Edwards is from an extended argument for the validity of the law in Exodus 22:16 on this point in an undated manuscript, "Some reasons . . . [for] the obligation of a man to marry a virgin that he had humbled." ANTS, Works of Edwards transcription. He also argued that such laws must be enforced both in civil society and through church censure, "the Good order decency and benefit of mankind in society, and especially their virtue & purity."

6. Joseph Hawley to Elisha Hawley, Northampton, Mass., January 16, 1749, Hawley Papers, New York Public Library, George Claghorn transcription. Edwards to John Erskine, July 5, 1750, *Works*, 16: 353.

7. Edwards to Speaker Thomas Hubbard, August 31, 1751, *Works*, 16: 403.

8. Edwards to Thomas Foxcroft, February 19/20, 1750, *Works*, 16: 323. Helping fuel the claims that Edwards was attempting to give himself dictatorial powers was that he had

revealed to an advisory ministerial council in December 1749 that he wanted to have veto power regarding church membership, which he said Solomon Stoddard had had. See Tracy, *Jonathan Edwards, Pastor,* 178.

9. Chester Williams to members of the Hampshire Association, February 20, 1750, as transcribed in "Narrative of the Communion Controversy," 599.

10. Jonathan Mayhew, *A Discourse Concerning Unlimited Submission* (Boston, 1750). [Elisha Williams], *The Essential Rights and Liberties of Protestants, A Seasonable Plea for the Liberty of Conscience . . .* (Boston, 1744), more directly connected eighteenth-century discussions of rights to the New Light controversies (see below).

11. Dwight, *Life,* 399–403, 421–27. Edwards to John Erskine, July 5, 1750, *Works,* 16: 352–53. Edwards to Thomas Gillespie, July 1, 1750, ibid., 386.

12. "The result of a council of nine churches, met at Northampton, June 22, 1750," in Dwight, *Life,* 399–401. (The tenth church, Cold Spring, was not officially represented, but Edward Billing was allowed to sit on the council and to vote.)

The council summarized the issue, saying that Edwards held that candidates for admission of members to full communion "should make a profession of sanctifying grace," and the church majority held "that the Lord's Supper is a converting ordinance, and consequently that persons, if they have a competency of knowledge, and are of a blameless life, may be admitted to the Lord's table."

13. Ola Winslow, *Jonathan Edwards, 1703–1758: A Biography* (New York: Macmillan, 1940), 256, quoting Diary of David Hall, MS in Massachusetts Historical Society, Boston.

14. *A Farewell Sermon Preached at the First Precinct in Northampton, After the People's Public Rejection of Their Minister . . . on June 22, 1750* (Boston, 1751), in *Reader,* 212–41.

15. Edwards to Erskine, July 5, 1750, *Works,* 16: 354. He also mentioned that despite the controversy, a few of the young people of the town had been hopefully awakened during the past year, p. 356.

16. Edwards to the Reverend Peter Clark, May 7, 1750, *Works,* 16: 346.

17. Edwards to John Erskine, July 5, 1750, *Works,* 16: 355.

18. Ibid., 355–56.

19. Edwards to Hawley, November 18, 1754, *Works,* 16: 648–49. Four years later, Edwards was clearly still fuming over these offenses and in no mood to forgive unless the town fully repented. See discussion of this letter below.

20. James R. Trumbull, *History of Northampton, Massachusetts, from Its Settlement in 1654,* 2 vols. (Northampton, Mass., 1898, 1902), 2: 235.

21. Edwards to Erskine, November 15, 1750, *Works,* 16: 364. Hopkins, *Life,* 61–62. Trumbull, *History of Northampton,* 2: 227, 235–36.

22. Dwight, *Life,* 449. Timothy Dwight Sr. to Thomas Foxcroft, October 12, 1750, Dwight Family Papers, box 1, Beinecke, Claghorn transcription, mentions Edwards' trip to Stockbridge. In the fall he may also have had a call from Canaan, Connecticut, Winslow, *Edwards,* 264. A sermon on Luke 15:10 is dated September 1750 and marked that he preached it in "Canaan/Westfield/Ipswich." Another sermon, Malachi 1:8, is marked October 1750 and Longmeadow. Stephen Williams, due to divided loyalties, stayed out of the controversy, but his invitation to his cousin to preach at his church is an indication of their continued loyalty and friendship.

23. Timothy Dwight Sr. to Thomas Foxcroft, February 17, 1751, Dwight Family Papers, box 1, Beinecke, Claghorn transcription. It is not clear what Dwight's office was at

this time. It is also not clear when the campaign for a separate church began. Possibly relevant to the latter is that in November and December Edwards preached several sermons at the home of a neighbor. Sermons, Proverbs 8:17, pt. 1, II Corinthians 3:18, pt. 2, and John 12:73 (Works of Edwards transcriptions) are dated November or December 1750 with notes that they were preached at "Neighbor Allyns" or "Sgt. Allyns," two indicating "Sabbath evening."

24. Winslow, *Edwards*, 262, 365n., quoting undated MS, Beinecke. Addressing their concerns to a number of Edwards' ministerial friends (Thomas Prince, Thomas Foxcroft, et al.), they concluded by remarking that if all else fails, his friends might inquire into founding an academy, adding (in a comment on Edwards' character) that they "put them all [the founders] in mind that Mr. Edwards dwell in a part of the country where provisions are plenty and cheap and avocations and diversions rare and unusual." Winslow, *Edwards*, 262.

25. Edwards to Hawley, November 18, 1754, *Works*, 16: 650–52.

26. Edwards to Joseph Sewall and Thomas Prince, April 10, 1751, *Works*, 16: 368–69, confirms his coolness to the plan for another church in Northampton.

27. Edwards to Hawley, November 18, 1754, *Works*, p. 651. Shortly after his decision was made to go to Stockbridge, Edwards was importuned to settle in Virginia by a delegation sent by Samuel Davies, a Presbyterian evangelist who was successfully promoting awakening in Virginia. Murray, *Jonathan Edwards*, 364–65.

28. *Misrepresentations Corrected, Works*, 12: 498, indicates that Northampton people had financed and distributed the publication.

29. Edwards to Foxcroft, May 24, 1749, *Works*, 16: 284–85.

30. [Williams], *Essential Rights and Liberties*. Although Williams' book included a defense of Stoddardeanism, Edwards loaned this book to his parishioners, noting it in his "Diary or Account Book," 27, as "Rector Wms. Seasonable Plea." Kevin Sweeney, "River Gods and Minor Related Deities: The Williams Family and the Connecticut River Valley, 1637–1790" (Ph.D. diss., Yale University, 1986), 441.

31. *Sibley's Harvard Graduates*, 5: 592–97, quotation p. 596; Sweeney, "River Gods," 387–93. His second wife, Elizabeth Scott, was a hymn-writer of some renown.

32. Cf. Hall, "Introduction," *Works*, 12: 69.

33. While the Northamptonites were waiting for Solomon Williams' published reply, they engaged Ashley to come and deliver some sermons opposing Edwards' views.

34. The other opponent was Chester Williams of nearby Hadley, a more distant cousin. His mother was a Chester and may have been related to the Chester sisters who were married to John Stoddard and Israel Williams. Chester Williams' grandfather was Samuel Williams of Roxbury, Massachusetts, where the clan originated. "Chester Williams," in Dexter, *Biographical Sketches*, 1: 546.

35. Solomon Williams, *The True State of the Question Concerning the Qualifications Necessary to Lawful Communion in the Christian Sacraments, Being an Answer to the Reverend Jonathan Edwards* (Boston, 1751), 5–8, as quoted in Hall, "Introduction," *Works*, 12: 70–71. For a summary of Williams' argument see ibid., 69–73.

36. *Misrepresentations Corrected, Works*, 12: 355–60.

37. Ibid., 502.

38. Joseph Hawley to David Hall, May 9, 1760. This letter was reprinted in a Boston newspaper at Hawley's request and is reprinted in Dwight, *Life*, 421–27. In this letter

Hawley also wrote, "I made the substance of almost all the foregoing reflections in writing, but not exactly in the same manner to Mr. Edwards and the brethren who adhered to him." Further, he affirmed, "I have reason to believe that he [Edwards], from his great candor and charity, heartily forgave me and prayed for me." Hawley and Edwards may well have met in Northampton and talked of the matter between 1755 and 1758.

Hawley's original letter of apology to Edwards is not extant. Edwards' reply of November 18, 1754, is found in *Works,* 16: 646–54. The draft of Hawley's response to Edwards, January 21, 1755, is located in the Hawley Papers, New York Public Library. In it he contritely detailed instances where he thought he had done wrong in the controversy and professed regarding Edwards' letter to have "received and read it without any the least resentment or uneasiness at you for the plainness and freedom you have been pleased to use in it." Earlier, between May 1751 and May 1752, the people of the First Church, North-ampton, Massachusetts, sent Edwards "Retractions" (Edwards Collection, folder 46, Beinecke) in which they softened some of the harsh language of their earlier Remon-strance regarding his behavior concerning a proposed separate church and allegations that Edwards was interfering with their efforts to settle a new pastor in their church. I am grateful to George Claghorn for his transcriptions of these documents.

In his later years Hawley was incapacitated by "seasons of depression" followed by "periods of great exaltation." Nevertheless, during the time he was agonizing over his injustices toward his cousin, he was also making himself into one of Northampton's most respected citizens. A successful lawyer, he was for decades the town's representative in the General Court of Massachusetts, even after his public confession. In the years leading up to the Revolution, he was considered a western counterpart to Sam Adams as a leading figure in the cause of liberty. Trumbull, *History of Northampton,* 2: 534–49; Dexter, *Bio-graphical Sketches,* 1: 709–12.

39. Winslow, *Edwards,* 242. Cf. Tracy's similar summary, *Jonathan Edwards, Pastor,* 186–87. See Trumbull, *History of Northampton,* for summaries of these men's careers. James F. Cooper, *Tenacious of Their Liberties: The Congregationalists in Colonial Mas-sachusetts* (New York: Oxford University Press, 1999), esp. 197–217, provides a nuanced exploration of the extent to which lay democratic interests might be found in the church controversies (including Northampton's) of the era of the awakening.

40. Tracy, *Jonathan Edwards, Pastor,* 186–87, 264.

41. Ibid., 188–94. The present analysis, see chapter 16, above, is similar on this point, adding that Timothy Edwards may be more important than Stoddard as a model for Edwards' old-fashioned paternalism.

42. Kenneth P. Minkema in "Old Age and Religion in the Writings and Life of Jona-than Edwards, *Church History* 70 (December 2001): 674–704, presents a valuable analysis of communicant membership patterns to demonstrate that Edwards' congregation had a much lower percentage of young people under age twenty-five in 1750 (11.5 percent) than in 1740 (38 percent). Minkema argues that it is the alienation of the older people that cost Edwards his pastorate. Clearly it is the case that the older people had more reverence for Stoddard and Stoddardeanism. The statistics also confirm that the "young folk's Bible" case marked the end of Edwards' success in winning younger converts. Minkema points out that he never had great success in gaining converts among older people.

43. Ava Chamberlain's observations in "Immaculate Ovum" and "Bad Books and Bad Boys: The Transformation of Gender in Eighteenth-Century Northampton, Massa-

chusetts" *New England Quarterly* 72, no. 2 (June 2002), 179–203, that Edwards was resisting new prerogatives associated with male sexuality are especially helpful on this point.
Tracy, *Jonathan Edwards, Pastor,* 193, sees him as more thoroughly backward-looking on
this issue. Edwards still viewed himself as having some authority over the whole community because he held to the National Covenant and was, as discussed in chapter 21, above,
ambivalent on the relationship of the Old Testament and New Testament models.

44. *Works,* 16: 380–87. The summary and quotations below are from these pages.

45. Peter Gay, *A Loss of Mastery: Puritan Historians in Colonial America* (Berkeley:
University of California Press, 1966), 91–116.

46. Edwards to Gillespie, July 1, 1751, *Works,* 16: 383.

## CHAPTER 23. The Mission

1. They are to be distinguished from the Mohegan Indians, a tribe in southern
Connecticut whom the seventeenth-century New England settlers encountered. James
Fenimore Cooper confused the matter by conflating the names and some of the history of
the two groups in his fictional works about the "Mohicans."

2. I am using "English" here, as it was at the time, as a language grouping. The
Williams family was Welsh in origin. The settlers were all from New England, and I am
using "New Englander" to refer to British or European settlers in New England, recognizing that Native Americans also lived in and had claims to what the settlers called "New
England."

3. Lion G. Miles, "The Red Man Dispossessed: The Williams Family and the Alienation of Indian Land in Stockbridge, Massachusetts, 1736–1818," *New England Quarterly*
67, no. 1 (1994): 46–49; "John Sergeant," in Franklin Bowditch Dexter, *Biographical
Sketches of the Graduates of Yale College,* vol. 1 (New York: Henry Holt, 1885), 394–97;
William Kellaway, *The New England Company, 1649–1776* (London: Longmans, Green,
1961), 269–73. Rachel Margaret Wheeler, "Living upon Hope: Mahicans and Missionaries, 1730–1760" (Ph.D. diss., Yale University, 1999), 47–76; Patrick Frazier, *The Mohicans
of Stockbridge* (Lincoln: University of Nebraska Press, 1992), 28–49. Governor Belcher
indicated privately that he hoped that the English settlers would intermarry with the
Indians, as did the French, to reduce their differences. Frazier, *Mohicans of Stockbridge,* 26–
27.

On New England views that civilizing Indians was the best first step toward evan-
gelizing them see James Axtell, *The Invasion Within: The Contest of Cultures in Colonial
North America* (New York: Oxford University Press, 1985), esp. 131–78. Axtell discusses
Stockbridge on pp. 162–63, 196–204.

4. Sarah Cabot Sedgwick and Christina Sedgwick Marquand, *Stockbridge, 1739–1974*
(Stockbridge, Mass.: Berkshire Traveller Press, 1974), 31.

5. Samuel Hopkins (the elder), *Historical Memoirs Relating to the Housatonic Indians*
(New York, 1972 [Boston, 1753]), 89. On Hannah Edwards, see Wheeler, "Living upon
Hope," 46.

6. Sedgwick and Marquand, *Stockbridge,* 31. The Mission House has been moved from
its hillside location to downtown Stockbridge not far from the site of Sergeant's original
house and the Edwards residence.

On eighteenth-century American interests in refinement and good taste, see Cary

Carson, Ronald Hoffman, and Peter J. Albert, eds., *Of Consuming Interests: The Style of Life in the Eighteenth Century* (Charlottesville: University Press of Virginia, 1994).

7. Edmund S. Morgan, *The Gentle Puritan: A Life of Ezra Stiles, 1727–1795* (Chapel Hill: University of North Carolina Press, 1962), 81.

8. Reprinted in Hopkins, *Historical Memoirs,* 107–11.

9. Frazier, *Mohicans of Stockbridge,* 96–97, 101.

10. Hopkins, *Historical Memoirs,* 145–54. Frazier, *Mohicans of Stockbridge,* 85, sets the number of English families at ten, which seems more reliable than the twelve or thirteen Hopkins estimates.

11. See Frazier, *Mohicans of Stockbridge,* 82–88, for account of Indian complaints prior to Edwards' arrival.

12. The following account and its documentation depends largely on Edmund Morgan's wonderful chapter 5, "Abigail" in Morgan, *Ezra Stiles,* 78–89. "More ways than one" is borrowed from p. 85. Morgan's volume is an example of biography at its best. Extracts from the exchange of letters between Stiles and Abigail Sergeant are found in *The Literary Diary of Ezra Stiles,* 3 vols., ed. Franklin B. Dexter (New York: Scribner's, 1901), 1: 210–11.

13. Edwards to Secretary Andrew Oliver, February 10, 1752, *Works,* 16: 424.

14. Kevin Sweeney, "River Gods and Related Minor Deities: The Williams Family and the Connecticut River Valley, 1637–1790" (Ph.D. diss., Yale University, 1986), 464–65.

15. Edwards to Sir William Pepperrell, January 30, 1753, *Works,* 16: 555.

16. Abigail Sergeant to Ezra Stiles, February 15, 1751, Stiles Papers, quoted in Iain Murray, *Jonathan Edwards: A New Biography* (Carlisle, Pa.: Banner of Truth Trust, 1988), 362.

17. Ephraim Williams Jr. to Jonathan Ashley, May 2, 1751, in *Colonel Ephraim Williams: A Documentary Life,* ed. Wyllis E. Wright (Pittsfield, Mass.: Berskire County Historical Society, 1970), 61–62.

18. Sweeney, "River Gods," 465–66. He also had Elijah do his preparatory studies with the strict Edward Billings of Cold Spring, one of Edwards' firmest supporters in the communion controversy, who soon lost his own pulpit for similar reasons.

19. Frazier, *Mohicans of Stockbridge,* xi, 117, 234–45. Cf. Alan Taylor, *William Cooper's Town* (New York: Vintage, 1995), 36, 19–40, 56. Eventually the Stockbridge moved again to Wisconsin. Cooper's history, like his portrayals of Indians, was very inexact. His "Mohicans" were a fictional composite, probably including some Mahican elements. For a critique of a too-close identification of the Mahicans of Stockbridge with Cooper's Mohicans, see the review of Frazier, *Mohicans of Stockbridge,* by Daniel K. Richter, *Pennsylvania Magazine of History and Biography* 119, nos. 1/2 (January/April 1995): 151–53.

20. Frazier, *Mohicans of Stockbridge,* 98–99.

21. Edwards to Speaker Thomas Hubbard, August 31, 1751, *Works,* 16: 394–98.

22. Ibid., 398. On Hendrick, see Milton W. Hamilton, *Sir William Johnson: Colonial American, 1715–1763* (Port Washington, N.Y.: Kennikat Press, 1976). The weather is from *The Diary of Ebenezer Parkman, 1703–1782* (Worcester, Mass.: American Antiquarian Society, 1974), 242, August 13, 1751 ("hot weather"), August 15–16 ("exceeding rainy and stormy" through the morning). Presumably the same system earlier went through Stockbridge, just a hundred miles to the west.

23. "To the Mohawks at the Treaty, August 16, 1751," in Wilson H. Kimnach et al., eds., *The Sermons of Jonathan Edwards: A Reader* (New Haven: Yale University Press,

1999), 105–10. On Edwards' view of the Indians, see Gerald McDermott, "Jonathan Edwards and American Indians: The Devil Sucks Their Blood," *New England Quarterly* 72, no. 4 (December 1999): 539–57.

24. Edwards to Hubbard, August 31, 1751, *Works*, 16: 394–405.

25. Edwards to Joseph Paice, February 24, 1752, *Works*, 16: 434–47.

26. Edwards to Sir William Pepperrell, November 28, 1751, *Works*, 16: 413.

27. These educational proposals are found in Edwards to Hubbard, August 31, 1751, and especially in Edwards to Pepperrell, November 28, 1751, *Works*, 16: 404, 407–13. Edwards to Jonathan Edwards Jr., June 2, 1755, *Works*, 16: 666–67, mentions the death of an Indian boy "who used to live at our house." Cf. Edwards to Thomas Prince, May 10, 1754, *Works*, 16: 638, that a Mohawk boy was living at their house and five others were at the home of Joseph Woodbridge.

28. Edwards to Paice, February 24, 1752, *Works*, 16: 442.

29. Edwards petitioned on October 5, 1751, to purchase land from the Indians for his homestead and other land near the town for wood. The former most likely was to provide more land for gardening, etc., around the home, as they had had in Northampton. Ola Winslow, *Jonathan Edwards, 1703–1758: A Biography* (New York: Macmillan, 1940), 278, 367.

30. Christopher W. Mitchell, "Jonathan Edwards's Scottish Connection," paper delivered at "Jonathan Edwards in Historical Memory" conference, Coral Gables, Fla., March 9–11, 2000. Edwards' Scottish friends also supplied him with many books that he requested, which made it possible for him to move to Stockbridge without intellectual isolation. Mitchell also documents that as late as February 1751 John McLaurin and John Erskine were still working on finding a position for Edwards in Scotland, though the Stockbridge call may have made that a moot point.

31. Edwards to Timothy Edwards, January 27, 1752, *Works*, 16: 420.

32. Quoted from Esther Burr, Diary, 1752, Beinecke, photostat in Stockbridge Library, in Frazier, *Mohicans of Stockbridge*, 94.

33. Robert L. Ferm, *Jonathan Edwards the Younger, 1745–1801: A Colonial Pastor* (Grand Rapids, Mich.: Eerdmans, 1976), 15–16. Jonathan Sr., however, declined to learn the Indian languages himself, believing that his time would be better spent teaching them English. Edwards to Pepperrell, January 30, 1753, *Works*, 16: 562. Clearly, he thought learning Indian languages a better investment for the young, eventually sending young Jonathan Jr. along on a mission to live among the Indians.

34. Edwards to Timothy Edwards, January 27, 1752, *Works*, 16: 420–21.

35. Dwight, *Life*, 487n.

36. Princeton University Library MSS, AM 9261, as quoted in Thomas Jefferson Wertenbaker, *Princeton: 1746–1896* (Princeton: Princeton University Press, 1946), 29. Esther remained sensitive about the subject. Her sister Lucy writing to her sister Mary on August 20, 1754, remarked, "how little able she was to bear to have any body say any thing as though they didn't like her way of marrying." Letter in *The Journal of Esther Edwards Burr, 1754–1757*, ed., Carol Karlsen and Laurie Crumpacker (New Haven: Yale University Press, 1984), 289.

37. Edwards to John Erskine, November 23, 1752, *Works*, 16: 540. Edwards to William McCulloch, November 24, 1752, *Works*, 16: 544.

38. Edwards to Jasper Mauduit, March 10, 1752, *Works*, 16: 451–52; Edwards to Secretary Andrew Oliver, May 1752, *Works*, 16: 476.

39. Gideon Hawley, "A Letter from Rev. Gideon Hawley of Marshpee, Containing an Account of His Services among the Indians . . . .," *Collections of the Massachusetts Historical Society*, 1st ser., 4 (Boston, 1794), 51, quoted in Wheeler, "Living upon Hope," 165. Ibid., 166, notes also his remark in *Original Sin*, *Works*, 3: 160, "I have sufficient reason, from what I know and have heard of the American Indians, to judge that there are not many good philosophers among them." The present account of Edwards preaching to the Indians depends closely on Wheeler's excellent analysis, pp. 131–207, as well as on my own samplings of some of the sermons.

40. This point and the preceding one are taken directly from Wheeler, "Living upon Hope," who quotes, p. 178, from David Brainerd, *Mirabilia Die Inter Indicos . . . a Journal . . .* (Philadelphia, 1746), 19.

41. Sermon outline, Revelation 3:30 (Beinecke), as quoted in Wheeler, "Living upon Hope," 177.

42. Ibid., 133–36, 198–201. Indian professions of faith, Works of Edwards transcription.

### CHAPTER 24. Frontier Struggles

1. "Joseph Dwight," *Sibley's Harvard Graduates*, 7: 56–66. His first wife was Mary Pynchon, from a leading Connecticut River Valley family.

2. It is not clear when Dwight arrived to settle, although it was probably in December 1751 or January 1752. As late as November 28, 1751, *Works*, 16: 413, Edwards was still writing that it was necessary that the girls school, which Abigail controlled, be put under the care of a resident trustee. Edwards' remarks on the Dwights and their relationship are found in his letters, especially to Secretary Andrew Oliver, February 18, 1752, and to Sir William Pepperrell, January 30, 1753, and in some others in the intervening period. Dwight was one of a committee of three appointed by the General Assembly to oversee the mission. According to Edwards, however, the other two, Col. Joseph Pynchon and Capt. John Ashley, were seldom there and allowed Dwight virtually full control. Edwards to Secretary Andrew Oliver, February 18, 1752, *Works*, 16: 423.

3. Edwards to Secretary Andrew Oliver, February 18, 1752, *Works*, 16: 423.

4. Ibid., 423–24.

5. Aaron Burr to Brigadier Joseph Dwight [June 1752], Jonathan Edwards microfilm, reel 8, II, 12 (10), Jonathan Edwards Manuscript Collection, ANTS, transcription furnished by George Claghorn. Aaron Burr to Jonathan Edwards [July-August 1752], Aaron Burr letterbook, ANTS (no date, file no. 1), apologizes for something he said to Abigail, which she turned against the Edwardses. Burr to Abigail Sergeant, Aaron Burr letterbook, [1752], ANTS, transcription furnished by Claghorn, deals with an incorrect report (perhaps on the same unspecified topic) that originated with Burr, that Abigail had blamed on Sarah Edwards. Edwards to Aaron Burr, May 6, 1752, *Works*, 16: 477–79, tells him that he believes that Burr was misrepresented in a report concerning something Burr supposedly said about Edwards' book on communion.

6. Edwards to Oliver, February 18, 1752, *Works*, 16: 422–30. Some details are in Edwards to Oliver, May 1752, *Works*, 16: 475. See Patrick Frazier, *The Mohicans of Stockbridge*

(Lincoln: University of Nebraska Press, 1992), 99–100, regarding Ephraim Williams' instructions to Elisha Williams in London that the land, supposedly a donation to the mission but actually to be a trade, not be legally registered there, since it was not to be recorded in Massachusetts. "In other words," writes Frazier, "the deed was illegal," p. 100.

7. Edwards to Isaac Hollis, July 17, 1752, postscript, summer 1752, *Works,* 16: 506.

8. Edwards to Jasper Mauduit, March 10, 1752, *Works,* 16: 456.

9. Edwards' most detailed critiques of Kellogg are in his letters to Speaker Thomas Hubbard, March 30, 1752, *Works,* 16: 461–68, and March 19, 1753, pp. 572–74.

10. Joseph Dwight and John Ashley, Report to General Court, November 22, 1752, from typescript from George Claghorn, from Massachusetts Archives (hereafter MA), 32: 299–309. Edwards claimed, to Sir William Pepperrell, January 30, 1753, *Works,* 16: 559–60, that he had called the meeting only to warn the Indians of the moral dangers of dispersing for the harvest and that Woodbridge had initiated the subversion of Kellogg's school. Dwight defended Kellogg as doing as well as could be expected (though alluding to some shortcomings) and criticized Hawley for not living at the boarding school. He also reported that the Mohawks left not only because of the school crisis, but also because of the newly profitable business harvesting ginseng. Edwards says the same to William McCulloch, November 24, 1752, *Works,* 16: 543.

Edwards, Dwight reported, had called the April meeting, but the minister had only advised the Stockbridge men not to go into the Dutch country during the wheat harvest because of the temptations, especially of drinking. He then turned to others to address the school question.

11. Edwards to Oliver, May 1752, *Works,* 16: 471–73. Edwards said that Dwight wanted to place his own son as head of the boarding school. Dwight had alleged that Edwards wanted to settle one of his daughters as head of the girls school, Edwards to Speaker Thomas Hubbard, March 30, 1752, *Works,* 16: 470n.

12. Edwards to Oliver, May 1752, *Works,* 16: 474–75. Edwards to Oliver, August 27, 1752, *Works,* 16: 526, alleged that Dwight planned to divert the king's bounty of £500 sterling through his own hands "to be dealt to the Indians out of his shop" for a "very great" profit.

13. Edwards to Colonel Timothy Dwight, June 30, 1752, *Works,* 16: 485. Edwards asked Dwight to help him sell some land at Winchester. Cf. Wyllis Wright, *Colonel Ephraim Williams* (Pittsfield, Mass.: Berkshire County Historical Society, 1970), 64.

14. Edwards to Oliver, August 27, 1752, *Works,* 16: 521.

15. E.g., ibid. Edwards was aware of Elisha's appointment as early as February 1752, see *Works,* 16: 423.

16. This is the account of Elisha Williams to Jonathan Edwards, August 19, 1752, Rhode Island Historical Society (hereafter RIHS), transcribed by George Claghorn. Williams affirmed that his wife could verify that this was close to an exact account.

17. Edwards to Sir William Pepperrell, January 30, 1753, *Works,* 16: 556, recounted his conversation with Abigail, which he thought was "altogether friendly." His fullest summary of his often expressed objections to Abigail's position is in Edwards to Oliver, April 13, 1753, *Works,* 16: 587–92.

18. Edwards to the Reverend Isaac Hollis, July 17, 1752, *Works,* 16: 493–509.

19. Edwards to Elisha Williams, August 15, 1752, and August 18, 1752, *Works,* 16: 512–19. Williams to Edwards, August 19, 1752, RIHS.

20. Edwards to Oliver, October 1752, *Works,* 16: 534 reports the incident. Abigail Dwight to Thomas Williams, November 1, 1752, in Wright, *Colonel Ephraim Williams,* 67. (September 2, 1752, was followed by September 14.)

21. In late November Brigadier Dwight presented to the Massachusetts General Court the report of the legislature's committee to oversee the mission. The committee, made up of Dwight and a nonresident ally, alleged that the mission had been going as well as could be hoped under Captain Kellogg until the disastrous interference by Edwards in introducing Gideon Hawley. Edwards and Hawley, supported by Timothy Woodbridge, who had the Indians' ear, undermined Kellogg's work with "violent opposition, affronts, and abuses" and defied the efforts of the committee to restore good order (This was Dwight's version of the three-hour shouting match with Hawley.) Multiple managements were destroying the school and the Mohawks were leaving, partly for that reason and partly because of the recent European craze for ginseng root, the profits from which lured them to the forests. The only hope for the schools was to rid them of the outside influence (i.e., Edwards). Dwight and Ashley, Report to General Court, November 22, 1752, MA. Edwards agreed that ginseng was part of the problem.

Edwards received full intelligence of these goings-on, probably from Timothy Woodbridge, still Stockbridge's representative in the Assembly. Anticipating Dwight's attack, Woodbridge presented a rebuttal signed by the male heads of almost every English and Mahican family in Stockbridge. Kevin Sweeney, "River Gods and Related Minor Deities: The Williams Family and the Connecticut River Valley, 1637–1790" (Ph.D. diss., Yale University, 1986), 477, referring to "a rebuttal" in MA, 32: 365–74. Edwards reported that two Stockbridge Indians told him that they had been taken by Captain Kellogg to Wethersfield and that there Elisha Williams and others had told them they had a bad minister and urged them to sign a petition against him, plying them with wine to do so. Edwards to Oliver, April 12, 1753, *Works,* 16: 590.

22. Joseph Dwight had indeed delivered a letter from Elisha Williams to Sir William Pepperrell, dated August 29, 1753, urging Pepperrell to write to Joseph Paice, one of the mission's principal promoters in London, in support of Dwight versus Edwards (concerning whose shortcomings Dwight was to fill in Pepperrell) from Williamsiana Collections, Williams College, as transcribed by George Claghorn.

23. Edwards to Pepperrell, January 30, 1753, *Works,* 16: 553–63. Cf. Edwards to Hubbard, March 19, 1753, *Works,* 16: 564–76, a more formal refutation of Dwight's charges, designed to be read to the legislature. Edwards had earlier written regarding his alleged "stiffness, etc." to Secretary Josiah Willard, July 17, 1752, *Works,* 16: 509–10.

24. Edwards to Elizabeth Scott Williams, October 30, 1755, *Works,* 16: 677. The occasion of this revealing letter is that shortly after the death of Elizabeth's husband, Elisha Williams, Edwards heard that she was casting aspersions on Edwards' character and temperament. Edwards pled with her to consider that her views might be prejudiced by her late husband and his relatives in America. Edwards, who valued honesty over tact, ended his epistle with brief condolences on the death of "your honorable consort," but said nothing else about his character or role in Edwards' life. Elizabeth Scott Williams, predictably, remained convinced of her earlier opinion, pp. 674–78.

25. Provincial Secretary Josiah Willard to Sir William Pepperrell, February 24, 1753, printed in Usher Parsons, *The Life of Sir William Pepperrell* (Boston, 1855), 252. Pepperrell to Willard, March 6, 1753, Ibid., 253.

26. Wright, *Colonel Ephraim Williams,* 68–69. Gideon Hawley, "A Letter from Rev. Gideon Hawley of Mashpee, Containing an Account of His Services among the Indians . . . ," *Collections of the Massachusetts Historical Society,* 1st ser., 4 (Boston, 1794), 55, says "There were many persons who supposed, with some grounds, that this house was set on fire by design." Edwards does not mention the accusation.

27. Edwards to Hubbard, March 19, 1753, *Works,* 16: 572. Edwards said that the Onohquaga Indians, who left at the same time, made clear that their disillusionment was with Dwight and Kellogg and not with Edwards or any of his supporters. Edwards to Thomas Prince, May 10, 1754, *Works,* 16: 633.

28. Edwards to Mauduit, March 10, 1752, *Works,* 16: 455.

29. Hawley, "Letter from Rev. Gideon Hawley," 61. Edwards to Oliver, April 12, 1753, *Works,* 16: 581–86, outlines this plan. Edwards also recommended that the Ashleys be included. The Ashleys, despite their family relationships (Benjamin was a brother of the Reverend Jonathan Ashley of Deerfield), were loyal to Edwards, had assisted Hawley at his school, and were popular with the Indians. Benjamin was accused of being a "separatist and great enthusiast" by Joseph Dwight (Dwight and Ashley, Report to General Court, November 22, 1752, MA), and even Hawley regarded him as "a fanatick," in Hawley, "Letter from Rev. Gideon Hawley," 56. On Hawley's career see "Gideon Hawley," *Sibley's Harvard Graduates,* 12: 392–411.

30. Hawley, "Letter from Rev. Gideon Hawley," 57–65, provides an account of the trip, drawing directly from a diary he had kept at the time.

31. Edwards to Dwight, July 5, 1753, *Works,* 16: 597–98; Edwards to Major Ephraim Williams Jr. et al., September 11, 1753, September 18, 1753, and November 19, 1753, *Works,* 16: 601–5, 611–17, deal with these issues. See also Williams Jr. to Edwards, May 2, 1753, in RIHS, George Claghorn transcription.

32. Edwards to Thomas Gillespie, October 18, 1753, *Works,* 16: 610. A glaring defect in the mission was that so many agencies were involved in its oversight that it was seldom clear who had what authority in Stockbridge. The inefficient arrangements also protected Edwards because it was difficult to control all the agencies.

33. Edwards to Willard, March 8, 1754, and Edwards to Prince, May 10, 1754, *Works,* 16: 626–27, 629–43.

34. Edwards to Prince, May 10, 1754, *Works,* 16: 637.

35. Ibid., 638–39.

36. There probably had been some earlier tensions between the Mahicans and the Mohawks. At first the Mahicans had welcomed their old enemies as needed allies and had lent a 200-acre tract of land on a beautiful bow of the river for the boarding school. The honeymoon between the two peoples soon was over and the fiasco in the English management of the boarding school or schools, and the preferential treatment of the Mohawks, cooled the Mahicans on the project. Since the school began in Newington, Captain Kellogg had always had some Mahican boys under his care. In Stockbridge, however, he did little for them. Eventually, as things were falling apart, their sachem warned Kellogg to stay off their land. They also drew up a lengthy petition to the government on this and other points, complaining of Dwight's unwillingness to entertain their complaints. This latter event indicates that Edwards' Mahican parishioners shared Edwards' and Woodbridge's view of Kellogg and Dwight. Edwards to Prince, May 10, 1754, *Works,* 16: 630–33.

Sarah Cabot Sedgwick and Christina Sedgwick Marquand, *Stockbridge, 1739–1974* (Stockbridge, Mass.: Berkshire Traveller Press, 1974), 39, 69–70.

37. Edwards to Secretary Josiah Willard, May 22, 1754, *Works*, 16: 644–45. The account of the incident is based on Edwards' letter and on the account in Frazier, *Mohicans of Stockbridge*, 105–6, which is the most complete based on multiple sources. Cf. Wright, *Colonel Ephraim Williams*, 74–75.

38. For a critical comparison of French and English missions, see James Axtell, *The Invasion Within: The Contest of Cultures in Colonial North America* (New York: Oxford University Press, 1985).

39. Milton W. Hamilton, *Sir William Johnson: Colonial American, 1715–1763* (Port Washington, N.Y.: Kennikat Press, 1976), Wright, *Colonel Ephraim Williams*, 74–75; Fred Anderson, *Crucible of War: The Seven Years' War and the Fate of Empire in British North America, 1754–1766* (New York: Knopf, 2000), 78–79. Frazier, *Mohicans of Stockbridge*, 103–4, says Hendrick sent a note of warning to Woodbridge after the incident. Hendrick did remain friends with Ephraim Williams Jr., who (although another Susquehanna investor) had been his patron and soon would be a close military ally. Wright, *Colonel Ephraim Williams*, 71–72.

Concerning the Pennsylvania side of the story and especially the role of mediators such as Conrad Weiser, see James H. Merrell, *Into the American Woods: Negotiations on the Pennsylvania Frontier* (New York: Norton, 1999), which provides a fascinating and illuminating account.

40. Frazier, *Mohicans of Stockbridge*, 83–84, and passim.

41. Edwards had a small investment in the Susquehanna Company, "Jonathan Edwards' Last Will, and Inventory of His Estate," taken from *Bibliotheca Sacra* 33 (1876): 438–46; the original is at Hampshire County Courthouse, Northampton. At the time of the inventory, July 25, 1759, his interest was listed as £2 14s., which can be compared to the £30 value of his best five acres, between his house in Stockbridge and the river. Most of Edwards' landholdings seems to have been for his own use. Presumably Edwards, who had only Woodbridge's side of the story, thought the Susquehanna deal honest.

42. Anderson, *Crucible of War*, 50–85.

43. Edwards to John Erskine, April 15, 1755, *Works*, 16: 662–63. Only during September was Edwards able to perform his full duties, preaching five sermons to the Indians and five to the English that month. Otherwise he preached none between late July and late November and not at all in January or February. Rachel Wheeler, "Living upon Hope: Mahicans and Missionaries, 1730–1760" (Ph.D. diss., Yale University, 1998), 162, lists the number of sermons to the Indians preached by months. The list of sermons to the English is provided by the Works of Jonathan Edwards and seems to confirm a similar pattern.

44. This account follows closely that of Frazier, *Mohicans of Stockbridge*, 107–9, who quotes, p. 107, the letter from Samuel Hopkins to Joseph Bellamy, September 3, 1754. Also Sedgwick and Marquand, *Stockbridge*, 73–75, for some detail. Also Edwards to Erskine, April 15, 1755, *Works*, 16: 663–64.

45. Hopkins to Bellamy, September 3, 1754, quoted in Frazier, *Mohicans of Stockbridge*, 109.

46. Edwards petition . . . October 22, 1754; in another hand but signed by Edwards. MA, 13: 581–82. Photocopy furnished by George Claghorn. Quotations are also found in

Sedgwick and Marquand, *Stockbridge*, 75. That Edwards had on hand "7 gal. of good West Indian rum" is an indication that prohibition of alcohol was not yet part of New England's Reformed culture.

47. Esther Edwards Burr to Lucy Edwards, November 4, 1754, in *The Journal of Esther Edwards Burr, 1754–1757*, ed. Carol Karlsen and Laurie Crumpacker (New Haven: Yale University Press, 1984), 292.

48. *Journal of Esther Edwards Burr*, November 8, 1754, 60–61. The "diary" is in the form of extended letters to her friend Sally Prince, daughter of Thomas Prince, in Boston. Esther's fears were shared by some of the most knowledgeable. On November 18, 1754, Colonel Israel Williams, who had succeeded his late uncle John Stoddard as the chief commander on the frontier, recommended more troops to protect Stockbridge because of fears of defection by the Stockbridge Indians. Joseph Dwight, on the scene, defended the Stockbridge Indians and feared more bad treatment of them from outsiders. Frazier, *Mohicans of Stockbridge*, 110.

49. In late November, in his first return to the pulpit after a second round of his illnesses, Edwards repreached to his English congregation a thanksgiving sermon that he had first preached "for victory over the rebels" in 1746. Probably the occasion was the successful reconciliation, negotiated by Joseph Dwight, of the government of Massachusetts with the Stockbridge Indians and the agreement of many of the Indians to be "received as soldiers in the province service." Edwards reminded his people that God often bestowed great temporal mercies to his covenanted nations, even when they were wicked, as he had often to ancient Israel. Such blessings were, no less than punishments, calls for repentance. Sermon, Exodus 33:19 (August 1746 and November 1754), Works of Edwards transcription.

50. Edwards to Joseph Dwight, February 26, 1755, *Works*, 16: 657–58.

51. Edwards to Thomas Foxcroft, June 3, 1755, *Works*, 16: 668, says, "I am yet in a low state as to my health."

52. Edwards to Thomas Prince, April 14, 1755, *Works*, 16: 659; and Edwards to Thomas Foxcroft, March 8, 1755, *Works*, 16: 658.

53. Timothy Dwight Sr. to Thomas Foxcroft, April 1, 1755. Dwight thought that Foxcroft might hear of plans for Edwards to leave. Dwight also wrote to Foxcroft regarding the Northampton situation and to Edwards on June 6, 1753, December 7, 1753, and February 22, 1754. In the latter he complained of Edwards' Northampton replacement, John Hooker, whom he thought lacked experimental religion and "lurches toward an Arminian justification." Beinecke, George Claghorn transcriptions.

54. Edwards to Foxcroft, June 3, 1755, *Works*, 16: 668. On the Indian delegate see Claghorn's note, *Works*, 16: 659n.

55. Hawley manuscript, Congregational Library, Boston, 4, November 20, 1755, quoted in *Sibley's Harvard Graduates*, 12: 396.

56. Edwards to Jonathan Edwards Jr., May 27, 1755, *Works*, 16: 666–67. Edwards to Foxcroft, June 3, 1755, *Works*, 16: 668.

57. Edwards to Thomas Prince, September 15, 1755, *Works*, 16: 673. By the next summer Edwards had moved his Stockbridge boys to the safer confines of Bethlehem, where his friend Joseph Bellamy taught them. Edwards to Joseph Bellamy, [June 1756], *Works*, 16: 688–89. Edwards to Joseph Bellamy, February 12, 1757, *Works*, 16: 700–701. Edwards to Joseph Bellamy, August 6, 1757, *Works*, 16: 724–25.

CHAPTER 25. Wartime

1. Esther Edwards Burr to Sally Prince, July 19, 1755, in *The Journal of Esther Edwards Burr, 1754–1757,* ed. Carol F. Karlsen and Laurie Crumpacker (New Haven: Yale University Press, 1984), 136.

2. Fred Anderson, *Crucible of War: The Seven Years' War and the Fate of Empire in British North America, 1754–1766* (New York: Knopf, 2000), 86–114, provides the most helpful account.

3. Esther Edwards Burr to Sally Prince, November 5, 1755, in *Journal of Esther Edwards Burr,* 163–64 and August 8–9, p. 142. Burr wrote almost daily to Prince in what is virtually a diary and is now an invaluable source.

4. Aaron Burr, *A Discourse Delivered at New-Ark, in New Jersey, January 1, 1755. Being a Day Set Apart for Solemn Fasting and Prayer, on Account of the Late Encroachments of the French* ... (Philadelphia and New York, 1755), 40 and passim. Burr closes with a peroration that anticipates American revolutionary rhetoric and illustrates the connection of liberty with Protestantism. " 'Tis high time, to awake ... every spark of *English* valour; cheerfully to offer our purses, our arms, and our lives, to the defense of our country, our holy religion, our excellent constitution and invaluable liberties. For what is life, without *liberty?* Without the enjoyment of the glorious *Gospel* of Christ."
I am indebted to Nathan O. Hatch, *The Sacred Cause of Liberty: Republican Thought and the Millennium in Revolutionary New England* (New Haven: Yale University Press, 1977), 34, for pointing out Burr's differences with Edwards, published in Aaron Burr, *The Watchman's Answer* ... (Boston, 1757). Esther Edwards Burr to Sally Prince, January 1 and 2, 1755, in *Journal of Esther Edwards Burr,* 76–77.

5. "An Account of Events Probably Fulfilling the Sixth Vial," in "Notes on the Apocalypse," *Works,* 5: 283. In another section of "Notes on the Apocalypse," titled "Events of an Hopeful Aspect on the State of Religion," Edwards last entry was March 25, 1755, *Works,* 5: 296–97.

6. Sermon on Psalm 60: 9–12, "Fast after General Braddock's Defeat," August 28, 1755. This is a repreaching of a sermon from August 1746, but the application concerning Braddock is new. Works of Edwards transcription.

7. Edwards to William McCulloch, April 10, 1756, *Works,* 16: 686.

8. Edwards et al., Petition to Colonel Israel Williams, September 4, 1755, *Works,* 16: 670. Cf. Edwards to Colonel Israel Williams, September 5, 1755, *Works,* 16: 671–72.

9. Anderson, *Crucible of War,* 118–20; Wyllis Wright, *Colonel Ephraim Williams: A Documentary Life* (Pittsfield, Mass.: Berkshire County Historical Society, 1970), 127–49.

10. Edwards to John Erskine, December 11, 1755, *Works,* 16: 680. James R. Trumbull, *History of Northampton, Massachusetts, from Its Settlement in 1654,* 2 vols. (Northampton, Mass., 1898, 1902), 2: 285.

11. Abigail Dwight to Abram Bookee, November 1755, as quoted in Sarah Cabot Sedgwick and Christina Sedgwick Marquand, *Stockbridge, 1739–1974* (Stockbridge, Mass.: Berkshire Traveller Press, 1974), 81–82. Cf. Edwards to Aaron Burr, March 16, 1756, *Works,* 16: 683, and Claghorn's note p. 669.

12. Wright, *Colonel Ephraim Williams,* 110–11, 153–61.

13. Edwards to John Erskine, December 11, 1755, *Works,* 16: 679–81.

14. Burr, *Journal of Esther Edwards Burr,* September 26 to October 11, 1755, pp. 153–58.

15. Burr, *Discourse Delivered at New-Ark*, 39.

16. Ola Winslow, *Jonathan Edwards, 1703–1758: A Biography* (New York: Macmillan, 1940), 287. George Claghorn in his "Character Summary: Gideon Hawley," furnished to the author, dates this as July 1754, Gideon Hawley, Journal, Congregational Library, Boston.

17. Burr, *Journal of Esther Edwards Burr*, March 10 to April 12, 1755, pp. 98–108.

18. Ibid., October 13, 1754, pp. 54–55.

19. Burr, *Journal of Esther Edwards Burr*, April 12, 1757, p. 257, cf. p. 248.

20. Edwards had been involved at a distance in the New York Presbyterians' struggles. His close friend Joseph Bellamy had received a much-disputed call to pastor the divided congregation in 1754 but finally turned it down. Bellamy, a large forceful man from the backcountry, would have been a bull in a china shop in this delicate situation. Further, New Yorkers put on English airs. "I am not polite enough for them," Bellamy told a friend. "I may possibly do to be a minister out in the woods but am not fit for the city." Quoted in Joseph A. Conforti, *Samuel Hopkins and the New Divinity Movement* (Grand Rapids, Mich.: Eerdmans, 1981), 10, from Glen P. Anderson, "Joseph Bellamy: The Man and His Work" (Ph.D. diss., Boston University, 1971), 466.

In July 1755 the congregation had called David Bostwick of Long Island and had designated Edwards as their next choice, should Bostwick turn them down. Esther believed her father, "will by no means do for 'em if he would come." and hoped he would not consider it ( *Journal of Esther Edwards Burr*, 132). When Edwards was in New York in October, Bostwick's coming (which eventually led to a schism) was still being hotly contested, and there is no evidence that Edwards had an interest in moving into another maelstrom.

21. On Edwards' travels, see Burr, *Journal of Esther Edwards Burr*, 156–58. She mentions a visit from "the oyster man," March 21, 1755, p. 102. We have record of a number of occasions when Edwards ordered chocolate. For instance, in a letter to Timothy Woodbridge, June 4, 1755, *Works*, 16: 669, he ordered it from John Henry Lydius, the New York trader with whom Woodbridge had devised the Susquehanna purchase the previous year. "Was Edwards a Chocoholic?" *Friends of Edwards*, "News from The Works of Jonathan Edwards at Yale University" (autumn 1999): 3, lists seven evidences of chocolate purchases.

22. "Gideon Hawley," *Sibley's Harvard Graduates*, 12: 396–97. Edwards to McCulloch, April 10, 1756, *Works*, 16: 684–87. On Johnson, see Milton W. Hamilton, *Sir William Johnson: Colonial American, 1715–1763* (Port Washington, N.Y.: Kennikat Press, 1976).

23. Joseph Bellamy to Jonathan Edwards, in Dwight, *Life*, 555–56. Bellamy also found the learning and the academic discipline of the boys disappointing.

24. The references describing this visit here and below are from Esther Burr to Sally Prince, August 16 to September 19, 1756, in *Journal of Esther Edwards Burr*, 217–24.

25. Anderson, *Crucible of War*, 154–55. As a result, the colonials called off their Crown Point expedition and moved into a defensive position, p. 157.

26. Edwards to Gideon Hawley, October 9, 1756, *Works*, 16: 690–91.

27. For the point of view of the Iroquois, see Daniel K. Richter, *The Ordeal of the Longhouse: The People of the Iroquois League in the Era of European Colonization* (Chapel Hill: The University of North Carolina Press, 1992), and "War and Culture: The Iroquois Experience," *William and Mary Quarterly*, 3d ser., 40 (1983): 528–59.

28. Gideon Hawley, Journal, Congregational Library, Boston, February 12, 17, 1757, as quoted in *Sibley's Harvard Graduates*, 12: 399, cf. 398–400. Later, when Hawley was settled

and determined to have a wife, he wrote: "Miss Lucy Edwards is a charming girl, but guess she would not be happy here scarcely with any man much less me." Hawley's Journal, March 1, 1759, quoted ibid., 400. Three months later he married another.

29. Ibid., 399–400. On Stockbridge, see Gideon Hawley, "A Letter from Rev. Gideon Hawley of Mashpee, Containing an Account of His Services among the Indians . . . ," *Collections of the Massachusetts Historical Society,* 1st ser., 4 (Boston, 1794), 55, and below.

30. Edwards et al., Petition to Lieutenant Governor Spencer Phips, et al., *Works,* 16: 693–94, and "Editor's Introduction," p. 693.

31. Thomas Jefferson Wertenbaker, *Princeton, 1746–1896* (Princeton: Princeton University Press, 1946), 38–40. Wertenbaker omits any reference to the revival which inaugurated the school's stay at Princeton.

32. Aaron Burr to Edwards, February 20, 1757, and Esther Edwards Burr to Edwards, February 21, 1757, as excerpted in Edwards to John Erskine, April 12, 1757, *Works,* 16: 703–4.

33. Ibid., 702–5.

34. Edwards to Thomas Foxcroft, February 11, 1757, *Works,* 16: 697.

35. Esther Burr to Sally Prince, March 1 to May 1, 1757, in *Journal of Esther Edwards Burr,* 250–58.

36. Anderson, *Crucible of War,* 191–99. Esther Burr to Sally Prince, August 12, 1757, in *Journal of Esther Edwards Burr,* 271. Edwards to Joseph Bellamy, August 6, 1757, *Works,* 16: 734–35. The bombardment at Gettysburg on July 3, 1863, was heard as far as some two hundred miles away at Pittsburgh. James M. McPherson, *Battle Cry of Freedom: The Civil War Era* (New York: Oxford University Press, 1988), 661.

37. Burr, *Journal of Esther Edwards Burr,* 273–74. Esther Burr to William Hogg, December 22, 1757, p. 299. Cf. "Introduction," 17, which says the fever was malaria.

38. Esther Burr to Sarah Edwards, October 7, 1757, and to Jonathan Edwards, November 2, 1757, in *Journal of Esther Edwards Burr,* 292–95. Edwards to Esther Burr, November 20, 1757, *Works,* 16: 730.

39. Richard Stockton to Jonathan Edwards, September 19, 1757, Beinecke, Works of Edwards transcription. Stockton was engaged to Annis Boudinot, a close friend of Esther.

40. Edwards to the Trustees of the College of New Jersey, October 19, 1757, *Works,* 16: 726. His own words are "I have a constitution in many respects peculiar unhappy, attended with flaccid solids, vapid, sizy and scarce fluids, and a low tide of spirits; often occasioning a kind of childish weakness."

41. Ibid., 725–30.

42. Edwards to Esther Burr, November 20, 1757, in *Journal of Esther Edwards Burr,* 298. Most of the trustees' concessions are found in Richard Stockton to Jonathan Edwards, November 4, 1757, Beinecke, Works of Edwards transcription.

43. Hopkins, *Life,* 78.

44. Edwards to Gideon Hawley, January 14, 1758, *Works,* 16: 737–38. Brainerd did not accept.

45. Hopkins, *Life,* 78. Edwards to Gideon Hawley, January 14, 1758, *Works,* 16: 737–38.


CHAPTER 26. Against an "Almost Inconceivably Pernicious" Doctrine

1. Edwards to Trustees of the College of New Jersey, October 19, 1757, *Works,* 16: 729.

2. *Freedom of the Will, Works,* 1: 437.

3. Joseph Hawley to Elisha Hawley, January 16, 1749, Hawley Papers, New York Public Library, George Claghorn transcription.

4. Conrad Wright, *The Beginnings of Unitarianism in America* (New York: Starr King, 1955), 63–72, provides a useful overview which I have followed. Wright mentions a number of other cases. Foxcroft's remarks are found in an editorial note in John Porter, *A Vindication of a Sermon Preached at Braintree, Third Parish, December 25, 1749* (Boston, 1751), 43–46, quotation p. 45.

5. Jonathan Mayhew, *Seven Sermons* (Boston, 1749), 38, and Mayhew, *Sermons, upon the Following Subjects . . .* (Boston, 1756), 27, both quoted in Clyde A. Holbrook, "Editor's Introduction," *Works*, 3: 10–11.

6. Edwards to Edward Wigglesworth, February 11, 1757, *Works*, 16: 698–700, and "Editor's Introduction," 697–98.

7. Edwards to Thomas Foxcroft, February 11, 1757, *Works*, 16: 695.

8. Wright, *Unitarianism*, 76–82; and Stephen J. Stein, "Editor's Introduction," *Works*, 15: 12–21.

9. Edwards to John Erskine, July 7, 1752, *Works*, 16: 491.

10. Edwards to John Erskine, November 23, 1752, says he is still not back to it, *Works*, 16: 541.

11. Edwards to John Erskine, August 3, 1757, *Works*, 16: 719–20.

12. For these observations I am closely following Charles Taylor, *Sources of the Self: The Making of the Modern Identity* (Cambridge: Harvard University Press, 1989), 143–98.

13. Among the large literature on this topic is Bernard Bailyn, *The Ideological Origins of the American Revolution* (Cambridge: Harvard University Press, 1967); Isaac Kramnick, *Republicanism and Bourgeois Radicalism: Political Ideology in Late Eighteenth-Century England and America* (Ithaca: Cornell University Press, 1990); Joyce Appleby, *Liberalism and Republicanism in the Historical Imagination* (Cambridge: Harvard University Press, 1992); and Gordon Wood, *The Radicalism of the American Revolution* (New York: Vintage, 1991).

14. Daniel Walker Howe sketches such trends in "Franklin, Edwards, and the Problem of Human Nature," in *Benjamin Franklin, Jonathan Edwards, and the Representation of American Culture*, ed. Barbara B. Oberg and Harry S. Stout (New York: Oxford University Press, 1993), 75–97.

15. In the conclusion to *Freedom of the Will* Edwards addresses the explicit tenets of the Arminian challenge to Calvinist doctrines: total depravity, unconditional election, limited atonement, irresistible grace, and perseverance of the saints. See *Freedom of the Will, Works*, 1: 430–39. Although assertions of "freedom of the will" are often identified more precisely as Pelagian, they are implied, in the sense that Edwards was concerned about them, in the denial of total depravity, irresistible grace, and perseverance of the saints.

16. Cf. Allen C. Guelzo, *Edwards on the Will: A Century of Theological Debate* (Middletown, Conn.: Wesleyan University Press, 1989), 11–13, and Norman Fiering, *Jonathan Edwards' Moral Thought and Its British Context* (Chapel Hill: University of North Carolina Press, 1981), 272–77.

17. *Freedom of the Will, Works*, 1: 164–65. Edwards particularly attacked three influential authors. Thomas Chubb (1679–1747) was a popular English opponent of much traditional doctrine, whose views had led to Deism. Daniel Whitby (1638–1726) was a Church of England clergyman who was more strictly an Arminian, having published in 1720 a famous attack on the five points of Calvinism that Arminians opposed. More surprisingly, Edwards included his former supporter, the famed dissenter Isaac Watts (1674–1748), who

had attempted to combine evangelical Calvinism with contemporary ideas of free will and morality. Edwards could have included countless others with similar views, but these three served to illustrate how writers from a wide spectrum of theological opinions all assumed the "modern prevailing notions" regarding the sort of freedom necessary to moral agency. Paul Ramsey "Introduction," *Freedom of the Will, Works*, 1: 66–118, deals with these opponents in detail.

18. *Freedom of the Will, Works*, 1: 163–64.

19. Ibid., 140–48, 172.

20. Ibid., 345–46.

21. Ibid., 157.

22. Ibid., 160.

23. Ibid., 357–71, 277–94.

24. Edwards summarized these points most succinctly in ibid., 431–32. He dealt with them and with many possible objections to them at length, pp. 375–429.

25. Ibid., 397–412.

26. Ibid., 430, 374. Edwards probably learned some version of such arguments from Locke, who was influenced by Hobbes. Ramsey, "Introduction," *Freedom of the Will, Works*, 1: 14, 47–65. Edwards' views also resembled David Hume's in some respects, although they arrived at their views independently. Ramsey, "Introduction," 14.

27. Edwards spells out this view of God's governance in Miscellany no. 1263 (Works of Edwards transcription). Cf. Ramsey's analysis, "Introduction," *Freedom of the Will, Works*, 1: 110–14.

28. If one were comparing men to machines, Edwards further observed, men would be inferior beings if governed by blind chance. "Whereas machines are guided by an understanding cause, by the skillful hand of the workman or owner; the will of man is left to the guidance of nothing, but absolute blind contingence." *Freedom of the Will, Works*, 1: 371.

29. Cf. Ramsey, "Introduction," *Freedom of the Will, Works*, 1: 111–12; and *Freedom of the Will, Works*, 1: 381–83. In *Original Sin*, see chapter 27, below, Edwards dealt more directly with the objection that the Calvinist system would make God guilty of causing human sin.

30. Ibid., 437–39.

31. Edwards to John Erskine, July 25, 1757, published as *Remarks on the Essays on the Principles of Morality and Natural Religion, by Lord Kames; in a Letter to a Minister of the Church of Scotland* (Edinburgh, 1758), in *Freedom of the Will, Works*, 1: 453–65, quotation p. 453. See Ramsey's introduction to this letter, pp. 443–52. By the early 1760s *Freedom of the Will* had been adopted at Yale by his old antagonist, President Thomas Clap. Hopkins, *Life*, 86.

32. Guelzo, *Edwards on the Will*, 1. See also Joseph A. Conforti, *Jonathan Edwards, Religious Tradition and American Culture* (Chapel Hill: University of North Carolina Press, 1995), passim.

33. Cf. philosopher Paul Ramsey's remark that "this book alone is sufficient to establish its author as the greatest philosopher-theologian yet to grace the American scene." Ramsey, "Introduction," *Freedom of the Will, Works*, 1: 2.

CHAPTER 27. Original Sin "in This Happy Age"

1. Hopkins, *Life*, 73.

2. "Book of Controversies," Beinecke, Works of Edwards transcription.

3. Edwards to John Erskine, July 7, 1752, *Works*, 16: 491.

4. *Misrepresentations Corrected*, *Works*, 12: 501–2. Cf. Clyde A. Holbrook, "Introduction," *Works*, 3: 20.

5. Paul Ramsey, "Introduction," *Works*, 8: 10–11. Ramsey points out that Edwards debated whether to put his discussion of moral sense in *Original Sin* or *True Virtue* (where he eventually put it, referencing in *Original Sin* that the other volume was forthcoming).

6. Quoted in Joseph A. Conforti, *Samuel Hopkins and the New Divinity Movement: Calvinism, the Congregational Ministry, and Reform in New England between the Great Awakenings* (Grand Rapids, Mich.: Eerdmans, 1981), 55.

7. Samuel Hopkins to Joseph Bellamy, January 19, 1758, quoted in Conforti, *Samuel Hopkins*, 55.

8. *Original Sin*, *Works*, 3: 102.

9. Ibid., 152–53, cf. 107–205.

10. Ibid., 183.

11. Ibid., 129, 190–91, 386–87.

12. Ibid., 380–85.

13. Ibid., 386.

14. Edwards discusses Romans 5 at length, versus Taylor's interpretations, in ibid., 306–49.

15. Edwards differed on this point from some Reformed theologians and from the apparent implication of the Westminster Confession of Faith, chap. 6:3, which speaks of the imputation of guilt as though it were a judicial act distinct from the transmission of a corrupted nature: "They [our first parents] being the root of all mankind, the guilt of his sin was imputed; and the same death in sin, and corrupted nature, conveyed to all their posterity descending from them by ordinary generation."

16. Ibid., 391n–92n.

17. Cf. Paul Ramsey, "Introduction," *Works*, 1: 118, on this point and his helpful discussion of related problems, pp. 99–118.

18. *Original Sin*, *Works*, 3: 395–409, with quotation on p. 409. Cf. Holbrook's discussion of some of the problems regarding Edwards' multiple levels of causality, Holbrook, "Introduction," *Works*, 3: 60–64. Some of Edwards' language, such as that "the existence of each created person and thing, at each moment of it, [must] be from the immediate *continued* creation of God," p. 401, might lead one to think that he regarded God as the efficient cause of everything. Yet he says elsewhere, in a typical statement, "A being may be the determiner and disposer of an event, and not properly an efficient or efficacious cause. Because, though he determines the futurity of the event, yet there is no positive efficiency or power of the cause that reaches and produces the effect; but merely a withholding or withdrawing of efficiency or power." "Concerning Efficacious Grace," in *Works of Jonathan Edwards*, ed. Hickman, 2: 557. Edwards must have had in mind a distinction between God's action in sustaining the sequences of "immediate *continued* creation" and the powers he grants to created persons and things to act as efficient agents within those sequences. Thus he says with respect to the crucial doctrine of efficacious grace, "we are not passive, nor yet does God do some, and we do the rest. But God does all, and we do all. God produces all, and we act all. For that is what he produces, *viz.* Our own acts. God is the only proper author and fountain; we only are the proper actors. We are, in different respects, wholly passive and wholly active." Ibid.

19. Entry 652, *Works*, 18: 192–93.

20. *Original Sin*, *Works*, 3: 435–37. Edwards' *The Great Christian Doctrine of Original Sin* was the least influential of his major theological works. In the nineteenth century even some of his admirers, such as the conservative Reformed theologians at Princeton Theological Seminary, were critical of his metaphysical theories regarding the divinely constituted identity of the race. See Joseph A. Conforti, *Jonathan Edwards, Religious Tradition, and American Culture* (Chapel Hill: University of North Carolina Press, 1995), 122–23.

21. Peter Gay, *A Loss of Mastery: Puritan Historians in Colonial America* (Berkeley: University of California Press, 1966), 91–116. Gay was challenging the emphases of Perry Miller, *Jonathan Edwards* (New York: William Sloan, 1949), who provides a powerful, if overstated, account of Edwards as a modern critic of the assumptions of modernity.

22. Mark A. Noll, *America's God: From Jonathan Edwards to Abraham Lincoln* (New York: Oxford University Press, 2002), provides an excellent recent account.

CHAPTER 28. Challenging the Presumptions of the Age

1. Edwards to Thomas Foxcroft, February 11, 1757, *Works*, 16: 696.

2. Edwards had developed the basic argument in earlier Miscellanies, such as nos. 445, 461 (1729–30) *Works*, 13, and 702 (1736–37), *Works*, 18.

3. Bellamy, for instance, published his sermon on *The Wisdom of God in Permission of Sin* in 1758, which Edwards had likely read and approved before he left Stockbridge. See Joseph Bellamy, *Sermons upon the Following Subjects, viz. The Divinity of Christ, The Millenium, The Wisdom of God in the Permission of Sin* (Boston, 1758).

4. Alexander Pope, *An Essay on Man*, ed. Maynard Mack ((London: Methuen, 1950 [1734]), Epistle 1, ll. 289–94, pp. 50–51; Epistle, 3, ll. 109–14, p. 103.

5. For some comparisons of Edwards with Gottfried Wilhelm Leibniz (1646–1716), see Paul Ramsey, "Introduction," *Works*, 1: 113–17.

6. Edwards uses the phrase "our modern freethinkers" in a reference to the antagonists to whom the dissertation is addressed, *Concerning the End for Which God Created the World*, *Works*, 8: 536.

7. See *An Unpublished Essay of Edwards on the Trinity*, ed. George P. Fisher (New York: Scribner's, 1903).

8. *Concerning the End*, *Works*, 8: 530, cf. 526–30.

9. Ibid., 531.

10. Ibid., 533 (quotation) and 534.

11. Norman Fiering, *Jonathan Edwards's Moral Thought and Its British Context* (Chapel Hill: University of North Carolina Press, 1981), provides by far the most comprehensive account of the context for Edwards' moral thought. Equally important are Paul Ramsey's extensive editorial comments, *Works*, 8, including his introduction, notes on the text, and lengthy appendices, especially appendix 2, "Jonathan Edwards on Moral Sense, and the Sentimentalists," 689–705, in which he takes serious issue with Fiering. My account is informed by these and many other works, though I do not think it follows any one closely, except as indicated.

12. Charles Taylor, *Sources of the Self: The Making of the Modern Identity* (Cambridge: Harvard University Press, 1989), 248–50.

13. Francis Hutcheson, *A Short Introduction to Moral Philosophy* (Glasgow, 1747), 16–17.

14. Cf. Roy Porter, *The Creation of the Modern World: The Untold Story of the British Enlightenment* (New York, 2000), 175–76. The idea that private vices beget public benefits was suggested by Bernard Mandeville and even by Alexander Pope in the first half of the century, well before one finds it in David Hume and Adam Smith.

15. Cf. Taylor, *Sources of the Self,* 248–302.

16. Ned Landsman, *From Colonials to Provincials: American Thought and Culture, 1680–1760* (New York: Twayne, 1997), 3–4. See also Ned Landsman, *Scotland and Its First American Colony, 1683–1765* (Princeton: Princeton University Press, 1985); Henry May, *The Enlightenment in America* (New York: Oxford University Press, 1976), 342–50. William Small, a Scottish advocate of Hutcheson's thought, came to the College of William and Mary in 1758 where he was Thomas Jefferson's most influential teacher. Garry Wills, *Inventing America: Jefferson's Declaration of Independence* (New York: Doubleday, 1978), 176–80. John Witherspoon, an orthodox Presbyterian Scottish moralist, became president of Princeton in 1766, taught James Madison, and was himself an influential signer of the Declaration of Independence.

17. Edwards to John Erskine, December 11, 1755, *Works,* 16: 679.

18. *The Nature of True Virtue, Works,* 8: 539, 560, 557, 551. Edwards recognized that almost all the contemporary philosophers included some mention of duty to God. Yet he regarded them as simply *adding* that on theories based "on benevolence to the *created system.*" "If true virtue consists partly in a respect to God," he countered, "then doubtless it consists *chiefly* in it." Ibid., 552–53.

19. Ibid., 540.

20. Francis Hutcheson, *An Essay on the Nature and Conduct of the Passions and Affections* (London, 1728), 210–11, quotation p. 211.

21. *True Virtue, Works,* 8: 611.

22. Ibid., 540.

23. Ibid., 568–72. On the subtle distinctions between Edwards' and other eighteenth-century formulations, see Fiering, *Jonathan Edwards's Moral Thought,* e.g., 345.

24. *True Virtue, Works,* 8: 613–14. Justice is an objective concept having to do with proportion, so anyone might appreciate it as a "secondary beauty," and even evil persons may promote justice. True virtue, on the other hand, has ultimately to do with motive. True benevolence to being in general will entail a hearty approval of all justice and benevolence. The difference is that true virtue is based on the most extensive love for persons, whereas a love for justice, without true virtue, is more like a love for the proportions of the shapes of nature or of music. Ibid., 568–73.

25. Ibid., 555–56.

26. Edwards made this point in the context of pointing out that "self-love" is not bad if it simply means to love our own happiness, which is simply to love what we love. The question is whether our happiness, or our disposition, is ultimately defined by private or selfish interests or by God's universal interests. Ibid., 576–77.

27. Whereas Hutcheson argued that natural humans had a moral sense, Edwards regarded only truly spiritual persons as having a "truly spiritual sense or virtuous taste." Ibid., 596. Edwards argued, for instance, that a gang of robbers will have a natural sense of gratitude to someone who warns them that the sheriff is about to raid their hideaway. So their natural moral sentiments are not to be relied upon to approve of that which is in the public interest. Ibid., 583.

CHAPTER 29. The Unfinished Masterworks

1. This and subsequent references to this letter are from Edwards to the Trustees of the College of New Jersey, October 19, 1757, *Works*, 16: 725–30.

2. Kenneth P. Minkema, "The Other Unfinished 'Great Work': Jonathan Edwards, Messianic Prophecy, and 'The Harmony of the Old and New Testaments,'" in *Jonathan Edwards's Writings: Text, Context, Interpretation*, ed. Stephen J. Stein (Bloomington: Indiana University Press, 1996), 53. I am grateful for Minkema's work on this topic, which I follow as well as borrowing part of his title.

3. Christoph Wolff, *Johann Sebastian Bach: The Learned Musician* (New York: Norton, 2000), 433. Cf. pp. 431–42, on the two late great works.

4. Cf. Stephen J. Stein, "Introduction," *Works*, 15: 1–2. I am indebted throughout this section to Stein's most helpful overview of Edwards' biblical work.

5. Cf. Stephen J. Stein's summary in "The Spirit and the Word: Jonathan Edwards and Scriptural Exegesis," in *Jonathan Edwards and the American Experience*, ed. Nathan O. Hatch and Harry S. Stout (New York: Oxford University Press, 1988), 121–22, which I am following closely.

6. On Edwards and the commentarial tradition, see Stein, "Introduction," *Works*, 16: 4–12.

7. Minkema, "Other Great Work," 58, 64n19. Edwards also classified these as "Miscellanies," but they were separate enterprises.

8. Mason I. Lowance, with David H. Watters, "Introduction," *Works*, 11: 183.

9. Minkema, "Other Great Work," 61.

10. Stein, "Introduction," *Works*, 15: 12–23. Robert E. Brown, *Jonathan Edwards and the Bible* (Bloomington: Indiana University Press, 2002), is especially valuable in documenting Edwards' engagement with the international discussions of this topic. On Bayle, see Richard H. Popkin, "Pierre Bayle," in *The Encyclopedia of Philosophy*, ed. Paul Edwards, vol. 1 (New York: Macmillan, 1967), 257–62. Cf. Richard H. Popkin, "Skepticism in Modern Thought," in *Dictionary of the History of Ideas*, ed. Philip P. Wiener, vol. 4 (New York: Scribner, 1973), 240–48.

11. "Controversies," notebooks, Works of Edwards transcriptions, p. 191.

12. Miscellany no. 1340, Works of Edwards transcription. This miscellany is published in nineteenth-century versions of Edwards' works as "The Insufficiency of Reason as a Substitute for Revelation." See, e.g., *Works of Jonathan Edwards*, ed. Hickman, 2: 479–85.

13. Miscellany no. 1340, Works of Edwards transcription.

14. "Efficacious Grace," book 2, pp. 62–63, Beinecke, as transcribed and quoted by Minkema, "Other Great Work," 57.

15. Jonathan Edwards, "Concerning Efficacious Grace," in *Works of Jonathan Edwards*, ed. Hickman, 2: 557.

16. "Types Notebook," 152, as quoted in Lowance, "Introduction," *Works*, 11: 179. Edwards goes on to deny the claim of some that things should be interpreted as types only if the Scripture explicitly so interprets them. "For by the Scripture it is plain that innumerable other things are types."

17. Stein, "Introduction," *Works*, 15: 15 and 15n, 423–69, 154–56.

18. Ibid., 11, points out that Edwards' typological approach also allowed him an easy way to answer the eighteenth-century critics of the morality of some biblical teachings. For

instance, God's command to sacrifice Isaac was intended to illustrate the substitutionary atonement, since the ram that was sacrificed in Isaac's place was a type of Christ.

For a general account and interpretation of the crisis concerning Scriputre history during this era, see Hans Frei, *The Eclipse of the Biblical Narrative: A Study in Eighteenth- and Nineteenth-Century Hermeneutics* (New Haven: Yale University Press, 1974), 1–85. Edwards' views that the texts should be taken at face value as history and his assumption regarding their overall unity centered typologically on Christ were unremarkable in the post-Reformation tradition, except that he proposed to explore the unities of Scripture more comprehensively than other interpreters had done. Brown, *Edwards and the Bible*, shows that, although his conclusions were consistent with the precritical views of earlier Reformed interpreters, Edwards himself was hardly precritical since he was so deeply involved in answering the critics of his era.

19. Miscellany no. 248, *Works*, 13: 361. See also Brown, *Edwards and the Bible*, who uses this quotation (p. 44) in developing this theme and also points out in a related note (p. 219) that Reformed theology typically divided evidences for Scripture into internal and external evidences.

20. *Religious Affections, Works*, 2: 303–4. Cf. p. 304: " 'tis unreasonable to suppose, that God has provided for his people, no more than probable evidences of the truth of the gospel."

21. Edwards to Trustees of the College of New Jersey, October 19, 1757, *Works*, 16: 727–28.

22. It was to begin with a section on "The being and nature of God," a second "Of created minds, free will etc.," and a third "Of excellency, Trinity, etc." That would be followed by "Creation: the ends of it." Then would come doctrines such as faith and justification. The preface, he noted, would "shew how all the arts and sciences, the more they are perfected, the more they issue in divinity" and would also (anticipating the *Two Dissertations*) "shew how absurd for Christians to write treatises on ethics distinctly from divinity as revealed in the Gospel." One can see here the essence of all Edwards' later arguments regarding God's method of governing the universe through the dispositions of moral agents as well as the centrality of the redemptive end for which God created the world. "A Rational Account of the Main Doctrines of the Christian Religion Attempted," *Works*, 6: 396–97.

23. These descriptions follow closely that of John F. Wilson, *Works*, 9: 546–47, who furnishes much other valuable information on the project.

24. Edwards had already written, in the 1740s, a discourse on the Trinity. This was later published as *An Unpublished Essay of Edwards on the Trinity*, ed. George P. Fisher (New York: Scribner's, 1903).

25. All the above quotations are from the "History of Redemption," Notebook A, Works of Edwards transcription. Cf. Wilson's very helpful analysis, *Works*, 9: 61–72.

26. See Gerald R. McDermott, *Jonathan Edwards Confronts the Gods: Christian Theology, Enlightenment Religion, and Non-Christian Faiths* (New York: Oxford University Press, 2000), for a full discussion of these topics. On Islam, see ibid., 166–75. See also Edwards' views from Miscellany no. 1334, republished in in nineteenth-century editions of his Works, such as *Works of Jonathan Edwards*, ed. Hickman, 2: 491–93.

27. Cf. Peter Gay, *A Loss of Mastery: Puritan Historians in Colonial America* (Berkeley: University of California Press, 1966), 88–117. Gay's astute observations are marred by his

dismissive tone and glib assumption that all truth must be on the side of the moderns. For an important recent analysis, see Avihu Zakai's forthcoming *Jonathan Edwards's Philosophy of History: The Re-Enchantment of the World in the Age of Enlightenment* (Princeton: Princeton University Press, 2003).

28. Edwards, *History of Redemption, Works*, 9: 284, quoted in Brown, *Jonathan Edwards and the Bible*, 164. Brown, esp. pp. 64–76, has a helpful discussion of this theme.

29. Quoted from Lessing, *Über den Beweis des Geistes und der Kraft* (1777) in *Encyclopedia of Philosophy*, 4: 445.

30. On this point I am indebted to Brown, *Jonathan Edwards and the Bible*, 182–83.

31. Cf. the very helpful analysis of Sang Hyun Lee, *The Philosophical Theology of Jonathan Edwards* (Princeton: Princeton University Press, 1988), esp. 211–14.

32. Christ's substitutionary atonement is a topic, like most other theological topics, that Edwards wrote on at some length. See "Concerning the Necessity and Reasonableness of the Christian Doctrine of Satisfaction for Sin," a compilation from the "Miscellanies" on the topic, beginning with no. 779. Edwards is concerned especially to show that it is reasonable that a lawmaker who announces a punishment for a crime must see the punishment carried out. *Works of Jonathan Edwards*, ed. Hickman, 2: 565–78. On the love expressed in Christ taking on the punishment for human sins, see the long sermon on Luke 22:44 (October 1739 and winter/spring 1757), published in ibid., 866–77. The dates of the preaching of the sermon suggest that Edwards was thinking of this topic as one that might be integrated into the "History of Redemption" discourse.

33. Cf. Miscellany no. 702, *Works*, 18: 292: "'Tis evident that all God's works, both of creation and providence, are subordinate to the work of redemption." In Miscellany no. 461, *Works*, 13: 502, he writes "that God delighteth in the creatures' happiness in the sense that he does not in their misery. 'Tis true that God delights in justice for its own sake, as well as in goodness; but it will by no means follow from thence, that he delights in the creatures' misery for its own sake as well as [in their] happiness. For goodness implies that in its nature, that the good of its object be delighted in for its own sake; but justice don't carry that in its nature, that the misery of those it's exercised about is delighted in for its own sake: as is evident, because justice procures happiness as well as misery." In a related Miscellany, no. 445, ibid., 493, he says that God does not create to exercise his justice, but "glorifying that attribute might be the motive for his giving himself occasion for the exercise of that attribute by making the creatures."

## CHAPTER 30. The Transitory and the Enduring

1. *New York Mercury*, April 10, 1758, p. 1.

2. Susannah Edwards to Esther Burr, April 3, 1758, ANTS, George Claghorn transcription. Cf. Dwight, *Life*, 581. Susannah also reported that for his sermon in Stockbridge he preached on Hebrews 13:14, "for we have no continuing city, but we seek one to come." The Scripture read was Acts 20, Paul's affectionate farewell to the Ephesian elders.

3. Hopkins, *Life*, 79.

4. Ezra Stiles, *The Literary Diary of Ezra Stiles*, 3 vols., ed. Franklin B. Dexter (New York: Scribner's, 1901), May 24, 1779, 2: 337, quoted in Ola Winslow, *Jonathan Edwards, 1703–1758: A Biography* (New York: Macmillan, 1940), 290.

5. Hopkins, *Life*, 79.

6. Esther Edwards Burr, *The Journal of Esther Edwards Burr, 1754–1757,* ed. Carol Karlsen and Laurie Crumpacker (New Haven: Yale University Press, 1984), 274.

7. Edwards to Aaron Burr, May 6, 1752, *Works,* 16: 478.

8. Burr, *Journal of Esther Edwards Burr,* May 2–June 16, 1757, pp. 260–64.

9. Shippen was also one of the architectural designers of the building. Thomas J. Wertenbaker, *Princeton, 1746–1896* (Princeton: Princeton University Press, 1946), 37–38.

10. William Shippen to Sarah Edwards, March 22, 1758, ANTS, George Claghorn transcription.

11. Hopkins, *Life,* 80n.

12. William Shippen to Sarah Edwards, March 22, 1758.

13. On the other hand, Hopkins' account, written seven years later, adds some last words that sound suspiciously conventional, especially as they were not included in Shippen's letter. According to Hopkins, near the very end when friends in the room were lamenting the effects of Edwards' passing, thinking he was beyond hearing them, he surprised them by saying these words, "TRUST IN GOD, AND YE NEED NOT FEAR." *Life,* 81.

14. It is, of course, possible that some things to the contrary were suppressed by his disciples and descendants who cared for and edited his papers. Yet nothing that has survived there or elsewhere points to such.

15. Sarah Edwards to Esther Burr, April 3, 1758, ANTS, George Claghorn transcription.

16. Sarah Edwards Parsons to Mary Edwards Dwight, April 18, 1758, in Burr, *Journal of Esther Edwards Burr,* 302–3.

17. Ibid.

18. Timothy Dwight Jr. to Gideon Hawley, April 5, 1758, Hartford Seminary Foundation, George Claghorn transcription.

19. Sarah Prince, entry in her private book of meditations, April 21, 1758, in Burr, *Journal of Esther Edwards Burr,* 307–8.

20. Edwards to Esther Edwards Burr, November 20, 1757, *Works,* 16: 730.

21. Samuel Hopkins, *The Life and Character of the Late Reverend Mr. Jonathan Edwards* (Boston, 1765), appendix, p. 97. (This appendix is not in the Levin republication from which other references to Hopkins, *Life,* are taken.)

22. Dwight, *Life,* 582. The two Burr children remained with the William Shippen family in Philadelphia until 1760 when Timothy Edwards, recently married, became their guardian, taking them first to Stockbridge and then in 1762 to Elizabethtown, New Jersey, where Timothy practiced law. The precocious Aaron Jr. graduated from Princeton in 1772 and then studied theology under Joseph Bellamy before turning away from his heritage during the American Revolution. See Suzanne Geissler, *Jonathan Edwards to Aaron Burr, Jr.: From the Great Awakening to Democratic Politics* (New York: Edwin Mellen, 1981), 102–23.

23. As another biographer has observed, the Edwards narrative ends like "a Shakespearean tragedy where bodies strew a stage." Elisabeth D. Dodds, *Marriage to a Difficult Man: The "Uncommon Union" of Jonathan and Sarah Edwards* (Philadelphia: Westminster Press, 1971), 201.

24. Stiles, *Literary Diary,* as quoted in Joseph A. Conforti, *Jonathan Edwards, Religious Tradition, and American Culture* (Chapel Hill: University of North Carolina Press,

1995), 3. Cf. Conforti, *Edwards,* 37, on his late eighteenth-century reputation in Scotland and America.

25. John Adams to Thomas Jefferson, November 15, 1813, in *The Adams-Jefferson Letters,* ed. Lester J. Cappon (Chapel Hill: University of North Carolina Press, 1959), 399, quoted in Geissler, *Jonathan Edwards to Aaron Burr, Jr.,* 1.

26. On the early resurgence of the Edwardsean heritage, see David W. Kling, *A Field of Divine Wonders: The New Divinity and Village Revivals in Northwestern Connecticut, 1792–1822* (University Park: Pennsylvania State University Press, 1993). Also see Mark A. Noll, *America's God: From Jonathan Edwards to Abraham Lincoln* (New York: Oxford University Press, 2002); Allen C. Guelzo, *Edwards on the Will: A Century of Theological Debate* (Middletown, Conn.: Wesleyan University Press, 1989); Bruce Kuklick, *Churchmen and Philosophers: From Jonathan Edwards to John Dewey* (New Haven: Yale University Press, 1985).

27. Conforti, *Edwards,* 87–107, summarizes the literature on Mount Holyoke and points out its specifically Edwardsean character, quotation, p. 104. See ibid., on Edwards' reputation generally.

28. Ibid., 1.

29. Ibid., 108–85.

30. Albert E. Winship, *Heredity: A History of Jukes-Edwards Families* (Boston, 1925). Originally published as *Jukes-Edwards: A Study in Education and Heredity* (Harrisburg, Pa.: R. L. Myers, 1900), 13–14, 43.

31. Henry B. Parkes, *Jonathan Edwards, The Fiery Puritan* (New York: Minton, Balch, 1930), 36, 63, 66–67, 253. Cf. Conforti, *Edwards,* 186–90 on Parkes, Vernon Parrington, and others of the Progreessive Puritan-bashers and passim on other biographies. I am also grateful to William Svelmoe for his help regarding Parkes and other Edwards biographies.

32. Winslow, *Edwards,* 297–98.

33. A. C. McGiffert, *Jonathan Edwards* (New York: Harper and Brothers, 1932). Joseph Haroutunian, *Piety versus Moralism: The Passing of the New England Theology* (New York: Henry Holt, 1932).

34. E.g., H. Richard Niebuhr, *The Kingdom of God in America* (Chicago: Willet, Clark, 1937), 101–3, 113–16, 135–45.

35. M. X. Lesser, who has published two volumes of annotated bibliography on Edwards, for example, lists more than five hundred publications just for the 1980s. M. X. Lesser, *Jonathan Edwards: An Annotated Bibliography, 1979–1993* (Westport, Conn.: Greenwood Press, 1994), 11–119. Lesser lists books, dissertations, articles, and reviews, including some works that touch on Edwards secondarily. Cf. M. X. Lesser, *Jonathan Edwards: A Reference Guide* (Boston: G. K. Hall, 1981), which includes publications from the eighteenth century through 1978. Lesser has also written a biographical overview of Edwards and his writings, *Jonathan Edwards* (Boston: Twayne, 1988).

36. Especially notable among recent works that have approached Edwards theologically are Robert Jenson, *America's Theologian: A Recommendation of Jonathan Edwards* (New York: Oxford University Press, 1988); Sang Hyun Lee, *The Philosophical Theology of Jonathan Edwards* (Princeton: Princeton University Press, 1988); Michael McClymond, *Encounters with God: An Approach to the Theology of Jonathan Edwards* (New York: Oxford University Press, 1998); Gerald McDermott, *Jonathan Edwards Confronts the Gods: Christian Theology, Enlightenment Religion, and Non-Christian Faiths* (New York: Oxford Uni-

versity Press, 2000); Stephen R. Holmes, *God of Grace and God of Glory: An Account of the Theology of Jonathan Edwards* (Grand Rapids, Mich.: Eerdmans, 2000); Amy Plantinga Pauw, *"The Supreme Harmony of All": The Trinitarian Theology of Jonathan Edwards* (Grand Rapids, Mich.: Eerdmans, 2002). For a helpful applied theology, see John Piper, *God's Passion for His Glory: Living the Vision of Jonathan Edwards* (Wheaton, Ill.: Crossway Books, 1998).

# Credits

ii    Joseph Badger, *Reverend Jonathan Edwards (1703–1758) B.A. 1720, M.A. 1723*, c. 1750–55. Yale University Art Gallery, Bequest of Eugene Phelps Edwards.

x–xi    Southeastern section of Cotton Mather's map of New England, 1696. Old Sturbridge Village. Photo: Thomas Neill.

16    East Windsor house. Photo: Lori L. Fast-Minkema.

46–47    John Harris (after William Burges), *A South Prospect of Ye Flourishing City of New York in the Province of New York in America* (detail), ca. 1719. The Phelps Stokes Collection, Miriam and Ira D. Wallach Division of Art, Prints and Photographs, the New York Public Library, Astor, Lenox and Tilden Foundations.

49    Detail of Harris, *A South Prospect of Ye Flourishing City of New York*.

88    The Commencement at New Haven in 1718. From Edwin Oviatt, *The Beginnings of Yale (1701–1726)*. New Haven: Yale University Press, 1916.

92    "A Plan of the Town of New Haven," engraved and published by Thomas Kensett, 1806, from General Wadsworth's map of 1748. The New Haven Colony Historical Society. Photo © 1996 The New Haven Colony Historical Society.

146    Anonymous, *Engraving of Gov. Jonathan Belcher*, n.d. Graphic Arts Collection. Department of Rare Books and Special Collections. Princeton University Library. Photo: Princeton University Library.

187    Third Meeting House—Erected 1737. From Solomon Clark, *Historical Catalogue of the Northampton First Church, 1661–1891*. Northampton, Mass., Gazette Print, 1891.

188    Seating plan of the main floor of the 1737 meetinghouse. Courtesy the Forbes Library, Northampton, Mass.

203    John Wollaston, *George Whitefield*, 1742. Courtesy the National Portrait Gallery, London.

241    Joseph Badger, *Mrs. Jonathan Edwards (Sarah Pierpont)*, c. 1750–55. Yale University Art Gallery, Bequest of Eugene Phelps Edwards.

270    Unidentified artist, *Charles Chauncy*. Courtesy the Massachusetts Historical Society.

292 Maitland de Gorgorza, Eighteenth-century Northampton. Courtesy the Forbes Library, Northampton, Mass.

303 John Dixwell, patch box. Yale University Art Gallery, Gift of M. C. Edwards.

322 The Edwards parsonage house at Northampton. Reproduced from *The Sunday at Home,* no. 1165, August 26, 1876.

329 The graves of David Brainerd and Jerusha Edwards. Photo: Kenneth P. Minkema.

367 Reuben Moulthrop (after John Smibert), *Reverend Elisha Williams,* 1795. Yale University Art Gallery, university purchase.

377 The Mission House, Stockbridge, Massachusetts. Courtesy the Trustees of Reservations.

384 Map of Edwards' world as the embattled American west. Bill Nelson.

386 Chief Hendrick. © Corbis.

397 Joseph Blackburn, *Brigadier General Joseph Dwight,* 1756. Courtesy the Berkshire Museum, Pittsfield, Mass.

418 F. C. Yohn, *Death of Colonel Ephraim Williams Jr.* Courtesy the Chapman Historical Museum, Glen Fall, N.Y.

421 Unknown, *Mrs. Aaron Burr (Esther Edwards Burr),* ca. 1750–60. Yale University Art Gallery, Bequest of Oliver Burr Jennings, B.A. 1917, in memory of Miss Annie Burr Jennings.

422 Edward Lamson Henry, *Johnson Hall,* 1903. Albany Institute of History and Art.

448 Unknown carpenter, Desk with later bookcases, 1700–1730. Yale University Art Gallery.

461 Edwards' library table. Stockbridge Library Association Historical Collection, Stockbridge, Mass.

484 Page of Edwards' "History of Redemption" notebook. Courtesy Beineke Rare Book and Manuscript Library, Yale University.

492 Henry Dawkins, Nassau Hall with a front view of the president's house, 1764. Rare Books Division, Department of Rare Books and Special Collections. Princeton University Library. Photo: Princeton University Library.

# Index

The abbreviation "JE" refers to Jonathan Edwards. Works are by Edwards unless otherwise noted. Page numbers in italics refer to photographs and illustrations.

Adams, Eliphalet, 140
Adams, John, 434, 499
Addison, Joseph, 7, 62
*Advice to Young Converts*, 225–26
Albany Congress, 408, 409
Alcohol. *See* Drunkenness
Allen, Timothy, 275
Alsted, John, 76, 526*n*54
American Revolution. *See* Revolution, American
Ames, William, 76, 102, 526*n*54
Anderson, James, 47
Anglicanism, 7, 35, 71, 83–87, 91, 93, 138–40, 145, 147, 161, 202, 204, 210, 527*n*5, 528*n*16, 537*n*21, 572*n*20
Antichrist, 12, 17, 47, 88–89, 90, 196, 198–99, 201, 314, 315, 337–38, 415, 485
Antinomianism, 279, 281, 287, 518*n*10
Aquinas, St. Thomas, 488
Arianism, 199, 339
Aristotle, 60, 61, 63, 70, 282
Arminianism, 86–87, 91, 137–41, 175–82, 199, 256, 274, 279, 318, 329, 330, 339, 358, 362, 368, 379, 430, 433–34, 439, 440, 444, 445, 448, 453, 521*n*5, 527*n*13, 537*n*19, 537*n*26, 557*n*2, 586*n*53, 590*n*17
Ashley, Benjamin, 404, 584*n*29
Ashley, Dorothy Williams, 177, 274, 345, 367, 544*n*27
Ashley, Jonathan, 176–77, 274, 280, 345, 361, 367, 380, 544*n*27, 576*n*33

Ashley, Rebecca Kellogg, 404
Augustine, St., 77, 78, 197, 283, 439, 460, 488, 505, 525*n*47, 547*n*41
Awakenings: in *1710s*, 25–29, 33–34, 117; social contributors to, 150–52; of *1734–35*, 155–73, 183, 184, 207, 214, 216–26, 228, 239–52, 260–67, 284, 291; and youth, 155–56, 158–59, 160, 216–18, 267, 270, 275, 276, 300–301, 307, 427, 491, 539*n*11, 575*n*15; skepticism about and opposition to, 161–62, 170–71, 193, 231–33, 236–38, 269–74, 278–83, 290; in England and Scotland, 171–73, 202, 280, 283–84, 292, 309, 311, 334–35, 337; and Whitefield, 172, 202–16, 219, 228, 231, 232, 242, 262, 267, 268, 269, 273, 306–10, 324, 331, 548*n*19; in Germany, 194, 201; Great Awakening, 201–52, 260–92, 284, 560*n*44; and children, 207, 214, 217, 266, 270; excesses and enthusiasms in, 211–12, 227, 228, 231, 233–34, 241, 260, 269–71, 272, 279, 281, 284, 285, 336, 560*n*44; physical effects of terrors and ecstasies during, 217–19, 228, 234, 240–49, 260, 269, 279, 282, 284; JE's sermons and writings on, 220–24, 231, 233–40, 263–67, 273, 275, 283–90, 334–38, 561*n*5; and Land Bank, 229–30; in colleges, 231–38, 249, 267, 427, 429, 491; signs of true awakening, 235; and Sarah Pierpont Edwards' ecstatic experience, 240–49, 497; and Indians, 258, 325; and Northampton Covenant, 260–63; and millennium, 265–66, 292, 338, 557*n*30; liberal backlash to, 434–36; Second Great Awakening, 499; "great awakening" as term, 549*n*13, 557*n*31. *See also* Conversion; *Faithful Narrative*

Bach, Johann Sebastian, 79, 129, 473
"Bad book" case. *See* "Young folks' Bible" case

Baptism, 29–30, 207, 351, 354–55, 378, 573*n*23
Baptismal renewals, 53, 521–22*n*14
Baptists, 30, 350, 519*n*15
Bartlett, Phoebe, 242, 249
Bayle, Pierre, 61–62, 475
Beecher, Lyman, 8, 499
Belcher, Jonathan, 145–49, *146*, 174, 205–6,
    227–29, 339–41, 375, 392, 405, 428, 429,
    538*n*51, 571*n*54, 578*n*3
Bellamy, Joseph, 239–40, 275, 317–18, 320, 324,
    336, 357, 410, 423, 428, 450, 451, 459, 483, 498,
    552*n*2, 555*n*5, 572*n*17, 586*n*57, 588*n*20, 588*n*23,
    593*n*3, 598*n*22
Berkeley, George, 73, 80, 139, 140
Bible, 30, 31, 81, 91, 120, 189–95, 298, 351–52,
    379, 430, 435–36, 445, 473–81, 514*n*4, 572–
    73*n*22, 573*n*25. *See also* God; Jesus Christ
Biblicism, 5, 514*n*4
Billing, Edward, 360, 575*n*12, 579*n*18
"Blank Bible," 133, 474
Bolton, Connecticut, 55, 56, 93, 95–101, 103,
    107, 526*n*61, 529*n*33, 531*n*28
"Book of Controversies," 447, 476
Boyle, Robert, 246
Braddock, Edward, 414–17, 587*n*6
Bradstreet, Anne, 249
Brainerd, David, 1, 53, 54, 233–35, 249, 250, 311,
    319, 320, 323–34, *329*, 337, 338, 341, 385, 393,
    431, 436, 446, 499, 524*n*31, 568–69*n*23, 569*n*29
Brainerd, Israel, 326
Brainerd, John, 326, 330, 339, 341, 348, 568*n*17,
    571*n*54
Breck, Robert, 170, 176–82, 210, 228, 236, 274,
    307, 344, 359, 361, 433, 543*nn*15–16
Briant, Lemuel, 434, 449–50
Brown, Daniel, 84, 85
Buell, Samuel, 244–45, 247, 249, 260, 269, 271,
    275, 317, 348
Bundling, 130–31, 296–97, 328
Burnet, William, 145, 147
Burr, Aaron, 324, 330, 339, 348, 381, 392, 397–98,
    415, 419–20, 427–30, 491, 493–95, 497, 511,
    512, 517*n*2, 581*n*5, 587*nn*3–4, 589*n*37
Burr, Aaron Jr., 423, 429, 493, 498, 499, 517*n*30,
    598*n*22
Burr, Esther Edwards. *See* Edwards, Esther
    (daughter of JE)
Burr, Sally, 415, 493, 498, 598*n*22
Butler, Joseph, 477

Calvin, John, 86, 196, 501, 514*n*3, 547*n*41
Calvinism, 4, 5, 7, 8, 35, 40, 47, 63, 72, 76, 86,
    116, 120, 138, 140, 259, 318, 436, 437, 499–501,
    514*n*3, 526*n*54, 527*n*13. *See also* Puritanism
Catholicism. *See* Roman Catholic Church

Chamberlain, Ava, 301, 577–78*n*43
*Charity and Its Fruits*, 190–92, 261, 545*n*15
*Charity Contrary to an Angry Spirit*, 560*n*39
Chauncy, Charles, 142, 216, 238, 265, 268–73,
    270, 280–83, 285, 287, 290, 307, 313, 315, 379,
    433, 436, 550*n*19, 557*n*3, 557*n*33, 560*n*34,
    560*n*41, 566*n*22, 566*n*27
Chauncy, Israel, 110
Chester, Sarah, 345
Children: discipline of, 20–21, 26–27, 251, 321–
    22, 517*n*24; death of, 26–27, 128, 187, 189, 320,
    412; baptism of, 29–30, 207, 351, 354–55;
    number of, in families, 150; conversion of,
    160, 242, 249; and awakenings, 207, 214, 217,
    266, 270; religious teaching for, 321, 394,
    543*n*14, 568*n*5; salvation of infants, 518*n*6. *See
    also* Education; Youth
Christ. *See* Jesus Christ
*Christian Happiness*, 521*n*52
*Christian History*, 279, 280, 284, 291, 298, 313–
    14, 332, 563*n*22
*Christian Knowledge*, 282, 560*n*40
*Christ the Light of the World*, 54–55, 522*n*18
Chubb, Thomas, 177, 590*n*17
Churches. *See* Ministers; *and specific denomina-
    tions*
Church of England. *See* Anglicanism
Civil War, 499, 589*n*36
Claghorn, George S., xviii, 523*n*11
Clap, Thomas, 176, 177, 179, 231–33, 235, 307–9,
    324, 330, 331, 529*n*3, 559*n*27, 568*n*8, 591*n*31
Clark, Deacon, 483
Clark, Elisha, 334
Clark, Joanna, 294, 300
Clark, John, 124
Clergy. *See* Ministers; *and specific ministers*
College of New Jersey (later Princeton Univer-
    sity), 2, 215, 277, 330, 339, 392, 427, 429–31,
    472, 486, 491, *492*, 495, 498, 598*n*9
Colman, Benjamin: Calvinism of, 117, 139–40,
    142–45, 434, 537*n*23; on S. Stoddard, 124;
    Boston church of, 139, 274; and Yale College,
    139–40; and Belcher, 147; JE's connections
    with generally, 149, 227; and awakenings,
    163–64, 170–73, 180, 183–85, 272, 279, 542*n*2;
    and Breck case, 178; and publication of
    *Faithful Narrative*, 180, 183–84; and White-
    field, 202, 204–5, 309; and JE's family, 214;
    and Davenport, 273; writings by, 275; and In-
    dian missions, 376, 377–78
Communion. *See* Lord's Supper
Conaughstansey, Abraham, 385, 387
Concert of Prayer, 318, 330, 334–35, 337, 338,
    339, 340
Conforti, Joseph A., 500

Congregationalists, 7, 8, 11, 86, 87, 216, 273, 275, 330, 436

Constantine, 196, 198, 485, 546nn28–29

Conversion: S. Stoddard on, 13, 118, 119, 122, 533n27, 534n49; T. Edwards on, 26–29, 57–58; steps toward, 26–29, 57–58, 518nn8–9, 522n24; regeneration compared to, 28, 519n11; of JE, 39, 40–43, 521n51; JE's doubts about own, 50, 57, 104, 105; of Sarah Pierpont Edwards, 108–9, 242; of Indians, 117–18, 120, 174, 258, 325, 378; of youth, 158–59, 225–26; of children, 160, 242, 249; difficulties in judging, 211, 234, 237, 262, 269, 279, 286, 350; definition of, 519n11. *See also* Awakenings

Cooper, James Fenimore, 382, 404, 578n1, 579n19

Cooper, William, 141, 144, 149, 179–81, 183, 216, 235–37, 265, 274, 279, 537n31, 544n34

Covenant in Northampton, 260–63, 291, 298, 350, 556n18

Cutler, Timothy, 35–36, 38, 39, 63, 83, 84, 87, 91, 101, 102, 161, 192–93, 215–16, 273, 520n37, 537n21, 540n18, 544n31

Dante, 94, 121

Davenport, James, 232–33, 269, 271–73, 275–76, 324, 558n17, 559n20

Davies, Samuel, 392, 576n27

Death: of children, 26–27, 128, 187, 189, 320, 412, 553n18; JE's worries about, 57; of young adults, 153–55, 327–29; suicides in Northampton, 163–69, 358, 540n22, 541–42n41, 544n29; of martyrs, 245–46; and women, 245; in Northampton (1745–48), 316, 318, 345, 566n29

*Dedication to God,* 522n17

Deerfield, Connecticut, 14–15, 16, 114, 115, 126, 127, 174–76, 274, 280, 317, 345, 378

Deism, 71, 77, 103, 130, 138, 139, 192, 199, 379, 433, 440, 443, 448, 476, 486, 487–88, 590n17

Delemotte, Elizabeth, 208

Depression (melancholy), 103–10, 111, 113, 127–28, 163–64, 242, 323, 332, 368, 430, 531n28, 541n38, 569n32, 577n38, 589n40

Descartes, René, 61, 71, 72, 74, 76, 438, 524n34

Devils. *See* Satan and devils

Diary of JE, 45, 46, 50–56, 80–82, 94–108, 111, 112, 116, 135, 522n21, 529n34, 530nn17–18, 531n28

Dickinson, Jonathan, 215, 324, 325, 330, 339, 495

*Distinguishing Marks of a Work of the Spirit of God,* 233–38, 263, 265, 309, 552nn20–21, 552nn26–27

*Divine and Supernatural Light,* 156–58, 162, 211, 286, 443, 540n16

Doddridge, Philip, 366, 474

Doolittle, Benjamin, 256, 258

Downing, Mary, 295

Drunkenness, 34, 102, 126, 130, 131, 296, 299, 404, 427, 538n51, 544n2, 582n10

Dudley, Joseph, 14

Dudley, Paul, 66

Dummer, Jeremiah, 35, 139, 140

Dwight, Abigail Williams Sergeant. *See* Williams, Abigail

Dwight, Joseph, 383, 387, 395–406, *397,* 411–12, 417, 427, 437, 581nn1–2, 582nn10–13, 583nn21–23, 584n27, 584n36, 586nn48–49, 586n53

Dwight, Mary Edwards. *See* Edwards, Mary (daughter of JE)

Dwight, Mary Pynchon, 396, 581n1

Dwight, Sereno, 66, 182, 246, 475, 534n46, 542n2, 544n28, 553n14

Dwight, Timothy (JE's grandson), 8, 195, 499

Dwight, Timothy Jr. (JE's son-in-law), 363, 364, 369, 391, 495–96, 511

Dwight, Col. Timothy Sr., 179, 358–59, 364, 369, 412, 575–76n23

Earthquake, 121–22

East Windsor, Connecticut, 7, 14, 15–24, 33–34, 127, 128, 162, 209, 260, 556n16

Education: of females, 18, 19, 144, 323, 390, 499–500; of Indians, 320, 377–78, 382–83, 387, 389–406, 412, 413, 417, 423, 581n2, 582nn10–11, 583n21, 584n36

Edwards, Abigail (sister of JE), 21, 214, 275, 510

Edwards, Anne (sister of JE), 21, 128, 132, 510, 520n29

Edwards, Daniel (uncle of JE), 109

Edwards, Elizabeth "Betty" (daughter of JE), 320, 411, 511

Edwards, Elizabeth "Betty" (sister of JE), 21, 510

Edwards, Elizabeth Tuthill (grandmother of JE), 22–23

Edwards, Esther (daughter of JE): childhood and youth of, 207, 251, 317, 322–23, 342, 517n24; and fear of Indians, 317, 411, 414–15, 423–25, 567n33; in Stockbridge, 391, 392, 423–25, 429; marriage of, 392, 512, 580n36; and French and Indian War, 414–15, 423–25, 428; children of, 415, 419, 423, 428, 429, 491; reading of novels by, 419; and social gatherings, 419–20; portrait of, *421;* and College of New Jersey revival, 427; and Belcher's death, 428; ecstatic experience of, 428–29; and husband's death, 428–29, 491, 497; in Princeton, 491; smallpox inoculation of, 493; death of, 495, 496; birth of, 511; slaves owned by, 555n5;

Edwards, Esther (daughter of JE) (*continued*)
and pastoral calling for JE from Long Island, 588*n*20

Edwards, Esther (sister of JE), 18, 21, 173, 342, 510, 516*n*18

Edwards, Esther Stoddard (mother of JE), 14–21, 24, 58, 108, 128, 209, 391, 413, 490, 520*n*29, 539*n*12

Edwards, Eunice (daughter of JE), 248, 307, 511

Edwards, Eunice (sister of JE), 21, 391, 510, 516*n*14, 520*n*29, 567*n*34

Edwards, Hannah (sister of JE), 18, 376, 510

Edwards, Jerusha (daughter of JE): birth of, 128, 511; and Whitefield, 207; virtues of, 214, 249, 251, 323, 327–28; and Hopkins, 251, 252, 293; in Boston, 322; and Brainerd, 325–26, 331, 568–69*n*23; death of, 327–29, *329*, 341, 343, 495, 511, 568*n*20, 571*n*1

Edwards, Jerusha (sister of JE), 18, 21, 94, 128, 190, 249, 510

Edwards, Jonathan: portrait of, *ii;* chronology on life and times of, xiii–xiv; biographies of, xvii, 9, 60–63, 251, 253, 501–2; death of, 1–2, 493–97, 598*n*13; significance and legacy of, 1–10, 498–505; as College of New Jersey president, 2, 429–31, 472, 491; theology of generally, 4–5, 6, 134, 514*nn*3–4; personality of, 5–6, 36–37, 51, 253–55, 349–50, 370, 402, 419–20; childhood and youth of, 7, 16–26, 33–58, 66, 82; parents of, 7, 17–29, 32–34, 37–38, 42, 55–58, 108, 123, 352, 413, 490, 491, 521*n*51; reading by, 7, 17, 62–63, 73, 134, 318; birth of, 13–14; homes of, *16*, 24, 124, 320–21, *322*, 383, 390–91, 400, 491, *492*; education of, during childhood, 17–18; physical appearance of, 18, 206; sisters of, 18–19, 68, 128, 172, 510; naming of, 24; preaching style of, 33–34, 119, 127, 206, 220–21, 239–40; spiritual struggles and spiritual rapture of, as youth, 34, 36–37, 39–44, 63, 520*n*45; as Yale student, 34–39, 46, 59, 62, 63, 72, 520*n*37; ill health of, 36, 108, 127–28, 169, 193, 223, 227, 251, 409–10, 419, 430, 490, 534*n*44, 589*n*40; and social relations, 36–37, 99, 105, 109, 134–35, 253–54, 349, 362, 419–20; recreation and walks by, 42, 77, 135–36, 185; sinfulness acknowledged by, 45, 50, 55–56, 57, 288, 373; spiritual life of, after conversion, 45, 48, 50–58, 69, 185; as New York City pastor (1722–23), 46–55, 59, 90, 123; and world affairs, 48, 90, 134; spiritual discipline of, 50–52, 82, 95–96, 288, 349, 490; daily schedule of, 51, 133–36, 252; eating habits of, 51, 53, 96, 107, 133, 135, 251, 420, 529*n*34, 530*n*18, 588*n*21; as Bolton pastor (1723–24), 55, 56, 93, 95–101, 103, 107, 526*n*61, 529*n*33,

531*n*28; full church membership for, 57, 522*n*14; ambition and calling of, 59–60, 110, 132, 133–34, 150, 200, 255, 437, 467, 482; and science, 59–81; writing and study as priorities of, 59–60, 349, 362, 430, 432–33, 447; travels and travel plans of, 60, 145, 169, 178, 215, 317, 535*n*57; as Yale tutor (1725), 63–64, 101–10, 278, 530*n*23, 530*n*25; Yale 1723 commencement oration by, 82–83, 87, 91, 93; love for Sarah Pierpont by, 93–95, 99, 105–9, 241–42, 254; depression of, 103–10, 111, 113, 127–28, 332, 430, 531*n*28, 541*n*38, 569*n*32, 589*n*40; salary for, 103, 110, 123–24, 301–3, 341, 343, 520*n*35, 530*n*23, 564*n*40; spiritual crisis of (1724–27), 103–10, 111–13, 531*n*28; courtship and marriage of, 105–12, 123–24, 208–9, 511; and sexuality, 106–7, 111; as Northampton assistant to Stoddard, 110, 112–25; ordination of, 110, 116; and children's births, 111, 128, 135, 172, 187, 207, 248, 307, 320, 363; property of, 124, 302, *303*, 317–18, 321, 364, 567*n*3, 580*n*29, 585*n*41; memory device used by, 136; family resentments against, 182–83, 274, 345, 366–67, 544*nn*27–33; childrearing by, 214, 251, 321, 323, 355, 412–13; students and protégés of, 239, 250–52, 323; and death of daughter Jerusha, 327–29, *329*, 343; doubts of, about pastoral abilities, 349, 362, 364; dismissal of, from Northampton pastorate, 359–61, 369–74; in Northampton after dismissal, 363–65; job possibilities for, after dismissal from Northampton, 364–65, 575–76*nn*22–24, 576*n*27, 580*n*30; finances of, 391–92, 400, 430; grandchildren of, 415, 419, 423, 424, 428, 429, 491, 492; desk of, *448;* unfinished masterworks by, 472–89; descendants of, 500–501; genealogy of, 508–10; letters of, 517*n*26. *See also* Awakenings; Diary of JE; Northampton, Massachusetts; Notebooks of JE; Sermons; Stockbridge, Massachusetts; *and specific sermons and other writings*

Edwards, Jonathan Jr. (son of JE), 256, 320, 363, 391, 399, 404, 412, 421, 423, 498, 511, 554*n*19, 580*n*33

Edwards, Lucy (daughter of JE), 172, 207, 411, 423, 424, 425, 491, 493, 494, 495, 511, 580*n*36, 589*n*28

Edwards, Lucy (sister of JE), 172, 510

Edwards, Martha (sister of JE), 18–19, 510, 516*n*20

Edwards, Mary (daughter of JE), 207, 251, 322, 355–56, 363, 364, 365, 391, 411, 424, 495, 511, 580*n*36

Edwards, Mary (sister of JE), 21, 33, 35, 116, 343–44, 510, 532*n*6

Edwards, Pierpont "Pinty" (son of JE), 363, 411, 511

Edwards, Richard (grandfather of JE), 22–24

Edwards, Sarah Pierpont (wife of JE): JE's love for, 93–95, 99, 105–9, 241–42, 254; virtues of, 93–95, 99, 108–9, 207–8, 242–52, 497; courtship and marriage of, 105–12, 123–24, 208–9, 511; and music, 106; conversion of, 108–9, 242; depression of, 109, 242, 323; and children's births, 111, 128, 135, 172, 187, 207, 248, 307, 320, 363; homes of, 124, 320–21, 322, 383, 390–91, 400; household duties of, 133, 135, 240, 251–52, 317–18, 320, 323, 343; clothing and possessions of, 163, 243, 302, 303; ecstatic experience of, 240–49, 266, 497; portrait of, 241; and submission to God, 242–49, 497, 563–64*n*33; ill health of, 247, 248, 251, 495, 554*n*19; childrearing by, 251, 321–23; and JE's salary, 301–2; in Northampton, 302, 563–64*n*33; and church membership, 348–49; in Stockbridge, 391–92, 394, 400–401, 411, 491, 580*n*27; grandchildren of, 415, 419, 423, 424, 428, 429, 491, 492, 498; and JE's death, 494–95, 497–98; death of, 498, 554*n*28; birth of, 511

Edwards, Sarah "Sally" (daughter of JE), 111, 207, 214, 251, 307, 317, 322, 341, 342, 363, 365, 483, 495, 511, 559*n*27, 564*n*34, 568*n*8

Edwards, Susannah "Sueky" (daughter of JE), 207, 423, 491, 511, 597*n*2

Edwards, Timothy (father of JE): ill health of, 17, 490; JE's relationship with, 17–18, 20–21, 37–38, 42, 55–58, 60, 95, 109, 132, 352, 391, 413, 521*n*51, 577*n*41; military service of, 17, 90; daughters of, 18–19, 21, 128, 510, 516*n*20; parents and grandparents of, 21, 22–23, 520*n*35; personality of, 22; as East Windsor pastor, 23–27, 30, 33–34, 216, 260, 520*n*35; at Harvard, 23, 517*n*23; marriage of, 23; on conversion, 26–29, 57–58; on Lord's Supper, 32–33, 123, 262, 352, 520*n*26; preaching style of, 33–34, 119, 533*n*29; and science, 66; and James Pierpont Sr., 93; and Whitefield, 209; death of, 491; writings by, 533*n*29

Edwards, Timothy (son of JE), 187, 207, 320, 342, 392, 415, 511, 598*n*22

Eliot, John, 174

Emerson, Joseph, 342, 571*n*3

*End for Which God Created the World*, 450, 460–64, 467, 474, 483, 514*n*1, 593*n*6

England: monarchy in, 7, 12, 84, 149, 314–15, 336, 360, 427; warfare between France and, 12–17, 89, 306, 310–14, 316–18, 338, 382, 383, 409, 414–28; heresy and lax morals in, 138, 527*n*12; and hymns, 143–45; awakenings and Whitefield in, 171–73, 202, 204, 208, 339, 366;

methodism in, 208; warfare between Spain and, 263; and Indians, 324, 382–83, 385, 387–88, 406–11, 414, 421, 426; Elisha Williams in, 366. *See also* Puritanism; *and specific wars*

*Envious Men*, 148, 539*n*53

Erskine, John, 329, 362, 427, 437–38, 445, 448–49, 466–67, 498, 580*n*30

Evangelicalism, 4, 8–10, 116–18, 141–45, 171, 259, 286, 289. *See also* Awakenings

Evil, 137, 168, 222, 266. *See also* Satan and devils; Sins

"Excellencies of Christ," 106

*Faithful Narrative*, 25, 172–73, 175, 183, 184, 193, 201–2, 204, 249, 280, 296, 309, 533*n*36, 542*n*6, 573*n*24

Families: patriarchal authority in, 3, 19, 21, 187, 248–49, 259–60; and childrearing, 20–21, 26–27, 251, 517*n*24; and divorce, 22–23; deaths of children in, 26–27, 128; average age for marriage, 105, 151, 530*n*11; number of children in, 150. *See also* Children

*Farewell Sermon Preached . . . in Northampton*, 361–62, 563*n*32

Father Râle's War, 115, 117, 174, 532*n*5

Fiering, Norman, 523*n*6, 593*n*11

Finley, Samuel, 277

Finney, Charles, 499

Flavel, John, 275

Fleet, Thomas, 280

Foxcroft, Thomas, 268, 279, 309, 315, 354, 366, 412, 434, 435, 459, 566*n*27, 572*n*21, 576*n*24, 586*n*53

Foxe, John, 245

France: and Huguenots, 12, 47, 281, 336; and Indians, 12–13, 115, 382, 385, 387, 407, 410, 414, 416, 421; monarchy in, 12, 47, 196, 197, 307; population of New France, 12; warfare between England and, 12–17, 89, 306, 310–14, 316–18, 338, 382, 383, 409, 414–28. *See also specific wars*

Francke, August Hermann, 194, 201, 202

Franklin, Benjamin, 9, 52, 85, 133, 163, 202–3, 206, 212–13, 235, 312, 333, 407–8, 419, 565*n*19

Franklin, James, 68, 85, 143, 280

Franklin, John, 312

*Freedom of the Will*, 1, 410, 437–48, 453, 454, 457, 459, 467, 590*n*15, 590–91*n*17, 591*n*28, 591*n*31, 591*n*33

Frelinghuysen, Theodore, 163

French and Indian War, 382, 409, 414–28, 435

Gay, Peter, 458, 593*n*21, 596–97*n*27

Gee, Joshua, 268, 279, 545*n*19

Gender roles, 3, 19, 21, 248–49, 301, 420, 530*n*15

Genealogy of JE, 508–10

Germany, 194, 201

Gillespie, Thomas, 371, 541*n*38

*Glorious Grace*, 46, 521*n*5

Glover, Peletiah, 23, 517*n*23

God: sovereignty of, 4, 5, 40, 45, 54, 63, 112, 439, 478; S. Stoddard on, 13; glory and excellency of, 41–44, 78, 95, 118, 157, 200, 266, 462–63; love of, 54–55, 137, 157, 191–92, 266, 393, 438, 443, 453, 460, 462–63, 467–68, 470, 488, 505, 521*n*52; and natural philosophy (science), 64–81; as Creator, 65–66, 71, 74–77, 81, 504; omniscience and wisdom of, 70, 443, 444; holiness of, 112, 138; anger of, 130, 136–37, 166, 222–23, 337–38, 393; Israelites' relationship with, 136, 166, 197, 315, 316, 351; evil and sin permitted by, 137, 168, 222, 372–73, 453, 505; redemptive work of, 193–95, 481, 481–89, 546*n*31, 597*n*33; as judge, 221–22, 352, 361–62, 393; mercy of, 221–22, 224, 393; government of universe by, 442–44, 455–56, 504–5; as eternal, 443, 444; and end of creation, 460–63, 467–68; mysteries of, 477–78, 504–5. *See also* Holy Spirit; Jesus Christ; Trinity

*God Glorified in the Work of Redemption*, 140–41, 537*n*28

*God Makes Men Sensible of Their Misery*, 136–37, 536*n*14

*God's Awful Judgment*, 344, 571*n*7

*God's Continuing Presence*, 541*n*41

Grace, 27, 28–29, 31, 86, 152, 249, 262, 288–89, 592*n*18

Great Awakening. *See* Awakenings

*Great Concern of the Watchman of Souls*, 564*n*35

Grey Lock, 115, 532*n*5

Guyse, John, 171–72, 201

Half-way covenant, 30, 31, 354, 355, 519*n*18, 573*n*23

Hall, David, 361

Halley, Edmund, 69

Hampshire Association, 116, 124, 134, 176–80, 187, 227–28, 256, 359, 551*n*8, 552*n*25

Handel, George Frederick, 246, 314–15

*Harmony of the Old and New Testament*, 430, 473–82

Haroutunian, Joseph, 501

Harvard College, 11, 14, 23, 35, 61, 63, 72, 87, 114, 139, 140, 142, 144, 145, 148, 177, 182, 232, 267, 279, 309, 330, 435, 517*n*23, 538*n*37

Hatheway, Deborah, 225–26

Hawley, Elisha, 358, 417, 572*n*11

Hawley, Gideon, 399, 402–4, 407, 408, 412, 419–21, 423, 425–26, 582*n*10, 583*n*21, 584*n*29, 588–89*n*28

Hawley, Joseph II, 163–67, 168, 171, 358, 417, 540*n*22, 542*n*3, 544*n*29

Hawley, Joseph III, 311, 358, 360, 365, 368–69, 433, 576–77*n*38

Hawley, Rebekah Stoddard, 163

Heaven, 98, 106, 191, 326–27

*Heaven Is a World of Love*, 191

"Hebrew Idiom," 479

Hell, 36, 40, 57, 119–21, 136, 161, 165–66, 219–24, 235, 335–36, 522*n*24, 533*nn*23–24, 536*n*15

Hendrick, Chief, 385, *386*, 403, 408, 414, 416–17, 421, 585*n*39

Henry, Matthew, 474

Hierarchies, 3, 19, 187, 209–10, 258, 259–60, 304

"History of Redemption" notebook, 483, *484*

*History of the Work of Redemption*, 193–96, 201, 204, 236, 258, 265, 430, 460, 463, 481–89, 556*n*11

Hobbes, Thomas, 73–74, 440, 443, 475, 591*n*26

Hollis, Isaac, 377, 378, 383, 396, 398, 400, 405, 413

Holmes, Oliver Wendell Sr., 500, 501

Holy Spirit, 28, 96, 152, 157, 158, 166, 197–98, 200, 236, 237, 311, 351, 480–81. *See also* Awakenings; Trinity

Hooker, Thomas, 22, 93

Hopkins, Esther Edwards. *See* Edwards, Esther (sister of JE)

Hopkins, Samuel (JE's biographer), 9, 62–63, 67, 135, 231, 249–56, 291, 293, 304, 321–23, 341, 410, 411, 425–26, 431, 450–51, 459, 491, 494, 497–99, 523*n*11, 535*n*1, 553*n*15, 555*n*31, 561*n*1, 562*n*7, 598*n*13

Hopkins, Samuel (JE's brother-in-law), 173–74, 323–24, 342, 375, 516*n*18, 543*n*23

Howe, Daniel Walker, 133

Hubbard, Jonathan, 399

Hubbard, Thomas, 387

*Humble Attempt*, 334–39

*Humble Inquiry*, 352, 572*n*21, 573*n*25, 573*n*28

Hume, David, 456, 458, 466–67, 487, 594*n*14

Humiliation, 27–28, 58, 284, 373, 522*n*24, 533*n*27, 534*n*49. *See also* Conversion

Hutcheson, Francis, 465–66, 467, 468, 594*n*27

Hutchinson, Abigail, 249

Hutchinson, Anne, 249, 281, 287

Hutchinson, Thomas, 229

Hymns. *See* Music

Hysteria, 247, 248, 554*n*19

"Images of Divine Things," 111. *See also* "Shadows of Divine Things"

*Impending Judgments*, 122, 533*n*26

Indians: Stockbridge mission for, 1, 110, 319, 324, 364, 375–428, 431, 437, 447, 580*n*33,

584*n*32; in eighteenth-century New England generally, 3, 4; attacks on colonists by, 11, 12–15, 17, 115, 316–19, 334, 410–11; captives taken by, 15–17, 114–15, 219, 249, 378; R. Edwards as attorney for, 23; and J. Stoddard, 115, 148, 173–75, 318–19, 324, 344, 376; conversion of, 117–18, 120, 174, 258, 325, 378; missions for, 117–18, 120, 173–75, 311, 319, 323–26, 332–33, 339, 342, 426; and S. Stoddard, 117–18, 120, 173, 515*n*9; and W. Williams, 118; treaty with (1735), 174–75; JE on, 257–58, 385, 394, 452, 481, 581*n*39; and awakening, 258, 325; Brainerd's mission to, 311, 319, 323, 325, 326, 332–33, 385; education of, 320, 377–78, 382–83, 387, 389–406, 412, 413, 417, 423, 581*n*2, 582*nn*10–11, 583*n*21, 584*n*36; Hawley's mission to, at Onohquaga, 404, 412, 420–21, 423, 425, 426; and land deals, 408, 585*n*39, 585*n*41; and French and Indian War, 414, 423–28; Hawley's mission to, at Mashpee, 426
Islam, 485–86

James, Elizabeth, 208
Jefferson, Thomas, 499, 594*n*16
Jesus Christ: and redemption, 28–29, 77, 136–37, 190, 192, 193–95, 197, 481–89, 505, 546*n*31, 597*n*32; love and beauty of, 42, 44, 77, 81, 106, 109, 155, 165, 166–67, 190, 209, 248, 266, 489, 505, 597*n*32; glory and excellency of, 45, 52, 54–55, 106, 157, 165, 190, 326–27, 435, 550*n*21; as mediator, 45, 54, 192, 439; church as bride of, 106, 111, 191, 209, 248, 353, 488, 531*n*29; incarnation of, 111; parables of, 122, 189–90, 212; Judas' betrayal of, 129; crucifixion of, 161–62, 166, 297, 354, 393–94, 488; types of, 194, 209, 353, 475, 479–80; and last judgment, 196, 198, 236, 361–62; miracles of, 236, 251; and millennium, 333–40; presence of, in communion, 353–54. *See also* Trinity
Jews, 48, 117, 485–86
Johnson, Samuel, 35, 80, 84, 85, 139, 523–24*n*14, 525*n*53
Johnson, William, 417, 421–23
Jukes, Max, 500
Justification by faith, 91, 177–78, 544*n*28, 544*n*33

Kames, Henry Home, Lord, 445, 466, 467
Kellogg, Joseph, 408
Kellogg, Martin, 378, 382, 387, 391, 396, 398–400, 404, 405, 408, 413, 582*n*10, 583*n*21, 584*n*27, 584*n*36
Kimnach, Wilson H., 522*n*22, 550*n*19
King George's War, 306, 310–14, 316–18, 336, 338, 343–45, 366, 378, 380, 395, 567*n*34
King Philip's War, 12, 117, 173, 249, 410

Kingsley, Bathsheba, 276–77
Kunkapaut, John, 376

Land Bank, 228–30, 551*n*3, 551*n*5
Latitudinarianism, 138, 448
Leibniz, Gottfried Wilhelm, 72–73, 462
Lesser, M. X., xviii
Lessing, Gotthold Ephraim, 487–88
*Letter to the Author of the Pamphlet Called an Answer to the Hampshire Narrative*, 180–82
*Life of David Brainerd*, 1, 53, 54, 329–33, 339, 436, 446, 499, 514*n*1
Light imagery, 54–55, 156–58, 162, 385–87, 443, 460, 463, 550*n*21
Lister, Martin, 66, 524*n*22
*Living Peaceably One with Another*, 97–98
*Living Unconverted Under an Eminent Means of Grace*, 127, 534*n*40
Locke, John, 7, 60–64, 67, 71, 73, 74, 76, 103, 278, 286, 438, 452, 456, 464, 475, 504, 523*n*6, 591*n*26
Logic, 90–91, 145, 349. *See also* Reason; Science
Lord, Hezekiah, 162
Lord's Supper: S. Stoddard on, 30–33, 122, 160, 262, 297, 298, 346, 348, 351, 368, 401, 519*n*18, 532*n*7, 572–73*n*22; overscrupulous avoidance of, 31–32, 540*n*23; warnings on partaking unworthily, 31–32, 216, 297; T. Edwards on, 32–33, 123, 262, 352, 520*n*26; Mathers on, 32, 572–73*n*22; E. Taylor on, 32, 33, 573*n*22; and JE, 122–23, 129, 160–61, 262–63, 297–98, 304–5, 346–54, 368, 370, 371, 449, 575*n*12; self-examination before, 262, 263; presence of Christ in, 353–54; S. Williams on, 365, 367–68
Louisbourg campaign, 310–14, 316, 318, 336, 366, 395, 433, 566*n*20, 567*n*34
Lowman, Moses, 196, 474, 546*n*29, 570*n*47
Luther, Martin, 374, 439
Lydius, John Henry, 408
Lyman, John, 248, 553–54*n*18
Lyman, Moses, 227, 228, 231, 276, 277
Lyon, Mary, 499

Maclaurin, John, 142
Madison, James, 498, 594*n*16
Malebranche, Nicholas, 73, 525*n*41
*Many Mansions*, 186, 545*n*9
Marriage. *See* Families
Mastricht, Peter van, 318, 488
Mather, Cotton: map of New England by, *x–xi*; on slavery, 20; children of, 26–27, 268; and T. Edwards, 26, 517*n*23; on Lord's Supper, 32; and Yale College, 35; self-examination by, 52; writing style of, 59–60;

Mather, Cotton (*continued*)
and science, 60, 61, 68–69; and smallpox inoculations, 68, 85; and Anglicanism, 84–85;
criticisms of, 85; and Harvard College, 87;
and Calvinist orthodoxy, 140; death of, 140,
171; and evangelism, 142; and hymns, 144,
538n36; preaching by, 538n38
Mather, Eleazar, 14, 32, 516n10
Mather, Esther Warham. *See* Stoddard, Esther
Warham Mather (grandmother of JE)
Mather, Increase, 32, 68, 84–85, 117, 124, 140,
275, 516n10, 517n23, 527n7, 572–73n22
Mather, Samuel, 179, 247, 248, 268, 269, 325,
358, 554n19, 557n2
Mayhew, Jonathan, 360, 433–36
McCulloch, William, 292, 309, 416
McGiffert, A. C., 51–52, 501
McLaurin, John, 334, 580n30
Meacham, Esther Williams, 219
Meacham, Joseph, 219–20, 275
Melancholy. *See* Depression (melancholy)
Metcalf, Abigail Edwards. *See* Edwards,
Abigail (sister of JE)
Metcalf, William, 214
Methodism, 173, 208, 243
Millennium, 265–67, 292, 315, 335–37, 343, 350,
415, 485, 557n30
Miller, Perry, xvii, 60–62, 182, 280–81, 501–2,
515nn2–3, 523n6, 537nn26–27, 593n21
Milton, John, 167
"Mind," 59, 78, 95, 103, 525n51, 526n61
Ministers: S. Stoddard on, 13, 210; authority of,
31, 116, 178, 209–10, 268, 515n2, 519n18; salaries of, 123–24, 301–3, 341, 343, 520n35,
530n23, 564n35, 564n40; unconverted, 210–11,
215, 231, 237, 262, 350; Whitefield on, 210–11,
215; itinerant, 215, 218, 228, 232–33, 244, 269,
271–72, 277, 279, 552n17; opposition to
awakenings by, 237–38, 269–74, 278–83, 290;
candidates for ministry, 254–55; ordination
of, 330, 356; JE on deaths of, 551n6. *See also*
*specific ministers*
Minkema, Kenneth P., xviii, 534n44, 555n10,
573n24, 577n42
"Miscellaneous Observations on Scripture,"
474
"Miscellanies," 59, 77, 91, 95, 98–100, 105, 106,
109, 111, 119, 129, 134, 472, 518n6, 520n39,
522n24, 526n55, 530nn13–15, 533n29, 534n49,
536n15, 545–46n21, 591n27, 593n2, 595nn12–13,
596n19, 596n26, 597nn32–33
*Misrepresentations Corrected, and Truth Vindi-
cated,* 368, 449
Mix, Elisha, 37, 183
Mix, Stephen and Mary, 35, 37

Moody, Joseph, 356
More, Henry, 72, 89, 142–43
Mount Holyoke Seminary, 499–500
Murray, Iain, xvii
Music, 79, 106, 129, 143–45, 245, 390, 538nn37–
38, 540n15, 553n12, 576n31

Native Americans. *See* Indians
"Natural History of the Mental World, or of
the Internal World," 78
Nature, 42, 44, 64–66, 69, 77–79, 97, 99–100,
111, 121–22, 135, 136, 153, 185, 443, 477, 489,
545n6. *See also* Science
*Nature of True Virtue.* See *True Virtue*
*New England Courant,* 68, 85, 143, 280
New England maps, *x–xi, 384*
New Haven map, *92*
New Lights, 238, 275–80, 283–85, 287, 306–10,
315, 324, 330, 331, 350, 354, 360, 366, 379–80,
381, 385, 392, 402, 404, 434, 436, 458, 499,
551n3, 551n5, 559n25, 559–60n31, 572n19
Newton, Isaac, 7, 60–65, 67, 68, 70–74, 79, 89,
440, 444, 486, 504, 550n20
New York City, 46–55, *46–47, 49,* 59, 90, 95,
123, 257, 420, 529n33, 588n20
Niebuhr, H. Richard, 501
Northampton, Massachusetts: and Indian attacks, 11, 316–19; S. Stoddard as pastor of,
11–13, 30–33, 114–26, 132, 150, 346, 370, 372,
373, 573n23, 575n8; E. Mather as pastor of, 14;
awakenings in, 25, 121, 155–73, 184, 189, 207,
214, 216–26, 228, 239–52, 260–67, 284, 291,
541n41; communion and church membership
in, 30–33, 122, 123, 160–61, 297–98, 304–5,
346–56, 370, 371, 449, 574–75n8, 575n12; sins
of residents of, 97–98, 122, 126–27, 130, 150,
185–89, 261, 296–97, 353; JE as assistant to S.
Stoddard in, 110, 112–25; J. Stoddard as magistrate and leader in, 114–15, 125–26, 343; JE's
sermons in, 120–22, 126–31, 148–49, 152, 156–
58, 165–68, 189–200, 224, 284–90, 361–62,
534n44, 545n19, 546n22; and earthquake, 121–
22; youth of, 122, 126–27, 150–53, 292–302;
and JE's salary, 123–24, 301–3, 341, 343,
530n23; JE's home in, 124, 320–21, *322;* political conflicts in, 125–26, 130, 186–87, 189, 261,
371, 533n36; temperament of people of, 125,
371; size of church in, 127, 160, 534n42,
573n24; premarital pregnancies in, 131, 534–
35n51, 543n14; tavern culture in, 131, 296, 299,
544n2; respect for JE as pastor in, 132, 291,
535n57; JE's daily schedule in, 133–36; pastoral role of JE in, 134–35, 164, 225–26, 254,
255, 263, 373; small group meetings in, 135,
155–56, 296, 539n11; and JE's travels, 145, 169,

178, 215, 317, 535*n*57; common lands versus private property in, 150–51, 291; hymns of worship in, 156, 245, 540*n*15, 553*n*12; illness and deaths in, 160, 163–69, 316, 318, 345, 358, 541–42*n*41, 544*n*29, 566*n*29; skepticism about awakening in, 161–62, 170–71, 193; accident in old meetinghouse in, 184–85; new meetinghouse in, 186–89, *187, 188, 292;* town house in, 189, *292;* Whitefield in, 206–9, 212–13; JE's preaching tours while pastor at, 239–40, 263, 275; Buell's preaching in, 244–45, 247, 249, 260; fires in, 248, 535*n*58, 553–54*n*18; covenant of, 260–63, 291, 298, 350, 556*n*18; "young folks' Bible" case in, 292–302, 345, 370, 371, 561–62*nn*6–7, 563*n*16, 563*nn*25–26, 577*n*42; opponents of JE in, 302, 343, 357–61, 363, 365, 369–74, 544*n*2, 563–64*n*33, 573*n*24, 577*n*42; and agrarian capitalism, 303–4; population of, 316, 534*n*42, 573*n*24; church government revision in, 345–47; profession of faith and church membership in, 347, 352–53, 575*n*12; JE's dismissal from, 359–61, 369–74; JE's farewell sermon in, 361–62; JE in, after dismissal, 363–65; campaign for separate church in, 364–65, 575–76*n*23; Hooker as pastor in, 586*n*53

Notebooks of JE, 59–60, 67, 73, 78, 81–82, 88, 90, 95, 103, 109, 111, 112, 136, 337–38, 432, 437, 447, 455, 472, 474, 476, 479, 483, *484*

"Notes on Scripture," 59, 103, 133, 474, 480

"Notes on the Apocalypse," 59, 103, 133–34, 197, 337–38, 587*n*5

*Nothing upon Earth can Represent the Glories of Heaven,* 98

Noyes, Joseph, 233, 565*n*3, 568*n*8

"Of the Prejudices of Imagination," 80

Old Lights, 238, 256, 273–74, 277–80, 284, 290, 306–10, 315, 330, 339, 379, 381, 435, 436, 559–60*n*31

Oliver, Andrew, 396

*Original Sin,* 450–59, 474, 581*n*39, 591*n*29, 592*n*5, 592*n*18, 593*n*20

Owen, John, 162

Paice, Joseph, 387–88, 390, 583*n*22

Park, Edwards A., 250–51

Parkes, Henry Bamford, 501

Parkman, Ebenezer, 252, 325, 545*n*19, 568*n*16

Parsons, Elihu, 363, 391, 483, 511

Parsons, Jonathan, 218

Parsons, Sally Edwards. *See* Edwards, Sarah "Sally" (daughter of JE)

Partridge, Oliver, 408

Paternity case, 358, 572*n*11

Paul (apostle), 208, 274, 451, 454, 457

*Peaceful and Faithful Amid Division and Strife,* 545*n*7

Pepperrell, William, 310, 402, 403, 582*n*10, 583*n*22

Perkins, William, 58, 518*n*8

"Personal Narrative," 45, 46, 53–55, 58, 99, 104, 108, 109, 112, 185, 222, 474, 517*n*2, 520*n*45, 522*n*22, 524*n*15, 531*n*28

Pettit, Norman, 569*n*23, 569*n*29

Philosophy, 281–82

Pierpont, Benjamin, 127, 132, 133, 176

Pierpont, James Jr., 87, 93, 105, 529*n*33, 530*n*12

Pierpont, Mary Hooker, 93

Pierpont, Sarah. *See* Edwards, Sarah Pierpont (wife of JE)

Platonism, 72, 77, 78, 89, 97, 142–43, 465

*Pleasantness of Religion,* 96

Pomeroy, Benjamin, 216, 218, 232, 269, 271, 275, 277, 556*n*16

Pomeroy, Ebenezer Jr., 358, 365, 572*n*15

Pomeroy, Elisha, 349

Pomeroy, Elizabeth, 294–95

Pomeroy, Seth, 179, 295, 311, 316, 358, 365, 369

Poole, Matthew, 474

Pope, Alexander, 460–61, 594*n*14

Popery. *See* Roman Catholic Church

*Poverty of Spirit,* 51, 521*n*12

Prayer, 27, 104, 133, 156, 247–48, 312, 325, 334–35, 539*n*11, 565*n*16, 570*n*39

Preaching. *See* Sermons

Premarital pregnancies, 131, 534–35*n*51, 543*n*14

Presbyterians, 7, 8, 30, 31, 46–47, 54, 86, 139, 163, 177, 178, 210, 215, 277, 278, 309, 311, 312, 330, 346, 354, 387, 420, 467, 536–37*n*19, 576*n*27

Prince, Sarah "Sally," 322–23, 415, 419–20, 423, 428, 493, 496–97

Prince, Thomas Jr., 279

Prince, Thomas Sr., 69, 141, 142, 144, 145, 147, 149, 205, 215, 227, 265, 272, 276, 279–80, 284, 291, 298, 309, 313–14, 323, 332, 337, 413, 415, 419–20, 434, 549*n*13, 576*n*24, 587*n*3

Princeton University. *See* College of New Jersey

Profession of faith, 347, 352–53, 394, 575*n*12

*Pure of Heart Blessed,* 560*n*39

Puritanism, 3, 4, 7, 8, 11, 19–21, 84, 86–87, 143, 156, 189, 196, 259, 261, 275, 278, 300, 350–51, 439, 500–501, 546*n*27, 563*n*28. *See also* Calvinism

Queen Anne's War, 12, 17, 90, 115

Ramism, 63, 64, 76, 128

Ramsey, Paul, 591*n*33, 592*n*5, 593*n*11

"Rational Account of the Main Doctrines of the Christian Religion Attempted," 134, 482, 483, 596*n*22

Reason, 282–83, 358, 434–37, 452, 475–76. *See also* Logic; Science

Redemption, 28–29, 77, 137, 192–98, 264, 481–89, 505, 546*n*31, 597*n*32

Reformation, 90, 168, 169, 172, 198, 199, 201, 236, 287, 314, 374, 439, 440, 464, 465, 485, 547*n*41

Reformed movement, 259, 514*n*3. *See also* Calvinism; Presbyterians

Reid, Thomas, 466

*Religious Affections*, 1, 284–90, 304–5, 331, 332, 348, 352, 446, 465, 481, 560*n*47, 564*n*45

"Resolutions," 50–52, 82, 95–96

*Resort and Remedy*, 230–31, 551*n*6

Revivals. *See* Awakenings

Revolution, American, 256, 274, 369, 498, 556*n*14, 577*n*38, 598*n*22

Reynolds, Peter, 243–44

Richardson, Samuel, 419

Robe, James, 283–84, 309, 311, 563*n*22

Rockwell, Abigail, 27

Rogers, Robert, 382

Roman Catholic Church, 3–4, 7, 12, 16, 17, 85–91, 117, 129, 138, 197–99, 311, 314–15, 336–38, 380, 415–16, 528*n*19, 570*n*47

Root, Martha, 358

Root, Simeon and Timothy, 293, 295, 298–300, 302, 563*n*25

Rowlandson, Mary, 249

Sacraments, 29–33, 352–56, 370, 381, 533*n*29. *See also* Baptism; Lord's Supper

Saints, 109, 157, 191, 287, 288, 326–27, 333, 536*n*15

Saltonstall, Governor, 84

Satan and devils, 69, 108, 117, 119, 121, 137, 160, 163–69, 171, 194, 196, 198, 204, 219, 221, 235–37, 247, 257, 273, 275, 284–89, 336, 371–75, 386, 427, 483, 486, 489, 540*n*22, 541*n*38, 546*n*29, 558*n*17. *See also* Hell; Sins

Saum, Lewis O., 570*n*34

Schafer, Thomas A., xviii, 526*n*55, 528*n*30, 529*n*39, 530*n*25, 534*n*44

Science, 59–81, 89, 103, 438, 464, 550*n*20. *See also* Nature

Scotland, 142, 173, 177, 280, 283–84, 292, 309, 311, 314, 324, 329, 334–39, 346, 354, 362–63, 371, 391, 437, 446, 448, 465–67, 498, 541*n*38, 580*n*30

Scott, Elizabeth, 366, 400–401, 576*n*31, 583*n*24

Scripture. *See* Bible

Searle, John, 349, 572*n*15

Seeman, Erik R., 518*n*6

*Self-Examination and the Lord's Supper*, 297, 563*n*18

Sergeant, Abigail Williams. *See* Williams, Abigail

Sergeant, John, 174, 175, 324, 375–79, 383, 396, 398

Sermons: election-day, 11, 12, 123, 262; by S. Stoddard, 11, 12, 119–20, 124, 125, 128; by T. Edwards, 33–34, 119, 533*n*29; JE's preaching style, 33–34, 119, 127, 206, 220–21, 239–40; for New York City church, 46, 51, 54–55; imagery and analogy in, 54–55, 97, 98, 222–23, 385–87, 550*n*21; structure and logic of JE's, 54, 90–91, 128, 546*n*22; for Bolton church, 96–99, 107; in Stockbridge, 110, 364, 383, 385–87, 392–94, 424, 539*n*4, 585*n*43, 586*n*49, 587*n*6, 597*n*2; on hell, 119–21, 533*nn*22–23; S. Stoddard's preaching guidelines, 119–20; by JE in Northampton, 120–22, 126–31, 148–49, 152, 156–58, 165–68, 189–200, 224, 284–90, 361–62, 534*n*44, 545*n*19, 546*n*22; fast-day, 121–22, 129–30, 167–68, 171, 312, 415, 565*nn*17–18, 566*n*24; communion, 122–23, 354, 540*n*26, 573*n*31; jeremiad, 126, 129–30, 211; JE's Boston, 140–41, 149, 192; political, 148–49; funeral, 153–55, 230–31, 326–28, 344–45, 428, 551*n*6; public lectures, 177–78, 192; JE's sermon series, 189–200, 284–90; Whitefield's preaching style, 206, 212; awakening, 220–24, 284–90; Yale commencement address (1741) by JE, 231–38; and lay preaching, 276, 277, 279; JE on good preaching, 282; thanksgiving, 316, 566*n*24, 586*n*49, 587*n*6; ordination, 356; JE's farewell sermon in Northampton, 361–62; JE's, after Northampton dismissal, 364, 575–76*nn*22–23. *See also specific sermons*

Sewall, Joseph, 142, 144, 279, 309, 434

Sewall, Judith, 142, 537*n*31

Sewall, Samuel, 12, 20, 84, 88, 118, 124, 142, 143, 526–27*n*4, 527*n*7, 538*nn*37–38

Sexuality, 106–7, 111, 130–31, 151, 208, 261, 293–301, 328, 358, 370, 534–35*n*51, 577–78*n*43

"Shadows of Divine Things" (later "Images of Divine Things"), 111, 136, 137

Shaftesbury, Anthony Ashley Cooper, third earl of, 62, 465

Shippen, Joseph, 392

Shippen, William, 493, 494, 598*n*9, 598*n*22

Shirley, William, 229, 266–67, 281, 319, 406, 412, 416

Shute, Samuel, 86

*Signs of God's Displeasure*, 126–27, 534*n*39

Sin and sins: pride as, 5–6, 45, 51, 56, 60, 130, 225, 233, 288, 371–72, 373; T. Edwards on, 34;

of youth, 34, 122, 126–27, 130–31, 150, 261, 293–302, 328; JE's acknowledgment of own sinfulness, 45, 50, 51, 55–56, 57, 288, 373; natural disasters, deaths, and war as judgments on, 69, 121–22, 163–69, 312, 533*n*26; hatred of, and love of sinners, 97; of Northampton residents, 97–98, 122, 126–27, 130–31, 185–89, 261, 296–97, 353; JE on, 126–27, 129–130, 219–24, 553*n*10; hypocrisy as, 129, 234, 286, 287, 289, 297; fornication as, 131, 297, 358, 534–35*n*51, 543*n*14; envy as, 148, 185; original sin, 199, 447, 450–59, 478; S. Stoddard on, 199; against Holy Spirit, 236, 237; guilt over, 438, 439, 454–55, 592*n*15; Hopkins on, 450–51; Bellamy on, 451, 593*n*3; Wesley on, 553*n*10. *See also* Drunkenness

*Sin and Wickedness Bring Calamity and Misery on a People,* 131, 535*n*52

Singer, Elizabeth, 145

Singing. *See* Music

*Sinners in the Hands of an Angry God,* 1, 219–24, 501, 550*nn*19–20

Slavery, 20, 47, 250, 255–58, 295, 300, 321, 407, 498, 555*nn*5–10, 567*n*3, 572*n*10

Smallpox inoculation, 68, 85, 493–94

Smith, Adam, 466, 594*n*14

Smith, Cotton Mather, 405

Smith, John, 47, 48, 55, 87, 523*n*9

Smith, Susanna, 47, 48, 53, 55, 123

Smith, William, 47, 87, 523*n*9

Socinianism, 199, 329, 433, 434, 448

*Some Thoughts Concerning the Present Revival,* 240–43, 263–67, 273, 275, 276, 278, 281, 283, 292, 338, 530*n*19, 556*n*22

Spencer, Elihu, 339, 341, 342

Spiders and spider imagery, 64–66, 95, 223, 550*n*19

*Spiritual Understanding of Divine Things,* 96–97

*State of Public Affairs,* 148–49, 539*n*54

Stebbins, Thomas, 164

Steele, Richard, 7, 62

Stiles, Ezra, 379–80, 433, 491, 498–99, 560*n*41

Stiles, Isaac, 38, 108, 380

Stockbridge, Mary and Phoebe, 258

Stockbridge, Massachusetts: mission for Indians at, 1, 319, 324, 364, 375–428, 584*n*32; JE's sermons in, 110, 364, 383, 385–87, 392–94, 424, 539*n*4, 585*n*43, 586*n*49, 587*n*6, 597*n*2; establishment of, 175, 375–76; and King George's War, 345; JE as pastor in, 364, 365, 375, 381, 383–413, 430–31, 437, 447, 580*n*33; English families in, 375–76, 379–82, 578*n*2, 579*n*10; Williams family in, 376–77, 379–82, 395–405; Mission House in, 377, *377,* 390–91,

578*n*6; schools for Indians in, 378, 382–83, 387, 389–406, 412, 413, 417, 423, 581*n*2, 582*nn*10–11, 583*n*21, 584*n*36; land ownership in, 379, 380*n*29, 381; opposition to JE's appointment as pastor in, 380–81; finances of, 398, 399–400, 406–7, 411, 413, 582*n*12; fire in, 403, 584*n*26; exodus of Indians from, 405, 406, 582*n*10, 583*n*21, 584*n*27; violence against Indians in, 406; and Indian attacks, 407, 410–12, 416, 426–27, 586*n*48; JE's resignation from, 431, 490–91

Stockton, Richard, 429, 589*n*39

Stoddard, Esther Warham Mather (grandmother of JE), 14, 15, 32, 343, 516*n*14

Stoddard, John (uncle of JE): military career of, 14, 114–15, 306, 316, 318, 320, 343, 395, 515*n*9; as JE's patron, 114, 123, 182, 227, 318–19, 343, 348; marriage of, 114, 344; as political leader, 114–15, 125–26, 148, 149, 343, 369, 371, 543*n*22, 571*n*8; and Indians, 115, 117–18, 120, 173–75, 318–19, 324, 344, 376, 515*n*9; and Belcher, 148; and Hawley, 163; and Breck case, 179, 344; and "young folks' Bible" case, 299, 302, 345; children of, 323, 344; and New Lights, 339–40; death and funeral of, 343–45, 346; and awakening, 344, 345; home of, 531*n*3

Stoddard, Prudence Chester (wife of John Stoddard), 344, 345, 531*n*3

Stoddard, Solomon (grandfather of JE): authority and influence of, 11–12, 32, 114, 118–19, 124, 210, 370, 515*n*2; dress of, 11; as Northampton pastor, 11–13, 30–33, 114–26, 132, 150, 346, 370, 372, 373, 573*n*23, 575*n*8; preaching by, 11, 12, 119–20, 124, 125, 128; on conversion, 13, 118, 119, 122, 533*n*27, 534*n*49; family of, 13–15, 19, 23, 32, 163; on taxation and defense, 13, 14; and awakenings, 25, 151, 160, 204; and Lord's Supper and church membership, 30–33, 122, 160, 262, 297, 298, 346, 348, 351, 368, 401, 519*n*18, 532*n*7, 572–73*n*22; and clergy's role in church government, 31, 116, 178, 515*n*2, 519*n*18; writings by, 31, 117, 118, 119, 204; as Harvard student, 61; JE as assistant to, in Northampton, 110, 112–25; and evangelism, 117, 142; and Indians, 117–18, 120, 173, 515*n*9; and earthquake, 121–22, 124; death of, 124; and hymns, 145; Whitefield on, 210, 262; on change, 352; and half-way covenant, 519*n*18

Stout, Harry S., 205, 549*n*13

Stowe, Harriet Beecher, 9, 250–51

Strong, Ebenezer, 126

Strong, Job, 339, 356

Strong, Nehemiah, 195

Stuart, Prince Charles Edward, 314, 315

Suicides, 163–69, 358, 540n22, 541–42n41, 544n29

Swift, Jonathan, 138–39, 181

Taylor, Edward, 32, 33, 126, 573n22

Taylor, John, 434, 435–36, 448–49, 451, 452

*Temptation and Deliverance*, 296–97, 563n17

Tennent, Gilbert, 163, 210, 215–16, 231, 232, 242, 250, 267, 269, 307, 324, 330

Tennent, William Sr., 215

*Threefold Work of the Holy Ghost*, 129, 534n50

Tillotson, John, 62

Tindal, Matthew, 476, 487

Toland, John, 71

*Torments of Hell Are Exceeding Great*, 533n23

Tracy, Joseph, 549n13, 559n20

Tracy, Patricia J., xvii, 369–70, 561–62nn6–7, 578n43

Treat, Robert, 103

*Treatise on Religious Affections*. See *Religious Affections*

Trinity, 71, 77, 191, 434, 435, 443, 462, 596n24. See also God; Holy Spirit; Jesus Christ

*True Grace Distinguished from the Experience of Devils*, 392

*True Saints, When Absent from the Body*, 326–27

*True Virtue*, 1, 419, 450, 460, 464–71, 592n5, 594n18, 594n24, 594nn26–27

Trumbull, James R., 530n25, 566n29

Tucker, Louis Leonard, 307

Turretin, Francis, 318, 488

Twain, Mark, 500

*Two Dissertations*, 450, 459–71, 498

"Types Notebook," 479, 595n16

Typology, 77, 106, 111, 194, 353, 415, 475, 479–80, 531n29, 595n16, 595–96n18

Umpeecheanah, Paul, 376

*Value of Salvation*, 521n5

Virtue and virtues: JE's cultivation of, 51, 349, 490; piety as, 93–94, 116–17, 128, 132, 141, 142, 156, 199, 248–49, 312, 333; of Sarah Pierpont Edwards, 93–95, 99, 108–9, 242–52, 497; of Jerusha Edwards (JE's sister), 94, 128, 249; and happiness, 98, 109, 141, 191, 289, 463, 468, 470, 536n15, 594n26, 597n33; of Jerusha Edwards (JE's daughter), 214, 249, 251, 323, 327–28; and submission to God, 242–249, 496–97, 563–64n33; as signs of true religious affections, 286–88, 304–5, 332; of Brainerd, 325, 327, 331–33; of J. Stoddard, 344, 345; Briant on, 434, 449–50; JE on true virtue, 450, 464–71, 594n18, 594n24; Hutcheson on,

465–66, 468; and benevolence, 469–70; of Esther Edwards Burr, 496

Voltaire, 461–62, 487

Wallis, Joshua Jr., 27

Warham, John, 23–24

Warner, Oliver, 293, 294, 295, 300, 562n13, 563n26

*Warnings of Future Punishment*, 120–21, 533n23

*Warning to Professors*, 297, 563n19

War of Jenkins' Ear, 263

Washington, George, 66, 409

Watts, Isaac, 143–44, 145, 147–49, 156, 171, 172, 183, 201, 202, 224, 245, 264, 493, 542n6, 590–91n17

Waunaupaugus, Solomon, 406

Wauwaumpequunnaunt, John, 392–93

Weber, Max, 51

Weiser, Conrad, 408

Wesley, John, 173, 192, 208, 235, 333, 458, 517n24, 553n10

Wheelock, Eleazar, 29, 216–18, 220, 221, 232, 276, 277, 320, 323, 556n16

*When the Wicked Shall Have Filled up Themselves in Their Sin*, 165–66, 541n37

Whetmore, James, 85

Whitefield, George: and awakenings, 172, 202–16, 219, 228, 231, 232, 242, 262, 267, 268, 269, 273, 306–10, 324, 331, 548n19; in England, 172, 202, 339, 366; and B. Franklin, 202–3, 206, 212–13, 419; and Colman, 202, 204–5, 309; portrait of, *203*; JE compared with, 206, 209–10; preaching style of, 206, 212; and JE's family, 207–8; marriage of, 208–9; on S. Stoddard, 210, 262; on unconverted ministers, 210–11, 215; JE's criticisms of, 211–12, 524n31; Clap's fears about, 330

Whitman, Elnathan, 278

Whittelsey, Chauncey, 324

*Wicked Men's Slavery to Sin*, 533n22

Wigglesworth, Edward, 435

Wigglesworth, Michael, 121

Willard, Josiah, 403, 407, 547n1, 583n23

Williams, Abigail, 376–82, 395–98, 400, 401, 404, 410, 417, 433, 437, 581n2, 581n5, 582n17

Williams, Chester, 243, 245, 359, 576n34

Williams, Eleazer, 176

Williams, Elijah, 381, 382, 405, 579n18

Williams, Elisha: as tutor, 35, 63, 524n14; as Yale rector, 102, 140, 179, 181, 537n23, 551n12; and Breck case, 179, 181; and awakenings, 183; on religious liberty, 278; and Northampton communion controversy, 357, 366, 367, 401; military service of, 366, 571n8; writings by, 366, 576n30; as JE's ally generally,

367; portrait of, *367;* as commissioner of missionary society, 396, 400, 582*n*15; and Stockbridge mission, 396, 400–401, 437, 581–82*n*6, 583*n*21; marriage of, to Elizabeth Scott, 400, 583*n*24; death of, 413, 583*n*24; philosophical ideas of, as youth, 523*n*12

Williams, Elizabeth Scott. *See* Scott, Elizabeth

Williams, Ephraim Jr., 380–81, 388, 400, 402, 404, 416–17, *418,* 585*n*39

Williams, Ephraim Sr., 175, 376, 379, 381, 396, 398, 400–405, 413, 417, 427, 581–82*n*6

Williams, Eunice (daughter of John Williams), 16, 219

Williams, Eunice Mather (daughter of S. Stoddard), 14, 15

Williams, Israel, 182–83, 274, 345, 358, 359, 367, 369, 402, 412, 416, 544*n*29, 544*n*33, 586*n*48

Williams, Jerusha, 15

Williams, John, 14–17, 115, 126, 127, 176

Williams, John Jr., 15

Williams, Roger, 30, 31, 519*n*15

Williams, Samuel, 576*n*34

Williams, Solomon, 116, 275, 276, 365, 366–68, 410, 447, 449, 532*n*6

Williams, Stephen, 33, 147, 168, 173, 174, 176, 178, 215, 219–21, 230, 232, 324, 325, 376, 516*n*14, 523*n*12, 568*n*23, 575*n*22

Williams, William, 115–17, 124, 171–73, 176, 179, 182–83, 207, 227–28, 230–31, 274, 367, 376, 396, 532*n*7, 532*n*10, 544*n*31, 544*n*33, 551*nn*6–8

Williams College, 417

Winslow, Ola, xvii, 369, 501, 562*n*14

Winthrop, John, 261, 267, 304, 545*n*10

Witchcraft, 68–69

Witherspoon, John, 498, 594*n*16

Women: husband's relationship with wife, 3, 19, 21, 187, 248–49, 276–77; education of females, 18, 19, 144, 323, 390, 499–500; JE's examples of, in sermons and writings, 19; piety of, 93–94, 128; and childbirth, 111–12, 245; and awakening, 240–49, 270; and submission, 242–49, 429, 496–97, 563–64*n*33; and death, 245; and gender roles, 248–49, 301, 420, 530*n*15; in churches, 249, 346; and small group meetings, 539*nn*11–12; and speaking in groups, 553*n*11. *See also* Families; *and specific women*

Wood, Gordon S., 514*n*2

Woodbridge, Timothy, 93, 174, 375–76, 378–80, 393, 398–99, 400, 404, 406, 408–9, 412, 413, 431, 529*n*33, 580*n*27, 583*n*21, 584*n*36, 585*n*41, 588*n*21

*Works of Jonathan Edwards,* xvii–xviii, 502

Yale, Elihu, 35

Yale College: JE as student at, 34–39, 46, 59, 62, 63, 72, 520*n*37; and Cotton Mather, 35; students' immorality and disorder at, 37–39, 101–2, 103; curriculum of, 61, 63, 103, 523–24*n*14; library at, 62, 63, 84, 93, 103, 139, 140; JE as tutor at, 63–64, 101–10, 278, 530*n*23, 530*n*25; Berkeley's donation to, 73, 139, 140; JE's M.A. oration at commencement of (1723), 82–83, 87, 91, 93; JE's valedictory oration at (1720), 82–83; Anglican apostasy at, 83–87, 93, 139–40, 527*n*5, 537*n*21; Commencement Day at, 83, *88,* 103, 107–8; Cutler's commencement address at (1722), 83, 84; daily schedule at, 102; and awakening, 231–38, 249, 267, 307, 324; Clap as rector of, 231–33, 235, 307, 324, 330, 331; JE's commencement address at (1741), 231–38; Brainerd as student at, 233–35, 324–25, 330–31; presidents of, 379, 491, 499

"Young folks' Bible" case, 292–302, 345, 370, 371, 561–62*nn*6–7, 563*n*16, 563*nn*25–26, 577*n*42

Youth: sins of, 34, 122, 126–27, 130–31, 150, 261, 293–302, 328; Yale students' immorality and disorder, 37–39, 101–2, 103; and age for marriage, 105, 151, 530*n*11; Sabbath night frolics by, 122, 126, 150, 151, 152–53, 154, 296, 328, 331; and bundling, 130–31, 296–97, 328; and premarital pregnancies, 131, 534–35*n*51, 543*n*14; social conditions of, 150–52; compliance of, with JE's preaching, 152–53; death of, 153–55, 327–29; and awakenings, 155–56, 158–59, 160, 216–18, 231–33, 267, 270, 275, 276, 300–301, 307, 427, 491, 539*n*11, 575*n*15; JE's private meetings with, 155, 217–18; conversion of, 158–59, 225–26; and Northampton covenant, 261; and Davenport's book and clothes burnings, 275, 276; and "young folks' Bible" case, 292–302, 345, 370, 371, 561–62*nn*6–7, 563*n*16, 563*nn*25–26, 577*n*42. *See also* Children